Believers Church
Bible Commentary

Douglas B. Miller and Loren Johns, Editors

BELIEVERS CHURCH BIBLE COMMENTARY

Old Testament
Genesis, by Eugene F. Roop, 1987
Exodus, by Waldemar Janzen, 2000
Judges, by Terry L. Brensinger, 1999
Ruth, Jonah, Esther, by Eugene F. Roop, 2002
Psalms, by James H. Waltner, 2006
Proverbs, by John W. Miller, 2004
Isaiah, by Ivan D. Friesen, 2009
Jeremiah, by Elmer A. Martens, 1986
Ezekiel, by Millard C. Lind, 1996
Daniel, by Paul M. Lederach, 1994
Hosea, Amos, by Allen R. Guenther, 1998

New Testament
Matthew, by Richard B. Gardner, 1991
Mark, by Timothy J. Geddert, 2001
Acts, by Chalmer E. Faw, 1993
Romans, by John E. Toews, 2004
2 Corinthians, by V. George Shillington, 1998
Ephesians, by Thomas R. Yoder Neufeld, 2002
Colossians, Philemon, by Ernest D. Martin, 1993
1-2 Thessalonians, by Jacob W. Elias, 1995
1-2 Timothy, Titus, by Paul M. Zehr, 2009
1-2 Peter, Jude, by Erland Waltner and J. Daryl Charles, 1999
Revelation, by John R. Yeatts, 2003

Old Testament Editors
Elmer A. Martens, Mennonite Brethren Biblical Seminary, Fresno, California
Douglas B. Miller, Tabor College, Hillsboro, Kansas

New Testament Editors
Willard M. Swartley, Associated Mennonite Biblical Seminary, Elkhart, Indiana
Loren Johns, Associated Mennonite Biblical Seminary, Elkhart, Indiana

Editorial Council
David W. Baker, Brethren Church
Derek Suderman, Mennonite Church Canada
Christina A. Bucher, Church of the Brethren
Eric A. Seibert, Brethren in Christ Church
Gordon H. Matties, Mennonite Brethren Church
Paul M. Zehr (chair), Mennonite Church USA

Isaiah

Ivan D. Friesen

HERALD PRESS
Scottdale, Pennsylvania
Waterloo, Ontario

Library of Congress Cataloging-in-Publication Data
Friesen, Ivan D.
  Isaiah / Ivan D. Friesen
       p. cm.—(Believers church Bible commentary)
  Includes bibliographical reference and index.
  ISBN 978-0-8361-9440-1 (pbk. : alk. Paper)
  1. Bible. O.T. Isaiah—Commentaries. I. Title.
  BS1515.53.F75   2009
  224'.107—dc22
                                                    2009005025

Except as otherwise indicated, Bible text is from *New Revised Standard Version Bible,* copyright 1989 by the Division of Christian Education of the National Council of the Churches of Christ in the USA, and used by permission. NIV indicates Scripture from the Holy Bible, *New International Version* ® Copyright © 1973, 1978, 1984 by the International Bible Society. Used by permission of Zondervan Publishing House. All rights reserved. Abbreviations listed on pages 6-7 identify other versions briefly compared.

No part of this publication may be reproduced, stored in a retrieval system, or transmitted in any form or by any means, electronic, mechanical, photocopying, recording, or otherwise, without the prior permission of the publisher or a license permitting restricted copying. Such licenses are issued on behalf of Herald Press by Copyright Clearance Center, Inc., 222 Rosewood Drive, Danvers, MA 01923; phone 978-750-8400; fax 978-750-4470; www.copyright.com.

BELIEVERS CHURCH BIBLE COMMENTARY: ISAIAH
Copyright © 2009 by Herald Press, Scottdale, PA 15683
   Released simultaneously in Canada by Herald Press,
   Waterloo, Ont. N2L 6H7. All rights reserved
Library of Congress Control Number: 2009005025
International Standard Book Number: 978-0-8361-9440-1
Printed in the United States of America
Cover and charts by Merrill R. Miller

15 14 13 12 11 10 09   10 9 8 7 6 5 4 3 2 1

To order or request information please call 1-800-245-7894 or visit www.heraldpress.com.

To my wife, Rachel

Abbreviations

ABD	*Anchor Bible Dictionary.* Edited by David Noel Freedman. 6 vols. New York, 1992.
AD	*anno Domini,* in the year of the Lord, indicating the Christian era since the time of Christ
ANET	*Ancient Near Eastern Texts Relating to the Old Testament.* Edited by James B. Pritchard. 3d ed. Princeton, 1969.
AT	author's translation
BC	before Christ
BDB	*A Hebrew and English Lexicon of the OT.* Edited by Francis Brown, S. R. Driver, and Charles A. Briggs. Oxford, 1906, 1952.
ca.	*circa,* approximately
CBA	*The Carta Bible Atlas.* Edited by Yohanan Aharoni et al. 3d ed. Jerusalem, 2002.
CCW	*The Christian Conscience and War.* A statement by theologians and religious leaders with an introduction by John Oliver Nelson. Washington, DC, 1950, 1953.
cf.	confer, compare
chap./chaps.	chapter/chapters
COD	*The Concise Oxford Dictionary of Current English.* 7th ed. Edited by J. B. Sykes. Oxford, 1982.
e.g.	*exempli gratia,* for example
esp.	especially
et al.	*et alia,* and others
etc.	*et cetera,* and the rest
f.	feminine
GKC	*Gesenius' Hebrew Grammar.* Edited by E. Kautzsch. 2d ed. Oxford, 1910.
GNB	Good News Bible = Today's English Version
HADOT	*Hebrew and Aramaic Dictionary of the OT.* Edited by Georg Fohrer. London: SCM, 1973.
Heb.	Hebrew text
HWB	*Hymnal: A Worship Book.* Edited by Rebecca Slough et al. Elgin, IL; Newton, KS; and Scottdale, PA, 1992.
JB	Jerusalem Bible
KJV	King James Version of the Bible
lit.	literally
LXX	Septuagint, Greek OT
m.	masculine
NASB	New American Standard Bible
NCV	New Century Version
NHBD	*The New Harper's Bible Dictionary.* Edited by Madeleine S. Miller and J. Lane Miller. New York, 1973.
NIV	New International Version of the Bible
NJB	New Jerusalem Bible
NOAB	*The New Oxford Annotated Bible, NRSV.* Edited by Bruce M. Metzger and Roland E. Murphy. New York, 1991.
NRSV	New Revised Standard Version of the Bible
NT	NT

ODCC	*The Oxford Dictionary of the Christian Church.* 3d ed. Edited by F. L. Cross. Oxford, 1997.
OT	OT
pl.	plural
PTCY	*Preaching Through the Christian Year.* Fred B. Craddock, John H. Hayes, Carl R. Holladay, and Gene M. Tucker. Valley Forge, PA: 1992 (Year A), 1993 (Year B), 1994 (Year C).
RSV	Revised Standard Version of the Bible
SAW	*Spiritual and Anabaptist Writers.* Edited by Angel M. Mergal and George H. Williams. Philadelphia, 1957.
sg.	singular
TBC	The Text in Biblical Context
TLC	The Text in the Life of the Church
TNIV	Today's New International version
trans.	translated by, translation
v./vv.	verse/verses
WPM	*The Writings of Pilgram Marpeck.* Classics of the Radical Reformation 2. Edited by William Klassen and Walter Klaassen. Scottdale, PA, and Kitchener, ON, 1978.
WT	*Worship Together.* Edited by Clarence Hiebert et al. Winnipeg, MB: Christian Press, 1995.

Pronunciation Guide for Hebrew Transliteration

ḥ	ch (Scottish *loch*)
ś	s
ṣ	ts
š	sh
ṭ	t

Contents

Abbreviations 6
Series Foreword 13
Author's Preface. 15

Introduction to Isaiah 17

Part 1 (Isaiah 1–12): Testimony and Teaching

Isaiah 1:1-31	Rebellion, Repentance, Redemption	29
Isaiah 2:1-22	Word of the Lord, Day of the Lord	37
Isaiah 3:1–4:6	Corrupt Leadership and Its Replacement	44
Isaiah 5:1-30	The Lord's Anger and Judgment	52
Isaiah 6:1-13	The Lord's Holiness and a Holy Offspring	60
Isaiah 7:1-25	Royalty and Remnant	66
Isaiah 8:1-22	Call to Hope in the Lord	74
Isaiah 9:1-21	Judgment and Hope	82
Isaiah 10:1-34	The Lord's Power and Majesty	90
Isaiah 11:1–12:6	The Lord's Deeds Among the Peoples	98

Part 2 (Isaiah 13–27): The Nations and the Whole Earth

Isaiah 13:1–14:32	Nations Manifesto: Babylon	109
Isaiah 15:1–16:14	Nations Manifesto: Moab	118
Isaiah 17:1–18:7	Nations Manifesto: Damascus	124
Isaiah 19:1–20:6	Nations Manifesto: Egypt	131
Isaiah 21:1–22:25	Manifestos of Doom	139
Isaiah 23:1-18	Nations Manifesto: Tyre	148
Isaiah 24:1–27:13	Whole Earth Manifesto	154

Part 3 (Isaiah 28–39): Weal and Woe

Isaiah 28:1-29	Woe, Ephraim!	169
Isaiah 29:1-24	Woe, Ariel!	177
Isaiah 30:1-33	Woe, Rebellious Children!	183
Isaiah 31:1–32:20	Woe, Champions of Egyptian Help!	192
Isaiah 33:1-24	Woe, Destroyer!	200
Isaiah 34:1–35:10	Edom and Zion	207
Isaiah 36:1–39:8	Hezekiah's Face-Off with Assyria	216

Part 4 (Isaiah 40–48): New Day Dawning

Isaiah 40:1-31	God's People Comforted	231
Isaiah 41:1-29	Cosmic Judicial Inquiry	240
Isaiah 42:1-25	A Light to the Nations	248
Isaiah 43:1-28	The Lord as Redeemer	255
Isaiah 44:1-28	The Restoration of Jacob-Israel	265
Isaiah 45:1-25	No Other God Apart from the Lord	275
Isaiah 46:1–47:15	Who Has the Power?	285
Isaiah 48:1-22	Listen to This!	294

Part 5 (Isaiah 49–57): Servant and Scaffold

Isaiah 49:1-26	A Covenant to the People	305
Isaiah 50:1-11	Sustaining the Weary with a Word	314
Isaiah 51:1-23	The Lord Will Comfort Zion	320
Isaiah 52:1–53:12	Crown Prince of God's Kingdom	328
Isaiah 54:1-17	Covenant of Peace	338
Isaiah 55:1-13	Everlasting Covenant and Sign	344
Isaiah 56:1–57:21	Access to the Lord's Holy Mountain	350

Part 6 (Isaiah 58–66): New Heavens and New Earth

Isaiah 58:1-14	Bona Fide Piety	363
Isaiah 59:1-21	The God Who Comes	370
Isaiah 60:1-22	Everlasting Light	378
Isaiah 61:1-11	Good News of Liberation	385
Isaiah 62:1-12	The Lord's Salvation	392
Isaiah 63:1–64:12	God's Mercy Remembered	398
Isaiah 65:1-25	Decision to Seek or Forsake the Lord	408
Isaiah 66:1-24	Comfort and Hope	416

Outline of Isaiah 423
Essays 438
    Apocalypse 438

Atonement (see also Redemption, Redeemer) 439
Composition of the Book of Isaiah 441
Day of the Lord................................ 443
Glory 443
Hebrew Poetry 444
Holy, Holy One of Israel........................ 445
Justice and Righteousness....................... 445
Literary Perspective 446
Messenger Formula 447
Messiah, Messianic Hope 447
Redemption, Redeemer 448
Remnant....................................... 449
Righteousness (see Justice and Righteousness) 445
Sabbath Observance............................ 450
Servant, Servants............................... 451
Shalom 451
Steadfast Love.................................. 452
War, Warfare................................... 452
Woe Announcement............................. 455
Wrath of God 455
Zion 457

Map of Palestine for Isaiah 459
Map of the Ancient Near East for Isaiah 460
Bibliography 461
Index of Ancient Sources 470
The Author 479

Series Foreword

The Believers Church Bible Commentary Series makes available a new tool for basic Bible study. It is published for all who seek more fully to understand the original message of Scripture and its meaning for today—Sunday school teachers, members of Bible study groups, students, pastors, and others. The series is based on the conviction that God is still speaking to all who will listen, and that the Holy Spirit makes the Word a living and authoritative guide for all who want to know and do God's will.

The desire to help as wide a range of readers as possible has determined the approach of the writers. Since no blocks of biblical text are provided, readers may continue to use the translation with which they are most familiar. The writers of the series use the *New Revised Standard Version*, the *Revised Standard Version*, the *New International Version*, and the *Today's New International Version* on a comparative basis. They indicate which text they follow most closely and where they make their own translations. The writers have not worked alone, but in consultation with select counselors, the series' editors, and the Editorial Council.

Every volume illuminates the Scriptures; provides necessary theological, sociological, and ethical meanings; and, in general, makes "the rough places plain." Critical issues are not avoided, but neither are they moved into the foreground as debates among scholars. Each section offers explanatory notes, followed by focused articles, "The Text in Biblical Context" and "The Text in the Life of the Church."

The term *believers church* has often been used in the history of the church. Since the sixteenth century, it has frequently been applied to the Anabaptists and later the Mennonites, as well as to the Church of the Brethren and similar groups. As a descriptive term, it includes more than Mennonites and Brethren. *Believers church* now represents specific theological understandings, such as believers baptism, commitment to the Rule of Christ in Matthew 18:15-20 as crucial for church membership, belief in the power of love in all relationships, and willingness to follow Christ in the way of the cross. The writers chosen for the series stand in this tradition.

Believers church people have always been known for their emphasis on obedience to the simple meaning of Scripture. Because of this, they do not have a long history of deep historical-critical biblical scholarship. This series attempts to be faithful to the Scriptures while also taking archaeology and current biblical studies seriously. Doing this means that at many points the writers will not differ greatly from interpretations that can be found in many other good commentaries. Yet these writers share basic convictions about Christ, the church and its mission, God and history, human nature, the Christian life, and other doctrines. These presuppositions do shape a writer's interpretation of Scripture. Thus this series, like all other commentaries, stands within a specific historical church tradition.

Many in this stream of the church have expressed a need for help in Bible study. This is justification enough to produce the Believers Church Bible Commentary. Nevertheless, the Holy Spirit is not bound to any tradition. May this series be an instrument in breaking down walls between Christians in North America and around the world, bringing new joy in obedience through a fuller understanding of the Word.

—The Editorial Council

Author's Preface

My first serious look at the book of Isaiah took place in a seminar taught by Professor Brian Peckham at Regis College in Toronto in the spring of 1982. I am indebted to Professor Peckham for his insistence on giving priority to careful analysis of the text apart from emendation and conjecture as the point-of-departure for serious thinking about the Bible. He always encouraged me to be patient with myself and with the biblical text.

I am interested in how the interpretation of the book of Isaiah is carried out and lived out today in communities of faith for whom the Bible is a central aspect of faith and life.

Two Old Testament editors of the Believers Church Bible Commentary series have given me guidance in the Isaiah commentary project. Elmer Martens, now Professor Emeritus at Mennonite Brethren Biblical Seminary in Fresno, California, read the first draft of the entire manuscript and offered constructive criticism at many places. I am indebted to his patience and encouragement. Douglas Miller, Professor of Biblical and Religious Studies at Tabor College in Hillsboro, Kansas, took over the editing of the Old Testament part of the commentary series in 2004. He has had to pick up my Isaiah commentary project midstream and see it through to completion. My wife, Rachel, an editor in her own right, read much of the commentary as I was working on it. Her insights and suggestions were always helpful to me.

I received encouragement for this project from two congregations that I have served in pastoral ministry with my wife, Rachel: the Oak Hill Mennonite Church in Winston-Salem, North Carolina; and the Hutterthal Mennonite Church in rural Freeman, South Dakota. In the

Freeman community I organized an Isaiah project working group made up of Mennonites from the Freeman congregations that read parts of the first draft of my manuscript and offered many helpful comments. The group met six times a year from late 1999 until early 2003 and included Anette Eisenbeis, Walter Epp, Monica Friesen, Harold Hofer, Phyllis Hofer, Lois Janzen Preheim, Les Rensink, and Deloris Stahl. Two other persons—Daryl Dockter and Gwen Ortman—were part of the group for a shorter period of time.

Our meetings were occasions of good and interesting discussions as we searched the book of Isaiah, asking it to yield its meaning to us. The search did not always succeed to the extent that we had wished. Always more can be found as we search the Scriptures.

—*Ivan D. Friesen*
Bluffton, Ohio

Introduction to Isaiah

The power of vision is still with us today. It may be the power to imagine alternative realities. It may be an exceptional occurrence that conveys a revelation. It may be extraordinary perception or foresight. Isaiah's vision is a party to all three.

Imagine calling a head of state to trust God's power rather than the power of weaponry. Picture a vision of the night or an astonishing disclosure by day revealing a message of judgment. Think of a time when clear-sighted discernment opened the future to unprecedented possibility. Isaiah's vision carries the reader into the heart of God's purposes in the world.

Light to the Nations

It is impossible to read the book of Isaiah without noticing both its geopolitical perspective and its preoccupation with a distinct people. The geopolitical perspective is especially concerned with the empires northeast of Palestine in the Tigris-Euphrates River system (Assyria and Babylon) and southwest of Palestine in the Nile River system (Egypt). Interest in these empires is evident throughout the book of Isaiah.

While these empires are important in the book's geopolitical perspective, they are not the controlling feature. The projection of imperial power, with its emphasis on warfare, as the lens through which to study history provides a warped view of the meaning of history. In the same way the projection of imperial power as the lens through which to understand the work of God in history contributes to the subjugation of God's work to imperial standards.

The focus of attention in the book of Isaiah is concern for a distinct people with a particular relationship to God in the context of imperial interests. The mediating agent in this concern is the larger circle of the Isaiah prophetic tradition.

The concern for a particular people is most clearly stated in the name of the Lord as *the Holy One of Israel* (1:4; 5:19, 24; 10:20; 12:6; 17:7; 29:19; 30:11, 12, 15; 31:1; 37:23; 41:14, 16, 20; 43:3, 14; 45:11; 47:4; 48:17; 49:7; 54:5; 55:5; 60:9, 14) [*Holy, Holy One of Israel, p. 445*]. This name indicates a relationship between *Israel* as people and *the Holy One* as deity. The emphasis on God's holiness in the book of Isaiah arises in the vision of God's exalted greatness on his kingly throne in Isaiah 6:1-4.

The Holy One of Israel may at first glance appear to be concerned only with Israel. The witness of the book of Isaiah, however, yields an altogether different picture. The Lord is not only the God of a particular people but also God of the nations. This overarching theme may be expressed as the Lord's universal kingship (Lind: 199) or as his monopoly of power over history (Mendenhall: 1973). There are many places in the book of Isaiah where this view is evident (7:18-25; 8:5-8; 10:5-19; 37:23-29; 40:21-24; et al.).

The rule of God is revealed in God's speech and in God's signs. God's speech is evident everywhere in the book. Generally it is speech mediated through prophetic vision. It is through speech that the rule of God is exercised in the life of a particular people (often identified in the book of Isaiah as Judah-Jerusalem or Israel-Jacob). It is through speech that the rule of God is exhibited among the nations.

The book of Isaiah may also be described as a book of signs (cf. Brueggemann, 1998a:69). A sign is a symbol or a signal, usually other than speech, that results in communication. Through the use of signs, God's speech is confirmed (7:11, 14; 8:18; 19:20; 20:3; 37:30; 38:7, 22; 44:25; 55:13; 66:19).

The overall purpose of the book is to show how God's rule among his own people becomes the means by which the nations of the earth receive the blessing promised to Abram in Genesis 12:1-3 and reaffirmed during Abraham's lifetime (cf. Gen 18:17-19; 22:15-18; 26:1-5). And what was that promised blessing? In the first place, the blessing was on Abraham and his family—to become a great nation with a great name (Gen 12:2). To achieve such greatness, Abraham is charged to "keep the way of the Lord by doing righteousness and justice" (Gen 18:19). Righteousness and justice are to be lived out among God's people [*Justice and Righteousness, p. 445*]. In Isaiah the same language is used to indicate the Lord's way for his people (cf. 1:27; 32:16).

Second, the blessing was to move through Abraham and his descendants to "all the families of the earth" (Gen 12:3). In the book of Isaiah

Introduction to Isaiah

the swords-to-plowshares text (2:1-5) and the Servant Songs (42:1-4; 49:1-6; 50:4-9; 52:13–53:12), for example, move the promise toward a new internationalist outlook. A political vision of peacemaking, including issues of security and justice, is made available and accessible to the nations (cf. I. Friesen, 2003:74). The focus of the promise is most clearly stated in Isaiah 49:6, where the Lord gives his servant as a light to the nations.

Other Themes

It should be clear to the reader that while "light to the nations" constitutes a significant theme in the book of Isaiah, there are other important themes that present themselves. I have already mentioned "righteousness and justice" and "the Lord's holiness." To these could be added the themes of "remnant," "pride," "idolatry," "rebellion," "judgment," and "peace," among others.

The noun "remnant" occurs some fifteen times in the book of Isaiah (esp. in chaps. 10, 11, 14, 37). Allusions to a remnant are found at 1:9; 6:13; 7:3 and elsewhere. In Isaiah the "remnant" is a small group of survivors who serve as the nucleus of new and transformed people (cf. Gold and Holladay: 880) [*Remnant, p. 449*].

Pride as a theme in the book of Isaiah is best represented by the elevation of what is human and created above the glory and majesty of God (Isa 2). Humankind "attributes infinite significance to . . . finite cultural creations, making idols of them, elevating them into matters of ultimate concern. The divine answer to [this] cultural hubris comes in the disintegration and decay of every great culture in the course of history" (Tillich, 1957:51).

Isaiah's castigation of idolatry has its background in the prohibition of carved images in the Decalogue (Exod 20; Deut 5). Thus idols and those who make them are mocked and ridiculed (cf. Isa 40:19-20). But in Isaiah there is also an awareness of what idols symbolize. Not only are they sometimes made of silver and gold; they also symbolize the replacement of God by the material security that silver and gold provide (2:7).

Rebellion against the Lord is introduced early in the book (1:2-4) and appears in various forms throughout. The spirit of this rebellion is captured in 30:1-5, where the people rely on the political power of Egypt for their security rather than on the protection of the Lord. Reliance on anything except God's power and grace constitutes rebellion.

The announcement of judgment figures prominently in the first three parts of the book of Isaiah (chaps. 1–12, 13–17, 28–39). The Lord's judgment falls upon Jacob-Israel because of its rebellion (cf. chaps. 1–12), but the nations around Jacob-Israel are also recipients of God's judgment (cf. chaps. 13–27). While this judgment is harsh (34:5), it is more often construed as just (3:13, 14; 26:7-11). Jacob-Israel are also recipients of God's judgment (cf. chaps. 13–23).

References to peace occur in all six parts of the book. The meaning of peace in Isaiah is varied rather than uniform [*Shalom, p. 451*]. As a theme in Isaiah, peace indicates well-being. This well-being has a wide variety of applications, including peace that is based on justice (cf. 32:17, 18).

Organization of the Book

The book of Isaiah consists of 66 chapters, including some 1,292 verses. Most scholars see a break in these 66 chapters after chapter 39, yielding a two-part book (chaps. 1–39 and chaps. 40–66). Within each of these two parts there is a wide range of opinion about further subdivisions based on literary and content criteria.

For purposes of commentary and interpretation, it is important to recommend an arrangement of the larger work into its essential parts. I see the book of Isaiah falling into six parts (cf. Seitz for parts 1–3; Kaufmann for parts 4–6). There is continuity from one part to the next even when there is a change of focus and subject matter:

I. Testimony and Teaching (chaps. 1–12)
II. The Nations and the Whole Earth (13–27)
III. Weal and Woe (28–39)
IV. New Day Dawning (40–48)
V. Servant and Scaffold (49–57)
VI. New Heavens and a New Earth (58–66)

In the first part the prophet is introduced and the various themes of the remainder of the book are presented. The rebellion of God's children in 1:1-15 serves as a prologue and clue to the content of what follows. The twin themes of judgment and renewal unify chapters 1–12. On the one hand is the Lord's anger at Israel's rebellion, which resulted in Israel's exile. On the other hand is a remnant of God's people purified by the exile and forming the basis of a new Israel. This "testimony and teaching" is present throughout the book but receives its definition at the beginning. The first part ends with a thanksgiving psalm in chapter 12.

The second part is characterized by messages concerning the nations and the whole earth (13–27). An outcry concerning Babylon in 13:1-22 introduces this part. Whereas the focus in the first twelve chapters is on judgment of *the nation* (Judah and Jerusalem), the focus in the second part is on judgment of *the nations* (the ancient Near East as a whole, including Judah and Jerusalem). The so-called "Isaiah Apocalypse" of

Introduction to Isaiah

chapters 24–27 forms the conclusion to part 2. This is so, in part, because of the conclusion's return to themes introduced in chapters 13–14.

In the third part, "Weal and Woe," there is a return to the Lord's judgment of his people (28–39). *Weal* is an old-fashioned noun meaning "soundness" or "health" or "well-being." *Woe* continues to be used in modern translations to indicate suffering or grief and despair. A prologue to the third part announces judgment on Ephraim (Northern Kingdom) in 28:1-13. The interplay of woe and weal with regard to God's people characterizes this part. This interplay is often confusing, but it represents the conviction of the book as a whole that the Lord is his people's relentless adversary as well as his people's only hope (Brueggemann, 1998a: 219). The historical conclusion in chapters 36–39 illustrates the interplay of weal and woe in Hezekiah's experience.

Parts 4 through 6 each comprise nine chapters (40–48, 49–57, 58–66). Parts 4 and 5 have virtually identical endings (48:22; 57:21). The absence of peace for the wicked stated in these endings stands in contrast to the peace of God surrounding those who look to him for their security.

The fourth part speaks to the new direction that God has in mind for his people (40–48). The contrast between the Lord's resplendence and human transience introduces this part (40:1-11). The first servant song illustrates the Lord's intention to bring justice to the earth through one who has received God's spirit (42:1-4). The lively refutation of idols indicates that idolatry is a serious barrier to the realization of the Lord's intention.

The fifth part, "Servant and Scaffold," highlights the servant's ultimate end (49–57). This part is introduced by the second servant song and its sequel (49:1-6, 7-13), and it includes the third and fourth servant songs as well (50:4-9; 52:13–53:12). The servant, introduced in 42:1-4, now comes on stage! With great poise and resolution, the servant confronts the powers that be with the truth of God's purpose for humankind.

Finally, in part 6, there is a proclamation of "New Heavens and a New Earth" (58–66). The subject of fasting introduces this last part of the book (58:1-14). Thus true piety lies in the *practice* of one's faith alongside worship forms. The last chapters of part 6 move through contrasting themes of good news and divine vengeance to the transformation of heaven and earth (65:17-25) and the comfort of God's people in the midst of God's judgment (66:1-24).

Isaiah among the Prophets

In the Hebrew Bible the Prophets section falls into two parts: the Former Prophets and the Latter Prophets. The Former Prophets consist of four scrolls: Joshua, Judges, Samuel, and Kings. These scrolls were not written by prophets as we use the term, but by historians and, in particular, historians under the influence of the book of Deuteronomy. Nevertheless it is fair to say that these historians wrote with the intention of giving testimony to God's message for their times. Moses himself is called a prophet, and the law that Moses received and proclaimed to Israel is the standard by which the behavior of God's people is measured in the Former Prophets.

The Latter Prophets also consist of four scrolls: Isaiah, Jeremiah, Ezekiel, and the Twelve. These four scrolls are further divided into Major Prophets and Minor Prophets. Isaiah, Jeremiah, and Ezekiel constitute the Major Prophets because of the large size of each scroll. The Minor Prophets are made up of twelve smaller writings that fit into one scroll.

Christian readers will understand that the OT, the first part of the church's Bible, includes some books among the Former and Latter Prophets that are not in the Prophets section of the Hebrew Bible. These include Ruth among the Former Prophets, and Lamentations and Daniel among the Latter Prophets. In the Hebrew Bible, these books are found in a third section, called Writings.

The book of Isaiah stands among the prophets as "pastoral prophecy" (Berrigan: 1-4). The word *pastoral* refers to the spiritual care and guidance of a community of God's people. *Prophecy* refers to the proclamation of God's will and purpose for this people.

The pastoral role in a congregation is focused on relationships. The pastor, for example, must be able to provide spiritual care to people with differing and different social and theological convictions. In the church the purpose of the pastoral role is the formation of a community life in which the centrality of Christ is lived out in word and deed.

Prophecy in the OT is not primarily prediction and prognostication. It is first of all proclamation of God's word in the present and for the present. Pastoral prophecy urges pastors and people to engage in an accurate interpretation of the signs of the times. The insights gleaned in this way prevail upon pastors and people to render an appraisal of the times in which they live. The purpose of such an appraisal is to speak truth to power and not simply to be swept along and away by cultural values. The combination of prophetic and pastoral practice pervades the book of Isaiah "with moral clear-sightedness and courage under the threat of disaster" (Berrigan: 1).

The book of Isaiah stands as a remarkable record of God's word to his people in troubled times. What better example of this pastoral prophecy than Isaiah's proclamation to Judah's political and religious leaders that their covenant with death means invasion and conquest (Isa 28)? What

Introduction to Isaiah

better example than the proclamation of comfort to God's people near the end of the exile (Isa 40)? This makes that word especially accessible to our own troubled times, when the Lord's word continues to be the guide that leads his people on their way.

Book of Isaiah: Unity in Diversity

Various proposals about how to read the book of Isaiah have evolved over the past two centuries. Some have focused on an interest in the discovery of sources and the isolation and analysis of small literary units. Others have tried to identify literary forms and to trace these forms back to a preliterary stage where each form had its living context. Others have tried to be more synthetic and to understand how the different parts of the book were put together to form larger complexes (I. Friesen, 1990:1-3).

Alongside these proposals is a more conservative orientation marked by traditional and sometimes static views of exegesis. The three-volume commentary on Isaiah by E. J. Young may serve as a representative of this orientation. On the question of authorship, Young's view is that the eighth-century BC prophet Isaiah was the sole author of the book bearing his name (Young, 1969:3). For reasons that I shall explain, such a view disregards the rich complexity of the book's composition. As a result, genuine attention is not given to historical and theological divergences within the book, under the mistaken notion that theological faithfulness requires it.

I am equally critical of many postmodernist approaches that focus on literary analysis but ignore the theological content of Scripture as well as historical context. I am convinced that Scripture directs its attention to the object of its witness: the purposes of God in the world (cf. Childs: 4).

My approach seeks to be synthetic rather than atomistic. I see the book of Isaiah as a composite unity. It is not a simple unity that disregards the diversity that any reader can immediately see. At the macroscopic level, this diversity may be seen in the contrasting perspectives of the period represented by the Judean kings Uzziah through Hezekiah (chaps. 1–39; cf. 1:1) and the period illustrated by the Persian Cyrus some two centuries later (chaps. 40–66; cf. 45:1). At the microscopic level, this diversity may be seen in the dissonance between the vision of an age of peace in 2:1-5 and the reality of punishment for pride and idolatry in 2:6-22.

Nevertheless I do not regard this diversity as a fragmenting diversity. The book is not made up of loosely arranged fragments strung together by an editor! An author formulated the various diverse parts into a carefully structured whole [*Composition of the Book of Isaiah, p. 441*]. By this I do not mean to imply *single* authorship. The composite unity of the book recommends more than one author. The authors of the book of Isaiah were part of a circle of prophetic writing and commentary that produced the final form of the book as we have it.

The fountainhead of the book of Isaiah lies in a late eighth-century BC prophet by that name (1:1). It is not as important to know precisely which parts of the book were written by this author as it is to see him as both author and catalyst. As author, the eighth-century Isaiah wrote about the rebellion of the Lord's people and the judgment that lay in store for them, naming Assyria as the Lord's agent of judgment. As catalyst, the eighth-century author inspired an unnamed prophet during the Babylonian exile in the mid-sixth century BC who restated and refocused what his predecessor had written. Instead of judgment, this sixth-century prophet spoke of comfort and restoration. Perhaps another unnamed prophet was inspired by his predecessors to write during the Persian period (late sixth century) to emphasize purification as the object of the Lord's judgment.

By way of summary, therefore, while the relevance of Isaiah's message for his eighth-century audience remains intact, the final form of the book was shaped by a sixth-century author for a sixth-century audience. So one can speak of the historical situation of Isaiah's worlds (see accompanying maps): an eighth-century world and a sixth-century world.

A major regional political interest in the eighth century BC world of western Asia was the control of trade along the eastern Mediterranean seaboard (Hayes and Irvine: 17). Assyria was a major player in the exercise of this control, and the kingdoms of Israel and Judah were seriously affected by Assyrian expansion and aggression. Internally, Israel and Judah disregarded the fundamental tenets of social justice combined with genuine piety prescribed in Israel's covenant (cf. Gottwald, 1985:377-79). Isaiah of Jerusalem understood this faithlessness as a major component in the moral weakness of Israel and Judah, contributing to an Assyrian invasion. Assyria, he said, was the rod of the Lord's anger.

The sixth-century world of Western Asia is also reflected in the book of Isaiah and especially in the later chapters. The most obvious sixth-century reference, found in 44:28 and 45:1, is to Cyrus the Persian. Much of Isaiah 40 and what follows assumes the Judean exile in Babylon as well as an end to that exile. The prophet who speaks here is unnamed, but his purpose is to interpret what Isaiah of Jerusalem said two centuries earlier for the situation of the exiles and the end of their exile.

The arrangement of the book into six parts (see above) provides coherence to the flow of thought by paying attention to major literary markers and concentrations of subject matter. Most of the book is written in poetic style, with the result that coherence and flow of argument often give way to passion of thought and expression. This is as it should be, but it creates obstacles for the reader who wishes for greater understanding of the thought lying behind the passion.

Use of Isaiah in the NT

Christian readers recognize the importance of the book of Isaiah in the NT. In Luke's Gospel alone are some 45 allusions to or quotations from the book of Isaiah. The other Gospels echo this interest. Paul often quotes or alludes to this book in his letters (e.g., some 33 times in Romans). References to Isaiah occur most frequently in the Revelation to John (some 135 times in 22 chapters). These various references raise the question of just how the NT, in presenting Jesus, used and understood the book of Isaiah.

It is necessary to speak to this question in general terms rather than in detail. The writers of the NT were clear that in order to understand what God was doing in Christ, it was necessary to know the Scriptures. For these writers the Scriptures meant the Hebrew Bible or its Greek translation, the Septuagint. The NT writers searched these Scriptures for evidence that Jesus' coming was no mere accident of history or chance occurrence. These Scriptures, and Isaiah in particular, yielded the evidence they were seeking.

In Luke's account of Jesus in the synagogue at Nazareth, for example, Jesus claims the words of Isaiah 61:1-2 and 58:6 as the foundation for his own political and spiritual agenda (Luke 4:16-30). In his letter to the Romans, Paul argues from several OT texts, including Isaiah 11:10, that Christ became a servant of the Jews in order to incorporate the Gentiles into God's people (Rom 15:9-12; cf. Toews: 341). In the Revelation of John, as a final example, the many references to the Lamb reflect the language of Isaiah 53:7, as well as other OT texts (cf. Rev 5:6; 6:1; 7:9; 13:8; 14:1; 17:14; 19:9; 21:14; 22:1; cf. Yeatts: 116).

Influence of Isaiah on Judaism and the Early Church

This assessment of Isaiah's influence on Judaism and the early church takes into account their different interpretations of the Hebrew Bible. Because the church saw in one person—Jesus of Nazareth—the fulfillment of Jewish messianic hopes, it reread the book of Isaiah through that lens.

Judaism, remaining unconvinced of Jesus as Messiah, continued to read the book of Isaiah through the lens of its ongoing messianic hope. The source of this messianic hope was the Hebrew Bible and the book of Isaiah in particular (Albright: 378). But the object of this hope remained undefined.

During the centuries after the exile various schools of thought arose in Judaism. The first-century AD Jewish historian Flavius Josephus identifies four main groups ("philosophies"): Pharisees, Sadducees, Essenes, and Zealots. The Sadducees, who accepted only the five books of Moses as authoritative, did not adopt beliefs found in the larger Torah (Hebrew Bible). The Zealots, hoping to rid the Jewish people of their Roman oppressors by force of arms, looked for a Messiah who would be a revolutionary figure. They held that the Messiah would be revealed by their revolutionary action (*NHBD*: 440-41; cf. Organ: 33-37). The Pharisees, with their emphasis on an oral Torah alongside the written Torah, read Isaiah and the prophets through the lens of the law and its requirements. Their conviction was that God would reveal the Messiah in his own time and that through this Messiah the Torah would be fulfilled (*NHBD*: 441).

It seems likely that the Essenes, identified by Josephus, and the Jews of the Dead Sea Scrolls community at Qumran are the same or at least closely related. Some nineteen copies of the book of Isaiah have been found at Qumran. Most of these consist of fragments, but among them are two especially valuable scrolls, one of which is nearly complete (Goncalves: 470-72). There are also fragments of Isaiah commentaries at Qumran. One of these fragments comments on the messianic passage in Isaiah 11 and understands it to refer to a priestly Messiah figure (Vermès: 226-27). There is good evidence that Isaiah was esteemed by the Dead Sea Scrolls community.

Part of the first-century Jewish community believed that the Messiah had arrived in Jesus of Nazareth (cf. Organ: 37). As these believers in Jesus gradually established their own identity separate from Judaism, they began to be called "Christians" (Acts 11:26). Their reading of the Scriptures convinced them that the portrait of the "suffering servant" in Isaiah had found its fulfillment in Jesus.

Part 1
Testimony and Teaching

Isaiah 1–12

OVERVIEW

The first twelve chapters of the book of Isaiah bind together the testimony (*te'udah*) and the teaching (*torah*) of the Isaiah tradition (Isa 8:16).

Testimony is usually understood as evidence by a witness in response to questions by a prosecuting attorney. The testimony in Isaiah 1–12 declares that the people and leaders of Israel do not know the Lord. The evidence of this lies in their pride, idolatry, wrong worship, and lack of justice.

Teaching means communicating knowledge with authority. Instruction typically takes place through precept, example, and experience. The teaching in Isaiah 1–12 features the call to repentance, the promise of God's presence, purification through judgment, restoration beyond judgment, a messianic king and kingdom, a new world order resting on the Lord's instruction, a remnant to form the nucleus of a new community, and the Lord in his temple.

Isaiah 1:1-31

Rebellion, Repentance, Redemption

PREVIEW

The book of Isaiah begins by inviting the reader to understand that it is written as a vision. The vision may refer to the whole book or to part of it or to only the first chapter; this issue need not distract us. What should attract our attention concerns the *vision* that Isaiah saw (1:1), described as a *word* in 2:1 and as an *oracle* in 13:1. In each case the prophet saw something. We are given the substance of what was seen by means of written, verbal communication.

The vision concerns Judah and Jerusalem (the Southern Kingdom). The vision looks beyond Judah and Jerusalem, across no man's land to Israel (the Northern Kingdom), across international borders to neighboring states, and beyond these states to the power centers of the Nile and the Euphrates (in the introduction see "Light to the Nations"). But it returns again and again to Judah and Jerusalem as sign and symbol of God's activity and to the response of God's people to that activity.

The first chapter presents a picture of the Lord's children in full-scale rebellion. The rebellion against God centers on a mixture of ethical transgression and wrong worship in equal parts. Dire consequences flow from this rebellion. But beyond rebellion and consequences comes the call to repentance and the promise that redemption flows from repentance. This picture of rebellion, repentance, and redemption serves as a prologue to the first part of the book (chaps. 1–12) and to the book as a whole.

OUTLINE

The Lord's Rebellious Children, 1:1-15
   1:1-3   Rebellion
   1:4-6   Woundedness
   1:7-9   Devastation
   1:10-15 Wrong Worship
Repentance and Redemption, 1:16-31
   1:16-20 Call to Repentance
   1:21-23 Greed Has Displaced Justice
   1:24-26 Threat and Promise
   1:27-31 Redemption Versus Rebellion

EXPLANATORY NOTES

The Lord's Rebellious Children 1:1-15

Two summons call the reader to attention, each beginning with the verb *Hear* (*šamaʻ*). The first (1:2) calls on heaven and earth to witness Israel's rebellion against the Lord and to announce the consequences of this rebellion (1:2-9). The focus lies on the Lord's children (rebellious and wounded) and their land (devastated). The second summons (1:6), addressed to Israel's rulers and people, describes the root cause of the rebellion as religious and ethical (1:10-15).

1:1-3 Rebellion

The vision commences with a brief introduction (1:1). The recipient of the vision is a son of Amoz named Isaiah. This prophet lived and worked during the reigns of four Judean kings in the eighth and seventh centuries BC. The first of these four kings was Uzziah (783-742) and the last Hezekiah (715-687; Childs: 11).

The introduction leads immediately into a summons of heavens and earth (1:2). The summons may be compared to a lawsuit in which witnesses are served with a subpoena to appear in court. The prophets sometimes depict the Lord in litigation with his people (Hillers: 124-42; cf. Deut 32; Isa 1:2-3; Mic 6:1-8; Jer 2:4-13). In Isaiah 1:2-3 and in Deuteronomy 32, for example, there are similar words and phrases (Rignell: 140-58). Both Isaiah and Deuteronomy call heaven and earth to witness (Isa 1:2; Deut 32:1). Both regard Israel as foolish and senseless (Isa 1:3; Deut 32:6). This suggests that Isaiah stands in solidarity with Moses, calling heavens and earth as witnesses to God's raising up of a people and to this people's failure to understand the One who sustained them (cf. Delitzsch, 1:55-59).

The opening scene of the book centers on rebellion against God and defines this rebellion as not knowing God. Knowing God, in the book of Isaiah, means understanding God in relationship to his people, characterized much like the relationship between parents and children in a family. As in human families, the relationship in God's family has social, economic, spiritual, and legal facets, all of them overlapping.

Not knowing God means rebellion; it means rejecting the relationship. It may mean, in fact, accepting only part of the relationship—the spiritual part, for example (see 1:10-15). But knowing God in the broader sense means accepting the relationship in its fullness.

With knowledge of God as its topic, 1:3 is made up of two sets of parallel lines that are deftly joined by the association of *know* (*yada'*) at the beginning of line 1 (in the Hebrew text) and at the end of line 1. Israel is compared unfavorably to an ox and a donkey, loyal and faithful animals.

1:4-6 Woundedness

From rebellion the scene shifts to terminal illness and woundedness. Both, unattended by the usual remedies, follow on the rebellion described in the first scene. The compact images here describe an apostate people as diseased and afflicted with festering wounds. Rebellion against God wreaks havoc and destroys wholeness.

Although scholars have tried to link this rebellion historically to events in 734 BC or 701 BC, it is difficult to make a convincing case for one or the other (see the synopsis of history in the second half of the eighth century BC in Hayes and Irvine: 17-49). The more productive lines of inquiry are literary and theological. The word *children* in 1:4 continues the reference to the children in 1:2. Rebellion in 1:2 now focuses on forsaking the Lord: apostasy. This apostasy, defined as sin (*hote'*), is missing the goal of right living and right worship. And apostasy entails guilt, injury, and destruction.

Rebellion is depicted as abandoning the Lord, which results in estrangement from the Lord. Instead of a "holy nation" (Exod 19:6) or a "great nation" (Deut 4:7-8), Israel is a *sinful nation* (Isa 1:4).

The parallel questions at the beginning of 1:5 ask in a plaintive way why the people (addressed in 1:4) invite new punishment by continuing their rebellion. What follows does not answer the questions; rather, it is a description of the seriousness of the apostasy—not beyond repair, perhaps, but deep and dangerous (1:5b-6).

1:7-9 Devastation

In another scene shift, envisioning the consequences of rebellion, the imagery moves from woundedness to a land devastated and desolate. The text reads like captions for a photographic essay of a battlefield, the daughter of Zion alone in the center of the ruined land [Zion, p. 457]. Sodom and Gomorrah represent the epitome of death and destruction (1:9; cf. Gen 18–19). Standing between life and death, as it were, are a few survivors, a remnant. So hope rests on the slenderest of reeds, a remnant, and yet it is the Lord who keeps hope alive, who kindles new hope.

1:10-15 Wrong Worship

The address to the leaders and people of Judah and Jerusalem as if they are the leaders and people of Sodom and Gomorrah moves the poetry toward a climax. At the center of the peoples' rebellion lies satisfaction with sheer quantity of sacrifices (1:10-11), toleration of offerings to God coexisting with wrongdoing toward people (1:12-13), and practicing prayer and violence simultaneously (1:14-15).

It is surely true that the law prescribes sacrifices and offerings (Lev 1–7) and presupposes prayer (cf. Gen 25:1). The prophets, however, opposed a formal external worship carried on dutifully but without an interior ethical consciousness about doing the right thing (cf. de Vaux, 1961b: 454-56). Such an ethical consciousness was not limited to a rigorous personal ethic; it included also and especially a vigorously effective and articulate social ethic.

Isaiah expresses the deep emotion that God feels when his people offer superficial worship that fulfills the letter of the law but not its spirit. Does this mean that God's answer to prayer is conditional on the character of the petitioner (Isa 1:15)? Without repentance, prayer serves as a convenient tool in the hands of unscrupulous operators while remaining ineffective as spiritual armor.

At the core of the prophetic protest lies a revulsion for the mere repetition of worship that ignores ethical issues. This revulsion for sacrifice as a substitute for truth and justice places Isaiah in solidarity with Hosea (6:4-6), Amos (5:21-25), Micah (6:6-8), and Jeremiah (7:21-26). This aversion to wrong worship anticipates Jesus' teaching that reconciliation needs to take place if worship is to be credible (Matt 5:21-26).

Repentance and Redemption 1:16-31

The analysis of rebellion in the first part of the chapter provokes a call to repentance and the promise of redemption in the second part. A call to repentance opens the section (1:16-20). This is followed by the complementary themes of indictment and judgment (1:21-23, 24-26). A statement of promise tempered by further threat and punishment closes the chapter (1:27-31).

1:16-20 Call to Repentance

The call to repentance may be arranged in three stanzas (1:16-17, 18, 19-20). The call commences with a staccato-like sequence of nine plural imperative verbs (1:16-17). The first five imperatives (*Wash yourselves, . . . learn to do good*) refer to cleansing that flows out of right worship. This cleansing is not merely ceremonial holiness but also ethical holiness (NHBD: 265). The last four imperatives (*seek justice . . . plead for the widow*) refer to equity that flows out of right living (cf. Brueggemann, 1998a:18-19).

Following the initial call to repentance is a call to be decisive about the fact that sins can be cleansed (1:18). The comparison of sins to words indicating redness alludes to blood-stained hands. This is also suggested by the use of the same Hebrew root for the words blood (*damim*) in 1:15 and for being red (*ya'dimu*) in 1:18.

People and leaders are faced with a choice (1:19-20). As in Deuteronomy 30:15-20 the choice is between life and death (Brueggemann, 1998a:20). Willingness and obedience means yielding to the call to repentance and the appeal to reason. The consequence is eating the good of the land, a settled and peaceful life (cf. Delitzsch, 1:82). Refusal and rebellion, on the other hand, means spurning repentance and reason. The consequence of this choice is to be eaten by the sword, an allusion to the ravages of war. The imprimatur at the end of 1:20 gives the highest possible authority to the call to repentance.

1:21-23 Greed Has Displaced Justice

An indictment of the once-faithful city, now described as a prostitute, echoes the reference to daughter Zion in 1:8. Isaiah, along with Jeremiah (3), Ezekiel (16), and Hosea (1–3), illustrates Israel's moral defection by pointing to prostitution. It is clear that prostitution as moral defection represents personal degradation. But Isaiah's revulsion for prostitution should not obscure his outrage concerning murder, thievery in high places, and bribery among the population as a whole. These represent the failure of society to provide justice and security for its people. Such injustices on a social plane are equal to prostitution on a personal plane. Since the powerless are not protected, society falls into ruin.

1:24-26 Threat and Promise

Now the mood shifts from indictment to threat moderated by promise. A messenger formula introduces this warning (1:24a). The names of God in the messenger formula are striking: *Lord, LORD of hosts, Mighty One of Israel* (RSV). They impress upon the reader the authority of the address that follows. This address stretches over seven lines, beginning with a threat (1:24b) but continuing with purification (1:25) and concluding with restoration (1:26a). My translation seeks to preserve the force of the Hebrew text:

[24b]Alas, I will console myself on my enemies;	1
let me avenge myself on my foes.	2
[25]Let me turn my hand against you;	3
I will smelt away your dross as with lye;	4
let me remove all your alloy.	5
[26a]Let me restore your judges as at the start,	6
and your counselors as in the beginning.	7

The intent of the Lord's judgment is purification and restoration so that the city can reclaim its former names: *city of righteousness* (*'ir haṣṣedeq*) and *faithful city* (*qiryah ne'emanah*; 1:26b). The name *faithful city* repeats the same name in 1:21, thus bracketing the section 1:21-23, 24-26.

1:27-31 Redemption Versus Rebellion

The promise of redemption and the threat of destruction sets the tone for the last part of the chapter. Redemption rests on giving "due process" (justice) by the community as a whole. It also rests on truthful living (righteousness) by those in the community who repent. The threat of destruction is aimed at rebels and sinners, those who forsake the Lord (1:27-28).

The last two stanzas describe this destruction poetically, using botanical language (1:29-30) and a tableau of drought and fire (1:31). Judgment by fire is mentioned elsewhere in Isaiah with some frequency (e.g., 1:7; 9:5, 18, 19; 26:11; 29:6; 33:11; 64:11; 66:15, 16, 24).

THE TEXT IN BIBLICAL CONTEXT

Judah and Jerusalem

In the book of Isaiah, encoded in the reference to Judah and Jerusalem is a perspective of several centuries. This perspective remembers Judah and Jerusalem as an independent state and capital city respectively, with land and temple and kingship intact although endangered (cf. 7:1-16; chaps. 36–39). It also harbors a more recent memory of Judah and Jerusalem with land and temple in ruins and kingship "on hold" (cf. 44:21-28; 54:1-8). Finally, the perspective portrays Judah and Jerusalem as a new community scattered abroad, without land, and with temple and kingship radically transformed (cf. 58:1-14).

In the NT, Judah and Jerusalem occur together in Matthew and Mark, the spelling *Judea* in Greek deriving from Aramaic *yehuday* (cf. Matt 2:1; 3:5; 4:25; Mark 1:5; 3:8). They also occur together in Luke-Acts (cf. Luke 5:17; 6:17; 21:20-21; Acts 1:8; 2:14; 8:1; 10:39; 11:1-2, 27-29).

Jerusalem and Judea are first of all geographical markers in the NT. Judea is a territory of the southern part of Palestine and the region occupied by the Jewish people. Jerusalem refers to the leading city of Judea. Jerusalem and Judea, however, also serve as religious markers. They are the source of crowds that come to Jesus. Often when Jerusalem is mentioned by itself, it is a place of suffering, the place that killed the prophets, and the place of Jesus' own death (Matt 23:37; Mark 10:32-34). In the book of Acts, Jerusalem and Judea represent the starting point of the early church's witness.

In addition, Jerusalem served as the residence of the apostles and the site of the early church's first council (Acts 15).

Knowing the Lord

The book of Isaiah opens with an assumption that Israel ought to know who God is (1:3). This "ought" means that God's self-revelation to Israel occurred in ways clear enough to be understood by them. The "ought" also means that Israel had the capacity to respond but did not do so (cf. "Revelation," in *NHBD*: 613-14). The prophet describes this knowing in terms of the relationship between God and his people. The relationship between God and humankind may be seen already at the beginning of the Bible, yet it takes on a new dimension in the story of Abraham and Sarah and the ancestors of Israel. With Moses and the exodus, the relationship takes a decisive shape in the form of a people united by a common experience of slavery and liberation and by the revelation of God's law at Mt. Sinai.

Alongside Isaiah, Jeremiah and Ezekiel add a prophetic perspective to this kind of knowing. Jeremiah compares God's people, who "do not know the requirements of the Lord" (NIV), with wild birds who know their migration times (8:4-7). Ezekiel's oft-repeated declaration "They/you shall know that I am the Lord" refers to the recognition that the Lord exercises ultimate authority over Israel and the nations (Lind, 1996:380-81).

In the NT the relationship takes a new turn in the coming of Jesus, because now the way to know God is rooted in a historical person. The idea that the Lord "owns" his people in Isaiah 1:3 is reflected in the figure of the good shepherd who owns his sheep in John 10. The people know their shepherd because they recognize his care for them in a direct way.

Repentance

The call to repentance lies at the root of Christian experience. This is so because the human condition presents an intractable inclination to follow the call to survival and retaliation, which characterizes the animal kingdom as a whole (humans included). Over against this "call of the wild" rests the biblical call to repentance. In the OT, the call to repentance signals a call to turn from evil (Jer 25), to seek the Lord (Amos 5), and to learn to do good (Isa 1). In the NT, John the Baptist and Jesus proclaim repentance as the starting point if the good news is to be embraced. Paul appeals to the church at Rome to be transformed by the renewal of the mind so that what is good can be discerned (Rom 12:2).

THE TEXT IN THE LIFE OF THE CHURCH

Repentance and Regeneration

The problem of repentance in the story of God's people is the problem of transforming human behavior in ways that testify to genuine change in a person's life (cf. Wallis: 4-5).

In the confession of faith, written at Dort (Dordrecht), Holland, in 1632, there is a clear Anabaptist statement on repentance and regeneration:

> We believe and confess, that, since the imagination of [the human heart] is evil from [its] youth, and, therefore, prone to all unrighteousness, sin, and wickedness, the first lesson of the precious NT of the Son of God is repentance and reformation of life, and that, therefore, those who have ears to hear, and hearts to understand, must bring forth genuine fruits of repentance, reform their lives, believe the Gospel, eschew evil and do good, desist from unrighteousness, forsake sin. (Braght: 40)

Repentance and regeneration begin with the biblical call to turn from what Paul calls "the works of the flesh" (Gal 5:19-21). Such a turning includes sorrow for the destructive behavior that opposes God's kingdom, but it goes beyond sorrow. There also must be a turning to "the fruit of the Spirit" (Gal 5:22-26). Without a genuine change of behavior that follows the act of repentance, the power of religious experience collapses into meaninglessness.

In Isaiah 1 and in the Bible as a whole there are clear social dimensions of repentance alongside the personal dimensions. The social dimensions of repentance are often not heard in the North American church today. Evangelists who define sin primarily in personal terms often lose interest in the way in which the Bible and the gospel address the collective misdeeds and outrages in modern life (cf. Wallis: 18-37). Isaiah's call to repentance in chapter 1 of his book serves as a corrective to this loss of interest.

Isaiah 2:1-22

Word of the Lord, Day of the Lord

PREVIEW

In a world familiar with terror and war, Isaiah's vision of a peaceable planet is astonishing. It calls peoples and nations to a new order of human existence. The vision is situated as a preface to the appalling scene of human perfidy that follows it, as if to say that only such a vision offers a hopeful alternative to human treachery.

The contrast between 2:1-5 and 2:6-22 expresses itself in the bipolar theme of the chapter, *Word of the LORD, Day of the LORD.* The literary suture that brings the contrasting parts together appears in 2:5-6. The first part ends with an appeal to the house of Jacob to come with the nations to the Lord's mountain (2:5; cf. Seitz: 38-39). The second part begins with an address to the Lord asserting that he has abandoned the house of Jacob (2:6).

The two parts taken together form the bipolar message of the chapter. *The word of the LORD,* on the one hand, inspires nations and peoples to seek the Lord's instruction. The house of Jacob receives a call to do the same (2:1-5). *The day of the LORD,* on the other hand, goes out as a warning that human pride and arrogance stand in the way of God's purpose for all of humankind (2:6-22). The house of Jacob is not excluded from this warning. In fact, this "house" illustrates the fullness of human rebellion, in which God's own people have abandoned his covenant.

OUTLINE

Disarm and Dismantle, 2:1-5
   2:1-3a   Nations and Peoples Coming to the Lord's House
   2:3b-5   Swords to Plowshares

The Day of the Lord, 2:6-22
   2:6-8   Land Replete with Wealth, Weapons, and Wizardry
   2:9-10   The Lord's Terror and Glory (I)
   2:11-16   The Day of the Lord
   2:17-1   The Lord's Terror and Glory (II)
   2:20-22   The Lord's Terror and Glory (III)

EXPLANATORY NOTES

Disarm and Dismantle 2:1-5

Here is a call for a new world order, shared with the prophet Micah (4:1-5). The theme of this call is Zion as a gathering place where the nations (including Israel) will be taught the Lord's strategy for peace on earth.

2:1-3a Nations and Peoples Coming to the Lord's House

The opening line reveals the recipient of the vision as Isaiah son of Amoz (2:1). The first part of the poetic vision sees the coming of nations and peoples to the Lord's house on the Lord's mountain (2:2-3a). They will stream to *this* mountain, the site of the Lord's temple, not to some other mountain honoring some other deity (Lind, 1996:327) [*Zion, p. 457*. They will come at their own initiative. The convocation will have parts to play for the Lord and for the nations. The nations anticipate being taught by the Lord. This teaching may be understood to include explaining, showing, and stating the Lord's ways. The nations understand that this instruction has a practical application. Walking in the Lord's paths emphasizes the essential steps of practice.

2:3b-5 Swords to Plowshares

In the second part of the poetic vision, the intention of the convocation becomes clear (2:3b-4). The Lord's instruction takes the form of arbitration and adjudication between nations and peoples. The goal and objective is justice and peace. The evidence that peoples and nations are serious about walking in the Lord's ways is seen in disarmament, including dismantling the tradition of learning the tactics and techniques of warfare (2:4b).

The vision ends with an appeal to the house of Jacob to join the nations in the practice of disarmament (2:5; cf. Seitz: 38-39).

The Day of the Lord 2:6-22

In one of the most powerful "day of the Lord" passages in the Bible, the prophet employs picturesque language to make the point that elevating anything above the worship of God is intolerable in God's economy.

2:6-8 Land Replete with Wealth, Weapons, and Wizardry

The larger passage (2:1-22) begins by pointing to the interconnection between wealth and weaponry (horses, chariots) on the one hand and wizardry and idolatry on the other. The land is described as full to overflowing with all that is intolerable to the Lord (for a different interpretation, see Hayes and Irvine: 86). The verb to *fill* appears in the first stanza (2:6) and then three times in the second and third stanzas (2:7, 8). *Divination* (NIV; *soothsayers*, NRSV) is the practice of seeking to know the future by means of magic. This practice is prohibited in the Holiness Code (Lev 19:26) and the Deuteronomic Code (Deut 18:10, 14).

The text of 2:6-22 is difficult, and nowhere more so than in 2:6. The issue here is what to do with the initial conjunction *For* (Heb. *ki*). This conjunction may be seen as a connecting word linking 2:6 to 2:5 (as the NRSV displays the text) or as a word giving emphasis to what follows. I take *ki* in the latter sense. The pronouns *you* and *your*, then, refer to the Lord, as the NIV has translated the text. It hardly makes sense to have the house of Jacob forsake its own people (*the ways of your people*, 2:6). Rather, it is the Lord who has forsaken his people for all the reasons given (2:6-8).

Brueggemann's comments on this text are full of insight. The house of Jacob has assimilated religious and economic practices that contradict the Lord's covenant. The result is the amassing of wealth, which requires weapons to protect it. Wealth and weapons are based on an ideology of self-sufficiency, which excludes trust in the Lord. Such idolatry, created by their own hands, explains the Lord's repudiation of his people (1998a:28-29).

2:9-10 The Lord's Terror and Glory (I)

The poetry here, terse and even cryptic, contrasts the human situation with the Lord's exaltedness. Attention has now shifted from the house of Jacob to humankind in general (cf. *'adam* in 2:9, 11, 17, 20, 22). The subject of the command in 2:9—*Do not forgive (naśa') them!*—is the Lord, as in 2:6. The counsel against forgiveness expresses the prophet's exasperation with human seduction by material security, including idolatry. "Let them reap the consequences of their actions" is the substance of his counsel.

The prophet's counsel to the people is to withdraw from the Lord's awesome power (2:10). The last two lines—*from dread of the LORD/*

and the splendor of his majesty! (NIV)—appear again at the end of the chapter (2:19, 21). This repetition signifies the importance of God's fearful strength in the face of human infidelity.

The Lord's *dread* and *splendor* (NIV) may allude to a time of terror when people were forced to go into hiding in order to save themselves from hostile armed forces (cf. Clements: 46). Here dread and splendor are clearly signs of judgment for the apostasy described in 2:6-8.

2:11-16 The Day of the Lord

The theme of human fallenness in striking contrast to the Lord's exaltation continues in this well-known *day of the LORD* passage. Clements (45) sees 2:11 as an addition that breaks the link between 2:10 and 2:12-16. But it is better to see 2:11, with its repetition of *'adam* from 2:9, as the start of grasping the consequences of human arrogance. Certainly the Lord's day of exaltation (2:11) leads directly into the Lord's day of opposition (2:12-16).

For the LORD of hosts has a day . . . introduces a series of ten words of antipathy, each of which opposes pride and arrogance. These references to trees, mountains, battlements, and watercraft serve as metaphors of human exaltation at the expense of divine exaltation.

The use of the verb *lift up* (*nś'* used here in the sense of *forgive*) from 2:9 is developed in 2:12-16, describing what the Lord has a day against. He is against human exaltation (2:12, *niśśa'*), which displaces genuine humility. Smug security (2:13, *hanniśśa'im*) is compared to sturdy cedars and oaks, which nevertheless can be cut or burned down. He is against arrogant condescension. Even high hills (2:14, *hanniśśa'ot*), apparently, look down snobbishly on lower hills.

Why all the fuss about pride and arrogance? The book of Isaiah sees human pride and arrogance as the spiritual cause of invasion and exile. In its most basic form, human pride is the refusal to trust in God's power to save. Brueggemann points out that the "capacity to secure our own existence has not been turned over to us. The Lord has retained that" (1982:57). Idolatry represented by pride insists on securing human existence by any means necessary.

2:17-19 The Lord's Terror and Glory (II)

Following the ten words opposing pride and arrogance, the prophet summarizes human dethronement by using language quite similar to 2:11. Here also the Lord's exaltation is projected onto the screen of a future time, using the prophetic formula *on that day*. With this exaltation, idolatry, first mentioned in 2:8, will pass out of sight.

Caves and holes serve as places of escape (see v. 10). Elijah found refuge in a cave on Mount Horeb to escape the power of an enraged monarch (1 Kings 18). But the Lord found him and displayed his awesome power to the incredulous prophet. Humankind retreats from the divine energy. Here the Lord's *terror* and *glory* emphasize the contrast between the awesomeness of divinity and the pretentious character of human pride.

2:20-22 The Lord's Terror and Glory (III)

After presenting and developing the theme of human pride and idolatry brought down on the day of the Lord's exaltation, all that remains is to draw the appropriate conclusions. Although humankind will at last abandon its idolatry when the Lord rises to shake the earth, the reader is warned to be wary of human frailty. Humankind, after all, depends on the air to breath and is of little account when measured beside the Lord's breathtaking brilliance. In this power differential, humankind is completely outclassed.

THE TEXT IN BIBLICAL CONTEXT

Swords into Plowshares

Micah 4:1-4 provides the most immediate parallel to Isaiah 2:1-5, although they are not "identical twins." Scholars offer differing interpretations of the relationship of the two texts (see Bailey: 51-61, for her comments on this discussion). James Limburg has a fine article describing the journey of the swords to plowshares texts in Isaiah and Micah through Western history in action and artistry (1997). As "fraternal twins" the Isaiah and Micah texts share much in common, including the conviction that God's intention for the whole of creation is a world order free of the weapons of war, free of war itself, and free of the planning and preparation for war.

At the center of Isaiah 2:1-5 lies an interest in the nations and the peoples of the earth coming to the Lord's mountain for instruction (Micah 2:2 says *many nations*; 2:3 says *strong nations far away*). This hope in God's universal purpose for humankind is found elsewhere in the OT (cf. Gen 12:1-3; 18:18; 22:15-19; 26:4; 28:14; 1 Kings 8:41-43; Isa 9:1-7; 11:1-9; 42:1-4; 45:22-25; 51:4-5; 55:1-5; 56:6-12; 60:1-3; 66:18-21; Zech 2:11; 8:20-23; 9:9-10). In Isaiah 2:1-5 this hope is focused in a powerful call to peacemaking that serves as a loud and clear call to all nations and peoples. The reversal of this imagery is used in Joel 3:10 to announce the Lord's word of judgment against Tyre and Sidon and Philistia for their treachery against the people of Judah and Jerusalem.

The NT refines two important themes from Isaiah 2:1-5. The first letter of John (1:5-7) develops the theme of "walking in the light," not by quoting Isaiah 2:5 but probably with this verse in mind. In John's letter "walking in the light" means being in fellowship (living in peace) with one another.

Another NT theme in the spirit of Isaiah 2:1-5 is the proclamation of repentance and forgiveness in the Messiah's name "to all nations" (Luke 24:47). Isaiah 2:1-5 does not mention repentance and forgiveness, and it does not mention the Messiah as such. Nevertheless the Lord's universal purpose for humankind hovers in the background.

The call to peacemaking has among its roots Isaiah's vision of peace and disarmament in 2:1-5. The opportunities for creative and imaginative peacemaking and peace-building are boundless. These include promoting peace-building behaviors among students in schools, fostering a spirituality of reconciliation among diverse religious communities, or advocating for legislation and funding priorities that reflect a culture of peace (cf. the book on peace-building by Holsopple et al.).

The Day of the Lord

The poet in Isaiah 2:6-22 is familiar with Amos' reinterpretation of the day of the Lord (5:18-20) and with Zephaniah's elaboration of Amos' teaching that the day of the Lord does not mean a day of sweetness and light but a day of doom and despair (1:14-18).

NT eschatology [*Day of the Lord, p. 443*] develops the Hebrew prophets' revelation of the day of the Lord, although the language and teaching of the NT is closer to the apocalyptic style of the OT than the prophetic style. Jesus refers to the day of judgment in Matthew's Gospel (10:15; 11:22-24; 12:36; chaps. 24–25). Paul in his Letter to the Romans warns of "the day of wrath, when God's righteous judgment will be revealed" (2:5). He also refers to "the day of Jesus" as the day of Jesus' return and the end of the present age (2 Cor 1:14; Phil 1:6, 10; 2:16). The day of the Lord coming as a thief in the night (1 Thess 5:2, 4) explains Jesus' warning in Matthew 24.

The eschatological hope in the NT, birthed by the OT prophets, means that God's people live at each moment in God's presence while also looking ahead to the end of history (Tillich, 1963:395-96). An element of foreboding always accompanies any meditation on the end of history. But in both Testaments the future lies in God's domain so that God's people can live in the present and in God's presence in the confidence that "He's got the whole world in his hands."

Isaiah 2:1-22

THE TEXT IN THE LIFE OF THE CHURCH

The Problem of War

Jean Lasserre's *War and the Gospel* denies to the OT any positive contribution to a solution of the problem of war. He says that for the most part the OT is bloodthirsty and without the regard for human life found in the NT.

Lasserre admits that there is another thread running through the OT that is universalistic and challenges the conventional wisdom of warfare. Isaiah 2:4 and Micah 4:3 are cited in this regard. But he believes that these are exceptions to the rule of violence in the OT and that a nonviolent ethic cannot be derived from the OT as a whole.

Lasserre's view represents and perhaps reinforces a widely held perception of the OT in the church today. But this perception will not stand up under scrutiny. It is possible to reread the OT story through the eyes of the remnant that grasped God's will for humankind as an alternative to the conventional wisdom of warfare. Such a rereading understands that there has always been a fascination with violence. Violence in modern life is reported because it makes good copy and sells newspapers, not necessarily because it is the most important thing that is happening in the world.

Those who denounce the OT as warlike and bloodthirsty as well as those who embrace the OT as a resource for the ideology of warfare are called to reexamine this appraisal in the light of the teaching in Isaiah 2:1-5. Let the OT as a whole be read through the lens of this powerful poetry!

Witness to Peace

A significant witness to peace arising from the believers church tradition is a sculpture entitled "Guns into Plowshares" in Washington. The District of Columbia Metropolitan Police Department collected thousands of handguns in the 1990s, part of a plan to reduce violence in that city. Esther Augsburger, a Mennonite sculptress in Washington, suggested a "Guns into Plowshares" sculpture, and the police accepted her suggestion. So she and her son Michael fabricated a large steel plowshare on which thousands of handguns were welded. On the base of the sculpture, the inscribed text of Isaiah 2:4 witnesses to the call to peacemaking, issued by one of the great prophets of the OT. In the late 1990s I remember seeing this sculpture in a farmyard near Harrisonburg, Virginia, before it was moved to its permanent site at D and Fourth Streets NW near Judiciary Square in the nation's capital. Someday I hope to make a pilgrimage to Washington, to see this sculpture again and to renew my own commitment to Isaiah's vision of an end to warfare.

Isaiah 3:1–4:6

Corrupt Leadership and Its Replacement

PREVIEW

I can imagine the prophet standing in a courtroom, manacled, trembling with rage and foreboding, declaring in even tones that mask his rage:

> *By what right do you crush my people*
> *and grind the faces of the poor?* (3:15 JB)

With the rebellion of the Lord's people unmistakably clear (1:1-31) and the Lord's day against the high and mighty still reverberating (2:6-22), a picture painted in bold strokes now emerges that gives the landscape a clearer definition (3:1–4:6). Something like anarchy opens the scene in which dishonorable male leadership is removed and indicted (3:1-15). Disgraceful behavior by the wealthy women of Jerusalem leads to the removal of their symbols of insolence in the scene that follows (3:16–4:1).

Before the curtain falls, an abrupt mood change occurs. Language of removal gives way to language of cleansing followed by images of security that recall the Lord's leading and protection of the exodus Israelites (4:2-6).

This theme of the Lord's security (4:2-6) recalls the nations (including the house of Jacob) finding security in the Lord's instruction (2:1-5). In this way the two passages serve as a frame for all the scenes of judgment between them. While it is not always clear how frames work, here the frame presents the scope of God's grace (2:1-5; 4:2-6) in order to

Isaiah 3:1–4:6

enclose scenes of God's judgment (2:6-22; 3:1–4:1) that offer limits to human conduct.

OUTLINE

Removal of Support and Staff, 3:1-15
    3:1-5   Removal of Leadership
    3:6-8   Defiant Tongues and Mutinous Deeds
    3:9-12   Oppressed and Misled
    3:13-15   The Lord's Judgment
Removal of Security, 3:16–4:1
    3:16-17   Pride and Penal Servitude
    3:18-24   Removal of Finery
    3:25–4:1   Lamentation and Mourning
The Lord's Security, 4:2-6
    4:2-3   The Lord's Branch
    4:4-6   The Lord's Canopy

EXPLANATORY NOTES

A scene of anarchy unfolds in chapter 3, with leadership of the community in disarray.

Removal of Support and Staff 3:1-15

3:1-5 Removal of Leadership

The theme of 3:1-5 is the removal of life support. This means, quite literally, basic *physical* needs (food and water) and basic *communal* needs (leadership).

In the first stanza the Lord is described as the One who removes support of every kind (3:1-3). This refers to positions considered essential to social stability. In the second stanza the Lord himself speaks (3:4-5). I take the first person singular "I" in 3:4 to have *the LORD of hosts* in 3:1 as its antecedent. The Lord announces the effects of the removal of *support and staff* in terms of communal oppression and exploitation.

This six-line stanza (3:1-3) is arranged in three pairs of lines, each pair identifying an example of social disintegration. Boys and infants, incompetent as leaders, will nevertheless be placed in leadership roles (3:4). Neighbors with much in common to unite them will capitulate to tyranny, without the restraints of just government (3:5a). Civility and graciousness will disappear (3:5b, cf. Watts, 1985: 41). These examples of scandalous behavior prompted by God show the reality of judgment where honoring God is lacking.

3:6-8 Defiant Tongues and Mutinous Deeds

The removal of support and staff is followed by defiance and noncompliance. Pictured here is the random choosing of a leader, anyone with even a vestige of wealth (a mantle) ruling over a ruined landscape (3:6). But the chosen leader refuses the leadership that is demanded (3:7). An explanation for this behavior follows (3:8).

Rejecting the demand to *be our leader* (*qaṣin*) in 3:6 would apparently be "I will not be your leader!" Instead, the response in 3:7 is *I will not be a healer* (*ḥobeš*). The paraphrase offered by the NIV, *I have no remedy*, provides a reasonable interpretation. Since the foundation for leadership (*bread* = material support; *cloak* = authority) is missing, there is no remedy, and leadership is refused.

The explanation in 3:8 may be rephrased: *Do not imagine that freedom and order flow out of anarchy. Stumbling and falling flow out of anarchy*. This explanation returns to the focus on Jerusalem and Judah from verse 1. Now, however, the emphasis is not on what *the LORD* is doing (as in 3:1), but on what *the people* have done.

3:9-12 Oppressed and Misled

Three stanzas make up this section. In the first there is the classical prophetic cry of woe against evil deeds (3:9). Judgment is defined as the evil that people bring upon themselves. There is no sense here that the people are unchangeably evil. Rather, both the righteous and the wicked encounter the consequences of their deeds (3:10-11). The final stanza defines the people's oppression in terms of disastrous leadership (3:12).

Whereas 3:6-8 reads as description and anecdote, 3:9-12 has more of a courtroom air to it. The prophet speaks as a prosecuting attorney. A certain shamelessness characterizes the people's deeds, a haunting reminder of the flagrancy of Sodom's sin (3:9).

In the interest of fairness, looking out over the courtroom as it were, the Lord instructs the prosecuting attorney to tell the *righteous* (NIV; *innocent*, NRSV) that they need not worry: *They shall eat the fruit of their labors* (3:10; *deeds*, NIV). While it is the deeds of Jerusalem and Judah that constitute prima facie evidence against them, it is the deeds of the righteous that constitute prima facie evidence in their favor. The adjective *righteous* (*ṣadiq*) in the courtroom setting has the sense of being innocent in ethical conduct and character.

3:13-15 The Lord's Judgment

The courtroom scene now takes a central place in the flow of the poetry. The theme of God's people unites the two stanzas (3:13-14a,

14b-15). The Lord acts as both judge and prosecutor in the trial scene, a dual role not impossible in Israelite court decisions (Watts, 1985:43).

The Lord wears the robe of a judge in the first stanza (3:13-14a). The lawsuit (or case, Heb. *rib*) brought by the judge is addressed to the elders and princes.

The voice of the Lord as prosecutor is heard in the second stanza (3:14b-15). Here the elders and princes receive a four-point indictment for their inept guidance. (1) Destroying (lit., *burning*) the vineyard tops the list, anticipating 5:1-7, where it is clear that the vineyard is a metaphor for God's people, Israel (cf. Ps 80:8-19). (2) Confiscating property from the poor comes next. This is followed in 3:15 by two other indictments: (3) suppression (Heb. *daka'*, *crush*), and (4) repression (Heb. *ṭaḥan*, *grind*). These may well refer to high interest rates and self-enrichment through the use of political power, privilege, and position (Hayes and Irvine: 92). The prophets keep a conscious watch over the way the poor are treated (cf. Jer 22:13-17; Ezek 16:49; 18:10-13; 22:29; Amos 8:4-6; Zech 7:8-14).

Removal of Security 3:16-4:1

3:16-17 Pride and Penal Servitude

The theme of pride and its downfall from 2:6-22 reappears here in a statement of the Lord's intentions concerning the daughters of Zion.

In Isaiah 1:8 the phrase *daughter* (sg.) *of Zion* refers to the city of Jerusalem. The phrase *daughters* (pl.) *of Zion*, used only here, in Isaiah 4:4, and in Song of Solomon 3:11, refers to the women of Jerusalem in particular. In Isaiah 3-4 it is the wealthy women of Jerusalem who are chided for their pride.

The Lord matches the threat of punishment to fit the offense of the wealthy women, humiliation as the reward for haughtiness (3:17; Clements: 51).

3:18-24 Removal of Finery

Removal (*taking away*) is an important theme in chapter 3: removal of support and staff (3:1) and now removal of finery (3:18). The list of finery to be removed charts a course from opulence to indigence. All the tokens of wealth that inspire arrogance and mask oppression will be removed and replaced by the reality of want and destitution. The items in the list compare the grim circumstances of imprisonment and poverty with the former affluence and prosperity.

At the end of 3:24 the NRSV adds the word *shame* in order to complete the phrase *instead of beauty*, which appears to be incomplete in the Hebrew Bible. The word *shame* is found in one of the Isaiah scrolls found at Qumran (Watts, 1985:44).

Several versions understand the opening Hebrew word (*ki*) in the last line of 3:24 as a noun meaning *burning* (KJV) or *branding* (NIV). But this requires changing the sequence established in the verse (BDB: 465; cf. Watts, 1985:44).

3:25–4:1 Lamentation and Mourning

The dashed hopes of the daughters of Zion are expressed in 3:25–4:1. In contrast to 3:16-17, where the verbs and suffixes are feminine plural, referring to the daughters of Zion, in 3:25-26 the verbs and suffixes are feminine singular, referring to the city of Jerusalem. The punishment of penal servitude on the women of Jerusalem is now applied to the city itself, as is also true in the book of Lamentations (Jones: 243).

The situation in Jerusalem-Zion is one of death and devastation. Men at arms fall in battle. Breaches in the walls permit the entry of besiegers who ransack the city. Watts comments wryly, "Sitting on the ground belongs to mourning. But it also is a necessity when nothing else remains to sit on" (1985:46). The account in 4:1 serves to illustrate a desperate situation (as in 3:6-7). The catastrophe of war creates a scarcity of men so that women have to resort to audacious measures.

The Lord's Security 4:2-6

4:2-3 The Lord's Branch

The collapse of all human security on the day of the Lord's judgment (2:6–4:1) now spawns the creation of a divine security canopy over Zion-Jerusalem. This is the very same Zion-Jerusalem elevated in 2:1-5 as the site to which peoples and nations stream, to be taught how to dismantle the weapons of war as well as how to unlearn the art of warfare.

The point of view in 2:1-5 and here in 4:2-6 is that Zion-Jerusalem is exalted because the Lord is there. The Lord's presence serves to hallow the city as a place of security even as human perversity and aggrandizement threaten to destabilize this security.

The first stanza embraces two images: *the branch of the LORD* (*beautiful and glorious*) and *the fruit of the land* (*the pride and glory of the survivors of Israel*; 4:2). The two images allude to the joining of the Lord's purpose and the survivors' prospect. The gloriousness of the branch (possibly but not necessarily a messianic term) invites comparison with the Lord's glorious presence in 3:8, which the people spurn. The pride (*ga'on*) of the survivor's fruit invites comparison with the majesty (*ga'on*) of the Lord in 2:10, 19, 21.

The second stanza refers to these survivors who are *recorded among the living in Jerusalem* (4:3 NIV; cf. Hayes and Irvine: 96).

4:4-6 The Lord's Canopy

In the first stanza it is clear that a cleansed remnant is in Zion-Jerusalem (4:4). This remnant can be called *holy* (4:3) because it has been *cleansed* (4:4).

The concluding stanza uses the imagery of *canopy* and *pavilion* to talk about the Lord's protection (4:5-6). The word *canopy* recalls the bridal suite in one of the psalms (19:5) and in Joel (2:16). Here it is a protective enclosure for those who have come to Zion-Jerusalem (Hayes and Irvine: 97). The word *pavilion* recalls the temporary shelter where a family lived during the festival of weeks (Lev 23). It is here, then, that the Lord will teach the nations, through the survivors of his people, how to walk in his paths.

THE TEXT IN BIBLICAL CONTEXT

Removal and Restoration

Verbs of removal draw the reader to attention in Isaiah 3–4. The Lord exercises his authority to take away the "supports" of human culture (3:1, 18) and let human pride and defiance run their course. This removal has a redemptive purpose to it because the Lord's spirit of judgment and burning brings about another kind of removal—a cleansing of human villainy (4:4).

Cleansing and removal are not God's sole prerogatives in Isaiah. The call to *God's people* to cleanse themselves and remove evil from themselves acts as an antidote to wrong worship in 1:10-20.

In language reminiscent of Isaiah 3:1, Ezekiel is told that the Lord will break "the staff of bread in Jerusalem" so that the people will experience and fear hunger and thirst (4:16). The purpose of this judgment is to bring about an acceptance of the Lord's word of power (Lind, 1996:56).

Leviticus 26:26 also uses the language of the Lord's breaking the staff of bread in order to discipline his people for their hostility to him. The intention of discipline in Leviticus is restoration. The refusal of discipline leads to punishment. But even in punishment there is a call to confession of sin, with the hope of restoration ever present (26:40).

The spirit of burning as both cleansing and punishment (Isa 4:4) is expressed in John the Baptist's call to repentance, where baptism with fire is a cleansing fire (Matt 3:11-12; Luke 3:16-17). Nevertheless burning with unquenchable fire is reserved for the chaff, those whom "he who is coming" will winnow (cf. Mal 3:2-3).

In both Testaments there is a harshness about the reality of punishment for solidly entrenched rebellion against God, a harshness that sometimes obscures the grace of God. But God's grace is there for the observant reader to see.

THE TEXT IN THE LIFE OF THE CHURCH

Celestial Canopy Versus Nuclear Umbrella

The text invites the reader to imagine God's security as a protective canopy over Mount Zion, where pilgrims and worshippers have assembled. It is a secure place because the Lord is there.

The official ideology of Canada and the United States invites its citizens to imagine human security as a nuclear umbrella over a continental landmass. It is supposed to be a secure place because the Bomb is here.

The biblical vision of security has been largely unable to penetrate either the church or the state. This vision, symbolized in Isaiah by the beating of swords into plowshares in chapter 2 and by the celestial canopy in chapter 4, trusts implicitly in God's power to save *apart from* the use or threat of weapons of mass destruction.

The swords-into-plowshares symbolism is a clear turning away from violence as a means toward an end. Its spiritual underpinning is a word of instruction from the Lord. This symbolism deserves much greater attention in synagogue and church, which have preserved it, than it has received.

The celestial canopy symbolism is inspired by the exodus narrative, where the Lord's presence is seen as a pillar of cloud by day and a pillar of fire by night (Exod 13–14).

The symbolism of a celestial canopy in Isaiah 4:5 in concert with the swords-into-plowshares symbolism of Isaiah 2:4 invites reflection on God's protection and how this security umbrella works in practical situations. Will not the invading barbarians simply flatten the umbrella? Is not Isaiah simply anticipating the arrival of an eschatological kingdom (Dekar: 329) rather than calling for a new community in the present based on a new ethic?

The model for the celestial canopy image lies in the marriage feast, which anticipates home and family. Security in that setting arises from faithful relationships and secure residence. Although the "right to bear arms" appeals to a kind of security that idealizes the recourse to lethal violence, this is alien to the foundation for home and family.

The model for swords-into-plowshares lies in an active disarmament, which anticipates the larger arena of peoples and nations. Security in that setting also arises from faithful relationships and secure residence.

Isaiah 3:1–4:6

Consider how faithful relationships and secure residence share common ground. Both have their home in a spiritual framework (the Lord's teaching on disarmament and the Lord's creation of a pavilion) where God's miracle is given first place.

Isaiah 5:1-30

The Lord's Anger and Judgment

PREVIEW

The breadth of emotion in this chapter stretches from love song at the beginning to death knell at the end. Between these extremes lie six woes (5:8, 11, 18, 20, 21, 22 NIV, KJV) spelling out the weary possibilities for living outside of God's justice and righteousness. Four *therefores* (5:13, 14, 24, 25) trace the consequences of this rebellion.

The vineyard song at the beginning quickly sours as it compares expectations with results (5:1-7). Woes and therefores detail the results and allude to the effects (5:8-25). To conclude the chapter, a vivid image of an invasion force combines with the image of a lion roaring as it captures its prey (5:26-30).

The agenda of Isaiah's text in chapter 5 spells out a verdict on the failure of justice in the social structures of the Southern Kingdom. This continues the courtroom scene and the vineyard imagery of 3:13-15, where social wrongs are identified. But it also harks back to 1:16-31, which concludes (like chap. 5) with an announcement of judgment.

The prophet draws attention to the causes of the exile. On the one hand these causes include a combination of wrong worship and general disregard of the Lord's deeds among the people. On the other hand they include the continuing practice of social injustice, which violates the covenant. Drawing attention to the causes of the exile serves to emphasize the theme of judgment as purification.

Isaiah 5:1-30

OUTLINE

The Vineyard, 5:1-7
    5:1-2   Song of the Vineyard
    5:3-4   Appraising the Vineyard's Harvest
    5:5-7   Removing the Vineyard's Defenses
Calamity, 5:8-25
    5:8-10   Woe! Greed
    5:11-17   Woe! Spiritual Indifference
    5:18-20   Woe! Deceptive Speech
    5:21-25   Woe! Graft and Corruption
Seizing Prey, 5:26-30
    5:26-28   Invading Force
    5:29-30   No Rescue

EXPLANATORY NOTES

The Vineyard 5:1-7

The vineyard portrait dominates the opening part of chapter 5, concluding with the vineyard falling into ruin (5:7).

5:1-2 Song of the Vineyard

Whether this is a song or a parable, the prophet speaks everywhere of the feelings of the bridegroom giving expression to disappointed love (Junker: 259-66). It is the first place in the book where the prophet speaks in the first person, which is distinguishable from the first-person speech of God (Seitz: 48).

The first stanza introduces and gives the opening lyrics of what is commonly referred to as the Song of the Vineyard (5:1). The prophet appeals to the reader for consent to sing a love song for his beloved. The opening lyrics of the song tell about a vineyard on a fertile hill. The *fertile hillside* (NIV; lit., *hill of oil*) indicates a prime location for producing fine grapes. The song's subject is the beloved's vineyard, but neither the beloved nor the vineyard are named.

The second stanza concludes the song, describing the preparations more fully and ending with dismay over the inexcusable harvest (5:2). The preparations included clearing the land of stones. Likely this does not mean *all* stones but mainly those that would hinder the development of healthy vines. The vines themselves were the choicest, indicating that no expense was spared to ensure an abundant yield. The watchtower added a further guarantee that sneak thieves or stray animals would be kept out.

With these preparations in place, the vine grower expected a yield of sweet-smelling grapes (*'anabim*). But to his dismay the vineyard yield a harvest of ill-smelling berries (*be'ušim*). So the reader's first impression is that of a determined effort on the part of a devoted vine grower to create a productive vineyard, yet without a harvest to reward effort with satisfaction. There is the moment of surprise at the end of the second stanza, when it is clear that all the work and care of preparation has gone for naught.

5:3-4 Appraising the Vineyard's Harvest

Now the vine grower himself, the beloved, speaks from out of the song, as it were, to the people of Jerusalem and Judah, asking for a verdict. The prophet Nathan's parable of the ewe lamb in 2 Samuel 12 offers a parallel. Nathan tells the parable to David, and David's answer reveals his guilt. Here the prophet sings a song that seems innocent enough to the people of Jerusalem and Judah. But then the prophet, speaking on behalf of his beloved, turns to the people for a ruling. The implied response of the people is that the vineyard should be demolished.

So the reader's second impression is that the relationship of endearment between the beloved and his vineyard has cooled. The vine grower in particular files a complaint that his vineyard has failed him. Was it the fault of the vine grower that there was a harvest of ill-smelling berries? Surely not!

5:5-7 Removing the Vineyard's Defenses

The vine grower then explains his next step: not destruction of the vineyard as such but a removal of its protective barriers so that it will be invaded by animals (5:5). The result will be the vineyard's return to its natural, wild state.

It seems clear that human culture is praised here; in this case it is viticulture. A question that may be asked is whether the natural order (represented by the untended vineyard) is disparaged. A short answer is that neither the book of Isaiah nor the Bible as a whole has a negative view of the natural order. The focus in the passage under consideration is the prophet's use of a dramatic vineyard image as he develops his main point about the identity of the vineyard, the vine grower, and the vineyard's fruit. So the vine grower's speech concludes in 5:6, describing the return of the vineyard to its natural state where hardy plants (briers and thorns), needing no cultivation, take over. Then, suddenly, the vine grower adds that he will withhold the rain. This represents the final blow to the agricultural project. It also represents the beloved's power over the forces of nature.

All becomes abruptly clear in the final stanza, where the prophet's voice reasserts itself, revealing the identity of the vine grower and the vineyard itself (5:7). The vine grower is the Lord of hosts, and the vineyard is the house of Israel and the people of Judah. The question is not simply one of identity, however, but a disclosure of substance. Justice and righteousness belong to the Lord (cf. Lev 19:9-18; Deut 10:12-22; 32:4; Pss 33:4-5; 72:1; 89:14; 97:2; 99:4; 145:17). At the center of the Lord's covenant with his people is the expectation that they will imitate God's justice and righteousness.

The people of Judah and Jerusalem, in fact, imitated the behavior of those who perpetrate violence and oppression. So the reader's third impression is one of the Lord's disappointment with his people. This disappointment is expressed in the play on words at the end of verse 7 between justice (*mišpaṭ*) and bloodshed (*mišpaḥ*), and between righteousness (*ṣedaqah*) and cry of distress (*ṣeʿaqah*).

Calamity 5:8-25

In the middle section of chapter 5, the interjection *Woe!* (NIV) introduces a cluster of four outcries against personal and social wrong rooted in spiritual disorientation (5:8-10, 11-17, 18-20, 21-25). These outcries form a pattern dominated by the theme of people and nobility alike in rebellion against the Lord and going into exile because of it.

5:8-10 Woe! Greed

The *Woe!* outcry in the first stanza addresses those who collect parcels of land into huge estates (5:8). The meaning of the harvest of bloodshed and cry of distress in the Lord's vineyard takes shape as an indictment of greed in the real-estate market, underscored by the Lord's pronouncement of an end to such greed. It concludes with an explanation (*until* . . .) that the result of this land amalgamation will be the destruction of the people.

The second stanza employs images of razed and untenanted houses and the meager harvest of an untended vineyard (5:9-10). The language of vineyard and poor yield echoes the song of the vineyard and its sequel in 5:1-7. The comparison between expectation and result at the end of 5:7 is now measured. The *ten-acre vineyard* (NIV) and the *homer of seed* refer to a square measure and a dry measure respectively. These ample quantities are placed under production. The *bath* and *ephah* refer to a liquid measure and a grain measure respectively; their scant quantities are wholly unable to support the conspicuous consumption of the wealthy elite.

5:11-17 Woe! Spiritual Indifference

The second *Woe!* outcry identifies those with a high regard for intoxicating drinks (5:11). The amassing of wealth encourages unrestrained self-gratification (cf. Brueggemann, 1998a:52).

Here is a correlation between the high regard for strong drink and the low regard for genuine faith. While unconcern for the Lord's work may be a result of other preoccupations and obsessions than calculated disregard, the effect remains the same (5:12). The prophet Amos has a similar estimate of the correlation between mind-altering drink and the abandoning of ethical behavior (6:5-6).

The next two stanzas, each introduced by the adverb *therefore*, state the consequences of disregard for the Lord's handiwork. The first *therefore* states the consequences in terms of exile (5:13). The phrase *lack of understanding* (NIV) does not mean simply being unaware of God's will but being unwilling to do it (Clements: 64). The second *therefore* employs vivid metaphors of Sheol to describe the extent and seriousness of this unwillingness (5:14). The people as a whole bear responsibility, but it is their leaders who are cited for special consideration.

The final stanza serves as a more general summary of the human condition (5:15-17). It restates the conviction from 2:9 about human ignobility in comparison to the Lord's nobility. In 5:15 Watts observes that humankind is brought into disgrace by Israel's behavior (1985:61). For the prophet, the Lord's just and righteous behavior stands as a beacon to both Israel and to humankind as a whole. The reference to justice and righteousness draws the reader back to the vineyard song and its sequel, where justice and righteousness define God's expectation. Lambs feeding among ruins alludes to the image of humankind finding comfort in the Lord's justice and righteousness (cf. 51:3). Bold imagery!

5:18-20 Woe! Deceptive Speech

The interjection *Woe!* appears twice in quick succession, focusing on those whose speech betrays their unfaithfulness. In the first stanza the *woe* addresses those who exhibit impatience with the hiddenness of God (5:18-19). They clamor for visible evidence of God's work. What is known has to be seen to be believed! The prophet describes them as people whose infidelity is persistent. The image of dragging (*mšk*) iniquity and sin along with ropes is hard to visualize. The image in the stanza as a whole is one of vigorous villainy cloaked in a disregard for the Lord's work.

In the second stanza the *woe* castigates those whose distorted speech destroys the truth (5:20). The first line constitutes a definitive statement about confusing good and evil. Lines 2 and 3 offer a poetic elaboration illustrating how moral confusion inspires muddled thinking in other areas as well.

5:21-25 Woe! Graft and Corruption

Three six-line stanzas make up this section. The first stanza opens with two Woe! interjections (5:21-23). The discounting of *those who are wise in their own eyes* (NIV) is not a judgment against wisdom as such but against wisdom rooted in arrogance and exalted self-importance. As in 5:11-17, where intoxicating drink leads to spiritual indifference, here strong drink leads to graft and corruption.

Two stanzas, each introduced by the adverb *therefore*, attach specific threats to outcries against wrong. In the first the subject is those whose self-satisfied wisdom and hard drinking lead to injustice (5:24). Consequences follow behavior! By cutting themselves off from the Lord's wisdom, in favor of their own, they put themselves under the Lord's judgment, like dry straw next to a fire.

In the second stanza the subject is the Lord, whose hand is stretched out in anger (5:25). Injustice brings on divine judgment! The last two lines of this stanza are heard again in identical form at the end of chapter 9 (9:12, 17, 21) and the beginning of chapter 10 (10:4).

Seizing Prey 5:26-30

A vivid poetic description of an invasion opens the last part of the chapter (5:26-28). Then the image shifts dramatically from an invading army to a lion capturing its prey (5:29-30). The effect is stunning!

5:26-28 Invading Force

The scene opens with an image of a draft call-up, a muster of forces, only here it is an enemy force that receives the prearranged signal to invade (5:26). The Lord, mentioned in 5:24-25, gives the signal. The next two stanzas have four lines of similar length, describing an invading force with no apparent deficiencies (5:27-28). Although the force is not identified, its identity is implied because of Assyria's reputation as having a well-disciplined army. To modern readers of Isaiah, the identity of the force is understood from the specific references to Assyria, especially in chapter 10, to which the poet has already alluded by means of the "refrain" in 5:25.

The closing scene of the chapter compares the roaring of the invading force to the power and ferocity of a lion seizing its prey and carrying it off (5:29-30). Here the inescapable allusion is to God's people going into exile and the image of Sheol swallowing this people (5:13-14).

Then, to make sure there is no misunderstanding, the image shifts to the roaring of the sea. The reader is invited to be a seafarer in a storm, looking for land and safety and seeing only stormy darkness illuminated by bolts of lightning.

THE TEXT IN BIBLICAL CONTEXT

The Fruit of the Vine

In the Bible the vineyard symbolizes the earth's bounty; it calls to mind the "land flowing with milk and honey" toward which the exodus Israelites were headed (Deut 26:15).

In the prophets the vineyard is used as a metaphor of God's people, with God as the vine grower. In Jeremiah, Israel as a choice vine degenerates into a wild vine (2:21). In the Lord's word to Ezekiel, the vine's wood is depreciated as worthless (15:1-8). Again in Ezekiel, the emphasis is on the withering of the vine's strong stem (19:10-14).

The psalmist, departing from the prophets' disparaging words about the vineyard, writes a lament pleading for the vine that the Lord planted and then abandoned (80:8-18).

Jesus' parable of the tenants employs vineyard language from Isaiah 5:1-7 but adapts it to his own ministry and message (Mark 12:1-12; cf. Matt 21:33-46; Luke 20:9-19).

The clearest reference to vineyard imagery in the NT is in John 15, where Jesus refers to himself as "the true vine." The people of God form the branches growing from the vine. God (the Father) is the vine grower. Vine grower, vine, and branches combine to produce a fruitful harvest. God's work of creating a people becomes a reality when that people bears the fruit of love. Love, defined by Jesus as the relationship of believers to one another on the model of the Father's love for the Son (John 15:9-17), complements the expected harvest of justice and righteousness in Isaiah 5.

In Galatians 5, then, Paul contrasts the works of the flesh with the fruit of the Spirit. The contrast between works and fruit is striking. Works are understood as death-giving; fruit is understood as life-giving. Those who belong to Christ bear the fruit of the Spirit.

THE TEXT IN THE LIFE OF THE CHURCH

Love and Justice in the Believers Church Tradition

The OT notion of justice in Isaiah 5 inspired the NT standard of love in John 15. The two texts together (in addition to other texts; e.g., Matt 25:31-46) provide the base line for a believers church social strategy. This social strategy, however, has often been characterized by sacrificial giving to people in need rather than challenging the powers that control access to and distribution of resources. "The imperatives to feed the hungry, to heal the sick, to visit those in prison, to be a 'neighbor' to those in need, which underlie and motivate the social concern of the church, are seen to derive from the ethic of love, not from the ethic of justice" (Brunk: 316). Brunk proposes to unite the two by defining justice as "nothing more than the proper distribution of love."

The movement among believers churches to bring love and justice together may be seen in Mennonite Central Committee's partnership in Wi'am (Arabic for "cordial relationships"), the Palestinian Conflict Resolution Center in Bethlehem, and in conflict-resolution teaching at believers church colleges. Christian Peacemaker Teams is an initiative among Mennonites, Church of the Brethren, and the Religious Society of Friends (Quakers); it supports violence-reduction efforts around the world (Chupp: 22-23). These are serious ventures in the believers church tradition to draw up and act upon a biblically literate notion of justice, which does not abandon the commitment to the biblical teaching on love of neighbor and love of enemy.

Isaiah 6:1-13

The Lord's Holiness and a Holy Offspring

PREVIEW

Four points of special importance highlight this chapter. Opening with a vision of the Lord's glory (6:1-4), the scene shifts to an account of the visionary's lips touched by fire at the hands of *seraphim* (6:5-7 RSV). The fiery touch produces a warrant to ensure that *this people* will reap the harvest of their disbelief (6:8-11). A fourth point moves beyond judgment to an accent on hope, a holy seed, to be seen against the reality of exile (6:12-13).

Often referred to as a call narrative, interpreters wonder why chapter 6 does not come at the beginning of the book, as any self-respecting call narrative should! The answer lies in the special *position* of this chapter in the composition of the book of Isaiah. Chapter 6 functions as a synopsis of chapter 1 by reemphasizing the ideas of hearing, knowing, and understanding the Lord's message. Chapter 6 also functions as a climax to chapters 1–5 by reiterating the Lord's holiness (5:16, 19, 24), the Lord's glory (3:8; 4:2, 5), and the Lord's exaltedness (2:12-14).

But the importance of chapter 6 is not only as a summary of the first 5 chapters of Isaiah. It also anticipates chapters 7 and 8 by announcing judgment. This is seen in 6:8-13, where judgment is described in terms of an empty land, a theme taken up in the following chapter (7:16).

Isaiah 6:1-13

OUTLINE

The Lord's Holiness, 6:1-4
Confession and Forgiveness, 6:5-7
Sending, 6:8-10
Exile and Hope, 6:11-13

EXPLANATORY NOTES

The Lord's Holiness 6:1-4

From a scene of roaring lions and a storm at sea (5:29-30), the reader is abruptly brought into a vision of a throne room, with the Lord seated among courtiers (6:1). The time of the vision is linked to the year of King Uzziah's death, which occurred not long after the middle of the eighth century BC (ca. 742). Uzziah reigned during a time of relative peace and material abundance in Judah. But the prophet Amos, a contemporary of Uzziah, understood the high price of this abundance. The high price was paid by a substantial majority of poor people, on whose backs Judah's prosperity was built (cf. Gottwald, 1985:345-48). The death of King Uzziah implies a negative value placed on kingship in the book of Isaiah. After Uzziah's death and throughout the reigns of Ahaz and Hezekiah, Judah had to face serious threats of invasion by external enemies. Kingship failed to deliver stable peace and security (cf. Conrad: 144).

The vision in Isaiah 6 begins with the prophet seeing the Lord seated on a throne. What does it mean that the prophet sees the Lord when it is stated elsewhere in the OT that a person cannot see God and live (e.g., Exod 33:20; cf. Judg 13:22)? The view prevails in the OT as a whole that God's magnificence and awesomeness rule out human visual observation. Even Exodus 24:9-11, which may be seen as an exception to this view, guards against the displacement of God's transcendence and mystery (Janzen, 2000:327-28). Thus in Isaiah 6:1 and 5 the prophet sees the Lord, but the text does not say that he sees the Lord's "face" (cf. Exod 33:23). Here too, therefore, the *seeing* of God is restrained and restricted.

The courtiers in Isaiah's vision are the *seraphim* (RSV; *seraphs*, NIV, NRSV). The "train" (KJV; lit., "skirts," as in Exod 28:33-34) that fills the temple would seem to be a reference to the Lord's robe (NRSV). The *seraphim* are resplendent creatures known only here in the OT (6:2). They may be understood as visionary transformations of the "olivewood cherubim" overlaid with gold of 1 Kings 6, lit up by the sun striking them (Lacheman: 71-72). The plural noun *seraphim* is derived from the verb *śarap* (*burn*), associated undoubtedly with the fiery ("venomous," NIV, NRSV) serpents of Numbers (21:6) and Deuteronomy (8:15).

The speech of the seraphim creates a momentous effect (6:3-4). The speech is marked by the noun *holy* repeated three times for emphasis:

Holy, holy, holy is the LORD of hosts;
his glory fills the whole earth.

The words *glory* [Glory, p. 443] and *holy* [Holy, Holy One of Israel, p. 445] have special importance in this speech. The glory of the Lord refers to the Lord's power and reputation (von Rad, 1962:239), just as the glory of the king of Assyria refers to his might and name (Isa 8:7). The Assyrian king's power, however, alludes to the power of the god Asshur transferred to an imperial power structure (Mendenhall: 45-47). In Isaiah, the Lord himself is king, but the power of the Lord does not translate into state power. It translates into holiness.

The Lord's holiness refers to his exaltation and therefore to his separateness from human perversity. In the Decalogue (Exod 20; Deut 5) and the Holiness Code (Lev 17–26), God's holiness is closely parallel to his standard of what is right and good. So the prophets were not inventing something new when they spoke of God's holiness in an ethical sense (Isa 5:16; 33:5; 61:8; Amos 2:6-8). Childs is right in saying that it is inadequate to deny an ethical quality to holiness in the OT (55).

The speech of the seraphim has an earthquake-like effect. The house (i.e., the temple) filled with smoke suggests the cloud often affiliated with divine appearances (Ezek 10:4). This first part of the vision in chapter 6 opens with a depiction of the Lord's robe filling the temple (6:1) and closes with the *seraphim* announcing that the whole earth is full of the Lord's glory (6:4). This image of fullness expresses both the completeness and sufficiency of God's presence.

Confession and Forgiveness 6:5-7

The prophet's response to the Lord's holiness is a recognition of impending danger and a "sense of displacement" (Seitz: 55), *Woe is me! I am lost . . .* (6:5). This is equivalent in value to a confession of sin. In the OT, God's holiness is encountered as mysterious power, posing a threat to human life. The Lord's warning to Moses that *no one shall see me and live* may be cited as an example (Exod 33:20). The sin is here identified as the human inclination toward wrongful speech; such speech compromises the relationship between God and his people.

The removal of this barrier requires a cleansing of speech. Fire is a means of cleansing (Mal 3:2-3). The fact that the fire is taken from the altar means that the cleansing arises from the symbol of the Lord's presence (6:7).

The seraph touching a live coal to the prophet's lips is a graphic and highly unusual method of cleansing (6:7). The prescribed way of experiencing forgiveness for sin was by means of offerings and sacrifices (Lev 1–7; esp. 5:1-13). Nevertheless the result is the same: the removal of guilt and sin by means of a symbolic action.

Sending 6:8-10

With his lips cleansed the prophet is qualified for service in the Lord's court as the Lord's spokesperson. Even so, the Lord does not issue an order to the prophet to fill that role. Instead, there is a request for volunteers, and the prophet steps forward (6:8-9). In the heavenly court scene in 1 Kings 22:19-23, a response to the call for volunteers comes from one of "the host of heaven," a spirit, not Micaiah, who has the vision. But in Isaiah 6, it is the prophet himself who replies to the call for volunteers.

The message given to the prophet often baffles the modern reader. The Lord, ever gracious and merciful toward his people, appears in this instance to prevent the peoples' turning and healing. An explanation lies in a careful observation of the text. The commission to the prophet begins with what must be spoken *publicly* as a warning *to the people* (6:9). This warning is enclosed in quotation marks in the NIV and the NRSV. Though the people keep listening and looking, their comprehension and understanding will lag behind. The people's unwillingness is part of the burden of the prophetic office (Seitz: 56).

Now the commission continues with what is spoken *to the prophet privately* in the throne room (6:10). Here the intent is pastoral. The prophet must not interpret the unwillingness on the part of the people to hear and comprehend his message as a sign of his failure or of God's malevolence.

Exile and Hope 6:11-13

The last part of the chapter includes the prophet's final query and the Lord's response (6:11). This is followed by a comment on the outcome (6:12-13).

The prophet's query *How long, O Lord?* suggests a degree of anxiety about the duration of such a commission (6:11). The Lord's reply does not focus on the duration of the commission, however, but on the dimensions of the penalty. The reply indicates that the dimensions are broad and deep. But it does not close the door on healing in the future.

The comment at the end of the chapter begins with a brief summary (6:12). The *emptiness* (from the stem *'zb*) of the land is an indication of the Lord's judgment upon it. This judgment theme is resumed in 7:16 by a further announcement of the desertion (from the stem '*zb*) of the land.

The conclusion of chapter 6, though obscure, points to a vestige of hope in an otherwise cheerless landscape (6:13). Both the *tenth* and the *stump* refer to a remnant in the land after everyone has been exiled. The holy seed (*zera'*) offers an alternative to the offspring (*zera'*) of evildoers in 1:4. The stump with its roots uncut symbolizes a surviving remnant (4:2-6), purified by fire yet miraculously with its faith intact, prepared to become a renewed people. This is a slender reed on which to build a theology of hope. Yet if one sees the root of hope *in God's purposes* for humankind, it is adequate!

THE TEXT IN BIBLICAL CONTEXT
Dullness of Mind

Preaching has the effect of intensifying deafness if the message or the messenger are unpopular. Does Isaiah 6:9-10 indicate a predetermined decision on the part of God to prevent repentance among those to whom Isaiah is sent? Does God's sovereignty make an end of human freedom?

When Moses and Aaron spoke to Pharaoh, seeking release of the Israelites from their bondage in Egypt, they were repeatedly denied permission (Exod 7–12). The "hardening" of Pharaoh's heart often focuses solely on God's predetermined decision to thwart Pharaoh's freedom to make up his own mind. An analysis of Exodus 7–12, however, discloses a complex interplay between Pharaoh's will and the Lord's purposes (Janzen, 2000:452-54).

In Ezekiel 3:4-11 the prophet and his message from the Lord are spurned by the house of Israel. Isaiah's challenge, like Ezekiel's, is how to communicate an unpopular message to a people who do not want to receive God's word of healing (Lind, 1996:92-93).

All four Gospel writers quote or allude to Isaiah 6:9-10 to illustrate the lack of receptiveness among Jesus' listeners (Matt 13:13-15; Mark 4:12; Luke 8:10; John 12:40). And in the book of Acts (28:26-27), Luke has Paul quoting Isaiah 6:9-10 to explain the Jews' unbelief. These examples, with the exception of John 12:40, rely on the Greek (LXX) translation of Isaiah 6:9-10, in which indicative verb forms (e.g., *For the heart of this people has become dull* . . .) are used rather than the imperative verb forms of the Hebrew Bible (e.g., *Make the heart of this people dull* . . . [Isa 6:10]).

Must human freedom and divine sovereignty be understood as simple alternatives? Is it not more true to the wide scope of the biblical witness that the two work interactively rather than alternatively? Thus God's sovereignty remains a clear tenet of biblical faith. But this sovereignty does not nullify human freedom. Divine sovereignty and human freedom are reciprocal rather than mutually exclusive.

THE TEXT IN THE LIFE OF THE CHURCH

"The Eye Made Blind by Sin"

Christian hymnals sometimes include the hymn "Holy, holy, holy," written by Reginald Heber in 1826 to the tune "Nicaea," composed by John B. Dykes in 1861. In Christian tradition this hymn appeals to the threefold *sanctus* (Latin for *holy*) of Isaiah to point to the oneness of God in three persons.

The text of this hymn contrasts the holiness of God with human sinfulness in verse 3: "Tho' the eye of sinful man/Thy glory may not see" (*Church Hymnal*: no. 28). In a more recent hymnal this line has been rewritten in inclusive language: "though the eye made blind by sin thy glory may not see" (*HWB*: no. 120). While similar in meaning, "the eye made blind by sin" shifts the message toward human responsibility for sin instead of a simple declaration of human sin.

That sin blinds the human eye to God's glory is well understood in the Bible. But the hymn does not assert that such blinding is without remedy. The saints take the initiative toward recovery of sight by letting their song rise to the Lord in worship (hymn, v. 1) and by acknowledging God's holiness and power as they cast "their golden crowns around the glassy sea" (v. 2), referring to Revelation 4.

A Template for Worship

It is sometimes said that Isaiah 6 suggests a template for worship (cf. Brueggemann, 1998a:58). Such a template may be seen in Isaiah 6:1-8. There is, first of all, (1) an expression of praise (6:1-4). In this praise the holiness of the Lord is given particular attention. Praise is followed by (2) confession (6:5). This is not precisely a confession of *sin*, but it is a declaration of profound unworthiness to stand in God's presence. (3) Forgiveness follows confession (6:6-7). The notion of forgiveness is captured by the "turning aside" and "blotting out" of sin and consequently a readiness to respond. (4) The response to forgiveness is a voluntary offering of oneself to be sent (6:8).

The content of the sending is located in the sequel that follows (6:9-13). This sequel is realistic about the difficulties involved in being sent by God. But it also hints at the promise that accompanies the sending.

Isaiah 7:1-25

Royalty and Remnant

PREVIEW

The book of Isaiah begins with a list of four kings of Judah: Uzziah, Jotham, Ahaz, and Hezekiah (1:1). King Uzziah is named in chapter 6. His death marks the year of the temple vision (6:1). King Ahaz is the subject of chapter 7, exemplifying nonreliance on the Lord. Ahaz ruled in Judah toward the end of the eighth century BC. Assyria was a serious threat during this period, and Ahaz faced internal pressure either to join Israel and Syria in a coalition against Assyria, or to form an alliance of his own with Assyria. Isaiah's counsel was to do neither but, instead, to pursue neutrality in external matters and to promote policies of social justice at home (cf. Gottwald, 1985:379). Ahaz refused Isaiah's counsel and followed the "wisdom" of conventional ancient Near Eastern politics, forming an alliance with Assyria.

Chapter 7 includes six segments arranged in pairs. The first four segments highlight the encounter between Isaiah and Ahaz. The first pair exhibits a contrast between *the fear* of Ahaz and his people, and the Lord's word through Isaiah to Ahaz *not to fear* (7:1-2, 3-4). The second pair combines the Lord's counsel through Isaiah to Ahaz to rely on God alone, followed by Ahaz's *nonreliance* and the *Immanuel* sign (7:5-9, 10-17). The last pair, then, portrays the description of an invasion and its aftermath (7:18-20, 21-25).

In the first part of the chapter, therefore, the counsel to Ahaz not to fear the enemies that threaten him occupies a central place, initially as a word from the Lord and finally as a sign from the Lord (7:1-17). In

Isaiah 7:1-25

the last part of the chapter, fearful images of an Assyrian invasion and its aftermath come into focus (7:18-25). Here the Lord brings disaster on king and people alike for their faithlessness. Nevertheless, for the Christian reader of the chapter, the figure of Immanuel rises above all else, directing attention to the ancient promise of God's presence with all who trust in him. This is Immanuel, both son and sign.

OUTLINE

Wind and Fire, 7:1-4
    7:1-2   Trembling Before a Storm
    7:3-4   Two Smoldering Stumps of Firebrands
Plot and Sign, 7:5-17
    7:5-9   Foiling the Plot
    7:10-17   Countersign of Immanuel
Invasion and Survival, 7:18-25
    7:18-20   Dispatch of Assyria
    7:21-25   Briers and Thorns

EXPLANATORY NOTES

Wind and Fire 7:1-4

The reality of fear is evoked with the image of trees trembling in a windstorm. The call to fearlessness is accompanied by the image of extinguished firebrands.

7:1-2 Trembling Before a Storm

The reference to Uzziah, grandfather of Ahaz, connects this chapter with chapter 6, where the temple vision takes place. A political crisis, first mentioned in 2 Kings 16:5, gives rise to fear on the part of Judah, both people and king. The NIV describes the crisis as an alliance of two regional powers, Aram and Ephraim. The Hebrew text is more graphic. *Aram has reached Ephraim* (JB)! Aram refers to the kingdom having Damascus as its center, situated northeast of Ephraim (Northern Kingdom). The coalition is ready to strike! Such a message strikes fear in the heart of Judah.

The 2 Kings 16 text indicates that Ahaz has introduced human sacrifice into the Judean political situation, making his own son "pass through fire" (16:3). In 2 Kings 16 this statement immediately precedes the account of kings Rezin and Pekah mounting an attack on Jerusalem (2 Kings 16:5 = Isa 7:1). In Isaiah 7 the attack on Jerusalem is immediately followed by the account of Isaiah and his son going to

Ahaz. "One son is sacrificed to the gods of war, another, signifying hope and endurance, accompanies his father on a mission of truth" (Berrigan: 36).

7:3-4 Two Smoldering Stumps of Firebrands

In the face of the king's paralyzing fear, the Lord sends Isaiah with his son Shear-jashub to Ahaz with an astonishing message. The Lord will not allow this hostile alliance to implement its plan.

The name of Isaiah's son, *Shear-jashub*, means *A remnant shall return*. This name is apparently intended to communicate the alternatives facing Ahaz. If Ahaz pursues the "wisdom" of conventional ancient Near Eastern politics and enters into an alliance with Assyria, there will be few survivors. *[Only] a remnant shall return*. But if Ahaz calms his fears and puts his trust in the Lord, there will be some survivors. *[At least] a remnant shall return* (Watts, 1985:90-91).

The advice not to be fainthearted (7:4) recalls the trembling hearts of king and people (7:2). The exhortation *Do not fear* runs like a thread through the Bible and the church as a pledge of God's presence (see TLC below). Here the pledge also rests on a realistic political assessment. Kings Rezin and Pekah have little power to carry out their scheme.

Plot and Sign 7:5-17

7:5-9 Foiling the Plot

Attention focuses on Aram and Ephraim in this segment. Their projected strategy was to set *the son of Tabeel* as a puppet king on the throne of Judah (7:5-6); he would mimic every policy dictated by Aram and Ephraim, allowing these invaders to exploit Judah. This strategy is unmasked by the Lord's word to Isaiah; it will fail (7:7-8). The Lord addresses a decisive word to Ahaz in the concluding lines of the last stanza (7:9):

If you do not stand firm in faith (ta'aminu),
   you shall not stand at all (te'amenu).

The verb *'aman* appears on both lines in different forms. Surely the essence of biblical faith finds expression in these words. In the face of invasion and war and death, the king insists on following his advisers and their conventional wisdom. "When push comes to shove," they might have said, "the sword is the basis of our trust. Trusting in the Lord will have to wait!" But Isaiah's words do not allow such evasive reasoning. Berrigan offers a powerful interpretation with his translation: "Hold on to the Lord; no other lifeline will hold" (37). The plural *you* of 7:9 contrasts with the singular *you* of 7:4, indicating that now both king and people are addressed (Watts, 1985:93). Security lies in the guarantee of God's adequacy rather than a frantic pursuit of military alternatives (Gray: 119).

The shattering of Ephraim in *sixty-five years* is placed in parenthesis in the NRSV. This indicates that an explanation in the form of a prediction is being provided, although the explanation is not clear to the modern reader. A frequent suggestion is that the prediction looks ahead to roughly 670 BC, when Assyria exiled many Ephraimites (cf. Childs: 65). Thus the Northern Kingdom, subjugated by Assyria in 721 BC, will finally be brought to a complete end.

7:10-17 Countersign of Immanuel

After Isaiah's initial meeting with Ahaz (7:3-4, 5-9), there is another meeting (7:10-17). In this second meeting, although Isaiah is not mentioned by name, he is surely intended as the bearer of the Lord's word to Ahaz.

Ahaz is offered a sign, which he refuses (7:10-12). In the OT a sign can be an ordinary (natural) event or an extraordinary (unusual) event of some kind. The language in 7:11 argues for something extraordinary, a miraculous sign. The context here indicates that the sign was intended to encourage Ahaz in his hour of decision. Scholars see in his refusal to *put the LORD to the test* a false piety (cf. Childs: 65). His refusal was actually a victory of realpolitik (the political art of the possible) over an alternative politics based on trust in the unseen power of God (the art of the imaginable). Ahaz is offered a sign from *the LORD your God*, thus giving him the benefit of the doubt regarding his piety (7:11).

In the second stanza the benefit of the doubt is removed in the reference to my God being wearied (7:13-14). This indicates an exasperation with Ahaz's faithlessness. Ahaz misunderstands the distinction between *testing* the Lord and *trusting* the Lord. The adverb *therefore* indicates that the sign to be given is a response to Ahaz's refusal of the first offer of a sign. The issues in 7:14 that continue to trouble interpreters include (1) the meaning of the sign, (2) the status of the young woman, and (3) the identity of Immanuel.

While the sign offered in Isaiah 7:11 is of the miraculous type, there is no indication that this is so in 7:14. The interpreter's interest surely lies in the sign in 7:14 since the earlier sign, refused by Ahaz, was never given. What did the sign of Immanuel mean for Ahaz? What did the sign of Immanuel mean for Isaiah? It was clearly a positive sign for Ahaz, a sign of assurance given to a king and people living in the dread of invasion and siege. The name *Immanuel* means "God is with us" (8:10), and since the Immanuel sign was given by a bearer of the Lord's word, it would have had authority as a word of assurance. For Isaiah, the sign of Immanuel is a visual and material affirmation of the essence of Israel's faith that God's presence displaces fear (cf. Brueggemann, 1998a:70).

In Isaiah 7 the emphasis rests on the birth of a son as a sign rather than on the identity or status of the son's mother (7:14; see TBC). The identity of neither the mother nor the son can be known from the evidence in 7:14. There have been numerous suggestions. One is that the mother-to-be was the wife of Ahaz and that the son-to-be-born was Hezekiah. This agrees with the context and offers the possibility for a messianic interpretation (Watts, 1985:99; see 98-104, where there are a number of useful essays on 7:14). Gottwald's argument that Immanuel was Isaiah's son is a plausible suggestion (1958:36-47). The church's interest in the identity of both mother and son in Isaiah 7:14 rises from its theology of incarnation. As such, it is a reinterpretation in "a new key" of the testimony in Isaiah (cf. Brueggemann, 1998a:70). Such reinterpretations update earlier revelations for new circumstances.

The third stanza moves from sign to promise (7:15-16). The *curds and honey* continue the promise of the sign by guaranteeing the survival of the Immanuel child. The withdrawal of the two kings (Resin and Pekah) means that they are forced to abandon their plot against Judah in order to defend their own borders from Assyrian aggression (Clements: 89). At the end of the stanza, the underlying lesson is that the apprehension concerning the two kings has no real basis in fact.

The fourth stanza identifies the larger field of concern in the Lord's word to Ahaz (7:17). The threat of Aram and Ephraim, the coconspirators of 7:1-16, recedes into the background. Assyria, not previously mentioned in the book, now makes its appearance. The Lord intends to engage Assyria as an agent of discipline upon the king and people of Judah.

Invasion and Survival 7:18-25

The last part of the chapter intensifies the language of threat. The adverbial phrase *on that day* introduces threats about what will happen to Judah in the future.

7:18-20 Dispatch of Assyria

The first threat, employing this adverbial phrase twice, focuses on an invasion. The reference to the *fly* from Egypt and the *bee* from Assyria means that the gathering storm will arrive from the great centers of imperial power rather than from the regional coconspirators (7:18). The fly from Egypt may be a reference to the Ethiopian pharaoh Pi (730-716 BC) (Watts, 1985:107).

The stanza that follows develops the pervasiveness of the invasion (7:19). The word *all*, employed as an adjective, pictures the extent of the force and the expanse of its occupation.

The last stanza indicates that the king of Assyria has arrived (7:20). The image of Assyria, humiliating prisoners of war by shaving off their hair, depicts the harsh treatment imposed on the Judeans by the Assyrian occupation forces (Hayes and Irvine: 139). The phrase *the hair of the feet* is a veiled reference to the genital organs (Clements: 90).

7:21-25 Briers and Thorns

Two more *on that day* adverbial phrases conclude the chapter by introducing conditions in Judah after the invasion. The first, in 7:21, introduces imagery of milk and honey introduced in 7:15-16. There curds and honey guarantee that the Immanuel child will have enough to eat (7:15). Here curds and honey guarantee the survival of the remnant in the land after the Assyrian devastation (7:22).

The second adverbial phrase, in 7:23, introduces the scorched-earth policy of marauding armies. Everything reverts to briers and thorns (7:23-25), as in the Song of the Vineyard (Isa 5:5-6).

THE TEXT IN BIBLICAL CONTEXT

Sign Language

In the Bible a sign is usually something material that signifies something spiritual. The Immanuel sign in Isaiah 7:14 signifies something that lies beyond the reality of a birth. The name stands for the truth of God's presence. In 7:13-14 the Immanuel sign trumps the refusal of Ahaz and the house of David to accept God's presence as a reality for political life. The authority of this sign asserts itself in later chapters of the book. In 8:5-10 Immanuel, referring now to Judah, is addressed (*O Immanuel*). A more general reference in 8:18 to the prophet and his children as *signs and portents* verifies the significance of names with special meanings.

Signs from God often occur in the Bible as guarantees of God's faithfulness. In the OT, signs describe ordinary phenomena, such as the rainbow in the clouds to signify God's covenant with Noah (Gen 9:12, 13, 17). Signs also accompany the Lord's extraordinary deeds in freeing the Israelites from slavery in Egypt (Deut 7:19; 26:8; 29:3; 34:11). Whether a sign is grasped as a sign *from God* depends less on whether it is miraculous than on whether it corresponds to the observer's inner faith and trust in God. For the person of faith, signs (extraordinary or otherwise) confirm the reality and power of God.

In the NT, Jesus' mighty deeds are designated as signs in John's

Gospel (2–11). The signs do not automatically generate faith, but they do reveal Jesus' true identity.

The Young Woman

The meaning assigned to the Hebrew word *ha'almah* in Isaiah 7:14 must take into account its various usages in the OT. The noun *'almah* means a sexually mature young woman (BDB: 761). Rebekah is referred to as an *'almah* in Genesis 24. The older sister of Moses (presumably Miriam) is called an *'almah* in Exodus 2. The book of Proverbs speaks of "the way of a man with a maiden" (*'almah*) as something beyond understanding (30:19). In each of these cases, the young woman's virginity is implied but not specifically stated.

When the Hebrew Bible was translated into Greek in the third century BC (a translation referred to as the *Septuagint*), the word used to translate the Hebrew *'almah* of Isaiah 7:14 was the Greek word *parthenos* (virgin). It is not clear why this word was chosen since the Hebrew word for virgin is *betulah*.

When Matthew (1:23) quoted Isaiah 7:14 in his account of Jesus' birth and infancy, he followed the Greek translation, in which he saw the announcement of a sign to Ahaz providing a suitable allusion to the wondrous birth of Christ. In this birth, God's intention was to liberate humankind by means of a powerless child rather than by the use of lethal force (cf. Watts, 1985:104).

THE TEXT IN THE LIFE OF THE CHURCH

Do Not Fear

The counsel not to fear occupies a prominent place in the Bible. From the assurance to Abram in Genesis 15 to the promise to John in Revelation 1 (and many places between), the counsel not to fear comes as a word from God.

People everywhere, in the church and outside it, experience fear in their lives. Often it is natural phenomena such as storms that inspire fear. John Wesley in his *Journal* tells about a storm at sea during an Atlantic crossing in 1735. He had observed the serious behavior of a group of Moravians (whom he calls "Germans") on board:

> If they were pushed, struck, or thrown down, they rose again and went away; but no complaint was found in their mouth. There was now an opportunity of trying whether they were delivered from the spirit of fear, as well as from that of pride, anger and revenge.
> In the midst of the psalm wherewith their service began, the sea broke over, split the mainsail in pieces, covered the ship, and poured in between

the decks, as if the great deep had already swallowed us up. A terrible screaming began among the English. The Germans calmly sang on. I asked one of them afterward, "Were you not afraid?" He answered, "I thank God, no." I asked, "But were not your women and children afraid?" He replied, mildly, "No; our women and children are not afraid to die" (35-36).

The absence of fear among these Moravians may be attributed to their centeredness in God's purpose for them.

Often fear arises out of terrifying human circumstances: national crises such as the invasion that Ahaz faced or personal crises such as people face who are robbed or raped or experience other horrors. In a Pax Christi filmed interview *A Nonviolent Response to Personal Assault*, two women, Angie O'Gorman and Maggie Pharris, talk about their experiences of facing personal assault nonviolently. Each situation entailed the element of fear. In personal assault situations, fear often triggers a response in the victim (anger, hostility, helplessness) that may actually escalate the violence. The victim should not be blamed for this. But in many cases the victim has the power to alter the situation and avoid a tragedy. Blocking the initial fear response becomes a priority so that this power can be used. In each of their cases, God gave them a word to calm their fears. Out of this calm center, then, they found words and actions to deescalate the violence.

Isaiah 8:1-22

Call to Hope in the Lord

PREVIEW

Speaking in the first person now, the prophet recalls three occasions when the Lord spoke to him. Each occasion has its own particular emphasis. The first lays stress on a child with a special name, interpreted as a reprieve from the threat posed by the Damascus-Samaria axis (8:1-4). The second focuses on warning Judah of an invasion by Assyria, and warning the invaders that God's presence can be discounted only at their peril (8:5-10). The third admonishes the people to fear the Lord rather than the Damascus-Samaria conspiracy (8:11-15).

Following these three occasions when the Lord speaks to the prophet, attention turns to the role of teaching and testimony in the prophet's circle of disciples (8:16-22). Testimony and teaching blend with waiting in hope for the Lord. This waiting in hope is to be lived out in the context of the Lord's hidden face and the people's confusion and distress.

The Hebrew text of chapter 8 has 23 verses. English translations end chapter 8 with verse 22 and assign verse 23 as the first verse of chapter 9 (see NRSV footnote). I follow the Jerusalem Bible (cf. NIV) in placing the first line of 9:1 in English—*Is there not gloom where there is anguish?*—as the conclusion to the thought of 8:21-22.

OUTLINE

Three Encounters, 8:1-15
    8:1-4   Name and Interpretation
    8:5-10   Submerging Flood

Isaiah 8:1-22

8:11-15   Admonishment to Fear the Lord
Teaching and Testimony, 8:16-22
  8:16-18   The Lord, Cause for Hope
  8:19-20   Hopelessness of Counsel from the Dead
  8:21-22   Trespassing Teaching and Testimony

EXPLANATORY NOTES

Three Encounters 8:1-15

In chapter 8 the poetry takes on an autobiographical cast. No auspicious grammatical feature separates the end of chapter 7 from the beginning of chapter 8. But there is something auspicious about the chain of *on that day* warnings in 7:18-25, preceding the personal revelation's poetic mode beginning in 8:1. The three encounters in 8:1-15 take the prophet's message to the people.

8:1-4 Name and Interpretation

The first encounter begins with an instruction to write a message on a large tablet in *common characters*. The writing surface is large, and the lettering is clear to all. Nothing needs to be hidden (8:1). The name *Maher-shalal-hash-baz* (*Spoil is speedy, prey hastens*) gives a thumbnail sketch of the hidden purpose of war.

The supplying of witnesses (Heb. root '*wd*) emphasizes the significance of the name (8:2). The priest Uriah is probably the same person spoken of in 2 Kings 16:10-16; Zechariah may have been the father-in-law of King Ahaz (2 Kings 18:2). Both were taken as witnesses because of the trust placed on them by their positions (Clements: 95). The allusion to witnesses also links the first part of the chapter with the second part, where the prophet's testimony (Heb. root '*wd*) is the foundation for a hope that rests in the Lord (8:16; cf. 8:20).

The prophetess refers to the prophet's wife (8:3). Their son's name corresponds to the name inscribed on the tablet. The name's interpretation is introduced with the conjunction *for* (8:4). The name signals not only the collapse of the Damascus-Samaria coalition at the hands of the king of Assyria; it also points to the brief time span before this collapse will take place. Assyria claims the coalition's wealth by right of conquest.

8:5-10 Submerging Flood

The autobiographical character of chapter 8 continues in the unfolding of another message of the Lord to Isaiah. The first part of this message focuses on the contrast between two *waters* (8:5-7a). *The gently flowing waters of Shiloah* (8:6 NIV) alludes to the Lord, whose gentle strength undergirds Judah's well-being. An intermittent supply of water flowed from the Gihon spring, on the eastern side of ancient Jerusalem, to the reservoir called the Pool of Siloam (Shiloah), on the southwestern side of the city. The *gently flowing waters* describes the apparent impotence of the Lord's promise in comparison to the power of Assyria (cf. Childs: 73). *The mighty flood waters of the River* (8:7 NIV) alludes to the Euphrates River and the Assyrian Empire, whose ample power will inundate Judah.

The people reject the Lord's strength because it appears insufficient (Gray: 146). They rejoice in the downfall of the coalition made up of Rezin, king of Aram (Syria), and Pekah, king of Samaria, but fail to notice the larger threat on the horizon. The Hebrew text refers to *the king of Assyria and all his glory* (8:7; *all his pomp*, NIV). Here the word *glory* likely refers to Assyria's allies.

The flood power of the river is expressed in poetic cadence (8:7b-8 AT):

1 *It will rise above all its streambeds*
2 *and overflow all its riverbanks;*
3 *it will inundate Judah, surge and swell;*
4 *until, reaching up to the neck,*
5 *its outstretched wings*
6 *will fill the breadth of your land, O Immanuel.*

Although the change from a flood metaphor to an avian metaphor is sometimes described as awkward (e.g., Clements: 97), its *outstretched wings* (line 5) continues its *streambeds* and its *riverbanks* (lines 1-2).

After addressing *this people* (Judah), the prophet now turns to *you peoples* (Assyria and its allies, 8:9-10). After their invasion, the invaders come face-to-face with a new and unanticipated reality described as the presence of God (*God is with us*). The invaders are taunted by the prophet to be discontented, to be terrified, to arm themselves, as well they might when they realize that *God is with us*. Their plans and threats mean nothing at all in the face of God's presence.

8:11-15 Admonishment to Fear the Lord

The third word comes to Isaiah individually (*to me* in 8:11) but the message itself addresses a group (*you* plural in 8:12-15). The persons addressed in the message seem to be Isaiah and his disciples. This is not stated in the text but may be inferred from the context.

The word *for* at the beginning of 8:11 provides a connection to *for*

God is with us at the end of 8:10. God's speech grows out of God's presence. The Lord's address to the prophet is accompanied by *his strong hand* (NIV). Watts suggests that *his strong hand* marks the passage as a hard saying (1985:120). It seems more likely that the phrase intends to emphasize the strength needed to banish fear and rely wholly on the Lord. On occasion Ezekiel refers to the hand of the Lord upon the prophet (1:3; 3:14, 22; 8:1; 33:22; 37:1; 40:1), and once it is the *strong* hand of the Lord (3:14). This follows Ezekiel's second commission, when the admonishment not to fear is emphatically stated (3:9).

In what follows, the focus of the Lord's speech lies in the application of two notions of fear. On the one hand Isaiah and his disciples are warned against fearing the *conspiracy* (8:12). Most likely this is a reference to the Damascus-Samaria alliance and perhaps also to the Assyrian threat.

On the other hand Isaiah and his disciples are exhorted to fear *the LORD* (8:13). This is a call to maintain a single-minded trust in God's strength. The specific language of trust rests on the notion of the Lord's holiness, which includes his kingship (Isa 6).

In the final stanza, warning and exhortation give way to consequences (8:14-15). Instead of the Lord as Rock of salvation for Judah and Israel, celebrated in the covenant with David (cf. Ps 89), the Lord becomes a stone to stumble over. The metaphor of God as a rock (of strength or refuge) is widely attested in the Hebrew Bible (e.g., Gen 49:24; Deut 32:4, 15, 18, 30, 31; 2 Sam 23:3; Ps 89:26). That this source of strength should become an impediment to faith is a commentary on the power of nationalistic ideology to displace the biblical vision of peace and security.

Teaching and Testimony 8:16-22

The last part of the chapter alerts the reader to Isaiah's teaching and testimony, which his disciples preserve.

8:16-18 The Lord, Cause for Hope

Testimony and *teaching* dominate the first stanza (8:16-17). *Testimony* (*te'udah*) occurs only here (8:16, 20) and in Ruth 4:7 (where it has a different meaning). Isaiah's testimony most likely has to do with attesting the name *Maher-shalal-hash-baz* (8:1-4) and the name's reference to the dissolution of the Damascus-Samaria alliance (Gray: 155). The word *teaching* (*torah*), in its broader sense, refers to the instruction of Moses. Here, in its narrower sense, it refers to the prophetic teaching of Isaiah. The securing of Isaiah's prophetic words gives rise to a time of waiting and hoping until the words are fulfilled.

The face of God, hidden from the house of Jacob (Northern Kingdom), shines through the children of the prophet, who are described as *signs and symbols* (NIV) because of their names (8:18; Clements: 101). Israel-Mount Zion refers to the Southern Kingdom. *I and the children* refers to the prophet and most likely to the children who are named in chapters 7 and 8. All of their names have meanings that attest to judgment in Israel for faithlessness as well as promise for a faithful remnant (Childs: 76).

8:19-20 Hopelessness of Counsel from the Dead

The difficulties of 8:19-20 are often magnified by commentators. It is best to grasp the seeking-out of the spirits of the dead as a contrast to the seeking-out of instruction and testimony. The conventional wisdom of the day argued for seeking the spirits of the dead in order to address the problems of the living. According to this wisdom, the taboo against consulting the dead may be set aside (8:19). By way of contrast, the unconventional wisdom of God lies in the instruction and testimony of God's prophet (8:20). The gist of this instruction and testimony is that waiting and hoping in the Lord occur among the living, distinct from recourse to the dead. *Surely, those who speak like this . . .* refers to those who advocate consulting the spirits of the dead (8:20). The phrase *will have no dawn* implies having no hope.

The reference to teaching and testimony in 8:20 echoes the same reference in 8:16 (in inverse order) forming an *inclusio* [*Literary Perspective*, p. 446].

```
8:16-17   testimony (te'udah) and law (torah)
   8:18   signs and wonders from the LORD of hosts
   8:19   consulting mediums and spiritists
   8:20   the law (torah) and the testimony (te'udah)
```

The purpose of an *inclusio* is often to emphasize the importance of a point at issue. In the two center lines (8:18-19), the point at issue is the contrast between hoping in the living Lord and consulting those who maintain contact with the dead.

8:21-22 Trespassing Teaching and Testimony

The first stanza alludes to the baleful consequences of violating the teaching and the testimony (8:21). Both the NRSV and the NIV add *the land* in 8:21 where the Hebrew text has only *it* (feminine singular). Interpreters have puzzled over this pronoun. The stanza depicts a person

Isaiah 8:1-22

in transit and under great distress of mind and body. Since there is a reference to *the land* (*the earth*) at the beginning of the next stanza (8:22), it is reasonable to add *the land* at the beginning of 8:21.

The second stanza concludes this dark outlook (8:22). I include the first line of 9:1 (8:23 in Heb.) as the last line of this stanza (AT):

> 8:22When they look toward the earth,
> they will see distress and darkness,
> gloom of anguish, thrust into thick darkness.
> 9:1Is there not gloom where there is anguish?

The language of gloom and anguish in the first line of 9:1 (as a rhetorical question) summarizes and concludes the mood and content of 8:22. The trespassing of God's *torah* leads to all kinds of rage and cursing, resulting in distress and darkness. Line 2 of 9:1 and what follows (beginning with *In the former time* . . .) introduce the passage in 9:2-7.

THE TEXT IN BIBLICAL CONTEXT

Teaching and Tradition

The writing down of a revelation (8:1) and its preservation (8:16) continues a custom found elsewhere in the biblical tradition. In Isaiah 30:8 the prophet is instructed to preserve his revelation in writing for future reference. Jeremiah (36:4-8) dictates words the Lord has given him to Baruch, who writes them on a scroll for public reading. Habakkuk (2:2) writes down a vision he has seen so that it may be read.

In the book of Deuteronomy, the Lord himself writes on the tablets of stone that Moses has carved (10:1-2). According to Deuteronomic law, the Israelite king is to "have a copy of this law written for him" (Deut 17:18), which he is to read and obey.

This self-conscious recording of what has been seen and heard finds expression in the NT as well. It is found in the introduction to Luke's Gospel (1:1-4) and in what may have been the original ending of John's Gospel (20:30-31).

Paul continues this practice when he appeals to the law of Moses, which was "written for our sake" (1 Cor 9:10). And the second letter to Timothy (3:14-17) reflects this tradition of writing down a revelation and declares that these revelations are inspired and useful for all who belong to God's people. Stated another way, the authority of Scripture rests on God's prestige rather than on human ingenuity.

Seeking the Counsel of the Dead

The prohibition against seeking the counsel of the dead through mediums and wizards appears at various places in the OT (e.g., Lev 19:31; 20:6, 27; Deut 18:9-14), including the story of Saul's visit to the medium at Endor in 1 Samuel 28. The exhortation in Isaiah 8:19-20 to shun such mediums and wizards, receiving the torah and the testimony instead, belongs to this genre of the OT's teaching. The polemic in the OT against consulting the dead rises out of a conviction that God and his messengers speak *directly* to and through the living, all who are open to hearing God's voice (Isa 6 may serve as an example here). Hearing God's voice *indirectly* through other voices, including voices from the dead, allows for development of practices antithetical to God's way (in this regard, compare Manasseh in 2 Kings 21:6 and Josiah in 2 Kings 23:24).

THE TEXT IN THE LIFE OF THE CHURCH

The Spirits of the Dead

The prohibition in the OT against seeking the counsel of the dead furnishes evidence for the Western church in its teaching against the occult. At the heart of the prohibition in the Bible and the church lies the concern that supernatural power must be observable if it is to be available and credible. Supernatural power must not be hidden and secret. If it is hidden and secret, it becomes indistinguishable from magic. Magical power, for weal or for woe, depends on the skill of the magician rather than the power of God. As a result, magical power is often capricious and arbitrary.

The prohibition against seeking the counsel of the dead, however, receives a quite different reading in African Christian spirituality, where the ancestors, the living dead, appear in dreams and visions, and their instruction is held in high regard. Anyone who has lived among the Batswana of southern Africa, will appreciate this difference of perspective. Belief in the ancestors seemed to the early Christian missionaries to be ancestor worship. But for many Batswana, ancestors are not worshipped; they are listened to for their guidance. In one of the Independent Churches in Botswana, the Spiritual Healing Church, for example, people understand the remembering of their ancestors to be similar to the Israelite remembering of their ancestors, honoring them but not deifying them. So the Spiritual Healing Church calls on the God of Abraham and Isaac and Jacob in prayer, regarding these ancestors of ancient Israel as the great ancestors of everyone (R. Friesen: 87-88).

What in one's culture can be kept and incorporated into Christian faith, and what has to be discarded? The occult, certainly, threatens both Western Christian spirituality and African Christian spirituality. For

Isaiah 8:1-22

Christian spirituality, the Bible remains a key witness in discerning questions of faith and culture. Whatever does not contradict the spirit of the Bible's teachings may be kept and added to the rich tapestry of Christian spirituality.

Isaiah 9:1-21

Judgment and Hope

PREVIEW

This chapter contains two contrasting themes: hope and despair. Hope is the initial theme (9:1-7). A Davidic child, rising like a phoenix out of fire and oppression, will establish justice. Despair follows hope (9:8-21). Here there is no Davidic child in sight, but only war and wickedness and wrath.

The first part was written to kindle hope in a future king whose authority would increase and who would be the author of peace (9:1-7). A positive image of a people seeing a great light, rejoicing in freedom from oppression, and embracing a messianic king and kingdom pervades this section.

The second part was written in the belief that the Lord's anger at Israel's disobedience resulted in Israel's exile (9:8-21). Here there is a negative image of an arrogant people refusing to turn to the Lord, led astray, fuel for the fire. From elsewhere in the book, the reader knows that the heat of angry emotion in 9:8-21 does not spell the end of Israel but the survival of a remnant as the basis for a new community.

The Hebrew text of chapter 9 has 20 verses, beginning with *The people who walked in darkness* . . . . English translations, however, begin chapter 9 with verse 23 of chapter 8 (in the Hebrew text), which then yields 21 verses. I follow the English translations, except that I begin chapter 9 with the second line of 8:23: *In the former time* . . . .

Isaiah 9:1-21

OUTLINE

Passion for Justice, 9:1-7
    9:1-3   A Great Light
    9:4-5   Boots and Uniforms Burned
    9:6-7   Davidic Child with Divine Names
Passionate Anger, 9:8-21
    9:8-12   Pride Goes Before the Fall
    9:13-17   Off with Their Heads!
    9:18-21   Fuel for the Fire

EXPLANATORY NOTES

Passion for Justice 9:1-7

A declaration that light has dawned on a people in darkness opens the first section (9:1-3). This dawning is illuminated first in terms of liberation from oppression (9:4-5) and then in terms of a Davidic child with divine names (9:6-7).

9:1-3 A Great Light

The chapter opens by contrasting a *former time* with a *latter time* (9:1). These times stand in relationship to *this time* (9:7). The former and latter times refer to chronological times of oppression and liberation for the regions named. Zebulun and Naphtali were formerly tribal allotments in the northern sector of Canaan. These territories were annexed by Assyria before the fall of Samaria in 721 BC (2 Kings 15:29). *He brought into contempt* refers to God's judgment on these territories for all the sins enumerated in 2 Kings 17. *This time* (9:7) refers to a present time that fully expects a hopeful future because of the Davidic child.

What follows is a reversal of the annexation reported in 2 Kings 15:29. Three geographical areas are mentioned. First is the great road from Egypt to Syria called the Via Maris (*the way of the sea*). The second is the region east of the Jordan River called Gilead (*the land beyond the Jordan*). The third is the territory of Zebulun and Naphtali itself (*Galilee of the nations*). God has made these areas important (glorious) because the people in them who walked in darkness have seen God's saving light.

The Hebrew verb *to make glorious* should probably be translated in the English present perfect tense, *He has made glorious*, meaning that now, in the latter time, a new opportunity for liberation has opened up as a result of a new initiative by God on behalf of his people.

The prophet uses imagery of deep darkness and great light to describe a people transformed by light (9:2). Elsewhere in Isaiah the Lord is the creator of light (45:7), or the Lord's justice is described as a light to the peoples (51:4), or the Lord himself is light (10:17; 60:1, 20), or it is the Lord who turns the darkness into light (42:16). But here, the light is a reference simply to the Lord's activity among his people.

The contrasts between former and latter times on the one hand, and darkness and light on the other, are resolved in the joy of a liberated people; the poet now speaks to God in an ode to joy. The joy expressed here is the extravagant joy of people who have brought in a harvest or won a victory (9:3). It is the Lord who increased the joy, so the joy is expressed before you (i.e., before the Lord).

9:4-5 Boots and Uniforms Burned

Now the joy of seeing a great light is declared in terms of political and military victory (9:4-5). Five images are evoked—yoke, bar, rod, boots, uniforms—to describe the joy.

The prophet uses the analogy of the Lord's victory over the Midianites under Gideon's leadership (9:4; cf. Judg 6–7). The reader sees the pattern for the Lord's breaking of yoke, bar, and rod—symbols of oppression—on behalf of his people. Gideon did not win his battle by means of military superiority but "by the miraculous intervention of Yahweh" (Lind, 1980:91). So also in Isaiah 9:4-5, the breaking of oppression is portrayed by means of the Lord's power. The particular oppression that the Lord has broken in the recent past is not mentioned. Some scholars say this is a reference to the long-standing domination of the Southern Kingdom by the North (Hayes and Irvine: 179). Others think the breaking of oppression refers to an Assyrian defeat, possibly during the reign of Josiah (Seitz: 86).

The important point is that the breaking of oppression is a reference back to the light mentioned in the first part (9:2) and forward to the birth of a child in the third part (9:6-7). If the Lord could liberate Israel in the past by means of a mere handful of unarmed men led by Gideon, he can liberate Israel in the present by means of a child.

The result of the Lord's power over the symbols of oppression is a disarmament that recalls the spirit (but not the vocabulary) of Isaiah 2:1-5. The prophet envisions the destruction of an important symbol of military force, the uniform, as the harbinger of an era of peace (cf. Clements: 107).

9:6-7 Davidic Child with Divine Names

The joy of seeing a great light is now declared in terms of a Davidic child with divine names (9:6-7). First the birth of a child endowed with authority and sanctioned with divine names is announced (9:6). The emphasis is on a child born *to us* and given *to us*, echoing the name of the child in Isaiah 7 and 8, *Immanuel*, whose name means *With-us-is-God* (AT). It is a child who will show the way beyond political and military liberation.

The names given to the child are usually called throne names because they are the names that a king would receive at his enthronement (Seitz: 86). *Wonderful Counselor* describes the king's wisdom in resolving interstate disputes. *Mighty God* asserts the king's power. *Everlasting Father* attributes long life to the king. *Prince of Peace* refers to the king as the source of economic, social, and political well-being.

After the announcement of the child's birth, attention focuses on the greatness of the child's authority (9:7). This authority shows its greatness by the child's facility to wage *endless peace* for the throne and kingdom of David. Using language from the Davidic monarchy, this term alludes to a messianic king. The messianic character of the text is further validated by the reference to the perpetual reign of justice and righteousness (cf. Childs: 81).

The movement from light and joy at the beginning of Isaiah 9:1-6 to a throne and a kingdom at the end is almost breathtaking! The signature at the end, *the LORD of Hosts*, finally makes perfectly clear who is the authority behind the text. Here is a confession of faith that the Lord himself will establish this messianic king to rule in perpetuity.

Passionate Anger 9:8-21

A sudden shift from joy and promise to rebellion and judgment characterizes the transition from the first part to the second part of chapter 9. The first part pictures the joy of those upon whom the Lord's light has shone and then develops this picture in terms of a messianic figure establishing peace (9:1-7); the second part portrays a spiraling decline into an abyss of violence (9:8-21). Identical "refrains" conclude each section in the second part: *Yet for all this, his anger is not turned away/his hand is still upraised* (9:12, 17, 21 NIV).

The literary character of this shift may be expressed in the form of a diagram:

A^{1-3} the people *rejoicing* (śmḥ) in the great light
$\quad B^{4-5}$ military gear is *fuel for the fire*
$\quad\quad C^{6-7}$ the Lord's *zeal* for a son and a kingdom
$\quad\quad C'^{8-12}$ the Lord's *word* against all the people
A'^{13-17} the Lord *not rejoicing* (śmḥ) in the people
$\quad B'^{18-21}$ the people are like *fuel for the fire*

9:8-12 Pride Goes Before the Fall

The second part of the chapter begins with a people whose pride and arrogance result in attack by enemies (9:8-12). This imagery of war stands in contrast to the endless peace of the previous part (9:6-7). The prophet wants to shift the reader's attention to the consequences of the people's rebellion.

The word of the Lord falling upon Jacob-Israel is featured in the first stanza (9:8-10). When the prophets bring a word from the Lord, this word usually includes a call to repentance. Such a call is implied here, especially in the revealing phrase that *all the people knew it* (9:9). The people knew that the Lord had sent a word against them, and they also knew for what purpose the word was sent. Yet there is entrenched resistance to the call to repentance in the form of the old human downfalls: pride and arrogance. The consequence of ignoring the sent word is a nasty dose of trouble from external enemies. This is described as an invasion by enemies who muster (stir up) their forces, deploy them (east and west), and launch the attack (to devour Israel; 9:11-12). The reference to the enemies of Rezin (king of Damascus), Arameans (Syria), and Philistines has to do with the incursion of surrounding kingdoms into the Israelite kingdom (Hayes and Irvine: 186-87).

Each stanza begins with the Lord acting in judgment (9:8, 11). The refrain at the end summarizes the ongoing nature of the judgment. All of this stands in contrast to the zeal of the Lord in giving a son and establishing a kingdom (9:7). On the one hand the Lord acts in judgment, which his people invite by their rebellion (9:8-12). On the other hand the Lord acts in hope and promise, inviting his people to live in justice and righteousness (9:6-7). These two ways of acting are presented as two sides of the same coin rather than as two different and incompatible coins.

9:13-17 Off with Their Heads!

The second part of the chapter continues by focusing on the people who did not respond to the Lord's discipline (9:13-17). Here the prophet explains the consequences of not seeking the Lord. This is a deliberate contrast to 9:1-3, where the people see a great light.

The refusal to repent and seek the Lord leads to loss of leadership (the cutting off of head and tail, 9:13-14). The prophet takes pains to explain the head-tail imagery in terms of corrupt leaders (9:15-16). Though the judgment is said to fall on all the people, it is the leaders who are blamed.

Finally, there is a return to the broader apostasy and the Lord's corresponding lack of compassion (9:17). The words *pity* and *pleasure* (NIV) are less-than-ideal translation choices for the Hebrew śmḥ, the word translated *rejoice* in 9:3. In 9:3 it is the people who rejoice in the light. In 9:17 it is the Lord who has no joy (or compassion) because of all the godlessness.

9:18-21 Fuel for the Fire

The second part of the chapter concludes by comparing the people to fuel for the fire because of their wickedness. Here the prophet emphasizes the contrast between the oppressors' boots and uniforms as fuel for the fire (9:5), and the people themselves as fuel for the fire (9:18).

The first stanza begins with a comparison of wickedness to a consuming forest fire (9:18). It continues with the imagery of burning, describing the Lord's anger at the people's insatiable violence (9:19-20a). And it concludes with an image of cannibalistic brutality due to total depletion of food supplies in time of siege (9:20b-21; cf. Lam 4:10). Ephraim and Manasseh, each named after one of Jacob's sons, were adjacent Israelite territories. The picture here is one of civil war.

The contrast of this part (9:18-21) with its counterpart at the beginning of the chapter (9:4-5) reinforces the two ways that the Lord acts. On the one hand, as a response to the people seeing a great light, the Lord consigns their enemies' uniforms to the fire. This is a way of saying that the Lord acts on behalf of those who seek him. On the other hand, as a response to wickedness, the Lord's wrath is unleashed, the land is burned, and the people themselves become like fuel for the fire. This is a way of saying that the Lord's capacity for mercy had reached its limit.

THE TEXT IN BIBLICAL CONTEXT

A Messianic King

The advent of a messianic king was a source of hope for the Judeans exiled in Babylon (9:1-7). On the one hand the hope was nurtured for a renewed national experience under a Davidic king. On the other hand there was an expectation, not always so visible, of a transnational kingdom of God that would embrace all the families of the earth (Gen 12:3). The hope for a renewed national experience may be seen in Ezekiel's vision in chapters 40–48. The notion of a universal messianic king and kingdom is expressed in texts such as Isaiah 11:1-9. The conviction of a universal messianic kingdom inspired the writing of the book of Jonah. And in the book of Daniel, God's kingdom embraces all peoples, nations, and languages (7:14).

In the NT, Isaiah 9:1-2 is quoted to show that Jesus' withdrawal to Galilee was a fulfillment of Isaiah's words (Matt 4:15-16). In Luke's Gospel, Zechariah alludes to Isaiah 9:2 to show how his newborn son

John (the Baptist) would prepare the way for the Lord to give light to those who sit in darkness and in the shadow of death (Luke 1:79). Luke 1:32-33 probably alludes to Isaiah 9:6 in the angel's word to Mary that her son will be given the throne of his ancestor David and an everlasting kingdom.

God's Anger

The theme of the Lord's passionate anger in 9:8-21 is echoed in Isaiah 5:24-30 as well as in 10:1-4. Beyond these texts, it is a theme found frequently in the prophets and beyond the prophets in the OT as a whole (cf. Zeph 2:2; 3:8). Often the anger of God is described as slow in developing and tempered by mercy and grace (as in Ps 103:6-14). Nevertheless it is nearly always expressed alongside a call to repentance. Even when the call to repentance is not highly visible, as here, it is present as a reminder of God's intention for his people.

In the NT, God's anger, although available in the present (cf. Rom 12:19 and 1 Thess 2:16), is more often a reality in the future as part of God's final reckoning with evil (e.g., Rev 6:16; 11:18; 14:10).

THE TEXT IN THE LIFE OF THE CHURCH

Messiah and Messianic Kingdom

The climax of Isaiah 9:1-6 comes in verses 6-7, where the birth of a child is announced. The church has understood this announcement as a prophecy concerning the coming Messiah and messianic kingdom [*Messiah, Messianic Hope, p. 447*]. And so it is! The prophecy has been expressed in the church's hymnody, in great musical compositions such as Handel's *Messiah*, and in the choice of texts for the season of Advent. What Isaiah records as a promise and a hope, the NT and the church joyously proclaim as a promise fulfilled in Jesus.

In this promise the church has focused on two themes: Israel's coming king and the king's righteous reign. Menno Simons, the Dutch Anabaptist leader in the sixteenth century, appealed to Isaiah 9:6 in the conviction that Christ is king of his believing church and not John of Leiden, who called himself "joyous king of all" (Menno: 35). In this conviction Menno was following the mainstream of Christian interpretation, proclaiming the kingship and kingdom of Christ.

When the church reflects on Isaiah 9:1-7, there is a temptation to focus on 9:6 and 7 to the exclusion of 9:1 through 5. This ought to be resisted by taking a bold look at the section as a whole. In the first part there is euphoric joy at the light that has broken through the darkness (9:1-3). Light overcoming darkness is a major theme in the creation

Isaiah 9:1-21

account in Genesis and in the Prologue to John's Gospel. And here too it stands out as a harbinger of an important announcement.

But first there is a reflection on the world of tyranny and oppression, where the Lord has broken the tyrant's power (9:4-5). The specific reference to the day of Midian is a pointed reminder that, like the crossing of the sea in Exodus 14–15, the victory is the Lord's. Two common assumptions may be addressed in this regard. One is that only soldiers and armies can solve the problem of oppression and tyranny. The other is that the refusal to participate in warfare leaves people helpless in combating tyranny (*CCW:* 10-13). Both assumptions fail to account for moral and political decisions based on a view of reality in which the source of security is not warfare and military force but rather God's kingship.

The birth of a child who is a king and whose kingdom is characterized by a passion for justice and righteousness (9:6-7) is a bold announcement with far-reaching implications. The child's "throne names" give a penetrating insight into the divine authority of this messianic king.

Isaiah 10:1-34

The Lord's Power and Majesty

PREVIEW

The wrath of God was not a theme from which the prophets shrank. The "wrathful refrain" at the end of 10:4 reminds the reader of identical refrains in 9:12, 17, 21, and earlier, in 5:25. With vigorous debate and a variety of conclusions, biblical scholars disagree about how these refrains relate to each other in the composition of the book. What is clear is that the Lord's anger and outstretched hand, exhibited in these "wrathful refrains," are directed against his people; the nation, as Walter Brueggemann has said, "has lost its center, its reference, its focus, its purpose, and its chance for well-being" (1998a:55). Chapter 10 as a whole illustrates a high view of God's role in international affairs. The Lord acts freely for weal or woe, against his own people when needed, against a foreign nation when required.

OUTLINE

Day of Infamy, 10:1-19
    10:1-4   Day of Visitation
    10:5-11   Assyrian Bravado
    10:12-15   Assyrian Brawn

Isaiah 10:1-34

10:16-19 Day of Burning
Day of Liberation, 10:20-34
  10:20-23 Return of a Remnant
  10:24-26 Destruction of Assyria
  10:27-28 Invasion Set in Motion
  10:29-34 Invasion Halted

EXPLANATORY NOTES

Day of Infamy 10:1-19

The first section of the chapter has a chiastic structure (A-B-B´-A´) [*Literary Perspective, p. 446*]. This structure may be displayed as follows:

A^{1-4} Judgment because of injustice
   B^{5-11} Assyria as the Lord's rod and staff
   $B´^{12-15}$ King of Assyria does not control the Lord
$A´^{16-19}$ Judgment because of arrogance

The first and the fourth parts describe scenes of judgment, but in neither place is the recipient of judgment named (10:1-4; 16-19). The second part portrays Assyria as the Lord's rod and staff, with the third part denying that rod and staff can control their user (10:5-11; 12-15).

10:1-4 Day of Visitation

It is not perfectly clear to whom the opening *woe* (NIV) is addressed. The immediately preceding text infers that the addressee is Jacob-Israel (9:8-21). The first stanza denounces unjust lawmakers and then lists the effect of unjust laws on the poor, those with little economic power (10:1-2). The opening *woe* indicates that the Lord demands just laws so that the poor have protection from unscrupulous operators.

The *day of visitation* (KJV; *reckoning*, NIV) alludes to a *day of punishment* from which escape is futile (10:3). Three penetrating questions highlight this futility (NIV). The last stanza describes captivity and death as unhappy alternatives (10:4). The Lord's outstretched hand is remarkable in that a similar expression (*outstretched arm*) is used in the exodus story to describe the Lord's liberation of the Hebrews from slavery (Exod 6:6). Here, however, the Lord's outstretched hand describes the Lord's anger and determination to punish and discipline his own people (Brueggemann, 1998a:87-88).

10:5-11 Assyrian Bravado

Rod and staff have different uses in the OT: as support for a traveler (Gen 38:18, 25), as implement for counting sheep (Lev 27:32), as symbol of authority (Isa 14:5), as tool for the farmer (Isa 28:27), or as truncheon for punishment (Ezek 7:11). The message here is that the Lord intends to discipline his people with rod and staff (10:5-6; see TBC). The infinitives *to take spoil, to seize plunder*, and *to tread them down* describe the nature of this discipline (10:5-6). It is caustic but not cutthroat. The description of *a godless nation* (10:6) alludes to the two Israelite kingdoms (Northern and Southern) as one. The identity of the speaker ("I"), Assyria, is not stated here but becomes clear as the poetry unfolds.

Assyria's intentions, as the reader learns, turn out to be cutthroat, and in the second stanza the infinitives *to destroy* and *to cut off* show the difference in perception of the appointed task (10:7). To make this point, the infinitives of destruction balance the infinitives of discipline.

The first Assyrian speech begins by illustrating the intention to obliterate all enemies (10:8-9). Each of the six city-states (Calno to Damascus) lies in ruins (Watts, 1985:149-50). Even with *many* gods on their side, these city-states could not stop the Assyrian onslaught. Can Jerusalem and Samaria, with *fewer* gods, really expect a different outcome?

In the Assyrian king's perception, Jerusalem and Samaria are two city-states (10:10-11). The declaration of the nation as *godless* in 10:6 denies divinity to the idols and images of Samaria and Jerusalem. The Assyrian implication that Jerusalem and Samaria have multiple gods, though fewer than their neighbors, has a double meaning. On the one hand it means that the Assyrians put Jerusalem and Samaria in the same polytheistic basket as their neighbors. On the other hand it also means that Jerusalem and Samaria have abandoned the Lord for other gods, an underlying theme of the prophets.

10:12-15 Assyrian Brawn

Now it becomes clear, if it wasn't before, that it is the Lord who put the rod and staff in Assyria's hand. The reference in 10:5-6 to the sending of Assyria against *a godless nation* is answered here by the Lord completing his work on Mount Zion and in Jerusalem (10:12). In the last two lines of 10:12, some translators (cf. NRSV) emend the text from *I will punish* to *he will punish*, following the LXX. Other translators (cf. NIV) add *he will say*, beginning a speech of the Lord that continues through verses 13 and 14. Either translation choice is acceptable. I follow the NIV here because the two speeches of the Lord (10:5-11, 12-14) complement each other.

The second Assyrian speech, then, is a quotation within the Lord's speech (10:13-14). First the king asserts his own autonomy and strength (10:13). Although the Lord claims to have authority over the Assyrian king, the Assyrian king claims to be his own authority and to have unrivaled power (Watts, 1985:151). Then the king compares his brawn to the ease with which a malicious child might rob a bird's nest and slaughter its helpless occupants (10:14).

The prophet's rejoinder comes in the form of a question and a disparaging comment (10:15). The question refers to an ax and a saw to point out the absurdity of a tool controlling the person using it. The disparaging comment that follows refers to a rod and a staff to make the same point. The nonsense of tools controlling their users makes the point that the Lord intended to control his "tool" Assyria, although Assyria had other ideas.

The interest in rod and staff lies not so much in the instruments of discipline themselves as in the one who has the prerogative to handle them or who assigns their use to an agent. From time to time, God places rod and staff in the hands of a designated agent, to administer discipline. The agent receives these instruments along with certain limitation on their use, limitations defined by the instruments themselves (see TBC).

10:16-19 Day of Burning

In response to the Lord's *sending* Assyria against a godless nation in 10:5-6, the Lord now *sends* emaciation against *his sturdy warriors* (10:16 NIV). By using the word *send* in both cases, the prophet wants to contrast an earlier sending *of* Assyria with a new sending *against* Assyria.

The alliteration in the Hebrew text of 10:16 (*wetaḥat kebodo yeqad yeqod kiqod 'eš*) is difficult to reproduce in English. It may be rendered *and under his brilliance a blaze bursts forth like a blaze of fire* (AT). The annihilation that Assyria had in mind comes back to haunt its sturdy warriors. Fire and flame devour the Assyrian military machine. The Lord's sturdy warriors are now his thorns and briers, his forest, and his orchards put to the torch (10:17-18a).

The image of burning then gives way to the image of wasting sickness, decimating the ranks of the once-powerful army (10:18b-19). The application of the words *day*, *write*, and *glory* (*kebod*) to Assyria in 10:17-19 repeats the same words applied to Israel in 10:1-4. Israel is not mentioned in 10:1-4, and neither is Assyria mentioned in 10:17-19. Nevertheless the context strongly suggests that both are intended.

Day of Liberation 10:20-34

In the second section of the chapter, the parts are arranged in pairs (A-B-A'-B'):

A$^{20\text{-}23}$ On that day a remnant will return
  B$^{24\text{-}26}$ Rod and staff lifted up against Assyria
A'$^{27\text{-}28}$ On that day the invasion begins
  B'$^{29\text{-}34}$ Invasion halts at Nob

The focus in the first two parts is on the remnant's reliance on the Lord and the Lord redirecting his anger against Assyria (A-B). In the last two parts there is a promise at the beginning and a threat of annihilation at the end (A'-B'). Between promise and threat lies a tersely reported sketch of an invading force, probably Assyria, threatening Jerusalem and then facing the prospect of its own annihilation.

10:20-23 Return of a Remnant

An adverbial phrase "on that day," a recurring theme in the prophets, opens the second section of the chapter and refers to a time of judgment when God will reveal himself. The reference to Israel and the house of Jacob in the first stanza means the Northern Kingdom (10:20). The word rely (NIV) carries the full weight of dependence and confidence, once centered upon Assyria but in the future to be centered upon the Lord.

The second stanza describes the return of a remnant (10:21-22a). The name of Isaiah's son in 7:3 (She'ar-jashub) is reproduced here in the phrase A remnant will return (še'ar jašub). The name and the phrase have a double meaning here as well as in 7:3. It can be a sign of judgment (Only a remnant will return) or a sign of promise (Surely a remnant will return). The emphasis here recalls the promise of descendants like the sand of the sea to Abraham and Jacob (Gen 22:17; 32:12). But the promise is now diminished because of God's judgment (Childs: 95).

The last stanza indicates that the decree of destruction remains a reality (10:22b-23). But the promise of a surviving remnant, relying on the Lord, continues intact.

10:24-26 Destruction of Assyria

The reference to the people living in Zion means Jerusalem in particular and the Southern Kingdom in general (10:24-25). The counsel not to fear the Assyrian threat rests on the assertion that the Lord's anger has now turned against his Assyrian disciplinarian. Two evocative images describe this reprisal for loss suffered (10:26). One has the Lord wielding

Isaiah 10:1-34

a whip. This reference alludes to the execution of the two Midianite captains at the rock of Oreb (Judg 7:25). The specific imagery of a whip is not used in Judges 7. Instead, the comparison lies in the Lord's victory over the Midianites, based on the element of surprise instead of numerical superiority.

The second image evokes the Lord's victory over the Egyptians when the exodus Israelites crossed the sea (Exod 14:16). The two images taken together describe the Lord's defeat of enemies in order to reassure God's people of the defeat of Assyria.

10:27-28 Invasion Set in Motion

Another *on that day* phrase opens the first stanza (10:27). I translate the four-line stanza as follows:

> *So it shall be on that day:*
> *his burden will be removed from your shoulder,*
> *and his yoke [will be removed] from your neck;*
> *the yoke will be broken because of fatness.*

The last line is often emended and joined to the first line of 10:28. Nevertheless it belongs with 10:27 even though it is difficult to translate. The masculine possessive pronoun in *his burden* and *his yoke* almost certainly refers back to Assyria in 10:24-25.

The second stanza portrays an invader entering the land (10:28). The context suggests that this is Assyria although Assyria is not specifically named. The place names (Aiath, Migron, Micmash), insofar as they can be identified, lie north of Jerusalem.

10:29-34 Invasion Halted

The poetry develops a picture of invincibility on the part of the invaders and terror on the part of those in the path of the invasion (10:29). Geba, Ramah, and Gibeah are also towns along the northern approach to Jerusalem.

The towns immediately north of Jerusalem (Gallim, Laishah, Anathoth, Madmenah) are in a panic (10:30-31a). Madmenah's retreat serves as an example to the others. All is lost!

The invasion reaches its goal upon its arrival at Nob, on the outskirts of Jerusalem (10:31b-32). Instead of siege and conquest, however, the invading force merely shakes its fist at the city. In language that is terse and direct, the poet depicts invincible power neutralized before the symbol of the Lord's presence, Zion-Jerusalem.

An image of destruction dominates the final stanza (10:33-34). The Lord, in the guise of a lumberjack wielding his ax in a display of invincible power, decimates the forest. The chapter's second part ends, therefore, as the first part ended (10:16-19). A forest representing the Assyrian military machine is overwhelmed by the Lord's superior power. In the last line Lebanon's majesty emphasizes its elevation and serves as an emblem of Assyria's fall.

THE TEXT IN BIBLICAL CONTEXT
Tools in God's Hands

The symbolism of rod and staff as instruments of national discipline is developed in the book of Isaiah (10:5-16). In the parable of the farmer (28:23-29), rod and staff carry out a separating function. The separation of seeds from their husks requires tools that can be used with restraint. Rod and staff serve this purpose well. By way of contrast, threshing sledge and cartwheel symbolize the use of unrestrained force.

Elsewhere in the prophets, Jeremiah thinks of war club and battle weapon as the Lord's instruments of judgment against Babylon, wielded by Media or Persia (51:20). Jeremiah also thinks of the sword as an instrument sent by the Lord, although it is not specified who wields it (25:15-29; cf. 50:35-38). Nations will fall by the sword because they are intoxicated (disoriented, overpowered) by the wine of the Lord's wrath (Martens: 164-65). In each case the Lord exercises authority over his tools of discipline and judgment, not the other way round.

In a change of idiom, the potter and the clay illustrate the power and authority of the sender over the one sent. In Isaiah 29:16 and 45:9, the prophet cannot conceive of the clay in any other position than being molded and shaped by the potter. Jeremiah 18 pictures the house of Israel as clay in the potter's (the Lord's) hand. The Lord's word portrays nations, too, as under God's authority.

In Romans 9:20-21 Paul argues against the clay having any authority over the potter. God has the freedom to include non-Jews in his plan of salvation. This principle, well-established in the biblical record, sees the various tools of discipline firmly in God's hands. God does not relinquish control of the tools he places in the hands of his representatives. To do so would be to allow these representatives to act on their own, purely on the basis of self-interest.

Isaiah 10:1-34

THE TEXT IN THE LIFE OF THE CHURCH

The Lord's Anger

The church confesses the righteousness of God, including the Bible's testimony that this righteousness includes anger. In Isaiah 10 God's anger vents itself in disciplinary action against his people. Jeremiah 18 speaks of this discipline as a disaster (NIV) or an evil (NRSV) that can be averted if there is repentance. The anger of God is restrained by his righteousness. Although the Bible often describes God's anger as thoroughgoing, it refrains from celebrating God's anger as unrestrained.

The intention of God's anger is to bring about fundamental change. Some people believe that anger, as in Isaiah 10, is God's primary way of convicting and correcting and calling to repentance. But the church, reflecting Jesus' life and teaching, takes refuge in God's love as the primary reality to which people respond, not his anger. The Bible as a whole, not only the NT, affirms this love of God over and over again.

God's love is primary, God's anger is secondary. One way to address the tension between love and anger is to think in terms of marriage, where strong anger is often the response to scorned love. Isaiah 54 speaks of God's anger arising from the anguish of scorned love. But Hosea is most well known for his portrayal of God as a husband whose love is spurned and scorned by Israel, represented as a wife who acts like a prostitute (cf. 2:2-13; 4:7-19).

Human Fallibility

The church confesses human fallibility. Isaiah 10 thinks of this fallibility as injustice and godlessness and arrogance. *The Confession of Faith in a Mennonite Perspective* states that

> through sin, the powers of domination, division, destruction, and death have been unleashed in humanity and in all of creation. They have, in turn, further subjected human beings to the power of sin and evil, and have increased burdensome work and barren rest. . . . Because of sin and its consequences, the efforts of human beings on their own to do the good and to know the truth are constantly corrupted. (31).

Human fallibility, however, may not be used as an excuse for continuing injustice. Sin and evil do corrupt human beings, including those who claim to put their faith in God. Nevertheless this faith in God, where it is active and living, reaches out to each person to convict and correct and call to repentance.

Isaiah 11:1–12:6

The Lord's Deeds Among the Peoples

PREVIEW

Isaiah 11:1–12:6 brings the first part of the book to a conclusion. The thanksgiving song in 12:1-6 serves two purposes: to celebrate the remnant's return (11:10-16) and to close the testimony and teaching in part 1 (Isa 1-12).

Chapters 11 and 12 are made up of three sections. The first portrays a prophetic vision of great power (11:1-9). Here a descendant of Jesse, endowed with the Lord's Spirit, announces peace on earth. Peace is not presented as an impossible ideal but as a tangible possibility when emanating from God's Spirit.

The second section envisions the remnant of Jesse's people, long in subjection, returning to claim its heritage of being a blessing for all the families of the earth (11:10-16). The blessing begins with the remnants' renunciation of their own internal hostilities.

In the third section the prophet gives a resounding call to this remnant to exalt the Lord's name (12:1-6). The call is presented in the form of a thanksgiving psalm celebrating the Lord as the source of salvation. Rebellion and refusal to repent characterize the texts of judgment in Isaiah 1–12. But in the concluding thanksgiving psalm is a personal testimony to reliance on the Lord, with a call to reclaim the exalted name of the Lord, which is the "bedrock" of faith.

Isaiah 11:1-12:6

OUTLINE

They Shall Not Hurt or Destroy, 11:1-9
    11:1-3   Delighting in the Fear of the Lord
    11:4-6   Deciding with Justice
    11:7-9   Declaring a Peaceable Kingdom
The Remnant, 11:10-16
    11:10-11   Recovery of a Remnant
    11:12-14   Harmony of the Gathered Remnant
    11:15-16   Return of the Remnant
The Lord's Salvation, 12:1-6
    12:1-3   Trust Without Fear
    12:4-6   Call to Give Thanks

EXPLANATORY NOTES

They Shall Not Hurt or Destroy 11:1-9

The picture in 10:33-34 of a forest, its trees chopped down with an ax, sets the scene for new growth from the stump of Jesse in 11:1-9 (Brueggemann, 1998a:97).

11:1-3 Delighting in the Fear of the Lord

The stump of Jesse refers to the house of David. The stump would appear to be dead, but its rootstock remains alive and able to produce new growth. This new growth is portrayed as a descendant of Jesse endowed with the Lord's Spirit (11:1-2). This Spirit echoes some of the names given to the Davidic child in 9:6-7, especially counsel and might. All of these "gifts of the Spirit" reflect a messianic figure (cf. Childs: 102). The fear of the Lord means the opposite of hearsay and appearances (11:3). The heir of Jesse sees and hears the issues of everyday life out of a centeredness in the Lord's purposes.

It seems unlikely that the reference to the roots and stump of Jesse indicates a hope on Isaiah's part that the Lord's salvation is based on promises to David's house (cf. Ollenburger: 125). Rather, the end of the Davidic dynasty makes it possible for something new to grow. It is not that the new has no connection with the old, but that the spirit of the Lord creates a new order out of the old.

11:4-6 Deciding with Justice

A six-line stanza comprising three pairs of lines continues the mandate of Jesse's heir (11:4-5 AT):

1 judge the destitute with righteousness
2 decide for the poor with justice
   3 strike the land
   4 kill the wicked
5 righteousness his belt
6 faithfulness his belt

The first two lines describe the heir of Jesse acting toward the poor out of a commitment to righteousness and justice [*Justice and Righteousness, p. 445*]. This commitment flows out of a delight in the fear of the Lord, not simply from personal preference. It may be startling to read in lines 3 and 4 that the heir of Jesse will *strike the earth* and *kill the wicked*. The word *earth* means the inhabitants of the earth who oppress the poor. The justice of Jesse's heir includes a decision *for* the poor as well as a verdict *against* those who oppress the poor (cf. Childs: 103). The last two lines describe the essence of Jesse's heir, not what he does. Righteousness and faithfulness are essential to this messianic figure.

The righteousness of Jesse's heir, complemented by justice and faithfulness, blends smoothly with the dense and vivid imagery of predators living in peace with their prey, led by a small child (11:6). Synonyms for children in 11:6 and again in 11:8 provide a further connection with 9:6-7.

11:7-9 Declaring a Peaceable Kingdom

This peaceful landscape continues in 11:7-8 with more images of predators and prey living together in harmony. The summary in 11:9 points back to the predators in particular. It declares the pacification of their survival instincts throughout *my holy mountain*. The *my* comes as a surprise here. It occurs previously in 10:5-6 and 24-25 and later in 12:1-2. In this stanza the Lord speaks in a direct way to emphasize the peaceable kingdom just described as the standard of his purpose for humankind (11:9).

All my holy mountain refers to more than simply Zion or the land of Judah. It corresponds to the earth and the sea as the *whole* of God's transformed world. This transformation rests on the *fullness* of the knowledge of the Lord (Watts, 1985:173). Chapter 11, therefore, comes full circle from chapter 1, where the accusation against the Lord's people is that they neither know nor understand the Lord. The peaceable kingdom is linked directly to knowledge of the Lord throughout the earth.

The Remnant 11:10-16

The notion of a remnant controls 11:10-16. The word *remnant* appears only in verses 12 and 16, but the idea of a remnant sets the tone for the section as a whole.

11:10-11 Recovery of a Remnant

The adverbial phrase *on that day* opens each of the two stanzas, announcing a coming time of blessing. The sprout growing from Jesse's roots at the beginning of the chapter now becomes simply *the root of Jesse* (11:10). The root of Jesse serves as a signal addressed to peoples and nations who come to inquire of the messianic heir of Jesse.

The second stanza is concerned with the Lord's dispersed people, who live among the peoples and nations (11:11). The list of nations in this stanza anticipates the longer section focused on messages against foreign nations (Isa 13–27). The extraordinary picture in 11:11 suggests that in the exodus from Egypt, the Lord acquired a people for himself. Now, *a second time*, the Lord is acquiring the remnant of his people from the places to which they have been dispersed (Gray: 225). The two great powers, Assyria and Egypt, lead the list of nations among whom the remnant dwells. But other nations are represented as well, and they appear to be listed in pairs:

Northeastern Africa (southwest of Palestine):
   Pathros (upper Egypt) and *Cush* (Ethiopia)
Western Asia (east of Palestine):
   Elam (western Persia) and *Shinar* (Babylonia)
Rim of the Mediterranean (north and west of Palestine):
   Hamath (western Syria) and *the coastlands of the sea*

11:12-14 Harmony of the Gathered Remnant

The first stanza has the Lord ("He") raising a signal for the nations (11:12). This provides an explanation for the Lord's hand movement in 11:11 (Watts, 1985:179). The word *reclaim* (NIV) or *recover* in 11:11 becomes more specific here as the remnant is collected from far and wide.

Animosity between the south (Judah) and the north (Ephraim) was legendary, at least since the formal division of a united kingdom into two kingdoms after the death of Solomon. The hope for a healing of this hostility rises to the surface in the second stanza (11:13; cf. Ezek 37:15-17). Reunited, their mastery of regional enemies looms on the horizon as a prospect (11:14).

11:15-16 Return of the Remnant

The theme of a return of the remnant comes to a conclusion at the end of the chapter. The Lord's Spirit and the Lord's hand, at work in the messianic "shoot" from Jesse's root system, combine to create a new Exodus (11:15). The people do not engineer their own rehabilitation. The *tongue of the sea of Egypt* refers to the sea that the Israelites crossed during the exodus. The allusion to *the River* means the Euphrates River, and the NIV has added *Euphrates* for clarification.

The second stanza envisions a highway from Assyria in the northeast on which the remnant will travel (11:16). The highway here is similar to the one in 19:23; 40:3; 49:11; and 62:10. There are other references to a "second exodus" in Isaiah (51:9-11) and Jeremiah (23:7-8).

The Lord's Salvation 12:1-6

A thanksgiving psalm concludes the section and the first part of the book of Isaiah. It consists of two groups of verses (12:1-3, 4-6). Each group begins with the adverbial phrase *in that day*. The first group focuses on trust in the Lord's salvation, the second on making the Lord's name and deeds known.

12:1-3 Trust Without Fear

In the first stanza the expression of gratitude refers to the time of the remnant's return from its dispersion among the nations near and far (12:1). The expression *in that day* clearly echoes the same phrase in 11:10 and 11 (NIV). The singular pronoun *you* addresses the remnant of God's people, mentioned in 11:16, collectively.

The word *comfort* in 12:1 is echoed in the last three parts of the book (40–48, 49–57, 58–66; cf. esp. 40:1), where it often refers to "homecoming from exile" (Brueggemann, 1998a:109). In Isaiah 12:1, however, *comfort* reflects back on the places in chapters 1–12 where the Lord's anger had not yet subsided (e.g., 5:25; 9:12, 17, 21; 10:4). But now thanksgiving is focused on the abating of this anger and the enlargement of the Lord's comfort.

Trust in God based on God's salvation forms the theme of the second stanza (12:2-3). The expression *the LORD, the LORD, is my strength and my song* (NIV) alludes to Exodus 15:2, which celebrates the Lord's victory over the Egyptians. Psalm 118:14 uses the same language to declare that it was God who gave the king victory in battle.

In the last part of the second stanza, the plural pronoun *you* is distributive, addressing the restored remnant (12:3; Gray: 230-31). It is as if to say, *With joy each of you will draw water.* . . . The speaker addresses the assembly of God's people, using the same language of salvation spoken to the individual worshipper in the first stanza. The imagery of water and springs understands the Lord's salvation as rising up from water-bearing rock deep in the earth. The new Exodus calls for an outpouring of joy. The identity of God's people is confirmed.

12:4-6 Call to Give Thanks

A new "on that day" adverbial phrase, continuing the plural pronoun of 12:3, now introduces imperative verb forms in the first stanza (12:4). The imperatives summon the people to *give thanks* and *to call*, *to make known* and *to proclaim*. Although a reference to God's name does not appear in the book until now, it is a significant theme in subsequent chapters (cf. 18:7; 24:15; 30:27; 48:1; 56:6; 60:9).

The final stanza borrows language from the book of Exodus to express joy for the Lord's work in the present (12:5-6). The opening line continues the imperative form of the previous stanza: *Sing praises to the LORD, for he has done gloriously*. The language of Miriam's song in Exodus 15:21 comes to mind here. "Sing to the Lord," she says, "for he has triumphed gloriously." It is no accident that language from the old exodus is employed to give thanks for the new exodus.

The concluding line emphasizes the indwelling presence of God among his people (12:6). This repeats a key theme in chapters 1–12. It also emphasizes the favorite name of God in the book of Isaiah, *the Holy One of Israel* [*Holy, Holy One of Israel*, p. 000]. God's holiness includes both judgment and redemption (Eichrodt, 1961:281). The name *the Holy One of Israel* brings judgment and redemption together in the concluding exclamation of Isaiah 1–12.

THE TEXT IN BIBLICAL CONTEXT

The Peaceable Kingdom

The tranquil landscape of 11:6-8 fires the imaginations of all who read it. The scene appears to stand apart from its context. In fact, however, the poetry flows without interruption from the just rule of the shoot from Jesse's stump (11:5) into the landscape of predators and prey at peace (11:6-8). Likewise, 11:9 gathers this scene of amity into an assertion of God's purpose in the earth, an earth free of violence.

Two other passages in the book of Isaiah join 11:6-9 in directing attention to God's creative intention for humankind in a world redeemed from violence. Isaiah 65:25, one of these passages, repeats 11:9 in an abridged form. The other is Isaiah 35, which uses language of reversal to speak of a renewed earth.

Habakkuk 2:14 employs language similar to Isaiah 11:9 in the context of a series of five curses on power laced with violence. Habakkuk sees an earth filled with the knowledge of God's glory as the antidote to the curses of human folly. Hosea (2:18-20) uses the language of betrothal to refer to a messianic age characterized by justice and righteousness based on knowledge of the Lord.

In the OT prophets as a whole, justice and righteousness distinguish the messianic age. Isaiah's peaceable kingdom crystallizes this vision.

Song of Salvation

Isaiah 12 contains elements that are at home in the Psalter. *The LORD, the LORD, is my strength and my song* (12:2 NIV) reflects Psalm 118:14. The language of 12:4-6 echoes the hymnlike introduction to Psalm 105. The exaltation of the Lord's name in 12:4 is similar to Psalm 148:13. In a way much like songs and hymns in the Psalter, Isaiah 12 calls on the remnant of God's people to give thanks for the Lord's wonderful works, and especially his work of liberation.

The Lord's Spirit

In OT thought God carries out his work in the world through his Spirit. Isaiah 11:2 illustrates this work in the giving of spiritual gifts to the descendant of Jesse. The gifts are not inconceivable or improbable. Rather, they are the gifts needed to build and sustain a community: wisdom, understanding, advice, strength, and knowledge, all attentive to the fear of the Lord.

God's Spirit works in a variety of ways: *hovering over the waters* at creation (Gen 1:2 NIV), lifting Ezekiel up and carrying him to the exiles at Tel-abib (Ezek 3:12-15), and bearing the Lord's words to his people through the prophets (Zech 7:12). The Spirit of the Lord takes possession of Gideon (Judg 6:34), comes upon David in power (1 Sam 16:13), and gives God's people rest (Isa 63:14).

The testimony of the NT is that God's Spirit is a personal reality whose unique role is to empower the new Israel as it lives and proclaims the lordship of Christ (1 Cor 12:3). The uniqueness of this role signified God's Spirit as "holy," and the designation Holy Spirit became commonplace in the NT (cf. *NHBD*: 265-66).

THE TEXT IN THE LIFE OF THE CHURCH

The Holy Spirit in the Life of the Church

The comprehension of a Holy Spirit, somehow distinct from God yet indivisible from God, became increasingly evident in early Christian thought (*NHBD*: 265-66). But a specific doctrine of the Holy Spirit, elaborated in a theologically refined way, did not emerge until the Council of Constantinople in AD 381 (*ODCC*: 783-84).

One of the points of contrast between the Western (Roman Catholic) and Eastern (Orthodox) creeds was the relationship of the Holy Spirit to the Father and the Son. In its creeds the Western church held that the Holy Spirit proceeds from the Father *and* the Son. This may be interpreted as giving priority to the Father and the Son, with the Spirit subject to both. The Eastern church said that the Holy Spirit proceeds from the Father *through* the Son. This formulation ties the Spirit's work more directly to that of the Son in discerning God's will. Many of the early Anabaptists followed the Eastern church in their understanding of the work of the Holy Spirit: the Spirit is working with the Son (representing the written Word) in order to discern the truth (Oosterbaan: 9-17).

The testimony of the church to the power of God's Spirit reaches back to this vision of Isaiah, where the Lord's Spirit endows a descendant of Jesse with the gifts necessary for the building of a peaceable kingdom. Such a kingdom is universal in nature and denies to human-centered nationalism its right to demand of citizens the loyalty to one nation above all others.

Part 2
The Nations and the Whole Earth

Isaiah 13-27

OVERVIEW

The poetry of Isaiah makes a sudden change-of-direction in chapter 13. Gratitude for the remnant's return in chapter 12 now yields to the language of outcry concerning the nations arrayed against God's people.

Sudden changes of direction in Isaiah's book no longer surprise the reader. They indicate the changing interests and perspectives in the development of the Isaiah tradition. But it should be observed that a change of direction generally relates in some way to the preceding text. Continuity from one part of the text to another is preserved.

In Isaiah 1–12, for example, the focus rests on the Lord's judgment of the nation, Judah and Jerusalem. *The nations* play a supporting role but not a lead role. They stream to the mountain of the Lord (2:2-3), or the Lord uses them as agents of judgment upon his own people (10:1-19), or the Lord raises a banner for the nations in order to gather his scattered people (11:12 NIV).

Now in chapters 13–27, the focus rests on the Lord's judgment of *the nations*. Judah and Jerusalem (*the nation*) play a supporting role but not a lead role. Here the nations and the whole earth receive special attention.

Although chapters 13–27 chart a new course, they remain in the same waters as chapters 1–12. These are the waters of judgment based on God's intention for his people and for humankind as a whole. So the change of direction turns out to be a shift of emphasis rather than something altogether new and unfamiliar.

Isaiah 13:1-14:32

Nations Manifesto: Babylon

PREVIEW

Many of the prophets speak to the issue of God's relationship to the nations (cf. Isa 13–27; Jer 46–51; Ezek 25–32; Amos 1–2; Zeph 2). In Isaiah this relationship is defined by the Lord's plan, drawn up on an international scale. Brueggemann is right in arguing that this plan is not a rigid map, changeless and determinate. Instead, the plan is adjusted to particular issues and needs, nevertheless always keeping the Lord's reign in focus (1998a:113).

I use the word *outcry* to draw attention to the prophet's vehement insistence that the Lord's plan for the earth has precedence over all nationalisms. Babylon appears first as the subject of Isaiah's outcry (13:1-22) followed by a parody on the king of Babylon as its sequel (14:1-23). Initially the outcry is generic, proclaiming the Lord's punishment of the whole earth. But in the end, Babylon is named, struck down in all its glory like Sodom and Gomorrah. The parody focuses on the king of Babylon as an object of scorn, and in an epilogue the Lord makes a personal declaration of Babylon's ruin.

Two concluding pieces, formally distinct from the preceding, are thematically integrated with it. The first is an oath against the Assyrians (14:24-27). This continues the direct speech of the Lord at the end of the preceding section. The second, an outcry against the Philistines, concludes this direct speech (14:28-32).

OUTLINE

Outcry Concerning Babylon, 13:1-22
    13:1-5   Marshaling Troops for Battle
    13:6-16   The Day of the Lord Proclaimed
    13:17-22   Babylon Overthrown
Parody on the King of Babylon, 14:1-23
    14:1-2   Prologue: Rest Versus Restitution
    14:3-21   Downfall of the Autocrat
    14:22-23   Epilogue: Babylon in Ruins
Oath Against Assyria, 14:24-27
Outcry Concerning Philistia, 14:28-32

EXPLANATORY NOTES

Outcry Concerning Babylon 13:1-22

A proclamation of the Lord's punishment of the whole earth opens the section (13:1-5). This proclamation continues under the rubric of the *day of the LORD* (13:6-8, 9-13, 14-16). A focus on Babylon concludes the section (13:17-22). The severity of Babylon's overthrow is indicated by its comparison to the overthrow of Sodom and Gomorrah.

13:1-5 Marshaling Troops for Battle

Translators sometimes use the word *oracle* to render the Hebrew noun *maśśa'* at the beginning of 13:1 and throughout chapters 13–23 (cf. NIV, NRSV). The noun *maśśa'* derives from the verb stem *nś'*, meaning *to lift up*. It is used here in the sense of the prophet *lifting up* his voice. It is, therefore, an utterance in the form of an outcry against nations who usurp the Lord's authority and sovereignty.

Isaiah *sees* this utterance rather than *hears* it. This is because Isaiah grasps God's message in the form of a motion picture of God's will and purpose, with simultaneous audio accompaniment. He both sees and hears the message.

The message is attributed to Isaiah son of Amoz (cf. 1:1; 2:1), who lived in the eighth century BC. But there is a long-standing debate as to whether the message in chapters 13 and 14 and what follows has its origin in the eighth century. There is an assurance in 14:1-2, for example, that Jacob-Israel will return to their land, assisted by strangers who in turn will be ruled by Jacob-Israel (Clements: 139; cf. Isa 61:5-7). Such a view is much more likely in the sixth century than in the eighth. Seitz (137) argues, convincingly I believe, that chapters 13 and 14 were written to say that in Isaiah's original vision of Assyria's destruction was the root of God's larger plan comprising Babylon's rise and fall.

The message opens with a signal going out to unidentified assailants (13:2). Equally mysterious is the identity of the *nobles* whose gates are being entered. The Lord's summons in 13:3 serves as a keynote to the first part of the chapter (13:1-5). It refers to *my holy ones* and *my warriors* (NIV), those who are signaled in 13:2. These, too, are not identified. What is of importance is that these assailants operate under the Lord's command.

After the summons comes the sound of troops mustering for battle (13:4a). They come from far and wide and serve as the Lord's instruments, to bring the whole earth into subjection (13:4b-5). The NIV and NRSV use the verb *destroy* in 13:5. The Hebrew verb *ḥabal* is not so forceful. It means *to spoil* or *to ruin*, and the sense *to bring the earth into subjection* reflects more accurately the force of the Hebrew verb (cf. Clements: 134). So the opening lines in chapter 13 unfold in four stanzas: a signal (13:2), a summons (13:3), a muster (13:4a), and an arrival (13:4b-5).

13:6-16 The Day of the Lord Proclaimed

The declaration of the Lord's intent to bring the whole earth into subjection now takes form as the day of the Lord [*Day of the Lord, p. 443*]. First the day is announced (13:6-8); then it is described (13:9-13). The announcement of the day begins with a cry of grief and despair (*wail*, NIV, NRSV). With Amos (5:18), Isaiah exposes the fallacious idea that the day of the Lord necessarily means salvation. A wordplay in 13:6 draws attention to the reason for wailing. The Hebrew word for devastation, *šod*, precedes an ancient name for God, *Shaddai* (Mighty). The announcement declares that humankind will be unable to withstand the devastation on the day of the Lord because the devastation comes from Shaddai.

The description of the day begins with the Lord's anger directed toward earth's sinners (13:9). The focus here goes well beyond Judah and Jerusalem in Isaiah 1–12 to include the whole earth. Ophir (13:12) likely refers to an area in southwest Arabia along the Red Sea and perhaps also across the that sea on the African coast (D. Baker: 26-27). The direct speech of the Lord gives special attention to pride as the epitome of human sinfulness (13:11-13; TLC below).

Flight and capture characterize 13:14-16. The picture in 13:15-16 may reflect the capture of Jerusalem by the Babylonians in 587 BC. If so, that event serves as a paradigm of the Lord's judgment on the day of his anger, when he comes to judge the earth. The wording of 13:16 is similar to Psalm 137:9. In both places revenge, typical of ancient and modern warfare, is exacted on innocent and guilty alike, without discrimination.

13:17-22 Babylon Overthrown

Now the tables are turned. The Lord stirs up the Medes to defeat Babylon. Babylon refers to the city located on the east bank of the Euphrates River. Babylonia refers to the country of which Babylon was the capital city.

The Medes, at home in the Iranian uplands, had helped Babylon conquer Assyria in 612 BC (Noth: 270-71). Then in the mid-sixth century, the Persian king Cyrus defeated the Medes and became king of the Medes and Persians. In 539 BC the army of Cyrus defeated the last Babylonian king, Nabonidus, and occupied the city of Babylon without a fight (Noth: 300-2). In Isaiah's vision all the nations are subordinate to the Lord, although the details of that subordination remain indistinct.

Parody on the King of Babylon 14:1-23

The beginning and end of this second section serve as prologue (14:1-2) and epilogue (14:22-23). The prologue identifies the singer of the taunt song in 14:3-21 as Jacob-Israel. The epilogue, by referring to the Lord's rising up against Babylon (14:22), recalls the declaration in 14:21 that the heirs of Babylon's king shall never rise again to subdue the earth.

The center of the section presents the case against the king of Babylon in four scenes (14:3-6, 7-11, 12-17, 18-21).

14:1-2 Prologue: Rest Versus Restitution

The first stanza means to say that the Lord's mercy toward his people (the house of Jacob) binds them to a policy of welcoming the stranger (14:1). The second stanza indicates the reluctance of his people (the house of Israel) to take up this calling (14:2).

The central meaning of these stanzas lies in this contrast between what the Lord will do and what his people will do. The Lord's work keeps coming back to a work of mercy toward his people. Seeing this, non-Israelites align themselves with an Israel whose hope rests on divine mercy.

When the house of Israel, on the other hand, finds itself once again in its land, it falls back on the conventional wisdom that conquest and captivity provide the only security available.

14:3-21 Downfall of the Autocrat

In this section the king of Babylon comes under the prophet's censure. A sequence of four scenes projects on the screen of history the end of Babylonian tyranny.

The first scene situates the background, names the speaker, and assigns the theme (14:3-6). The background takes into consideration two important changes. One has to do with the *end* of Israel's servitude (14:4 NIV). Most likely this alludes to the end of the Babylonian exile. The other has to do with *the symbol* of Israel's servitude, the king of Babylon, who now faces the uncertain future of all ex-tyrants.

The references to the pronoun *you* (sg.) in 14:3-4a allude to Jacob-Israel, identified in the prologue. From its position of rest (in the land), Jacob-Israel cannot resist lifting up a mocking song (*taunt*) against its oppressor.

The theme never moves far from the Lord as one who exercises power. The Lord gives rest to his people (14:3-4a). The Lord breaks the rod of the oppressor (14:4b-5). The Lord subdues nations (14:6).

The next scene pictures the king of Babylon going into Sheol (14:7-11). The first scene opened with Jacob-Israel at rest (*nwh*). Now the second scene opens with the whole earth at rest (*nwh*). The earth is overjoyed that the king of Babylon has been struck down. Even the trees join the jubilation (14:7-8). Tyrants use vast quantities of natural resources to maintain their power (Clements: 141-42). Sheol, the place of the dead, welcomes the deceased king (14:9). In a similar graphic portrayal, Ezekiel (32:17-32) pictures Pharaoh being received by the residents of Sheol. Here the residents of Sheol join in the taunt (14:10). The *singing* (*rinnah*, v. 7) at the beginning of the scene turns into *maggots* (*rimmah*) at the end (14:11).

The third scene offers a graphic portrayal of Babylon's fall (14:12-17). Using language reminiscent of Assyrian claims in 10:13-14, the prophet accuses the Babylonian king of usurping God's place in the universe (14:12-14). In 14:12 the title *Day Star, son of Dawn* (Heb. *helel ben-šahar*) probably refers to the planet Venus. Canaanite mythology may have included a deity represented by Venus who attempted a hostile takeover of the highest throne. If so, the prophet uses this myth as an analogy for the death of the king of Babylon (Clements: 142-43).

In 14:12 the KJV renders *helel ben-šahar* as *Lucifer*, following the Vulgate. So this passage is sometimes associated with Satan, with *Lucifer* as Satan's proper name, even though the king of Babylon is clearly intended.

Sheol levels the pretentious and powerful and reduces them to weakness (14:15-16a). At the end of the scene, the king of Babylon is the defendant, derided by a ruffian band of plaintiffs (14:16b-17). A tyrant has an obligation to respect the earth and its citizens, even if they are his captives.

The stanzas of the third scene suggest the following pattern:

Stanzas	Verses	Topics
1	12	cast down to the earth
2	13a	"I will ascend"
3	13b-14	"I will ascend"
4	15-16a	brought down to Sheol
5	16b-17	shaking the earth

This pattern compares the arrogance of the king of Babylon (stanzas 2, 3) with his humiliation (stanza 5). The accusation specifies arrogance as the cause of the fall from the heavens (stanzas 1, 4).

The fourth scene reflects on the extent of the Babylonian king's fall (14:18-21). It begins as the second scene ended, with a reference to *all the kings of the nations* (JB). The central meaning of this scene lies in the declaration of the Babylonian king's ignominy. He becomes the pariah of the biblical story, symbolic of evil, unworthy of burial (14:18-20; cf. Jer 22:18-19). The full end of the king and his progeny is declared in the final stanza (14:21).

14:22-23 Epilogue: Babylon in Ruins

A clear word of the Lord confirms the words of the prophet in the epilogue. Four times the Lord speaks his mind on Babylon's end (*I will . . .*). Three times the Lord's signature (*says the LORD*) brings authority to the text. The outcry against Babylon comes to a conclusion in this final word of judgment.

Oath Against Assyria   14:24-27

The sudden reference to Assyria seems out of place here. Babylon and the king of Babylon loom large in what precedes. Why mention Assyria at all? A verbal connection provides one clue. In 14:5 the prophet refers to the king of Babylon as *broken* by the Lord. In 14:25 the Lord promises that he *will break* the Assyrian in his (the Lord's) land.

A thematic connection provides another clue. Babylon's downfall has just been celebrated at some length. But Assyria was the forerunner of Babylon. Assyria, named as the Lord's agent in 10:5-6, receives the Lord's denunciation in 10:12-15. The reminder of Assyria's experience here puts the finishing touch on Babylon's demise. Jeremiah (50:18) brings the Assyrian and Babylonian experiences together in a similar way: "I am going to punish the king of Babylon and his land, as I punished the king of Assyria."

The real focus of this section, however, rests on the Lord's plan (see TBC). The Lord has a plan, and this plan has to do with all the nations of the earth. An earlier reference to the Lord's plan and his hand stretched out in judgment against Judah occurs in 5:18-25. In Isaiah 1–12 as a whole, that plan has in mind the restoration of God's people, or at least the restoration of a remnant of God's people. The plan begins with judgment but has in its view the rehabilitation of the people in a new community.

The Lord's plan then shifts to Assyria (7:17-20; 8:1-10; 10:5-19). Assyria is the Lord's agent at first and then the Lord's adversary.

Now the plan extends to all the nations of the earth. In 10:14 the power of Assyria's rule *gathered all the earth*, but in 14:26 the power of the Lord's rule involves a plan *concerning the whole earth*, with Assyria's rule broken. There are no limitations on what the Lord may do. His plans cannot be weakened or destroyed by anyone. His sphere of activity lies among the nations (the whole earth) as well as among his own people. His decisions cannot be rescinded (Erlandsson: 67).

Outcry Concerning Philistia 14:28-32

At about the time that the Israelites entered Canaan from the plains of Moab, the Philistines entered Canaan from the Mediterranean Sea. Many of the Philistines came from Crete (Caphtor, Amos 9:7), and Palestine took its name from the Philistines. During the time of the Judges and the early period of kingship, the Israelites and Philistines competed for land and livelihood, and contacts between them were often tense (Katzenstein: 326-28).

The year of King Ahaz's death, probably 725 BC, inspires a message directed to the Philistines (Clements: 148). The other historical allusions are impossible to establish with certainty. The context (following 14:24-27) suggests that the Assyrians represent the rod and the snake. Although Assyria has been broken (a possible reference to the death of Tiglath-pileser III in 727 BC), its power is not spent. It will return and vent its fury again. All of 14:30 refers to the fate of the Philistines. The *root* (royal house) and *remnant* (upper classes) will bear the brunt of this fury. The poor and needy, less likely targets of conquest, will be spared (Hayes and Irvine: 237).

The demand to *wail* (14:31) recalls the demand *Do not rejoice* (14:29). These demands are a warning not to be consoled by the apparent death of Tiglath-pileser III since his successor will intensify Assyrian tyranny (Childs: 128). *The nation* in 14:32 probably refers to the *Philistine* nation. But the question no longer addresses the Philistines. The prophet now crafts an answer to the Philistines. In this answer the Lord provides the basis for Zion's security (and Philistine security). Zion's security does not lie in alliances or rebellion or military force. Zion's security rests on trust in the Lord.

THE TEXT IN BIBLICAL CONTEXT
The Lord's Plan

The notion in 14:24-27 that the Lord works according to a plan strikes a familiar chord in the Bible. There are a number of places in the OT where God frustrates the evil plans of others (e.g., Neh 4:15; Pss 21:11; 33:10; Isa 19:3; Jer 19:7). Elsewhere the Lord's deliverance from those who plan evil is requested (Ps 140:2).

More often the OT portrays God as one who acts according to a definite plan. At times this plan conveys judgment against someone (e.g., Assyria and all the nations, Isa 14:24-27; God's own people, Jer 18:11; Babylon, Jer 50:45; 51:12; Edom, Jer 49:20; many nations, Mic 4:12). At times God's plan conveys salvation. In Isaiah, the Lord's plan is that his people find their security in him (22:8-11; 25:1-5; 30:1-5; 31:1-3). In Jeremiah, the Lord's plans include a future with hope for his people (29:10-14). Proverbs acknowledges that while humans are good at making plans, the Lord's purpose will be established in the end (19:21).

The NT certainly sees God's planning behind the coming of Jesus (e.g., Acts 2:23; Eph 1:10; 3:9). And when the apostles face a death sentence for their witness to Jesus, the liberal rabbi Gamaliel argues before the Sanhedrin that if the plan of those who exalt Jesus "is of human origin, it will fail." On the other hand, "if it is from God," it cannot be defeated (Acts 5:38-39 NIV).

The evidence of Scripture portrays God as working from a plan rather than acting capriciously. God acts in his own people's best interest even when acting in judgment. Although God's plan cannot be defeated, yet the details of God's plan remain part of the discernment of God's people. This, however, does not leave out the larger community of nations. They too are part of God's plan for humankind and are called to the mountain of the Lord, to be taught his ways (Isa 2:1-5).

THE TEXT IN THE LIFE OF THE CHURCH
Human Pride

Isaiah 13 and 14 identify pride as one of the causes, if not the principal cause, of Babylon's fall. Isaiah 2:6-22 leads the way in portraying pride as the bane of humankind in general. Accordingly, pride falls under God's judgment. In the synagogue and the church, pride stands as a profound threat to faith.

In solidarity with the denunciation of pride in Isaiah, the church has understood pride as inordinate self-esteem, which translates into conceit. Such pride leads to disdainful behavior toward others and, often, shameful treatment of others. The fruit of pride, therefore, constitutes the offense, although the motive behind the offense must also be taken seriously.

The motive of pride lies in the exaltation of the self above the reality of God. The human inclination to act the part of God, or to place oneself above God, or to be self-sufficient so that one no longer needs God—yielding to such an inclination constitutes pride.

Self-esteem is a good thing, and the loss of self-esteem is always to be lamented. But like many good things, self-esteem moves easily into arrogance, haughtiness, superiority, and condescension. The spiritual defense against pride rests on true humility. Thomas Merton speaks to the sin of pride and the dangers of false humility in his *Seeds of Contemplation*. True humility frees a person from servitude to reputation, he says. Such freedom leads to the discovery that real joy arises only when self recedes into the background. It is "only when we pay no more attention to our own life and our own reputation and our own excellence that we are at last completely free to serve God in perfection for His own sake alone" (37-38).

Isaiah 15:1–16:14
Nations Manifesto: Moab

PREVIEW

Israel's close neighbor Moab, in the highlands east of the Dead Sea, now comes under prophetic scrutiny. Contact between Israel and Moab is noted elsewhere in the OT (e.g., Num 22–24; Ruth; 1 Sam 14:47-48; 22:3-5; 2 Sam 8:2-12).

The manifesto concerning Moab contains three parts. Each part speaks to the tragedy of Moab's devastation although the connections between the parts are not completely clear.

The first part employs language of weeping and suffering (15:1-9). Moab's destruction generates immense pain as refugees flee for their lives. The second part describes a Moabite embassy seeking advice and shelter in nearby Judah (16:1-5). This part unites a plea for shelter with an announcement of messianic hope. The third part combines a description of a ravaged Moab with an assessment of the cause of Moab's fall (16:6-14). Arrogance and insolence in particular figure into the reasons for Moab's demise.

OUTLINE

Outcry Concerning Moab, 15:1-9
    15:1-2   Destruction of Moab
    15:3-5a   Lament for Moab
    15:5b-6   Rampant Destruction
    15:7-9   Plight of the Survivors

Isaiah 15:1–16:14

Moabites in Judah, 16:1-5
    16:1-4a   Compassion for the Moabites
    16:4b-5   Davidic Rule
Grieving for Moab, 16:6-14
    16:6-11   Hushing the Shout of Joy
    16:12-14   Moab's Demise

EXPLANATORY NOTES

Outcry Concerning Moab 15:1-9

15:1-2 Destruction of Moab

The second extended manifesto in part 2 of Isaiah's book names Moab as its subject. The manifesto alludes to a nighttime attack on Moab, although the aggressor is not named (15:1). Five important cities in Moab are named—Ar, Kir, Dibon, Nebo, and Medeba. These cities bore the brunt of the attack. The high places of 15:2, mentioned again in 16:12, refer to places of worship.

15:3-5a Lament for Moab

Signs of grief appear everywhere. Sackcloth as an indication of mourning occurs with some frequency in the OT (e.g., Gen 37:34; 2 Sam 3:31; 1 Kings 20:31; 2 Kings 6:30; Neh 9:1; Ps 35:13; Jer 4:8; Ezek 27:31). Words for weeping abound in this anguished outcry (15:3). The poetry and imagery speak forcefully. Five more place names in Moab are mentioned: Heshbon, Elealeh, and Jahaz in the north (15:4); Zoar and Eglath-shelishiyah in the south (15:5a). The phrase at the end of 15:4, *His soul trembles*, summarizes the plight of Moab. The soul of Moab, not merely the souls of the combatants, trembles under the tragedy of the destruction. The prophet, the author of the manifesto, speaks in 15:5: "My heart cries out for Moab."

15:5b-6 Rampant Destruction

The lament continues with an image of refugees fleeing the destruction, inconsolable (15:5b). The image of flight shifts to a description of the countryside (15:6). The waters of Nimrim, probably on the southeastern shoulder of the Dead Sea, are deserted. All vegetation disappears, contributing to the scene of devastation.

15:7-9 Plight of the Survivors

The *Wadi of the Willows* (*Wady Hesa-Kerahi* in Smith: 371) marks the border between Moab and Edom. It is referred to as Wadi Zered in the book of Numbers (21:10-12; cf. *CBA*: 107, map 141). The first stanza has the refugees from the destruction fleeing pell-mell across this border with their possessions (15:7-8). Their cries of grief and despair, echoing all the way back to the towns of Eglaim and Beer-elim in the northwest part of Moab, reflect the national character of the disaster (Clements: 153).

The second stanza features an otherwise unknown town of Dimon (15:9). The NRSV takes this to be a reference to Dibon, the well-known town mentioned in 15:2. This may be so, but some geographers believe Dimon was another town (Smith: 372). The last part of the stanza seems to be more of a threat than a lament: *But I will bring still more* (NIV). The prophet, speaking in the Lord's name here, alludes to a future disaster. The stanza as a whole draws the curtain on a scene of appalling anguish at the calamity that has fallen upon Moab.

Moabites in Judah 16:1-5

16:1-4a Compassion for the Moabites

Now the scene shifts to neighboring Judah, and the focus is on a plea from the Moabites for sanctuary. It is not possible to link this scene with a particular historical event. If the prophet had wanted to do so, it could have been done. Instead, there are themes and images that invite interpretation, as is the case for the subject matter of chapter 15 as well.

The NIV paraphrases the first line of 16:1 to read *Send lambs as tribute* because a more direct translation yields less sense. Tribute as the price of protection, however, goes beyond the simple meaning of the text. Rather, a symbolic gift is to be sent from Sela, a Moabite town, to the king of Judah, with the prospect that Judah will provide safe haven for Moabite refugees. *The mount of the daughter of Zion* usually means the temple in Jerusalem, although in this case it appears to refer to the city of Jerusalem (Clements: 153).

In the second stanza the reference to the daughters of Moab links them to the daughter of Zion in the first stanza. The daughters of Moab stand in need of refuge at the fords of the brook Arnon (16:2).

The request for safe haven is made in the last two stanzas (16:3a, 3b-4a). Moab as the weaker party appeals for compassion to Judah as the stronger party. Their traditional antagonism is now being put to the test.

16:4b-5 Davidic Rule

Whether 16:4b-5 represents a continuation of the plea (Seitz: 139) or a reply to the plea (Clements: 153) cannot be determined with certainty. It seems best to take 16:4b as a proclamation that the devastation of 15:1-9 has ended. The end of destruction precedes a messianic vision that Moab's hope and Judah's hope are the same (16:5). Both await a messianic ruler embracing steadfast love, faithfulness, justice, and righteousness (Oswalt, 1986:343; cf. Isa 9:6-7).

Grieving for Moab 16:6-14

16:6-11 Hushing the Shout of Joy

The manifesto concludes with a reprise, continuing the lament of 15:1-9 but introducing the theme of pride, also a major point in the Babylon manifesto (13:13-14). Three uses of the adverb *therefore* punctuate the reprise (16:7, 9, 11).

The opening stanza focuses accusingly on the pride of Moab (16:6). The next three stanzas, introduced by the first *therefore*, state the repercussion of this pride (16:7, 8a, 8b). The focus of this repercussion is the destruction of Moab's vineyards and viticulture. The *raisin-cakes of Kir-Hareseth* symbolize Moabite prosperity. These raisin cakes are not cakes baked with raisins but raisins pressed into blocks, possibly for sale or export (16:7; cf. Gray: 291). Viticulture has long been important to the economy of Kir-Hareseth (probably modern Kerek in the Hashemite Kingdom of Jordan). Sibmah was known for its vineyards (16:8a, 8b; cf. Jer 48:32).

A second *therefore* extends the image of viticulture in the next three stanzas (16:9a, 9b-10a, 10b). It portrays Moab's grief over its economic loss in the wake of the invasion. The prophet enters into this grief with his tears (16:9a). The usual joy of the harvest is stilled (16:9b-10a). In 16:10b the Lord speaks through the prophet's words.

With a third *therefore* the prophet concludes his lament (16:11). Mood and language recall 16:7, where the lament for Moab and Kir-Hareseth begins. The prophets, with the exception of Jonah, did not delight in pronouncing judgment (cf. Mic 1:8; Jer 9:1, 18). They pronounce judgment with tears and lamentation.

16:12-14 Moab's Demise

The reference to the high place in the first stanza (16:12) recalls the high places at the beginning of chapter 15 (15:2). The weeping and lamentation and shaved head and beard in 15:2 all receive their interpretation here. In its places of worship, Moab is unable to find consolation for the devastation it has experienced. This indicates that the religious leaders of Moab could not give a theological interpretation of the disaster. No sense could be made of such a terrible event in Moab's history.

The focus of the second stanza rests on the contrast between the

Lord's word from the past and for the future (16:13-14). The word from the past consists of the manifesto concerning Moab in 15:1–16:11. This word describes Moab's defeat and devastation in the past with an indication that the theological reason for the defeat was Moab's pride. The word for the future contemplates an even greater disaster, when *her survivors will be very few and feeble* (NIV). The reference to three years indicates a brief time period before the onset of this disaster.

THE TEXT IN BIBLICAL CONTEXT

Lament

Weeping and lamentation are part of the human experience. So it is not surprising that there is a rich literature of lamentation in the OT. Well over a third of the psalms in the Psalter are laments, individual (e.g., 22, 42–43, 139) and communal (e.g., 44, 80). Most of these follow a lament form that moves through complaint and petition to a testimony of praise at the end (Anderson, 1974:56-58; Martens: 301-2). Chapters 3 and 5 of the book of Lamentations follow this lament form.

The laments in Isaiah 15:1-9 and 16:6-11 present the *experience* of lament, but not its formal character. This experience is described by using the words and emotions of grief and despair (weeping, wailing, mourning, tears). Moab is both the subject and the object of lament.

What is in view here is a national lament, not merely for the loss of wealth and possessions, but also for the loss of a homeland. The means of production is gone. Security is gone. Well-being is gone. Darfur provides a modern comparison. The tragedy is all but impossible to imagine.

THE TEXT IN THE LIFE OF THE CHURCH

The Plight of Refugees

When the South Africa Council of Churches (SACC) held its national conference at St. Barnabas College in Johannesburg in July of 1987, I attended as a Mennonite Central Committee observer. The theme of the conference was "Refugees and Exiles: Challenge the Churches." Three challenges to the churches captured my imagination. One was a challenge to rewrite the definition of "refugee" and to find ways and means of resolving the root causes of refugee production.

In 1987 some five million refugees existed in Africa alone, but millions more lived as refugees within their own borders and so were not counted. Rewriting the definition of *refugee* and resolving causes of refugee production are a continuing challenge to the church.

The second challenge to the churches emphasized the biblical perspective, with its call to be motivated by justice. "But that is really only the point of entry," said one of the speakers. "More importantly, we must be motivated by solidarity and brotherhood and fellowship with refugees. That is the foundation. The energy for this solidarity has to come from our grasp of the power of the resurrection. If we are not a resurrection community," he said, "we might as well 'call it a day.'"

The third challenge to the churches was to play a much larger role in advocacy. By this was meant calling sister churches, especially those in the Northern Hemisphere, to become involved in the refugee issue.

If the manifesto concerning Moab in Isaiah 15 and 16 has no other impact on the church, at least it should be a wake-up call to the plight of refugees in the twenty-first century. The refugee crisis is as lamentable today as it was in 1987. The challenge to the church is to address conditions that create refugees. Among these conditions are the problem of war and the social and economic conditions that lead to war.

Isaiah 17:1–18:7

Nations Manifesto: Damascus

PREVIEW

Damascus, although named in the opening line of chapter 17, plays only a supporting role in this manifesto. Ephraim (the Israelites) emerges as the more pivotal player. It has been suggested that by naming Damascus while focusing on Ephraim, the author intended to classify Ephraim as one of the nations (Seitz: 142). Ethiopia and the world at large complete the manifesto's addressees.

Ephraim's status as one of the nations comes about because its people have forgotten the Lord. But Ephraim still has a role to play in spite of its forgetfulness, because it represents the place and the memory of the Lord's name. Nations will come to that place even if Ephraim has abandoned it.

The first part of the manifesto speaks of the decline of Damascus and Ephraim to remnant status (17:1-14). They are faded remnants of a former glory. The prophet addresses the root cause of Ephraim's desolation. The many raging peoples, perpetrators of Ephraim's desolation, are themselves scolded and scattered.

The second part of the manifesto addresses Ethiopia in particular and the world in general (18:1-7). The world at large represents the commonwealth of nations who are addressed and challenged to heed the Lord's word to the prophet. The messengers, sent by the Lord to one of these nations, elicit a positive response to the Lord.

Isaiah 17:1-18:7

OUTLINE

Outcry Concerning Damascus, 17:1-14
   17:1-3   Remnant of Aram
   17:4-6   Remnant of Jacob
   17:7-11   Too Little, Too Late
   17:12-14   Rebuking the Peoples
Woe, Land of Whirring Wings, 18:1-7
   18:1-2   Go, Swift Messengers!
   18:3-7   Listen, Earthlings!

EXPLANATORY NOTES

Outcry Concerning Damascus 17:1-14

The first part of the manifesto exhibits a definite structure, although finding it requires patience. There is a pattern at the beginning because of the messenger formula [*Messenger Formula, p. 447*] *says the LORD* in 17:3 and 6. Each messenger formula sanctions the idea of a remnant and stresses the common nation status of both Damascus (Aram) and Jacob (Ephraim). The Damascus-Jacob alliance follows a course to oblivion in 17:7-9, and Jacob receives special censure in 17:10-11. At the end the tables are turned, however, and sudden terror descends on the peoples who plundered Jacob (17:12-14).

17:1-3 Remnant of Aram

Ephraim and Damascus appear side by side as casualties of some calamity. Clements (158) argues that this calamity refers to the Syro-Ephraimite war of 734-732 BC (cf. Isa 7). Ephraim refers to the territory in the Northern Kingdom (Israel), with Shechem as its most important city. Damascus refers to the capital city of Syria (also known in the Bible as Aram; cf. Pitard: 5-7).

The clue to 17:1-3 lies in the second stanza (17:3). The chiasm [*Literary Perspective, p. 446*] in the first four lines may be stated as follows:

    A—fortress . . . Ephraim
       B—kingdom . . . Damascus
       B'—remnant of Aram
    A'—glory of the Israelites

The transformation of Ephraim-Israelites from fortress to glory (A-A') "frames" the transformation of Damascus-Aram from kingdom to remnant (B-B′). There are no verbs used in presenting the picture of Damascus-Aram (B-B′). The verbs *will disappear* and *will be like*, describing Ephraim's fate, are in the "frame" (A-A′) and govern the fate of Aram. The phrase *the glory of the Israelites* (NIV) refers to a glory that once was.

Aroer (17:2 NRSV footnote) alludes to a city of Moab on the Arnon River, some 180 miles due south of Damascus. It seems strange that Aroer should be mentioned here rather than a place name closer to Damascus. As a result most scholars and translations emend the text to read *Her cities will be forever deserted* (Kaiser, 1974:75) or something similar. The NIV translates the Hebrew literally, yet the problem of geography remains, without a clear solution at hand.

17:4-6 Remnant of Jacob

Now the picture of Damascus-Aram fades, and in its place appears a portrait of Jacob. The glory of the Israelites in 17:3 becomes the glory of Jacob in 17:4. The opening line of 17:4, *On that day*, refers to a time in the future, and the next two lines emphasize the fading and emaciation of Jacob (17:4). Two figures of speech drawn from the grain and olive harvests paint a new picture of Jacob's diminished state (17:5-6). The Valley of Rephaim lies southwest of Jerusalem, in the territory of Judah (cf. Josh 15:8). The final line, *says the LORD God of Israel*, puts the stamp of the Lord's authority on the prophet's message.

17:7-11 Too Little, Too Late

In the first stanza it seems that a return to the Lord will save the day (17:7-8). The central meaning of the stanza lies in the contrast between the Holy One of Israel as the *Creator* of humankind (*ha'adam*), and humankind as the *creators* of altars to other gods. Here humankind seems to refer to Aram and Ephraim in particular rather than to humankind in general. Although a return to God's plan is envisioned, the consequence of abandoning the Lord for other gods runs its course (17:9). The NIV follows the Hebrew text more closely in reading *places abandoned to thickets and undergrowth* here (cf. NRSV, emending the text by following the LXX: *deserted places of the Hivites and the Amorites*). Either way, responsibility for abandoning the Lord falls on the Israelites, to whom the promise was given.

The last stanza addresses the Israelites directly (17:10-11). Having lost sight of the God of their salvation, they took up the easier path of alien gods. The Rock as a metaphor for God appears in Deuteronomy 32 and elsewhere in the Bible. The two references to *in/on the day* in 17:11 clearly echo the two references to *in/on that day* which open 17:7 and 9.

17:12-14 Rebuking the Peoples

The last part of the section is separated from the first three parts because of the lack of specific vocabulary to tie them together. The image of peoples raging and roaring uncontrollably and then fleeing when they hear a rebuke from the Lord lies at the center of this part. The one who rebukes the peoples refers to the Lord, whose name occurs in the preceding stanzas.

The identity of the peoples remains an enigma. Whoever they are, they bear responsibility for making Damascus a heap of ruins and for snuffing out the glory of the Israelites (17:1-3). They represent the harvester who leaves little behind (17:5-6) and the enemy who drives out the inhabitants of secure cities (17:9).

Now the tables are turned. Those who made terrified people flee now find themselves fleeing sudden terror. The prophet, speaking for the faded glory of Jacob, adds a word of personal triumph that those who have imposed their will on the people of God will now pay for their imposition (17:14).

Woe, Land of Whirring Wings 18:1-7

18:1-2 Go, Swift Messengers!

The poetry of chapter 18 opens with the word *woe* (NIV), a familiar word among the prophets and Isaiah in particular (last noted in chap. 10) and often used in conjunction with a tragedy or disaster. As an interjection, *woe* indicates displeasure and reprimand. Ambassadors from Ethiopia receive the reprimand directed against their country. Ethiopia lies southwest of Palestine, in northeastern Africa, bordering on Egypt and the Red Sea. The *land of whirring wings* may refer to the movement of insect wings (BDB: 852). But it is more likely, following the Septuagint, that the "whirring wings" refers to boats, possibly to the flapping of sails (cf. Clements: 164). The Ethiopians would have used boats in travel up and down the Nile River.

But who are the swift messengers (*mal'akim qallim*) sent to a land divided by rivers? Are they the Ethiopian *ambassadors* (*ṣirim*)? The swift messengers seem to be the Lord's messengers, heading for Assyria, a land divided by rivers (the Tigris and Euphrates; cf. Janzen, 1972:60-61). Although the evidence points to Assyria, Assyria is not named.

18:3-7 Listen, Earthlings!

Now the focus shifts from swift messengers to the world at large. This means the nations, and they are to pay attention when the alarm is sounded (Gray: 313).

The Lord's word to the nations comes through the prophet. As in chapter 8, the word comes *to me*; autobiography resurfaces momentarily. In a brief message, the prophet hears the Lord declare his quiet observation of the nations. This quiet observation stands in contrast to the raging of the peoples as well as to the Israelites' bitter harvest of grief and pain (18:4).

The Lord's word to the nations lies in the imagery of pruning before the harvest. Submitting to the Lord's discipline of pruning results in a bountiful harvest (18:5).

It seems clear that one of the nations, *a nation mighty and conquering*, hears this word and responds by bringing gifts to the place where the Lord's name dwells. This recalls the nations streaming to the mountain of the Lord's house in 2:1-5. There they receive the Lord's instruction and determine to walk in his paths (cf. Mic 7:16-17).

THE TEXT IN BIBLICAL CONTEXT

Why *Do* the Nations Rage?

The image of nations raging appears in one of the messianic psalms, Psalm 2, as well as elsewhere in the Psalter (cf. Ps 46). In Psalm 2 nations and peoples rage against the Lord, only to be warned to serve the Lord with fear in order to avoid his anger. Psalm 2 concludes with a blessing on all who take refuge in the Lord. In Isaiah, the nations' raging (17:12) is followed by the Lord's quiet answer (18:4).

In Isaiah 5:30, after the vivid description of an invasion, the invading nation roars like a lion and like the sea. And the peoples rage and roar in Isaiah 17:12-13. Jeremiah reflects this same imagery in 6:23. The Lord uses this raging of the nations to judge the earth (Isa 13:4-5). But the Lord also censures this raging when the raging gets out of hand, scattering the nations (Ps 83).

The nations' raging lies in their preoccupation with economic power and military force and utter self-interest. Plunder and pillage, whether by military forces or by civil governments, often results (Isa 17:14).

The Nation and the Nations

With the call to Abraham and Sarah, Genesis 12 strikes the keynote of nationhood in the Bible. God calls them and promises to make them a great nation and to bless them with a great name so that all the families of the earth might be blessed. Over against this "great nation" stands the nations of the world.

The Hebrew word for "nation" (*goy*) refers specifically to the descendants of Abraham and Sarah (Gen 17:4-6, 16). It refers, in particular, to

Israel and Judah in a number of texts (Isa 1:4; 10:6; Jer 5:9, 29; 7:28; 9:8; 12:17; Exod 19:6; Deut 4:6; Josh 3:17). But *goy* often refers to non-Israelite peoples as well (Exod 9:24; 34:10; Lev 25:44; Num 14:15; Deut 15:6; Isa 11:10, 12).

The promise to Abraham and Sarah to make them a great nation came to be understood narrowly as chosenness. Isaiah's word of judgment addresses the great nation and the nations on equal terms. All the nations (including Israel) will be judged.

Forgetting God

Human forgetfulness is proverbial. People forget appointments and anniversaries. People who were once poor forget to open their hands to the poor once their own wealth increases. People forget God.

In Isaiah 17:10-11 the adoption of a foreign god accompanies the forgetting of the God of Israel. Not only this. The people of Israel also seek other gods *because* they have forgotten the God of Israel. There is a void to fill, and a spurious spirituality fills the void of the God, now forgotten, who brings salvation and provides refuge. It is not, however, simply a case of mental lapse that causes forgetting of God. In the Bible the emphasis is that people have a choice whether or not to be faithful to God.

Jeremiah declares with some frequency and heat that God's people have forgotten him (2:32; 3:21; 13:25; 18:15; 23:26-27; 50:6). They trust lies rather than trusting the Lord, he says (13:25; 23:26-27). Hosea, too, places an accent on the reality of Israel forgetting God (2:13; 4:6; 8:14; 13:6).

Deuteronomic teaching warns against forgetting God (Deut 4:9, 23; 6:12; 8:11, 14, 19; 32:18). In Deuteronomy, as in Isaiah 17:10-11, forgetting corresponds with not remembering; it is a choice and an act of the will to forget.

The Bible expresses an awareness that many distractions and amusements clamor for attention in human life. Many of these distractions and amusements lead to grief and despair. Loyalty to the God who pledges salvation and refuge demands a cancellation of these distractions and amusements or at least a counterbalance to them. It demands a conscious and deliberate determination not to forget God.

THE TEXT IN THE LIFE OF THE CHURCH

A Great Nation

Synagogue and church and mosque continue to face the challenge of becoming *a great nation*, according to the promise given to Abraham and Sarah (Gen 12:2). The temptation has always been to become "like other nations," raging and roaring like the sea, demanding divine legitimacy for the plunder and pillage of war (1 Sam 8:5, 20).

In his book *The Tenth Generation*, George Mendenhall provides a superb critique of religious systems that fail the promise:

> It seems valid to conclude that the biblical tradition has always been most creative and socially functional during periods when the community was without any great political or economic power. Conversely, the most shocking and corrupt periods in the history of religion generally occur when the religious system is identified with a monopoly of force. It is then that the religious and political tribalisms reinforce each other to create the atrocities for which religion is usually blamed. Religion should be blamed—but it is not the normative biblical tradition that has gained the ascendancy when such atrocities occur. Rather, it is the natural pagan religion of unregenerate man that identifies the distinction between good and evil with an arbitrary political boundary line, and in so doing identifies God with the political monopoly of force. (xi-xii)

Isaiah 19:1–20:6

Nations Manifesto: Egypt

PREVIEW

After manifestos concerning Babylon (13–14), Moab (15–16), and Damascus (17–18), the fourth manifesto begins with a requiem for Egypt and ends with an acted-out parable directed at Egypt and Ethiopia (19–20).

A menacing tone characterizes the first part of the manifesto concerning Egypt (19:1-15). Then menace resolves into blessing (19:16-25). A final warning to Egypt and Ethiopia brings the manifesto to its conclusion (20:1-6).

How do these changing moods—threat, blessing, warning—fit together in a coherent pattern? There are two "signals" indicating mood changes. The series of *on that day* expressions beginning in 19:16 constitutes the first signal. At 19:16 the text turns from menace and moves toward a new outlook, with blessing as its consummation. The second signal comes into view at 20:1. Here again expressions of time (*in the year, at that time, on that day*) mark a transition from blessing to warning.

OUTLINE

Outcry Concerning Egypt, 19:1-15
    19:1-4   Civil War in Egypt
    19:5-7   Drying Up the Nile
    19:8-10   Fishers and Weavers Lament
    19:11-15   Sages and Princes Deceive Egypt
Egypt's Repentance and Blessing, 19:16-25
    19:16-18   Terror in Egypt

19:19-22	Egypt's Repentance
19:23-25	Blessing on Egypt, Assyria, and Israel

Warning to Egypt and Ethiopia, 20:1-6

20:1-2	Parable of Sackcloth and Sandals
20:3-4	Egypt and Ethiopia in Captivity
20:5-6	Judah's Plight

EXPLANATORY NOTES

Outcry Concerning Egypt 19:1-15

Egypt has always played a critical role in the region, as much today as in antiquity. The wealth of the Nile has provided Egypt with a powerful economic base for millennia. The land's fertility, as Isaiah knew it, depended on the regular flooding of the Nile, making agriculture possible in Egypt (cf. Noth: 185).

The section begins with domestic turmoil in Egypt and concludes with a perspective on the senseless advice given to Pharaoh, which brought Egypt to this state of affairs. Within this section a theme can be discerned that gives it coherence. This theme rises to the surface in the contrast between the plans of Egypt and the Lord's plan. The critical question of interpretation lies in the meaning of these contrasting plans.

19:1-4 Civil War in Egypt

Ugaritic poetry describes *Baal as the Rider of the Clouds* (ANET: 132). The poet in Isaiah 19 describes the Lord as *riding on a swift cloud* as he arrives in Egypt. The language of ancient Near Eastern spirituality cannot be denied to the Hebrew prophets. The writer uses the Canaanite imagery of God as cloud rider to assert the Lord's authority beyond Palestine in Egypt.

Beginning in 19:2, the Lord's arrival strikes fear into the Egyptian deities and the Egyptians themselves. The Lord speaks in the first person. Egyptian fear leads to political chaos initiated by the Lord himself. This chaos, then, leads to a ravaging of the Egyptian spirit (19:3). When the spirit of a nation is ravaged, spiritism easily replaces spirit (Oswalt, 1986:368). So it is here. Egyptian plans, which the Lord confuses, rest on the intention to find meaning and direction in conjury and sorcery. The Egyptians themselves bear responsibility for seeking this path of spiritism. In the end the political life of Egypt collapses (19:4).

First the Lord *stirs up* the Egyptians by dividing them against each other. Then the Lord *confuses* their plans, which are leading them in a misguided search for meaning.

19:5-7 Drying Up the Nile

This segment and the next stand apart from what precedes and follows as examples of the magnitude of the Egyptian calamity. The Nile itself, source of economic life and stability, fails. First the waters in the Nile dry up (19:5-6), then the fields irrigated by the Nile dry up (19:7).

19:8-10 Fishers and Weavers Lament

Those who earn their livelihood as fishers on the Nile will be among the first to experience the impact of the Nile's failure (19:8). Those who ret the flax grown in the fields along the Nile and those who weave the flax into linen will soon follow (19:9-10). Both laborers and artisans will suffer when the labor-intensive linen industry fails.

The Nile itself and those who depend on it for their livelihood receive attention in these examples. The Lord's displeasure with Egypt expresses itself in the assertion of his authority over the Nile, on which the Egyptians depend (Clements: 168).

19:11-15 Sages and Princes Deceive Egypt

Zoan (named Tanis by the Greeks) lay in the northeastern part of the delta region of the Nile. Once the capital of Egypt, it nourished the wisdom tradition of the Nile (cf. Watts, 1985:254). The train of thought in chapter 19 returns to the main theme of the Lord's plan as it relates to Egyptian plans. The three stanzas in 19:11-15 highlight the poor advice that Egypt has received from its leadership. The first stanza focuses the question (19:11). In dramatic fashion the prophet asks the princes and counselors how they have the temerity to remind Pharaoh of their prudence and position (Gray: 329).

The second stanza raises the ante another notch (19:12-13). The prophet taunts the Egyptian advice-givers with a rhetorical question: *Where now are your sages?* The answer continues the taunt. *Let them tell you* the Lord's plan against Egypt if they are so wise. Egypt's reputation for its wisdom is legendary (ANET: 412-25). Yet with one sweep of the hand, the prophet in Isaiah 19 dismisses this wisdom as having no sense. It has no rootage in the plan of the Lord. The princes of Memphis and Zoan, the architects and carriers of the Egyptian wisdom tradition, depend on plans resting on the way things *are* rather than on the way things *might* be if informed by the wisdom of the Lord.

The result fills stanza 3 (19:14-15). Because their own wisdom cannot help them, the princes and rulers create havoc in Egypt. Nothing can be done for Egypt unless, it may be said, Egypt receives the wisdom of the Lord at the mountain of the Lord's house (2:2).

Egypt's Repentance and Blessing 19:16-25

Modern translations place Isaiah 19:16-25 as well as chapter 2 in a prose format (cf. NRSV, NIV, JB). Maintaining a poetic format is also possible with the additional benefit of providing a sense of continuity with what precedes and follows (cf. Watts, 1985:248-49, 256-57, 262-63).

19:16-18 Terror in Egypt

Now the scene shifts from mere *result* of the deception of Egypt's leaders; it now focuses on *discipline* leading to wisdom, which rests on knowing the Lord. This scene and those that follow emphasize Egypt's deliverance and blessing.

The adverbial phrase *on that day* introduces the first stanza (19:16). This stanza features the hand of the Lord poised to strike, and shows Egyptian terror at this uplifted hand. Throughout Isaiah 1–12 the stretched-out hand of the Lord signifies the Lord's anger directed at his people (5:25; 9:12, 17, 21; 10:4). Here, though, the raised hand of the Lord targets the Egyptians, who recoil in terror. The second stanza stresses Egyptian terror, which now focuses on the Southern Kingdom (Judah) as the Lord's agent (19:17). The Lord's plan against Egypt is not spelled out for the reader, but the Egyptians know it and fear it.

Another *on that day* expression introduces the third stanza (19:18). The five cities in Egypt are not identified except for the *City of Destruction* (NIV). As a place name *City of Destruction* ('*ir haheres*) boasts weighty Hebrew manuscript support but lacks clear sense in its context. Some Hebrew manuscripts read *Sun City* (NRSV), probably Heliopolis (ancient On), which yields better sense but lacks solid manuscript support. Jeremiah mentions four places in Egypt where Judeans lived: Migdol, Tahpanhes, Memphis, and the land of Pathros (44:1). Jewish residents in Egypt attracted Egyptian adherents, who united with Egyptian Jews and used Hebrew (the language of Canaan) in their worship (Clements: 171). Among these Jewish communities was the city mentioned in 19:18, but it is not clearly identifiable.

19:19-22 Egypt's Repentance

A third *on that day* expression introduces this section. At some period of time in the future, says the prophet, symbols of the Lord's authority (altar and pillar) will be present in Egypt (19:19). The second stanza focuses on the importance of altar and pillar as sign and witness (19:20). Here the language recalls the book of Judges (cf. 3:9). But now those who *cry to the LORD because of oppressors* are the Egyptians. In the second stanza the focus rests on the Egyptians, who appeal to the Lord for help.

The third stanza emphasizes this Egyptian allegiance to the Lord of hosts *on that day* (19:21). Allegiance here means knowing the Lord. The prophet uses the language of knowing the Lord as it is used in the plagues narrative in Exodus 7–12. In that narrative the plagues serve as signs to the Egyptians so that they will know the Lord's power. Here knowing the Lord means that the Egyptians turn to the Lord and identify themselves with him (Clements:172). Commitment to the worship of the Lord makes this identification clear.

The final stanza emphasizes Egypt's healing (19:22). The idea of striking in order to heal seems counterproductive and excessive. Exodus employs the Hebrew word for *strike (ngp)* to refer to the plagues. In Exodus and here, however, the term implies that strong defiance demands strong discipline. The Lord's plan includes discipline for Egypt, discipline in order to bring healing. And when the Egyptians turn to the Lord, the Lord heals them.

19:23-25 Blessing on Egypt, Assyria, and Israel

Two final *on that day* adverbial phrases conclude the series and the section as a whole. The first announces a highway connecting Egypt and Assyria so that they can worship together (19:23). The second includes Israel and announces a tripartite blessing (19:24-25 AT; cf. NIV):

> my people, Egypt
> my handiwork, Assyria
> my inheritance, Israel

Using language normally reserved for Israel, the prophet brings the great powers on the Nile and the Tigris-Euphrates into a new relationship with each other and with Israel.

Warning to Egypt and Ethiopia 20:1-6

20:1-2 Parable of Sackcloth and Sandals

A sudden shift in mood and subject takes the reader to the time when the Assyrian king Sargon laid siege to Ashdod (one of the five main Philistine cities) and captured it in 711 BC (20:1; *ANET*:286; cf. Clements: 174).

Here the Lord speaks to Isaiah the son of Amoz again. Previously the prophet's name and patronymic have occurred in 1:1; 2:1; and 13:1. Later they appear in 37:2, 21 and 38:1. Lacking reference to a vision proper, there is simply a command for Isaiah to go and disrobe. A note of compliance follows the command (20:2). Whether Isaiah disrobed *completely* or only removed his outer garments cannot be determined. Even the latter would have exposed him to insult and indignity (Gray: 346).

The Lord's bidding to Isaiah to disrobe appears to forecast the despoiling of Ashdod. Although this acting out of the forecast occurred at the time of Assyria's conquest of Ashdod, Isaiah probably did not wait until the meaning of his action was clear before explaining it (Clements: 173).

20:3-4 Egypt and Ethiopia in Captivity

The original acted-out parable receives a new interpretation in the next two stanzas. Here the parable focuses on the people of Egypt and Ethiopia, who will be led into captivity without even the clothes on their backs. An introductory clause forms the first stanza (20:3). The acted-out prophetic sign continues for three years. No doubt this represents the time when there was a quest for Egyptian aid by Judah. A main clause forms the second stanza, beginning with *so shall the king of Assyria* . . . (20:4). Here the acted-out prophetic sign drives its point home. Egyptians and Ethiopians, as ill-clad prisoners of war, face an uncertain future in Assyrian hands.

20:5-6 Judah's Plight

The first stanza seems to point to the people of Judah who sought military help from Egypt and Ethiopia (20:5). In the eighth and seventh centuries BC, Ethiopia conquered Egypt and formed the twenty-fifth Egyptian Dynasty. It may have been Tirhakah, one of the kings of this dynasty (*ANET*: 293), to whom Judah appealed for help against Assyria (cf. *NHBD*: 175). Egypt and Ethiopia could not provide help and deliverance from the Assyrian king.

In the second stanza it seems best to identify *the people who live on this coast* (NIV) with the perplexed and terror-stricken people along the Mediterranean coast, including Judah, who were betrayed by Egypt (20:6; cf. Brueggemann, 1998a:168). It is true that they were betrayed by Egypt. But also Judah in particular was betrayed by its own leaders, who sought Egyptian help in defiance of the prophet's word from the Lord that Egyptian help was against God's plan for his people (cf. Isa 30:1-5).

THE TEXT IN BIBLICAL CONTEXT

Acted-out Prophetic Signs

Acting out a message, rather than simply speaking it, belongs to the prophetic movement in ancient Israel and to the witness of the NT. In Isaiah 20 walking naked and barefoot signifies the impending captivity of

Egypt and Ethiopia. Jeremiah buys a linen loincloth and buries it. When he digs it up and finds it ruined, he perceives that in the same way the Lord will ruin the pride of Judah and Jerusalem (Jer 13:1-11). The book of Jeremiah has other examples of messages acted out (e.g., 16:1-9; 19:1–20:6; 27:1–28:17; 32:1-44; 35:1-19; 43:8-13; 51:59-64). In a series of symbolic actions (a pantomime in three scenes) followed by a sermon, Ezekiel portrays the impending siege of Jerusalem (4:1–5:17). Pantomime and sermon together aim to bring Israel to accept "the power of the Lord's word to determine their future" (Lind, 1996:56).

Jesus' triumphal entry into Jerusalem shortly before his death is best understood as an acted-out parable signifying the nonviolence of his kingship (Mark 11:1-11).

The story of Agabus in Acts 21:7-14 begins with a symbolic action that captures the attention and the imagination of the people in Philip's house. An explanation, using the messenger formula common to the Hebrew prophets, follows the symbolic action. The explanation removes any doubt about the meaning of the action.

These symbolic actions serve to make God's message to his people and to the nations poignant, piercing the armor of human pride and prejudice, touching the spiritual fabric of human life.

On That Day . . .

The expression "on that day" occurs at many places in the OT, often in clusters. The phrase may refer simply to specific days marking certain events (e.g., Judg 20:15, 21, 26, 35, 46). In Deuteronomy 31 it appears in the Lord's words to Moses near the time of his death. The forecast is that after Moses' death, the Israelites will forsake the Lord and turn to other gods. The Lord says, "My anger will be kindled against them in that day" (Deut 31:17).

The prophets in particular use "on that day" language to refer to something that will happen at some time in the future, either for weal or for woe (e.g., Amos 8:3, 9; Hos 2:18, 20, 22; Isa 2:11, 17, 20; 19:16-24). The prophets' emphasis on God's judgment leaves the impression that they have forgotten about God's mercy. In fact they have not forgotten about God's mercy because the call to repentance remains inseparable from the proclamation of a day of judgment.

THE TEXT IN THE LIFE OF THE CHURCH

Egypt, Assyria, Israel

The Quaker study *Search for Peace in the Middle East* was a bold effort by one of the peace churches to express concern and to affirm hope for the region after the Six-Day War in 1967. Can the political powers on the Nile and the Tigris-Euphrates River systems come together with the political power on the land bridge linking Africa, Asia, and Europe? The Quaker study proposed that they could and suggested practical steps for accomplishing it.

The first step urged psychological and emotional disengagement to prepare the way for a settlement. The second step pressed for military disengagement to reduce violence in the region. The third step urged the structuring of a political settlement embracing the rights of all the parties in the dispute. The fourth step strongly advocated development of a frame of mind in the region conducive to the growth of peace.

The Quaker study received widespread criticism along with much widespread acclaim in the 1970s. The editor of a collection of responses to the Quaker study commented that the "difference between the Quakers and their critics is that the Quakers are willing to hope while its critics have abandoned hope" (Solomonow: 78). At the center of the prophecy in Isaiah 19:23-25 lies a blessing for establishing cordial relations between sworn enemies. The Lord works as an arbitrator, announcing hope where most human beings simply abandon hope.

Acted-out Prophecy Today

Prayer vigils in public places can be effective acted-out prophecy today. At noon on Good Friday each year, South Dakota Peace and Justice holds a service at the South Dakota State Penitentiary in Sioux Falls to protest the death penalty. People of many ages and creeds call for an end to the death penalty by meeting on Good Friday, when the church commemorates the death of Jesus—which happened by public execution.

Isaiah 21:1-22:25

Manifestos of Doom

PREVIEW

Chapters 21 and 22 paint a picture of upheaval and destruction in the Fertile Crescent, a geographical region encompassing the Tigris and Euphrates Rivers, Palestine, and the Nile delta. Babylon falls to the armies of Elam and Media (21:1-10). The Arabian desert oases of Dumah, Tema, and Kedar suffer attack and defeat by an unnamed enemy (21:12-17). The valley of vision, probably referring to Jerusalem, hosts enemy chariotry (22:1-14). Jerusalem itself serves as a microcosm of regional upheaval. Shebna faces disgrace, and Eliakim takes his place in the palace, but not for long (22:15-25).

These manifestos are public announcements, sometimes declaring a warning, sometimes a word of judgment. Where does the reader find illumination in these pictures?

OUTLINE

Outcry Concerning the Desert by the Sea (Babylon), 21:1-10
    21:1-5   News of an Invasion
    21:6-7   Observing the Invaders' Arrival
    21:8-10   Fall of Babylon Announced
Outcries Concerning Desert Regions, 21:11-17
    21:11-12   Dumah
    21:13-17   Tema and Kedar
Outcry Concerning the Valley of Vision (Jerusalem), 22:1-25
    22:1-4   Empty Joy

22:5-8a	Bitter Weeping
22:8b-11	Pointless Preparations
22:12-14	Reveling Instead of Repentance
22:15-19	Shebna's Banishment
22:20-25	Transfer of Authority to Eliakim

EXPLANATORY NOTES

Outcry Concerning the Desert by the Sea (Babylon) 21:1-10

Chapters 13–27 of the book of Isaiah fall into two parts, chapters 13–20 and 21–27, each part with 129 verses. Each part begins with a message concerning Babylon's fall. In chapter 13 Babylon appears in the first line. Here in chapter 21 *the Desert by the Sea* (NIV) in the first line conceals Babylon's name.

The first manifesto features the Hebrew verb for *tell* (*nagad*). It begins with a harsh vision which *is told to me* (21:2) and ends with a disclosure of the vision sender (the God of Israel) and the message, which *I tell to you* (21:10 NIV). Midway through the manifesto, the Lord instructs the prophet to post a watchman with instructions to *report* (= *tell*) *what he sees* (21:6 NIV).

21:1-5 News of an Invasion

The *Desert by the Sea* in the NIV gives a more specific rendering of the Hebrew text than the *wilderness of the sea* in the NRSV. A desert by the sea suggests the Babylonian Empire, stretching from sea (Mediterranean Sea) to shining sea (Persian Gulf). The whirlwinds in the first stanza refer to the invaders, *Elam* and *Media* (aided by Persia), lying immediately east of the Babylonian Empire (21:1). They are the plunderers and destroyers mentioned in the second stanza (21:2). The last line of the stanza—*I will bring to an end all the groaning she* [Babylon] *has caused* (21:2 NIV)—is best interpreted as a remark by the commander of the invasion forces, speaking in the prophet's vision.

In the next two stanzas the speaker, though not identified, is likely the prophet himself, appalled at the upheaval that has accompanied the demise of the empire (21:3-4). With the oblique reference to *the twilight I longed for*, the prophet has in mind Babylon's downfall, long imagined by Babylon's victims, but nevertheless a terrifying spectacle when it happens (21:4).

The call to arms goes out to the Babylonian officers enjoying themselves (21:5). Oiling the shields, in addition to making them less easily pierced, served as a religious rite, consecrating them before employing them in battle (cf. Clements: 178).

21:6-7 Observing the Invaders' Arrival

A messenger formula addressed to the prophet (*me*) introduces the brief dialogue in 21:6-7. Following the news of an invasion comes a time of anxious waiting for a report of the invasion force's arrival. Although the Lord instructs the prophet (*me*) to post a sentinel, the sentinel appears to be the prophet himself (21:6). Clements (178) finds support for this conclusion in Ezekiel 33:1-9, which depicts the prophet as a sentinel in ancient Israel.

21:8-10 Fall of Babylon Announced

The cry of the sentinel fills the first two stanzas (21:8, 9). The Hebrew Bible reads *'aryeh* (lion) in 21:8, and the KJV translates this line *And he cried, A lion!* Modern versions follow the textual evidence in the Dead Sea Scroll of Isaiah, which has the word *haro'eh* (sentinel) instead of *'aryeh* (lion). The sentinel, watching day and night, observes the approach of a herald, who then speaks, announcing not only the fall of Babylon but also the fall of Babylon's gods. Historically, Babylon fell to invaders from the East under Cyrus the Persian in 539 BC. The alliance of the Babylonian Empire and its deities meant that when one fell, the other fell with it.

This point is not lost on the Judean exiles in Babylon, whom the prophet addresses in 21:10. They understand that the Lord disciplines his people, sometimes by means of invasion and exile. And in Babylon they have learned that although the kingdom of Judah fell to the Babylonians, the God of Israel did not fall with it.

Outcries Concerning Desert Regions 21:11-17

The scene shifts away from Babylon now and to three desert regions where the shadow of Babylon's power has fallen. In three terse poetic statements, the prophet paints a picture of the terrors of war. According to Genesis 25 the twelve sons of Ishmael include Dumah, Tema, and Kedar. Ishmael was Abram's firstborn son (by Hagar). When Isaac was born (by Sarah), he was a half brother to Ishmael (Gen 16–17). Jacob and Esau, then, were nephews of Ishmael.

21:11-12 Dumah

The oasis of Dumah in northern Arabia begins the scene shift. The prophet understands someone calling to him from Seir (south of the Dead

Sea, extending almost to the Gulf of Aqabah, on the east side of the rift). Seir refers to the mountainous area known as Edom, the traditional home of Esau.

An Edomite asks the question *Watcher, what of the night?* (AT) and then repeats it to emphasize the question's importance. The reference to the night refers metaphorically to the night of oppression (Clements: 180). When will it be over (21:11)? The watcher's reference to the coming of morning suggests that the oppression will soon be over (21:12). Although the oppressor remains unspecified, Babylon, whose fall the previous section announces, qualifies as the most likely candidate. But all is not well because the return of night after the coming of morning indicates a new oppressor on the horizon.

21:13-17 Tema and Kedar

A second outcry concerns the desert, known today as the Arabian Desert. The oasis of Tema, some 160 miles south-southwest of Dumah, provided food and water for Dedanite caravans plying the caravan routes of the Fertile Crescent (Ezek 27:15, 20).

An inscription from the Neo-Babylonian Empire gives an account of Nabonidus' (555-539 BC) conquest of Tema (*ANET*: 313-14):

> . . . He started out for a long journey,
> The (military) forces of Akkad marching with him;
> He turned towards Tema (deep) in the west.
> He started out the expedition on a path (leading) to a distant
>   (region). When he arrived there,
> He killed in battle the prince of Tema,
> Slaughtered the flocks of those who dwell in the city (as well as)
>   in the countryside,
> And he, himself, took his residence in [Te]ma, the forces of Akkad
>   [were also stationed] there.
> He made the town beautiful, built (there) [his palace]
> Like the palace in Su.an.na (Babylon), he (also) built [walls]
> (For) the fortifications of the town and [. . .]
> He surrounded the town with sentinels [. . .]

While not immune to conquest, the desert served as a refuge for people fleeing conquered territories. The residents of Tema and the Dedanite traders were called upon to give provisions to these refugees (21:13-15).

A messenger formula introduces a final brief remark focusing on the desert (21:16-17). This remark indicates that a time, soon to come, will bring devastation to Kedar (a region in Arabia east of Transjordan, now in Saudi Arabia). The word *glory* means *abundance* or *honor* or *riches* (AT). The word of the Lord to the prophet indicates that Kedar's material wealth (*glory*) will disappear, and its military power will be decimated.

Outcry Concerning the Valley of Vision (Jerusalem) 22:1-25

A military campaign against Babylon resulting in Babylon's fall opens this manifesto (21:1-10). The shadow of Babylon's military campaigns into the desert falls on the memory of those who survived (21:11-17). Now the recollection of Babylon's military campaign against Jerusalem assaults the senses (22:1-25).

22:1-4 Empty Joy

A question, almost a taunt, opens the first stanza (22:1-2). The feminine singular *you* addresses the *Valley of Vision* (NIV), understood to be Jerusalem. This cryptic reference complements the other cryptic references in the manifesto (*Desert by the Sea*, 21:1; Dumah, 21:11; the desert, 21:13). This valley may refer to the valley of Hinnom, lying southwest of Jerusalem (Gold and Holladay: 893; cf. Jer 7:30-34). Jubilation abounds in the valley of vision, perhaps in anticipation that Jerusalem's army will be victorious. But this joy turns out to be unfounded.

The second stanza describes a scene of futile escape and certain capture (22:3). Woundedness and death have resulted from the escape attempt. Instead of defending the city, the army has been overwhelmed and its soldiers taken as prisoners of war. The tone of the description by an unnamed observer is one of disapproval if not taunt.

The prophet speaks in the last stanza, addressing those who fill the city with their ill-advised jubilation (22:4). With his people in captivity and the city destroyed, what is there to celebrate?

22:5-8a Bitter Weeping

The reply uses language of invasion (*tumult, trampling, and turmoil*) side by side with language of the day of the Lord (22:5 AT). This language matches the reference to the day of the Lord against every fortified wall in 2:15. The day has come to pass in the destruction of Jerusalem's walls. The *cry for help to the mountains* may refer to the cry of the city's people for help that echoes on the neighboring hills (Gray: 366).

The general description of the conquest of Jerusalem becomes more specific in the second stanza (22:6-8a). Elam and Kir probably represent contingents in Nebuchadnezzar's army when it entered Jerusalem in

587 BC. Elam occupied an area east of the Tigris River and northeast of the Persian Gulf. The location of Kir is disputed (Clements: 185).

The reference to *your choiceest valleys* alludes to Jerusalem's surrounding valleys, now filled with enemy chariotry. They arrive at Jerusalem's gates after having destroyed all the defensive positions in Judah.

22:8b-11 Pointless Preparations

Now the poetry shifts from an address to *the Valley of Vision* in particular (second-person f. sg.) to an address to the people of Jerusalem in general (second-person m. pl.; 22:8b-9):

> And you [2d f. s.] looked in that day
>   to the weapons in the Palace of the Forest;
> ⁹ you [2d m. pl.] saw that the City of David
>   had many breaches in its defenses;
> you [2d m. pl.] stored up water
>   in the Lower Pool. (NIV)

The Palace of the Forest alludes to the royal palace in Jerusalem, which served as an arsenal (Gray: 371). The references to *you* and *your* have the people of Jerusalem in mind. The energy employed to buttress the walls and to secure the water supply stands in contrast to the lack of attention to the vital signs of faith. These signs include recognizing God's power as the real power that needs to be embraced by the people of Jerusalem.

The leading idea of 22:8b-11 comes at the end of verse 11, where disregard for the Lord's plan dominates. It is characteristic of the human obsession with security and survival that it resorts to weaponry and elaborate defensive measures as the solution. The fear inside a city surrounded by enemy chariotry should not be discounted. Even so, the people failed to realize that an alternative to paralyzing fear lies in a renewed commitment to God's power and purpose.

22:12-14 Reveling Instead of Repentance

The prescription for honoring the Lord's plan is repentance (22:12). That the Lord *called* for repentance indicates a summons, a notification rather than mere encouragement. The phrase *on that day* appears at the end of the second line (as in NIV; in contrast to 22:20, 25). As an adverbial phrase, here it does not refer to a particular *day* of the Lord but rather to a general time.

The specific behavior of the people of Jerusalem is exhibited in the next stanza (22:13). Instead of repentance, there is festivity centering around reckless revelry, with the prospect of death in view.

The Lord announces his verdict to the prophet (22:14). *This sin* (NIV) refers to disregarding the Lord's plan by resorting to the politics of violence. The outcome will be death.

22:15-19 Shebna's Banishment

The last part of the chapter reports on two officials of Hezekiah's court: Shebna (22:15-19) and Eliakim (22:20-25). Shebna appears in Isaiah 36 and 37 (cf. 2 Kings 18–19), during the reign of Hezekiah, but as a secretary rather than as a steward. Watts (1985:290-91) assumes that the same Shebna is intended in Isaiah 22 and 36–37. Jerusalem's people have been inattentive to the vital signs of faith (22:11b). Now Shebna, displaying the same inattentiveness to the vital signs of faith, prepares his own tomb while Jerusalem faces approaching destruction.

The prophet receives a word from the Lord to visit Shebna at a burial ground and confront him with the impropriety of hewing out a tomb for himself (22:15-16). The Lord's response is framed in language evoking images of athletic skill (22:17-19). This response includes the opposite forces of holding and hurling, followed by an explanation. The holding refers to the preparation for hurling, much as a pitcher on a baseball team rubs the ball and gets a sign from the catcher before throwing a pitch. Continuing the baseball metaphor, as a good fastball with good location results in a strikeout and perhaps a riled batter, so the hurling refers to throwing a people into an exile of some kind, accompanied by disgrace and disaster. Shebna's behavior is a pointed example of corrupt government (Seitz: 161).

22:20-25 Transfer of Authority to Eliakim

Four concluding stanzas complete the section (22:20-21a, 21b-22, 23-24, 25). The "I" in the first three stanzas may be the Lord speaking or the speech of the king. Two *on that day* phrases frame the section at the beginning and at the end (22:20, 25). In the prophets the expression *on that day* indicates a future favor or misfortune. Here it is first favor, then misfortune.

Eliakim is mentioned with Shebna in Isaiah 36 and 37 (cf. 2 Kings 18–19) during Hezekiah's reign. Eliakim assumes the position vacated by Shebna. Robe, sash, and scepter (implied by *your authority*), formerly belonging to Shebna, now designate Eliakim's rank (22:20-21a). His designation as *father* to the people of Jerusalem and Judah means that he will care for their needs (22:21b-22; cf. Gray: 380). Likewise, the *key to the house of David* indicates his authority.

The reference to a *peg . . . fastened in a secure place* (22:25) summarizes the esteem accorded to Eliakim (22:23-24). This esteem is tied to the Davidic throne (his ancestral house, 22:23).

The final stanza, however, indicates that this security and esteem will not last (22:25). Although no reason is given, it is clear that the fall of the Davidic throne is anticipated (cf. Childs: 162). The peg that was thought to be firmly anchored cannot bear the weight placed upon it.

THE TEXT IN BIBLICAL CONTEXT

The Fall of Babylon

In Isaiah 13 and 21, Babylon's fall serves as a paradigm of God's judgment on the nations who hinder the Lord's design for the earth (cf. Watts, 1985:186-89). Jeremiah 51, where Babylon's evil with respect to Zion receives special attention, illustrates this paradigm (51:24). Babylon serves the Lord's purposes among the nations for a time, but then it exceeds its commission (51:7). So the Lord turns against Babylon and determines to make it a heap of ruins (51:37).

The Key to the House

The reference to the key to the house of David on Eliakim's shoulder in Isaiah 22:22 receives special attention at two places in the NT, Matthew 16:19 and Revelation 3:7-8. In Matthew 16 Jesus promises to give Peter the keys (pl.) of the kingdom of heaven, in a context where binding and loosing play a critical role. Matthew (and Jesus) appear to have Isaiah's reference to opening and closing in mind. As the key to the house of David signifies Eliakim's authority, so the keys promised to Peter give him authority.

In Revelation 3, John the Revelator quotes Isaiah 22:22 to show that it is the Lord who has the key of David and who has the authority to open and shut. The Lord sets before the church in Philadelphia an open door to continued faithfulness.

These three references to keys are used in vastly different settings. The common theme in all of them lies in the authority the key symbolizes.

THE TEXT IN THE LIFE OF THE CHURCH

Apostolic Succession Versus Binding and Loosing

The framing of a doctrine of apostolic succession occurred already at the end of the first century AD by Clement of Rome. The doctrine was understood at first to refer to *all* bishops as successors to Peter through the ordination of *all* the apostles. The crucial text was Matthew 16:18-19, with its reference to Jesus' giving to Peter the keys of the kingdom.

Some five centuries later, Pope Leo I (440-461) declared that since Peter ranked first among the apostles, Peter's successors should rank first among the bishops (Noss: 640-41). The effect was to transform a more general notion of apostolic succession not based on rank into a specific notion of apostolic succession based on Peter's special status among the apostles.

The believers churches growing out of the Reformation abandoned this definition of apostolic succession since the succession had been broken when the severance from the Roman Church took place. In any case the believers church reading of Matthew 16 yields an altogether different understanding of the text, especially when this chapter stands alongside Matthew 18. The doctrine of apostolic succession is seen as a product of church tradition rather than as arising out of a faithful reading of the text. The keys to the kingdom have to do with the church's authority to bind and loose, with "binding" meaning to withhold fellowship and "loosing" meaning to forgive. When the church as a whole or a particular congregation practices this kind of binding and loosing, they may be said to be exercising their claim to be the body of Christ.

Isaiah 23:1-18

Nations Manifesto: Tyre

PREVIEW

This manifesto, the last of Isaiah's messages against the nations in chapters 13–23, deals with the Phoenician commercial empire. It touches on commerce and industry and the haughtiness that easily accompanies success. Historically separate, the Phoenician coastal cities of Tyre and Sidon appear interchangeably in 23:1-13. The last part of the chapter focuses on Tyre itself (23:14-18).

OUTLINE

Outcry Concerning Tyre, 23:1-14
    23:1-3   News of Tyre-Sidon's Demise
    23:4-5   Anguished Response to the News
    23:6-9   Plan Behind the News
    23:10-14   Destruction of Sidon
Testimonial for Tyre, 23:15-18
    23:15-16   Tyre Forgotten
    23:17-18   Tyre Remembered

EXPLANATORY NOTES

Outcry Concerning Tyre 23:1-14

A lament engages the reader's attention in 23:1-14. Imperative verb forms punctuate the lament: *wail* (23:1, 6, 14), *be still* (23:2), *be ashamed* (23:4), *cross over* (23:6, 10). But the poetry goes beyond mere lament to specify the power of God at work to thwart the ambitions of nations.

23:1-3 News of Tyre-Sidon's Demise

Although the outcry addresses Tyre, Sidon hears the call to be silent. It seems likely not only that these two cities are closely allied but that Sidon, in particular, represents all the Phoenician coastal inhabitants (cf. Clements: 194).

Ships of Tarshish may refer to ships bound for Tarshish or a particular type of ship (23:1; cf. Hayes and Irvine: 290-91). The NIV interprets them as *trading ships* at several places (e.g., 1 Kings 10:22; 22:48; 2 Chron 9:21; Isa 2:16). A reference to wrecked ships of the Tarshish type at Ezion-geber is found in 1 Kings 22:48. The location of Tarshish itself remains disputed. From the testimony of Jonah 1:3, it must lie in the Mediterranean Sea region. Sardinia, off the west coast of Italy, is a likely possibility (*CBA*: 89, map 117). Some scholars identify Tarshish with Tarsus, in southwestern Asia Minor.

A calamity has fallen on the Phoenician coast, decimating the infrastructure of a once-prosperous region (23:2-3). The seafarers who pilot the ships of Tarshish know that the loss of Tyre-Sidon means great personal loss for them. The importance of grain from Egypt in particular is noted. *Shihor* refers to the upper Nile River in Egypt (*CBA*: 88, map 115).

23:4-5 Anguished Response to the News

The sea and *the fortress of the sea* are best understood to be one and the same (23:4a). The sea is represented as speaking; its speech brings shame on Sidon. The sea's denial that it has had children implies that the sea no longer provides Sidon, and probably Tyre as well, with the produce to enrich its merchants. From Egypt in the south comes a cry of grief and despair at the tragedy in Tyre and along the Phoenician coast (23:4b-5).

23:6-9 Plan Behind the News

The command to the inhabitants of the Phoenician coast, *Cross over to Tarshish—wail!* indicates the far-flung impact of the Tyre-Sidon collapse (23:6). Now the coastal inhabitants hear a rhetorical question addressed to them: *Is this your exultant city / whose origin is from days of old / whose feet carried her / to settle far away?* (23:7). It is indeed their city! Tyre, already an ancient city when Isaiah was written (cf. Noth: 262; *CBA*: 16, map 9), carried on a prosperous trade throughout the Mediterranean region. It founded various colonies to enhance its production of wealth, Carthage on the Mediterranean coast of Africa being the most important of these (*CBA*: 89, map 117).

Now the people hear a taunt against their *exultant city* in ruins. Was this simply the work of fate, or the misfortune of history? Who would contemplate the ruin of such a thriving economy? Who would calculate the fall of such a cosmopolitan city? The prophet, silent about fate and fortune, claims that it was the Lord's intervention that brought about Tyre's end (23:8-9). The prophet, in the tradition of Isaiah 2:6-22, states that the Lord of hosts opposes all that is proud and lofty, including nation-states that exceed their prescribed roles. Here is a central theme of the book; that the Lord controls history and carries out his purpose in it (cf. Childs: 168).

23:10-14 Destruction of Sidon

A poetic rendition in three stanzas evokes the destruction of Sidon. The first stanza addresses Sidon directly but not by name (23:10-11). The Phoenician coast (Sidon's land) will no longer benefit from the trade with Tarshish (probably Sardinia) and the Nile valley (Egypt) because the Lord has intervened against it. The assertion of the Lord's intervention in this stanza (following a similar assertion in 23:8-9) constitutes a central confession of faith. The Lord uses his power over the sea as he did in the exodus from Egypt (Exod 14). The Lord has no rivals in his authority over the nations.

In the second stanza the Lord addresses Sidon directly by name (23:12-13a). Sidon will not find refuge in Cyprus or in the land of the Chaldeans (Babylonia), he says, so there is no cause to look hopefully in those directions.

In the third stanza Assyria appears as the enemy laying siege to Sidon (23:13b-14; cf. NRSV which says *it was not Assyria*; I accept the NIV translation here). The section as a whole moves between different historical periods (Babylonian and Assyrian) just as it moves between different geographical locations (Tyre and Sidon).

Treating the text as a whole rather than cutting it into pieces means refusing to force historical and geographical harmony upon the text. Rather, a comparison of the two parts of the Outcry Concerning Tyre (23:1-3, 4-5 and 23:6-9, 10-14) provides a key to understanding the section:

Isaiah 23:1-18

	Stanzas	Cities	Topics	Litanies
part 1	23:1	Tyre	lament	Wail, you ships . . . (AT)
	23:2-3	Sidon	past prosperity	
	23:4a	Sidon	the sea's speech	
	23:4b-5	Tyre	no offspring	
part 2	23:6-7	[Tyre]	lament	Wail, you settlers . . . (AT)
	23:8-9	Tyre	the Lord's plan	
	23:10-11	[Sidon]	the Lord's command	
	23:12-13a	Sidon	no rest	
	23:13b	[Sidon]	invaded by Assyria	
	23:14	[Tyre]	lament	Wail, you ships . . . (AT)

The sea's speech in the first part and the Lord's command in the second part provide a vivid contrast (cf. Brueggemann, 1998a:182-85). The sea has the power to deny wealth and prosperity (using a denial-of-offspring metaphor) to Tyre-Sidon. The Lord, on the other hand, has the power to deny a peaceful existence (using the metaphor of rest) to Tyre-Sidon.

Testimonial for Tyre 23:15-18

Two communiqués about Tyre's future, each concerning seventy years, complete the Tyre manifesto (23:15-16, 17-18).

23:15-16 Tyre Forgotten

The first communiqué opens with two references to seventy years, recalling the years of Israel's exile (23:15; cf. Jer 25:11-12; 29:10; Dan 9:2; Zech 1:12; 7:5). The *seventy years* probably signifies a prolonged period rather than an exact number of years (cf. Watts, 1985: 308).

What follows is a song mocking a forgotten prostitute who still hopes that her former customers will seek her out (23:16). The prophet compares Tyre's mercantile fame to the career of a prostitute because of Tyre's willingness to do anything for a profit (Clements:195).

23:17-18 Tyre Remembered

The last reference to seventy years indicates that Tyre will once again take up its mercantile ways and accompanying prosperity (23:17). But now Tyre's prosperity will support the Lord's people. It is surprising to see the harlot's *earnings* (NIV) dedicated to the Lord (23:18). Nevertheless, as Brueggemann writes, what is imagined here is a transformation of the "world system" so that economic life does not exist for the enrichment of the few but for the benefit of all (1998b:186-87).

THE TEXT IN BIBLICAL CONTEXT
Tyre

Tyre plays a special role in Kings and Chronicles as supplier of materials and skills for Solomon's building projects (cf. 1 Kings 5:1; 7:13-14; 9:11-12; 2 Chron 2:3, 11, 14). In Isaiah and Ezekiel, however, this special role disappears, and judgment sets in. In Ezekiel, this judgment comes about because of Tyre's willingness to plunder Jerusalem and because of Tyre's pride (Ezek 26–29). In Isaiah, Tyre's pride comes under the Lord's scrutiny as well.

Seventy Years

The reference in Isaiah 23:15-18 to Tyre's seventy years finds an echo in Jeremiah and Daniel and Zechariah. In Jeremiah, the seventy years refers to the extent of Babylon's power in the region (25:11, 12; 29:10; cf. Martens: 164, 308). Daniel interprets Jeremiah's seventy years as a reference to the duration of *the desolation of Jerusalem* (9:2 NIV). By this is meant the duration of the exile. But in Daniel's vision, while he is praying, Gabriel reveals *seventy "sevens"* (9:24 NIV) as a time period (often defined as 490 years) during which faithful Jews devote themselves to the issues of sin and restoration (Lederach: 213).

Zechariah, in the late sixth century, does not refer to Jeremiah but understands the exile as a seventy-year experience (1:12; 7:5).

THE TEXT IN THE LIFE OF THE CHURCH
Merchants and Traders

Tyre's economic power around the rim of the Mediterranean was legendary during the time that the book of Isaiah was written. Can such economic power fit into the kind of order envisioned in God's kingdom? It is clear that the Bible does not oppose economic activity as such. Rather, the Bible assumes that economic activity of some kind is necessary for individuals and communities to survive and prosper. But the Bible does concern itself with the quality of economic activity that takes place. Is the economic activity exploitative? Profit may be the bottom line, but is it the only line? Is cutthroat competition necessary in order to survive? As the church's primary source for faith and life, the Bible provides guidelines, which the church ignores at its own peril.

John Woolman, the eighteenth-century American Quaker, thought a good deal about economic activity with moral restraints. In his *Plea for the Poor*, first printed in 1793, Woolman reflects on the larger purpose of economic activity:

> The Creator of the earth is the owner of it. He gave us being thereon, and our nature requires nourishment from the produce of it. . . . By the agreements and contracts of our predecessors, and by our own doings, some enjoy a much greater share of this world than others; and while those possessions are faithfully improved for the good of the whole, it agrees with equity; but he who with a view to self-exaltation, causeth some to labor immoderately, and with the profits arising therefrom employs others in the luxuries of life, acts contrary to the gracious designs of Him who is the owner of the earth; nor can any possessions, either acquired or derived from ancestors, justify such conduct. (Woolman: 239-40)

In the early twenty-first century a spokesperson with similar concerns is the Canadian Mennonite economist Henry Rempel. In his book *A High Price for Abundant Living*, Rempel identifies seven "sacred values" that serve as a critique of "the worship of abundance" in a capitalist economy. The seven sacred values include (1) human dignity, (2) living together with others, (3) work as a form of creative participation, (4) sharing responsibility for ongoing creation, (5) honoring the Sabbath, (6) building community with fairness, and (7) making peace possible. Rempel does not see these values as comprehensive but as a baseline to encourage further discussion.

Isaiah 24:1–27:13

Whole Earth Manifesto

PREVIEW

The whole earth manifesto brings the preceding nations manifestos to a conclusion by presenting God's judgment on human pride and trust in military force. This presentation is often referred to as the Isaiah Apocalypse. This is so because some of the language and images that it employs are common to apocalyptic literature [*Apocalypse, p. 438*].

The portrayal of earth's devastation in chapter 24 has many points of similarity to the beginning of chapter 13 (e.g., 13:5, 9; 24:1, 3; cf. Seitz: 118-19). A picture of the sun and moon in disarray appears in both places (13:10; 24:23). Judgment on pride is evident in both places (13:11; 25:11). It is legitimate, therefore, to take chapters 13 through 27 as a unified section in the book of Isaiah. The whole earth manifesto brings the nations' manifestos to a conclusion by insisting on the distinctive manner of the Lord's work and way in the world. It is a way that combines judgment and hope, to the exclusion of neither.

The section may be read in six parts. Unmitigated judgment dominates the first part (24:1-13). But this is not the final word. Although earth's brokenness continues in the second part, now a word of hope founded on the Lord's reign is heard (24:14-23). The Lord's name is exalted in prayer and promise in the third part (25:1-12). The fourth part is a victory song (26:1-6). A prayer combining elements of confession and lament makes up much of the fifth part (26:7–27:1). The last part concludes the section with an affirmation of the Lord's ongoing relationship with his people (27:2-13).

Isaiah 24:1–27:13

OUTLINE

Desolation Everywhere, 24:1-13
    24:1-3   Earth Laid Waste
    24:4-6   Earth's Inhabitants Decimated
    24:7-13   City of Chaos
Trembling of Earth's Foundations, 24:14-23
    24:14-18a   Singing and Pining
    24:18b-20   Treachery and Terror
    24:21-23   Called to Account
A Feast Prepared, 25:1-12
    25:1-5   Hymn of Praise to the Lord
    25:6-8   A Great Banquet
    25:9-12   Hand, Hands
Song of Trust, 26:1-6
    26:1-3   Strong City Exalted
    26:4-6   Lofty City Humbled
Confession of the Lord's Work, 26:7–27:1
    26:7-11   Waiting for the Lord
    26:12-15   Acknowledging the Lord's Name
    26:16-19   Confession of Failure
    26:20–27:1   The Lord's Judgment
Root of Jacob, 27:2-13
    27:2-6   Vineyard Song
    27:7-11   Jacob's Atonement
    27:12-13   Great Gathering

EXPLANATORY NOTES

Desolation Everywhere 24:1-13

24:1-3 Earth Laid Waste

The eye-catching feature of the opening lines rests on the inclusive character of the Lord's judgment. No one dare think that provision will be made for exemption in special cases (24:1).

Six comparisons are presented (*as with . . . so with*); in all six, judgment falls on rich and poor alike, on the privileged and those lacking entitlement, without preference (24:2-3). Alongside the inclusive character of the judgment stands its thoroughness. Though the judgment is both inclusive and thorough, the announcement gives no motive for it. The absence of any reason for the judgment is probably a deliberate move, inviting the reader to further explore the Lord's ways in the world.

24:4-6 Earth's Inhabitants Decimated

The opening stanza continues the theme of earth and world wasting away (24:4). Earth refers in particular to the soil that can be cultivated to support human life. The world refers more broadly to the earth with its inhabitants and everything on it. The *exalted of the earth* (NIV) identifies more particularly those who exercise power and control the earth's resources.

A motive for earth's decimation surfaces in the second stanza (24:5). The word *polluted* refers at the same time to the breaking of God's laws and statutes and to the devastation of the environment (cf. Brueggemann, 1998a:192). The *everlasting covenant* is likely an allusion to Genesis 9:16 and indicates the universal character of the judgment. Clements (202) points out that the breach of God's everlasting covenant with Noah refers in particular to human violence and bloodshed. The third stanza emphasizes the disaster in terms of human ecology (24:6).

24:7-13 City of Chaos

Two images appear next, the image of vine and wine and the image of a city. The vineyard symbolized prosperity in ancient Israel, so the absence of a vineyard's produce (in the form of wine) symbolized adversity (24:7-9).

The image of a city appears with some frequency in chapters 24–27 (24:10, 12; 25:2; 26:1, 5; 27:10). The first reference to a city, a *city of chaos*, appears to signify any concentration of human power (cf. Childs: 179) rather than a specific historical city (24:10-12). The word *chaos* (Heb. *tohu*) describes the formless state of the earth at the dawn of creation (Gen 1:2).

The comparison of the earth to an olive tree and a vineyard after the harvest indicates emptiness (24:13). The earth no longer has fruit, though the production of fruit in the future remains a possibility.

Trembling of Earth's Foundations 24:14-23

24:14-18a Singing and Pining

A song of gladness celebrates the Lord's glory (24:14-15). The identity of those who sing cannot be known with certainty. The earth and the nations in the previous stanza (24:13) suggest the subject of *they*, a wider identity than only Israel. The main point is that the Lord's glory [Glory, p. 443] is recognized (cf. Watts, 1985:324-25).

The song continues in the next stanza but abruptly turns to lament (24:16). The prophet's lament, *I waste away, I waste away! Woe to me!* (NIV), ends the celebration with a reminder that human treachery always threatens to overwhelm the voices glorifying the Lord's name.

The final stanza elaborates the threat, creating an image of the futility of efforts to escape (24:17-18a). The language of Isaiah's vision here is similar to that of Jeremiah 48:43-44. Jeremiah directed the threat to Moab, but in Isaiah the threat is directed to the people of the earth.

24:18b-20 Treachery and Terror

Now the reader is taken into the midst of a cataclysm in which the earth is wracked by flood and earthquake (24:18b-19). The expression *windows of heaven* refers to openings in the sky through which rain pours in a destructive way, as in the story of the flood (Gen 7:11; 8:2). Judgment is characterized as a return to the chaos of the flood (G. E. Wright: 65).

The second stanza pictures the earth as staggering and swaying on unsteady legs (24:20). This picture of earth's fall is intended to describe God's judgment on humankind.

24:21-23 Called to Account

Now the prophet formulates a picture of a day when the Lord will call to account rebellious beings on earth and in heaven. Their imprisonment is envisioned before the accounting (24:21-22). The relevant texts for the background of *the host of heaven* are Deuteronomy 4:19 and 17:3, which prohibit seeing the sun, moon, and stars as objects of human worship. In these texts the stars and the earth's moon seem to be the patron angels allotted to the nations (cf. Gray: 422). These heavenly powers, along with their earthly counterparts, represent the domain of evil; they will be imprisoned and finally punished by the Lord (Hayes and Irvine: 304).

With the moon and the sun in their prescribed orbits as lesser and greater lights, the Lord's glorious reign on Mount Zion and in Jerusalem indicates his preeminence over all beings, heavenly and earthly (24:23). The reference to the elders on Mount Zion recalls Exodus 24, where the elders experience the presence of God on Mount Sinai (Clements: 206).

A Feast Prepared 25:1-12

25:1-5 Hymn of Praise to the Lord

The prophet's awe at the *glorious* character of the Lord's reign in 24:23 (NIV) now prompts a hymn of praise to the Lord. The hymn has similarities to Psalm 145, especially the references to the Lord's exaltation and his works.

In the first stanza the hymn addresses the Lord as the God who does marvelous deeds and forms definite plans (25:1). The reader already knows that the Lord has a plan for the earth and its people, whom he has created (cf. Isa 14:24-27; 19:11-15, 16-18). This plan is expressed here in a confession of faith.

The second stanza defines the Lord's plan in terms of the ruins of a fortified city (25:2). The city is not named (as also in 24:10-12). While it may refer to Babylon, its main significance is as a symbol of oppression and arrogance (Brueggemann, 1998a:197; cf. Watts 1985:318-19, excursus on "The City").

The last three stanzas contrast those who are ruthless with the picture of God as a refuge (25:3-4a, 4b, 5). The adverb *therefore* introduces these stanzas, indicating the consequence of what has just been said. Peoples and nations will respect the Lord because of his justice and compassion. The motive for this respect lies in the Lord's power to silence the ruthless. This power is presented alongside the Lord's strength of compassion. Compassion is not viewed as weakness, nor is naked power presented as unqualified strength. The Lord's power overshadows and overwhelms human power so that even ruthless nations fear him.

25:6-8 A Great Banquet

The praise hymn in 25:1-5 confessing the wonderful things the Lord has done (*'aśah*) now unfolds into a sketch of what the Lord will do. The Lord will prepare (*'aśah*) a feast for all the peoples (25:6). *On this mountain* certainly refers back to Mount Zion in 24:23. All peoples emphasizes the universality of the guest list planned by the Lord.

The menu at the feast receives a startling interpretation in the next two stanzas (25:7-8). The feast offers as its entrée the destruction of the shroud and the sheet covering peoples and nations (25:7). The word *destroy* in the NIV and NRSV translates the Hebrew *bl'*, which means *swallow*, as in 25:8 (NIV, Heb.; in 25:7 NRSV). The shroud and sheet that the Lord will swallow are a wrap signifying mourning. The mourning is probably not about the fact of death itself but about the curse mentioned in 24:4-6, because the earth and its people have scorned the Lord's everlasting covenant (24:5; cf. Gen 9:16).

The reference to *the everlasting covenant* links Isaiah 24 with the flood story in Genesis 6–9, where an everlasting covenant is first mentioned. The reason for the flood was earth's corruption and violence (Gen 6:11-12). The everlasting covenant was the antidote to the flood, insuring a perpetual relationship between God and the earth, with its living creatures, human and nonhuman alike (Gen 9:15-16). But humankind, as reported in Isaiah 24:4-6, scorned this covenant, presumably with the same corruption and violence named in Genesis 6:11-12. The cataclysm of Isaiah 24 shows the Lord's response. Following the cataclysm, there is the Lord's promise to swallow shroud and sheet. This is a promise to swallow the death, to wipe away the tears, and to take away the disgrace. The use of the definite article with *death* (*the death, hammawet*) indicates a specific idea (Watts, 1985:331). That idea is the replacement of death with life, of mourning with elation, of disgrace with esteem (cf. Seitz: 190).

Scholars have debated whether *his people* limits the promise to Israelites only, or whether it includes *all* peoples (25:8). The context strongly suggests that all peoples are included in the promise, in the spirit of Isaiah 19:25, where the Lord blesses *Egypt my people, and Assyria the work of my hands, and Israel my heritage* (Seitz: 190-91).

25:9-12 Hand, Hands

The concluding section of chapter 25 begins with a confession of faith, possibly spoken by a representative of the nations (25:9). The confession gives testimony to the Lord's salvation and calls all and sundry to rejoice in that salvation. The confession also affirms the Lord's hand (power and blessing) on Mount Zion. There is an echo of Isaiah 2:1-5 in this stanza and the preceding section (25:6-8).

It is not clear why Moab receives special attention in the last two stanzas (25:10-11a, 11b-12). The reference to Moab's pride recalls the Moab manifesto in Isaiah 15–16 (cf. Jer 48:29). It also recalls the great tirade against pride in Isaiah 2:6-22. The effect is to contrast the joy of the nations in the Lord's salvation, alongside Moab's wretchedness in its pride and cleverness.

Song of Trust 26:1-6

In this short hymn the prophet pictures a city with two personalities, one sturdy and stalwart, and the other diminished and depressed.

26:1-3 Strong City Exalted

The strong city, though unidentified, undoubtedly refers to Jerusalem (26:1). *The one who makes salvation* (NIV) refers to the Lord, whose name appears in 26:4. The singers of the song would be the people in Judah who address the gatekeepers (26:2-3). The address recalls Psalm 24, although there the gates are opened so that the King of glory may come in. Here a righteous nation who trusts in the Lord receives an invitation to enter.

The central concern in 26:2-3 rests on the theme of a righteous nation that keeps faith and trusts in the Lord. Needless to say, this does not refer to the nation-state as such, ancient or modern, but to God's people in the world. The song of trust in 26:2-3 stresses the heart of biblical faith: trust in the Lord founded on a radical and profound grasp of God's will for peace [*Shalom*, p. 451].

26:4-6 Lofty City Humbled

The motive for trust in the Lord lies in the Lord's power to topple the city with its proud inhabitants (26:4-5a). The NIV captures the prophet's social consciousness in its translation:

> *Feet trample it down—*
>   *the feet of the oppressed,*
>   *the footsteps of the poor.* (26:6)

The Lord topples the city, but it is the feet of the oppressed that trample it down (26:5b-6). No doubt this trampling refers to the reversal of fortunes for the poor. Such a hope finds expression in the Song of Hannah (1 Sam 2:1-11) and in Mary's Song (Luke 1:46-55).

Confession of the Lord's Work 26:7–27:1

The power of the prophet's words in this section lies in the personal address to God, sometimes in faith, sometimes in despair. There are four parts in the section. The flow of the text through these four parts follows the teaching on the peril of human pride, contrasting with the security of trusting the Lord in the previous section (26:1-6). The first two parts confess the Lord's way and work above all other alternatives (26:7-11, 12-15). The last two parts ponder the meaning of failure and judgment, but not without an attending word of hope (26:16-19; 26:20–27:1).

26:7-11 Waiting for the Lord

Those who long for the way of the Lord reflect the Lord's moral integrity (26:7-8). The confession of the Lord's integrity continues the theme of 26:4-6, where the Lord acts on behalf of the poor and needy. The Lord's name and reputation in 26:7-8 also recall the Lord's name and wonderful deeds in 25:1-3. The significance of the Lord's name cannot be underestimated. As in Exodus 3, the name of God should not be understood in an abstract sense, but in an active sense: One who acts to save and One who sits in judgment (Janzen, 2000:63-65).

Out of the communal confession of faith rises a solo voice with the same theme and using the same language (26:9-10). The longing for the Lord begins in a personal way but moves quickly into a longing for social justice (26:9). Personal piety in the prophets is never far away from the longing for a just social order. Nevertheless this personal piety and social justice are realistic about the world (26:10). Evil continues to be a reality to contend with, not one that can be easily overcome.

The last stanza concludes the theme of evil in the world (26:11). The wicked do not recognize the Lord's power; the prophet seeks their awakening even though the consequences of their evil continue in effect. By conceding the question of evil to God, the prophet acknowledges the biblical claim that vengeance belongs to the Lord (cf. Lev 19:18; Deut 32:35; Matt 5:39; Rom 12:19; Heb 10:30).

26:12-15 Acknowledging the Lord's Name

Direct address to the Lord continues with an opening confession of confidence that the Lord will provide peace (26:12-13). This confidence rests on a conviction that the achievements of God's people stem from God's providence. Nevertheless God's providence is linked to a resolute faith in the Lord's name on the part of God's people. This is so even in times of political domination by *other lords*.

The dead and departed spirits (*shades*) in the next stanza refer to these *other lords* (cf. Clements: 215), whose very memory the Lord has erased (26:14). The Hebrew noun that the NRSV translates *shades* derives from a verb used figuratively to mean losing heart or energy and abandoning or letting go (BDB: 951-52). In the Hebrew Bible the dead are thought of as having a sinking and shadowy existence.

On the other hand, God's people (here referred to as *the nation*; Heb. *goy*) are moving in a different direction (26:15). As in 26:12, the nation's achievements stem from the Lord's energy directing and nurturing human existence.

26:16-19 Confession of Failure

In this part and the next the meaning of failure and judgment is pondered. The subject of *they* is not named in the first stanza (26:16-17). It seems to be God's people (*the nation* in 26:15, understood collectively) who sought him in their distress. But when the Lord responded with discipline, the people responded not with prayer (as the NIV and NRSV have it) but with magic (cf. Watts, 1985:337, 341). Their offense does not lie in seeking the Lord but in abandoning the mode of prayer for doing so. Pain and anguish characterize their outcry, therefore, rather than a change of heart.

The confession of sin that follows admits that magic does not give birth to revelation but only to hot air (*wind*, 26:18)! The confession goes on to lament the failure to be bearers of salvation on earth. While the Hebrew *yešu'ot* may be translated *victories* (NRSV), the sense of the passage here does not justify it. The result of the failure to be bearers of *salvation* (NIV) has been the further failure to advance the rebirth of hope among the world's people.

The portrayal of birth in the previous lines is given a striking interpretation in the final stanza (26:19). However difficult the Hebrew text and its translation may be, here is a testimony to the resurrection of the dead (as also in Dan 12:2-3; cf. Brueggemann, 1998a:208). Childs' assessment that "God's light penetrating into the land of the shades" is heard clearly for the first time in this passage is worth noting (192). There is a bold sense of joy that in God's providence *the earth will give birth to her dead* (NIV).

26:20–27:1 The Lord's Judgment

It seems best to include the first verse of chapter 27 with the last two verses of chapter 26, forming three stanzas. The first stanza opens with an imperative, calling God's people to hide themselves while his judgment of the earth takes place (26:20). This hiding is due not to terror (as in 2:10, 19, 21) but to foresight, so as to prevent unintentional harm to God's people (Gray: 449).

The last two stanzas, then, employ imagery of the Lord's final judgment of the earth (26:21; 27:1). The *serpent Leviathan* has been identified with Assyria (Hayes and Irvine), Tyre (Watts), and Babylon (Seitz), among others. Leviathan is a mythological sea monster common to the ancient Near East (cf. ANET: 137-38). The monster, who symbolizes evil, engages in battle with the good and eventually is defeated by the good (Day: 295-96). The prophet uses imagery from this myth to declare the Lord's triumph over all his enemies.

Root of Jacob 27:2-13

The final part in the nations section of the book of Isaiah has a distinct structure and outlook. The structure may be depicted as follows:

    A   The Lord watching over the vineyard (27:2-6)
        B Jacob's guilt atoned (27:7-11)
    A´   The Lord gathering his people (27:12-13)

The two exterior sections (27:2-6, 12-13) enclose the interior section (27:7-11). The enclosure allows the prophet to emphasize the Lord's ongoing relationship with the people of Israel (A-A´) while insisting that the response to atonement [*Atonement, p. 439*] lies in the ongoing rooting out of idolatry (B).

27:2-6 Vineyard Song

The concluding section of the whole-earth manifesto (24:1–27:13) begins with a vineyard song that has clear points of contact with the vineyard song in 5:1-7. There, however, the emphasis is on preparation of the vineyard and expectation of a sweet harvest. Here the vineyard is already in place, and the emphasis is on guarding it (27:2-3).

The NRSV and NIV offer bewildering translations in the second stanza (27:4-5). Admittedly, the Hebrew is difficult to translate. But the sense of it is that while the Lord's anger toward his people has ceased, unfruitful behavior (represented by thorns and briers) will not now be tolerated. Nevertheless the people are encouraged to come under the Lord's protection. Under that protection his people receive an invitation to make peace with him. This reference to peace (*šalom*) between God and his vineyard recalls the earlier allusions to peace in 26:2-3 and 26:12, where it stands in contrast to the chaos of the surrounding world (cf. Brueggemann, 1998a:202-3).

The agricultural language of the previous stanzas appears again in the last stanza (27:6). The fruit that is promised refers, no doubt, to peace between God and his people on a small scale, which is the pattern for peace between peoples on the larger scale of world affairs. Jacob-Israel's fruit filling the world suggests Abram's blessing by God so that all of earth's peoples will be blessed through him (Gen 12:1-3).

27:7-11 Jacob's Atonement

The questions opening the first stanza ask whether the punishment of *them* (= Jacob-Israel in 27:6) has equaled the punishment of their enemies (27:7-8). The NIV correctly supplies *the LORD* as the subject of *struck* in 27:7. The implied answer to each question is "no," meaning that Jacob-Israel's punishment has not been as severe as the punishment of their enemies. Instead, the Lord *struggled against them*, removal from the land being the means of conducting the struggle. The reference to the east wind may well be an allusion to the Assyrian and Babylonian invasions, which brought so much suffering and displacement for Jacob-Israel (Clements: 221).

The second stanza follows with an explanation of this suffering and displacement (27:9). The purpose of suffering and displacement was that God's people might atone [*Atonement, p. 439*] for sin (cf. G. E. Wright: 68). God's atoning work and Jacob's repentance belong together as a single act of reconciliation. God's atoning work inspires Jacob's repentance, and Jacob's repentance inspires God's atoning work.

There is an ongoing debate about the identification of the *fortified* (beṣurah) city in the third stanza (27:10). A strikingly similar setting presents itself in Isaiah 1, where daughter Zion is presented as a besieged (neṣurah) city because the people lack understanding (1:3, 8). Childs (198) is on the right track when he sees the contrast between Isaiah 27:7-9 and verses 10-11. In the first two stanzas the discipline and atonement of Jacob-Israel is maintained (27:7-8, 9). In the last two stanzas the sequestered city stands for a people unwilling to understand the ways of the one who formed them (27:10, 11).

27:12-13 Great Gathering

The expression *on that day* introduces each of the last two stanzas (27:12, 13). The expression signals a return to the vineyard song at the opening of the section (27:2-5). There the stress was on the Lord's continual watch over his fruitful vineyard. Here the stress lies on the Lord's gathering of his people (27:12). This is followed by the people's response of worship (27:13). It is typical in this chapter that words of hope are placed next to words of judgment (cf. Hos 1:8-9 with 1:10). The explicit reason for the words of judgment is that Israel has sinned. The implicit reason for the words of hope is that God is gracious.

THE TEXT IN BIBLICAL CONTEXT

Apocalypse and Eschaton

Chapters 24–27 of the book of Isaiah have been called the Isaiah Apocalypse [*Apocalypse, p. 000*]. Because of their apocalyptic tone, these chapters are often described as being unrelated to their context (Gold and Holladay: 895). Such a view, however, ignores the clear points of contact between these chapters and what precedes them (13–23; cf. 24:7 and 11 with 16:10; 25:4 with 14:32; 26:17 with 13:8; 27:12-13 with 19:21, 23, 24-25). This commentary sees the nations manifestos (13–23) flowing directly into and being completed by the whole-earth manifesto (24–27).

The language of apocalypse and *eschaton* [*Day of the Lord, p. 443*] characterizes the section as a whole, especially chapters 13–14 and 24–27. Eschatological language, language directed to the future (*on that day . . .*), occurs with some frequency. Apocalyptic writing is characterized by a move from the plane of history to the end of history. This literature addresses the ultimate outcome of the struggle between evil and good. Within this framework of eschatology appears language about the future that encompasses more than simply the nation or the nations. Rather, the whole earth finds itself the object of cosmic judgment and catastrophe.

The meaning of this eschatological and apocalyptic language lies in the nature of prophecy, which has an eye on the future while preaching repentance in the present. The future cannot be known in detail. But God's will for the future can typically be seen in a prophetic vision. The prophet announces this future as the point of departure for a call to repentance and change. The prophets who venture into an apocalyptic style of writing see that future more clearly in cosmic and dualistic terms. When the end time comes, God's judgment will fall on the whole earth, and a new eon will emerge from the old.

THE TEXT IN THE LIFE OF THE CHURCH

Confession of Failure

One of the themes of the book of Isaiah—salvation—derives from the meaning of the prophet's own name, *salvation of Yahweh*. In a luminous moment the Israelite community confesses (in 26:18):

> *We have not practiced salvation on the earth,*
> *and the inhabitants of the world are not born.*(AT)

When the church defines *salvation* in static terms, it thinks of a once-and-for-all accomplishment in Christ. So the notion of *practicing* salvation seems surprising. Alongside of this lies the confession that the community has failed in its commitment to be an agent of God's salvation. The result of this lack of practice is that the world's people are not born. The world's people are not brought to faith. Such a confession commends itself to the church when tempted with a triumphalist missiology. Salvation belongs to the Lord. The church testifies to the Lord's salvation and calls people to be saved.

A clear part of the church's testimony and call is the day-to-day practicing of the salvation that it espouses. In the NT that call finds expression in Jesus' word to Zacchaeus: "Today salvation has come to this house" (Luke 19:9); or in Paul's counsel to the Philippians: "Work out your own salvation with fear and trembling" (2:12). By this, Paul does not refer to a salvation by works but rather to salvation as a testimony that needs to be practiced.

Confession of Faith

A confession in the form of a prayer in Isaiah 26:12 testifies to a specific understanding of God in the Bible:

> O LORD, you provide peace for us;
>> for indeed, all that we have done you have accomplished for us. (AT)

This confession does not deny human activity. Instead, it surrounds human activity with the reminder of God's activity *for us*, which gives meaning to human activity. This confession may be seen as a prototype of confessions of faith elsewhere in the Bible (e.g., 1 Tim 6:11-15).

The confession of faith remains a cornerstone of Anabaptist faith and life. It supplies guidance for interpreting the Scriptures, counsel for faith and practice, and encouragement for unity, among other things (*Confession of Faith in a Mennonite Perspective*: 8).

Making Use of an Apocalyptic Agenda

A global perspective dominates the worldview of Isaiah 24–27. The whole earth is subject to death and decimation, and parallels to a range of twenty-first-century issues come to mind. These issues call the church to turn away from an outline of salvation that stresses spiritual life and afterlife to the exclusion of concern for the material conditions of life on this planet (cf. Berrigan: 66-67).

Isaiah 24:1-13 speaks to the issue of ecology in the twenty-first century. The pollution spoken of in 24:5 does not refer to outrages against law and covenant in a purely spiritual sense. With Brueggemann (1998a: 192), I maintain that breach of God's law includes blatant disregard for the created order.

The reference in 25:10-12 to Moab's pride brought down suggests the nationalistic pride that characterizes modern nations. When citizens submit to the state as their highest loyalty, they surrender their loyalty to the God who was in Christ, reconciling the world to himself (2 Cor 5:19).

A third region of convergence between Isaiah 24–27 and the church's mission is that of secularism. In 27:2-6 and elsewhere lies a worldview with God's watchful presence at its center. In much of modern thought, however, the earth sustains itself apart from any regard for divine presence or spiritual reality.

Part 3
Weal and Woe

Isaiah 28–39

OVERVIEW

In a sequence of judgment announcements (each introduced with the interjection *Woe*, NIV), the book of Isaiah returns to the Lord's judgment of his people in part 3, variously named *Ephraim*, *Ariel*, *Jerusalem*, *sinners in Zion*, and *people of Israel* (28–33). Located within the announcements of judgment against Israel-Judah are assurances of hope (28:23-29; 29:22-24; 30:19-26; 32:1-8, 14-20; 33:17-24; 35). So the judgment is not incessant, but it is persistent.

At the outset, the agent of the judgment on Ephraim is not named but is described with imagery that points unmistakably to Assyria (28:1-13; cf. 28:2 with 8:5-8). Assyria is specifically named as the recipient of the Lord's judgment in Isaiah 30:31 and 31:8.

The sequence of judgment announcements is followed by an exposition of vengeance as judgment and salvation (34–35) and a historical review on the meaning of relying on the Lord for guidance and security (36–39). This review also names Assyria as the agent of judgment on Judah. Highlighted here is the role of the prophets as God's messengers to speak truth to power.

For both Ephraim and Judah, the interplay of weal and woe serves as a strategy for the formation of God's people by means of discipline (woe) as well as restoration (weal), threat as well as promise. Through it all is a consistent testimony to the Lord's power and to the urgency of reliance on the Lord for freedom and preservation.

Isaiah 28:1-29

Woe, Ephraim!

PREVIEW

The second part of the book of Isaiah presents an international, even cosmic, outlook (Isa 13–27). Now in the third part of the book, the prophet returns to the more restricted view of the first twelve chapters by addressing his own people again (Isa 28–39).

The prophets use a variety of idioms to communicate the Lord's word given to them. In Isaiah the idiom of drunkenness dominates the first part of chapter 28 (28:1-13). An inebriated Ephraim, petty kingdom in the shadow of a conqueror on the march, is about to be swallowed alive.

The idiom of a covenant with death dominates the second part (28:14-22). This covenant on the part of Jerusalem's rulers issues in a decree of destruction from the Lord of hosts.

The final part presents a parable that would be at home in the Bible's wisdom literature but is used here to illustrate careful listening to God's instructions (28:23-29).

OUTLINE

Drunkards in Ephraim, 28:1-13
    28:1-4   Proud Crown
    28:5-6   Crown of Glory
    28:7-10   No One to Teach
    28:11-13   Snared and Taken
Scoffers in Jerusalem, 28:14-22
    28:14-17   Covenant with Death

28:18-22   Overwhelming Scourge
Parable of the Farmer, 28:23-29
    28:23-26   Seedtime
    28:27-29   Harvest

EXPLANATORY NOTES

Drunkards in Ephraim 28:1-13

The prophet uses the image of drunkenness to describe the people as a whole in Ephraim (the Northern Kingdom) and the erring counsel of priests and prophets in particular in the years before the Assyrian conquest (28:1, 3-4, 7-8). Interspersed are reminders of the Lord's discipline (28:2) and the Lord's remnant (28:5-6), with a concluding word about captivity (28:11-13).

28:1-4 Proud Crown

The *proud crown* (AT; *garland*, NRSV) in 28:1 and 3 is best seen as having a double meaning (Clements: 225). It refers to the city of Samaria, capital of the Northern Kingdom, and it also refers to flower garlands worn by revelers.

In both cases (of the city as invincible, and of the people as inattentive to the Lord's justice), "pride goeth before . . . a fall" (Prov 16:18 KJV). The agent of the Lord's judgment (Assyria) is not named here but is described with powerful imagery (28:2). The alert reader will recall some of the same imagery in Isaiah 8:5-8, where Assyria is named.

28:5-6 Crown of Glory

The Lord as a *glorious crown* (NIV) for a faithful remnant stands as a promise of regal presence among those who remain true to the Lord's vision for his people (28:5). The same crown imagery is used here as in 28:1. But now it is a glorious crown of the Lord's presence, not a fading crown of Ephraim's debauchery.

The glorious-crown imagery continues in the second stanza (28:6). The crown, closely associated as it is with the Lord of hosts, is a symbol of moral authority that embodies a *spirit of justice* and is a *source of strength* (NIV).

28:7-10 No One to Teach

The allusion to drunkards in 28:1-4 continues here, with a frenzy of images depicting drunkenness (28:7). The religious leaders, entrusted with teaching the Lord's way, offer only confused and addled thinking. This thinking is all the more insidious because it is drug induced. It is often asserted that this, now, is a reference to the religious leaders of Judah rather than Ephraim. But it is more likely that the reference to Ephraim continues through 28:13.

A despairing word about Ephraim's leadership crisis follows (28:8-9, 10). One question of interpretation is the identity of the pronoun he in 28:9. Is it the Lord? Is it the prophet? Childs' suggestion is useful (206). Isaiah's opponents are laughing at him. The translations enclose verses 9 and 10 in quotation marks to indicate what the priests and prophets have to say about Isaiah. It is not complimentary. Does Isaiah think they are children? Does he have nothing better to do than to criticize their stockpiling of precepts to support their judgments?

The intent of the words in 28:10 remains indistinct. The Hebrew words ṣaw laṣaw ṣaw laṣaw/qaw laqaw qaw laqaw/ze'er šam ze'er šam sound like an elementary singsong recitation of some letters of the Hebrew alphabet (cf. Brueggemann 1998a:223-24). The priests and prophets probably saw themselves as too worldly-wise to listen to Isaiah's words. So they mimicked Isaiah's teaching with a singsong satire.

28:11-13 Snared and Taken

Isaiah's reply in verses 11-13, signaled by the opening Hebrew conjunction *ki* (*Truly*; *Very well then*, NIV), incorporates a message from the Lord to Ephraim as a whole: *this people*. The speaker ("he") of the message is now the Lord (28:11, RSV). The message that Ephraim is urged to hear is one of accepting the Lord's rest (28:12; cf. Exod 33:14). Such rest for Ephraim means a place to live and security in that living place (Watts, 1985:364).

The chaismus [*Literary Perspective, p. 446*] in 28:12 is noticed by Watts (1985:359, 364). My translation follows:

> A . . . to whom he had said:
>   B "This is the resting-place.
>   C Give rest to the weary.
>   B´ And this is the quiet-place."
> A´ But they were not willing to listen.

The pronoun "this" points to the offer of salvation (cf. 30:15), trusting in the Holy One of Israel. The idea of rest, then, alludes to the Lord's plan, announced by Isaiah, of holding to a resolute neutrality in spite of urgent appeals to join a conspiracy against Assyria (cf. Clements: 228).

In the final stanza the Lord imitates the satire of 28:10 in order to announce Ephraim's captivity (28:13). Since Ephraim has refused to listen, the Lord will communicate through people who speak another language (cf. Brueggemann, 1998a:224). The words describing this captivity recall a similar account in 8:15. So there is a rough correspondence between the portrayal of the agent who brings about this captivity at the beginning of chapter 28, and the depiction of this captivity at the end of the first section. The Lord's agent will come like a storm (28:2), and the Lord's people, Ephraim, will be overcome like someone *snared* in a net (28:13).

The explanation of 28:1-13 that yields the most sense, then, is to take *this people* in 28:11 as referring to Ephraimite leaders and people who choose the path of revolt against Assyria, with the result being defeat and captivity.

Scoffers in Jerusalem 28:14-22

Now the scene shifts from Ephraim in the north to Jerusalem in the south. The leaders in the north point the nation in the wrong direction. And in the south the situation is no better. Leaders north and south are making bad decisions. The address to scoffers in 28:14 is echoed the command *Do not scoff* in 28:22.

28:14-17 Covenant with Death

The adverb *therefore* connects the forthcoming judgment and execution of sentence on Jerusalem to the previous survey of Ephraim's ruin. The first stanza begins a word of the Lord, first addressing the scoffers in Jerusalem who boast about their *covenant with death* (28:14-15). This boast clearly is a parody of their spirited self-assurance. The *covenant with death*, then, refers to a foreign military alliance, possibly with Egypt. The word from the Lord implies that the scoffers' plans for protection through military alliance will utterly fail (cf. Childs: 208).

A repetition of the adverb *therefore* continues and concludes this word of the Lord (28:16-17). In deliberate contrast to the covenant with death representing false security, a foundation stone stands, representing true security (28:16). Many explanations of the *tested stone* (NRSV, NIV) have been proposed in the history of interpretation. In its context here, it is surely a reference to Zion as a place of refuge for those whose faith is in the Lord. The *tested stone* links the Lord's promises with Zion's security as a firm foundation stone (Ollenburger: 117-18). Trusting in the Lord rather than giving way to panic is the key to faithfulness.

The imagery of *line* and *plummet* continues the theme of testing (28:17). The Lord confirms justice and righteousness as the only suitable models by which to gauge right and wrong (Watts, 1985:370). The focus of 28:14-17 lies in the contrast between the fear-inspiring image of a covenant with death, and the fear-allaying picture of a foundation stone in Zion, a secure place upon which to stand.

28:18-22 Overwhelming Scourge

The focus of 28:18-22 is a message of destruction on Judah. It seems best to see this as the prophet's reflection on the word of the Lord just concluded. The message begins with a direct address (28:18). The pronouns *you* (pl.) and *your* (pl.) refer back to the rulers of Jerusalem in 28:14. Their spirited self-assurance is swept away by the warning that they will be subjugated and defeated. The language is similar to Isaiah 8:7-8, 10, where Assyria is the agent of destruction.

The second stanza continues the same theme with special emphasis on the *sheer terror* upon understanding the message (28:19). *The message* alludes back to 28:9, where the priests and prophets were taunting the prophet. Here, however, the message refers to the shock of what the Lord is about to do.

Picturesque metaphors of a short bed and a narrow blanket are introduced in the third stanza (28:20-21a). These metaphors of inadequacy portray Jerusalem and its leadership exposed to the overwhelming scourge, with no place to hide (Brueggemann, 1998a:227). Two comparisons follow: one with Mount Perazim and the other with the valley of Gibeon (28:21). *Mount Perazim* refers to David's defeat of the Philistines at Baal-perazim, as described in 2 Samuel 5:17-21. David seeks the counsel of the Lord as to whether he should attack the Philistines, and after the Philistines are defeated, he ascribes the victory to the Lord. But the concept of deliverance by means of the Lord's miracle lies in the background (cf. Lind, 1980:116-17).

The *valley of Gibeon* refers to the defeat of a coalition of kings opposing the Israelites and the Gibeonites (Josh 10:1-15). In that narrative the concept of deliverance by means of the Lord's miracle is in the foreground (cf. Lind, 1980:83).

The Lord's action of rising up in agitation is described as *strange* and *alien* (28:21b NIV). Watts (1985:371) argues convincingly that the rulers of Jerusalem thought of the Lord's work as delivering Israel from her enemies. It is a strange and alien idea to them that the Lord will work to devastate their land and exile their people.

The direct address that began in 28:18 now ends with the command to stop scoffing (28:22; cf. 28:14). The rulers of Jerusalem have made their bed, so to speak, in a covenant with death, and now they will have to lie in it. The prophet intends to convey the message that vengeance belongs to the Lord, who will act against those who scoff at the wisdom of God in their dealings with enemies.

Parable of the Farmer 28:23-29

A parable concludes the chapter by presenting an argument from common sense to counteract the foolishness of Ephraim and the rulers of Jerusalem. It describes a farmer who listens to God's instruction.

28:23-26 Seedtime

The parable begins with a call to listen. This call seems to be addressed to the drunkards and scoffers of 28:1-22. The implied answer to both of the questions in the first stanza is "No, of course not" (28:23-24). Farmers do not focus only on the preparation of the soil for seeding. The second stanza also includes rhetorical questions indicating that farmers must give attention to the placement of crops with an eye to maximum yield (28:25-26). Farmers know when to stop preparing the soil as well as when and how to plant the seed. This knowledge comes from God, who in the proper way (lammišpaṭ) teaches the farmer how to produce food from the earth. The point is that if the farmer, with God-given common sense, knows what to do and how to do it, should not the leaders of Ephraim and Judah know the proper way to guide their people?

28:27-29 Harvest

The second part of the parable shifts to the grain harvest. The methods of threshing depend on the grain being threshed (28:27). The wise farmer threshes with the proper implements so as not to damage the grain.

Threshing serves as a word picture for discipline (28:28-29). Lest the reader interpret the first part of the chapter to mean that the Lord plans to destroy his people, the parable stresses the Lord's disciplinary interest. The Lord disciplines his people but does not destroy them. The Lord of hosts, wonderful in counsel and excellent in wisdom, has advice that the leaders of Ephraim and Judah should take to heart.

THE TEXT IN BIBLICAL CONTEXT

A Sure Foundation

The prophet visualizes God's way of salvation as a foundation stone (28:16, 17). Such a foundation can be trusted because it will not fail under stress. In Isaiah 8:14-15 the Lord is a stone against which Israel collides ('eben negep); by contrast, in Isaiah 28:16 the Lord lays a stone (yissad . . . 'eben) as a sure foundation. It is clear in this context that the foundation stone refers to Zion as the symbol of the Lord's presence as king, to the exclusion of all other kings. The Lord's kingship, then, carries with it the promise of security as well as the demand for trust (Ollenburger: 120).

Illustrations of a strong foundation often appear in the Bible. The author of 1 Kings describes the foundation of Solomon's temple as made of "huge stones" (1 Kings 7:10). As a figure of speech, Psalm 102:25 refers to the foundation of the world as laid by the Lord. Again as a metaphor, Psalm 89:14 characterizes justice as the foundation of the Lord's throne. These images come from the everyday life of building construction, where a sure foundation provides the basis for a lasting structure.

Jesus' comparison of the wise and foolish builders adapts the image to his kingdom (Matt 7:24-27; cf. Luke 6:46-49). Paul in 1 Corinthians 3:11, a passage clearly indebted to Isaiah 28:16, sees Jesus as the foundation par excellence. Paul goes on in 3:12-15 to expand on the value of such a foundation as the basis on which to build a life's work.

The sure foundation envisioned by Isaiah and illustrated by Jesus, therefore, places great emphasis on hearing the Lord's word and faithfully acting on that word.

A Remnant of God's People

One of the theological messages of this chapter is that, alongside the realities of corrupt and cynical leadership in political and religious life, there is an alternative model. This model, a faithful *remnant* (cf. Isa 28:5), calls people and leadership back to the vision for being a people of God.

A remnant of survivors as the basis of a new community forms an important theme in the book of Isaiah as a whole. God's judgment will yield a purified remnant, with a renewed sense of calling to hear and abide by God's justice and righteousness, through living in God's presence (Isa 4:2-6; 10:20-23; 11:10-16; 37:30-32).

In the NT book of Romans (chaps. 9 and 11), Paul appeals to the idea of a remnant. In Romans 9:27-28 he refers to Isaiah 10:22-23 (following the Septuagint but not quoting it verbatim) to say that a faithful remnant was saved. His argument is that God's call to the Jews (Rom 9:24-26) also applies to the Gentiles. In Romans 9:29 he quotes Isaiah 1:9 (again from the Septuagint) to make the same point.

Paul's remnant argument in Romans 11 appeals to the story of Elijah in 1 Kings 19. It was not a matter of *only* seven thousand who had not followed Baal. It was a matter of *fully* seven thousand who had remained faithful. "The remnant is a promise of a larger whole to come" (Toews: 275).

THE TEXT IN THE LIFE OF THE CHURCH
Christ as Foundation Stone

The church has understood the reference to the foundation stone in Isaiah 28:16, through the lens of Paul in 1 Corinthians 3:11, as a hopeful anticipation of the coming of the Messiah. The hymn "How Firm a Foundation" (*WT*: 576) expresses the fulfillment of that hope.

Menno Simons, the sixteenth-century Dutch Anabaptist, included 1 Corinthians 3:11 on the title page of all his writings: "For other foundation can no man lay than that is laid, which is Jesus Christ" (Menno: 32). In several of Menno's writings this text receives special attention. His *Foundation of Christian Doctrine*, written in 1539, includes an "Exhortation to the Magistrates," in which he admonishes them concerning the primacy of Christ the foundation over legislative assemblies, over scholarship, over the use of lethal force (Menno: 192).

In his treatise *Why I Do Not Cease Teaching and Writing*, also written in 1539, Menno pleads with his readers to weigh all the doctrines that people have written, including his own. "Is it the Word of God which I teach?" he asks. If it is, they must accept it. If it is only human doctrine, they must reject it. "For other foundation can no man lay than that is laid by the apostles, which is Christ Jesus. 1 Cor. 3:11" (Menno: 312).

Isaiah 29:1-24

Woe, Ariel!

PREVIEW

Two cries of woe (NIV) punctuate this chapter. The first addresses Ariel (29:1-14). The second addresses those who try to hide their plans from the Lord (29:15-24).

The first *woe* brings the reader into the familiar territory of God's conflict with his people. This conflict works itself out through a vast host of enemies, but these enemies, in turn, see their successes dissipate like a dream. Even so, Jerusalem's leaders remain confused and remote from the Lord.

The second *woe* is a disparagement of those who suppose that the Lord does not know their plans. This view undergoes a pronounced transformation: at the end of the chapter the house of Jacob comes to accept the Lord's instruction.

OUTLINE

Conflict and Confusion, 29:1-14
    29:1-4   Ariel Besieged
    29:5-8   Ariel's Enemies Dispersed
    29:9-10   Deep Sedation
    29:11-12   Vision Unrevealed
    29:13-14   Lip Service
Understanding the Lord's Deeds, 29:15-24
    29:15-16   Illusion of Eluding the Lord
    29:17-21   Day of Justice for the Poor
    29:22-24   Jacob Comes to Understanding

EXPLANATORY NOTES

Conflict and Confusion 29:1-14

The *woe* (NIV; *ah*, NRSV) that introduces this section falls on Ariel most pointedly. Nevertheless the fallout of the woe settles on Ariel's enemies as well.

29:1-4 Ariel Besieged

The Lord takes the field against Ariel in the opening part of chapter 29. Ariel is a title meaning *lion of God*, and it almost certainly refers to Jerusalem in this context. The NIV translates Ariel as *altar hearth* (29:2; cf. NRSV footnote). The Hebrew noun *Ariel* is almost identical in spelling to a noun found only in Ezekiel 43:15, which in that context means "altar hearth." Clements (236) is probably right in seeing this as a play on words to indicate that Jerusalem (*'ari'el*) will become an altar (*'ari'el*) on which her residents will be the sacrifice.

The first stanza opens with an allusion to David's conquest of the city (29:1-2a). In spite of popular respect for David and veneration of the city he conquered, the prophet maintains the unpopular view that Ariel has no immunity to siege or subjugation (29:2b-3). Although its citizens may try to placate God through their festivals, the fact is that Ariel (Jerusalem) is vulnerable.

In 29:4 the threat of Ariel's near extinction echoes the language of Isaiah 2. Now Ariel speaks from the dust of subjugation with muted voice.

29:5-8 Ariel's Enemies Dispersed

The host of Ariel's enemies dominates this section. The first stanza characterizes them as blowing dust and swirling chaff (29:5-6). The visitation of the Lord upon these enemies takes the form of earthquake, storm, and fire. But instead of the expected cataclysm, the legions of Ariel's enemies dissipate like a dream (29:7). Empty and faint, they abandon the fight (29:8). With poetic power the prophet restates a strong conviction that Mount Zion, though vulnerable, has a continuing role to play in God's plan. Mount Zion's enemies serve as the Lord's agents to remind and punish when necessary. But they too fall under the Lord's discipline when their work is complete.

29:9-10 Deep Sedation

In this part the scene shifts back to the festivals in 29:1. The participants in Jerusalem's festivals, indirectly addressed there, now are addressed forthrightly. They, leaders and people, do not grasp the gravity of the Lord's discipline (29:9). Torpor has descended on those with special responsibility to discern and warn (prophets and seers). When the prophet says that the Lord has *poured out . . . a spirit of deep sleep,* he means that the Lord has resigned himself to his people's blindness rather than that he has designed the blindness or commanded it.

29:11-12 Vision Unrevealed

Leaders and people continue to be addressed in the next part. Literate people are addressed first (29:11). *This whole vision* (NIV) refers to Isaiah's larger vision. This vision (in the book as a whole) is concerned with the formation of a people of God through discipline (often received as judgment) and restoration (often received as promise). Such a vision, as it becomes Scripture, has no use if it is sealed (Watts, 1985:386).

An example of people who lack the benefits of reading follows (29:12). Readers and nonreaders alike flounder when Scripture cannot be interpreted.

29:13-14 Lip Service

The reference to *this/these people* in both of the following stanzas indicates the Lord's annoyance with his people. A fundamental tenet of prophetic faith rests on the conviction that mere lip service based on intellect or mindless repetition fails the test of true worship (29:13). True worship requires a heart close to God (Deut 4:29; Jer 29:13). True worship requires convictions based in the emotions as well as in the intellect.

Because the people fail the test of true worship, the Lord engages in direct action, using wondrous events to bring his people back to right worship (29:14). But the supposedly wise and knowing fail to understand. Their investment in wisdom and insight rests on a foundation of reason and common sense, which resists meeting revelation halfway.

The Lord's discipline of his people and their ongoing confusion characterize the first part of the chapter (29:1-14). While the enemies of God's people disappear like a vision (*hazon,* 29:7) of the night, Jerusalem's seers (*hozim,* 29:10) are blinded by poor judgment, and a guiding vision (*hazut,* 29:11) for the people remains hidden.

Understanding the Lord's Deeds 29:15-24

The second *woe* in chapter 29 addresses those intent on hiding their plans from the Lord (29:15-16). Then the prophet turns to another concern, a coming day when hiding from the Lord will be displaced by joy *in the LORD* (29:17-24).

29:15-16 Illusion of Eluding the Lord

The first stanza deals a blow to those who conceal their deeds from the Lord (29:15). They understand God as finite regarding sight and knowledge.

The second stanza scoffs at such a limited view of God (29:16). The reference to the potter and the clay reminds the reader of Jeremiah 18. There the point is that the potter has freedom with regard to the created vessel. Here the point is the potter's authority with regard to the clay. The two rhetorical questions [*Literary Perspective, p. 446*] affirm the superiority of the Lord to his creation. No one can hide from God.

29:17-21 Day of Justice for the Poor

The question mode continues here, but in a different direction (29:17). A new day comes into view on the horizon. Lebanon, known for its cedars, and Carmel, known for its orchards, serve as symbols of this new day. The Hebrew word *karmel* (orchard) refers both to a place name (Carmel) and to an orchard. *That day* signals a reversal of an earlier time when the vision was sealed (29:11-12). Now when the words of a scroll are read, even the deaf and the blind will understand them (29:18).

This reversal moves without hesitation into the social and political spheres, where the ruthless, the scoffer, and all who lead people into sin disappear (29:19, 20-21). The emphasis now is on the return to a system of justice where the poor receive fair treatment. They receive fair treatment because the rich, who have the means to manipulate the legal system, have faded away.

The theological explanation for lifting up the poor and cutting off the ruthless lies in God's justice (e.g., Isa 5:1-7; Mic 6:6-8). It does not lie here specifically in God's command. Even so, the command to do justice is deeply embedded in the law (cf. Exod 23:1-3, 6-8; Lev 19:15-18; Deut 16:18-20; 19:15-21).

29:22-24 Jacob Comes to Understanding

The last two stanzas summarize the new day dawning. In the first stanza the Lord addresses the house of Jacob (29:22). In the book of Isaiah, Jacob often refers to the people of Israel as a whole. Jacob's shame alludes to his idol worship. Jacob's pale face alludes to fear of attack and dispossession. Shame and fear have come to an end.

The second stanza focuses on Jacob's recognition of the Lord's hand and power (29:23-24). This results in a return to an understanding of God that had been lost (29:14). The lip service and loss of under-

Isaiah 29:1-24

standing in 29:13-14 are replaced by true worship and renewal of understanding in 29:22-24.

THE TEXT IN BIBLICAL CONTEXT

A Spirit of Deep Sleep

The Hebrew word for deep sleep (*rdm*) occurs fourteen times in the OT. In five of the occurrences, it refers to a state of physical unconsciousness yet spiritual consciousness in which the Lord reveals himself in some way (Gen 15:12; Job 4:13; 33:15; Dan 8:18; 10:9).

Even in the places where deep sleep does not result in the receiving of a message from the Lord, it has some special purpose. In Judges, Sisera lies fast asleep before he is murdered (Judg 4:21). Jonah needs to be awakened from his sound sleep as the ship begins to break up (Jon 1:5-6).

In 1 Samuel 26:12 and Genesis 2:21 (and probably Gen 15:12), the Lord causes the deep sleep. This is so in Isaiah 29:10 as well. The phrase *a spirit of deep sleep*, found only here in the OT, stands in contrast to a word of revelation and refers metaphorically to the obstruction of vision in prophets and seers.

When the Septuagint translates *rdm* in Isaiah 29:10, it uses the word *katanyxis*. Paul uses the same word in Romans 11:8 to describe a *spirit of stupor* (NIV) that God gave those in Israel who did not submit to God's righteousness. Both texts describe people who are spiritually unconscious. In such a state the Lord is not able to bring new vision and new insight.

THE TEXT IN THE LIFE OF THE CHURCH

Lip Service

The Bible draws a fine but clear distinction between the need for repetition in worship and the danger that this repetition will become vain. It goes without saying, and yet it does not hurt to say it again, that at the heart of worship lies a recital of God's gracious work among his people. This recital takes place again and again, just as spouses recite their love for each other again and again, not just once.

The difficulty, when it becomes one, rests in keeping the recital fresh and new. Recitals tend to become flippant. The Bible uses the language of the heart to inspire worship without vanity. The heart that stays close to God enables the speech of worship to arise out of love and obedience, not simply out of duty or fear.

In his treatise *True Christian Faith*, Menno Simons speaks eloquently of faith, even duteous faith, proclaimed but not lived:

But as surely as faith is in the mouth only, so certainly, no righteousness, no change, no renewed spirit, no penitent life follows; no, nothing but unbelief, hypocrisy, and lies. . . . In this it is evident that where sincere and true faith exists, . . . there through the blossoming tree of life all manner of precious fruits of righteousness are present, such as the fear and love of God, mercy, friendship, chastity, temperance, humility, confidence, truth, peace, and joy in the Holy Ghost. For where a sincere, evangelical, pious faith is, there also are the genuine evangelical fruits in keeping with the Gospel. (Menno: 342)

Isaiah 30:1-33

Woe, Rebellious Children!

PREVIEW

The chapter begins with words of judgment against rebellious children who take refuge in Egyptian power rather than trusting God's power (30:1-18). Turning aside from the Lord's path receives the prophet's censure here; it is all the more shameful because the Lord's mercy remains available.

The center of the chapter develops this reference to mercy with the promise of teaching and healing for the people of Zion (30:19-26).

For peoples in general and Assyria in particular, however, the Lord reveals himself as a devouring fire in the concluding section (30:27-33). In the chapter as a whole, words of healing lie between images of judgment:

A judgment: Israel in flight (30:1-18)
  B healing: day of healing for Zion-Jerusalem (30:19-26)
A′ judgment: Assyria set ablaze (30:27-33)

The realities of retribution and restoration move side by side throughout the book, almost like a pair of figure skaters in a routine. The modern reader may find this blending of retribution and restoration disconcerting. But the prophet insists on keeping them together, reminding the reader that they belong together. In life, as in the book of Isaiah, discipline and renewal move side by side.

OUTLINE

Rebellious People, 30:1-18
    30:1-5   Seeking Egypt's Shelter
    30:6-7   Egypt's Worthless Help
    30:8-11   Witness Against Rebellious Children
    30:12-14   Breaking, Collapsing Wall
    30:15-18   Remnant in Flight
The Lord as Teacher and Healer, 30:19-26
    30:19-22   The Lord as Teacher
    30:23-26   Day of Healing
The Lord as Devouring Fire, 30:27-33
    30:27-28   Breathing Fire
    30:29-30   Descending Blow
    30:31-33   Assyria Shattered

EXPLANATORY NOTES

Rebellious People 30:1-18

30:1-5 Seeking Egypt's Shelter

The cry of despair, *Woe!* (NIV), now falls on those who take refuge in the military power of Egypt, likely to ward off the Assyrian threat. The reference to *rebellious children* dominates the first stanza (30:1). By the rebellious children, the prophet means the leaders and people of Judah. The rebellion consists in forging plans and alliances contrary to the Lord's intention. The assertion that they *make an alliance, but against my will* has the literal sense that *they pour out a libation, but not by my Spirit* (cf. NIV). The treaty was sealed by a sacrifice of some kind, witnessed by the gods. The sin is failure to rely on the Lord (Ollenburger: 113).

In the second stanza, Egypt and Pharaoh enter the spotlight (30:2). Judah has made an alliance without consulting the Lord. The offense of the alliance lies in the deficiency of trust in the Lord as refuge and shelter.

The third stanza announces that Judah's dependence on Egypt shall be transformed into Judah's mortification (30:3-4). *Refuge* and *shelter* in the second stanza become *shame* and *humiliation* in the third. Scholars often interpret *his* officials and envoys to mean those sent by Hezekiah (cf. Clements: 244). But the context suggests that *his* officials and envoys refers to those sent by *Pharaoh*. Zoan refers to the city that the Greeks called Tanis, on the lower Nile Delta (*CBA*: 45, map 47). Hanes (pronounced *ha-NASE*) corresponds to Heracleopolis, near modern Fayyum, upriver (south) from Tanis (*CBA*: 112, map 147; 139, map 182). Pharaoh's ambassadors await the emissaries coming from Judah.

The final stanza emphasizes the humiliation of seeking Egyptian help (30:5). The empty help and benefit offered by Pharaoh's envoys leads to the twin lessons of shame and disgrace.

30:6-7 Egypt's Worthless Help

It seems clear that the word of the Lord introduced in 30:1 comes to an end in 30:5. In what follows (30:6-7, 8-11) the prophet gives his own commentary, rooted in the language of the word in 30:1-5.

The outcry (*oracle*, NIV, NRSV) refers the reader back to the nations section of the book (Isa 13–23). There the outcries indicated the Lord's displeasure with the nations arrayed against his people. Here his people form the object of his displeasure.

The outcry concerns the wild Negeb animals, which heighten the risk of travel. Yet the larger focus of the outcry pertains to the transport of tribute to *a people that cannot profit them*, referring to Egypt in the following line. Domestic animals transport Israel's tribute (*riches/treasures*, NIV, NRSV) demanded by Egypt in exchange for its promise of military help. The tribute, however, will not buy the security Israel seeks.

In the prophet's view, Egypt will sit on this tribute rather than come to Israel's help. *Rahab* in the expression "*Rahab who sits still*" (cf. NIV, "*Rahab the Do-Nothing*") does not refer to the resident of Jericho in the book of Joshua (Josh 2:1, 3; 6:17, 23, 25). The spelling, though the same in English, is different in Hebrew. The prophet compares Rahab, a mythical sea monster, to Egypt. Rahab, once a power to be reckoned with, no longer has any power (cf. Isa 51:9).

30:8-11 Witness Against Rebellious Children

The prophet continues speaking and arranges for a recording of his message in a book for future reference (30:8). One of the purposes of prophetic writing is to establish a prophet's "alternative vision of reality" (Brueggemann, 1998a:79) as an authoritative word for the future. This may be compared to Isaiah 8:16, where the prophet's testimony and teaching are bound and sealed for a later time, as evidence of the prophet's word and the people's resistance to it.

Although the prophet does not give the content of the message in 30:8, probably it consists of his name for Egypt, *Rahab who sits still* (cf. Hayes and Irvine: 340-41). The name implies that Egypt, though a dragon, is a sitting dragon (!), not one that will be of any help.

In the second stanza the prophet specifies the motivation for recording his message in a book (30:9). When Egyptian help fails to materialize, the faithless people will know that the prophet warned them, but they did not give heed to his warning.

The Lord's warning typically comes through seers and visionaries who have the obligation of envisioning and proclaiming the Lord's way for his people and confronting those who abandon that way (30:10a). The people's faithlessness consists in preventing the seers and visionaries from doing their job (cf. Amos 2:12).

The Lord's way lies in truth and justice and right, not in illusion and deception (30:10b-11). But the people are intent on suppressing the Lord's instruction and blocking the prophet's message. *The Holy One of Israel* is a preferred name for the Lord in Isaiah's vision (found over two dozen times in chaps. 1–66). The Lord's holiness stands in contrast to the people's rebellion and faithlessness and deafness (30:9).

30:12-14 Breaking, Collapsing Wall

Now the prophet returns to the direct speech of God. In the first stanza the reference to *this word* means the prophet's warning (*Woe!* in 30:1 NIV) that Egypt's help will prove useless (30:12). The second-person plural language here echoes the same language in 30:3.

The people trust and rely on oppression and deceit. The verb *to trust* (*baṭaḥ*) is used in parallel with the verb *to lean* (*šaʿan*). In the second stanza *this iniquity* refers in particular to the absence of trust in the Lord's power (30:13). The breaking wall provides a visual illustration of this absence of trust.

The third stanza shifts the imagery from a collapsing wall to the smashing of a clay pot, to emphasize the utter ruin, spiritually and materially, arising out of the lack of trust (30:14). The smashing will be so thorough that not even a potsherd large enough to dip water or carry fire will remain. The rejection of the Lord's *word* by an act of the people's *iniquity* is no small thing. It is rebellion against God; like all sin, it brings its consequences with it.

30:15-18 Remnant in Flight

Four stanzas bring the first part of the chapter to a close. The Holy One of Israel speaks in the first stanza (30:15 AT):

> *In repentance and rest you shall be saved;*
> *in quietness and trust shall be your strength.*

This counsel serves as a summary of Isaiah's entire vision. The word *repentance* (*šubah*) in this context implies the renunciation of war as a means of security. The option is clear-cut: reliance on God, or reliance on military power. *Rest* (*naḥat*) signifies quiet patience (Watts, 1985:396).

Isaiah 30:1-33

Both repentance and rest define a liberating spirituality attentive to the voice of God and confident in God's power to save.

The word quietness (*hašqeṭ*) means to enjoy peace based on justice (cf. Isa 32:17). Trust (*biṭḥah*) indicates reliance on God. Quietness and trust are evidence of strength, not weakness.

The next two stanzas indicate the cost of not following this path (30:16, 17). The reference to reliance on horses for flight anticipates the prophet's opposition to the strategy of going down to Egypt for military help in 31:1. The prophet sees flight and decimation as the outcome of seeking strength in horses.

The final stanza concludes the passage with a blessing (30:18), affirming the promise in 30:15. The words *gracious* and *mercy/compassion* characterize God's energy. God energizes his people and, through them, calls humankind to redemption and restoration. In turn, God's grace and compassion flow out of his *justice*, which is God's unerring competence to stand firm for what is right.

The Lord as Teacher and Healer 30:19-26

30:19-22 The Lord as Teacher

A shift in tone and emphasis takes place beginning at 30:19. This shift is sometimes taken to signal the beginning of a commentary on 30:18 (cf. *NOAB*: 906). The NRSV and the NIV place 30:19-22 and 30:23-26 in a prose format, but there is no compelling reason to depart from the poetry of 30:1-18.

The four stanzas in 30:19-22 include a pairing of words in each stanza: *Zion* and *Jerusalem* (stanza 1, v. 19), *bread* and *water* (stanza 2, v. 20), *right* and *left* (stanza 3, v. 21), and *idols* and *images* (stanza 4, v. 22).

The first stanza addresses people in Zion and residents in Jerusalem (30:19). *Zion* and *Jerusalem* are in a parallel arrangement here and have an equivalent meaning. The address to their people promises that the Lord will hear and answer their cry. The inclination on the part of God to reach out to humankind in distress, as in Exodus 3 and elsewhere, finds expression here.

The focus of the second stanza lies in the contrast between the misfortune allotted by the Lord and the appearance of *your Teacher* (30:20). The prophet uses the symbols of plenitude (*bread* and *water*) to characterize hardship! Hardship, reflecting the Lord's hiddenness, is replaced by the Lord's self-disclosure as *your Teacher*. The word *Teacher* appears as a plural in the Hebrew Bible. Its translation as a singular, parallel to *the Lord*, is based on the singular verb *hide himself*. The sense of the stanza rests on the affirmation that while the Lord allows misfortune, he reveals himself as Teacher in order to interpret the meaning in misfortune.

The instruction to walk in the Teacher's way lies at the center of the third stanza (30:21). The first stanza contains the assertion that the Lord hears the cry of Jerusalem's people (30:19). In the second stanza the Lord reveals himself as Teacher (30:20). Now in the third stanza the person addressed hears a word, probably a word from the Teacher. This word comes from *behind you*, meaning that the speaker remains unobserved. The prophet creates the image of a herdsman giving instructions from behind to keep to the path and not to stray.

Hearing the word results in the decisive rejection of carved *images* (30:22). Carved images give a counterfeit symbol of God's presence because they materialize God in space and time (cf. Watts, 1985: 401). The prophet expresses their disposal with a single contemptuous command, *Out!* (AT; "*Away with you!*" NIV, NRSV).

30:23-26 Day of Healing

Although the message of 30:23-26 continues to be addressed to Jerusalem's people, the emphasis now shifts to the natural order and especially to a day when healing will take place. First the Lord gives rain, allowing the seed to produce an abundant harvest (30:23a). The result is that livestock flourish on the harvested grain (30:23b-24). The reference to *that day* indicates a day in the future when the people's fortunes will be reversed.

The theme of prosperity continues with water flowing from mountain streams (30:25). The prophet links this prosperity to a day of *great slaughter* and falling towers. The word *slaughter* derives from a Hebrew word that implies ruthless violence. The image of falling towers depicts earthquake destruction.

Both images clash with the prosperity theme. The prophet has in mind a "great eschatological day of God's victory" over his enemies (Clements: 251). This will occur even as his people experience great prosperity.

Great brightness characterizes the day of the Lord (30:26). This brightness emphasizes the wonder of God's healing power. The Lord has disciplined his people through much war and suffering, leaving many wounds and bruises. Now the Lord moves to heal those injuries and remind the people of his love behind the discipline.

The Lord as Devouring Fire 30:27-33

30:27-28 Breathing Fire

The coming of the name of the Lord from afar indicates a visible demonstration of the Lord's power and purpose on Israel's behalf. A dense shroud of smoke represents the Lord's anger (30:27). Human characteristics of lips set in anger and tongue speaking fiery words are attributed to God.

The imagery changes from fire to water in the next stanza (30:28). The Lord's breath is compared to an overflowing stream (cf. 8:5-8). The word picture of a sieve of destruction for the nations invites comparison with a screen through which particles of various sizes may be washed to separate what is fine from what is coarse. Here the coarser nations remain in the screen, to be discarded. In another change of imagery the Lord's breath becomes a bit or bridle, leading peoples astray.

30:29-30 Descending Blow

The beneficiaries of the previous judgment scene are now identified (30:29). The second-person plural *you* addresses the people of Zion-Jerusalem, who were previously addressed in verse 19. The song, sung on a nighttime pilgrimage to the temple, expresses joy that an enemy has received its due reward.

The demonstration of the Lord's power now takes the form of a great storm (30:29). Voice and arm represent the Lord's word and power unleashed in an immense tempest.

30:31-33 Assyria Shattered

The auditor of the Lord's voice is now revealed as Assyria (30:31-32). Assyria "hears" the Lord's voice in an intensity of sound that is shattering. Rod and staff of discipline follow the devastating acoustics. The rod and staff given to Assyria in order to discipline God's people (Isa 10:5-6) are now taken back in order to discipline Assyria (cf. Seitz: 220). The musicians who play *tambourines and harps* (NIV) are not identified.

Topheth (30:33 NIV) refers to a place in the valley of Hinnom outside of Jerusalem where rubbish was burned, and it was associated with human sacrifices (Clements: 253; cf. 2 Kings 23:10). The Lord's discipline comes as fire on a sacrificial altar, with the Assyrian king the first to be placed upon it. *The breath of the LORD* ignites the sacrifice.

THE TEXT IN BIBLICAL CONTEXT

Rebellious Children

The epithet of God's people as rebellious children finds expression at several places in Isaiah (cf. 1:1-6; 30:1, 9-11). The noun *children* does not mean young people between infancy and youth. It means God's spiritual offspring. The adjective *rebellious* indicates that God's spiritual offspring fail to keep their side of the covenant and reject God's attempts at correction.

Ezekiel uses the expression *rebellious house* some fifteen times. The OT speaks about rebellion and stubbornness in the same breath. Jeremiah equates stubbornness and rebellion against the Lord with acting corruptly and judging unjustly (5:23; 6:28). Hosea compares Israel to a stubborn heifer (4:16).

This preoccupation with rebelliousness underlines the seriousness with which the Bible understands behavior that deliberately renounces God's rule. At stake is not an angry God imposing his will on errant humanity. The issue, rather, is the fullness of life that God intends for humankind. The renunciation of this fullness, in favor of violence and life centered on the self, requires drastic measures. God's intention is disciplinary and restorative in nature.

Idols and Molten Images

The English word *idol* derives from the Greek word *eidos*, meaning "form" or "kind." The word *idol* signifies the image or likeness of something used as an object of worship. In the ancient Near East, images were often cast metal objects or melted metal poured over an inner core (Curtis: 376-81).

The primary symbol of human rebellion against God in the OT is the idol. The Decalogue describes the idol as "the form of anything" fabricated and utilized as an object of worship (Deut 5:8). The discarding of these fabrications in Isaiah 30:22 serves as a symbol of repentance and returning to God.

Nowhere in the OT does the Lord authorize a material representation of himself (see von Rad's helpful discussion of "The Veto on Images in the OT"; 1962:212-19). The ban on representing the Lord by an image rests on the experience at Mount Sinai, where Israel heard the Lord's voice out of the fire but did not see his visible form (Deut 4:9-20).

Isaiah 44:9-20 speaks boldly to the reasons behind the ban. First, the fabricators of images are sinful humans. Can such persons create an image of a holy and wholly sinless God? Second, images are formed from commonplace materials (wood, metal). Can such materials represent the extraordinary spiritual character of God? An idol represents the fixed presence of divinity as an object with strength, yet under human control. The OT thought could not reconcile such a representation of divinity with the Lord's revelation of himself at Mount Sinai through speech and words (von Rad, 1962:217).

THE TEXT IN THE LIFE OF THE CHURCH

Christ and Culture

The problem of images, as in Isaiah 30:22, confronted ancient Israel throughout the OT period. The NT church followed Palestinian Judaism in its careful observance of the ban on images (*ODCC*: 820). A relaxation of the ban on images seems to have developed as Christianity became assimilated into Greco-Roman culture. The opposition to images in the early centuries of the church was met, however, with a stress on the theological importance of the incarnation, in which God became visible by taking human form in the person of Christ. In the Eastern (Orthodox) Church, icons, paintings or mosaics depicting Christ, continue to be important in Orthodox Christian spirituality. In the Western (Catholic) Church, the veneration of images, including statues, is a significant component of Catholic spirituality. The Council of Trent (1545-63) denied to the image any virtue inherent in itself and claimed only that in the image the person is honored (cf. *ODCC*: 820-21).

The problem of images reasserted itself as Christian missionaries came into contact with image-based religious systems in various parts of the world at various times. The Mennonite church in Japan provides a modern example. In 1955 several new Christians in Nichinan decided to publicly burn some of the books and objects symbolizing their old religion. One woman in particular, a widow, brought her family god-shelf, where the spirits of her husband and ancestors were said to be enshrined. Her neighbors warned her of the consequences of such an act of desecration; sometime after the burning, this woman had a stroke that paralyzed half of her face, confirming her neighbors' warnings.

But the new Christians refused to accept this cause-and-effect explanation. They knew the testimony of James 5:13-16 that sick people in the church could be healed through prayer and anointing with oil. So there was a prayer meeting at the woman's bedside, an anointing with oil, and a claim of the Lord's victory. Within a few days the woman was healed from the stroke and paralysis. Juhnke (116-17) says that "there was never a doubt in the Japan churches that to become a Christian involved a decisive break with old ways."

Isaiah 31:1–32:20

Woe, Champions of Egyptian Help!

PREVIEW

The theme of trust is the focus of this section. In the first part the prophet laments the policy of seeking military help from Egypt (31:1-9). Trust in chariotry and horsemen, he says, contradicts the quest for the Lord's will (31:1).

The second part moves in the direction of a habitat of peace (32:1-20). *Trust* serves as an image of what life lived without fear will be like (32:17-18).

Trust provides an orientation to the whole of 31:1–32:20. False trust at the beginning becomes true trust at the end. In between, the prophet cajoles and coaxes his people to choose the right kind of trust.

OUTLINE

Idolatry of Military Power, 31:1-9
    31:1-3   Egyptian Powerlessness
    31:4-5   The Lord's Protection of Jerusalem
    31:6-9   Assyrian Collapse
Habitat of Peace, 32:1-20
    32:1-8   A King Ruling with Justice
    32:9-13   Women at Risk
    32:14-20   Righteousness and Peace

EXPLANATORY NOTES

Idolatry of Military Power 31:1-9

31:1-3 Egyptian Powerlessness

The opening *woe* (NIV) continues the series of woe texts that began in chapter 28. The play on words with *help* binds this part together. In the first stanza, seeking help from Egypt constitutes the offense (31:1). This help consists of military hardware and personnel. Clements (253) thinks that the prophet does not criticize militarism as such but only a specific time in Hezekiah's reign when a military solution would not work. A principled objection to military solutions seems more likely here. A fundamental inconsistency exists between trusting in chariots and horsemen for security, while at the same time claiming to trust in the security of the Lord's power.

The *helpers* in the second stanza refer to Egypt (31:2). It is clear that *the house of the evildoers* and *those who work iniquity* are the rulers of Judah who go to Egypt for help, not the Egyptians (Ollenburger: 109). The Lord fights against his own people (cf. 63:10).

In the third stanza the helper again refers to Egypt, and the one helped means Israel (31:3). The emphasis on the humanity of the Egyptians and the limitation of their horses deliberately contrasts Egypt's weakness with the Lord's strength. The extension of the Lord's hand serves as an image of the Lord's power throughout the book of Isaiah.

31:4-5 The Lord's Protection of Jerusalem

The menacing tone of the previous section continues in the first stanza of the next section (31:4). The consequence for those who *go down* (*yarad*) to Egypt seeking counterfeit help (31:1) is that the Lord *will come down* (*yarad*) to Mount Zion, fighting against it (Clements: 257). The Hebrew verb with its preposition (*liṣbo' 'al*) may be translated to *fight upon* or *to do battle on* (NIV). But the verb and its preposition elsewhere are always translated *to fight against* and should be so understood here as well (cf. Num 31:7; Isa 29:7-8; Zech 14:12).

The second stanza changes the imagery and compares the Lord to birds keeping watch overhead, to protect and rescue vulnerable fledglings (31:5). Now it is the protection of Jerusalem that is in view.

These contrasting images can be confusing, and there have been many attempts to harmonize them (cf. NRSV, NIV). The unity of 31:4-5, however, rests in the assertion that the Lord is capable of both discipline and deliverance in relating to his people.

31:6-9 Assyrian Collapse

The opening command to *turn back to [the LORD]* addresses those who trust in Egypt's strength (31:6-7). This call to repentance rests on the promise of Jerusalem's protection in 31:5. The anticipation that they will reject idolatry recalls the same expectation in Isaiah 2:20, and beyond this, the prohibition against gods of gold and silver in Exodus 20:23. Evidence of repentance follows on the act of repentance as the rainbow follows the shower.

The imagery of the Lord's sword dominates the second stanza (31:8). References to Assyria's overthrow open and close the stanza. But the agent of this overthrow is the Lord's sword. The prophet uses innuendo to refer to the Lord, whose name appears clearly enough in 31:9.

The degree of Assyria's fall as well as the One authorizing the fall conclude the section (31:9). The specific agent of Assyria's collapse is not named. But it is clear that Assyria's military defenses and defenders are incapacitated by the overwhelming power that they face.

Habitat of Peace 32:1-20

32:1-8 A King Ruling with Justice

In chapter 31 the prophet declared the idolatry of leadership relying on military power; now in chapter 32 the prophet sketches a profile of wise and noble governance. Four six-line stanzas paint a picture of rulers and ruled seeking what is good, although the temptation to foolish and ill-advised behavior is always close at hand.

King and princes offering protection furnish the key image in the first stanza (32:1-2). Figures of sanctuary from windstorm lie parallel to figures of refreshment in the desert. These images portray a positive role for leadership in a social order under God's rule. This role offers refuge for the helpless and powerless as its central feature, rather than power based on lethal violence.

In such a social order, human dignity is upheld, and this prompts good judgment and clear speech (32:3-5). Eyes, ears, mind (heart), and tongue, receptive to wisdom, are servants of righteousness and justice. Foolishness and villainy are no longer celebrated or tolerated. Instead, the fool and the villain come under close scrutiny in the following stanzas.

The third stanza describes the fool as the perpetrator of injustice through carelessness that leads to deliberate discrimination against the powerless (32:6). Foolish speech accompanied by the practice of evil leads to practical atheism and confusion about God's order.

The villain comes under examination in the fourth stanza (32:7-8). The villain willfully plans evil against the powerless. The honorable per-

Isaiah 31:1–32:20

son stands in contrast to fool and villain. The planning of noble things by the people in 32:8 rises from a just and righteous rule by king and princes in 32:1.

32:9-13 Women at Risk

From king and princes pictured as shelter and refuge in the previous section, the prophet now turns to a picture of the women of Judah as *complacent* (*trustful*, AT) and *secure* (NIV). Hayes and Irvine (357) are correct in arguing that neither of these words suggests overconfidence or arrogance. The women are naively trustful and unaware of distress on the horizon.

This reference to naive trust contrasts with the misguided trust in Egyptian arms at the beginning of the section (31:1-3). It also contrasts with the faithful trust rising out of justice-based peace at the end of the section (32:17-18). The interaction between misguided trust, naive trust, and faithful trust characterize the section as a whole.

The first stanza includes three urgent imperatives addressed to the women: *rise up*, *hear*, and *listen* (32:9). What follows is a warning of an impending calamity (32:10). *In little more than a year* means that after the current crop year, there will be crop failure (cf. Clements: 262).

The third stanza (32:11) includes a chain of commands similar to the first stanza. The sense of these commands is that mourning of a drastic sort needs to be undertaken by the women of Judah. Removal of everyday clothing and dressing in sackcloth were marks of death or disaster (Watts, 1985:417) as well as repentance (cf. Jonah 3).

The picture of mourning continues in the fourth stanza, but now with an emphasis on the aftermath of the distress (32:12-13). The theme of lamentation refers to the harvest failure in 32:10. Joyful houses will become choked with wild overgrowth. Not only will they be emptied of vitality; they also will be filled with bereavement.

32:14-20 Righteousness and Peace

The final part of the chapter begins with a retrospective lament (32:14). The distress of households (32:9-13) is mirrored in the plight of palace and watchtower. They are empty shells; wild donkeys will delight in them.

But from this retrospective lament, the prophet looks forward to an outpouring of justice and righteousness from God (32:15-16; Heb. *from on high*). This stanza and the next (32:17-18) abound in the language of messianic hope [*Messiah, Messianic Hope, p. 447*]. Justice, righteousness [*Justice and Righteousness, p. 445*], peace [*Shalom, p. 451*], quietness, and trust characterize this hope.

Childs (241-42) represents a Protestant consensus when he sees "this eschatological vision of the future" in a symbiotic rather than an adversarial relationship with the nation-state. He sees the place for a prophetic witness to the state, to be sure, but he stays away from any notion that this prophetic witness stands over against the state. This would be "radical sectarian polarity," which belongs to the "heirs of Pietism."

In the last stanza the reference to forest and city is threatening in tone (32:19-20). The first line of 32:19 in the Hebrew Bible reads *And it will hail when the forest comes down* (NRSV footnote). The meaning of the Hebrew is uncertain, and the need for a clear translation probably cannot be met. What is clear, however, is that in the first two lines of 32:19, forest and city correspond to city and undeveloped land (caves, pasture) in 32:14, forming an inclusion [*Literary Perspective, p. 446*]. The inclusion "frames" the messianic vision in the intervening stanzas (vv. 15-16, 17-18). The last two lines of the stanza give a blessing to the messianic vision in the two inner stanzas. Sowing beside streams and free-ranging stock serve as symbols of this messianic vision.

THE TEXT IN BIBLICAL CONTEXT

Reliance on Egypt

The immediate context for Israel's reliance on Egypt for military aid may be seen in Isaiah 30:1-18 and 36:4-10 (cf. 2:7). In Isaiah 30 the prophet reprimands those who seek the protection of Egypt, protection understood as reliance on military support. In Isaiah 36 the Rabshakeh taunts the short-sighted policy of Israelite reliance on Egypt against Assyrian military power.

Ezekiel 17:11-21 refers to Israelite rebellion against the Lord in its request for armed help from Egypt. Israel's covenant at Sinai requires full reliance on the Lord. Sending ambassadors to Egypt to get horses and an army violates this covenant (cf. Lind, 1996:144-46).

The so-called law of the king in Deuteronomy 17:14-20 forbids the return to Egypt to acquire horses. Indeed, the acquiring of many horses from anywhere indicates an infringement of the law.

The reliance on a power other than the Lord constitutes a fundamental betrayal in the Law and the Prophets. The reliance on horses and armed forces *from Egypt* has special significance because it was out of Egypt that the Israelites were freed from bondage. To return to a new form of bondage *in Egypt* was unthinkable.

The Assyrian threat in Isaiah 36 and Isaiah's reply in chapter 37 are best understood as alternative realities. The Assyrian threat, *Thus says the great king, the king of Assyria* (36:4, framed in the prophetic messenger formula "thus says the Lord") offers a thinly disguised menace based on military force. Isaiah's reply, *Thus says the LORD* (37:5), on the other hand, is a call to Judah to risk a resolute faith in the Lord's word (cf. Brueggemann, 1998a:285). This word proclaimed Israel's clear-cut understanding of warfare, that obedience to the Lord's word and reliance on his miracle are alone decisive (Lind, 1980:171).

King of Righteousness

The origin of the vision of a righteous king lies in the prophet Nathan's promise to David in 2 Samuel 7, a promise that extends beyond the immediate future (7:16). In this promise to David, the prophets saw the promise of a messianic king and kingdom in the course of time.

Isaiah 9:6-7 in particular anticipates a *Prince of Peace* from the throne of David, who will rule with justice and righteousness. In Isaiah 11:1-5 a branch from the stump of Jesse will rule with righteousness and equity. Isaiah 32 (vv. 1-8, 14-20) continues this theme.

How does such a vision of a righteous king progress through the Bible? First of all, other OT prophets extend Isaiah's notion of a future king of righteousness. Jeremiah speaks of the Lord raising up a righteous Branch from David's line (23:5-6; 33:15-16). In Ezekiel, a future Davidic king will be a shepherd to his people (34:23-24; 37:24-28). Zechariah speaks of a coming righteous king who will sweep away horses and chariots and battle bows (Zech 9:9-10). This king will proclaim "peace to the nations."

A second instance is the way in which the psalmist speaks of a righteous king who brings prosperity and defends the powerless (72:1-4). Beyond this, the sages in the book of Proverbs allude to upright kings (8:15-16; 14:35; 16:12; 25:5; 29:14). And the Chronicler publishes a prayer of David acknowledging the Lord's pleasure in the righteous king (1 Chron 29:10-19).

The cumulative evidence of the OT contemplates such a king when God's rule will become a reality [*Messiah, Messianic Hope, p. 447*].

THE TEXT IN THE LIFE OF THE CHURCH

Reliance on God

The truth of the motto "In God we trust" on American coins and paper currency is open to question. What, after all, does it mean to trust in God? Does it mean trust in God *to the exclusion of* various types of defensive and offensive weapons? Or does it mean trust in God *alongside of* such weapons? And if trust in God is to be seen as complementary to trust in defensive and offensive weapons, do both of these "trusts" carry equal weight?

In the Bible the notion of reliance on God is understood to be restrictive rather than admitting of multiple allegiances, with God included among them. The prohibition against worshipping other gods in the Decalogue (Exod 20:3; Deut 5:7) has its counterpart in the prescription to trust in the Lord (e.g., Pss 25:1; 31:14; 37:3; 44:6, 7; 56:3, 4, 9-11; 92:2; 115; 125:1; Prov 3:5; Isa 12:2; 26:4).

The obstacle to this trust in God alone lies in the impulsive sinfulness of the human race. This sinfulness expresses itself especially in the "will-to-live" (cf. Macgregor: 120). The will-to-live by itself is not sinful. The creation of humankind in God's own image includes the will-to-live, because God wills to live. But in its human form, the will-to-live has been corrupted by pride and the choice of power over others. So there is a predisposition in our human experience to make our own will-to-live the foremost aim and purpose of our lives. We know and believe that love of God and of neighbor is the key to eternal life (Luke 10:25-28); yet with the apostle Paul, we still see in ourselves "another law at war with the law of [our minds]" (Rom 7:21-25).

Does this "other law" then mean an abandonment of reliance on God and a taking on of violent power in our own self-defense? It would mean this if it were not for the victory over the power of sin that is possible in Christ (cf. Rom 6). This victory in Christ makes it possible for us to seek alternatives to violence.

Justice, Righteousness, Peace

The churches that claim to be part of the Anabaptist stream of the Reformation sometimes think of themselves as being neither Catholic nor Protestant (Klaassen: 1-10). As in Catholic teaching, Anabaptists understand the church to be essential. But as in Protestantism, Anabaptists believe that no individual church can claim universal allegiance. Rather, the church is a new community of the Spirit, proclaiming the lordship of Christ in contrast to all earthly loyalties, whether of governments or any other earthly institutions (cf. Kraus: 80-83). From this new community grows a strategy of relating to the world at large that exhibits the qualities of justice, righteousness, and peace.

Political movements and parties often employ the language of justice, righteousness, and peace as part of a strategy to achieve political objectives. The strategy of the church as a new community of the Spirit, however, binds justice, righteousness, and peace to the kingdom of God and to a king, Jesus the Messiah, endowed with God's Spirit.

The difference between these strategies lies in their underlying motives. In the realm of political life based on the balancing of competing interests, justice, righteousness, and peace are often simply convenient slogans for achieving limited goals. But where the underlying motivation is the kingdom of God and a king endowed with God's Spirit, justice, righteousness, and peace belong to the order of God's plan for humankind and for the world.

Isaiah 33:1-24

Woe, Destroyer!

PREVIEW

Each of the first two parts of the chapter begins with an interjection. The Hebrew interjection *hoy* (*Woe!* NIV) opening the first part sounds the death knell for an unnamed enemy bent on a policy of destruction and betrayal (33:1-6). In striking contrast to this death knell comes a plea to the Lord for salvation based on the Lord's reputation as salvation giver.

The Hebrew interjection *hen* (*Look*, NIV) opens the second part (33:7-16). Here the prophet paints a picture of the futility of war but also charts a course for the future based on obedience to the law.

The last part visualizes a messianic king and kingdom as an alternative community of God's people (33:17-24). People will have enough for their needs because there will be no war.

OUTLINE

The Lord's Salvation Open to View, 33:1-6
Acknowledging the Lord's Might, 33:7-16
    33:7-9   Lament for People and Land
    33:10-12   The Lord's Response
    33:13-16   Right Living
Promise of Salvation, 33:17-24
    33:17-19   A Future Under a Righteous King
    33:20-22   The Lord as King in Zion
    33:23-24   Postscript

Isaiah 33:1-24

EXPLANATORY NOTES

The Lord's Salvation Open to View 33:1-6

The last of the *Woe* (NIV) sections addresses an unnamed destroyer. The content of the four stanzas alternates between threat and promise:

A Threat: The Lord announces the destroyer's demise (33:1)
  B Promise: The Lord's people plead for salvation (33:2)
A′ Threat: The Lord's voice scatters the nations (33:3-4)
  B′ Promise: Ode to the Lord (33:5-6)

Lying behind the first stanza is the prophetic conviction that God employs world powers as his agents but also judges them for going beyond what they are authorized to do (cf. Isa 10:5-7, 12). Although the agent is unnamed here, Assyria and Babylon are implicated (Clements: 265; cf. similar language in Isa 21:2; 24:16).

Following a threat in the first stanza comes a promise constituted as a prayer in the second (33:2). The Lord's grace and salvation surround his arm, as it were. An *outstretched arm* signifies the Lord's power from the time of the exodus onward (e.g., Exod 6:6; Deut 26:8; 1 Kings 8:42; 2 Kings 17:36; Ps 136:12; Jer 27:5; Ezek 20:33, 34).

The prophet's prayer continues with *the thunder of your* [sg.] *voice* (NIV) in the third stanza (33:3-4). But the allusion to *your* [pl.] *plunder* (NIV) that immediately follows seems most likely to address the peoples and nations previously mentioned.

The allusion to *your* [sg.] *times* in the last stanza remains unclear (33:5-6). Various changes have been suggested, none fully satisfactory. The prophet appears to address an individual in Zion, and this person may be the king himself, in David's line, who has received the promise of the Lord's faithfulness (cf. Ps 89).

The central meaning of the passage as a whole lies in its clear declaration that salvation belongs to the Lord. Destruction follows the destroyer as betrayal follows the betrayer. Destruction and betrayal reap their own rewards. But salvation belongs to the Lord.

Acknowledging the Lord's Might 33:7-16

The Hebrew interjection *hen* (*Look*, NIV) opens the second part of the chapter and complements the *hoy* (*Woe!*) at the beginning of the first part. The three sections that make up this part employ vivid imagery to emphasize the Lord's salvation in 33:1-6.

33:7-9 Lament for People and Land

Like the beginning of the chapter, this section opens with a lament. Although war is not specifically mentioned, its signs can be seen easily enough: failure of peace talks, withdrawal of people from commercial thoroughfares to the relative safety of their homes, the breakdown of the rule of law (33:7-8). The disruption of war is regional, and the devastation of war is lamented. This devastation is described with metaphors of shame and atrophy (33:9; cf. Watts, 1985:423).

33:10-12 The Lord's Response

The Lord now addresses combatants and noncombatants alike. In the first stanza (33:10) the Lord declares his intention to remedy the situation pictured in the previous lament (33:7-9). An adverb of time (*now*) repeated three times indicates the nearness of the remedy. Three verbs of similar meaning (*arise, exalt, lift up*) serve to emphasize the energy of the Lord's intention, anticipating perhaps the tiresome arguments to justify war.

The remedy is an outburst on the utter futility of war (33:11-12). Images of fire and burning indicate the human tragedy that results from war (cf. Watts, 1985:423-24). War is a scourge that devours its perpetrators. There is no hint of war as an instrument of justice here.

33:13-16 Right Living

The imperative *Hear* opens a new plea to acknowledge the Lord's deeds of power (33:13-14). The prophet refers to peoples and nations *far away* but still within hearing distance; those *near* means Israelites within easy hearing distance. Those described as *sinners* and *godless* clearly are the Israelites. Stricken by terror, they ponder the question as to who can survive the scourge of war.

The answer emerges in a recipe for right living. The recipe includes (1) right conduct, (2) honest speech, (3) renouncing profit based on violence, (4) refusing bribes, (5) shunning bloodshed, and (6) avoiding evil (33:15-16). These six prescriptions show the way to justice and nonviolence. The person who abides by these prescriptions *will live on the heights* (*rwm*). The same word (*rwm*) refers to the Lord lifting himself up in 33:10. The Lord will champion those who seek justice and nonviolence, providing for their needs.

Promise of Salvation 33:17-24

33:17-19 A Future Under a Righteous King

Although the previous section addresses a group or groups of people, this section addresses an individual (*your, you,* sg.). The individual is not named, but it is likely the person (referred to in vv. 15 and 16) who follows the recipe for right living. To see a resplendent king means to visualize a king ruling in righteousness, as in 32:1-2. Seeing *a land that stretches far away* means to picture this king in a vast domain (33:17). This view of things, however, is interrupted by a phantasm of an earlier time of great fear, when rapacious occupation troops looted and pillaged Judean resources (33:17-18; cf. Brueggemann, 1998a:265).

Using language reminiscent of Isaiah 28:11-13, there is an assurance in the second stanza that the experience of foreign invaders has come to an end (33:19). The concern of both stanzas (33:17-18, 19) is with a messianic king serving as "an earthly representative of Israel's true heavenly king" (Childs: 248).

33:20-22 The Lord as King in Zion

From a resplendent king and an extensive domain, attention now turns to Zion-Jerusalem. The words *look on, your eyes,* and *see* link the two sections. The prophet addresses the same individual as in 33:17-19, but focusing now on Zion-Jerusalem as a permanent residence for God's people (33:20). The sense of this is that those who follow God's way find themselves in a secure place. The reference to *stakes* and *ropes* is similar to the *cords* and *stakes* of Isaiah 54:2. Both emphasize the permanence of the Zion-Jerusalem axis. The reference to *festivals* means that the axis has to do with the celebration of peace, not the recourse to war.

The idea of power dominates the second stanza (33:21). The Lord as *our Mighty One* (NIV) is in the city, and *no galley,* or *mighty ship* (NIV; probably armed enemy transports), can ply the rivers that flow through it. Rivers and streams symbolize abundance, even though Zion has no permanent rivers or streams.

The climax comes in the last stanza (33:22). Zion acclaims the Lord as political leader. His designation as agent of salvation repeats this theme from the beginning of the chapter (33:1-6).

33:23-24 Postscript

The concluding section seems anticlimactic after such a moving acclamation of the Lord as king. The subject turns to things nautical and belligerent, serving as a postscript to the chapter.

The first three lines of 33:23 address the galley in 33:21 as if it were a person. The lines include information about the deficiencies of the warships barred from Zion's rivers. The last four lines add more information to the reference to spoil in 33:4 (see NRSV). In addition they appear to refer to the Zion of 33:20-22 with a comment about the physical and spiritual health of Zion's inhabitants.

THE TEXT IN BIBLICAL CONTEXT
Waiting for the Lord

The confession of faith *We wait for you* (33:2) has a larger context in the book of Isaiah itself as well as in both Testaments. In Isaiah, waiting for the Lord means expectant waiting in hope for salvation (8:17; 25:9; 51:5). Sometimes it means focusing on God's name (26:8; 60:9) or the longing for renewal (40:31).

Other prophets as well see such waiting as crucial to the human relationship to God (e.g., Hos 12:6; Mic 7:7; Zeph 3:8). The psalmist prescribes patient waiting for the Lord (25:3, 5, 21; 27:14; 31:24; 37:7, 9, 34; 38:15; 39:7; 130:5). Such waiting will result in an answer or in God's action.

The language of waiting changes in the NT, where people wait for "the gift my Father promised" (Acts 1:4 NIV) or for "adoption" and "redemption" (Rom 8:23). With the waiting for the coming of the Messiah over, the early church began a new waiting "for our Lord Jesus Christ to be revealed" (1 Cor 1:7 NIV) or for "the righteousness for which we hope" (Gal 5:5 NIV).

Salvation

The verb *to save* (*yš'*) occurs some 19 times in the book of Isaiah. The noun *salvation* (*yešu'ah*) occurs some 29 times, including 16 times as part of the name *Isaiah*, which means "salvation of the Lord."

In the Bible both the verb *to save* (*yš'*) and its various noun derivatives refer to preservation from loss and, more actively, rescue or deliverance or liberation from material bondage and from spiritual bondage.

Liberation from material bondage finds expression in the OT identification of God's favor with material well-being (e.g., Exod 14:13; 1 Sam 9:16; 2 Kings 19:34; Pss 6:4; 7:1; 22:21). In the NT, Jesus' compassion for the poor and their suffering indicates a similar identification (e.g., Luke 4:16-30).

Both Testaments present salvation from spiritual bondage as a common teaching. Salvation that leaves sin in command is not salvation at all (*NHBD*: 636-37; cf. O'Collins: 907-14). Human rebellion against God and alienation from God appear as major problems in the Bible. They are problems not simply because they offend God in some sense but also because they devalue human life. God demands justice and righteousness, for example, because of who God is; moreover, the alternatives lead to destruction. The OT sees repentance and return to God as the way to well-being.

The NT proclaims salvation through faith in Christ and his redemption of humankind from sin. Freedom from the power of sin lies at the base of a life of wholeness. Such a life does not end at death but goes on in perpetual life with God.

THE TEXT IN THE LIFE OF THE CHURCH

Success Versus Wholeness

In part 2 of his book *Between God and History*, the Quaker author Richard K. Ullmann (137-43) discusses the subject of doing the will of God. Although he does not specifically refer to the characteristics of moral goodness in Isaiah 33:15, his argument rests on a similar foundation.

The doing of good, Ullmann says, does not rest on scientific method, where repetition of experiment results in a physical law. It rests on the ethics of the person making a decision. A good action may not have its intended consequences. Many morally good actions fail to be politically successful. And morally evil actions may produce morally good results. Even if war sometimes pays big dividends, to take one example, it is nevertheless true that war is wrong and evil and sinful and against the will of God. "The simple truth is that what is morally wrong . . . remains morally wrong, however politically right it may prove to be, and what is morally right remains morally right, however dismally it may fail in fact" (139).

Success or failure in history requires omniscience, which we do not have. Nevertheless we must always consider the possibilities of the success or failure of our actions. The means we use must be judged both as to their effectiveness and to their morality.

Success is not a religious category. Such things as wholeness and the fruit of the Spirit are religious categories, but neither depends on success. Holiness is their "success." Success and failure lie outside the spiritual goal that Jesus attained with the acceptance of the cross.

Bonhoeffer writes, "It was precisely the cross of Christ, the failure of Christ in the world, which led to His success in history, but this is a mystery of the divine cosmic order, and cannot be regarded as a general rule even though it is repeated from time to time in the suffering of His Church" (Ullmann quoting Bonhoeffer: 16).

Even with the best of goodwill, we may choose inappropriate methods of conveying it. Or our best intentions may be misunderstood by others so that acts of goodwill estrange rather than reconcile. It often happens that goodwill produces goodwill. But goodwill does not guarantee success.

The language of God-as-refuge is used in Isaiah 33:16 to describe the well-being of the morally upright person. This is not will-of-God language, as Ullmann uses it, but it is comparable to it. Adopting habits of action and speech that are good as well as refusing practices supporting oppression and bloodshed that are evil—all this places a person in God's favor. The precise interpretation of these habits and practices is outside the scope of the text although it is available in the larger aggregate of biblical teaching. But success or failure as a result of these habits and practices is not primary; what is primary is their faithful observance.

Isaiah 34:1–35:10

Edom and Zion

PREVIEW

The two parts of Isaiah 34:1–35:10 paint contrasting pictures. The picture of Edom in the first part is everywhere punctuated with gory details (34:1-17). The Lord's rage is against nations in general and Edom in particular. Edom is soon bereft of its people and is populated by birds and animals of prey.

The picture of Zion in the second part is of a land and a people bursting with joy (35:1-10). The Lord's glory and salvation shine through each poetic line.

The theme that joins the two contrasting parts is the word commonly translated *vengeance* (34:8; 35:4). The vengeance of the Lord in 34:8 anticipates a day of punishment for Edom. The vengeance of God in 35:4 anticipates reparations for Zion after a time of oppression (Mendenhall: 99-100).

There is controversy around chapters 34 and 35 in the history of interpretation. Childs' summary is useful in order to understand the various conflicting views (253-56). He sees the two chapters taken together as a bridge between what goes before (Isa 1–33) and what follows (40–66), with chapters 36–39 anticipating the onset of exile and projecting God's purposes for his people beyond exile.

OUTLINE

The Lord's Vengeance Destroying His Enemies, 34:1-17
    34:1-4   The Lord's Anger

34:5-7	Judgment on Edom
34:8-10	End of Edom
34:11-15	Edom Abandoned
34:16-17	Judgment Completed

The Lord's Vengeance Saving His People, 35:1-10
35:1-4	Rejoicing in the Lord's Glory
35:5-7	All Nature Sings!
35:8-10	Everlasting Joy

EXPLANATORY NOTES

The Lord's Vengeance Destroying His Enemies 34:1-17

The portrayal of Edom's demise stretches over five brief scenes. The first two move from a general description of the Lord's rage against the nations as a whole to a specific designation of Edom as the focus of that rage (34:1-4, 5-7).

The last three scenes emphasize the duration of Edom's demise and the extent of its desolation (34:8-10, 11-15, 16-17).

34:1-4 The Lord's Anger

The first scene opens with the Lord addressing nations and peoples (34:1). Earth and world, representing the larger sphere of God's creation, are invited to listen in (cf. Watts, 1987:316-17, "Excursus: The Land").

The content of the address takes shape in the second stanza (34:2-3). The issue is the Lord's anger focused on the nations. This is similar to the theme of the second section of the book of Isaiah (13–27). In 34:2-3 this wrath is directed against *all the nations*. Since *nations* is a plural noun, in the first line translators generally render the singular *ṣeba'am* in the second line as a collective noun (*their hoards*, or *their armies*, NIV) rather than an abstract noun (*their warfare*), which might be expected here. The Lord's fury appears to be against the nations usurping the vengeance that belongs to the Lord (cf. Deut 32:35, 43, and Watts, 1987:17-18).

The word *doomed* (34:2) translates the Hebrew word for banned (*ḥerem*), which places this passage in the holy war tradition [*War, Warfare, p. 452*]. The carnage that ensues is described in vivid detail (34:3). What is in view here is the nations' use of warfare as a tool of conquest. Later in the chapter it becomes clear that the Lord's anger is focused on the nations' conquest of Zion.

In the final stanza, *all the host* (*ṣaba'*) *of heaven* refers to the sun, moon, and stars (34:4; cf. BDB: 839). The reference to *the skies* indicates that the whole created order suffers because of the warfare of the nations.

34:5-7 Judgment on Edom

In a sudden switch to the first person, the Lord himself speaks a word of judgment directed against Edom, followed by the beginning of an interpretation of this word (34:5-6a). That his sword *has drunk its fill in the heavens* means that the judgment originates with the Lord, in heaven's domain. As in 34:2 the word *doomed* (34:5) translates the Hebrew word for banned, continuing the language of holy war. The expression *to judgment* has the meaning of "for good cause" (Watts, 1987:10), not merely on circumstantial evidence. The sword's work, described in gory detail, leads into the theme of sacrificial slaughter in the next stanza.

The sword of the Lord, primed and ready, falls specifically on Edom (34:6b-7). Brueggemann speaks for other commentators in seeing Edom's particular role in Zion's suffering as representative of the nations in general and their opposition to the Lord's purposes (1998a:270).

In the second scene the prophet describes the judgment of Edom by using the twin themes of sword and sacrifice. *The LORD has a sword* (34:6), and *the LORD has a sacrifice* (34:6-7). The sword is the *instrument* by which sacrificial animals are slaughtered. The sacrifice, in turn, constitutes the *means* by which people make gifts to God (de Vaux, 1961b:452). Here, however, the tables are turned, and the focus of the sacrifice is on the slaughter itself. Bozrah, a commanding city in northern Edom, symbolizes the lifeblood of Edom's culture and economy poured out because of Edom's sin.

What would that sin be? Most likely it refers to Edom's behavior in the destruction of Jerusalem in 587 BC. Ezekiel (25:12-14) states that Edom acted in revenge on that occasion, thus incurring the Lord's anger. According to Genesis 36, Esau, Jacob's brother, was the ancestor of the Edomites, who settled southeast and southwest of the Dead Sea. So Edom and Israel had blood ties and might have been expected to help each other in times of need. But their relationship as neighbors and "cousins" during the biblical period was seldom friendly and never cordial.

34:8-10 End of Edom

During the first two scenes a threefold repetition of phrases has alerted the reader to a cataclysmic judgment:

1. The Lord has wrath (*ki qeṣep layhwh*, 34:2).
2. The Lord has a sword (*ḥereb layhwh*, 34:6).
3. The Lord has a sacrifice (*ki zebaḥ layhwh*, 34:6).

Now in the third scene the crescendo of judgment reaches its climax (34:8-9): *the LORD has a day of vengeance* (*ki yom naqam layhwh*,

34:8). The day of vengeance in this case is an exercise against Edom as a vindication for Zion (34:8-9). The Hebrew word translated as "vindication" or "retribution" (*šillumim*) derives from the root *šlm*, which in its noun form is often translated as peace or health or security (*šalom*). *Zion's cause* (34:8) stands in contrast to Edom's *judgment* (34:5). The language of this judgment suggests the cataclysm that descended on Sodom and Gomorrah as a way of indicating its severity (Gen 19).

Although Edom is not named here, it is assumed from 34:5-6. The sacrifice (34:6) is a holocaust that destroys Edom's land and streams in addition to her people and domestic animals (34:9).

Four words and phrases of finality emphasize Edom's end (34:10). There is one word or phrase on each line: *night and day* (line 1), *forever* (line 2), *from generation to generation* (line 3), and *ever . . . again* (line 4 NIV).

34:11-15 Edom Abandoned

Vengeance on Edom, it turns out, does not take place by literal slaughter and fire but by the land's return to wilderness (34:11-12). *The measuring line of chaos* as well as the *plumb line of desolation* (NIV) recall the primordial formless void named in Genesis 1:2. The chaos and desolation extend to Edom's leaders (nobles and princes) as well. It is best to render the last two lines of the stanza (34:12) as follows (AT):

> Its nobles will not call anything there a kingdom,
> and its princes will all become nonexistent.

In the following stanzas a vision of the land's abandonment becomes foremost in the prophet's mind. The language is similar to that found in Isaiah 13:17-22, describing the devastation imposed by the Medes on Babylon (Childs: 257). Edom's citadels, overgrown by nettles and thistles, will be occupied by birds and beasts (34:13). Other wildlife will use the citadels as a lair, including a creature called *Lilith* (34:14). This word may be closely related to the Hebrew *laylah* (night), and so the NIV renders it simply *night creatures* (cf. Watts, 1987:13-14). The final stanza completes the picture, naming birds of prey in an otherwise abandoned countryside (34:15). The passage as a whole intends to describe a catastrophe greater than any previous calamity.

34:16-17 Judgment Completed

Two stanzas bring 34:1-17 to a conclusion. The first includes a curious reference to *the scroll of the LORD* (34:16 NIV). The identity of this scroll remains a mystery. Perhaps the prophet has in mind other prophetic declarations of Edom's fall in Jeremiah 49:7-22 and Ezekiel 25:12-14 (cf. Clements: 274). The most immediate reference point of *these not missing* is the birds of prey in the previous stanza (34:15). The Lord himself has put them in Edom's abandoned citadels.

The second stanza emphasizes the long-term character of Edom's destruction (34:17). Here the prophet concludes the section by using language from previous stanzas. The reference to the *line* portioned out to Edom recalls the *line of confusion* over Edom's leadership in 34:11. But here it means that the birds of prey have been allocated to Edom as boundary lines are allocated (Ps 16:6; cf. Clements: 274). The phrase *from generation to generation* recalls the same phrase in 34:10. Both refer to the perpetual time frame of Edom's destruction.

The Lord's Vengeance Saving His People 35:1-10

The second part of Isaiah 34:1–35:10, celebrating a land and people bursting with joy, stands in stark contrast to the first part. The first part moves toward complete devastation of Edom's land and people (34:1-17). The second part moves toward complete restoration of Zion's land and people (35:1-10).

35:1-4 Rejoicing in the Lord's Glory

The mood of joy, introduced here, pervades the whole part. Although Edom drops out of the picture, wilderness and desert probably refer to the rift valley south of the Dead Sea, part of Edomite territory (*CBA*: 109, map 144; cf. Watts, 1987:14-15). In the first stanza the prophet envisions this disputed area as bursting with life (35:1-2a):

> The wilderness and the dry land shall be glad;
> the desert shall rejoice and blossom;
> like the crocus it shall blossom abundantly,
> and rejoice with joy and singing.

He compares it to the productivity of the coastal plain along the Mediterranean (Sharon) and the green vegetation of the mountainous areas farther north (Carmel and Lebanon). Coastal plain and mountains take on the attributes of glory and majesty often reserved for God.

The glory and majesty of God take their proper place in the second stanza (35:2b). God's glory and majesty reflect backward to three verdant areas—Lebanon, Carmel, and Sharon—symbolizing the rebirth of wilderness and wasteland.

But God's glory and majesty also cast their light forward to energize those with weak hands, to stabilize those with trembling knees, and to call those with fearful hearts to courage and fearlessness (35:3-4). The prophet expresses God's salvation in terms of God's coming with vengeance and retribution. This vengeance calls to mind the Lord's vengeance against Edom in 34:8, which the prophet clearly has in mind here. How does God bring about salvation through vengeance? By "setting right an unjust situation" in which suffering is relieved and liberation from fear and impoverishment is achieved. There is no sign of satisfaction in seeing an enemy or oppressor punished or eliminated (Mendenhall: 100).

35:5-7 All Nature Sings!

Now the prophet addresses these empowered people with two images of salvation. In one image persons with physical afflictions find health and well-being (35:5-6a). The fourfold list of those being saved (blind, deaf, lame, mute) may be compared with similar lists in Isaiah (29:18-19; 32:3-4) and Matthew (15:30). They indicate the intervention of God's salvation in human history.

In a second image, desert landscapes begin to support life-bringing surface water (Isa 35:6b-7). The healing of the earth parallels the image of human health and well-being.

35:8-10 Everlasting Joy

The celebration of land and people bursting with joy concludes with three final stanzas. The first speaks of a highway across this transformed landscape on which those who have been healed may travel (35:8). The focus is on both a physical highway (*derek*) as well as a spiritual Way (*derek*; cf. 2:3). The unclean and fools are excluded from this pilgrimage, but they are not prevented from being cleansed and from being unburdened of their foolishness.

The second stanza describes this highway in terms of its safety and those qualified to use it (35:9). The absence of wild animals invites comparison with Edom, where wild animals dominate a land once occupied by humans. This word for *redeemed* (*ga'al*) occurs here for the first time in the book of Isaiah and is frequently used in the last three parts of the book (40–48, 49–57, 58–66).

The third stanza focuses on the return of the ransomed of the Lord to Zion (35:10). *Redeemed* and *ransomed* serve as parallel terms for those who have been delivered from physical and spiritual bondage and now find themselves returning to the place from which they have been exiled.

THE TEXT IN BIBLICAL CONTEXT

Paradigms of Judgment and Salvation

The major prophets after Isaiah include Edom among the nations listed in their foreign nations sections (Jer 49:7-22; Ezek 25:12-14). Among the minor prophets, Edom figures prominently in Amos (1:11-12), Obadiah (1-21), and Malachi (1:2-5).

Isaiah includes a brief, cryptic reference to Seir (Edom) in the nations section as well (21:11). Scholars have often disregarded this reference although an annotation to Isaiah 21:11-12 gives it more weight (*NOAB*: 892). The extended reference to Edom in Isaiah 34 retrieves this cryptic reference and develops it in greater detail.

Something like this happens in Ezekiel as well. In his nations section, Ezekiel records a brief message of judgment against Edom (25:12-14). Ezekiel 35, then, retrieves the brief message and develops it in greater detail. Ezekiel makes it clear why Edom qualifies as the paradigm of God's judgment:

> Because you [Mount Seir] cherished an ancient enmity, and gave over the people of Israel to the power of the sword at the time of their calamity, . . . therefore, as I live, says the Lord GOD, I will prepare you for blood, and blood shall pursue you; since you did not hate bloodshed, bloodshed shall pursue you. I will make Mount Seir a waste and a desolation. (35:5-7)

In both Isaiah and Ezekiel, Edom serves as a paradigm of God's judgment upon the nations: the reality of God's judgment finds expression in his judgment on Edom. If you want to understand God's character as judge, look at Edom.

Both Isaiah and Ezekiel contrast Edom's judgment with Israel's salvation. The exaltation of Zion in Isaiah 35 follows the judgment scene against Edom in Isaiah 34, much as the blessing on Israel in Ezekiel 36:1-15 follows the judgment of Edom in Ezekiel 35.

Zion's exaltation represents the reality of God's salvation. If you want to understand God's salvation, look at the miracle of Zion's restoration.

THE TEXT IN THE LIFE OF THE CHURCH

The Vengeance of God

Since at least the fourth century, the church has taken the OT evidence of the harsh side of God's nature as a moral if not theological justification for war. War, it is argued, is one way that God uses as a means of judgment upon sin. Isaiah 34:8, for example, speaks of God's vengeance to punish Edom for its sins. So should not Christians, in imitation of God, be justified in emphasizing God's vengeance as well?

Before the church can answer this question, it must answer a prior question: What is the nature of God's purpose in creation, and how does this purpose address the problem of evil in general and human sin in particular? (Macgregor's chapter on "The 'Wrath' of God" has influenced my thinking here.) One of God's purposes in creation may be said to be the formation of a moral order of free persons and the bringing of these persons into a right relationship both with their fellow humans and with God. The principle of this moral order, for Christians and for the church, is love. This moral order is so constructed, however, that persons are free to assert their independence from God, to live for self alone, and to ignore the principle of love. This is the essence of sin. The spiritual law of cause and effect states that "the soul that sins shall die" (Ezek 18:4). The Lord's response to this law says, "Have I any pleasure in the death of the wicked, . . . and not rather that they should turn from their ways and live?" (Ezek 18:23).

In speaking of God's vengeance, the prophets think of events, actual or expected, conceived as the inevitable consequence of sin. God's vengeance is the effect of human sin. God's mercy, on the other hand, is not the effect of human goodness, but is inherent in the character of God.

Jesus, in continuity with the OT, regards vengeance as God's prerogative, as Luke attests in 18:7. Paul, too, sees vengeance as belonging to God, whereas the doing of good belongs to humankind (Rom 12:19-21). Although Jesus does not ignore the harsh side of God's nature, he emphasizes the merciful side of God's nature for his followers to imitate.

The duty of Christians and of the church is not to imitate God's vengeance but to point to God's way of redemption revealed in Christ. If the church would expand and deepen its view of God as judge, its members would be less inclined to take it upon themselves to act as judge. If God's anger falls on *all the nations*, why should one nation think that it should bring judgment on another? The refusal to meet force with force does more than anything else to make the gospel credible to a world in bondage to cynicism and fear.

The vengeance of God often raises questions in the reader's mind about the violence of God. In her book *God and Violence*, Patricia McDonald is concerned with violence attributed to God in the Bible, as her title indicates. She maintains that it is unfair "to claim that the Bible depicts violence as an attractive option" (18). God shows partiality toward those who are not able to raise themselves up by trampling others down, or who give up that alternative (71).

Human Wasteland

In Isaiah 34 the description of an Edom abandoned due to war suggests the modern image of a wasteland or no-man's-land. My experience of living adjacent to such a wasteland in Jerusalem after the Six-Day War in 1967 gives this image renewed vigor. This unoccupied territory lay alongside the Mennonite Central Committee house in Jerusalem as a reminder of the ravages of war. Although it had been cleared of land mines, it remained uninhabited except by the occasional Bedouin family. In 1968 and in the years that followed, this area served as a reminder of the ongoing conflict between Israelis and Palestinians, a scar of land in a land of scars.

Isaiah 36:1–39:8

Hezekiah's Face-Off With Assyria

PREVIEW

King and prophet (Hezekiah and Isaiah) figure prominently in all three "panels" in Isaiah 36–39: (1) 36:1–37:38; (2) 38:1-22; and (3) 39:1-8 (cf. 2 Kings 18:13–20:19). Each of the panels begins with a time reference. Each panel has a particular focusing theme.

The first panel provides a specific time reference: *the fourteenth year of King Hezekiah*. It focuses on an Assyrian invasion of Judah, with special emphasis on Assyrian intimidation and an urgent exchange of communications between Hezekiah and Isaiah (36:1–37:38). Isaiah's message to Hezekiah reassures the king that Assyria will not carry out its threats against Jerusalem.

The second panel begins with a general time reference, *in those days*, and concentrates on Hezekiah's illness and recovery (38:1-22). This time Isaiah has a word of hope for the king himself. The king will not die as expected.

The third panel provides another general time reference, *at that time*, and then gives a brief account of a visit to Hezekiah's court by an official delegation from the Babylonian court (39:1-8). After the visit, Isaiah comes to Hezekiah, much as Elijah came to Ahab, without invitation and with a word of judgment against Hezekiah's indiscretion.

Isaiah 36:1-39:8

OUTLINE

Assyrian Advance and Retreat, 36:1–37:38
    36:1-3   Assyrian Advance
    36:4-22   Sennacherib's Threat
    37:1-4   Hezekiah's Appeal
    37:5-7   Isaiah's Reply
    37:8-13   Sennacherib's Threat
    37:14-20   Hezekiah's Prayer
    37:21-35   Isaiah's Reply
    37:36-38   Assyrian Retreat
Hezekiah's Illness and Restoration, 38:1-22
    38:1-3   Impending Death and Bitter Weeping
    38:4-6   Fifteen Years Added to Hezekiah's Life
    38:7-8   A Sign for Hezekiah
    38:9-20   Hezekiah Reflects on His Life
    38:21-22   Of Figs and Figures
Envoys from Babylon, 39:1-8
    39:1-4   Hezekiah Shows All
    39:5-8   Bondage in Babylon

EXPLANATORY NOTES

Assyrian Advance and Retreat 36:1–37:38

The paragraph form of the story in the first panel fails to create an image in the reader's mind of the major dramatic scenes. The following diagram locates the main contours of the story within the outer framework of Assyrian advance and retreat; it shows that the greatest consideration (judged by length) is given to the speeches about the Assyrian threat. The maneuver of intimidation quickly thickens the plot.

    A Assyrian advance (36:1-3)
        B Sennacherib's threat (36:4-22)
           C Hezekiah's appeal (37:1-4)
              D Isaiah's reply (37:5-7)
        B´ Sennacherib's threat (37:8-13)
           C´ Hezekiah's prayer (37:14-20)
              D´ Isaiah's reply (37:21-35)
    A' Assyrian retreat (37:36-38)

36:1-3 Assyrian Advance

Scholars disagree on the date of Hezekiah's accession to the throne. If his reign began in 715 BC, as is often assumed (e.g., Watts, 1987:25-26), the fourteenth year of his reign would have fallen in 701 BC. Sennacherib ruled in Assyria from 704-681 BC (*ANET*: 287). Sennacherib's account of the invasion of Judah provides detail not found in the biblical account:

> As to Hezekiah, the Jew, he did not submit to my yoke, I laid siege to 46 of his strong cities, walled forts and to the countless small villages in their vicinity, and conquered (them) by means of well-stamped (earth-)ramps, and battering-rams brought (thus) near (to the walls) (combined with) the attack by foot soldiers, (using) mines, breeches as well as sapper work. . . . Himself I made a prisoner in Jerusalem, his royal residence, like a bird in a cage. (*Annals of Sennacherib*, in *ANET*: 288)

Isaiah's account does not concern itself with these details but instead focuses on the theological importance of the Assyrian threats and the Israelite rejoinders.

A personal representative of the enemy presents himself to a delegation from Hezekiah's court (36:2-3). The word *Rabshakeh* does not denote a personal name but the title of a high-ranking officer in the Assyrian army. The convocation assembles at the same place where Isaiah was instructed to meet Ahaz and his son Shear-jashub some years earlier (7:3).

36:4-22 Sennacherib's Threat

The Rabshakeh serves as the mouthpiece for Sennacherib's threat. The opening part of his speech focuses on the theme of reliance (36:4-10). If reliance on the Lord their God characterizes their faith, he asks, how can they also depend on such an unreliable ally as Egypt (36:4-6)? If reliance on the Lord distinguishes their faith, he continues, how can they maintain their loyalty to their king, who has removed the Lord's altars and high places (36:7-9)? There is irony in the Rabshakeh's use of the same word for "trust" and "reliance" (*baṭaḥ*) that Isaiah uses elsewhere (cf. 14:30; 26:4; 31:1; 32:17). The Rabshakeh concludes with a coup de grâce, claiming that the king of Assyria has come up against Judah at the Lord's behest (36:10).

Now the reader learns that the Rabshakeh has been speaking in Hebrew to the Hezekiah delegation and onlookers (36:11-12). The Rabshakeh rivets the attention of the Hezekiah delegation as well as onlookers with his grasp of Judean politics and theology. The delegation wants the speaker to express himself in Aramaic, which the onlookers do not understand. This request is denied, and the Rabshakeh continues in Hebrew.

The closing part of the Rabshakeh's speech focuses on the theme of

Jerusalem's liberation (36:13-20). The specific intent of his speech is to dissuade the onlookers from the belief that the Lord can save them. The Lord, he says, has no more power than the gods of other nations. This is a critical part of his argument, that none of the gods of the nations around Judah have been strong enough to prevent an Assyrian invasion. So why should Hezekiah think that his God can do so (36:18-20)?

Modern readers have the advantage of access to maps of the ancient Assyrian Empire. A gently curved line about three hundred miles in length can be traced on a map, beginning at Arpad in the far north. From Arpad the line moves in a south-southwesterly direction through Hamath, Sepharvaim (site unknown but probably near Riblah), Damascus, and on to Samaria (*CBA*: 96, map 127; 102, map 136; 112, map 147; 115, map 150). Jerusalem lies only another fifty miles south of Samaria. Arpad, Hamath, Sepharvaim, and Samaria are already in Assyria's power, so the Rabshakeh's argument is not only theological; it also has the weight of historical and geographical evidence.

Now there is quite a dramatic moment in the narrative. Where a counterclaim to the Rabshakeh's argument might be expected, the Judean reply is only chilly silence (36:21-22). There are royal orders to abstain from giving a response. The Judean delegation, however, is visibly shaken. Their torn clothing, when they report to Hezekiah, indicates their grief and despair concerning the vulnerability of Judah's situation (Watts, 1987:29).

37:1-4 Hezekiah's Appeal

Hezekiah responds by tearing his own clothing in dismay. He then goes to the house of the Lord (the temple), where he dispatches a delegation to the prophet Isaiah, briefing him on the disturbing news and imploring *him* to pray.

When Hezekiah's envoys address Isaiah, they use the messenger formula common to the prophets: *Thus says Hezekiah . . .* [*Messenger Formula, p. 447*]. The messengers speak on behalf of the message sender. In his message to Isaiah, Hezekiah appeals for a word from the Lord reprimanding the Rabshakeh for his words denouncing the Lord's power to save.

37:5-7 Isaiah's Reply

Isaiah replies promptly and tersely. Using the messenger formula of prophetic speech, *Thus says the LORD*, he conveys a watchword for the king. The antidote to fear of Sennacherib's threat lies in the Lord's intention *to put a spirit in* Sennacherib, who will return home, where he will meet his death (37:7). This spirit may well have been the news of an uprising at home, which actually did result in Sennacherib's assassination later (Isa 37:36-38; cf. 2 Kings 19:35-37).

37:8-13 Sennacherib's Threat

After Isaiah's reply to Hezekiah, the Rabshakeh returns to Sennacherib's fighting forces at Libnah (37:8; cf. *CBA*: 122, map 158). When Sennacherib receives a scouting report that an Ethiopian force is on the march against him, he sends messengers to Hezekiah with a further threat (37:9-13). This threat has less persuasion in it than the Rabshakeh's speech, and more menace.

It is no doubt designed to hold off Hezekiah, or even confuse him, while Sennacherib diverts his energies to meet the Ethiopians. It repeats the theme of reliance on the Lord from the Rabshakeh's speech and denounces such reliance. It repeats the theme of the hopelessness of deliverance from the king of Assyria and equates the Lord with the gods of the nations in being powerless. The threat concludes with two rhetorical questions (37:12, 13). The nations and their gods have all been overpowered by the Assyrian military machine. How can Hezekiah think that he will escape conquest?

37:14-20 Hezekiah's Prayer

Hezekiah's response to this threat has less of a passionate tone than his response to the first threat. The reader learns that the threat comes to Hezekiah by letter rather than by messenger. The king goes to the house of the Lord with the letter and presents it to the Lord as evidence of the seriousness of Sennacherib's threat (37:14). This time the king himself prays to the Lord (37:15). The first part of the prayer is an affirmation of the Lord's sovereignty (37:16-17). Hezekiah opens his prayer with a confession of God's oneness. This oneness is exhibited in the creation (Heb. *'aśah*) of the universe (37:16). Hezekiah calls on the Lord to hear Sennacherib's words insulting the living God (37:17). It is clear that Sennacherib's insults are outrageous in the larger perspective of the Lord's creation (cf. 29:16).

The second part of the prayer maintains trust in the Lord's power to save (37:18-20). Here Hezekiah makes a concession to Assyrian power but notes the powerlessness of the gods in the lands overrun by Assyrian military might (37:18-19). The description of these gods as *fashioned* (NIV; from *'aśah*) by human hands is a deliberate contrast to the Lord as the one who *made* (*'aśah*) earth and sky (37:16).

37:21-35 Isaiah's Reply

Although Hezekiah and Isaiah never actually speak face to face, they remain in contact with each other. Isaiah learns of Hezekiah's prayer and sends him the Lord's word on the subject of Sennacherib's threat (37:21-35). This word from the Lord to Isaiah falls into two parts. The first part addresses Sennacherib with a word of judgment (37:22b-29). The second part addresses Hezekiah with a word of promise (37:30-35).

The word of judgment against Sennacherib concludes in 37:28-29 with an echo of the earlier promise to Hezekiah that the king of Assyria would return to his own land (37:7). This is a word of disapproval concerning Sennacherib's arrogance and miscalculation of the Lord's strength. The arrogance of Sennacherib's "I" in 37:24-25 stands in contrast to the confidence of the Lord's "I" in 37:26-29. This amounts to a comparison of powers that control history and a dismissal of Sennacherib's power as insignificant.

Although this poetry of dismissal is addressed to Sennacherib, Sennacherib is not present to hear it. Elsewhere in Isaiah, an enemy is addressed but not present (e.g., the king of Babylon in 14:4-21 and Tyre in 23:1-13). These words of judgment against an enemy function as encouragement to God's people in times of threat and insecurity (cf. Hayes and Irvine: 377).

The word of promise to Hezekiah begins with a sign (37:30). This sign, like the sign of Immanuel to Ahaz in 7:10-17, provides encouragement to Hezekiah in his time of crisis. Unlike the sign of Immanuel it is a natural rather than an unusual event. In three crop years, agriculture in the countryside will recover from the looting and plundering of the Assyrian army (37:30). Survivors of the siege will return to their lands, confirming the truth of the sign (37:31-32; cf. Watts, 1987:45). The second-person singular *you* in 37:30 refers to Hezekiah. Although he is not specifically mentioned here, his name appears at the beginning of Isaiah's reply (37:21).

Following the sign comes a message concerning the king of Assyria (37:33-35). Introduced by a messenger formula, the message uses language similar to that at the end of the word addressed to Sennacherib in 37:29. The difference here lies in the emphasis on *this city*, referring to the city of Jerusalem. The king of Assyria will return to his own land by the way that he came. He will not enter Jerusalem because the Lord will prevent him. The limited power of Sennacherib is dwarfed by the magnitude of the Lord's power.

37:36-38 Assyrian Retreat

The withdrawal of Assyrian forces in 37:36-38 balances the advance of these same forces in 36:1-3, as can be seen below:

> 36:1 *king of Assyria* attacks, captures walled cities of Judah
>   36:2 *king of Assyria* sends the Rabshakeh to Jerusalem
>   36:3 emissaries of Hezekiah *go out* to the Rabshakeh
>   37:36 angel *goes out* and decimates the Assyrian camp
>   37:37 *king of Assyria* returns to Nineveh
>   37:38 Esar-haddon exercises *king*ship in his place

The withdrawal takes place because a catastrophe carried out by an angel of the Lord falls upon the Assyrian forces. The focus of the entire account of the Assyrian threat to Judah and Jerusalem is the teaching about relying on the Lord for guidance and security. The people of Judah and Jerusalem are not needed as combatants in the Lord's response to the Assyrian threat (cf. Watts, 1987:47). The departure of the Assyrians and the death of their king remind the reader of the power of the Lord's miracle.

Hezekiah's Illness and Restoration 38:1-22

The second panel concentrates on Hezekiah's illness and recovery. The key to the interpretation of this panel lies in the relationship between Hezekiah's reflection on his life (38:9-20) and the narratives that precede and follow this reflection (38:1-8, 21-22).

38:1-3 Impending Death and Bitter Weeping

This paragraph emphasizes three events: (1) Hezekiah's terminal illness, (2) Isaiah's announcement of Hezekiah's approaching death, and (3) Hezekiah's prayer highlighting his own faithfulness. Hezekiah's bitter weeping signifies the depth of his sorrow, similar to Peter's bitter weeping after his denial of Jesus (Matt 14:72; Luke 22:62).

38:4-6 Fifteen Years Added to Hezekiah's Life

The Lord's word to Hezekiah through Isaiah echoes the Lord's word to Moses in Midian: I have *seen*, I have *heard*, I have come down *to deliver* (Exod 3:7-8). Hezekiah receives a twofold answer to his prayer: the addition of fifteen years to his life, and deliverance of himself and *this city* from the Assyrian menace. The Lord *hears* Hezekiah's prayer but does not commend him for his faithfulness. It may be that the Lord was not impressed with Hezekiah's faithfulness. It is Hezekiah's tears and their bitterness, which the Lord *sees*, that moves him. The reference to *this city* recalls 37:34-35, where the Lord states that he will defend the city for his own sake and for David's sake, and thus not (by implication) for anyone else's sake.

38:7-8 A Sign for Hezekiah

Hezekiah receives a sign to guarantee the word of the Lord spoken through Isaiah. The sign to Hezekiah recalls the sign offered to and rejected by Ahaz in 7:11-12. The reference to Ahaz in 38:8 deliberately contrasts his unfaithfulness and Hezekiah's faithfulness (Conrad: 44). The Hebrew text highlights the contrast by using a form of the Hebrew word meaning *to ascend* in both passages. In 7:11 the offer of a sign high (*ma'lah* from *'lh*) *as heaven* comes to Ahaz. In 38:8 the word *steps* (*ma'alot* from *'lh*) occurs five times, indicating the sign of the thing promised. The text implies a contrast between Ahaz in the past (unfavorable) and Hezekiah in the present (favorable).

38:9-20 Hezekiah Reflects on His Life

The introductory clause identifies the poem that follows as a writing from Hezekiah's pen. Both the NRSV and the NIV indicate that it was written *after* his sickness and recovery. The Hebrew text may be translated *after*, but it seems better to translate *when* he was sick and recovered. This reflects the mood and flow of the poem itself more accurately.

Hezekiah's reflection begins with words of despair (38:10-15). This despair reflects back on Isaiah's severe words about Hezekiah's impending death (38:1), and the mood reminds the reader of lament psalms such as 27, 39, and 102. Hezekiah focuses on himself, his resignation to death, and working through his grief.

As in the psalms of lament, despair gives way to praise and thanksgiving as Hezekiah finds himself beyond the crisis of his illness and still alive (38:16-20). Hope and praise replace lament, and the emphasis now rests on the Lord's faithfulness rather than Hezekiah's own faithfulness.

The declaration *You have cast all my sins behind your back* (38:17) reflects an ancient view that sickness and sin are related. An illness implied that a person had sinned against God, even if that sin (as here) is not clearly known or stated (cf. Clements: 292). It is enough to know that God's power to save is demonstrated in the restoration of one's health and in the pardoning of one's sins.

That *Sheol* (or *the grave*, 38:18 NIV) cannot praise the Lord means simply that the dead are separated from God and cannot take part in worship among those who live (Watts, 1987:61). A place of punishment after death is not in view here.

38:21-22 Of Figs and Figures

The question at the end of the paragraph seems awkwardly placed (38:22). The importance of the question, however, does not lie in its placement but in its repeated reference to the sign (37:30 and 38:7) and to the house of the Lord (37:1, 14; 38:20). Hezekiah expresses openness to understand the sign's meaning for himself in each case where it is found. He gives deference to the temple in each case where it is found. Both the sign and the temple summarize Hezekiah's piety.

Isaiah's prescription of figs pressed on a boil simply indicates an agreement between the healing power of the Lord's word and the power of conventional means of treatment (cf. Clements: 293).

Envoys from Babylon 39:1-8

The third panel gives an account of a visit to Hezekiah's court by an official delegation from the Babylonian court. Readers wonder about Hezekiah's role as betrayer-of-national-security-secrets in this panel. Hezekiah's role seems out of character with his role in chapters 36-38.

39:1-4 Hezekiah Shows All

The first paragraph recounts Hezekiah's welcome of the envoys and his open sharing of information regarding his wealth and his military power. This is followed by Isaiah's unannounced visit with Hezekiah.

The most important observation about this visit is that Isaiah's views are not solicited by Hezekiah; the prophet comes without invitation to confront the king. The right of the prophet to do so is based on Israel's understanding that the king is accountable to God, and the prophet as God's spokesperson has the prerogative to speak truth to power (cf. Lind, 1990:109-19).

39:5-8 Bondage in Babylon

Isaiah's interview with Hezekiah continues in the second paragraph. Now, however, Isaiah calls Hezekiah to account for his indiscretion. Hezekiah hears the prophet's censure but reassures himself that judgment will not fall during his lifetime.

Is Hezekiah's self-confidence simply a realistic acceptance of God's mercy, or is it insolent complacency? Seitz argues the former (261-66). As with Josiah before him, Hezekiah is exempted from God's judgment during his lifetime. This, however, contradicts a straightforward reading of the chapter. Such a reading declares that, although Hezekiah will escape judgment, his kingdom will not. As an institution, Davidic kingship will end, and in its place something new will be born (Conrad: 143-52). Hezekiah's disregard for these consequences lends doubt to his faithfulness.

THE TEXT IN BIBLICAL CONTEXT

Synoptic Accounts

Isaiah 36:1-39:8, 2 Kings 18:13-20:19, and 2 Chronicles 32:1-31 tell the same story from different perspectives and with considerable differences of detail. Of the three, Isaiah 36-39 and 2 Kings 18-20 are most alike. The most important difference of detail in the Kings and Isaiah accounts is the inclusion of a psalmlike poem attributed to Hezekiah in Isaiah 38:9-20. The account in 2 Chronicles 32 provides an abridgment of the account in 2 Kings, yet with some additions to the story.

The author of 2 Kings 18-20 based the story of Hezekiah's reign on records in the Judean royal archives. The story was then incorporated into the larger history (Genesis-2 Kings). Of the kings following Hezekiah, only Josiah distinguished himself as faithful to the Lord. After Josiah, the Southern Kingdom moved quickly to its end in 587 BC. The story of Hezekiah's reign in 2 Kings 18-20 serves as some reprieve from the direction in which the story moves.

The story of Hezekiah in Isaiah 36-39, on the other hand, belongs to the larger vision of Isaiah. Although this vision also points to the failure of kingship, it moves on to a new era, portrayed in chapters 40-66, when the Lord will do a new thing (40:19).

The author of the two books of Chronicles, usually referred to as the Chronicler, has a later, postexilic outlook, which focuses attention on the temple and its sacred space. The story of Hezekiah in 2 Chronicles 29-32 illustrates its differentiation from the story in Isaiah and 2 Kings quite well. For the Chronicler, Hezekiah's legacy lies in the restoration of temple worship. His faithfulness in foreign policy receives less acclaim.

THE TEXT IN THE LIFE OF THE CHURCH

Terminal Illness

Hezekiah's experience with terminal illness in Isaiah 38 suggests themes related to dying and death that the church can learn from in its ongoing spiritual life. Following his diagnosis, the king resorts to prayer accompanied by bitter weeping. He then receives a reprieve with an accompanying sign, and this is followed by a reflection on his life that moves from despair to hope. The reality of a terminal illness might well begin with a reflection on Hezekiah's experience.

Hezekiah responds to his diagnosis with what may be interpreted as anguish (Isa 38:1-3). An outcry to God about the injustice of it all is an understandable response. How could it be otherwise than to weep bitter tears in the aftershock of such an announcement?

A reprieve may or may not follow the diagnosis of a terminal illness. Sometimes there is a remission, but not always. Sometimes a diagnosis falls wide of its mark, and a person lives much longer than anticipated, as in Hezekiah's case. Sometimes there are signs accompanying extended life or speedy death (Isa 38:4-6, 7-8).

Whatever the outcome, the diagnosis of a terminal illness offers an opportunity for reflection on one's life (Isa 39:9-20). The first part of Hezekiah's reflection, which includes elements of prayer, takes the torment of the diagnosis seriously and concedes the depression and doubt that go with it (Isa 38:10-15; cf. Roth: 116). The reality of the anguish that accompanies a diagnosis of terminal illness ought to be met, not suppressed. Hezekiah expresses himself through personal lament, and lament remains a resource of healing for those in the Christian community. In the distress of his lament, Hezekiah also appeals to God: *Come to my aid!* (38:14 NIV). He does not feel abandoned by God.

The second part of Hezekiah's reflection centers on hope (Isa 38:16-20). Here the expression of hope rests on a cure. People everywhere, Christian or otherwise, face serious illness and hope for a cure. The expression of hope in the life of the church, however, goes beyond a cure, stretching to hope of the resurrection because "all will be made alive in Christ" (1 Cor 15:22). This is not intended to gloss over the pain of death but to set our eyes on a reality beyond death. There is hope beyond death, whether or not the miracle of physical healing occurs.

The brief narrative at the end of chapter 39 (vv. 21-22) provides the briefest of indications that the art of medicine and the hope for God's miracle are not mutually exclusive.

Prayer

King Hezekiah testifies to the importance of prayer, personal and corporate, in times of crisis. His prayer for deliverance in time of war illustrates his piety as a governing authority (37:16-20). Hezekiah's prayer for deliverance from illness and death depicts his recourse to prayer in time of personal need (38:3, 9-20).

Late in his life (after 1550), Menno Simons (1068-70) wrote "Prayer in the Hour of Affliction," when serious illness prevented him from carrying on his ministry. The prayer moves from (1) lament and a plea for the Lord's grace and comfort, to (2) a reflection on human frailty, and (3) Menno's submission, confession of sin, and resignation. From resignation the prayer turns to (4) confession of faith, (5) a plea for recovery, and (6) a concluding petition for prayer on his behalf. Menno's prayer recognizes and encourages the practice of prayer among believers churches. The practice of prayer in the life of the church, though always and everywhere lauded, often remains neglected. The church practices the outward form of prayer, but the inward power of prayer awaits full utilization. The urgency of the call to prayer continues to be felt in the life of the church.

Part 4
New Day Dawning

Isaiah 40–48

OVERVIEW

The flow of prophetic poetry from Isaiah 40 through 66 is unmatched among the Hebrew prophets in its power to evoke God's creative work through his servant, in company with his people, engaging the nations. This poetry pauses briefly at the end of chapter 48. And it pauses again at the end of chapter 57, before flowing on to the end of the book.

Part 4 opens with a prologue announcing good tidings (40:1-11) and closes with something like a praise hymn, followed by an aphorism of sober reality (48:20-22). Between opening and closing lies a poetic discourse encompassing a theology of hope resting on a foundation of the Lord's power and presence. Much of this discourse, as Clements (30-38) has argued, is an effort to persuade and convince reluctant exiles in Babylon (whom I refer to as Jacob-Israel) to accept the good tidings heralded in the prologue.

Although the prologue announces a "New Day Dawning," this is not unremitting comfort and encouragement. Comfort and encouragement are freely given along with down-to-earth reminders of the obstacles lying in wait to make faithful people stumble. There is the ongoing expectancy of spiritual blindness and disobedience (42:13-25). Everywhere are challenges to God's rule by a host of idolatries (41:21-29; 44:9-20; 46:1-13).

Nevertheless the Lord's presence is a convincing reality. This presence is abundantly evident in the servant, who is authorized to bring justice to the nations (42:1-4). It is also evident in the Lord's redemption of his people (43:1-4, 14-21; 44:6-8, 21-28) and in a variety of other ways.

Isaiah 40:1-31

God's People Comforted

PREVIEW

Poetry of arresting power confronts the reader in Isaiah 40. A prologue of announcement leads the way in the first part of the chapter (40:1-11). The announcement centers on the Lord's coming with power and glory among humankind. The poet proclaims the good news of this coming with unrestrained exuberance and joy.

Exuberance and joy give way to a Job-like battery of questions demanding answers from those uncertain of the Lord's power (40:12-31). In a concluding flourish, the poet discredits Jacob-Israel's despair about the Lord's hiddenness and affirms the Lord's gift of power to the faint (40:27-31).

Chapter 40 continues and enlarges the earlier vision of Isaiah; it does not start something completely new. In the prologue, for example, the Lord's comfort of his people (40:1) echoes another word about comfort (12:1). And in the ode to the Creator, the emptiness of the nations (40:17) restates what has already been said about the nations sifted for judgment (29:7).

On the other hand, the joy and the confidence of chapter 40 does bring the reader into a new dimension of the vision. This newness rises above the streambeds of chapters 36–39, overflows the riverbanks of chapters 40-48, and sweeps on to the end of the book.

Many scholars have concluded that Isaiah 40–66 derives from one or more anonymous authors who nevertheless stand in the same tradition as Isaiah of Jerusalem. Thus, despite the likelihood of multiple authors, the book of Isaiah can be understood as a unity [*Composition of the Book of Isaiah, p. 441*].

OUTLINE

Prologue of Announcement, 40:1-11
    40:1-5   Revealing the Lord's Glory
    40:6-8   All People Are Grass
    40:9-11   The Lord Coming with Might
Ode to the Creator, 40:12-31
    40:12-14   God Without Equal
    40:15-17   Pretension of Nations
    40:18-20   God Without Image
    40:21-24   Posturing of Princes
    40:25-26   The Lord's Power
    40:27-31   Power to the Faint

EXPLANATORY NOTES

Prologue of Announcement 40:1-11

40:1-5 Revealing the Lord's Glory

The prologue commences with an announcement of exceptional power, in which the prophet sketches an outline of what the Lord has revealed to him. The sketch begins in the Lord's court with words of consolation to be announced to *my people/Jerusalem* (40:1-2a). The gist of this consolation follows in three breathtaking assertions: (1) the people's *hard service* (NIV) has come to an end, (2) punishment for their sin has been accepted, and (3) they have received generous discipline for their sins (Knight: 10). The idea of a *double* penalty here is that the penalty for Jerusalem's sins is discharged (Whybray: 49). Though the prophet does not specifically mention the Judean exile to Babylon, the reference to *hard service* is best understood as an allusion to the exile.

How the discharge of the people's penalty unfolds remains to be seen. A voice in the Lord's court responds to the words of consolation with a cry that such an announcement merits special preparation. A way/highway for the Lord's coming must be prepared so that the Lord's glory [*Glory, p. 443*] may be revealed (40:3, 4, 5).

Desert and *wilderness* (NIV) describe the location of this highway. The Hebrew term for *wilderness here*, '*arabah*, refers in particular to the part of the rift valley extending from the Dead Sea southward to the Gulf of Aqaba. Mount Seir rises to the east of this wilderness valley (CBA: 15, map 8). In the blessing of Moses, the Lord comes from Sinai, from

Seir, from the south (Deut 33:2). Now the voice envisions the Lord again coming from the south, through the Arabah, then on into Jerusalem (cf. Watts, 1987:80). As in Ezekiel 43, the Lord returns to Jerusalem and resumes his residence there. He returns through the Arabah, with all its natural barriers removed.

The voice concludes with a soul-stirring revelation of the Lord's glory in sight of all humankind (40:5). The word *revealed* (*galah*) has a double meaning. It may indicate the revealing or uncovering of something hidden, but it may also indicate going naked and exposed into exile. Here the revelation of the Lord's glory signifies the end of his people's exile and, by extension, the end of exile for all peoples (cf. Isa 2:1-5).

40:6-8 All People Are Grass

A second voice in the Lord's court speaks. This voice commands the prophet to proclaim a message, and the prophet demands to know the content of the message: *What shall I cry?* (40:6). *All people are grass* begins the message that is an answer to the prophet's question (Whybray: 51). The answer is a disparaging discourse on human transience (40:6b-8). All humankind has seen the Lord's glorious return to Jerusalem and perhaps has been impressed by it (40:5). But will all humankind welcome his return? Probably not. The NIV translates the Hebrew *ḥasdo* (from *ḥesed*) with the word *glory* (40:6) [*Steadfast Love, p. 452*]. But the noun *ḥesed* means "loyalty" or "piety" rather than "glory." Treated as loyalty in the sense of faithfulness, a translation such as *their constancy is like the flower of the field* (NRSV) is possible, but since the subject is "people," what is at stake here is an evaluation of human piety. A fading and transient piety characterizes humankind's response to the Lord's coming.

The prophet emphasizes the fleeting quality of human life, but at the end he affirms the stability of God's word (40:8b). The fact of human transience only serves to highlight the stability of God's word. The prophet echoes the reference to *our God* from the first voice speaking in the Lord's court (40:3).

40:9-11 The Lord Coming with Might

Now the prophet announces what the second voice (40:6) has told him to announce. *My people-Jerusalem* from 40:1-2a appear as *Zion-Jerusalem* here: the Judean exiles returned from Babylon. With poetic flourish the prophet commands them to tell their good news from a high mountain so that all may hear (40:9). He instructs them to tell the people in Judah who did not go into exile that *your God is here* (Knight: 16). This announcement affirms the presence of God in the sense of God's *renewed* presence. It is good news!

The prophet proclaims God's coming *with might* (40:10). He comes as divine conqueror. The Babylonian deities have not displaced him.

The reference to God speaking tenderly to Jerusalem has opened the prologue. Now at the end of the prologue, God gently leads his people like a shepherd (40:11). God's gentleness does not contradict his might. God's might indicates his sovereignty and power as Creator and sustainer of the earth. God uses his might on behalf of his people. The OT and other ancient Near Eastern texts refer to kings and deities as shepherds (Jer 23:1-4; Ezek 34; cf. *ANET*: 443).

Ode to the Creator 40:12-31

Following the prologue of announcement, the prophet composes a hymn on the Lord's power. The hymn employs a question-answer format. Three sets of programmatic questions move the instruction forward to its goal. The goal is an impressive testimony about God's power available to his people.

40:12-14 God Without Equal

The first set of questions acknowledges the Lord's sovereignty, beginning with the wry perception that no one but the Lord can measure and weigh heaven and earth (40:12). This perception flows from the last stanzas in the prologue, where the Lord comes with might (40:10) and leads his flock like a shepherd (40:11). Endowed with power, this mighty Shepherd has acted decisively in creation.

The Lord did so with neither inside advice nor outside help. "No one" remains the only admissible answer to each of the two questions in 40:13-14. The outlook in these questions is similar to that of the wisdom literature of the OT (cf. Job 21:22; 38:4-41; Prov 8:22-31). Both questions aggressively refute the possibility that God acted in concert with other intelligent beings. He did not! The questions confirm the Lord's acting on his own knowledge and enlightenment.

The words *marked off* (40:12) and *directed* (40:13) translate the same Hebrew word (*tikken*). In both places the English word *estimated* (or perhaps *calculated*) serves as a better translation of the Hebrew. To ask *Who has estimated the mind* (NIV) *of the LORD?* (AT) means that the Lord's mind defies appraisal.

40:15-17 Pretension of Nations

"Surely nations have considerable power and knowledge in God's sight, do they not?" The exiles might have asked some such question in response to the prophet's testimony to the Lord's measureless knowledge and power. Their own experience of Babylon's conquest of Judah and Jerusalem would have suggested such a question. The prophet's answer may have shocked them. Nations have no such weighty status in God's sight (40:15). In God's estimate they appear as weightless as dust. The nations as dust (40:15) recalls the dust of the earth in 40:12.

Even mountainous Lebanon, rich in resources, cannot confer status to the nations. The nations count as emptiness in God's sight (40:16-17). The word *emptiness* employs the language of Genesis 1:2, which describes the earth as *formless and empty* (NIV). The order provided by nation-states falls so far below God's intention that it resembles the emptiness before creation.

40:18-20 God Without Image

The second set of questions acknowledges God's transcendence. The questions address *you* (pl.), speaking in all likelihood to exiles in Babylon. No one and nothing can be compared to God. El, the name of God found here, refers to the true God of Israel (cf. Whybray: 55). To introduce the concept of God's transcendence, the prophet challenges his hearers to think of ways to describe God (40:18-19). He offers an image (or idol) as a possibility, but it is clear that an image made by human hands will fail the test.

The word for "image" (*pesel*) repeats the same word found in the second commandment (Exod 20:4). The polemic against images here rests firmly on the ancient Israelite prohibition against depicting God in human form or any other form. An image crafted by an artisan certainly cannot be compared to God (40:20). Elsewhere in Isaiah is sharp criticism of idol making (cf. 44:9-20). Some of the same rhetoric of God's incomparability and the foolishness of idol production is found in Jeremiah (e.g., 10:1-16).

40:21-24 Posturing of Princes

Four questions (NIV) follow the lesson on images. Each question has its implied answer, as shown below:

Do you not know? (Of course you do!)
Have you not heard? (Of course you have!)
Has it not been told you from the beginning? (Of course it has!)
Have you not understood since the earth was founded? (Of course you have!)

The prophet asks these questions of the exiles with a sense of disbelief (40:21). They ought to know very well the prohibition on images of God and the reality of God's power.

The perception of God sitting above the horizon indicates God's greatness and majesty; likening people to grasshoppers indicates their finite character (40:22; cf. the spies' reference to grasshoppers; Num 13:33). The language in this stanza has similarities to Psalm 104:2, a hymn to God the Creator.

Concern with the heavens now shifts to concern with the earth (40:23-24). Here Princes and rulers are regarded with as little merit as all the nations in 40:17. They have no stability, no durability. For all their pomp and ostentation, they are like the rest of humankind, which withers like the grass (40:7). God himself brings about the rise and fall of princes and rulers.

40:25-26 The Lord's Power

The third set of questions acknowledges the Holy One's strength. A question similar to the one in 40:18 opens the set. Now, however, the Holy One speaks in person, and the comparison shifts from human-made images to God's creative power, illustrated by *the starry host* in *the heavens* (40:25-26 NIV). This reference to the heavenly host (sun, moon, stars) as part of God's creation indicates that these bodies are not themselves gods. The Babylonians worshipped the heavenly host as gods in control of history (Whybray: 57). The prophet countered this dogma with the testimony that the heavenly host has no power. Only God who created this host has power.

40:27-31 Power to the Faint

The prophet, now addressing the exiles in a personal way as Jacob-Israel, quotes them directly (40:27). They wonder why their legitimate interests are ignored by the Lord. This may be paraphrased with the disparaging statement, "The Lord has grown weary of our waiting for him."

The response begins with the same questions found in 40:21 and then continues with a reference to four convictions basic to the faith of Israel (cf. Whybray: 59). (1) The Lord as *the everlasting God* refers to past time as well as to the indefinite future of God's activity. (2) The Lord as *Creator* alludes to Genesis 1:1, where God's creative power for all time is established. (3) The confession that the Lord *does not faint or grow weary* indicates the inexhaustible nature of his strength. And finally, (4) the Lord's *insight* (AT) eludes human comprehension (40:28). These four tenets commend the Lord's ongoing life and vitality to the exiles. The surprising corollary to these convictions is that the Lord directs his inexhaustible strength toward his people for their use, especially for the faint and the powerless (40:29).

The Lord does not withhold his strength from his people but makes it available to those who seek him (40:30-31). To *run and not be weary* points to the promise of physical energy, at one level. But in the OT "run" is also used in the sense of "living one's life" (cf. Hab 2:2, which should be translated, "so that the one reading it may run" = "go on with life").

THE TEXT IN BIBLICAL CONTEXT

Comfort and Hope

The beginning of the prologue, which speaks of the Lord's comforting his people (40:1), as well as its end, which depicts the feeding and gathering of his flock (40:11), find common ground in Jeremiah 31:10-14. There, in opposite order, the Lord gathers and keeps his flock (31:10) and comforts his people (31:13; cf. Ezek 14:23; 16:54). The books of Isaiah and Jeremiah preserve the memory of an Israel dispersed among the nations but gathered and comforted as a nation. Jeremiah uses the words *ransom* and *redeem* to describe this gathering (cf. Martens: 192). Isaiah uses the words *reward* and *recompense* (40:10).

The Lord's Power in Creation

In Isaiah 40:12-31 the prophet joins other writers of the biblical story in giving voice to the Lord's power in creation. The narrative of creation in Genesis 1—especially days three, four, and five—serves as the fountainhead of all these various expressions.

The Lord's compassing of heavens and earth in Isaiah 40:12 brings to mind the Lord's speech to Job out of the whirlwind, reminding him of the one who fixed the limits of the sea (Job 38:8-11). The psalmist, quoted by the author of Hebrews (1:10-12), emphasizes the perishability of heavens and earth in contrast to the Lord's permanence (Ps 102:25-27).

Isaiah speaks of the Lord stretching out the heavens (40:21-22), using the same metaphor employed by Job (9:8) and the psalmist (Ps 104:2). Isaiah speaks of the Lord calling the stars by name (40:26) in remarkable similarity to the psalmist in Psalm 147:4.

The Lord as Creator, everlasting and measureless in understanding, completes the hymn on the Lord's power (Isa 40:28). This, too, finds expression in the Psalms. Psalm 90:2 says of the Lord, "From everlasting to everlasting you are God." And the poet in Psalm 147:5 says that the Lord's "understanding has no limit" (NIV).

The poets and prophets of the Bible, drinking from the fountainhead of creation, continue to rephrase and refresh their conviction about the Lord's power in creation.

Isaiah and John the Baptist

The relationship between the Testaments is exhibited with great poignancy in the Gospel writers' portrayal of John the Baptist with reference to Isaiah 40:1-5. At the beginning of Isaiah 40, God addresses his heavenly court with the good news that the penalty for Jerusalem's sins has been paid (40:1-2). A voice from the court then urges the removal of obstacles in the way of the Lord, who comes to reveal himself to his people (40:3-5).

All four Gospel writers place these words, especially Isaiah 40:3, at the beginning of Jesus' public ministry. Matthew and Mark restrict themselves to a nearly literal quotation of Isaiah 40:3 (Matt 3:3; Mark 1:3). Luke (3:4-6) quotes most of Isaiah 40:3-5, and John (1:23) uses a paraphrase of Isaiah 40:3 in his presentation of John the Baptist.

All four Gospel writers quote the LXX version of Isaiah 40, which is punctuated differently from the Hebrew text. In the Hebrew text a voice calls for the preparation of a highway in the wilderness for God's coming. The LXX version, on the other hand, has the voice calling out *in the wilderness* for the preparation of a highway. The Gospel writers interpreted John the Baptist as this voice in the wilderness.

THE TEXT IN THE LIFE OF THE CHURCH

Gospel

The gospel (*good news*) of God's kingdom lies at the center of Jesus' coming, according to Mark 1:14-15. The English word *gospel* renders the Greek word *euangelion*, which translates the Hebrew word stemming from *baśar* (*good tidings*) in Isaiah 40:9.

Jesus' use of the word *gospel* signaled both his rootedness in the OT Scriptures and his readiness to begin a new thing. The church understands the gospel as the foundation made by God in Christ for the salvation and transformation of humankind. The gospel serves as the instrument for restoring a transparent relationship between God and humankind as well as creating reconciliation between and among people. The church sees the gospel as the gift of God's grace for sinful humanity (cf. *NHBD*: 232).

Dietrich Philips, in his essay "The Church of God" (ca. 1560), writes that the gospel

> is the joyful message of Jesus Christ, the only begotten Son of God, the only Redeemer and Saviour, . . . who gave himself for us that we might be ransomed from the power of Satan, sin, and eternal death, and made us children and heirs of our Heavenly Father, to be a royal priesthood, . . . to be a holy people and an elect race and a possession of God in the Spirit. . . . Now, all who . . . turn away from their sinful life and godless being and with penitent heart believe the gospel and accept Jesus Christ as their Saviour . . . are born

anew of God by his eternal Word . . . and in the power of his Holy Spirit. (SAW: 236-37)

Isaiah 40 in Handel's *Messiah*

George Frideric Handel (1685-1759) composed the *Messiah* in 1741. The three parts of the *Messiah* correspond roughly to (1) the Messiah's birth and early ministry; (2) his death, resurrection, and exaltation; and (3) the meaning of the Messiah's life for humankind.

Throughout the *Messiah*, Old and New Testament texts are woven together in the telling of the story. After the overture, the *Messiah* begins with three pieces from Isaiah 40: a tenor recitative "Comfort ye, my people," from Isaiah 40:1-3 (no. 2); a tenor air "Ev'ry valley shall be exalted," from Isaiah 40:4 (no. 3); and a chorus "And the glory of the Lord," from Isaiah 40:5 (no. 4).

Two other pieces from Isaiah 40 are employed in part one: an alto air and chorus "O Thou that tellest good tidings to Zion" (40:9 with 60:1; no. 9), and "He shall feed his flock like a shepherd" (40:11; no. 20). The messianic hope in the book of Isaiah found its fulfillment in Jesus of Nazareth. The NT writers understood this clearly, as did artists such as Handel throughout the history of the church.

Isaiah 41:1-29

Cosmic Judicial Inquiry

PREVIEW

A judicial inquiry of cosmic proportions dominates chapter 41. The Lord calls two sets of defendants into the heavenly courtroom. The nations receive a summons first (41:1-20). If the nations have an answer for the judge's queries, their answer does not appear. Instead, the judge addresses Israel as his servant, but not as the plaintiff. Israel is simply present at the judicial inquiry as a witness.

The gods receive the second summons (41:21-29). They also do not speak. This is because they cannot speak. Their silence exposes them as counterfeit.

OUTLINE

Nations Called to Judicial Inquiry, 41:1-20
    41:1-4   Call and Query
    41:5-7   Fear and Trembling
    41:8-10   Israel's Servanthood
    41:11-16   Enemies Disgraced and Scattered
    41:17-20   Promise to the Poor
False Gods and Their Images Called to Judicial Inquiry, 41:21-29
    41:21-24   Call and Query
    41:25-29   No Answer

Isaiah 41:1-29

EXPLANATORY NOTES

Nations Called to Judicial Inquiry 41:1-20

Nations and peoples gather before the Lord in a judicial inquiry. In several brief scenes the Lord presents his case as power broker of the world. Israel receives the call as the Lord's brokerage agent.

41:1-4 Call and Query

The Lord speaks to islands and peoples, representing nations on the rim of the Mediterranean (41:1). The invitation to these nations to renew their strength links the beginning of chapter 41 to chapter 40, where renewal of strength comes to those who wait for the Lord (40:31). Here the nations need strength in order to participate in a judicial inquiry, with the Lord acting as judge. Though invited to speak, the nations themselves do not speak.

The Lord opens the proceedings with a rhetorical question: *Who has stirred up one from the east, whom victory meets at every step?* (41:2a NIV footnote). The implied answer would be, "I, the Lord, did this!" Although the one from the east whom the Lord stirs up remains unnamed, scholars in rare consensus argue that Cyrus the Persian (reigned 550-530 BC) is meant (Isa 44:28; 45:1). Cyrus takes the world stage as conqueror at the Lord's bidding, not his own.

Undoubtedly Cyrus sees himself as entirely responsible for his own success (41:2b-3). But the prophet knows that the Lord has a plan including Cyrus and his empire (cf. God and Nebuchadnezzar, Jer 49:30).

In case the reader has missed the point, the final stanza identifies the Lord as the one who has done it (41:4). The prophet presents the Lord as one who calls people into his service. The Lord, who revealed himself to Moses as the "I AM" (Exod 3:6, 14; 6:2) now reveals himself to the nations in the same way (cf. Knight: 29).

41:5-7 Fear and Trembling

A recess in the court proceedings may be surmised here. This gives the nations an opportunity to draw conclusions about what has been said. They respond with fear and trembling (41:5). Whom or what do they fear? The Lord? Cyrus? They fear both. Fear grips the islands because the Lord has called them to silence. The whole earth trembles because of the conqueror from the east (Cyrus) about whom the Lord speaks.

They buttress their courage by reinforcing their confidence in images of deity, illustrating how people "will whistle in the dark to keep their courage up" (Knight: 30). The NIV supplies *idol* in 41:7 from its usage in 40:18-20. The experience of creating a golden calf illustrates, from Israel's own experience, the recourse to idolatry when faced with anxiety and uncertainty (Exod 32). The body politic, never very tolerant of patient waiting, sought a substitute for the One who delivered them from slavery in Egypt.

41:8-10 Israel's Servanthood

After the court recess the Lord addresses Israel as his servant [*Servant, Servants, p. 451*] for the first time (41:8-9a). He compares his servant Israel to the patriarch Jacob, grandson of Abraham. The Jacob-Israel word pair occurs repeatedly in Isaiah 40–48, always referring to the exiles in Babylon. Here in 41:8 the word pair appears in reversed order as Israel-Jacob, drawing attention to Jacob's new name: Israel. The clauses *whom I have chosen* and *whom I took* both refer to Israel-Jacob. The Lord's calling of Israel-Jacob corresponds to his calling of the conqueror from the east (Cyrus, implied in 41:2). These are not callings in the sense of "the divine right of kings" but in the sense of opportunities for service on behalf of the King of kings.

The Lord repeats his interest in the Judean exiles (*my servant*) in the second stanza (41:9b-10). The Lord's solidarity with his people comes with a rock-solid guarantee of divine presence, divine help, and divine strength. The power behind Cyrus' victory (ṣedeq in 41:2) now opens to full view as the Lord's *victorious [ṣedeq] right hand* (41:10 JB, NRSV); here the NIV prefers the more traditional *righteous right hand*. Salvation speeches with the admonition not to fear are found throughout the Bible (Gen 46:3; Josh 11:6; Isa 43:1, 5; Jer 1:8; Ezek 2:6; Luke 1:13, 30; John 6:20; etc.). The exhortation not to fear is part of the bedrock of faith.

41:11-16 Enemies Disgraced and Scattered

The Lord continues to address the exiles in the setting of the judicial inquiry. Jacob-Israel faces three categories of opponents in its own ranks: adversaries, antagonists, warlords. The adversaries, *those who oppose you* designates those who engage in endless legal disputes (41:11 NIV). The antagonists, *your enemies*, suggests those who encourage active hostility between factions (41:12 NIV). The warlords, *those who wage war against you*, need not refer to external enemies but to those who advocate internecine violence (41:12). The Lord declares that these opponents have no future among God's people.

The focus of the address then shifts to the foundation of Israel's spiritual power (41:13-14). This foundation rests on two assurances: (1) the assurance of the Lord's help, and (2) the assurance that Israel need not fear. The *right hand* of God (41:10) grasping the *right hand* of God's servant (41:13) indicates the flow of power in the relationship between God and people. The answer to the opponents in 41:11-12 lies in the assurances in 41:13-14. The reference to Jacob as a worm seems intentionally derogatory (41:14). I see it as a word with double meaning, indicating Jacob's fragility yet addressing Jacob with the courage-building words *Do not fear*. The instruction not to fear, repeated from the previous verse, rests on the Lord's character as *Redeemer*. *Redemption* signifies setting something or someone free. So the Lord as Redeemer commends freedom from fear among God's people because the Lord's help is always near.

The threshing and winnowing of mountains and hills in 41:15-16, then, refers to the troubles that Jacob-Israel will overcome by God's help (cf. Knight: 37). The *threshing sledge*, dragged over grain on a threshing floor, removes the grain from the husk (41:15). The reference to mountains and hills indicates Canaanite worship centers in general and idolatry in particular. So threshing them means resisting them. The wind and tempest, representing the Lord's control of the storm, scatter all things idolatrous (41:16).

The theme of nothingness in 41:11-12 finds expression in chaff blown away by the wind in 41:16. The kernels of grain are the goal and joy of the harvest, the chaff a by-product. The last two lines of verse 16 have the people praising and rejoicing in the Lord because of the grain harvest. Having suppressed false worship, Jacob-Israel moves on to fulfill its calling to worship the Lord alone as God.

41:17-20 Promise to the Poor

The Lord continues to speak in the setting of the judicial inquiry. Now, however, the Lord does not speak *to* the exiles but about them, referring to them as *the poor and needy*. What is said may be described as a hymn (G. E. Wright: 102). Its theme centers on the Lord's response to the poor and needy in terms of new opportunity.

The first stanza of the hymn poses the problem of the poor and needy requiring water and receiving a promise that their need will be met (41:17). The last two lines of the stanza refer to *the LORD, the God of Israel* (NIV), the promise maker.

The second stanza extends the promise in specific terms: water in the wilderness (41:18). This alludes to the wilderness wandering described in the book of Numbers, when the people needed water (cf. Num 20). The hymn refers to rivers and fountains that the Lord will open. It mentions pools and springs that the Lord will make. All are signs of life and hope.

The third stanza extends the promise in terms of trees in the wilderness (41:19). Water comes first, but shelter follows closely. The fourth stanza brings the hymn to a close (41:20). The Lord gives water for life and trees for shelter so that the poor and needy will realize on whom they depend. The last two lines of the stanza refer to *the LORD, the Holy One of Israel* as the one with the power to keep the promise [*Holy, Holy One of Israel, p. 445*].

False Gods and Their Images Called to Judicial Inquiry 41:21-29

Although a word for *images* occurs only at 41:29, a summons to gods represented by images is clearly implied already in 41:21. The NIV adds *your idols* in 41:22 to make this clear.

41:21-24 Call and Query

The plural imperative verbs here imply that the Lord calls gods and their images to the judicial inquiry to give evidence of their claim that they are a force to be reckoned with (41:21-22a). The reference to the Lord as *Jacob's King* (NIV) occurs only here in the OT (41:21). The Lord as Jacob's King, calling the gods and their images to account, recalls Genesis 35, where God instructed Jacob to make an altar at Bethel. In response, Jacob required his household to dispose of their foreign gods, which Jacob hid under an oak tree near Shechem (35:1-4).

Now *Jacob's King* demands that the gods chart the future on the basis of the past (41:22b-23a). If they are able to chart the future, this would confirm their legitimacy as deities. Then the Lord demands that they do anything at all, good or bad, that can be noticed and observed (41:23b-24). Their lack of response, however, indicates their nonexistence. All who choose such gods are loathsome. The conjunction *But* does injustice to the Hebrew word at the beginning of 41:24 (NIV). *See here!* or *Pay attention!* does a better job of indicating this imminent pronouncement from the head of the judicial inquiry. The verdict declares the nonexistence of the gods and expresses extreme disgust with all who choose such gods.

41:25-29 No Answer

The shift back to the first-person singular (cf. first-person speech in 41:1-20) signals the beginning of the Lord's case that he is God (41:25). His claim rests on his competence to envision future events, which only the Creator of these events could bring about (cf. Whybray: 69). Knowledge of the conqueror *from the north* serves as an example of this competence. The stirring up of a conqueror recalls 41:2. There the conqueror comes from the east, here from the north and the east. In fact, Cyrus began his campaign in Persia, to the east of Babylon, marched into Armenia to the north, then descended into Babylon from the north (cf. Watts, 1987:118; *CBA*: 127, map 166).

The reference to Cyrus as one *who calls on my name* (NIV, following the Heb.; cf. NRSV footnote) implies that Cyrus worshipped the Lord. This is a difficult text because Isaiah 45:3-5 clearly states that Cyrus did not worship the Lord. Various emendations and explanations have been offered (cf. Watts, 1987:118). Although it is not possible or even desirable to resolve every difficulty, this particular case may well be one of Cyrus as conqueror recognizing the Lord as Israel's God without acknowledging (worshipping) the Lord *besides [whom] there is no other* (45:6). The comparison of Cyrus to a mason or a potter indicates his intention to do as he pleases with the nations he defeats (41:25).

No one foresaw Cyrus' rise to power except the Lord himself (41:26-27). The point is that none of the gods could exhibit their competence by foretelling the rise of Cyrus. The Lord alone announced it to Zion-Jerusalem, who received the announcement as good news.

The final stanza denies once and for all the gods' claim to existence (41:28-29). With a commanding call, *See them all!* in 41:29 (AT), the gods and their images alike are declared to be a *delusion*. They cannot speak. They cannot give counsel. They are like the heavens and earth before creation.

THE TEXT IN BIBLICAL CONTEXT

Mountains and Hills

Mountains and hills form a word-pair some 32 times in the OT. One fourth of these word pairs occur in the book of Isaiah, including the reference in 41:15.

Among these 32 word-pairs, 18 occur in situations of promise or blessing (Num 23:9; Deut 33:15; Isa 2:2; 40:12; 54:10; 55:12; Ezek 36:4, 6; Joel 3:18; Amos 9:13; Mic 4:1; Hab 3:6; Pss 72:3; 114:4, 6; 148:9; Prov 8:25; Song of Sol 2:8). The other 14 of these word pairs occur in situations of judgment, mostly but not exclusively judgment on idolatry (Deut 12:2; Isa 2:14; 41:15; 42:15; 65:7; Jer 3:23; 4:24; 17:2-3; Ezek 6:3; 35:8; Hos 4:13; 10:8; Mic 6:1; Nah 1:5).

Ancient Near Eastern peoples often thought of mountains and hills as holy places. On a mountain, Sinai, Moses received the law. The Lord called his dwelling place Zion, a hill. But the Hebrew prophets carried on a relentless campaign against Canaanite worship centers built on mountains and hills since these places encouraged beliefs and practices contrary to the Lord's instruction. The beliefs included the worship of images representing God. The practices embraced behavior in violation of the Ten Commandments and the other law codes of the Pentateuch.

False Gods

At the beginning of Isaiah 41 (vv. 1-7) and at the end (vv. 21-29) the gods of the nations are called upon to present their case that they are true gods. The test is whether the gods understand the past or know the future and whether they can take action in the present. The conclusion is quickly reached that the gods fail the test and that this failure indicates their falseness.

This test was applied in the setting of the exile in Babylon and the challenge posed to the Judean exiles by the Babylonian religious system. The Babylonian gods were closely tied to Babylonian imperial interests (cf. Mendenhall: 47). The message of Isaiah 41 counters the exiles' serious temptation to see these gods as true and powerful. After all, their representative, the king of Babylon and his army, invaded and defeated the kingdom of Judah.

The intention of Isaiah 41 is to convince the Judean exiles that their future does not lie with the religious system of Babylon. The only voice its gods have is the voice given to them by Babylonian imperial interests. Once the empire fades away, its gods fade away as well. They have no transcendence beyond the material reality of the empire. They are mere puppets, manipulated by their human creators.

THE TEXT IN THE LIFE OF THE CHURCH

Foundation of Spiritual Power

Any interpretation of Isaiah 41 needs to focus on the biblical foundation of spiritual power found in verses 11-16. The thought of these six verses moves in pairs.

The first pair of verses declares the "principalities and powers" vulnerable and overthrown (41:11-12). While these principalities and powers refer to Israel's opponents in the OT story, there are NT equivalents to choose from as well. A number of NT letters (1 Tim 1:10; Phil 1:28; 1 Pet 5:8) use the same or similar adversarial language as Isaiah 41.

The second pair of verses proclaims the Lord's redemption founded on his help and his encouragement (41:13, 14). Here there is a focus on the Lord's encouragement not to fear. Alongside this encouragement stands the promise of the Lord's help. The hymn "Precious Lord, Take My Hand" (*WT:* 611) was inspired in part by Isaiah 41:13. Verse 2 of the hymn includes the appeal to God to "Hold my hand lest I fall."

The Lord as Redeemer gathers all the strands of verses 13 and 14 into one center of significance. *Redemption* means to set free. A Redeemer is the agent of such freedom. God as Redeemer sets people free from the fears and anxieties that plague them.

The third pair of verses announces the peoples' situation inside the Lord's encouragement and promise (41:15, 16). Various applications of the role of God's people in church and society today come to mind. The twin focus of threshing and rejoicing offers an opportunity to call God's people to faithful living. The question to be asked is whether threshing means a frontal attack on the evil of worldly powers, or whether, in the light of Jesus' life and teaching and death, it means dying rather than submitting to the powers' evil commands (cf. Wink: 10-14).

The threshing and winnowing of mountains and hills are best interpreted as resistance to the idolatries that tempt humankind in the twenty-first century. Such idolatries begin with pride and arrogance (Isa 2:6-22). The shattering of pride (threshing) prepares the way for faith that has integrity (rejoicing).

Monotheism

In the context of a cosmic judicial inquiry (Isa 41; cf. 43:8-13 and 45:18-25), the case is made for asserting that there is but one God. The primary issue in this assertion is God as a source of power. This is in contrast to the gods, depicted as human-made images, who are extensions of their makers' personalities and therefore powerless (Barton: 74).

The word "power" is not used in Isaiah 41, but it is clear that the ability to tell about events, past and future, is critical to the case for monotheism. Alongside this competence in telling about events is the ability to advise and answer questions.

It is not, therefore, simply a question of God's power; it is also a question of the nature of the power that God wields. In Isaiah 41 the case for monotheism rests on the creative power of the Lord's words and deeds rather than on the Lord's ability to carry out lethal violence (cf. Lind, 1990:154-55).

In ancient polytheistic thought, the ability of the gods to carry out lethal violence is exhibited in the power of the king, who represents the gods through his "monopoly of force." In this worldview the most important fact of human history is the political state, based on a "deification of [lethal] force" (Mendenhall: 64-66). The biblical worldview completely discredits this view of history. And it does so by basing its monotheism on an alternative view of power, as exhibited in Isaiah 41, in which one God exercises power through his word to his community, formed to be a blessing to the nations.

Isaiah 42:1-25

A Light to the Nations

PREVIEW

The cosmic judicial inquiry in chapter 41 concludes with a denial of the gods' claim to existence and to any kind of power. Now in chapter 42, the Lord presents an "answer" to the spurious gods: his servant as "the messenger of the heavenly court" (Watts, 1987:119) constitutes this answer. The beginning of Isaiah 42 focuses entirely on the Lord's servant and his mission (42:1-12). In three deft strokes the prophet draws the reader into the Lord's purpose for his servant. The Lord's introduction of his servant comes first (42:1-4). Then follows the servant's presentation by the Lord (42:5-9). A song in praise of the Lord's glory concludes the announcement of the servant's mission (42:10-12).

The second part continues the judicial tribunal, with the Lord pondering the blindness of his people (42:13-16, 17-20) and with the prophet pondering the consequences of the people's disobedience (42:21-23, 24-25).

OUTLINE

The Lord's Spirit upon His Servant, 42:1-12
    42:1-4   Justice in the Earth
    42:5-9   Light to the Nations
    42:10-12   Glory to the Lord
The People's Blindness and Disobedience, 42:13-25
    42:13-16   The Lord's Guidance
    42:17-20   Calling Deaf and Blind to Account

Isaiah 42:1-25

42:21-23   The Lord's Guidance Spurned
42:24-25   Disobedience and Discipline

EXPLANATORY NOTES

The Lord's Spirit upon His Servant 42:1-12

The noun *servant* appears previously in the book with reference to Isaiah (20:3), Eliakim (22:20), David (37:35), and Israel (41:8). In Isaiah 41:9, Israel is addressed collectively. The address itself in 41:10 incorporates words of salvation for the exiles (cf. Brueggemann, 1998b:33).

In Isaiah 42, the noun *servant* begins to be used in a way that is distinctive in the book. I am referring to a cluster of passages in Isaiah 42–53 called the Servant Songs (see "Servant of the Lord" in TBC below) [*Servant, Servants, p. 451*]. There are four of these songs (42:1-4; 49:1-6; 50:4-9; and 52:13–53:12). They were not necessarily written as songs; they are songs by virtue of a poetic style that is accessible to musicians (I. Friesen, 2003:63).

42:1-4 Justice in the Earth

The first of the Servant Songs introduces the servant's mission. The Lord works through a servant, an emissary, to deliver *justice to the nations* (42:1). What does it mean to deliver justice? The Hebrew word for *justice* (*mišpaṭ*) has many meanings in the OT, including "judgment" and "right" and "custom." Here *justice* refers to the idea of a right way to live [*Justice and Righteousness, p. 445*]. Its application to *the nations* means that the Lord intends nations to work together in peace and harmony (Knight: 44). The production of justice for the nations rests on the Lord's *Spirit* (NIV) being present and active among them. The nations have confidence in the Lord's servant just as adversaries in a conflict must trust a mediator to bring peace and healing.

The second stanza discloses the personal character of this servant (42:2-3a). The character of the Lord's Spirit reveals itself in the servant's behavior. The Lord describes the servant, not as one who bellows and bleats and blubbers, but as one who demonstrates sensitivity to the weak (bruised reed) and sympathy to the faint (dimly burning wick). The servant moves about with gentle poise, secure in the knowledge that the nations will one day imitate God's justice [*Justice and Righteousness, p. 445*]. They will do so as they see it put to the test and lived out in the servant's life (Hanson: 46).

The third stanza indicates the servant's resolution and perseverance in executing his mission (42:3b-4). The word *faithfully* indicates that the servant lives in obedience to the Lord's Spirit. The stanza closes with parallel lines, *earth* and *coastlands* showing the global scope of the work. *Justice* and *teaching* identify the means of accomplishing the work. The term *teaching* (Heb. *torah*) captures the essence of the Lord's will and way.

42:5-9 Light to the Nations

Following the introduction to the servant's mission, there is a presentation of the servant himself in 42:5-9. A declaration *Thus says God, the LORD* [*Messenger Formula, p. 447*] introduces four active Hebrew participles (*creating, stretching, spreading* out, *giving*) describing the Lord's sovereign power in heaven, on earth, and among humankind (42:5). That the Lord gives breath and spirit to earth's people simply means that people receive the gift of life.

The presentation itself encompasses two seven-line stanzas (42:6-7, 8-9), with each stanza beginning with the identifying phrase *I am the LORD*. In the first stanza the Lord addresses the servant personally (*you* sg.). Since the Lord put (gave) his Spirit upon his servant, he now presents (gives) his servant for a particular task. Two parallel lines give a synopsis of the task. The servant is to be *a covenant for the people* and *a light for the Gentiles* (NIV). Certainly *people* refers to the people of the earth in the previous verse. And *nations* refers to the nations for whom the servant is to bring forth justice (cf. 42:1). The servant's commission is global in scope. The servant assumes the role of God's agent to bring God's *covenant* (relationship) and *light* (salvation) to the nations and the whole earth (Hanson: 46-47).

In the last stanza the Lord speaks to the exiles (*you* pl.; 42:8-9). The Lord gives his Spirit to his servant (42:1 NIV). He gives both breath and spirit to earth's people (42:5). He gives his servant as covenant and as light to earth's people and nations (42:6-7). But he does not give his glory to anyone. That he does not give his praise to idols means that he does not share his divinity with idols. Idols have no divinity.

The *former things* and the *new things* refer to earlier announcements and fresh announcements. In the time before the exodus, the Lord had announced his name to Moses (Exod 3). Throughout the time before the exile, the prophets spoke tirelessly against idol worship. The *new things* in Isaiah's vision now include a clear expression of God's oneness, embracing "a distinct moral quality" (Lind, 1990:153).

42:10-12 Glory to the Lord

A song in praise of the Lord's glory concludes the announcement of the servant's mission. The first stanza begins with the prophet calling earth's peoples (pl. imperative) to *sing* a new song (42:10). Populations along seacoasts and those who ply the seas are identified. The announcement of new things requires *a new song*. The prophet's contagious joy rings through the stanza.

The focus of this joy lies in earth's inhabitants attributing glory and praise to the Lord alone (42:11-12). Here inland inhabitants are represented by Kedar and Sela. Kedar is a region in Arabia east of Transjordan, now in Saudi Arabia; Sela is a city of the Edomites southeast of the Dead Sea (*CBA*: 89, map 116; 103, map 137). Even these ancestral enemies join in singing the new song (Knight: 51)!

The People's Blindness and Disobedience 42:13-25

From the announcement of the servant's purpose and mission early in the chapter, the judicial tribunal now moves to a declaration of the Lord's deeds and demands concerning his people.

42:13-16 The Lord's Guidance

The prophet affirms the Lord's strength by using battlefield imagery in the first stanza (42:13). In the second line the word *fury*, or *zeal* (NIV), translates a Hebrew word meaning jealousy (*qn'*). In the OT this jealousy occurs as a characteristic of God, often in passages where idolatry is denounced (Exod 20:5; Deut 5:9; Josh 24:19; 1 Kings 14:22; etc.; cf. *NHBD*: 303).

In the following stanzas the Lord himself speaks, his jealousy expressing itself in his leadership of his people (42:14, 15, 16). This jealousy of his people begins with the comparison to a woman giving birth (42:14). Patient waiting gives way to the crisis of birth. New things announced by a new song await imminent delivery.

The signs of imminent delivery lie in the sheer power of the Lord to transform the landscape (42:15). The Lord denudes hills and mountains and dries up surface water. The signs also recall Israel's experience of being led through trackless wilderness after the exodus from Egypt (42:16).

The pledge to do these wonders recalls the prologue, where a way is prepared for the Lord (40:3-5). Here a way is prepared for the blind (cf. Jer 31:8-9). I take this to be a reference to the exiles, whose way back to their land the Lord now prepares.

42:17-20 Calling Deaf and Blind to Account

The Lord continues speaking in 42:17-20. The contrast between the Lord's strength in 42:13 and the shame of trusting in false gods in 42:17 could not be greater. The Lord presents idol and image as lethargic and shiftless, utterly unable to provide help.

The hopelessness of idolatry leads to a call to faithfulness. The Lord urges those who do not understand the futility of idols and images to listen and see (42:18-19a). Do the blind and deaf refer to people in general or to the Israelites in particular? Since in 42:16 the reference to those who are blind appears to indicate the exiles in Babylon, it is best to take the deaf and blind in 42:18 as these same exiles. They continue to trust in illusions. The question *Who is blind . . . and deaf?* speaks about the Lord's servant, the exiles collectively understood, as in 42:1. Israel remains blind and deaf to the peril of idolatry. Hearing and seeing and renouncing the reality of idolatry continues as a test of faithfulness.

42:21-23 The Lord's Guidance Spurned

Now the prophet speaks again. The Lord's original intention for Israel bursts into bloom. His instruction (*torah*) was intended to be at the center of his people's life (42:21). Instead, they wandered far from the Lord's instruction, and the prophet uses word pictures to describe the consequences of this wandering: *plundered, looted, trapped, imprisoned* (42:22a NIV).

The proof of their captivity lies in the absence of anyone to loose the chains of their bondage (42:22b-23). The question in 42:23 addresses the exiles personally. The prophet throws out a challenge to his people. Will anyone listen?

42:24-25 Disobedience and Discipline

The questions continue (42:24). The first question asks, Who allowed this looting and plundering of Israel? The reply comes in the form of a rhetorical question [*Literary Perspective, p. 446*]: *Was it not the LORD, against whom we have sinned?* The last two lines of 42:24 are parallel to each other [*Hebrew Poetry, p. 444*]. The first represents the refusal to live rightly (orthopraxy), and the second represents the refusal to worship rightly (orthodoxy). The "we" in 42:24 means that the prophet includes himself in the corporate sin of the people.

In the NT the apostle Paul writes, "The wages of sin is death" (Rom 6:23). The tragedy of the human experience lies in the unwillingness or the inability to learn from the past (Isa 42:25). The Lord's judgment, always moving toward restoration rather than revenge, fails to convince the people of the error of their ways.

Isaiah 42:1-25

THE TEXT IN BIBLICAL CONTEXT

Servant of the Lord

The idea that the Lord has servants who are answerable to their master is common to both Testaments. Thus Abraham and Moses and David in the OT are designated servants of the Lord. And in the NT, Paul and James and John are called servants of God.

It is not surprising, therefore, that there are references to the Lord's servants in the book of Isaiah. The Lord calls David *my servant* in 37:35, and Isaiah himself is called *my servant* in 20:3. What is striking in the book, however, is the special way in which the designation *my servant* is used in Isaiah 41–53. In these chapters are four Servant Songs [*Servant, Servants, p. 451*] as well as other references to the servant of the Lord.

The servant in the Servant Songs is distinguished from the servant elsewhere in Isaiah 41–53 by the practice of "giving" (cf. I. Friesen, 2003:63-74). In the first song the Lord gives (*natan*) his spirit to his servant (42:1). In the second song the Lord promises to give (*natan*) his servant as a light to the nations (49:6). In the third song the servant reflects on the talent for encouraging speech that the Lord has given (*natan*) him (50:4). The "gift" in the fourth song is that the servant makes (*natan*) his grave with wrongdoers (53:9).

These "gifts" provide a thumbnail sketch of the servant's character and destiny in Isaiah 41–53, beginning with the gift of God's spirit resting on him (42:1-4). His mission to Jacob-Israel was as a teacher and comforter (50:4-9), and to the nations as a light bringing salvation (49:1-6). The substance of this salvation is the servant's living out of God's reign by accepting suffering rather than inflicting it (52:13–53:12).

Jesus' Baptism

A comparison of the language in Isaiah 42:1 with that in the Gospel accounts of Jesus' baptism shows some interesting similarities (Matt 3:13-17; Mark 1:9-11; Luke 3:21-22; cf. John 1:29-34). In Isaiah 42:1, for example, the Lord puts his Spirit upon his servant; in the four Gospels, God's Spirit descends upon Jesus at his baptism.

In the first three Gospels the voice from heaven refers to Jesus as "the Beloved [*ho agapētos*]." The word used of the servant in Isaiah 42:1 is *my chosen* (*ho eklektos*, LXX). The two words have points of similarity although they are not completely equal in meaning.

In the first three Gospels the voice from heaven describes Jesus as one with whom God is well pleased (*eudokēsa*). In Isaiah 42:1 the servant is one in whom the Lord takes pleasure (*rṣh*). The LXX, which may be following a different Hebrew text here, uses the word *prosedexato* (from *prosdechomai*, meaning "receive" or "welcome"). The Gospel writers were aware of the similarities between the servant introduced in Isaiah 42:1 and the Son introduced at his baptism in the Jordan River.

THE TEXT IN THE LIFE OF THE CHURCH

Spirit-Led Community

The conferral of the Lord's Spirit upon the servant in Isaiah 42:1 serves as a sign and anticipation of the Lord's Spirit breathed upon the church (John 20:22). As the early church surveyed the body of Scripture that it shared with Judaism (which Christians call the OT), it understood and accepted the Spirit of God present in creation itself (Gen 1:2). It took for granted that this same Spirit enabled Balaam to bless Israel (Num 24:2) and Saul to prophesy (1 Sam 10:10). The church recognized God's Spirit upon the prophets, who were appointed to speak the Lord's word (Ezek 2:2). The church was especially conscious of God's Spirit upon a future messianic king (Isa 11:1-2) and upon the servant of the Lord (Isa 42:1; *ODCC*: 783-84).

The early church recognized the Spirit of the Lord coming upon Jesus at his baptism (Mark 1:10). John's Gospel states this forcefully in John the Baptist's testimony that the Spirit came down from heaven as a dove and "remained on" Jesus (John 1:32). The outpouring of the Spirit at Pentecost marked a rite of passage for the early church. Now, for the first time in a public way, the Lord's Spirit entered upon the life of the church (Acts 2:1-18, 38).

During the next four centuries, an elaboration of a doctrine of the Holy Spirit took place in the church, East and West, in the writings of Tertullian, Origen, Basil, Augustine of Hippo, and others (*ODCC*: 783-84). This doctrine, enshrined in the church's creeds, became the standard by which the church's understanding of the Spirit's work was guided. The Apostles' Creed enjoins intellectual assent to the existence of the Holy Spirit and to the work of the Holy Spirit in the conception of Jesus. The Nicene Creed goes beyond intellectual assent and provides a fourfold definition of the Holy Spirit: (1) the Lord and giver of life, (2) proceeding from the Father and the Son, (3) to be worshipped and glorified together with the Father and the Son, and (4) who spoke by the prophets.

Neither creed clearly speaks about the Spirit's work at Pentecost, shaping a new community of the Spirit. The challenge of the church lies in its self-understanding as a *Community of the Spirit* (Kraus: 24-30). Spirit-led individuals make up the church. But such individuals do not receive Christ's Spirit in isolation. Instead, their self-identities are shaped by the community commissioned by Christ's presence. Such a community may become a light to the nations.

Isaiah 43:1-28

The Lord as Redeemer

PREVIEW

In Isaiah and in the Bible, the reality of God rests on two pillars: (1) God's self-revelation through his messengers, and (2) human testimony to God's activity in everyday experience. Isaiah 43 focuses on the first of these pillars: God's self-revelation through his prophetic messenger. The Lord speaks throughout the chapter.

The first part centers on the Lord's work of redemption (43:1-13). The Lord as Redeemer and as gatherer prepares the way for the people as witnesses to the Lord as the only savior.

The second part centers on the Lord's doing of a new thing (43:14-28). The new thing portrays the next steps in the Lord's plan for his people, including their new exodus and their declaration of his praise. The rebellion of his people does not go unnoticed, but it is offset by the Lord's pardon; yet the consequences of the rebellion take their toll.

OUTLINE

The Lord's Saving Presence, 43:1-13
    43:1-4   Redemption of Jacob-Israel
    43:5-7   Gathering from East, West, North, South
    43:8-13   The Lord's Witnesses
Doing a New Thing, 43:14-28
    43:14-21   The Lord as Redeemer
    43:22-24   Burdened and Wearied
    43:25-28   Sins Blotted Out

EXPLANATORY NOTES

The Lord's Saving Presence 43:1-13

Three aspects of redemption [*Redemption, Redeemer*, p. *448*] emerge in the first part of the Lord's discourse. The opening statement focuses on the Lord's *redeeming love* for his people (43:1-4). The second statement stresses the Lord's *gathering* of his people (43:5-7). The last statement emphasizes this people as *witnesses* of the Lord's oneness (43:8-13).

43:1-4 Redemption of Jacob-Israel

Four special words in the first stanza reveal the length and breadth of the Lord's relationship with his people: *created, formed, redeemed, called* (43:1). The words *created* and *formed* reach back to Genesis 1–2, where they refer to God's creation of the universe and of humankind within that universe (Gen 1) and his formation of the first human beings in the garden (Gen 2). The fashioning of Jacob-Israel compares to the creation story itself, where God calls everything into being and where the first human names (calls) the living creatures. The fashioning of Jacob-Israel has that kind of importance in the Lord's perspective.

Creation and *formation* define the indispensable relationship of Jacob-Israel to the Lord. With this relationship established, the Lord can say, *Do not fear; . . . you are mine*. Between the command not to fear and the declaration of God's ownership stand the assertions of *redemption* and *calling*.

The words *redeemed* and *called* bring to mind Jacob's redemption and name change in Genesis. Jacob's name change in Genesis 32:22-32 signified a new self. No longer the deceptive one (*Jacob*; 25:26 + footnote), his name now signified God's perseverance or God's rule (*Israel*; 32:28 + footnote). Near the end of his life, Israel blessed his grandsons Ephraim and Manasseh (48:15-16). In that blessing he recalled that he himself was redeemed from harm by God. In Isaiah 43:1 the prophet recalls those experiences of redemption and calling from the past. They serve as a reminder of what the Lord plans to do in the near future (Whybray: 82).

The redemption and the calling of Jacob-Israel center on God's promise to be with his people in times of trouble (43:2). God's promise to *be with* his people stands as a fundamental promise in the Bible (Hanson: 63; see TBC). This promise refers to a solidarity between God and people based on a prior covenant that makes the relationship binding.

The identity of the Lord as the savior of Jacob-Israel dominates the third and fourth stanzas (43:3, 4). The central meaning of these stanzas rests on the Lord's recovery of Jacob-Israel for a ransom. Jacob-Israel lies in bondage but has a Redeemer who will pay a price to purchase its freedom (Smart: 97).

The stanzas form parallel statements:

> v. 3a I am . . . your savior
> > v. 3b I give . . . in exchange for you
> v. 4a Because you are precious . . . and I love you
> > v. 4b I give . . . in exchange for your life

It is not advisable to push the meaning of this exchange too far. What is in view here is the extravagant language of God's love lavished upon Jacob-Israel (cf. Brueggemann, 1998b:53-54), rather than a closely argued rationale for the Lord's behavior toward Egypt, Ethiopia, and Seba. Elsewhere Isaiah envisions all the nations receiving the Lord's instruction at the mountain of the Lord's house (2:2-4). But there is a high cost for Israel's redemption and a high value on Israel in God's sight (Childs: 334-35).

43:5-7 Gathering from East, West, North, South

The foundation for the instruction not to fear in 43:1 lies in the Lord's claim on his people (*You are mine*). The Lord has both redeemed his people and called them by name. In 43:5 the basis for the instruction *Do not fear* lies in the Lord's presence with his people: *I am with you*. Redemption, calling, and presence represent three aspects of God's saving relationship with Jacob-Israel.

The Lord's presence carries with it a promise of gathering his people from the four points of the compass (43:5-6a). The *east* refers to exiles in Babylon as well as places closer to Judah after 587 BC (Jer 40:11-12). The *west* refers to exiles in Greece and the rim of the Mediterranean (cf. Joel 3:4-8). The *north* refers to exiles *beyond Damascus* (Amos 5:27). The *south* refers to exiles in Egypt after 587 BC (Jer 43:1-7). But beyond these places of exile, the compass points are a poetic convention meaning a gathering from everywhere. The stanza focuses on the repatriation of God's exiled people to their homes. *I will bring . . .* means that the Lord will inspire their return to the land, though the promise does not include a return to political power (Watts, 1987:133).

The same thought continues in the final stanza (43:6b-7). To whom does the Lord speak when he says *Bring* [f. sg.] *my sons . . . and my daughters*? Probably he speaks to the last-mentioned points of the compass (north, south, both f. sg.) as a way of addressing all points of the compass. They are *all* to yield up the Lord's sons and daughters. In any case, the reference to sons and daughters presumes God as their father, after whom they are named (i.e., *the Holy One of Israel*, 43:3). The threefold reference to *name* and *create* and *form* brings the reader back to the beginning of the chapter, where the order is *create, form,* and *name* (43:1).

43:8-13 The Lord's Witnesses

Following the declaration of Israel's repatriation in 43:5-7, the Lord's speech turns to a judicial inquiry mode similar to that found in chapter 41. There the Lord summoned nations and gods to the inquiry, to establish the fact of the gods' powerlessness. Here the inquiry focuses on Israel as the Lord's witnesses.

In the first stanza the declaration of God's people as blind and deaf means that they are unmoved by the prophetic word (43:8-9a; cf. Lind, 1990:155). In spite of these impediments, however, they are called to appear in court. It is well known that the blind and deaf have or develop extraordinary powers of perception to compensate for the loss of sight and hearing.

In court the nations are challenged to produce witnesses to prove their case (43:9b). The gods of the nations are the implied witnesses whom the Lord invites to affirm the truth of his powerful word to interpret the past. The Lord expects no answer and receives none. Instead, he turns to his own blind and deaf people and declares that they are his witnesses, and they are also his servant (43:10a). Though blind and deaf to the prophetic word, their calling continues to lie in knowing and believing and understanding the Lord's power behind the prophetic word. Knowing, believing, and understanding represent three significant ways of grasping this reality. *I am he* means that the Lord alone interprets past events in such a way that his word of power is seen in them.

The Lord's uniqueness, which may be designated by the English noun *monotheism,* is the focus of the third stanza (43:10b-12a). Monotheism is the belief in but one God. In a world replete with gods, such a testimony declares that divine plurality is a fiction. The Lord does not intend to say that he was formed before the formation of the gods. The Lord was not formed at all but proclaims himself as uncreated and existing from the beginning (Whybray: 85). The word *savior* indicates the Lord's character as one who delivers his people in time of need (BDB: 446-47).

In 43:12b-13 is a return to the focus of the inquiry: Jacob-Israel as the Lord's witnesses to his oneness and saving power. The NIV follows the Hebrew text in placing the phrase *I am God* at the end of 43:12 rather than at the beginning of 43:13 (as in NRSV, JB). Brueggemann is right in pointing out the connection between *the theological claim* of the Lord and *the witness* of Israel. Without Israel's witness that the Lord is God, the world will not grasp this saving claim (1998b:57).

The Hebrew adverb *gam* (*Yes*, NIV) introduces the climax of the section (43:13). With a repetition of the announcement *I am he*, the Lord rests his case that he is the only God (cf. Clements: 86, 61).

Doing a New Thing 43:14-28

The second part of the Lord's discourse reflects on the new thing (see TBC) that the Lord is doing among his people after he has gathered them together. The first comment pictures the exiles on their way to a safe place (43:14-21). The second and third comments contemplate the persistent rebellion that brought on the exile, as well as the Lord's saving grace within that rebellion (43:22-24, 25-28).

43:14-21 The Lord as Redeemer

The Lord declares his redemption of Jacob-Israel at the start of the chapter (43:1). Now the Lord refers to himself as *Redeemer* alongside the name often used in the book of Isaiah: *Holy One of Israel* (43:14; cf. 1:4; 5:19; 10:20; 12:6; 17:7; 29:19; 30:11; 31:1; 37:23; 41:14; 45:11; 47:4; 48:17; 49:7; 54:5; 55:5; 60:9).

A message of liberation for the exiles stands between two notices of the message sender's identity (43:14-15 NIV):

messenger formula:	*This is what the LORD says—*
	your Redeemer, the Holy One of Israel:
message:	*"For your sake I will send to Babylon*
	and bring down as fugitives
	all the Babylonians,
	in the ships in which they took pride.
message sender:	*I am the LORD, your Holy One,*
	Israel's Creator, your King."

The Hebrew text of the message resists easy translation. The Lord addresses his people *for your sake*, so the message focuses on what the Lord will do for his people in exile in Babylon. The verb *to bring down* indicates a blessing on the exiles at the expense of the Babylonians.

The messenger formula at the beginning and the identity of the message sender at the end form brackets (an *inclusio*) that endorse the Lord's character as one who acts on behalf of his people. Message and message sender overlap at the end (43:15).

A new messenger formula introduces the second stanza (43:16-17). Two relative clauses (*who makes, . . . who brings out*) define the Lord's power, recalling exodus language *of the sea* and *of chariot, horse, army,* and *warrior* (Exod 15). The Lord rules over the sea's fury as well as over land-based armed forces. The last two lines of the stanza refer specifically to the demise of armed forces. Armed force occupies no decisive place in God's strategy (cf. Watts, 1987:134-35).

A portrait of the Lord's redemption follows (43:18-19, 20-21). The admonishment against remembering the *former things* refers to crossing the sea during the exodus from Egypt, alluded to in the previous stanza. The Lord does not mean that these *things of old* should be forgotten but that they will appear less important in comparison with the *new thing* that he is doing (Whybray: 88; see TBC). *A way in the sea* (from Egypt to Sinai) allowed the Israelites a way of escape in the past (43:16). *A way in the wilderness* (from Babylon to Palestine) grants the exiles a new exodus in the present (43:19; Knight: 67).

The rhapsody that concludes the section sees wild animals at home in the wilderness, honoring the Lord (43:20-21). The water provided for them is enough to share with the exiles passing through. With a final flourish the prophet recites the Lord's intention that Jacob-Israel will fulfill its purpose *declare my praise*. This is an allusion to Israel's mission, stated in a more direct way in Isaiah 55. God's purpose is no less than the redemption of Israel itself, and beyond Israel the redemption of the whole of humankind (cf. Knight: 189). The quenching of thirst is for God's people in 43:20. The quenching of thirst is for everyone in 55:1.

43:22-24 Burdened and Wearied

The address to Jacob-Israel, with which the chapter began, now brings the chapter to an end. But the difference in meaning could not be more striking. In 43:1 the Lord speaks of Jacob-Israel as the flower of his creation, *called* by name. In 43:22 the flower of his creation lies wilted, disinclined *to call upon* him.

Two words stand out in the accusation: *burdened* (used twice) and *wearied* (used three times). The reply to the Lord's creation and calling of Jacob-Israel (43:1) is apathy and complaint (43:22). God expects more than this. God expects the fruits of a personal relationship: gifts and sacrifices, by which love is communicated (43:23; cf. Hanson: 77-78). Gifts and sacrifices are not imposed as burdens but invited as expressions of love.

The reader is drawn to the contrast between 43:22-24 and 40:27-31. In chapter 40 the Lord's strength empowers Jacob-Israel, who is weary and faint. Here in Isaiah 43, it is the Lord who experiences weariness and heaviness as a result of the sin and offense of Jacob-Israel. How is it that *the everlasting God* (Isa 40:28) can experience weariness and burden because of his people's transgressions? There is a picture of God's suffering, in Isaiah 43:22-24 and in the closing lines of the chapter, which is full of pathos. The Lord gazes over Jacob-Israel, as it were, looking for a sign that his people are serious about a covenant relationship. There is sorrow, here, because there are no expressions of affection and warmth (Hanson: 78; cf. Fretheim: 140).

The focus of God's suffering is that Jacob-Israel responded to the Lord's creation and calling with its sins and iniquities (43:24). It is wearisome to the Lord that Jacob-Israel does not express love for God. It is burdensome that sins and iniquities characterize its life.

43:25-28 Sins Blotted Out

The sin and rebellion of Jacob-Israel conclude the section and the chapter. The first stanza employs language of forgiveness (43:25-26). This forgiveness takes place *for my own sake*, because it is the Lord's character to forgive. The word that binds verses 25 and 26 into a stanza is the verb *remember* (zakar; *remembers, review*, NIV). Forgiveness (not remembering) is God's nature. But this does not mean that God's people receive the benefit of the doubt regarding transgressions and sins. God's grace is free but not cheap.

The second stanza reflects on the beginnings of disobedience and its end (43:27-28). The *first father* (NIV) refers to the patriarch Jacob himself, the original model of treachery (Gen 27). The *interpreters* probably alludes to the prophets (Whybray: 93). The history of sin and rebellion goes very deep. The result is that the Lord expelled the priesthood and handed Jacob-Israel over to destruction. The destruction refers figuratively to the Lord's handing Judah over to the Babylonians for punishment rather than Judah's annihilation (BDB: 356).

THE TEXT IN BIBLICAL CONTEXT

"I Will Be with You"

The promise of God's solidarity with his people spans both Testaments as an underlying theme: *I will be with you!* (as in Isa 43:2). This cardinal pledge echoes from one generation to the next in the OT. The promise of the Lord's presence came to Isaac and Rebekah, living among the Philistines (Gen 26:3). The Philistines saw the Lord's presence in Isaac (26:28). The Lord was with Joseph in Potiphar's house (Gen 39).

The promise came to Moses at the burning bush (Exod 3:12). Moses conveyed the promise to all Israel (Deut 31:6). Joshua witnessed to the promise after the spies' return from Canaan (Num 14:9). He received the promise of the Lord's presence before leading the Israelites into the Promised Land (Josh 1:5).

The prophets, Isaiah and Jeremiah in particular, announce this promise. In addition to 43:2, 5, Isaiah speaks this word in the Immanuel passages in 7:14 and 8:8, 10. Jeremiah's call features the reassurance that the Lord will be with him in his prophetic ministry (1:8, 19).

In the Psalms (23:4; 46:8, 12) and in the Chronicler (2 Chron 13:12), the confession "The Lord of hosts is with us" shines like a beacon from a lighthouse.

The NT reflects this same light when Matthew quotes Isaiah 7:14 in his announcement of the birth of Jesus (1:23), which is clearly echoed at the end of the gospel in Jesus' commission to his disciples and his promise to be with them always (28:20). Mary receives the promise of the Lord's presence when the angel appears to her (Luke 1:28). In Luke's account of the beginnings of the church, he notes that "the hand of the Lord was with [the men of Cyprus and Cyrene], and a great number became believers and turned to the Lord" (Acts 11:21). In Paul's letter to the Romans, he writes, "If God is for us, who is against us" (8:31)? Nothing, he says, "will be able to separate us from the love of God in Christ Jesus our Lord" (8:39).

These are the raw materials for a theology of God's presence. In spite of the danger that this theology may be employed to support a politics of nationalism, it remains a foundation of the relationship between God and his people.

"A New Thing"

The announcement of "a new thing" in Isaiah 43:19, in contrast to "the former things" (43:18), echoes through the OT Prophets (cf. Jer 31:22; 31–34) and on into the NT. In his *OT Theology*, Gerhard von Rad pins his understanding of what the prophets were up to on this announcement of "a new thing" (1965:243-50). *The former things* (Isa 41:22; 42:9; 43:9, 18; 44:7; 46:9; 48:3) means the history beginning with Abraham's call, continuing with the exodus event, and ending with the subjugation of Jerusalem. *A new thing* means the salvation seen by the prophet, which the Lord will undertake in the future.

The contrast between the old and the new in the NT is quite evident, although not necessarily directly dependent on Isaiah. In Jesus' teaching (Matt 9:14-17; cf. Luke 5:33-39; Mark 2:18-22), the old and the new stand in tension with each other. Jesus identifies his teaching and movement with new wine, warning of the problems inherent in combining old and new. Elsewhere, however, Jesus sees those who proclaim the good news as drawing on the original vision of God's revelation to Israel (the old) as well as interpreting this original vision in light of God's revelation in Jesus' own life and witness (the new; Matt 13:52; cf. Gardner:

218). Jesus in John's Gospel refers to the new commandment of love (13:34-35). In 1 John 2:7-11, however, this commandment to love is understood as an old commandment renewed in Jesus.

The theme of the old and new is taken up by other NT writers. Paul speaks of the person who is *in Christ* as being part of a new creation (2 Cor 5:16-21) and as having a new nature (Eph 4:22-24; Col 3:5-11), putting off the old. The concept of a new covenant in the letter to the Hebrews (8:8-13; 9:15-22; 12:18-24), though drawn from Jeremiah 31:31-34, has its larger frame of reference in *the new thing* of Isaiah 43:19.

THE TEXT IN THE LIFE OF THE CHURCH

Walking Through Fire

Braght's *Martyrs Mirror* (570-73) includes a letter written by a youth named Algerius and the account of his execution by fire in Rome in AD 1557. Algerius was from the kingdom of Naples in present-day Italy and a student at Padua. An Anabaptist brother came to Padua, and Algerius inquired of him about the Lord's will and way. Accepting this way and confessing faith, Algerius was baptized. Sometime afterward, he was imprisoned at Padua and wrote to brothers and sisters in Italy from his prison cell.

From Padua he was transferred to Venice, where attempts were made to convince him to renounce his newfound faith. But Algerius held firm and was sent to Rome; after hard imprisonment, he was executed there by officials pouring boiling oil over his head and body.

A letter, written on July 12, 1557, while he was still in prison in Padua, tells of his buoyant faith:

> In a state of misery I have had very great delight; in a lonely corner I have had most glorious company, and in the severest bond, great rest. All these things, my fellow brethren in Jesus Christ, the gracious hand of God has given me. Behold, He that at first was far from me, is now with me. . . . Is there any like God the Most High, who sustains and refreshes those that are tempted? He heals them that are bruised and wounded, and restores them altogether. Isa 41; 43:20. None is like Him. Learn, most beloved brethren, how sweet the Lord is, how faithful and merciful; who visits His servants in trial (Isa 43:2); who humbles Himself and condescends to be with us in our huts and humble abodes. He gives us a cheerful mind and peaceful heart.

Although Algerius walked through fire and died a martyr's death, the fire did not consume his spirit, and his faith remained strong to the end.

To this kind of perseverance, God called Israel to be his witnesses

(Isa 43:8-13, 21). Jesus commissioned his disciples to be his witnesses (Luke 24:44-49; Acts 1:7-8). Men and women throughout the Bible were called to persevere in their faith (Heb 10:32-39; 11:1-40). The church stands in this biblical tradition, witnessing to God's work of redemption in Jesus Christ.

Isaiah 44:1-28

The Restoration of Jacob-Israel

PREVIEW

The three parts of this chapter form an inclusio [*Literary Perspective,* p. 446], which may be represented in the following way:

    A The Lord's Chosen Servant Jacob-Israel (44:1-8)
        B Ashes of Idolatry (44:9-20)
    A´ The Lord's Redeemed Servant Jacob-Israel (44:21-28)

The first and last parts (A, A´) open and close the chapter with a similar theme: Jacob-Israel as the Lord's servant. The similarity of the beginning and end of the chapter argues for the coherence of the chapter as a whole.

The middle part (B) presents a contrasting theme: the folly of idolatry. Far from destroying the unity of the chapter, however, the middle part strengthens the theme on either side by reducing idolatry to absurdity.

OUTLINE

The Lord's Chosen Servant Jacob-Israel, 44:1-8
    44:1-5   Choice of Jacob-Israel
    44:6-8   The Lord's Uniqueness

Ashes of Idolatry, 44:9-20
    44:9-13   Artisans of Idolatry
    44:14-17   Raw Materials of Idolatry
    44:18-20   Folly of Idolatry
The Lord's Redeemed Servant Jacob-Israel, 44:21-28
    44:21-23   Redemption of Jacob-Israel
    44:24-28   The Lord Speaking as Redeemer

EXPLANATORY NOTES

The Lord's Chosen Servant Jacob-Israel 44:1-8

44:1-5 Choice of Jacob-Israel

Chapter 44 opens with the same expression (*But now* . . .) as at the opening of chapter 43. In both places the expression introduces a contrast to what was written immediately before it. In 43:22-28 the Lord laments the rebellion of Jacob-Israel. The *But now* . . . of 44:1 brings the reader back to the underlying fact that it was the Lord who formed Jacob-Israel in the first place.

Words of preference are employed in the address to Jacob-Israel in the first stanza (44:1-2). The phrase *my servant, . . . whom I have chosen* in the first two lines balances the same phrase in the last two lines. Taken together, they indicate God's singling out Jacob-Israel for a special purpose (cf. 42:1). The word *Jeshurun* in the last line appears only here, in the Song of Moses (Deut 32:15), and in the Blessing of Moses (Deut 33:5, 26) in the OT. It is a poetic name for Israel, meaning "upright one," possibly referring to the ethical pattern that Israel was to follow. *Thus says the LORD* [Messenger Formula, p. 447] at the center of the stanza establishes the Lord's foundational character as both Creator and helper. The instruction not to fear flows from God's character. This means that God comes to the aid of his creation rather than abandoning creation to fate. What fear does Jacob-Jeshurun harbor that elicits the Lord's instruction not to fear? The context implies that Jacob-Jeshurun fears the uncertainty of an adequate food supply because of drought (44:3a) and a future in which the Lord's Spirit and blessing may no longer nourish the children (44:3b).

The promises in the second stanza speak to these fears (44:3-4). Jacob-Israel need not fear because the Lord will act on its behalf. Twice the verb *I will pour* indicates that the Lord will quiet their fears. The parallel words *water* and *streams* in the first two lines promise refreshment for dry land. Rainfall and streams to channel the rainfall promise material resources adequate for the preservation and enlargement of God's people. The parallel words *my Spirit* (NIV) and *my blessing* in the second pair of lines promise spiritual renewal for future generations. The last pair of lines in the stanza compares this renewal to luxuriant grass and trees (44:4).

Voices from among Jacob-Israel speak in the final stanza (44:5). The exiles in Babylon, estranged from the Lord, reclaim their identity as Israelites and their allegiance to the Lord (Watts, 1987:144-45). The text may also be read to include proselytes entering the family of God. God's people are more than a kinship group bound together by blood ties. They are all those who bind themselves to the Lord's name and cause (Knight: 76-77).

44:6-8 The Lord's Uniqueness

Now a messenger formula introduces a group of three stanzas, which serve as a response to the Israelites' and proselytes' renewed identity and allegiance. The response begins with a reaffirmation of the Lord's uniqueness (44:6). Three expressions of the Lord's name open the stanza: *the King of Israel, Redeemer,* and *the LORD of hosts*. The Lord as Israel's King refers to the immediacy of the Lord's political leadership, a leadership unmediated by human kingship (Lind, 1990:143). The Lord as Redeemer refers to both material deliverance and spiritual salvation, redemption from the spiritual mastery of sin (Vriezen: 272). The Lord of hosts expresses the majesty of the Lord's power (Whybray: 96). The word *hosts* means literally armies, in the sense of heavenly beings under God's command.

The Lord's self-revelation as *the first* and *the last* opens the direct speech in 44:6. *The first* refers to the Lord as Creator at the beginning of history, thus unlike the Babylonian gods, and without genealogy (Whybray: 61). *The last* indicates the Lord's presence at the end of history. The Lord's uniqueness and the nonexistence of other gods within human history remain nonnegotiable.

Those who see the Lord as an imitation of Babylonian deity are questioned in the second stanza (44:7). *Who is like me?* combines rhetorical question with defiant challenge. At issue is whether any deity combines a long-term relationship to a particular people with a long-term vision of the future. The Lord asserts his ability to know the future and to reveal it. The question, then, is whether the Lord knows the future in minute detail, or whether the Lord knows the future in terms of its outcome. If the Lord knows the future in minute detail, then the course is set toward a deterministic view of history. What is meant here and elsewhere in the Bible, however, is that the Lord knows the outcome of history and invites humankind to live in the confidence of that outcome.

The answer in the final stanza assures the people of the Lord's dominion (44:8). The counsel not to fear repeats the assurance of 44:2;

this is standard advice in the Bible for those who find themselves in difficult situations (cf. Gen 15:1; Pss 27:1; 46:2; 91:5; 118:6; Isa 7:4; 8:12-13; Luke 1:30; John 14:27; Acts 18:9). The declaration to the exiles that they are the Lord's witnesses recalls 43:8-13. A witness is someone who testifies in a cause or who has personal knowledge of something that can serve as evidence or proof. God's people have personal knowledge of the Lord's uniqueness, and they have a responsibility to give evidence of this uniqueness.

Ashes of Idolatry 44:9-20

The direct speech of the Lord concludes with the declaration that other gods besides the Lord have no existence (44:6, 8). Now the prophet, as if to dispute what could be raised as counterargument, turns his attention to the idols that dominate the Babylonian religious scene (Hanson: 88). What follows is a polemic against idol production.

44:9-13 Artisans of Idolatry

A focus on the artisans, their idols, and those who worship the idols comprises the first stanza (44:9). The artisans themselves are described as *nothing*, the same Hebrew word (*tohu*) used to describe the nothingness into which God spoke the creation into being (Gen 1:2). The combination of negative adverbs and rhyming verb endings in the next three lines echo this nothingness:

tohu	emptiness
bal-yo'ilu	they benefit nothing
bal-yir'u	they see nothing
bal-yede'u . . . yebošu	they know nothing, . . . are a shame

The artisans' products, the idols themselves (*the things they treasure*, NIV), have no value. The *witnesses* of the idols refers to those who worship them. That they see nothing and know nothing indicates that there is no divine reality behind the idols. The Lord also has witnesses who are addressed in 44:8. These witnesses declare the Lord's oneness and saving power (cf. 43:12).

Three further statements about the artisans of idolatry follow the opening statement. The first gives attention to the *shame* of the artisans (44:10-11). Something of the "futility and self-deception of idol worship" (Watts, 1987:146) finds expression here.

A particular artisan is the focus of attention in the second statement: *the ironsmith* (44:12). The prophet describes how an ironsmith works the metal with his own strength and grows weary as a result. The reader will recall that the prophet uses the same language to describe the Lord as Creator of the earth, *not* growing weary, but giving strength to the faint (40:27-31). The contrast between the limited human strength of the iron-smith as worker and the boundless divine strength of the Lord as Creator cannot be overstated.

Another artisan, the woodworker, appears in the third statement (44:13). The prophet portrays the carving of a piece of wood into a human figure, whose purpose is to depict a god. The last two lines (*he makes it* . . .) offer a comparison with the creation narrative in Genesis. There, God makes humankind in God's image and likeness (1:26). Here, the woodworker makes an idol according to a human pattern. The contrast between divine competence in the creation of humankind and human cleverness in the fabrication of an idol makes itself felt.

44:14-17 Raw Materials of Idolatry

Next the prophet turns to the woodworkers' raw materials. The first stanza sketches a picture of harvesting specialty woods (44:14). That the woodworkers themselves harvested the wood seems unlikely though not impossible. Cedar, the wood of preference, had to be imported, probably from Lebanon (Knight: 80). Perhaps because of the cost of transportation and tariffs, cedar trees were planted in Babylon as a source of raw materials for woodworkers.

The picture is developed with more than a touch of absurdity in the second stanza (44:15). The stanza focuses on using part of the wood for material purposes and part for fashioning an idol to represent what is immaterial. The prophet clearly has the commandment against making carved images in mind (Exod 20:4-6). The prophets as a whole firmly refused to recognize any divine reality behind carved images (cf. G. E. Wright: 12).

The third stanza (44:16) explains the first half of verse 15, on the raw materials of idol making used for food preparation and warmth. Now the woodworker speaks for the first time, expressing contentment with the warmth generated by the fire. The sense of this is that the woodworker has been misled into thinking that a material object good for warmth and food preparation can represent divinity.

The fourth stanza (44:17) expands upon the second half of verse 15, the worship of a carved image. Here the woodworker speaks a second time. With the wood for burning, he expects warmth and contentment; but from the carved image he has made with his own hands, he expects salvation! So he addresses the carved image with a plea to deliver him.

44:18-20 Folly of Idolatry

A cluster of negative statements brings the section on idolatry to a close. The first stanza berates all who see and perceive in human-made idols the representation of divinity (44:18). That their eyes and minds are hindered from the truth refers to the value placed on material culture as the highest form of reality. Those who see ultimate spiritual reality in their material culture end up creating gods of wood and metal, to use in worshipping this culture.

The lack of insight leading to the creation of such gods is lamented in the second stanza (44:19a). A negative statement opens the lament: *No one stops to think* (NIV) means, literally, "He does not return to his heart." The Hebrew word for "heart" refers to the inner person, where knowledge, thought, memory, conscience, and moral character reside. Not returning to one's heart indicates a renouncing of one's conscience. Such renunciation means that *no one has the knowledge or understanding* (NIV) to tell the truth about the futility of idolatry. The prophet recalls the language of 44:16, but the spirit is now one of despair rather than contentment.

A prophetic polemic against idolatry comprises the last stanza (44:19b-20). Many modern translations render the two lines of 44:19b as questions (T/NIV; cf. N/RSV, N/JB, KJV). But the Hebrew does not suggest questions and ought to be translated as follows:

The rest of it I make into an abomination;
  I bow down to a block of wood! (AT; cf. NASB, NCV, GNB)

Those who make and bow down to idols in 44:19-20 repeat the sentiments of the woodworker in 44:15-17. Now, however, those who make and bow down to idols see them as an abomination, something despicable. *He feeds on ashes* graphically portrays the folly of idolatry, realizing the absurdity of it, yet continuing in it. The final line may be a proverb that the prophet's listeners know and that he employs to rest his case (Knight: 81). The idol worshipper says, *Is not this thing in my right hand a lie?* (NIV). As a rhetorical question, the implied answer rings loud and clear, "Of course it is a lie!" And yet those who worship idols find themselves so deluded by them that they cannot free themselves from their grip.

The Lord's Redeemed Servant Jacob-Israel 44:21-28

The prophet now returns to the theme of 44:1-8, the Lord's redemption of Jacob-Israel. But the focus of 44:21-28 lies in the Lord's credentials as Redeemer-in-action rather than on the Lord's oneness as Redeemer (as in 44:1-8).

44:21-23 Redemption of Jacob-Israel

The first stanza consists of the Lord's direct address to Jacob-Israel (44:21-22). The counsel to *remember these things* refers to the polemic just completed against idolatry. But *these things* reminds the reader of the chapter's beginning, where the redemption of Jacob-Israel comes into focus. The Lord's redemption [*Redemption, Redeemer, p. 448*] has the specific meaning here of not forgetting Jacob-Israel and of wiping away rebellions and sins. The word *redeemed* translates a Hebrew legal term for buying something back or setting someone free, as in Leviticus 25 and 27 (Unterman and Shogren: 650-57). In the book of Exodus (6:6; 15:13) the word refers to the Lord's act of freeing Israel from Egyptian bondage. Here it alludes to the Lord's act of freeing Israel from Babylonian exile. When the prophet breaks into song, he follows the structure of a hymn in the Psalter (Isa 44:23; cf. Anderson, 1974:99-104). A threefold summons opens the hymn: *Sing for joy, . . . shout aloud. . . . Burst into song* (NIV). Within the summons and again after it, the prophet states the motive for singing (prefaced by the word *for*):

> *for the LORD has done it . . .*
> *for the LORD has redeemed Jacob,*
> *[for the LORD] will be glorified in Israel.* (NRSV)

44:24-28 The Lord Speaking as Redeemer

This entire section consists of one continuous thought developed by means of a series of subordinate participial clauses (NRSV, NIV). The Lord speaks throughout. The Lord's glory, from the last line of 44:23, may be seen in action here. The first stanza combines the particular with the general (44:24). The Lord's formation of a particular people was an initial step in the liberation of humankind as a whole. The Lord's single-handed creation of all things testifies to divine power at work in the world at large, not merely among a particular people.

The second stanza focuses the Lord's activity negatively, by thwarting foolish counselors; and positively, by enabling the Lord's representatives (44:25-26a). The *false prophets* and *diviners* (NIV) refer in particular to the Babylonian practice of trying to predict the future by supernatural means (e.g., Ezek 21:21). Through *the learning of the wise* (NIV), the Babylonians wanted to foretell the future by rational means (Whybray: 103). The Lord thwarts both these means of determining the future.

Instead, the Lord offers an alternative. As in Deuteronomy 18:9-22, so here also, the Lord speaks through the prophet who has the Lord's words in his mouth. The Lord does not speak through those who practice human sacrifice or divination or sorcery or witchcraft or consultation with the dead (Deut 18:10-11).

The NIV reads the plural *servants* (instead of the singular *servant* in the Hebrew Bible) to supply a parallel to *messengers* (44:26a). The singular *servant*, however, ought to be kept, as in the NRSV. This is the same servant referred to in 44:1, 2, 21, either Jacob-Israel or the servant of the Servant Songs (cf. Whybray: 103-4). Alongside this servant stand the prophets as the Lord's messengers. Both people and prophets as bearers of the Lord's word stand in opposition to Babylonian diviners and sages, whose knowledge rests on a foundation of foolishness. The word and counsel of the Lord through people and prophets (44:26b) rest on the Lord, who created all things in the first place (44:24b).

The Lord now addresses the specific situation of Jacob-Israel in exile (Hanson: 97). In 44:26b-27 he begins by proclaiming the repopulation of Jerusalem and the rebuilding of Judah's cities (44:26b). The restoration of Judah and Jerusalem must have come as a powerful promise to the exiles in Babylon. This promise combined spiritual renewal with material reconstruction, forming a new vision for the future.

The promise is followed by the Lord addressing *the watery deep* (NIV; Heb. *ṣulah*) with the command to be dry and announcing his drying up of the streams flowing along the seabed (44:27; cf. Knight: 85). This appears to be an allusion to the Lord's power over Babylon, to bring about its end (cf. Jer 50:36; 51:37).

The Lord as Jacob-Israel's Redeemer in the first stanza (44:24) makes a remarkable promise in the last stanza (44:28). This promise identifies the agent of the Lord's redemption as Cyrus (cf. TBC), whom the Lord calls *my shepherd* (44:28a). This is the first specific reference to the Persian king Cyrus (reigned 550-530 BC) in the book of Isaiah. The only other specific reference to Cyrus is in Isaiah 45:1. Calling Cyrus as *my shepherd* associates him with Israelite kings, who were called shepherds (cf. Jer 23; Ezek 34). This means that the Lord has designated Cyrus as the political leader of Israel's redemption. The Lord's statement that Cyrus was being called upon to carry out *my purpose* indicates a leading role for the Persian king in the relationship between the Lord and Jacob-Israel. An adjunct to announcing Cyrus as the Lord's shepherd is the announcement that Jerusalem and its temple will be rebuilt (44:28b).

Isaiah 44:1-28

THE TEXT IN BIBLICAL CONTEXT

Cyrus

Two references naming the Persian king Cyrus appear in the book of Isaiah (44:28; 45:1). Elsewhere in the OT he appears in the books of Daniel, 2 Chronicles, and Ezra.

The book of Daniel places the career of Daniel in Babylon during the Judean exile, a span of some sixty or seventy years (Lederach: 17). The Babylonian king Nabonidus suffered a military defeat in 539 BC at the hands of the army of Cyrus. Babylon itself was not destroyed, and the Persian king Cyrus entered the city, welcomed as a liberator by many Babylonians (Noth: 301-2). So Daniel lived as a resident of Babylon during the first years of Cyrus' rule (Dan 1:21; 6:29; 10:1).

The book of 2 Chronicles ends and the book of Ezra begins with an almost identical reference to the edict of Cyrus to the exiled Judeans, inviting them to rebuild their temple in Jerusalem. This edict was proclaimed in 538 BC, after Cyrus' armies had subdued the kingdom of Babylon.

As a chronicle of the Israelite experience of the monarchy, and particularly of the line of Davidic kings, 1 and 2 Chronicles touches on the exile only at the end (2 Chron 36). The edict of Cyrus enters the narrative only in the last two verses (2 Chron 36:32-33). The book of Ezra, on the other hand, describes the Israelite experience at and after the end of the exile in Babylon. Cyrus figures prominently in the book of Ezra as the Persian king who decreed the rebuilding of the temple in Jerusalem (1:1, 7, 8; 3:7; 4:3, 5; 5:13-17; 6:3-5, 14).

In the parts of the book of Isaiah that originate in the period of the exile (cf. 44:28; 45:1), Cyrus is presented as the Lord's shepherd and anointed one. This regard for Cyrus rests on his policy of repatriating conquered peoples to their former homes and rebuilding these peoples' ruined sanctuaries (*ANET*: 316).

THE TEXT IN THE LIFE OF THE CHURCH

Doctrine of God

In its history and theology the church has proclaimed God's unity in a trinity of persons. The evidence of the Scriptures has played an essential role in unfolding this Christian doctrine of God. Interacting with the role of the Scriptures were the various disputes with Jews, pagans, and nonconformists (usually branded heretics) as well as the influence of Greek philosophy on the early church (*ODCC*: 1641-42). The result was a doctrine that "the one God exists in three Persons and one substance" (*ODCC*: 1641). The three-part Apostles' Creed, for example, pays attention to the doctrine of three persons and one substance (cf. *HWB*: 712; cf. 120).

In his *Confession of the Triune God* (the shorter title), written in 1550, Menno Simons voices his essential conformity with the church's consensus on this issue (489-98). Menno goes out of his way to emphasize God's unity. He uses language from Isaiah 44:6-8: "Besides this only, eternal, living . . . Lord we know no other" (495). He also draws from Isaiah 42:8 and 48:11: "God does not give His glory to another" (494). But God's unity is always a unity in a trinity of persons. While Menno's doctrine of God uses some of the terminology of philosophy, his language borrows liberally from biblical words and expressions.

Attention to a correct formulation of a doctrine of God has played an important role in the life of the church. This is so because of the different variations and interpretations implicit to a doctrine of the Trinity. Christian orthodoxy has consistently maintained, however, that its Trinitarian formulation of the godhead upholds a monotheistic view of God (cf. *ODCC*: 1105).

The formulation of Christian doctrine in general has tried to limit doctrinal variation. One result of the emphasis on doctrine has been to maintain that it is what a person believes (in one's head) that determines whether one is a Christian, not essentially how one lives. In this understanding, faith is an inward attitude expressed as compliance with orthodox Christian doctrine (cf. Kraus' argument against this view: 20-24). The Anabaptist movement, on the other hand, tries to fuse right belief with right action.

Isaiah 45:1-25

No Other God Apart from the Lord

PREVIEW

In this chapter the Lord makes bold claims about himself. Among these claims, *I am the LORD* serves as a drumbeat at the beginning and end of the chapter (cf. 45:3, 5, 6, 8, 18, 19, 21, 22).

Scholars sometimes combine the last part of chapter 44 with the first part of chapter 45 because Cyrus appears at both places (Whybray, Hanson). The significance of Cyrus, however, should not be overstated. Cyrus plays a moderately important role in the overall scheme of the book. But Cyrus' significance pales in comparison to the Lord's role as mover and shaker in the exilic period. The word of the Lord addressed to Cyrus in the first part of chapter 45 is, nevertheless, quite startling (45:1-13).

In the second part of the chapter, the Lord's word to the exiles remains the focus of the chapter as a whole (45:14-25). Not only is Jacob-Israel saved, but the Lord's intention also is to implement the ancient promise to Abraham that through his descendants "all the families of the earth shall be blessed" (Gen 12:3).

OUTLINE

The Lord's Word to Cyrus, 45:1-13
    45:1-4   Cyrus as the Lord's Anointed
    45:5-7   The Lord's Witness to Cyrus

45:8-10	Doxology and Disputation
45:11-13	Cyrus Summoned

The Lord's Word to the Exiles, 45:14-25

45:14-17	Israel and the Promise of Salvation
45:18-19	Earth as Habitat for Humanity
45:20-21	No Other God Besides the Lord
45:22-25	Earth Called to Turn and Be Saved

EXPLANATORY NOTES

The Lord's Word to Cyrus 45:1-13

45:1-4 Cyrus as the Lord's Anointed

Cyrus, introduced by name at the end of the previous chapter (44:28), is now addressed. In the opening stanza the Lord speaks of Cyrus as *his anointed* (45:1). The word *anointed* (from *mšḥ*) means setting someone apart for an office. In the book of Isaiah, the root *mšḥ* is applied to people only here and in 61:1 (cf. the same word in 21:5: *Oil the shield!*). In this context the word means being strengthened (45:1) and equipped for a particular assignment, even though Cyrus does not *know* the Lord (45:4-5), even though Cyrus "knows" Marduk (*ANET*: 316).

Accompanying the reference to Cyrus as *his anointed* is the act of *grasp*ing Cyrus' *right hand* just as the Lord grasps the right hand of Jacob-Israel, his servant, in 41:13. There is a transfer of power in this act, but the one transferring the power maintains his sovereignty even though his power has been shared. Two infinitives indicate the scope of the power delegated to Cyrus: *to subdue* and *to open*. The Lord will enable Cyrus to triumph over nations, and the Lord will open doors for Cyrus to reach his goals.

Three signs of the Lord's power in the opening stanza (speaking, subduing, opening) are enhanced in the three stanzas that follow (45:2, 3, 4). The author uses an *inclusio* [Literary Perspective, p. 446] to make his point clear:

    A the Lord *says to* Cyrus (45:1)
      B the Lord *subdues* nations (45:1)
        C the Lord *opens* doors (45:1)
        C' the Lord *breaks down* doors (45:2)
      B' the Lord *gives* him treasures (of nations) (45:3)
    A' the Lord *calls* him by name (45:4)

What the Lord will do for Cyrus (B-C-C'-B') is framed by what the Lord says to Cyrus (A-A'). The Lord, not Cyrus, stands at center stage.

45:5-7 The Lord's Witness to Cyrus

In the first stanza (45:5-6a) and from this center-stage position, the Lord continues to address Cyrus with the word *I am the LORD*. Though Cyrus does not know the Lord (cf. 45:4), the Lord knows Cyrus and equips him. I am using the word *equips* to refer to all of the ways in which the Lord has strengthened Cyrus (45:1-4). The goal of that equipping was to set the Judean exiles free (45:13). The equipping of Cyrus takes place *so that they may know . . . that there is no one besides me* (45:6). It is not clear who *they* might be. The NIV substitutes the word *men*, meaning people in general. But this is conjecture. The more likely antecedent for *they* would be Jacob-Israel (45:4). But why would the Lord's equipping of Cyrus make it possible for Jacob-Israel to know that there is no one besides the Lord? The answer lies at the end of 45:1-13. Cyrus will permit Jerusalem to be rebuilt; Cyrus will set the Judean exiles free (45:13). Jacob-Israel will know that the Lord has delegated power to Cyrus but that it is *the LORD's* power that needs to be reckoned with.

The phrase *I am the LORD* opened the first stanza and now it opens the second (45:6b-7). This is followed by parallel lines describing the Lord as

> *forming light and creating darkness,*
> *making peace and creating distress.* (45:7 AT)

These lines employ language from Genesis 1 and 2 (*forming, creating, making*). In the second line the Lord lays claim to making peace as well as creating distress (*ra'*). The Hebrew noun *ra'* has a range of meanings (cf. *evil*, KJV; *disaster*, NIV; *woe*, NRSV; *calamity*, JB). It is a mistake to elaborate a theology of God as the creator of evil from this text (see "Creating Evil" in TLC below).

The main point in the witness to Cyrus in 45:5-7 is the Lord's singularity (no one else) and his activity (doing all these things). God's power may be seen in creation and in history. God's sovereignty is over Cyrus; Cyrus does not control God.

45:8-10 Doxology and Disputation

Although the Lord is no longer addressing Cyrus in 45:8-10, he still has Cyrus in mind. In the opening stanza the Lord's call to the heavens and the clouds to *rain down righteousness* (*ṣedeq*) indicates a powerful intention to see right prevail (45:8 NIV). Righteousness describes God's character as one who does the right thing, what is morally right.

Then the Lord calls upon the earth to open *that they may bring forth salvation* (NRSV footnote). *They* seems to refer to earth's inhabitants and especially, perhaps, Jacob-Israel. Righteousness (*ṣedaqah*) and salvation (*yeša'*) are parallel terms. They represent the human response to God's righteousness raining down from above. *I the LORD have created it* serves as a signature on the last line of the stanza. The masculine-singular pronoun *it* refers to the whole of the natural order.

An abrupt change of mood from doxology to disputation characterizes the next stanza (45:9-10). The interjection *woe* occurs only here in the last three parts of Isaiah (40–48, 49–57, 58-66). Three illustrations, with Cyrus in mind, express the ill-advised criticism by a product of its producer (Whybray: 107-8). The first chides the person who quarrels with the one who has commissioned him (45:9a). The second scolds the one (the clay) who quibbles about the potter's competence (45:9b). The third criticizes the one who questions his birthright (45:10).

45:11-13 Cyrus Summoned

The stanzas that follow offer an answer to this criticism. A messenger formula clarifies the identity of the speaker as Israel's *Holy One* and *Maker* (45:11). From the general argument that a product has no authority to find fault with its producer (45:9-10), the prophet, speaking in the Lord's name, charges the exiles with exactly this faultfinding (Whybray: 108):

> *Do you ask me of things to come about my children?*
> *Do you give me orders about the work of my hands?* (AT)

The questions serve as a reprimand to Jacob-Israel [you] for taunting the Creator (Brueggemann, 1998b:79).

The two final stanzas return to the emphasis on creation and righteousness introduced in 45:8. The reference to the Lord as Maker of the earth and Creator of humankind serves to remind Jacob-Israel of the power at work in history (45:12). This is not power that can be controlled or regulated. Wherever there are references to God as one who creates, it is understood that God for his own purposes brings into being what was previously unimagined or unimaginable.

In the final stanza the pronouns *he, him, his* must refer to Cyrus, though Cyrus is not named (45:13; NRSV and NIV insert Cyrus where Heb. has only a pronoun). Cyrus is named, of course, at the beginning of the chapter. The word *righteousness* here does not refer to the righteousness of Cyrus (to clarify this point, NIV reads *my righteousness*, though "my" is not in Heb.). Whybray is surely correct in suggesting that *righteousness* means *in accordance with my purpose* (74, 61). The

Lord's purpose is in view here. Though Cyrus will rebuild Jerusalem and set the exiles free, the Lord remains the one in charge of history.

The Lord's Word to the Exiles 45:14-25

45:14-17 Israel and the Promise of Salvation

The Lord addresses Jacob-Israel in 45:14. The content of this address has to do with a promise to the exiles (cf. Childs: 351). The pronouns *you* and *yours* are second-person feminine singular pronouns, whose antecedent is *my exiles* (f. sg. noun in 45:13). The Lord promises that African (Egypt and Ethiopia) and Asian (Sabeans, from southern Arabia; Smart: 130; cf. *ANET*: 284-86) nations will submit themselves to the exiles. This does not mean that these nations come in abject surrender. They come to accept the Lord's dominion displayed in Jacob-Israel's freedom from exile (Childs: 354-55). The nations will come to recognize that God and no other god is with Israel and, in fact, that *there is no other god* (NIV). The *wealth* of Egypt and the *merchandise* of Ethiopia probably represent the people themselves (45:14; Whybray: 109).

In 45:15 the nations—Egypt, Ethiopia (*Cush*, NIV), and the Sabeans—speak, addressing God (AT):

> *Truly you are God, O Hidden One,*
> *God of Israel, O Savior!*

God's hiddenness means hidden from view rather than absent. God's hiddenness stands in contrast to the visibility of the idols, which can be manipulated and managed. The reference to God's hiddenness may also be an indication that Isaiah's audience found it difficult to imagine how God is at work in history. The Lord's choice of Cyrus as *my shepherd* and *his anointed* is a case in point, showing the mystery of God's work. The prophet goes on to single out the artisans who carve the images as objects of disgrace (45:16).

The confession of God as Israel's Savior receives special mention in the last stanza (45:17). Israel's *everlasting salvation* (NIV) reaffirms what the nations say in 45:14: *Surely God is with you* (NIV). Addressing Israel, the prophet declares that shame and disgrace will never fall upon an Israel that embraces the Lord's salvation.

45:18-19 Earth as Habitat for Humanity

Beginning with a messenger formula, the first stanza contrasts creation and chaos (45:18a). The language and concerns here reflect the creation account in Genesis 1, where both the verb *create* and the noun *chaos* occur. The Hebrew word for *chaos* (*tohu*) also means *emptiness, without inhabitants*. The prophet, speaking in the Lord's name, insists that the Lord created the earth as a habitat for humanity and not as a cradle for chaos.

The message itself is lodged in the second stanza (45:18b-19). The message includes four assertions. The first declares that no divinity exists other than the Lord (45:18b). This has already been stated in 45:5-6. The negative statement *There is no one else* (AT) emphasizes the positive statement *I am the LORD*, rejecting all forms of idolatry (Young, 1972:212). The English word monotheism is not used here or anywhere else in the Bible. Nevertheless the main idea of monotheism, that there is but one God, is central to the vision and testimony of Isaiah 45.

In the second assertion the Lord denies speaking in secret (45:19a). The word *secret* serves as a clarification of God's hiddenness (Childs: 355). Though God is not visible to be manipulated and controlled, he does speak openly to all who prepare themselves to listen.

The third assertion denies that the descendants of Jacob are to seek the Lord *in chaos* (45:19b NRSV; *in vain*, NIV). In its immediate context, chaos stands in contrast to the inhabited earth (45:18). In Genesis 1 God spoke the earth into being out of chaos, with a view to his ongoing interaction with creation. So in Isaiah 45:19b, not seeking the Lord in chaos means not reverting to an emptiness devoid of God (cf. 44:9).

The declaration *I, the LORD* (NIV) opens the final assertion (45:19c). What follows is a manifesto of the Lord's trustworthiness. *Truth* and *right* characterize the Lord's speech, not secrecy.

45:20-21 No Other God Besides the Lord

Now the poetry moves into the form of a trial speech (TBC below). The prophet continues to speak in the Lord's name, calling together the refugees of the nations living in Babylon (Watts, 1987:162). This would have included various exiles of nations conquered by the Babylonians, including the exiles of Judah. Those *who have no knowledge* means those who, because of their idolatry, do not know the Lord (45:20).

After calling the refugees of the nations together, the Lord invites them to answer two parallel questions (45:21a AT):

> *Who proclaimed this long ago?*
> *Who declared it in the past?*

These questions echo questions in the previous trial speeches (41:2, 4; 41:22, 26; 43:9). The questions in all the trial speeches aim to establish once and for all the Lord's superiority over idols made by human hands.

45:22-25 Earth Called to Turn and Be Saved

The Lord calls the whole earth to turn; it is a command to turn in worship to the Lord rather than a command specifically to turn from sin. Is this an offer of salvation to all of humankind, or is it meant for the exiles alone? Wherever the phrase *all the ends of the earth* is found in the OT, it refers to the whole created world, including humankind. This is so here as well. Turning in worship to the Lord is exhorted because of the Lord's credentials: he has no rivals, and he keeps his promises (45:22-23a).

Every knee and *every tongue* in the stanza that follows indicate the result of a universal turning (45:23b-24a; cf. Rom 14:10-12; Phil 2:6-11). The word *right* or *righteousness* (from the root ṣdq, found 8 times in Isa 45), occurs here for the last time in the chapter (45:24). It is *in the LORD alone* (NIV) that human compassion founded on God's righteousness can be combined with God's strength for faithful living. This constitutes a foundational statement about God's character.

The chapter concludes with a twofold affirmation (45:24b-25). First, there is a statement about the repentance required of all who come to the Lord. The *all* in verse 24b reflects the *all* in verse 22a. The idea of shame indicates consciousness of unbecoming behavior toward the Lord. Second, Israel's descendants will, in fact, be righteous and self-confident in the Lord (v. 25). *In the LORD* means considering the Lord as the foundation for action.

THE TEXT IN BIBLICAL CONTEXT

Trial Speeches

Part 4 of the book of Isaiah (40–48) contains several trial speeches. These include 41:1-7, 21-29; 43:8-13; 45:20-25. The addressees vary from one speech to another. In the first one the Lord addresses the nations, represented as islands (41:1). In the second, the false gods are called upon to present their case (41:21). The Lord addresses the exiles, represented as a people blind and deaf, in the third speech (43:8). And in the fourth speech the Lord addresses the refugees of the nations, including the exiles (45:20).

The trial speeches pose critical questions to the defendants. These questions demand that the defendants produce evidence that their idols and images have power to explain the meaning of past events or to predict future events (Whybray: 68). The defendants do not answer the ques-

Every Knee Shall Bow

The cosmic declaration that *every knee shall bow* and *every tongue shall swear [allegiance]* to the Lord finds expression in Isaiah 45:23. Psalm 95, celebrating God's kingship, calls upon the Israelite congregation to "kneel down" and to "bend the knee" before the Lord (vv. 6-7). As in the "no other gods" commandment (Exod 20:3), all possibilities of worshipping other gods are abolished by the Lord's convincing reality (Brueggemann, 1998b:85).

In the NT, Paul focuses on the *every knee* and *every tongue* of Isaiah 45:23 to teach against sitting in judgment upon or scorning a fellow believer (Rom 14:10-12). Here Paul interprets Isaiah 45:23 to mean that since all people will be accountable to God, all people ought to exercise restraint in opinions of judgment.

In Philippians 2:10-11 Paul interprets Isaiah 45:23 quite differently. Here he takes *every knee* and *every tongue* as applying to Christ's lordship. Paul can make use of the same text for different purposes.

It is true elsewhere in both Testaments that an original text is open to multiple interpretations. Take, for example, Jeremiah's reference to seventy years as the time of captivity in Babylon (25:11-12; 29:10). In 2 Chronicles 36:17-21, Jeremiah's seventy years are given a Sabbath interpretation. Daniel 9:1-2, 24-27 takes those seventy years into a numerical interpretation (70 weeks of years means $70 \times 7 = 490$ years).

Psalm 95, with its emphasis on God's kingship, serves as a bridge between Isaiah 45 and Paul's testimony in Romans 14 and Philippians 2. Yet it is the universal character of the call to repentance and salvation in Isaiah 45 that inspired the early Christian hymn writer in Philippians 2.

THE TEXT IN THE LIFE OF THE CHURCH

Turning and Being Saved

The English word *turn* in Isaiah 45:22 translates the Hebrew word *panah*. In the translation of the Hebrew Bible into Greek (the LXX) several centuries before the birth of Christ, the Greek word *epistrephein* translates *panah*. The NT writers used this term as one of the words for conversion (along with *metanoein*).

Repentance as turning stands at the fountainhead of Jesus' call to discipleship in the Gospels. This turning includes the idea of remorse but goes well beyond it to mean changing one's mind and therefore changing one's behavior. This is conversion in a religious and ethical sense.

In the preaching of John the Baptist and Jesus, repentance (*metanoein*) is the stipulation for gaining access to the kingdom of God (Matt 3:2; 4:17; Mark 1:15). At Pentecost, repentance and baptism are prescribed as the response to God's work in Israel and through Jesus of Nazareth (Acts 2:38). In Acts 3:19 Peter, speaking to a Jewish audience in the Jerusalem temple, says, "Repent [*metanoein*], therefore, and turn [*epistrephein*] to God, so that your sins may be wiped out." From this text especially, the church understands turning to mean turning from sin as well as turning to God.

In its history the church has often focused on *turning* as sorrow for sin committed and confession of guilt (*ODCC*: 1384). This has resulted in an understanding of repentance as the ongoing position of one who, though regretting one's sins, expects to continue in them under the weight of the human condition and because of social pressure (*CCW*: 9).

Pilgram Marpeck, one of the voices of the Radical Reformation, speaks of true repentance in a letter of 1550, "Five Fruits of Repentance." The fourth fruit is the resolution not to allow sin to rule (*WPM*: 492). Becoming a prisoner of God replaces slavery to sin. If slavery to sin remains, then repentance is in vain.

Creating Evil

When Hans Denck wrote his tract at Augsburg in 1526 entitled *Whether God Is the Cause of Evil*, the first text that he cited was Isaiah 45:7 (*SAW*: 89). Denck argued that some writers explain this text to mean that God is the cause of evil. "'Since God is in all creatures,' they say, 'he works in them all good and evil, . . . virtue and sin.'" Denck's tract refutes such a conclusion.

His refutation begins with the assertion that since God is good, he cannot create anything but the good. From that assertion Denck poses a series of twenty-three objections, for which he provides rejoinders. This question-answer format covers a wide range of topics on the Christian life that go well beyond the initial query as to *Whether God Is the Cause of Evil*. The subject of Denck's inquiry is not so much whether God creates evil but whether humankind can do anything good. Denck responds to this with a question: "But can God do good?" In response to an affirmative answer, Denck replies: "So let him do what he wills to do. . . . If you . . . will not concede to him that he do it, you thereby prove that you have no contentment in him, which is an arrogance, which God has not created, as Scripture says" (93).

Denck's tract includes the well-known saying about the Christian life:

"No one can truly know Christ except one who follows him in life. And no one can truly follow Christ except one who already knows him" (paraphrased from German; cf. 108).

Isaiah 46:1–47:15

Who Has the Power?

PREVIEW

Humankind has a flair for creating gods in its own image. In ancient Babylon, Bel and Nebo were these kinds of gods. So the prophet launches into sarcasm as he holds up these fragile images in contrast to the reality of the Lord of hosts.

Chapters 46 and 47 belong together. Isaiah 46 contrasts the burdensome character of Babylon's idols with the burden-bearing character of Israel's God. This is not simply an exercise in contrasts. The debunking of Babylon's idols serves as an attack on the ideological foundation of Babylon as empire.

Chapter 47, in the pattern of Isaiah 13–14, announces the demise of Babylon in the form of a lament. Babylon, addressed as a woman, faces wrack and ruin.

OUTLINE

Bel, Nebo, and the God Who Saves, 46:1-13
    46:1-2   Bel and Nebo as Burdens
    46:3-8   Jacob-Israel Carried by the Lord
    46:9-13   Remembering the Lord's Counsel
Lament over Babylon, 47:1-15
    47:1-3a   Babylon Shamed
    47:3b-5   Babylon Silenced
    47:6-7   Babylon's Lack of Mercy
    47:8-11   Babylon Overtaken by Disaster

| 47:12-13 | Taunting Babylon |
| 47:14-15 | Deriding Babylon's Astrologers |

EXPLANATORY NOTES

Bel, Nebo, and the God Who Saves 46:1-13

The chapter begins with an object lesson on the helplessness of the Babylonian gods (46:1-2). Then the Lord addresses Jacob-Israel, employing the object lesson in order to distinguish authentic deity from reasonable facsimiles (46:3-8). Leaving the object lesson behind, the Lord reminds the exiles that he alone has the ability to bring to fulfillment what he has promised (46:9-13).

46:1-2 Bel and Nebo as Burdens

The object lesson features two Babylonian deities, Bel and Nebo, belonging to the cities of Babylon and Borsippa respectively. These cities lay on the east bank of the Euphrates River, Borsippa some fifteen miles south-southeast of Babylon. Bel and Nebo were part of a larger pantheon of Babylonian gods and goddesses, Nebo being the son of Bel (*ANET*: 303, 306, 311; cf. Noth: 292). Most important, they were imperial deities, giving divine sanction to the self-interest of the Babylonian Empire.

The point of the object lesson lies in characterizing Bel and Nebo as burdens, as burdensome. The images of Bel and Nebo must be carted from one place to the next. Neither the gods nor their images have any power intrinsic to themselves (see TLC, "Modern Imperial Gods").

46:3-8 Jacob-Israel Carried by the Lord

The object lesson in 46:1-2 offers an opportunity for the Lord to address Jacob-Israel with a teaching about credible deity. The first part of the teaching focuses on the Lord's disposition as a burden-bearer (46:3, 4). From cradle to grave, the Lord bears his people's burdens. What does this mean? This burden-bearing centers on the Lord's character as Creator and Redeemer. *Creator* and *Redeemer* are comprehensive terms that signify unmediated power. This imageless deity wields power that cannot be manipulated. The Lord is a free agent. Therefore humankind is not caught in the cross fire resulting from the intrigues and power struggles of gods in a pantheon.

The last part of the teaching illustrates further the powerlessness of image-based deities (46:5-8). Created by humans, they share the powerlessness of humans to save. Jacob-Israel, referred to as rebels, is called

Isaiah 46:1-47:15

to abandon its trust in the imperial gods and embrace the Lord (cf. Brueggemann, 1998b:87).

46:9-13 Remembering the Lord's Counsel

Departing from the object lesson, the Lord reminds the exiles that he alone has the ability to bring to fulfillment what he has promised (46:9-10a). The imperative *Remember!* means more than simply recollection of the past. It contains an exhortation to vigorous response (cf. Childs: 361). The *former things* refers to Israel's history. The allusion is to the disclosure in Israel's history of the Lord's incomparable being and performance. The language reflects but goes beyond the Lord's revelation of his name to Moses in Midian (Exod 3:13-15) and the prohibition of other gods in the law-giving at Mt. Sinai (Exod 20:1-6). Now it includes the Lord's ability to comprehend history from beginning to end.

This comprehension takes on meaning in the next stanza (46:10b-11). Here, recalling language reminiscent of 44:24-28, the Lord attests to a purpose and a plan that he intends to carry out. The plan includes mustering *a bird of prey from the east*. Although Cyrus is not named, the similarity of language to 41:2; 44:28; and 45:3-4 suggests that Cyrus is intended. The Lord has a plan that includes Cyrus, who will give the exiles breathing space in their land of origin.

The concluding stanza reminds the reader that the Lord continues to address a people that resists the implementation of his plan (46:12-13). The hyphenated *stubborn-hearted* (NIV) recalls the phrase *Take it to heart* (NIV) in 46:8. The metaphor of the heart refers to human intellect and emotion. The Bible understands the heart as the storehouse and command center of thoughts and feelings (*NHBD*: 247-48).

The people have distanced themselves from *righteousness*. The English word *righteousness* translates the Hebrew noun ṣedaqah, which includes "truthfulness," "salvation," and "right" among its meanings. Some translations take ṣedaqah to mean *deliverance* (RSV, NRSV; cf. Whybray: 118). Even though deliverance is not unrelated to righteousness, I take righteousness to refer more specifically to moral discernment in 46:13. Knight argues that ṣedaqah refers to the human response to God's action (92). He further defines this righteousness as *love to others* and *creative love* and *new creative way of life* (104-5). With its richness of meaning, including truthfulness, salvation, and right, it is not a very large leap to include love as a component of righteousness (46:12).

The Hebrew text of 46:13 employs assonance, the similarity of sounds in words or syllables. A remnant of this assonance comes through in translation in the threefold repetition of the pronoun *my*:

> I have brought *my righteousness* near, it is not far away;
>   and *my salvation* is not far behind;
> in Zion I shall give salvation,
>   to Israel *my splendor*. (AT)

There is a sequence here that bears mentioning. The Lord's salvation follows in the train of the Lord's righteousness. Or, to state it another way, as people imitate God's ethical standards, the Lord's saving grace flourishes. Then, as icing on the cake, the Lord confers his splendor on the people who bear his name.

Lament over Babylon 47:1-15

From object lesson and instruction, the poetry moves to lament in chapter 47. The lament, addressed to Babylon, moves through six stages. The first two stages focus on Babylon's disgrace (47:1-3a, 3b-5). In the next two stages, Babylon's arrogance emerges as the cause of her downfall (47:6-7, 8-11). The end of the lament taunts Babylon to continue in her futile ways, in which there is no salvation (47:12-13, 14-15).

47:1-3a Babylon Shamed

In the first stage, Babylon is depicted as feminine and directed to sit in the dust, mourning her subjugation (47:1). The previous chapter portrays the gods of Babylon as powerless and unable to save (46:7). Now these gods have abandoned Babylon to her fate (cf. Hanson: 116-17). This appears to be a mock lament spoken by the Lord, whose interest lies in refashioning his own people.

The second stanza addresses Babylon as a violated virgin (47:2-3a). The former queen faces the life of a commoner, suffering the indignities of life and labor.

47:3b-5 Babylon Silenced

The Lord speaks throughout chapter 47, but in 47:3b and again in verse 6 the speech is more personal. In this second stage of the lament, the statement *I will take vengeance* means that the Lord will impose a penalty on Babylon (47:3b-4). The speaker's name bears the right of genuine sovereignty, whose dominion rests on redemption (Hanson: 118). Vengeance and redemption stand side by side as an entitlement of the Lord of history.

The penalty imposed is removal of Babylon's status as imperial mistress (47:5). Silence and darkness replace Babylon's lusty past.

47:6-7 Babylon's Lack of Mercy

The reason for Babylon's silence and darkness becomes clear in the third stage of the lament. The Lord gave his people into Babylon's power in order to discipline them. Although Babylon's appointed task was disciplinary, her application of that task was punitive. The elderly of Israel are singled out for special mention because they are vulnerable (47:6).

Babylon saw an opportunity to crush God's people and keep them in bondage forever (47:7). But she did not consider the judgment of history on such behavior (Watts, 1987:171). The Lord judges imperial powers for their arrogance. This is a theological statement about the judgment of history. A review of world history shows that all empires rise and then go into a period of decline and collapse. Whether one understands this as God's judgment or simply the judgment of history depends on prior understandings of spiritual reality.

47:8-11 Babylon Overtaken by Disaster

The cause of Babylon's downfall continues to be expressed in the fourth stage of the lament. *Now then, listen* (NIV), in the first stanza, introduces the announcement of disaster upon the virgin daughter of Babylon (47:8; cf. 47:1). Secure in her conviction that she is accountable to no one, Babylon has no suspicion of a disaster. Instead, she claims divine status that rivals that of the Lord (cf. 45:5, 6, 18, 22; 46:9). She claims exemption from the twin calamities of widowhood and loss of children. But Babylon is not the *I AM* of history, in spite of her claims to the contrary in the ancient Near East (cf. Esarhaddon, 680-669 BC, in *ANET*: 290).

Babylon's claims, in fact, are turned on their head in the second stanza (47:9). Whybray is right in concluding that, as in 47:1, an exchange of roles between Babylon and Zion-Jerusalem is announced (122). Babylon, though still in power, will experience the deprivation that the exiles continue to experience. Although the Hebrew verb is the simple *bw'* (to enter, to come), the context gives it a more forceful meaning. Calamity will *overtake* her and *come upon* her (47:9 NIV). This will happen in spite of Babylon's recourse to *sorceries* (see TLC, "Modern Imperial Gods"). Sorcery will be ineffective against the overwhelming power of the Lord (cf. Brueggemann, 1998b:97).

In the third stanza (47:10) this sorcery is named as evil (*wickedness,* NIV, NRSV). *No one sees me* indicates that the empire, though replete with pseudo-religious practices, trusts in its own power and not in any divine power outside itself. Claiming to be unseen by God, the empire proceeds to implement strategies of power based on self-interest. No one representing God's power calls (or is allowed to call) the empire to account. Babylon claims the *I AM* role of history, which belongs to God alone. Such hubris, the claim to be in charge of the future, ignores the reality that God holds the future and has a plan and purpose for it.

Evil in the form of *calamity* and *catastrophe* will descend upon Babylon as a result of the evil she has nurtured (47:11 NIV). Babylonian knowledge cannot address the issues that drive the empire toward disaster. And when disaster comes, bewilderment about the causes of it will be rampant.

47:12-13 Taunting Babylon

The fifth stage of the lament moves from announcement of disaster to a sarcastic encouragement of the religious underpinnings leading to disaster. The first stanza looks back to the *sorceries* and *enchantments* of 47:9 and reverses their order (47:12; as an *inclusio* [*Literary Perspective*, p. 446]). The indoctrination of youth into religious practices that lead nowhere anticipates the same theme in 47:15. The sarcastic use of the adverb *perhaps* continues and concludes the stanza.

The sarcasm continues in the second stanza (47:13). *All the counsel* (NIV) refers to the use of astrology to predict the future. The Babylonians worshipped the stars as gods, controlling human life (Whybray: 125). The impotence of these gods points to the real source of salvation: the Lord of hosts.

The sarcasm directed against magic and astral religion in 47:12 and 13 recalls the admonishment not to seek the counsel of the dead in 8:19-20. Both texts censure any religious expression outside of the worship of the Lord and count such as misleading and destructive.

47:14-15 Deriding Babylon's Astrologers

The adverb *surely* (NIV) introduces a final word of judgment on Babylonian astrologers and beyond them on the empire itself (47:14). The astrologers are compared to stubble. Stubble has value in soil conservation, but it is not this value that concerns the prophet here. Rather, its flammability makes it a symbol of the astrologers' end. Their false religion has no power to save because it is based on fixed patterns in the stars rather than on the dynamic power of the Creator. The imagery of sitting by a fire to warm oneself recalls 44:9-20. There the woodworker uses one part of a piece of wood to make an idol while with the other part he builds a fire to warm himself. Here there is no warming fire to sit by—only the consuming fire of judgment.

The *you* of 47:15 is feminine singular, referring to Babylon addressed as a woman at the beginning of the chapter. Babylon's astrologers wander in circles. Babylon cannot be saved by such an unsure foundation.

THE TEXT IN BIBLICAL CONTEXT

Babylon

References to Babylon occur thirteen times in the book of Isaiah (13:1, 19; 14:4, 22; 21:9; 39:1, 3, 6, 7; 43:14; 47:1; 48:14, 20). In 39:1 and 3 the narrative simply reports the visit of Babylonian envoys to Hezekiah's court. In 39:6 and 7, however, the references to Babylon imply that Babylon serves as the Lord's instrument of judgment on Judah. This may also be seen in 13:1-16, where Babylon functions as the Lord's agent, to bring the earth into subjection. The reader knows from chapter 10 that Assyria, who received the Lord's authority to serve as disciplinarian, abused this authority and became the object of the Lord's discipline. Now Babylon follows the same pattern.

In the book of Isaiah, most references to Babylon have to do with the Lord's judgment on it. Babylon becomes the prototype of empires that are corrupted by their own power. This corruption leads to their demise. In Jeremiah, where Babylon (including Chaldea and Chaldeans) is mentioned sixty-nine times in chapters 50–51, the root of the corruption is arrogance (50:31-32; being "proud," RSV). Martens is justified in seeing Babylon as a symbol of evil in the OT (272; see TBC).

References to Babylon occur twelve times in the NT. In Matthew's Gospel (1:11, 12, 17) and in the Acts of the Apostles (7:43), Babylon refers simply to the site of the deportation, after Jerusalem's fall in 587 BC. In the other NT references, however, Babylon serves as a pseudonym for Rome. These references are all in the Revelation of John (except one reference in 1 Pet 5:13). The angelic announcement of Babylon's (Rome's) fall in Revelation 14:8 and 18:2 echoes the announcement of Babylon's fall in Isaiah 21:9.

In the Revelation of John the references to Babylon all occur after the vision of the two beasts in chapter 13. The beast from the sea represents the Roman Empire, and the beast from the earth represents the emperors or a particular emperor enforcing emperor worship. John's vision in Revelation 13 makes it clear that the beasts are not autonomous but receive power from God, who remains the source of all power.

THE TEXT IN THE LIFE OF THE CHURCH

Despising the Voice of God

The Chronicle of the Hutterian Brethren commences with a sketch of creation drawn from several biblical creation texts. The sketch draws special attention to God's power through speech to bring the earth into existence. When God speaks, his will is put into effect. *The Chronicle* (2) illustrates this Word of power by alluding to various places in Isaiah 43–46 where the prophet, speaking for God, says, *I am the LORD; I alone made all things, and there is none beside me* (cf. Isa 44:6, 24).

In 1539, when Menno Simons wrote his *Why I Do Not Cease Teaching and Writing*, he despaired of a world that despises the voice of God and prefers other voices (314). This world includes Christendom as well as the world's people in general. The other voices include the voice of arrogance based on wealth, as exemplified by Tyre (Ezek 27:3); and the voice of pride, in which Babylon equated itself with God (Isa 47:8). God's most terrifying anger is exhibited, Menno writes, in the removal of his divine Word. Plagues, including disease, famine, and war, are troubles which God hands out for our correction and so that we may learn wisdom.

> But when He deprives us of His Word, all is lost. For if we have not the Word, we verily have nothing but unbelief, blindness, error, disobedience, conceit, bitterness, an unclean, foolish, and adulterous spirit, and eternal death. (318)

In the church the preference for voices other than the voice of God goes hand in hand with God's removal of his divine Word. Individuals and congregations will benefit from reflection on how the voice of God can be truly heard while we are surrounded by the general babble of modern life.

Modern Imperial Gods

The imperial gods and sorceries of Babylon find their reincarnation in the imperial gods and sorceries of Western civilization. Only the names have changed. The idols of Isaiah 46 and the sorceries of Isaiah 47 are imperial deities and ideologies giving divine sanction to the Babylonian Empire.

Modern Western sensibilities have long ago abandoned the use of idols of wood or stone or metal to symbolize matters of "ultimate concern" (Tillich, 1951:11-15). Nevertheless other idolatries serve to give divine sanction to imperial self-interest. The ideologies of communism, fascism, national socialism, and capitalism dominated the twentieth century.

The conventional wisdom of socialism, "from each according to one's ability, to each according to one's need," became hardened, in its Soviet form, into a system of government in which one party controlled the means of production. Religious expression under Communist ideology was circumscribed, and the state became, for all practical purposes, the focus of "ultimate concern."

Fascism and national socialism (Nazism), each with its own ideological distinctives, shared an autocratic form of government and exalted nation and race above the individual and above any religious loyalty. The supremacy of the leader under Fascism and Nazism inspired loyalty and devotion similar to the worship of God.

Capitalism in its European and North American forms is an economic system in which capital goods are not owned by the state but by private or corporate entities. This free-market system has been successful in creating an abundance of material goods. But in doing so, the market has become a god, and abundance has become an object of worship (Rempel: esp. 48-66). Alongside the worship of abundance is the worship of the political powers that guarantee this abundance. This worship takes the form of civil religion, the conviction that the nation-state and its political power are the ultimate embodiment of transcendent elements that control the future; they are the ultimate focus of loyalty.

Isaiah 48:1-22

Listen to This!

PREVIEW

The appeal to listen comes to Jacob-Israel with some force in chapter 48, echoing similar appeals in Isaiah 40–47. The appeal in 48:1-11 focuses on Jacob-Israel's indifferent hearing and knowing. The declaration in 48:8 that Jacob-Israel has neither heard nor known throws strong light on the questions in 40:21 and 28: *Have you not known? Have you not heard?*

The appeal in 48:12-22 instructs Jacob-Israel about the Lord's creative and redeeming power. This instruction has clear roots in Isaiah 40–47, where creation serves as a testimony to the immensity of God's power available for his redeeming purpose in Israel and the nations (cf. Vriezen: 270-74).

The appeal to listen in chapter 48 serves as a drumroll, calling Jacob-Israel to believe in the Lord's name and to pursue the way of truth and righteousness and peace. A warning to the wicked in 48:22 concludes the chapter and part 4 as a whole (40–48). An almost identical warning, it will be seen, concludes part 5 of the book (49–57). Chapter 48 shifts dramatically from declarations of God's superiority over idols and of Babylon's destruction, to critical words of warning addressed to God's people.

OUTLINE

Hearing and Knowing, 48:1-11
    48:1-2   The Lord's Name

Isaiah 48:1-22

48:3-5	Former Things
48:6-8	New Things
48:9-11	For the Sake of the Lord's Name

Creation and Redemption, 48:12-22

48:12-13	The Lord's Preeminence
48:14-16a	The Lord's Speech
48:16b-19	The Lord's Way
48:20-22	Redemption Aplenty

EXPLANATORY NOTES

Hearing and Knowing 48:1-11

Chapter 48:1-11 begins with the prophet addressing Jacob-Israel concerning the disparity between confession of faith and actual practice (48:1-2). The Lord himself takes up the address where the prophet leaves off, but moves on to speak about new things soon to take place (48:3-11).

48:1-2 The Lord's Name

The imperative *Hear this* opens a six-line stanza addressing the house of Jacob and Israel (48:1). A strict distinction between Jacob and Israel should not be made. By combining them with a hyphen, I am representing Jacob-Israel as God's people.

After addressing Jacob-Israel, the prophet gives a brief synopsis of the relationship between God and his people. The synopsis begins with a reference to Judah and his descendants. The Hebrew Bible reads *waters of Judah* (KJV), but modern translations emend the text to read *line of Judah* (NIV), *loins of Judah* (NRSV), or *seed of Judah* (JB). The *waters of Judah* is an awkward expression, although not impossible. Beginning with the reference to Judah, the prophet highlights the bond between Jacob-Israel and the Lord. The bond, however strong it once was, became unglued over time. The last line of the stanza expresses this unfaithfulness as the profession of loyalty to the God of Israel while not living this loyalty out in honesty and candor.

The second stanza completes the prophet's description of Jacob-Israel's self-proclaimed relationship to the Lord (48:2). Nevertheless the last lines of the first stanza (48:1) reveal the truth of the relationship. While invoking the name of the Lord remained central, reliable evidence was lacking that the confession resulted in right behavior.

48:3-5 Former Things

The Lord's address begins abruptly, without an introductory formula. The first stanza focuses on how the Lord announced events in the past and then acted to make them happen (48:3-4). This announcement-performance strategy, however, failed to convince God's people to recognize the Lord's power. Nevertheless the text does not assume that God's people were predestined to be stubborn from the beginning, from which position they were powerless to free themselves.

The second stanza defines *for whom* the announcement of past events was intended (48:5). The announcement was intended for Jacob-Israel. From the time of the exodus onward, the temptation of Jacob-Israel was to attribute the power behind events to images of deity rather than to the Lord, who was not to be represented by images. The prohibition of idols in the second commandment of the Decalogue (Exod 20:4-6; Deut 5:8-10) was intended to preserve the power of God's word from the eroding effect of image-based deity. The second commandment lies in the background of Isaiah 48:5.

48:6-8 New Things

Hearing and knowing, the theme of 48:1-13, comes to a climax in the announcement of unheard-of new things (48:6-8). In the first stanza the Lord's power behind events in the past now yields to something new (48:6-7). The central meaning of this stanza lies in the juxtaposition of first things (past events, *former things*) from 48:3-4 and *new things* (events about to happen) in 48:6-7. The Lord announced past events before they happened in order to discourage people from attributing power to image-based deities. Now the Lord announces new things before their occurrence in order to prevent the excuse that they are already known, implying that the power of knowing the future lies in the people's hands.

The *new things* are not enumerated although it seems clear that they refer to Jacob-Israel's release from exile in Babylon (cf. Hanson: 124). But beyond this time-based reference to liberation, God's dominion is displayed in his ability to bring about the new. The new is God's accommodation to the human limitations of time. Idolatry and egocentrism, on the other hand, seem to stem from the same source, the refusal to give credence to God's power beyond the power of human achievement.

In the second stanza the mood shifts from suspicion to accusation (48:8). Ignorance of the Lord's power to control events in the past and in the future, combined with the people's refusal to obey what they knew about God, has led to treachery and rebellion from Jacob-Israel's beginning.

48:9-11 For the Sake of the Lord's Name

That the Lord responds to treachery and rebellion with restraint rather than unbridled anger *for [his] name's sake* echoes the view in Ezekiel 20:8-9, 44 (see TBC). The significance of this motive lies in God's compassion for his people rather than a compulsion to exercise judgment whenever an offense has occurred. God has the right to punish yet may choose to relinquish that right.

The focus of God's compassion is on restorative justice rather than punitive justice (48:10-11; see TLC). The phrase *though not as silver* (NIV) has puzzled commentators. It seems that the text should read *I have refined you as silver (is refined)*, where refining silver to remove impurities serves as a metaphor for purifying people, perhaps by suffering (cf. Dan 11:35; 12:10; cf. Mal 3:2-3). But the phrase *though not as silver* appears to mean simply that the purifying of the people has not taken place to the extent that silver is refined.

Restorative justice does not have its basis in any merit an offender may have accrued, but rather in the mercy a judge (acting for the victim) bestows. Compassion characterizes God's name and reputation. To act with revenge *on principle* would be to sully God's own name. God's punishment is disciplinary in nature, seeking repentance, seeking restoration, having "no pleasure in the death of anyone" (Ezek 18:32).

Creation and Redemption 48:12-22

Although the Lord's address to Jacob-Israel in 48:12-22 continues the address in 48:3-11, there is here a renewed call (cf. 48:1) to listen, a call that appeals to the Lord's role as Creator and Redeemer.

48:12-13 The Lord's Preeminence

The renewed appeal to listen moves immediately into the Lord's disclosure of his preeminence (48:12). As in 44:6, the Lord as *first* and *last* has a special meaning here. The Lord as *the first* refers to the Lord as Creator, at the beginning of history and without genealogy. The Lord as *the last* indicates the Lord's presence at the end of history and without peers.

The Lord's preeminence as *the first* finds expression in his role as Creator (48:13). The creation of earth and heaven took place at the Lord's call. The reader will notice that just as the Lord called creation into being, so the Lord called Jacob-Israel to be his people. The two callings stand in the same order of significance, the one establishing physical space and the other designating a particular people.

48:14-16a The Lord's Speech

Although the addressees (*you* pl.) of 48:14 may be thought of as nations and peoples in general, it makes more sense to think of them as Jacob-Israel since it is Jacob-Israel to whom the renewed call to listen is addressed in 48:12. The NIV interprets the pronoun *them* in the second line of 48:14 to mean *the idols*. But *them* probably refers to earth and heaven in the previous stanza. In other words, Has anyone in earth or heaven announced these things that are about to happen?

The pronoun *these things* looks ahead to the following lines. The implied answer is "No one has announced them." Instead of an announcement, there is a tour de force against Babylon by someone whom the Lord loves. Who might this be? Cumulative evidence in Isaiah 41–48 points to Cyrus. The argument for inferring Cyrus at places such as this, where he is not named, rests on language similar to or identical with language in 44:28 and 45:1, where he is named. In 44:28 Cyrus is to accomplish the Lord's whole purpose toward Jerusalem and the temple. Similarly, in 48:14 he (Cyrus) is to carry out *his* (the Lord's) *purpose* against *Babylon*. While not conclusive, the argument for Cyrus in 48:14 is reasonable. In 48:15 the pronoun *him* continues the reference to Cyrus, including his calling by the Lord (cf. Isa 45:3-4).

The plural addressee continues in 48:16. In 48:14 the Lord addressed Jacob-Israel in order to announce the downfall of Babylon at the hand of Cyrus. In 48:16 the Lord addresses Jacob-Israel again, reminding his people the evidence for his action in history has never been hidden from view (cf. 45:19).

48:16b-19 The Lord's Way

The passage in 48:16b-19 remains difficult to understand. The focus of the difficulty lies in the pronoun *me*. To whom does this refer? The prophet himself has been suggested (Knight, Clements) or an anonymous leader (Watts). The immediate context suggests that *me* refers to the servant of the Lord, named in Isaiah 49:1-6 (cf. Childs: 377-78). The servant, formally introduced in the first servant song (42:1-4), unveils a communiqué from the Lord here.

This communiqué falls into two parts. Beginning with the preamble *I am the LORD your God*, 48:17 expresses the two central tenets of the Lord's purpose among his people: teaching and leading. *Teaching* aims at imagining the future, starting from a firm foundation in the Lord's instruction. *Leading* signifies living in the present, starting from the imagined future expressed in teaching.

The second part of the communiqué, standing in juxtaposition to the first, indicates that teaching and leading have been discarded (48:18-19). The words *If only . . .* (NIV) announce a situation that has not been realized. Peace, righteousness, and offspring represent the fruit of listening to the Lord's teaching and leading.

48:20-22 Redemption Aplenty

The communiqué from the Lord by servant's mouth extends into 48:20. Now the exiles hear a command to leave Babylon, bearing the testimony of Jacob's redemption. This redemption, flowing from the Lord's work as Redeemer (48:17), means that God's people are once again free to move into the future with confidence (see TLC).

The narrative of the exodus from Egypt (Exod 17:1-7) serves as evidence of the Lord's redemption (48:21). Just as the exodus Israelites received water on their journey, so the people about to embark on a new exodus will receive provisions for their journey.

The last line of the stanza is sometimes judged to be unrelated to its context (48:22; cf. Whybray: 134). Yet in 48:22 the reference to the absence of peace (šalom) calls to mind the reference to unattained peace (šalom, or *prosperity*, NRSV) in 48:18. In my judgment, the two references to peace are related. And more is involved than the mere repetition of the same noun, *peace*. Due to inattention to the Lord's commands, peace did not unfold for Jacob-Israel (48:18). This refers to the correspondence between the spiritual life of Jacob-Israel based on the Lord's instruction, and the well-being and wholeness (peace) of Jacob-Israel flowing from that spiritual life. The same framework of meaning applies to the statement in 48:22. Those who have no roots in the Lord's instruction (the wicked) cannot experience the spiritual and material benefits of well-being and wholeness.

THE TEXT IN BIBLICAL CONTEXT

For My Name's Sake

In Isaiah 48:9 and 11, and earlier in 43:25 and 37:35, the Lord acts *for my name's sake* or *for my own sake* rather than for the sake of Jacob-Israel. This thought, mentioned infrequently in the book of Isaiah, finds expression elsewhere in the Hebrew Bible.

Two psalms, for example, speak in this way. In Psalm 25:11 the psalmist asks God *for your name's sake* to pardon his guilt. Again, in Psalm 106:8 the Lord is said to have saved the Hebrews from slavery in Egypt *for his name's sake*. The motive for the Lord's liberation in each case does not rest on compassion for the distressed but on concern for the Lord's own reputation.

A remarkable narrative in the book of Numbers illustrates this perspective (14:13-19). When ten of the twelve spies, sent by Moses into Canaan, brought an unfavorable report, there was much lamentation and complaint among the exodus Israelites. The Lord's reply to this lamentation and complaint was a resolve to make an end of the people. Moses, however, interceded for the Israelites. He argued that if the Lord destroyed the people whom he had led out of Egypt, the nations would draw the conclusion that he had no power. Moses' argument said, in effect, that even if the Lord would rather put an end to his people, even if they deserved to be struck down, the Lord should not do it for the sake of his own reputation.

The prophet Ezekiel, however, expresses the insight most clearly that the Lord acts for the sake of his name (chaps. 20, 36). The Lord acts for the sake of his name in the sense that he does not want his name to be sullied in the opinion of the nations (cf. Lind, 1996:290). Ezekiel makes it clear that the Lord's self-restraint toward Israel rests neither on Israel's virtue nor on the Lord's love for Israel. Instead, his self-restraint rests on his own self-regard. Walter Brueggemann comments that there is much more to the Lord than merely *self-giving* love; there is also *self-regarding* majesty (1998b:103-4).

THE TEXT IN THE LIFE OF THE CHURCH

Redemption

Two specific cases in ancient Israel illustrate the right of redemption. Jeremiah bought the field of his cousin Hanamel to prevent the loss of family property (Jer 32). Boaz bought the land of Elimelech that Naomi offered for sale (Ruth 4). In each case the right of redemption meant an obligation to assist and safeguard family members in need (de Vaux, 1961a:21-22). These cases form the background to the OT view that God acts as the Redeemer of his people. This view is especially represented in Isaiah 40–48, 49–57.

In this sense redemption refers to liberation that humankind experiences because of God's grace. God brings this liberation about because he provides the necessary path to set humankind free from sin and enslavement to sin (cf. *NHBD*: 605-6.).

The exodus from Egypt is the primary historical source in the Bible for an understanding of redemption. Although God did not "buy" Israel from Pharaoh, the language of redemption is used explicitly in Exodus 6:6 and 15:13, and implicitly elsewhere (cf. 7:4; 18:8).

In the history of the church there have been a variety of expressions and explanations of the redemption of Christ. In the eleventh and early twelfth centuries, Anselm of Canterbury argued that God's justice, which demands adequate satisfaction for sin, requires redemption by the death of one who was both God and human. In the thirteenth century Thomas Aquinas denied the necessity of redemption expressed in this way. He said that redemption meant a restoration of original righteousness, which enabled the repentant sinner to cooperate with God's grace, leading to justification and sanctification (*ODCC*: 1373).

Sixteenth-century Reformers rejected this view and maintained that they were returning to the teachings of Paul, with a heavy accent on the forgiveness of sin and justification by faith alone (*ODCC*: 1373). The Radical Reformation, in all its diversity, took a path that rejected works-righteousness on the one hand and faith without works on the other. Michael Sattler, an important voice in the early Anabaptist movement, speaks clearly to this point. In an essay "On the Satisfaction of Christ," Sattler argues against those who say that a person can be saved by Christ whether or not there are works of faith. "They reject works without faith," he says, "in order to raise up faith without works." When one speaks of justification through Christ, "one must also speak of that faith, which cannot be without works of repentance, yea, not without love" (Yoder, 1973:117, 115).

Creeds and Deeds

The opening lines of Isaiah 48 indicate that Jacob-Israel invoked the Lord's name without expressing this invocation in lives of truth and justice. Such a disparity between faith and practice lies behind the reluctance of believers churches to emphasize creeds.

Donald Durnbaugh, in his definition of the believers church, says that while believers churches accepted the tenets of the creeds, they held that formal adherence to the creeds tended to make them (the creeds) "a substitute for living faith" (207).

Furthermore, the creeds, in their silence concerning the life and teachings of Jesus, have little or nothing to say about the blending of Christian faith and practice. The concern for creedal orthodoxy combined with truthful living in Isaiah 48 commends itself to the ongoing life and witness of the church.

Restorative Justice

The Lord expresses the deferral and restraint of his anger toward his people as well as his refusal to blot them out (48:9). Then he uses language of purifying to speak of his intention for Jacob-Israel (48:10-11). This suggests a fundamental interest in restorative justice rather than punitive justice.

In its history the church has often accepted the concept of retributive justice practiced by the state. As the church became more closely allied with the state, especially after the fourth century, the church began to mimic the state's understanding of retributive justice. Howard Zehr shows how canon law in the Western church grew out of Roman law. Canon law, in turn, further refined retributive justice, which was then adopted by secular legal systems (110-13).

An alternative model of justice—restorative justice—waits to be recovered and developed. Such an alternative model is already functioning in the Victim-Offender Reconciliation Program (VORP). The movement began in Canada (Elmira, Ontario) in 1974 by Mennonites as a response to frustration with the system of retributive justice (Zehr: 158-60). From this beginning VORP has expanded to over three thousand similar programs worldwide. In the VORP model, offenders take responsibility for their crimes by participating in mediation, with the aim of entering into a restitution agreement with their victims. In this agreement, restitution may be monetary or symbolic; it may include work for the victim or community service or anything that creates a sense of justice between the victim and the offender.

Part 5

Servant and Scaffold

Isaiah 49–57

OVERVIEW

The prophetic poetry that paused at the end of Isaiah 48 (*"There is no peace," says the LORD, "for the wicked,"* 48:22) continues in chapters 49–57. In the first three chapters the Lord's servant, introduced in part 4, is now onstage with a twofold mission: the gathering of dispersed Jacob-Israel and the giving of light to the nations (49–51).

The next three chapters announce the peace and salvation at the center of God's kingdom, with the Lord's servant appearing onstage once more, followed by God's assuring his promise of a covenant of peace with his people (52–54). The servant embraces the vision of God's reign, bringing good out of evil and refusing to retaliate against evil with more evil (52:13–53:12). The scaffold, however, looms as a sign of the alternative spirituality that Israel offers to the nations. It is a spirituality that embraces life but that also attracts deep opposition to it, where idolatry and immorality and violence remain unfettered.

If the reference to Jesus "taking the very nature of a servant" (Phil 2:7 NIV) refers to the fourth servant song (esp. the reference to the servant in Isa 52:13 and 53:11), as it seems to do, then the vision of Isaiah already carries a clear anticipation of a future Messiah, who lives within the limits of experience and knowledge and who also exceeds and surpasses these limits.

The call to seek the Lord and to find refuge in him brings part 5 to a close (55–57). In the spirituality that Israel offers to the nations, the Lord is exalted, but the Lord also resides with all those who honor him (57:15).

Isaiah 49:1-26

A Covenant to the People

PREVIEW

Figurative language and the power of poetry grip the reader from the very first word of the chapter; imagery of marriage and children, of labor and childbirth, of nursing and child-rearing—these are all employed to convey the emotion of nurturing God's people to faithfulness.

The first half of the chapter focuses attention on the Lord's servant (49:1-13). The second servant song [*Servant, Servants, p. 451*], in which the servant describes his prenatal calling and his mission, opens the chapter (49:1-6). The sequel to the song features the Lord addressing his servant (49:7-13). The content of the address focuses on the guidance and compassion that the Lord has for his people.

The second half of the chapter gives attention to the Lord's response to Zion's complaint (49:14-26). The complaint is that God has abandoned Israel (49:14). In reply the Lord draws on language of infancy and early childhood to console Zion that her interests are secure. There is no need to worry.

OUTLINE

Servant Song and Sequel, 49:1-13
    49:1-3   The Servant's Calling
    49:4-6   The Servant's Mission

49:7-11	The Lord as Faithful One
49:12-13	The Lord's Comfort and Compassion

Redemption of Jacob-Israel, 49:14-26

49:14-18	Not Forgotten
49:19-21	Children of the Exile
49:22-23	Signal to the Peoples
49:24-26	Savior Who Saves

EXPLANATORY NOTES

Servant Song and Sequel 49:1-13

The song opens with imperative verbs appealing to faraway peoples to grasp the significance of the servant's calling (49:1). The song's sequel ends by calling attention to the coming of faraway peoples, followed by imperative verbs calling heaven and earth to notice the Lord's comfort and compassion for his people (49:12-13). Between these bookends lies a vision of the Lord's servant as one who declares the Lord's salvation.

49:1-3 The Servant's Calling

The servant addresses coastlands and faraway peoples with an announcement of his prenatal divine calling (49:1; cf. Jer 1:5; Gal 1:15). I take the coastlands and faraway peoples as a poetic allusion to the surrounding nation-states on the rim of the Mediterranean as well as the empires on the Nile and Tigris-Euphrates River systems. It is difficult to determine how the servant would have addressed these nations. Perhaps it was to an assembly of exiled Judeans in Babylon that he spoke. I do not assume that the nations are in attendance at such an assembly.

The servant's calling has to do with the use of his voice (49:2-3). The metaphor of his mouth as a *sharp sword* indicates that his message has a cutting function. He will cut through prevailing assumptions about how Jacob-Israel understood its mission. One of these assumptions, given the Lord's word in 49:5 concerning the servant's mission, may have been that the Lord had no mission beyond his own people.

The metaphor of the servant as a *polished arrow* indicates that his message has a "reflecting" and a "piercing" function. The message is to reflect the Lord's light; the servant's mission will penetrate Jacob-Israel's consciousness. That the mission is hidden from sight simply means that its time has not yet come. Nevertheless the servant's call by the Lord is clear. The call identifies the servant with Israel.

The role of the servant is to reflect the Lord's *splendor* (NIV), nothing more, nothing less (cf. Knight: 127). How is that splendor reflected?

Most likely it is reflected by persistent attention to the cultivation of justice (Isa 42:1-4) and to the fostering of reconciliation (Isa 49:5).

49:4-6 The Servant's Mission

The servant's response to the call to reflect the Lord's splendor indicates a mixture of discouragement and confidence (49:4). The complaint that his strength is exhausted in a lost cause summarizes the discouragement. The servant's discouragement, however, overlays a fundamental trust that his *cause* and his *reward* remain rooted in the Lord.

A conjunction and adverb (*And now*) introduces the Lord's reply to what the servant has just said (49:5). The testimony of the servant's call frames the statement of his mission (NIV):

> **call**   he who formed me in the womb to be his servant
>   **mission**   to bring Jacob back to him
>   and to gather Israel to himself,
> **call**   for I am honored in the eyes of the LORD
>   and my God has been my strength . . .

The servant understands his mission to begin with the gathering of dispersed Jacob-Israel. This means reshaping the exilic Jacob-Israel into a new people. The old Jacob-Israel experienced the exodus from Egypt and the calling at Mount Sinai to be a covenant people. Now a new people will be built up from the old.

A question may be raised: How can the servant be Israel and yet have the authorization to bring Israel back to God? One possibility is that the servant is the remnant of Israel (Roth: 142; Elmer Martens, private correspondence). The idea of a remnant is mentioned elsewhere in the book (cf. 10:21, 22; 11:11, 16; 28:5; 46:3; et al.). The relationship of the remnant to the people as a whole may be compared to that of yeast to bread. Yeast is mixed with flour, giving life and vitality and spirit to the bread (cf. Luke 13:20-21). It goes without saying that without yeast, the bread is hard and heavy and largely lifeless.

The Lord's message, strictly speaking, begins in 49:6. Here the Lord repeats the servant's mission of reshaping the exilic Jacob-Israel into a new people. To this mission is added the gift (*give*, v. 6) of being *a light to the nations* and of extending the Lord's *salvation . . . to the end of the earth*. The question is whether this gift simply continues the mandate to gather the exiles, or whether the Lord gives his servant the task of going beyond the frontiers of Jacob-Israel to the Gentiles (see TBC, "Was There a Mission to the Gentiles?").

49:7-11 The Lord as Faithful One

The sequel to the second servant song begins with a messenger formula [*Messenger Formula, 447*] presenting the Lord as *Redeemer* and *Holy One* (49:7a). The verb *to redeem* (*ga'al*) in the OT indicates the act of assisting a next-of-kin, as in Ruth 4:1 [*Redemption, Redeemer, p. 448*]. The epithet *Redeemer* suggests not only that the Lord promises to assist his people but also that he is, in a manner of speaking, their next of kin (Whybray: 65).

The Lord as Israel's Holy One, on the other hand, refers to God as sovereign and free. The designation of the Lord as *Holy One of Israel* is characteristic of the book of Isaiah. The adjective *holy* indicates that the Lord is unfettered by human frailty, corruption, and wrongdoing (cf. BDB: 872). The Lord as Redeemer and as Holy One bring together God's immanence and transcendence, present and available yet also wholly other.

The Lord addresses a message to his servant, who is despised and abhorred. The language here alerts the reader to the description of the servant in 52:13–53:12. There, also, kings come to understand the despised servant, who is set apart by God. This cross-reference points to the important theme of the servant's suffering in Isaiah 49–57 (cf. Childs: 386).

Kings and princes do not give obeisance to the servant but to the Lord (49:7b). They do so because they perceive the Lord's integrity. They are convinced of the Lord's integrity because of the integrity of the servant whom the Lord has chosen.

The messenger formula of 49:8 resumes the same formula in 49:7. The servant's mission was to lift up Jacob-Israel and to be a light to the nations. Now the servant receives a specific authorization as *a covenant to the people*. This raises a question: To whom does *the people* refer? The context suggests that *the people* refers to both Jacob-Israel and the nations. That the servant is the agent of God's covenant indicates that through Jacob-Israel a covenant relationship will be realized between God and all of humankind (Smart: 85).

It is no accident that exodus language is used to describe this covenant (49:8-11). The release of prisoners and bringing people out of darkness refers both to the restoration of the Judean exiles and to the redemption of the nations.

49:12-13 The Lord's Comfort and Compassion

The sequel to the second servant song concludes by calling attention to the coming of people from distant places (49:12). The location of *Syene* may be understood from Ezekiel, 29:10 where it refers to southern Egypt, modern Aswan (so NIV; *NHBD*: 712-13).

A hymn of praise calls on heaven and earth to rejoice in the Lord's comfort and compassion (49:13). This ode to joy is universal in scope. The Lord's people, *his suffering ones*, encompasses all those mentioned in the servant song and its sequel: peoples (v. 1), Jacob-Israel (vv. 4, 5), the nations (v. 6), and the people (v. 8).

Redemption of Jacob-Israel 49:14-26

The connection of 49:14-26 with the first half of the chapter is not readily apparent. In 49:14 Zion intentionally contradicts the Lord's comfort of his people in 49:13. This contradiction, however, serves as a foil for a new focus on the Lord's redemption of Jacob-Israel.

49:14-18 Not Forgotten

Zion-in-exile experienced the Lord's relationship as one of abandonment (49:14). Her complaint expresses the ongoing despair concerning her servitude in Babylon. The words *forsaken* and *forgotten* appear to annul the promise of comfort and compassion in 49:13 (Brueggemann, 1998b:116).

The Lord's reply to Zion's complaint, however, denies the thought of abandonment and forgetting with a forceful rhetorical question (49:15). Would the Lord forget his people or withdraw his compassion from them? Surely not! Such a thing is as repugnant as the thought of a mother forgetting her nursing child.

Why will God not forget his people? The response follows immediately in the next stanzas. The idea of the Lord inscribing Zion on his hands suggests the act of remembering (49:16-18a). What is the content of the Lord's remembering? He remembers *your walls*, the walls of Jerusalem destroyed by the Babylonians. The Lord has in view the building of a new city, and inscribing Zion on his hands reminds him of his intention (Whybray: 144). He remembers *your children* (*sons*, NIV), the Judeans who fled the city of Jerusalem ahead of the Babylonian army (cf. the NRSV which reads *your builders*, giving a different meaning to similar-sounding Hebrew words). He remembers *your pillagers* (*those who laid you waste*, NIV, NRSV), the Babylonians who destroyed the city.

The three nouns (*walls, sons, pillagers*) describe a history worth forgetting. But the Lord remembers this history because his people suffered through it. Now the Lord has in mind a healing of this history, if only Zion will open her eyes and see. Zion's eyesight has to do with her eyes of faith. Zion is invited to see that all her children are gathering and coming to her.

A great deal hinges on the purpose of this gathering and coming. If the gathering is for the purpose of reconstituting a political power base from which to rule nations and peoples, this is one thing. If, on the other hand, the gathering is for the purpose of being instructed by the Lord, this is another thing altogether. The verb *to inscribe* (*ḥqq*) in 49:16 indicates that the latter is intended. The noun form of this verb (*ḥoq*) is usually translated *statute*, referring to God's regulations and instruction to the Israelites. God wants to instruct his people.

The Lord's word is that Zion shall wear all of her children as ornaments are worn by a bride (49:18b). This metaphor suggests that Jacob-Israel's return to Zion means a new era of prosperity, with the Lord as Zion's husband.

49:19-21 Children of the Exile

The return of Jacob-Israel to Zion will mean crowded living conditions in the ruined city (49:19). While this may appear to be disheartening, it is not intended to be. It indicates, rather, that without the Babylonian military occupation there will be freedom and opportunity to rebuild.

Zion, whose children were taken from her at the Babylonian conquest, now hears the offspring of these children jostle for living space (49:20). Astonished, she wonders from where they have all come (49:21). Zion speaks as a mother robbed of her children, who like Job finds that she has more than she ever had before.

49:22-23 Signal to the Peoples

An explanation for the return of Zion's children follows in 49:22-23 and 24-26. The explanation begins with a messenger formula followed by a demonstrative particle (*See,* NIV). The nations and peoples, among whom Zion's sons and daughters live, release them at a signal from the Lord and bring them to Zion (49:22). The Lord's *hand* and *signal* indicate his authority to command the attention of the nations (cf. 11:10-12). It is not possible to know the precise meaning of these indicators. By them the peoples understand that the Lord is the power behind his people's restoration (cf. Brueggemann, 1998b:118).

The next stanza indicates that Zion's redemption has a broader purpose (49:23). *I* and *me* at the end of 49:23 correspond to *I* and *my* at the beginning of 49:22. The Lord's authority and integrity are unimpeachable. The sons and daughters of Zion (*you*) will know the Lord because he has gathered them out of their dispersion. But beyond this, the nations and peoples who put their hope in the Lord will be glad they did so. The conventional language of nations groveling in subservience to Zion indicates the rescinding of their power (Mic 7:16-17; Ps 72:9;

cf. Hanson: 134). The broader purpose of this submission does not lie in Zion's significance as such. It lies in the recognition of Zion's significance as the place where the Lord's law is taught (Isa 2:3).

49:24-26 Savior Who Saves

As earlier, Zion doubts the Lord's integrity (49:24; cf. 49:14). Specifically, she questions the Lord's power to rescue the oppressed. There is a rhetorical question, here, that expects a negative answer. The Lord's word in reply, however, answers the question positively (49:25). The impossible will be accomplished because the Lord will do it (cf. Whybray: 147).

The reference to the oppressors' cannibalism reflects the horrors of warfare, although the reference may be metaphorical rather than literal (49:26). The main point, however, rests in the contrast between the oppressors eating *their own flesh* and the announcement that *all flesh* will come to know the liberating power of the *Mighty One of Jacob* [*Redemption, Redeemer, p. 448*].

THE TEXT IN BIBLICAL CONTEXT

Healing of Brokenness

The Great Commission in Matthew's Gospel (28:19) has its roots in the OT agenda of charting God's reign on a worldwide scale. The servant song in Isaiah 49 illustrates this agenda. The gathering and restoration of Jacob-Israel's fractured and dysfunctional kinfolk in Isaiah 49 implies a healing of what has been broken (cf. Roth: 139-42).

Jacob-Israel refers broadly to the ancestral history in the book of Genesis, beginning with Abraham and Sarah. Alienation and estrangement have pursued their descendants. The half brothers, Ishmael and Isaac, both sons of Abraham, were separated and sundered (Gen 21). The sons of Keturah, Abraham's wife, were sent away to the east (Gen 25). The twin sons of Isaac and Rebekah, Jacob and Esau, were alienated from each other (Gen 27). Jacob's sons turned against their brother Joseph (Gen 37).

The servant receives the mandate in Isaiah 49 to heal the alienation and separation of the past and to bring together again the descendants of Abraham and Sarah. Simeon's blessing of the child Jesus in Luke's Gospel draws on Isaiah 49:6 to emphasize this healing aspect of God's salvation (Luke 2:29-32). In Paul's defense before Agrippa in Caesarea, he appeals to Isaiah 49:6 to proclaim its fulfillment in Christ (Acts 26:23).

Jesus' commission to the eleven to "make disciples of all nations" includes the authority for healing and peacemaking granted to the servant of Isaiah (Matt 28:19; cf. 2 Cor 5:16–6:2, where Isa 49:8 is quoted).

Was There a Mission to the Gentiles?

Christian scholars often emphasize the servant's mission in Isaiah 49:6 as a universal mission to the larger Gentile world (cf. Hanson: 130-31; Childs: 385-86; et al.). The questions to ask here are questions of strategy. Is the servant's mission to offer restored Jacob-Israel *as an example* to the nations so that they will be drawn to Israel's faith? Or is the servant's mission *to be sent* to the nations with a message of salvation for the Gentiles?

Both strategies are represented in the book of Isaiah. Isaiah 2:1-5 provides an affirmative answer to the first question. There is no hint there of a mission to the nations. The *mountain of the LORD's house* is a "light" to which the nations come, seeking the Lord's teaching. Jacob's challenge is to walk *in the light of the LORD* (2:5). Isaiah 42:1-4 provides an affirmative answer to the second question. Here the servant is given the Lord's spirit in order to *bring justice to the nations* (NIV). The nations do not come to him; he is sent to them.

The narrative of Jesus' birth in Luke's Gospel includes Jesus' presentation in the temple (2:25-35). In Simeon's blessing, Luke includes words from Isaiah 49 and 52 to indicate that the early church understood these texts as a mandate to take the gospel beyond the frontiers of Israel.

In Acts 13 Luke tells about the missionary work of Paul and Barnabas at Antioch of Pisidia. At the synagogue in Antioch, they meet with strong opposition from the Jews. In this connection they quote Isaiah 49:6 as the warrant for turning to the Gentiles, thus turning from a mainly Jewish mission (Acts 13:47).

THE TEXT IN THE LIFE OF THE CHURCH
Reading the Good News

Since the fourth century the church has assigned particular texts of Scripture to be read at public worship on particular days (*ODCC*: 962-63). The church calls the collection of these texts *lectionaries*, from the Latin *lectio*, "reading." The church inherited the regular and disciplined reading of the Scriptures from its Jewish forebears.

Lectionaries have traditionally assigned Isaiah 49:1-7 to the Tuesday of Holy Week. The call and mission of the Lord's servant in Isaiah 49 brings to mind Jesus' journey to the cross. This is particularly true of 49:7, which the lectionaries have added to the second servant song for this purpose.

Isaiah 49:1-7 is also sometimes read on the second Sunday after Epiphany. The church understands the prophet's call to be a light to the nations as a prophecy fulfilled when the evidence of Jesus' birth became clear to the Magi. In Matthew's Gospel the Magi represent the Gentiles (nations) coming to the child born king of the Jews.

Isaiah 49:1-26

So the church has placed the fulfillment of Isaiah's prophecy in the narrative of Jesus' birth as well as in the account of events leading to his death. Isaiah's prophecy and especially the Servant Songs serve to annotate the course of Jesus' life.

Isaiah 50:1-11

Sustaining the Weary with a Word

PREVIEW

"Weariness" is a word that sometimes describes people in the peace movement. Swimming against the current of war making and weapons development without adequate spiritual resources will exact a heavy toll. This toll may be expressed in despair, hopelessness, despondency, rage.

The third of the Servant Songs of Isaiah is a study in spiritual resources in times of despair. In the song itself the servant reflects on the Lord's gift of speaking and listening as well as the Lord's help in a time of distress (50:4-9). The servant's nonviolence shines out as evidence of the Lord's will for his people.

In the preface to the song, the Lord addresses his people with the reality of his strength to save (50:1-3). The sequel to the song counsels God's people to fear the Lord and warns them about the consequences of walking only in their own light (50:10-11).

OUTLINE

The Lord's Strength to Save, 50:1-3
The Servant in Crisis, 50:4-9
    50:4-6   Gift of Speaking and Listening
    50:7-9   Help Under Affliction
Call to Faithfulness, 50:10-11

Isaiah 50:1-11

EXPLANATORY NOTES

The Lord's Strength to Save 50:1-3

A word of the Lord introduced by a messenger formula serves as a preface to the chapter (50:1-3). This word simulates a trial in which an accusation against the Lord is implied. In the trial the Lord defends himself against the accusation. This trial, although not closely connected to the servant song that follows, serves to prepare the ground for the song. That is, those who oppose the servant in the song itself are the very ones whose sins and transgressions are exposed in the preface.

The Lord sets the tone of the trial with two rhetorical questions [*Literary Perspective, p. 446*] addressed to the exiles (50:1a):

> *Where is your mother's certificate of divorce? . . .*
> *Or to which of my creditors did I sell you?* (NIV)

The first question indicates that the Lord did not divorce Jacob-Israel (your mother) when he sent her into exile (Knight: 143). The evidence—a certificate of divorce—is lacking. The second question indicates that the Lord did not sell Jacob-Israel. If there was a sale, there would be creditors being satisfied.

The rhetorical questions receive further explanation in the stanza that follows (50:1b-2a). The absence of creditors indicates that there was no financial transaction. Rather, there was a moral transaction in which Jacob-Israel reaped the consequences of her own sins. Whybray says that there was no sale but only a temporary delivery of Jacob-Israel to the Babylonians (149). The absence of a certificate of divorce indicates that there was no divorce but only a separation. The point at issue, however, is who bears responsibility for this difficult situation. Was it God's fault that his people went into exile? Or does fault lie with Jacob-Israel's rebellion? The fault lies with Jacob-Israel. God's coming and calling may be understood to refer to the prophets, warning and calling to repentance but without response (cf. Jer 25:3-7).

Two rhetorical questions close the stanza:

> *Was my arm too short to ransom you?*
> *Do I lack the strength to rescue you?* (NIV)

Both questions require negative answers. The idiom about the Lord's hand not being too short recalls the Lord's hand outstretched to bring the Israelites out of Egypt (Deut 7:19; cf. Brueggemann, 1998b:120-21). The reference to the Lord's strength reminds the reader not only that the

Lord has strength to save but also that he gives strength to those who wait for him (Isa 40:27-31).

The final stanza illustrates the Lord's power to redeem (50:2b-3). Four verbs (NIV: *dry up, turn, clothe,* and *make*) reply to the four rhetorical questions at the end of the first two stanzas (Brueggemann, 1998b:121). The reference to the sea drying up points to the Lord's power on behalf of the Israelites, especially at the exodus from Egypt (Exod 14:21-22; cf. Pss 66:6; 106:9). Turning rivers into desert refers to the Lord's power over nature more generally (cf. Nah 1:4). The dying and rotting fish recalls the first plague in Egypt (Exod 7:20-24). Clothing the heavens with darkness recalls the ninth plague (Exod 10:21-23). The making of sackcloth to cover the heavens emphasizes the darkness of the ninth plague. Childs is correct in seeing the imagery of God's judgment on Egypt later falling on Jacob-Israel (394).

The Servant in Crisis 50:4-9

The third servant song consists of two parts. The first part centers attention on the servant's gifts of speaking and listening (50:4-6). The second part emphasizes the Lord giving help to the servant (50:7-9).

The word *servant* does not appear in the third song. Nevertheless scholars agree that this song belongs with the other Servant Songs (Watts, 1987:117). In the third song the servant reflects on the Lord's endorsement of his nonviolent behavior.

50:4-6 Gift of Speaking and Listening

The song begins with the servant's testimony to the Lord's gift of speech and listening (50:4). The gift of speech has the particular goal of encouraging those who are exhausted. This oblique reference to the exiles in Babylon gives further detail to the servant's commission in the first two Servant Songs. The critical question in this stanza is the rendering of the twice-occurring Hebrew adjective *limmudim* (lit., *those who are taught,* NRSV footnote). Both students and teachers qualify *as those who are taught.* Among the qualities of students and teachers is constructive speech and attentive listening. Here the Lord gives both to his servant.

The song continues with the servant's testimony to the practical results of his openness to the Lord's word (50:5-6). Four verbs highlight these results. The first two affirm the servant's submission when the Lord spoke (50:5):

> . . . I was not rebellious,
> I did not turn backward.

These verbs indicate that the servant listened carefully to the Lord and did not rebel against him.

The last two verbs show a second result of the servant's obedience. When his enemies mocked and abused him, he followed a strategy of nonviolence growing out of his submission to the Lord (50:6):

> *I gave my back, . . . my cheeks; . . .*
> *I did not hide my face. . . .*

The servant ran the gauntlet of violence and outrage. A political strategy of nonviolence grew out of a spirituality that was open to the Lord's will and way.

50:7-9 Help Under Affliction

The second part of the song emphasizes the Lord's giving help to the servant. The Lord's help comes in the form of a shield against humiliation (50:7-8a). The purveyors of violence offer insults, but the servant remains untouched by them. The expression *to set my face like a flint* indicates a determination to follow a course of action. The Lord's word not to offer violence in exchange for violence becomes a pillar of the servant's life. Although his enemies treat his nonviolence as shameful, he knows that he stands in the Lord's will. *He who vindicates* translates a Hebrew participle based on the verb ṣadaq (*to be just*). The Lord's help and the Lord's justice surround the servant with confidence.

A four-line stanza incorporates two confident questions and two bold replies (50:8b):

> *Who then will bring charges against me?*
>   *Let us face each other!*
> *Who is my accuser?*
>   *Let him confront me!* (50:8 NIV)

The servant's nonviolent courage is such that he can challenge his opponents to bring their case against him into a courtroom.

The final stanza puts the finishing touches on the challenge (50:9). The servant does not bear the guilt of violence. His nonviolence grows out of the spirituality of the Lord's help. The comparison of his opponents to a moth-eaten and worn-out garment stands in contrast to the servant's resolution to stand firm against the insults of the violent. Rather than demanding vengeance on his enemies, the servant speaks with self-assurance that the Lord's goals will survive all human attempts to subvert them (cf. Whybray: 152).

Call to Faithfulness 50:10-11

The song itself does not refer to the servant, but the servant is mentioned in the sequel to the song. At the beginning of the sequel, the speaker is no longer the servant but the prophet himself.

A question of exhortation opens the first stanza (50:10). The prophet exhorts the exiles (*you* pl.) to trust in the Lord. This trust in the Lord cannot be separated from listening to what the Lord's servant says. The *voice of his servant* calls attention to the servant's *instructed tongue* in 50:4 (NIV). The servant's voice does not differ from the Lord's purpose. So the servant calls those who walk in darkness to depend on the Lord.

Those who do not depend on the Lord are referred to as *firebrands* (50:11). In this stanza words of fire and burning dominate the first four lines. The word for firebrand (*zeq*) is used only here (twice) and in Proverbs 26:18. In Proverbs it refers to a *madman* (NIV) using lethal weapons against a neighbor and calling it a joke. Here *firebrands* are people who see violence as a source of strength and protection.

The twofold use of the verb *walk* provides the clue to the meaning of the passage as a whole. Those who walk in darkness may yet rely on God to bring them to safety (50:10). But those who walk in the light of their own fires will be burned from the heat (50:11).

THE TEXT IN BIBLICAL CONTEXT

Is Anything Too Hard for the Lord?

Two rhetorical questions in Isaiah 50:2 express the conviction that nothing is too hard for the Lord:

> *Was my arm too short to ransom you?*
> *Do I lack the strength to rescue you?* (NIV)

This conviction surfaces at several points in the Bible. In Genesis, Abraham and Sarah entertain three divine visitors, who announce that Sarah will have a son in her old age. When Sarah, taken aback by such a rash statement, laughs at the prospect, one of the visitors says to Abraham, "Is anything too hard for the LORD?" (18:14 NIV). As in Isaiah 50, God's power is affirmed in the face of tangible doubt.

In a prayer at the time of the Babylonian siege of Jerusalem, Jeremiah doubts the Lord's instruction to buy a field even as he confesses, "Nothing is too hard for [the LORD]" (32:17 NIV). Martens notes the language of the Lord's outstretched arm in this passage as signifying his power (202). In his reply to Jeremiah, the Lord repeats Jeremiah's confession but in the form of a rhetorical question (32:27).

Isaiah 50:1-11

The NT echoes this theme of God's power to save in response to reasonable doubt. At the annunciation, in Luke's birth narrative, Mary asks, "How can this be . . . ?" (1:34). At the end of the angel's reply to her, he says, "Nothing is impossible with God" (1:37 NIV).

When Jesus' disciples express disbelief that anyone might qualify for entrance into the kingdom of heaven, Jesus says, "For God all things are possible" (Mark 10:27; cf. Matt 19:26; Luke 18:27). When Jesus is facing his death, he is deeply grieved and agitated. His prayer in the garden of Gethsemane is that God would take the cup of suffering from him. He knows that God is able to do this as he prays, "For you all things are possible" (Mark 14:36).

THE TEXT IN THE LIFE OF THE CHURCH

Renouncing Retaliation in Kind

The preface to the second part of the *Martyrs Mirror* refers to the prophet Isaiah, who "lamented already in his time that he who departed from evil had to be everyone's prey and derision" (357). This reference does not identify the servant's testimony in Isaiah 50, but it seems to have this and other parts of the book in mind.

The *Martyrs Mirror* gives the testimony of a minority view in the Christian tradition. This testimony, with its roots in the OT and its stem in the NT, argues that retaliation in kind violates fundamental tenets of the Judeo-Christian belief system. In the OT these tenets include God's creation of humankind in his image and, in the Ten Commandments, the sixth commandment's prohibition of killing. In the NT the life and teaching of Jesus in particular calls for a renunciation of violence even at the risk of suffering.

The Christian Church, especially since the fourth century, has found various ways to circumvent the Bible's teaching on nonretaliation in kind. An important spokesperson in the twentieth century for this circumvention was Reinhold Niebuhr. Niebuhr argued that because of the weight of human sin, Jesus' call to nonretaliation in kind remains an impossible ideal (see the summary of Niebuhr's argument in Macgregor: 117-26).

Soon after the American-British bombing of Afghanistan in the fall of 2001, the managing editor of *Christianity Today* (in the October 22, 2001, issue) revived Niebuhr's argument for use in the twenty-first century. Niebuhr's argument continues to enable the church to steer clear of Jesus' teaching on nonretaliation.

ISAIAH 51:1-23

The Lord Will Comfort Zion

PREVIEW

The command to listen in 51:1 opens a new subject, as it does elsewhere in Isaiah 40–66 (cf. 44:1; 48:1, 12; 55:2, 3; 66:5). The previous chapter ends by asking, *Who among you* (pl.) *fears the LORD* (50:10)? Chapter 51 begins by addressing *you* (pl.) . . . *who seek the LORD* (NIV).

The first part of the chapter (51:1-16) abounds in imperative verbs. The command to listen introduces each of the first three sections (51:1-3, 4-6, 7-8). A doubling of the command to awake opens the fourth section (51:9-11). A doubling of the pronoun I announces the fifth section (51:12-16). The people's comfort throughout is based on the Lord's impending and unending salvation and righteousness.

The second part (51:17-23) begins with another doubling of imperatives: *Awake, awake!* (NIV). Now, however, the subject shifts from comfort to a celebration of Jerusalem's release from bondage. The doubling of imperatives gives emphasis to the commands (cf. GKC, sec. 110: 324-26). There is an urgency in the address to the Lord (51:9) and to Jerusalem (51:17) that permeates the last three parts of the book of Isaiah (chaps. 40–48, 49–57, 58–66). God is urged to act on behalf of his people. God's people are urged, in turn, to wake up to the good news of deliverance.

Isaiah 51:1-23

OUTLINE

Comforting the Lord's People, 51:1-16
    51:1-3   Tidings of Comfort and Joy
    51:4-6   Everlasting Salvation
    51:7-8   Righteousness and Salvation
    51:9-11   Old Exodus, New Exodus
    51:12-16   Fear and Forgetfulness
Loosening the Bonds of Oppression, 51:17-23
    51:17-20   Jerusalem Receives the Cup
    51:21-23   Jerusalem's Enemies Receive the Cup

EXPLANATORY NOTES

Comforting the Lord's People 51:1-16

Each of the first three parts of this section begins with an imperative form of the verb *to listen* or *to pay attention* (51:1-3, 4-6, 7-8). In each case the addressee is Israel in exile, called by the Lord to accept his comfort.

In the fourth part Israel in exile addresses the Lord, calling the Lord to exercise strength to rescue his people (51:9-11). The Lord addresses his people again in the last part (51:12-16). There the Lord challenges his people to place the truth of his power ahead of the reality of their fear.

51:1-3 Tidings of Comfort and Joy

The Lord's summons to listen addresses a people with the twin calling of pursuing righteousness and seeking the Lord (51:1). It comes as no surprise that pursuing righteousness and seeking the Lord belong together. Pursuing righteousness means living one's material life according to the Lord's instruction. Seeking the Lord means cultivating a spiritual life of worship and prayer. Both are centered in God's salvation. The invitation to look to the rock and to the quarry holds a clue to the next stanza.

The imperative *Look* opens the second stanza (51:2). Abraham and Sarah represent the rock and quarry alluded to in the first stanza. When the Lord's promise came to Abraham in Genesis 12:1-3, he was few in number and of no consequence in the political life of his day. He was *but one*, a single drop in the sea of humanity. By the Lord's blessing he became numerous. The point here is that God will fulfill his promise to the exiles as he did to Abraham and Sarah.

The third stanza translates summons into promise (51:3). The comfort of Zion recalls Isaiah 40:1. Brueggemann notes that to "comfort is to make new life possible" (1998b:126). For the exiles *comfort* meant that the Lord would restore Zion so that Zion would again experience joy beyond the pain of exile.

51:4-6 Everlasting Salvation

The Lord's summons to pay attention to his law and justice opens the next sequence of stanzas (51:4, 5, 6). The Lord's law proceeds from him (51:4). This law is the Lord's instruction; it portrays the Lord's justice (cf. Isa 2:3). The Lord's teaching and justice, then, are intended to enlighten earth's peoples. Scholars often note the similarity of the first servant song in 42:1-4 to 51:4-6, although the servant is not mentioned here.

The reference to *my people*, *my nation*, and *my justice* in the first stanza should be compared to *my righteousness*, *my salvation*, and *my arm* (NIV) in the second stanza (51:5). The emphasis on the Lord's power to be a light to earth's peoples is cumulative. The Lord's purpose now embraces peoples and coastlands, representing the whole earth, as in the second servant song (49:1-6).

Three illustrations capture the reader's attention in the third stanza: *smoke*, *a garment*, and *gnats*, or *flies* (NIV; 51:6). These illustrations depict the transience of material creation in order to elevate the Lord's everlasting purpose (cf. Whybray: 156). That air and sky will vanish like smoke indicates their fleeting character compared to the Lord's endurance. Likewise earth's impermanence lies in contrast to the Lord's constancy. And death remains the lot of earthlings, people and pest alike. But the Lord's salvation and righteousness (NIV) remain when all else fails.

51:7-8 Righteousness and Salvation

The Lord addresses Israel in exile with a third summons to *listen* (51:7). This summons is similar to the first one in 51:1. Now, however, the Lord's teaching in their hearts means that they can withstand the taunts and defamation of their enemies, whether fellow exiles or Babylonians. The call for confident courage in the face of torment is a common theme in the biblical story. The basis for courage lies in a firmly rooted spirituality and not simply in firmly resolved self-will.

As in 51:3 the final stanza commences with the conjunction *for* (51:8). An image of fabric consumed by a moth gives a graphic illustration of the fate of those who taunt and revile God's people. The stanza closes on the Lord's declaration of the infinity of his righteousness and salvation (cf. 51:6, 8). Knight is correct in noting that the Lord's transcendence is expressed in terms of time (living eternally) rather than in terms of space (dwelling outside the universe) (154).

51:9-11 Old Exodus, New Exodus

Isaiah 51:9 begins a sequence of passages in which a doubling of opening words occurs (51:12, 17; 52:1, 11). Here the words *Awake, awake* introduce a prayer that addresses the *arm of the LORD*, a reference to the Lord's strength (cf. 51:5). The prayer appeals to the past, when the Lord scuttled the sea's infamous dragon (cf. Isa 27:1; Pss 74:14; 89:10; Job 26:12). The Lord is understood to be victorious over Rahab the dragon in an ancient Near Eastern mythological battle (see TBC below, "Mythology and the OT").

The second stanza of the prayer speaks to the Israelite experience of the Lord's miracle at the sea (51:10). As in the previous stanza, so here the question addressed to the Lord serves as an affirmation of faith. Of course it was the Lord who vanquished Rahab! Of course it was the Lord who dried up the sea! The purpose of the miracle was to give the exodus Israelites a safe passage out of Egypt.

Now in the prayer, this safe passage receives a new explanation as a promise to the exiles in Babylon (51:11). The anticipation of a second exodus creates an immense outpouring of joy at the conclusion of the prayer (cf. Brueggemann, 1998b:130).

51:12-16 Fear and Forgetfulness

The first person pronoun *I* is doubled as the first stanza opens, lending emphasis to the Lord's speech (51:12-13a). Here the Lord speaks with an assurance of comfort, as in 51:3. He addresses Israel as *you* (pl.), a collective of individuals to whom the Lord speaks comfort individually (cf. Knight: 149, 155). If the word of assurance has taken root, why do *you* (sg.) continue to fear? The singular form of the pronoun *you* in 51:12-16 refers to Israel as a corporate structure, made up of individuals responsible to each other (cf. Knight: 155). The answer lies in the people's inclination to forget the Lord's power in creation, power shared with his people. When this power is remembered, fear can be mastered. Even though people forget God, God does not forget them.

The source of the people's fear—the oppressor's rage—emerges in the next stanza (51:13b-14). Reference to the *oppressed* prepares the reader for a later elaboration of being loosed from that oppression (51:17-23). The promise of release from oppression does not discount the real aftermath of an oppressor's rage. This may include suffering and death. The question at the center of the stanza, *But where is the fury of the oppressor?* (51:13), implies that it is nowhere. This does not mean that it does not exist but rather that it exists in an unfavorable relationship to the Lord's comfort.

The antidote to fear becomes clear in the last stanza (51:15-16). The reference to the sea recalls the confession of the Lord's power over the sea in 51:9 and 10. This power serves to illustrate God's power over the oppressor and over fear inspired by oppression.

The first two lines of 51:16 are often taken to be out of place (Whybray: 161). There is no compelling reason to agree with this assessment. Employing imagery similar to that addressed to the servant in 49:2-3, the Lord now addresses his people with the same promise of words to speak and protection from enemies. In 49:3 the Lord says, *You are my servant . . .* ('abdi-'attah). Here the Lord says, *You are my people* ('ammi-'attah). The people who receive the servant's call also accept the servant's commission to rehabilitate Jacob-Israel and to be *a light to the nations* (Childs: 404-05).

Loosening the Bonds of Oppression 51:17-23

Another double imperative opens the second section (see 51:9). These imperatives focus on a new future for Jerusalem.

51:17-20 Jerusalem Receives the Cup

The section opens with a picture of Jerusalem under judgment. A stirring call to wake up from the listless repose brought on by suffering comprises the first stanza (51:17). Just as a person may drink from a goblet of wine, so Jerusalem is pictured as drinking the wine of God's wrath. The resulting suffering is deserved. The image of the Lord's cup of wrath appears elsewhere in the prophets (see esp. Jer 25; Ezek 23) and once in Lamentations (4:21). In the Lamentations passage the cup passes from Jerusalem to her foes.

The second stanza describes Jerusalem as leaderless (51:18). Intoxicated by the cup of the Lord's wrath, Jerusalem's children stand helplessly by.

Now the prophet addresses Jerusalem with two consequences of her faithlessness (51:19). The consequences are presented in pairs: *ruin and destruction*, and *famine and sword* (NIV). The first pair describes the material destruction of the means of production. The second pair describes the loss of human life. Each of the two questions, *Who can comfort you?* and *Who can console you?* (NIV), implies a negative answer.

The final stanza paints a picture of Jerusalem's utter desolation (51:20). In the first stanza Jerusalem has emptied the Lord's cup of wrath (51:17). Here Jerusalem's children are full of the Lord's wrath and lying under God's rebuke. They have arrived at the low watermark in their course of life (cf. Knight: 158).

51:21-23 Jerusalem's Enemies Receive the Cup

The adverb *therefore* introduces a renewed address to Jerusalem, the *afflicted one* (51:21-22a NIV). Simple drunkenness is bad enough; the drunkenness of deserved suffering is worse. Yet the renewed address to Jerusalem now includes a word of the Lord defending his people. In Jerusalem's darkest hour, the Lord comes to his people's aid (cf. Knight: 158).

The interjection *See!* introduces a new stanza, confirming this aid (51:22b). The Lord's word in 51:22b reverses the description of 51:17 and removes the cup. My translation (below) preserves the line order of the Hebrew text (note the repetition of words in italics):

> [17]you [f. sg.] who have *drunk* from the *hand* of the Lord
> *the cup of his wrath,*
> *the bowl-shaped cup of reeling*;
> you [f. sg.] have *drunk* [it] to the dregs.
> [22]See! I have taken from your [f. sg.] *hand*
> *the cup of reeling,*
> *the bowl-shaped cup of my wrath*;
> you [f. sg.] shall *drink* [it] no longer.

The feminine singular pronouns address Jerusalem as a woman in much the same way that we use a feminine pronoun for a modern city.

The concluding stanza completes the picture of the cup of wrath (51:23). The Lord will put the cup into the hands of Jerusalem's tormentors. The Hebrew verb underlying the noun *tormentors* means *to suffer*. Tormentors are those who cause suffering. Here they are the Babylonians, acting out the orders of the Babylonian Empire. Those who walked on (Heb. *passed over*) the backs of the Judean exiles are now made to drink the cup of the Lord's wrath.

THE TEXT IN BIBLICAL CONTEXT

Mythology and the Old Testament

The Hebrew Bible takes mythological language such as that in Isaiah 51:9 and redefines it for its own purposes (cf. Childs: 403-4). Having said this, it is important to offer a definition of "mythology" before suggesting its redefinition in the OT.

The terms "myth" and "mythology" are a subject of debate among scholars. The noun "myth" is derived from the Greek *mythos*, "story." Sometimes "myth" is defined simply as "a story having to do with supernormal (often supernatural) persons, objects, or events" (Noss: 27). At other times "myth" has the more narrow purpose of legitimizing "tribal traditions, rituals, and sacred sites" (27). The NT employs the term five times in the pastoral letters and general epistles (1 Tim 1:4; 4:7; 2 Tim 4:4; Titus 1:14; 2 Pet 1:16), always portraying it as a misrepresentation of truth.

The OT does not denounce mythological language, but neither does it assimilate mythological language without redefining it. The reference to the dissection of Rahab and the piercing of the dragon in Isaiah 51:9 has echoes of the mythological combat between Tiamat and Marduk in the Babylonian *Creation Epic* (ANET: 67) and between Baal and Yamm in the Ugaritic *Poems about Baal and Anath* (ANET: 130-31). But in Isaiah 51:9, as elsewhere in the OT, ancient Near Eastern myth and mythological language are subordinated to the Lord's power in history (cf. Weiser: 57-59).

Isaiah 51:9-11 serves as a paradigm, therefore, of the OT's approach to mythological language. The Lord's power over the dragon of ancient Near Eastern myth is the prophet's point of departure (51:9). Then, instead of rehearsing the myth, the prophet offers its theological meaning in terms of Israel's redemption at the sea (51:10). Finally, the outcome of this redemption lies in a new people of God experiencing *everlasting joy* (51:11; cf. Knight: 154-55; Childs: 403-4).

THE TEXT IN THE LIFE OF THE CHURCH

Ideological Persuasion

In Isaiah 51:13 the prophet, speaking the Lord's word, asks *But where is the fury of the oppressor?* In its history, the church at various times has had to face the fury of the oppressor. The book of Revelation refers to persecution, probably during the rule of Domitian, due to refusal by early Christians to worship the Emperor (Rev 13). The early church faced intermittent persecution under Roman rule during its first three centuries (*ODCC*: 1257-59).

After the church became closely allied with the state in the fourth century, the church began its own persecution, especially of those in its own household who offered alternative views of faith. Augustine in the late fourth and early fifth centuries demanded physical punishment for dissenters. During the Middle Ages dissenters were deemed a threat to the underpinnings of society. The common punishment for dissent was death (*ODCC*: 1629).

The *Martyrs Mirror* provides an account of Christians who suffered for their faith. The first part consists of a chronicle of persecution and martyrdom during the first fifteen centuries of church history. A chronicle of persecution and martyrdom in the sixteenth century and up to 1660 makes up the second part. During the Reformation, Anabaptists and other dissenters received cruel punishment at the hands of Protestants and Catholics alike.

For the church in the twenty-first century, the issue is less one of toleration of religious dissent than the nourishing of religious belief in light of the secularization of life (*ODCC*: 1630). Walter Brueggemann observes that the church in the Western world finds it difficult to grasp the imagery of an oppressor. This does not mean that none exists, but the idea of an oppressor needs to be understood in terms of ideologies that enslave people. He names two such ideologies that seduce Christians and the church away from the gospel: the *market ideology of autonomy* and the *state ideology of conformity* (1998b:131). As Jim Wallis notes in his book *The Call to Conversion*, the threat to the church in the Western world is not persecution but seduction (117).

Isaiah 52:1–53:12

Crown Prince of God's Kingdom

PREVIEW

The power and influence of Isaiah 52:1–53:12 on the writers of the NT is well known. At least twenty-five NT passages (7 direct quotations and 18 probable allusions) reflect this impact, especially the impact of the servant song in Isaiah 52:13–53:12.

The immediate context of the servant song is Isaiah 52:1-12. Here Zion-Jerusalem is inspired to fulfill the announcement of consolation made in 40:1-2a (cf. Watts, 1987:217-18). The transition from 52:1-12 to 52:13–53:12 is not seamless. The two parts belong together on the order of similar fabrics with contrasting patterns in adjacent quilt blocks. The similar fabrics refer to the correspondence of language between the two parts (cf. *taken away* in 52:5; 53:8; and *my people* in 52:4, 5, 6; 53:8). The contrasting patterns refers to the shift of mood from 52:12 to 52:13.

Isaiah 52:13–53:12 is the fourth and last of the Servant Songs of Isaiah. This song begins with the Lord speaking about his servant. He speaks of this servant in terms suggesting royalty, the figure of a crown prince (52:13-15). Nations and kings are startled and stunned at the demeanor and disfigurement of this crown prince. Here is something new and bewildering.

A *we* passage follows in which kings and nations wonder aloud whether their testimony will be accepted (53:1-6). They understand the servant's suffering as somehow related to their rebellion, but they have no clear sense of guilt on their part.

Something like a theological interpretation of the servant's death follows the we passage (53:7-10). The prophet himself may be speaking here, explaining the death of the crown prince in God's larger design.

The Lord speaks again at the end of the song (53:11-12). The servant's life is summed up as an offering for sin, nothing more, nothing less.

OUTLINE

Messenger of Salvation, 52:1-12
    52:1-2   Jerusalem Freed of Chains
    52:3-6   Knowing the Lord's Name
    52:7-12   Salvation for Jerusalem
Servant Song, 52:13–53:12
    52:13-15   Demeanor and Disfigurement
    53:1-6   The Servant's Suffering
    53:7-10   The Servant's Death
    53:11-12   Bearing the Sins of Many

EXPLANATORY NOTES

Messenger of Salvation 52:1-12

52:1-2 Jerusalem Freed of Chains

A double command *Awake, awake!* opens the first stanza (52:1). This double command addressed to Zion-Jerusalem is the same verb used to demand the Lord's awakening in 51:9. Alongside the double command to awake comes the double command to *put on* garments of strength and splendor. These commands rally Israel in exile to wake up and see the demise of their captors (cf. Brueggemann, 1998b:136). The *uncircumcised* and the *unclean* refer to those who are ritually unclean, here probably the Babylonians.

A second series of commands inspires Jerusalem-Zion to take the first steps toward liberation by throwing off the bonds of captivity (52:2). Jerusalem's release has been achieved by the Lord (51:21-23). Now it is Jerusalem's turn to act, letting the Lord's strength become her strength (Hanson: 148). *Loose the bonds* does not mean to engage in revolt but rather to undo the psychological chains of bondage (cf. Brueggemann, 1998b:136).

52:3-6 Knowing the Lord's Name

Two words from the Lord, each introduced with a messenger formula, give credence to the commands just issued. The NRSV displays

52:3-6 in a prose format, but there is no convincing reason why these verses should not be presented poetically (cf. NIV).

In the first word, the Lord mentions the bondage from which Zion-Jerusalem will be retrieved (52:3). That she was sold *for nothing* (*ḥinnam*) indicates that Judah went into exile because of conquest. The Lord did not sell her into slavery. The Lord did not sell her for a profit. As a consequence, her redemption will be achieved without a monetary payment (Watts, 1987:216). The purpose of the exile was to discipline God's people.

The second stanza presents another word of the Lord, which does not address God's people but tells about their history of bondage, first in Egypt and later in Assyria (52:4). The expression *without cause* (Heb. *be'epes*) seems to contradict what is said in Isaiah 10:5-6 and elsewhere. Perhaps *without cause* means that the oppression exceeded what the Assyrians were authorized to do.

Two uses of the phrase *says the LORD* (NRSV) punctuate the third stanza (52:5). The first follows a question that reads literally, *And now what to me here?* (*And now what do I have here?* NIV). *Here* refers to Babylon, where the Judean exiles remain in captivity (Whybray: 166). The adverb for *nothing* (*ḥinnam*) echoes the same adverb in 52:3. Both reflect the purpose of discipline to bring about repentance. The howling (Heb. *yll*) of rulers suggests the Babylonian oppressors (cf. Brueggemann, 1998b:137). One of the realities of the exile was the contempt heaped on the Lord's name.

Two uses of the adverb *therefore* usher in the final stanza (52:6). Because of the oppression experienced by God's people (52:4) and in spite of the mockery of her oppressors (52:5), God's people will recognize the Lord as one who speaks. A similar reference to the Lord who identifies himself (*It is I*) and who speaks occurs in 48:12-16. God's self-disclosure constitutes evidence for God's people to know his name.

52:7-12 Salvation for Jerusalem

Scholars note the connections between this passage and the prologue of announcement in 40:1-11 (esp. 40:9-11; cf. Whybray: 167). Like the prologue, this passage reads like a vision in that there is a seeing (*r'h*) of the Lord's coming and of God's salvation (52:8, 10; cf. 40:5).

The first stanza focuses on messenger and message (52:7). The messenger remains anonymous but clearly is the bearer of good news (cf. 40:9). The good news of peace and salvation refers to the bursting in of the reign of God (Childs: 405). The message states a recurring confession of faith in God's kingship in ancient Israel. Here is the heart of ancient Israelite spirituality. The declaration *Your God reigns* means that the God of Israel controls history and the forces of nature. This is good news in Israel's immediate situation because it means that there are limits to exile and punishment. It is also good news in a universal sense because it offers humankind, along with Israel, a foundation for salvation and peace on earth.

The second stanza pictures sentinels awaiting the messenger's arrival (52:8). They give a ringing cry when they see the Lord's return to Zion [*Zion, p. 457*. What does this part of the vision mean? The prophet perceives that the Lord's presence in Zion has, until now, been restricted. The banishment of the people in exile and the withdrawal of the temple vessels indicate this restriction. The lifting of the restriction, therefore, occurs when news arrives of the impending return of temple vessels and long-lost exiles. It is not as if the Lord is limited by time and space, but that the Lord's presence is recognized in the presence of his people and the temple artifacts.

First the sentinels give a ringing cry; now the ruins of Jerusalem are instructed to give a ringing cry (52:9). Since the Babylonian destruction of Jerusalem in 587 BC, the city has lain in ruins. The *ruins of Jerusalem* may also refer to residents of the city despairing of a future (cf. Brueggemann, 1998b:139). They also are part of the redemption story. In his vision the prophet sees these ruins breaking into a song of joy because of the Lord's renewed presence in the city. The word *comfort*, as in 51:3 and 40:1, means to make new life possible for God's people. The comfort of God's people and the redemption of Jerusalem appear in parallel lines.

Isaiah 52:9-10 serves as a two-stanza praise hymn. The call to worship at the beginning of 52:9 gives way to the motive for worship in 52:10. The baring of the Lord's holy arm (a metaphor of power) before the nations indicates that Jerusalem's salvation is a public event. The Lord discloses himself to the nations through his redemption of his people.

The concluding stanzas recall the beginning of the chapter (52:1-2; cf. Childs: 406-07). There it is Zion-Jerusalem who is instructed with a double imperative to *Awake, awake!*. Here a double imperative *Depart, depart!* instructs the exiles to vacate the city and country of their exile. The instruction addresses in particular those who carry the emblems of the Lord's presence (52:11). They are to observe the purity rituals associated with those emblems.

Like the old exodus from Egypt, the Lord goes before (Exod 13:22) and behind the people (14:19) in the new exodus from Babylon (Isa 52:12). Unlike the old exodus with the Hebrews leaving in haste ahead of the pursuing Egyptians, however, the new exodus does not take place in haste. The initiator of the new exodus authorizes the exiles to go. The Lord's protection assures them that they are safe.

Servant Song 52:13–53:12

The beginning and end of the fourth servant song indicate that through the servant's witness the nations will see the power of nonviolence, which undergirds God's reign and is the condition for peace on earth (52:13-15; 53:11-12). The description of the servant's suffering and death occupies the center of the song. This suffering and death illustrate the power of one person, solidly obedient to God's will, inspiring future generations to faithfulness (53:1-10).

52:13-15 Demeanor and Disfigurement

Two contrasting impressions etch themselves on the reader's consciousness at the beginning of the song: the servant's demeanor and the servant's disfigurement. By *demeanor* I mean the outward manner in which the servant bears himself in the face of aggression and brutality. The Lord's word, spoken by the prophet, presents the servant's demeanor in terms of prosperity and dignity (52:13). The meaning of the Hebrew verb *śakal* (*prosper; act wisely,* NIV) is *to have insight* or *to have success.* Such is the demeanor of royalty. So kings and nations are astonished that a mere servant should exhibit prosperity and dignity. Nevertheless the reader is invited to interpret the song with the servant's demeanor in mind.

The disfigurement provides an image, a preview really, of what the servant experienced under due process (52:14-15). Kings and nations express surprise at the sight of the Lord's servant disfigured yet resolute. His mission to the nations rests on the shock effect of a royal figure submitting to suffering rather than inflicting it. Kings and nations represent the sentinels of law and justice. What they see and understand, however, shocks them into silence (52:15). They are shocked because they realize that in this disfigured servant lies the power of God to bring healing and forgiveness and reconciliation to the world (cf. Hanson: 154-55). But does this new awareness lead to behavior characterized by a change of heart? The history of kings and nations suggests otherwise.

53:1-6 The Servant's Suffering

The *we* section of the fourth song portrays the suffering of the Lord's servant as perceived by a collective voice (53:1-6). Who might this be? The answer is not obvious. Two possibilities present themselves in 52:13-15. One is the *many who were appalled* (52:14 NIV), which may be an oblique reference to Israel's collective voice. The second is the *many nations* and *kings* in Israel's peripheral vision (52:15). They would be attentive to the growth and development of a royal figure. At the same time they would be shocked by alternative behavior or appearance exhibited by such a royal figure.

The opening stanza expresses disbelief at the news of the servant's fate (53:1-2). The reason for this disbelief lies in the unpretentious and commonplace upbringing of the crown prince. In every way this person grew up among his peers as an equal, without distinction and without deference. There is no hint here of repulsiveness, only the absence of notable features that might have raised some eyebrows. The phrase *before him* in the expression *He grew up before him* indicates the servant's spiritual formation in the religious tradition of Israel's worship of the Lord. That formation has no remarkable features. Nevertheless it stands as a significant clue to the servant's remarkable strength of perseverance later on.

The disclosure of the servant's abuse begins in the second stanza (53:3). It may be asked whether the disclosure expresses "detached sympathy" (Berrigan: 147) or genuine regret. If it expresses genuine regret, there is no evidence in the song as a whole that regret has led to repentance, and repentance to transformation of life (cf. Berrigan: 148). The Hebrew nouns *mak'obot* and *ḥoli* are translated as *sorrows* and *suffering* in the 53:3 NIV. The noun *ḥoli* in particular may be translated *infirmity*, with the NRSV, referring to the outcome of abuse (cf. Whybray: 174).

The reference to *sorrows* and *infirmities* (NIV) is repeated in the third stanza in order to accent the servant's bearing of them (53:4). The adverb *surely* introduces a sobering thought. The verb *borne* (NRSV) is derived from the same Hebrew word as *lifted up* in 52:12. There the temple vessels are lifted up (carried). Here the collective voice asserts that the servant lifts up pain and disease in the sense of bearing them. The last two lines of the stanza provide a suggestion about the official view of God's punishment. Conventional theology had it that God was directly responsible for administering punishment for sin. But here it seems that God's servant took on himself others' diseases and pain caused by their own sin (Brueggemann, 1998b:145).

Now the collective voice adds *our* transgressions and *our* iniquities to the list of offenses borne by the servant (53:5). Both the NIV and the NRSV translate the Hebrew preposition *min* as *for* (*for our transgressions, for our iniquities*), indicating the servant's suffering as a substitute for the sin of God's people. It may be argued that the preposition *min* means *because of*, indicating the servant's suffering as a result of the sin of God's people (BDB: 580; cf. Whybray:175; also Watts,1987:231), but note that verses 4 and 6 suggest substitution.

The servant bears *the punishment that brought us peace* (53:5 NIV). Is this an indication that well-being (peace) often rests on injustice (punishment)? If so, then it may be said that the servant absorbs the grievances of those who suffer from injustice as well as the guilt of those whose peace rests on the fruit of injustice. Many people experience well-being because an innocent person or group has suffered unjustly. In such cases peace may be said to be ironic rather than genuine.

The *we* section closes with a stanza that gathers up what has been said into a brief summary (53:6). It is a confession of guilt to be sure. Following one's own path rather than paying attention to God's way is endemic in the Bible. Nevertheless the Lord is named as the one who bears responsibility for the servant's suffering. It is the Lord who lays the sin of God's people on his servant.

53:7-10 The Servant's Death

After the collective voice, an individual voice, perhaps the prophet himself, offers a theological explanation of the servant's death. The first stanza takes pains to point out the absence of protest on the servant's part (53:7). The closest comparison to the servant's silence in the face of abusive power and distressing anguish is the demeanor of sheep confronting slaughter. This silence complements the picture of God's people straying like sheep by their silence in the face of injustice (53:6).

The legal status of the servant's fate is emphasized in the second stanza (53:8). The NRSV translates the first line *By a perversion of justice he was taken away*. It would be better to translate this line *By coercion (me'oṣer) and by sentence (umimmišpaṭ) he was taken away*. As in the death of Christ, legality often rests on the power of the state to do as it pleases rather than on the moral basis of law. Being *cut off from the land of the living* almost certainly indicates a mortal wound to the servant, and being *stricken* has the sense of a paralyzing wound. Taken together, they speak of the servant's imminent death. The individual voice asserts that this disablement took place *for the transgression of my people* (or perhaps *because of the transgression*; cf. 53:5) [*Atonement, p. 439*].

The third stanza reports rather than describes the servant's death (53:9). The first two lines identify *the wicked* with *the rich*. The allusion to the servant's burial intends to place him among those who formed an alliance to ensure his death. The servant's nonviolence and truthfulness were the very qualities that threatened the wicked and the rich. Emending the text, as some translators do, to read *doers of evil* instead of *rich*, forming a more acceptable parallel with *the wicked*, is self-serving (cf. Smart: 212).

The fourth song emphasizes the "gift" of burial with evildoers: *He was assigned* [Heb. *given*] *a grave with the wicked* (53:9 NIV; cf. I. Friesen, 2003:72-73). The servant who is *given* the Lord's spirit to bring justice to the nations in 42:1 is here given a burial with evildoers, though he himself was no evildoer. Through it all, obedience to the Lord inspired the servant to accept suffering rather than inflict it. With obedience the servant followed the vision of God's reign, defying both worldly wisdom and human cowardice (Hanson: 160).

The Lord's resolve (*ḥapeṣ*) *to crush him and cause him to suffer* (53:10 NIV) is startling. The crushing indicates a mortal wound accompanied by suffering. The *offering for sin* (*guilt offering*, NIV) in the second line means, as in 53:4 and 12, a bearing of sin.

The point here is that at his own discretion the Lord accepted the life of the servant as the way of bringing forgiveness to Israel. The servant's suffering on behalf of others is critical to the prophet's message (Childs: 418). The move from suffering to exaltation occurs in the reference to offspring. Although there may be a hint of the servant's resurrection here, this is not clearly stated. But the servant does experience a reversal of fortune that results in seeing offspring and old age (Childs: 419). The last line in 53:10 indicates that through the servant's life, the Lord's resolve (*ḥepeṣ*) will flourish.

53:11-12 Bearing the Sins of Many

A final word from the Lord concludes the fourth servant song. First is an indication of the twofold intention of the Lord's servant: *to make many righteous* and *to bear their iniquities* (53:11). God works even through his people's rebellion to bring good out of evil intent.

Because of his servant's obedience, the Lord exalts him (53:12). Because the servant *poured out himself to death* rather than inflict death, he was able to bear the sin of all who call upon the Lord out of their rebellion.

THE TEXT IN BIBLICAL CONTEXT

The Reign of God

The announcement of the reign of God in Isaiah 52:7-12 takes up a theme found elsewhere in the OT. In the book of Isaiah itself, the theme finds expression in the temple vision of chapter 6.

The Song of Moses in Exodus 15 concludes with a ringing cry that "The Lord will reign forever and ever" (v. 18). In the triumph of the miracle at the sea, Moses and the Israelites celebrated the reign of God as a standard for their life together. During the period of the judges, therefore, Gideon rejected the offer of kingship because he believed that the Lord alone was to rule over Israel (Judg 8:23). Samuel understood the demand for a king to govern Israel as a rejection of the Lord as king (1 Sam 8:7).

The Psalter includes a number of praise hymns celebrating God's reign (47, 66, 93, 96, 97, 99, 103, 146). The praise hymns exalt God for his majesty as Creator and Leader of history (Anderson, 1974:98). Isaiah 52:7-10 may itself be an adaptation of a praise hymn (Whybray: 166).

The resolve to keep the reign of God in mind during the OT period bore fruit in Jesus' frequent reference to the kingdom of God in his life and ministry (some 54 times in Matthew's Gospel, 19 in Mark, and 44 in Luke). God's kingdom was a central feature of Jesus' message.

Announcement-Appearance-Assurance

The fourth servant song lies between an announcement of peace and salvation at the center of God's kingship (52:7-12) and God's promise of a covenant of peace with his people (54:1-17). Having just read of the announcement of God's kingship in 52:7, the reader now meets the crown prince of God's kingdom in Isaiah 52:13-53:12. The change of mood from 52:7-12 to 52:13-15 is startling. Suddenly the crown prince enters the picture; but what an inauspicious entry! Disfigurement and suffering lead to death and burial. Following the servant's death and tribute, the prophet moves again to a mood of hope and joy (54:1-17).

The location of the fourth servant song between chapters 52 and 54 is significant because of the sequence of announcement, appearance, and assurance. In Isaiah 52:1-12, and particularly in 52:7-12, the Lord *announces* a messenger of peace and salvation who will testify to God's kingship. This messenger, however, remains anonymous. One may therefore ask of this text, What form will this messenger take?

The answer emerges in Isaiah 52:13–53:12, where the Lord's servant *appears*. The crown prince of God's kingdom takes the form of a servant who opens to view God's pattern of servant leadership. Such servant leadership does not idealize suffering and death. Neither does it evade the harsh reality of following the servant leadership pattern. The refusal to retaliate against evil with more evil illustrates the pattern. Servant leadership faces even death with nonviolence. This is how God's messenger testifies to God's kingdom.

The *assurance* of hope and joy in 54:1-17 seems impossible after the testimony in 52:13–53:12. And yet it complements the announcement of salvation for Jerusalem in 52:7-12. Between these two expressions of happiness lies the servant's song of grief, but not despair, in 52:13–53:12. The servant portrays God's purpose for his people. They are to give evidence to God's way in the world. The servant's nonretaliation appears as a sign of God's strength in him. Such is the vocation of God's people.

And so the sequence of four Servant Songs comes to an end. In the first song the Lord's servant is introduced. By his patient endurance of suffering, the servant teaches justice to the nations; he exhibits the pattern of justice in his own life (42:1-4). The servant testifies to his calling in the second song. It is a twofold call: to Jacob-Israel and to the nations (49:1-6). The servant's teaching in the third song is directed to his own people. His teaching (theory) balances his nonviolence (practice), although both are discredited by his own people (50:4-9). The fourth song, then, gives evidence of the suffering servant's witness to Israel and the nations, witness concerning the power of nonviolence to bring peace on earth as underlying God's reign (52:13–53:12). The four songs show the servant's mission as a teaching mission flowing in two streams: to Jacob-Israel and to the nations (I. Friesen, 2003:63-74).

THE TEXT IN THE LIFE OF THE CHURCH

The Servant as Paradigm

At least since Luke's account of Philip's meeting with the Ethiopian on the road to Gaza, Isaiah 53 has been of immense interest to the church. In Luke's account the Ethiopian was reading from the scroll of Isaiah when Philip met him. Reading Isaiah 53:7-8, the Ethiopian posed a question to Philip: "About whom . . . does the prophet say this, about himself or about someone else?" (Acts 8:34) [*Servant, Servants, p. 451*].

Luke says that beginning with Isaiah 53:7-8, Philip proclaimed the good news about Jesus to the Ethiopian. Philip, by the Spirit's prompting, seized on the clarity of this text to announce its new meaning for the early church. The suffering servant of Isaiah 53 is seen by the NT writers as corresponding to Jesus. This means that the servant's destiny to *justify many* (53:11 NIV) and [*to bear*] *the sin of many* (53:12) opens the way for an interpretation of fulfillment in Jesus [*Atonement, p. 439*].

Isaiah 54:1-17

Covenant of Peace

PREVIEW

Isaiah 54 recalls and resumes chapters 51 and 52:1-12. There Jerusalem and Zion are clearly addressed by name. Here Jerusalem and Zion are also addressed, but not by name. Chapter 54 is written as a word of consolation to God's people in exile.

The Lord speaks throughout the chapter. The first two parts compare devastated Jerusalem first to a barren woman who receives children, and then to a widow whose husband returns (54:1-3, 4-6).

Interpretations of this comparison are given in the last three parts of the chapter (54:7-10, 11-14, 15-17). The covenant with Noah (Gen 9) is restated as a covenant of peace for Jerusalem (54:7-10). Zion, where the Lord is extolled (Ps 99), is reflected in the bejeweled city established in righteousness (54:11-14). And Jerusalem's security will be based on the Lord's protection (54:15-17).

OUTLINE

Barren Woman Blessed, 54:1-3
Widowed Woman Called, 54:4-6
Covenant of Peace, 54:7-10
Bejeweled City, 54:11-14
Safety and Security, 54:15-17

EXPLANATORY NOTES

Throughout the chapter the Lord addresses *you* (f. sg. pronoun) without identifying the pronoun's antecedent. In this case it is necessary to supply the antecedent from the context. Earlier, Zion is addressed with the words *Your* [f. sg.] *God reigns* (52:7). There Jerusalem is addressed with two feminine singular imperatives: *rise, sit enthroned, O Jerusalem* (52:2 NIV). It is reasonable to assume, therefore, that Zion and Jerusalem are implied in chapter 54. *You* and *your* refer to the exiles in Babylon and the citizens of Judea who did not go into exile. These pronouns also refer more literally to the city itself that was destroyed. It is not always clear which of these references is intended.

Barren Woman Blessed 54:1-3

The barren woman alludes to Zion as the exiles in Babylon. Three feminine singular imperatives that address Zion—*Sing! Burst into song! Shout!*—open the first stanza (54:1). These imperatives correspond to the threefold description of the woman as one who was *barren*, who *never bore a child*, and who was *never in labor* (NIV). The occasion for joy lies in the promise of children. These children refer to the exiled Judeans living in Babylon, who will be repatriated. The reference to *her who has a husband* (NIV) has Babylon in mind.

Now a sequence of five imperatives instructs Zion to prepare for the increase (54:2). A tent, enlarged to accommodate an influx of people, provides a colorful metaphor to communicate this instruction.

The verb *spread out* has a stronger force in Hebrew of *bursting through* (54:3). Zion's increase will be not merely expansive but also explosive! The fulfillment of the promise to Abraham and Sarah in Genesis finds expression in the language and metaphors of these verses.

Widowed Woman Called 54:4-6

Now the metaphor shifts from Zion as a barren woman to Zion as a widowed woman (54:4). Widowhood here refers to the shame and disgrace of exile. Widowhood is added on to barrenness, *the shame of your youth*. Widowhood, of course, does not mean simply the *loss* of a husband but also the *death* of a husband. The use of the metaphor of widowhood indicates the grimness of the exile. This grimness will not be recalled and rehearsed.

The removal of shame somehow relates to the Lord's names (54:5). Of the three names modified by the pronoun *your* (*Maker, husband, Redeemer*), *Redeemer* relates most closely to the removal of shame. As in the story of Ruth, the redeemer is the kinsman who frees the widow from the shame and insecurity of exclusion from society (cf. Brueggemann, 1998b:152).

Instead of continuing to live under the cloud of shame and insecurity, Zion is reassured of her calling (54:6). The Lord as Zion's husband calls her into a restored relationship of covenant faithfulness.

Covenant of Peace 54:7-10

Although the Lord speaks throughout the chapter, his speech becomes more direct after 54:6. The Lord's abandonment of his people seems startling here because the word *abandon* suggests a complete disinterest in the fate of what is given up. It suggests desertion and renunciation of a relationship. In this case, however, the abandonment is momentary and disciplinary (54:7-8). *In overflowing wrath* describes God's capacity for anger [Wrath of God, p. 455]. But this anger is not sustained anger. The Lord's hidden face indicates a certain self-consciousness about the danger of anger becoming unbridled. In any case, compassion, love, and redemption overshadow anger (Exod 34:6-7).

The second stanza turns to the example of Noah and the flood in Genesis 6–8 (54:9). This example endorses the emphasis on God's compassion in the previous stanza. As God established a covenant with Noah never again to send a flood to destroy the earth, so the Lord promises never again to vent his anger by abandoning his people.

This promise finds expression in a *covenant of peace* based on the Lord's *unfailing love* (54:10 NIV) [Steadfast Love, p. 452]. The covenant language of Genesis 9 has influenced this stanza. Here the covenant *of peace* means more than simply the absence of war. It means material and relational well-being as well as the larger scope of God's intention for his people and for humankind through his people.

Bejeweled City 54:11-14

A gap in the poetry indicates a shift of topic. Now the Lord addresses Zion no longer as the desolate woman but also as the personified city of Jerusalem (Childs: 427). Presumably this is because the exiles have returned to Jerusalem. Her status as *afflicted*, *storm-tossed*, and *not comforted* indicates her ruinous condition (54:11-12). The Lord promises, however, the building of a new Jerusalem. The gemstones signifying the city's unsurpassed beauty are entirely secondary to the Lord as skilled worker who lays them in place.

The city's beauty does not refer to physical beauty but to the beauty of her inhabitants, who are taught by the Lord (54:13-14). The substance of this teaching results in a peaceful existence. The foundation of this teaching lies in righteousness and the absence of violence (Childs: 430), conforming to the Lord's standard of right behavior. The indicative phrase *You shall be far from oppression . . . and from terror* is imperative in Hebrew, thus meaning, *Stay away from oppression . . . and from terror!* Although some commentators choose to emend the text, Whybray defends the imperative as an emphasis on the assurance of God's promise (189).

Safety and Security 54:15-17

The Lord's address to Zion as the personified city of Jerusalem continues in 54:15-17. The Hebrew of 54:15 resists easy translation. The sense seems to be that the Lord does not bear responsibility for internal dissension that arises in the new Jerusalem. On the contrary, the people's perseverance in the Lord's righteousness will enable them to stand firm against those who create dissension; their dissension will collapse.

The word *See!* points to a conclusion drawn from what has just been said. The expression *It is I* (a personal pronoun in Hebrew) occurs twice (NIV) to add emphasis to the verb *created* (54:16). Creation, not chaos (dissension), belongs to the Lord. The Lord is the creative force behind the skill of the blacksmith. The *smith*, however, bears responsibility for creating weapons of war. The *destroyer* (NIV) created by the Lord almost certainly alludes to the story of the flood in Genesis 6-9. The Lord's decision to destroy the earth with water resulted in a determination not to do so again (cf. 54:9).

The weapons of war will not succeed against a people clothed with the Lord's righteousness (54:17). God's people will confound those who seek their extinction by legal means.

A summary statement with the Lord's word as its guarantee (*declares the LORD*, NIV) draws the chapter to a close. *This is the heritage . . .* refers both to what has immediately preceded and to the chapter as a whole. This heritage refers above all to the Lord's servants, those characterized by right behavior (righteousness). The word *vindication* here and the word *righteousness* in 54:14 reflect the same Hebrew noun (ṣedaqah). They indicate the compassionate love of God, which God's people are invited to imitate in their faith and practice (cf. Knight: 187).

THE TEXT IN BIBLICAL CONTEXT

Vision of the New Jerusalem

The bejeweled city of Isaiah 54:11-12 finds a renewed expression in John the Revelator's vision of the new Jerusalem (Rev 21:18-21). John does not quote Isaiah 54, but his language suggests his awareness of this text.

Isaiah's city is resplendent. It refers to a restored Jerusalem (though not named as such) inhabited by a restored people. In a later chapter this restored Jerusalem becomes more defined, with walls rebuilt by foreigners (60:10), gates always open (60:11), and the Lord providing light for the city (60:19-20).

John's city exudes unrestrained beauty and artistry. The new Jerusalem comes down out of heaven, a tableau representing the church (Rev 21:2). The city is portrayed as a cube, perfect and magnificent.

My Covenant of Peace

The reference to *my covenant of peace* (54:10) invites an inquiry into the broader meaning of the phrase in its biblical context. This phrase also occurs in Numbers 25:12 (although the word configuration is slightly different in Hebrew). There, on the plains of Moab in the context of an outbreak of what was probably the black plague, the Israelites failed to obey the stipulations of their covenant with the Lord (Mendenhall: 105-21). This failure took the form of sexual contact between Israelite men and Moabite women, which was probably intended to put an end to the plague. The specific case of an Israelite man and a Moabite woman is "resolved" when Phinehas son of Eleazar murders the two offenders, and the plague is averted. The Lord commends Phinehas for the murder and establishes a covenant of peace with him.

What is striking about this incident is that there is no record of carrying out the orders given by the Lord and by Moses. Instead, Phinehas carries out the punishment on his own authority. Mendenhall regards this as an instance of the transition from covenant law to royal law (Mendenhall: 105-21). Covenant law seeks to make things right based on the needs of victim and offender. Royal law seeks the punishment of the offender.

Ezekiel refers to *a covenant of peace* in 34:25 and 37:26. In both cases the prophet, speaking for the Lord, makes a covenant of peace with the house of Israel. The covenant includes the promise of adequate rainfall and food. It includes God's presence among the people. It includes prosperity as well as domestic security and freedom from outside attack. And in Malachi a variation of the phrase *my covenant of peace* indicates the Lord's covenant with the priestly tribe of Levi (2:5 NIV).

THE TEXT IN THE LIFE OF THE CHURCH

Mendelssohn's *Elijah* Oratorio

In Mendelssohn's *Elijah* oratorio the story line follows the text of 1 Kings 17–19, 21 and 2 Kings 2. Passages drawn from other parts of the OT,

Isaiah 54:1-17

then, comment on or complement the story line. Part 1 of the oratorio tells the story of Elijah's preservation from a drought and the contest on Mount Carmel between the prophet Elijah (representing the Lord) and the prophets of Baal. During the contest Elijah calls the people of Israel near as he repairs the altar and offers a prayer (1 Kings 18). To present this episode, the baritone (Elijah) sings a recitative and air, *Draw near, all ye people* (no. 14). The solo is followed immediately by a choral piece, *Cast thy burden upon the Lord* (no. 15), from Psalm 55:22. For Mendelssohn, Psalm 55:22 captures the emotion and spiritual burden that Elijah felt in the contest.

Part 2 of the oratorio tells the story of Elijah's escape to Mount Horeb, where he meets God. A chorus and baritone recitative, *Go, return upon thy way* (no. 36), describe what follows the meeting. The chorus sings the word of the Lord to Elijah that he is not alone in his faithfulness to the Lord. Elijah responds with a confession of faith drawn in part from Psalm 16:9. Mendelssohn then puts the words of Isaiah 54:10, *For the mountains shall depart* (no. 37), into Elijah's mouth. Isaiah 54:10 serves as a further confession of faith in the Lord's word in response to 1 Kings 19:15, 18, that 7,000 in Israel have not bowed the knee to Baal.

Isaiah 55:1-13

Everlasting Covenant and Sign

PREVIEW

The promise of a covenant and a permanent sign in chapter 55 follows on the promise of the Lord's perpetual steadfast love (*ḥesed 'olam*) and his covenant of peace in chapter 54 (esp. vv. 8, 10).

The Lord's everlasting covenant with his people (*berit 'olam*), modeled on the covenant with David, begins the chapter (55:1-3). All and sundry are invited to live under this covenant. It is a general invitation and available for a broader interpretation by Jesus and the early church (cf. John 4:14; 7:37; Rev 22:17).

The Lord's ways and word constitute the center of the chapter (55:4-11). The focus is on the superiority of God's ways and plans to those of humankind. A key part of that focus is the power of God's Word to bring about what it intends. This Word is not "idle chatter" or "religious fantasy," as Brueggemann points out (1998b:161). It is stalwart speech, full and free.

The chapter concludes with the promise of an everlasting sign (*'ot 'olam*) heralded by exuberant joy and song (55:12-13). There is no hint of diffidence here; only confidence and expectation.

OUTLINE

Everlasting Covenant, 55:1-3
The Lord's Ways and Intentions, 55:4-9

The Lord's Word, 55:10-11
Everlasting Sign, 55:12-13

EXPLANATORY NOTES

Everlasting Covenant 55:1-3

The chapter opens with an interjection, *hoy* (*Ho*, NRSV). Elsewhere in Isaiah *hoy* is often translated *woe!* or *alas!* as an expression of dismay and judgment (cf. Isa 5, 28–31, 33). But sometimes, as here, *hoy* expresses wonder or astonishment.

An invitation to find refreshment at God's banquet table constitutes the first stanza (55:1). The Lord calls out the invitation to *all* (NIV) who thirst. The nearest referent for all would appear to be *the servants of the LORD* in 54:17 (Childs: 434). The call urges the Babylonian exiles to disengage themselves from the seduction of Babylonian culture and to drink from the wells of salvation (cf. 12:3). The call has a wider appeal as well to the peoples and nations to whom the exiles are to be a light. Plural imperative verb forms dominate the stanza: *come, buy, eat*. The waters represent the source of all life, and milk and wine the abundance of this life.

The invitation of the first stanza resolves into a plea in the second stanza (55:2). Here the emphasis is on food, representing both spiritual and material things (cf. Whybray: 191). To what might the parallel phrases *not bread* and *does not satisfy* refer? Surely the nonsatisfying food refers to what is not God (*not bread*), the worship of idols (Smart: 223). The worship of idols includes, among other things, Babylonian civil religion, "the bread of the empire" (Brueggemann, 1998b:159). This bread stands in contrast to the bread and abundance of the Lord's offer. That offer is presented as a banquet table to which the Lord's servants are invited (cf. Ps 23:5).

The plural imperative verb forms of the first two stanzas continue in the third stanza (55:3). The invitation *Come to the waters* in the first stanza now clearly means the invitation *Come to me* (the Lord). The invitation to life under God's rule reflects a common theme in the OT (e.g., Deut 30). This life finds expression in an everlasting covenant that has the promises to Noah, to Abraham and the patriarchs, to David, and to Jacob-Israel as a whole as its model (e.g., Gen 9:16; 17:7; 2 Sam 23:5; Ps 105:10; Jer 32:40; Ezek 16:60). God's steadfast love enshrined in this covenant tradition has now been handed over to the servants of the Lord, who accept his invitation to the banquet table.

The Lord's Ways and Intentions 55:4-9

As the interjection *Ho!* (*hoy*) captures the reader's attention in 55:1, so the interjection *See!* (*hen*) in 55:4 and repeated in 55:5 (NIV translates *hen* as *Surely* in 55:5) alerts the reader to something new.

The metaphor of coming to the Lord's table in the first part of the chapter now gives way to the metaphor of nations running to the Lord's people (55:4-5). David serves as the bridge between the two parts. The Lord's everlasting covenant with David (2 Sam 23:5) turns out to be more durable than David's dynasty, which has ended. David's role as witness to and leader-commander of *the peoples* indicates the extension of the everlasting covenant beyond David's house to the wider human family (cf. Hanson: 179). Israel summoning nations and nations running to Israel does not indicate an Israelite world empire (Kaufmann: 116). The significance of the nations coming to Israel lies in Israel's *Holy One*, not in Israel's political domination (for a similar perspective see Isa 2:1-5).

The plural imperatives of 55:1-3 resume in 55:6-7, summoning Israel and the nations to seek the Lord. The summons includes a call to repentance in the biblical sense of turning (v. 7b). The *way* of the wicked refers to customary behavior that is unresponsive to the Lord's way. The *thoughts* of the evil person include plans for evil growing out of the thought process. Unregenerate behavior works hand in hand with malignant plans. The turning means a change of behavior that will inspire God's pity and pardon. It is not cheap grace in the sense of forgiveness without repentance and change.

The ways and plans of humans differ substantially from the ways and plans of God (55:8-9). This difference is already indicated in the previous stanza by the human impulse to wrongdoing and the Lord's impulse to compassion.

The Lord's Word 55:10-11

An affirmation of the reliability of the created order to distribute water over the earth to nourish the soil opens the first stanza (55:10). The accent falls on the descent of rain and snow to carry out their intended purpose (Young, 1972:383). The purpose of this nourishment lies in food production to sustain life.

This affirmation is used in the second stanza to argue for the reliability of the word that goes out from God's mouth to carry out its intended purpose (55:11). Here one can imagine God's word at the dawn of creation. The word calling for light flowed from God's mouth. The creation of light accomplished the purpose for which the word was spoken. The word returned with a judgment that the light was good (Gen 1:3-5). God's word has that kind of resolve and purpose. The Lord's word operates in this way in Isaiah 55:11, where it gives rise to *a new future for exilic Israel* (Brueggemann, 1998b:161). Such a future rests on the Lord's promise of life. The promise is not an empty word but a word of honor. That word will accomplish its purpose when God's people respond to it in faith and trust.

Everlasting Sign 55:12-13

The reader may catch the correspondence between the word *going out* of the Lord's mouth in 55:11 and the people *going out* in joy in 55:12. Both references to *going out* indicate an assurance of the result. The reader may also recall the command to go out from exile in Babylon in 52:11-12. There the exiles are not to go out *in haste*. Here they are to go out *in joy*. An outburst of metaphors illustrates the joy. Mountains and hills sing for joy! Trees applaud!

The concluding stanza compares the cypress and myrtle of freedom with the thorn bush and brier of exile (55:13). Cypress and myrtle serve as a *memorial* (lit., *name*) of the promise that the Lord has made (Whybray: 195). This everlasting sign (*'ot 'olam*) may be compared to the everlasting covenant (*berit 'olam*) in Genesis 9:16. Both sign and covenant emphasize the Lord's enduring faithfulness.

THE TEXT IN BIBLICAL CONTEXT

Everlasting Covenant

The notion of an everlasting covenant (*berit 'olam*) occurs three times in the book of Isaiah. In 24:5, in a setting of judgment corresponding to the flood story in Genesis 6–9, earth's inhabitants stand in opposition to God's everlasting covenant. This alludes in particular to human violence and bloodshed (Clements: 202). Isaiah 55:3 addresses the promise of an everlasting covenant to all who thirst. This refers to the Lord's servants but it also has a wider appeal to the peoples and nations to whom the Lord's servants are to be a light. Isaiah 61:8 promises an everlasting covenant to the descendants of the exiles, whom nations and peoples will recognize as blessed by the Lord.

An everlasting covenant appears at several places in the book of Genesis (Gen 9, 17). The covenant with Noah in Genesis 9 includes the first reference to an everlasting covenant in the OT, a covenant with "all flesh" (9:16). In that setting the bow in the clouds serves as a sign of the Lord's faithfulness to his everlasting covenant (cf. Isa 54:7-10).

The covenant with Abram in Genesis 17 includes a reference to an everlasting covenant (17:7, 13, 19). Here the sign of circumcision accompanies the covenant. This covenant has a more particular focus, established between "God Almighty" (Heb. *'El Shaddai*) and Abram's household.

An everlasting covenant appears again in the book of Exodus (Exod 31). There, as in Genesis, a sign accompanies the covenant. Now it is the Sabbath that functions as a sign marking the Lord's creation of the earth and resting from his labor. Sabbath-keeping by the Israelites verifies their commitment to the Lord of creation (cf. Janzen, 2000:369).

In 2 Samuel 23 and in 1 Chronicles 16 are references to an everlasting covenant. The reference in 2 Samuel 23:5 appears in the last words of David, where the dying king reminds those who survive him of the everlasting covenant that God made with him (2 Sam 7:8-15; cf. Ps 89:29). In 1 Chronicles 16:17 the Lord's everlasting covenant with Jacob-Israel appears in a psalm of thanksgiving attributed to David. One of the sources of this psalm is Psalm 105:8-22.

Both Jeremiah and Ezekiel refer to the promise of an everlasting covenant that the Lord will make with his people (Jer 32:40; 50:5; Ezek 16:60; 37:26). Ezekiel 37:26 in particular presents the everlasting covenant as a covenant of peace, referring to God's presence among his people (cf. Lind, 1996:307).

Finally, in the NT the author of the letter to the Hebrews speaks of the "blood of the eternal covenant" (13:20). This is a profound reinterpretation of the OT texts where an everlasting covenant is mentioned. The testimony that God raised Jesus from the dead by "the blood of the eternal covenant" shows the continuing power of the covenant idea to produce new revelations. The testimony is a new revelation in Hebrews because now covenant includes a person, Jesus the Messiah, in a way that is different from all the OT antecedents (cf. Hillers: 179).

THE TEXT IN THE LIFE OF THE CHURCH

Hymns of Invitation and Joy

Isaiah 55, with its engaging poetic style, provides a rich resource for the church's music. The Moravians in the *Moravian Book of Worship*, for example, have at least five hymns inspired by Isaiah 55. A recent Lutheran hymnal, *With One Voice*, has three hymns from Isaiah 55.

The hymnal shared by Mennonite and Church of the Brethren congregations, *Hymnal: A Worship Book*, has included four marvelous hymns based on Isaiah 55. Each of these hymns focuses on a different aspect of the chapter. The hymn "O let all who thirst" (495) expresses the invitation in Isaiah 55:1-2 to drink from the waters of God's life and live. Jesus' invitation and promise to all "that labor and are heavy laden, and I will give you rest" (KJV) in Matthew 11:28 echoes through the hymn.

Two hymns draw on the imagery of the Lord's ways and plans in Isaiah 55:6-9. "Great God of wonders" (*HWB*: 149) takes the theme of the Lord's abundant pardon in 55:7 and sees in it the pardon "bestowed through Jesus' blood!" The Mennonite hymn writer J. Harold Moyer in his hymn "I sought the Lord" (*HWB*: 506) explores the call to *seek the Lord*, found in various passages, including Isaiah 55:6. The hymn focuses on the reciprocating nature of the search for God. That is, even as *all who thirst* are urged to seek the Lord, the Lord seeks the people of his earthly domain. The second verse of the hymn draws on the portrait of Jesus reaching out his hand to catch Peter, who was sinking in the waters of the Sea of Galilee (Matt 14:29-31).

The hymn "You shall go out with joy" (*HWB*: 427) gives voice to the exuberance of Isaiah 55:12 for those who follow Jesus, even though Jesus is not specifically mentioned.

Water as a Source of Life

Both Testaments teem with references to water. Water serves both as a physical necessity to support life as well as a symbol with a variety of religious or spiritual meanings. So it is not surprising in Isaiah 55 to find that water serves as a symbol of the grace that God offers (cf. Whybray: 190). The Lord's call to *come to the waters* in the first stanza (55:1) is completed by the call to come *to me* [the Lord] . . . *that you may live* in the third stanza (55:3).

The word of the Lord to Jeremiah is that he (the Lord) is "the spring of living water" (2:13; 17:13 NIV). In Zechariah 14:8 living waters flow from Jerusalem in an apocalyptic end-time victory.

In the NT the Gospel of John and the Revelation of John employ similar language of water symbolizing God's grace. In the Gospel of John, Jesus speaks to the woman of Samaria about himself as "living water," an allusion that she does not grasp at first (4:10-11). At the Feast of Tabernacles in John 7, Jesus uses language of Isaiah 44:3 and 55:1 and perhaps also Joel 3:18 and Zechariah 14:8 to announce the Spirit to be given after his glorification.

Several passages in the Revelation of John (21:5-6 and 22:16-17) have the offer of the water of life to the thirsty at their center. A careful study of Isaiah 55 helps to account for language usage in the book of Revelation. An understanding of *the water of life* in Revelation 21 and 22 is deepened and enriched when this message is read alongside the offer in Isaiah 55:1-3.

Isaiah 56:1–57:21

Access to the Lord's Holy Mountain

PREVIEW

Chapters 56 and 57 conclude part 5 of the book of Isaiah. They do so by means of a simple rhetorical device: the repetition in 57:21 of the phrase *There is no peace . . . for the wicked* from 48:22. The word *peace* in 48:22 follows the words *your peace* in 48:18 (NIV), concluding chapters 40–48. Now the word *peace* in 57:21 follows the words *peace, peace* in 57:19, concluding chapters 49–57 (cf. Kaufmann: 91).

The first section of chapters 56–57 centers on Sabbath keeping (56:1-8). The outlook of Isaiah 55 shapes the practices recommended in 56:1-8. The second section identifies key practices that exhibit the absence of Sabbath keeping (56:9–57:13). Here the reality of threats to Israel's faith and practice receive special attention. The third section contemplates the Lord as one who, though exalted, dwells with those who honor him (57:14-21).

OUTLINE

Keeping Sabbath, 56:1-8
    56:1-3   Doing the Right Thing
    56:4-5   Including Those Who Please the Lord
    56:6-8   Including Those Who Love the Lord's Name

Practices Leading to Death, 56:9–57:13
   56:9-12   Corruption
   57:1-2   Forced Removals
   57:3-5   Sorcery and Child Sacrifice
   57:6-8   Sexual Immorality
   57:9-13   Idolatry
Comfort and Hope, 57:14-21
   57:14-17   The Lord as High and Holy
   57:18-21   The Lord as Healer

EXPLANATORY NOTES

Keeping Sabbath 56:1-8

Sabbath keeping served as a defining characteristic of the Jewish community in exile [*Sabbath Observance, p. 450*]. Here it serves as the doorway permitting entrance into Jewish religious life.

56:1-3 Doing the Right Thing

A messenger formula (*Thus says the LORD*) indicating a message from the Lord introduces the first stanza (56:1). The verbs in the message are plural: *Maintain justice and do what is right* (NIV), addressed to exilic Jews. The safeguarding of justice (*mišpaṭ*) and right (*ṣedaqah*) means that each person receives what is needed, and the Lord receives the honor [*Justice and Righteousness, p. 445*] (cf. Vriezen: 326). The last half of the stanza reflects the words and spirit of 46:13 and 51:5. The accessibility of the Lord's righteousness and salvation means they are available for imitation by God's people.

The word *justice* in English is often thought of as an abstract noun meaning "impartiality" or "fairness." The Hebrew word (*mišpaṭ*) is employed in a more active sense. Justice is something that one does, often followed by specific instructions (Limburg, 1977:81-85; cf. Jer 7:5 followed by v. 6; Ezek 18:5 followed by vv. 6-9).

A beatitude introduces the second stanza (56:2). As in the first stanza, the emphasis falls on behavior. Doing the right thing finds its particular application in observance. The parallel lines

   who keeps the Sabbath without desecrating it,
     and keeps his hand from doing any evil (NIV)

indicate the parallel relationship between the spiritual obligation and the moral obligation.

Two examples of candidates for blessing, foreigner and eunuch joining themselves to the Lord, are cited in the third stanza (56:3). Each one in turn expresses serious doubt about inclusion in the Israelite community. The foreigner is the non-Israelite, often regarded as a threat to Israel's faith. The eunuch is an emasculated male whose participation in Israelite worship was prohibited in Deuteronomy 23:1 (*NHBD*: 176, 204-5). The Lord speaks to these outsiders, who express doubt about their status, with a promise that the foundation for their inclusion lies in their decision to belong to the Lord.

56:4-5 Including Those Who Please the Lord

A new messenger formula introduces the promise to eunuchs and foreigners in a more specific way. The poet uses chiasm [*Literary Perspective, p. 446*] to tie verse 3 to verses 4-7:

foreigner and *eunuch* (v. 3)
eunuchs (vv. 4-5) and *foreigners* (vv. 6-7).

In each case one stanza introduces the group (vv. 4, 6), and the following stanza furnishes the promise (vv. 5, 7).

Eunuchs as a group are presented in 56:4. Keeping Sabbath and pleasing the Lord through cherishing his covenant appear not as a condition of inclusion but as a conscious decision on the part of eunuchs.

In response to this decision, the Lord will give them a memorial and a name (56:5). The focus of this promise lies in access to the spiritual life of Israel (cf. Watts, 1987:249). The promise of access to the spiritual life of Israel replaces the prohibition in Deuteronomy 23:1 as well as the discouraging word of Isaiah 56:3 (Brueggemann, 1998b:170).

56:6-8 Including Those Who Love the Lord's Name

Foreigners as a group are presented in 56:6. These are converts to Judaism whose commitment to the Lord includes three things: *to minister to him*, in the sense of worship, *to love the name of the LORD*, in the sense of loyalty to the one God, and *to be his servants*, in the sense of working for him. Keeping Sabbath and cherishing the Lord's covenant serve as signs of this commitment.

The Lord responds to this commitment with a promise to receive foreigners into his house (56:7). The language is highly inclusive: bringing in, creating joy, acceptance. Foreigners joined to the Lord are welcome to the central symbols of Israel's faith: *my holy mountain, my house of prayer*, and *my altar*. The phrase *all peoples* gives a universal stamp to the whole passage. The motive for including outsiders lies in the Lord's

Isaiah 56:1-57:21

original promise to Abraham that in him "all the families of the earth shall be blessed" (Gen 12:3).

The concluding stanza provides the "signature" of the message sender: *The Sovereign LORD declares* (56:8 NIV). The verb *to gather* occurs three times in this stanza. Its significance cannot be overestimated. Brueggemann refers to the Lord as one who abolishes exile and gathers exiles for homecoming. This is homecoming in both a spiritual and a material sense: homecoming to communion with the Lord, but also homecoming in the physical sense of security for all peoples (1998b: 173).

Practices Leading to Death 56:9–57:13

From the emphasis on keeping Sabbath in 56:1-8, the poet now turns to five practices depicting the absence of Sabbath keeping.

56:9-12 Corruption

The corruption of leadership is the first of these practices. The beasts of field and forest, sarcastically invited to come and dine on God's people, indicate the nations (56:9-10). The nations wreak havoc because no one raises an alarm. The sentinels, entrusted with the task of warning, have neither sight nor sense. Ezekiel uses the word *sentinels* (e.g., 33:7) to refer to the prophets, and this is also its use here. The blindness and ignorance of the prophets means that they do not obey the Lord's *torah* and, as a result, provide no teaching that God's people can use to ward off evil. They appear as inept guard dogs. Their inclination is to sleep, offering no warning of approaching danger.

When awake, they gorge themselves, neglecting their duty (56:11). The shepherds, too, offer inept leadership. In the OT the designation *shepherds* often refers to the kings and rulers of Israel (cf. Jer 23, 25; Ezek 34). Without insight these shepherds pursue profit based on violence. Prophets and kings alike drug themselves with alcohol and mindless carousing, putting off until tomorrow the forewarning that needs to be done today (56:12).

57:1-2 Forced Removals

The second practice leading to death is forced removals. A result of corrupt leadership is structural injustice in which the righteous are removed without a trace, and no one understands the catastrophe (51:1). The first four lines of the stanza describe this momentous situation:

> *The righteous perish,*
> *   and no one takes it to heart;*
> *the devout are taken away,*
> *   while no one understands.*

The last two lines sharpen the social analysis even more. Watts translates these lines as follows:

> Indeed, when confronting the evil,
>   the one in the right is taken to prison. (1987:252)

Watts interprets removal as imprisonment, which is probably correct. More important, he translates the Hebrew *mippene* in the first of these two lines as *when confronting*. In this way, the one in the right does not act merely as a victim. Instead, the one in the right acts to confront evil. Removal by the authorities rests on this action. If only, we hear the authorities say, the one in the right would be content to be a victim.

Those who walk uprightly (57:2) indicates those who, though incarcerated, remain confident in the justice of their cause. The phrase *enter into peace* probably refers to the dawn of a just social order, when people will be able to rest on their beds.

57:3-5 Sorcery and Child Sacrifice

The third practice, witchcraft and the slaughter of children, begins with a sharp address: *But as for you . . . .* The first stanza addresses those who scorn the righteous (57:3-4a). The prophet brands the mothers of these scorners as promiscuous and utterly immoral. The righteous represent those who have remained faithful to the Lord in spite of pressures to adopt the gods of the nations: Baal, Marduk, Ishtar, and others (Hanson: 199).

The practices of those who worship these gods receive special attention in the second stanza (57:4b-5). The expression *burn with lust* indicates sexual fertility rites. These rites sought to guarantee the fertility of the land through sexual relationships between priests and priestesses (cf. Noth: 280-81; Gottwald, 1979:694-95).

In the ancient Near East children were sometimes sacrificed in times of great trouble, when such an offering was understood to placate the anger of the gods (Smart: 242). That Israel adopted this practice at times is indicated by Josiah's reform: he defiled Topheth, where children were sacrificed (2 Kings 23:10; Jer 7:31-32).

57:6-8 Sexual Immorality

The fourth practice leading to death is sexual immorality. Beginning here the addressee is feminine singular, the exilic community spoken to collectively as a prostitute. The first stanza appears as a statement about offerings and concludes with a question (57:6). The theme here is offerings to idols, although idols are not specifically mentioned. The reference to *smooth stones* seems to be to a valley where such stones were worshipped. The offense does not lie in the offerings themselves since various offerings are prescribed in the Israelite law codes (cf. Lev 22; Num 28–29). The problem is with their use in idol worship (cf. Whybray: 203-4). The question at the end of the stanza carries a hint of sarcasm, as if to say: *Should I be comforted by my people's idolatry?*

In the second stanza the prophet turns from valley to mountain (57:7-8a). The exilic community continues to be spoken to collectively as a prostitute. Mountains were thought to be auspicious as places to implore a deity's favor. The reference to *your bed* indicates that the deity's favor was sought by means of sexual liaisons of some sort. The prostitute sets up both bed and *symbol*, the symbol referring most likely to an image representing deity.

The Hebrew text of the third stanza remains difficult to translate clearly (57:8b). It seems that whereas in the previous stanza the prostitute *makes* her bed, here *she lies in it!* In other words, some kind of sexual immorality in worship is intended, the details of which are not clear. Six verbs (*uncover, go up, make wide, make a bargain, love,* and *gaze*) portray the scope of the immorality.

57:9-13 Idolatry

The second-person feminine singular address continues in 57:9-13, but now with idolatry, the fifth practice leading to death, more in focus. The first stanza has the harlot traveling to Molech with a gift of oil (57:9). The Hebrew text reads *melek* (*king*), which may be an alternate spelling of Molech (so NRSV, NIV; cf. Whybray: 205). Molech was a deity who was worshipped by forcing children to pass through fire. Here harlot Israel seeks out Molech, using fragrances of enticement to please the deity. This search for alternative spiritualities leads to distant places. Such a search is a downward spiral into death (*Sheol*, NRSV; cf. Smart: 242).

The second stanza indicates the persistence of the quest to find meaning in idolatry (57:10). The quest yields enough strength to allow it to continue.

Accusation replaces description in the next stanza (57:11a). The accusation is in the form of a question. The implied answer to the question is that Molech became an object of worship, and the Lord ceased to be remembered. Other prophets also complained about Israel forgetting God (e.g., Jer 18:13-17; Ezek 22:6-12).

The Lord now provides the motive to explain his people's quest for alternative gods (57:11b-12). The Lord appears to invoke his own silence as the cause of his people's faithlessness (57:11b). This is curious. The Lord's silence may be taken as a sign of patience with his people's quest for alternative gods. It is not patient resignation, however, but patient waiting, as in the father's waiting for his lost son (Luke 15:11-32). The Lord continues to expose their so-called righteousness and works, founded as they are on idolatry, but they will be of no use to them because their gods are impotent (57:12).

The final stanza contrasts the helpless idols with the Lord's implicit power (57:13). The context requires the phrase *of idols* even though it is not present in the Hebrew text. The word *breath* (*hebel*) also has the figurative meaning of something that is worthless or insubstantial (traditionally, "vanity" in Ecclesiastes). By way of contrast, the Lord asserts himself as one with the right to give land and to inhabit his holy mountain. To seek refuge in the Lord opens the door to everything in life that has dignity and value and worth.

Comfort and Hope 57:14-21

In this final section of the chapter the Lord speaks as one who, though exalted, dwells with those who honor him.

57:14-16 The Lord as High and Holy

The opening stanza recalls Isaiah 40:3, where a way for the Lord's coming must be prepared so that the Lord's glory may be revealed (57:14-15a). Here, however, a voice from the Lord's court enjoins the preparation of a way for *my people*. This bidding serves to announce the redemption of the exiles under the Lord's mandate (cf. Brueggemann, 1998b:181). It is clear that the voice from the court speaks for the Lord because notice is given that the Lord himself will now speak. The notice describes the Lord as the *high and lofty One* (NIV), restating the description of the Lord's glory and holiness in Isaiah 6:1-4.

The Lord's word commences in the second stanza (57:15b). The Lord declares himself as one who inhabits a high and holy plain yet who identifies with the humble and repentant. The theological terms *transcendence* and *immanence* describe this characteristic of the biblical understanding of God. Though residing in a high and holy place, beyond time and space, yet God also resides among those who acknowledge his presence and power (cf. Isa 66:1-2).

The conjunction for introduces the last stanza (57:16). The Lord's residence among the repentant and humble enables his understanding of human weakness. Although anger and accusation belong to God, God does not exercise them with impunity but with compassion. The wearying of the human spirit must be taken into account.

57:17-21 The Lord as Healer

A thematic shift takes place at 57:17. Now the Lord reflects on his anger against his people (them) as well as the consequences of exercising that anger with impunity (57:17-18a). The cause of the Lord's anger lies in his people's profit based on violence. The Hebrew (*beṣaʻ*) is much stronger than the English *wicked covetousness* (NRSV) or *sinful greed* (NIV). It means profit made by violence (profiteering; cf. BDB: 130; Isa 33:15; 56:11). The Lord, it seems, struggles with his anger and resolves to pursue the way of healing, in spite of his people's continuing penchant for backsliding.

Comfort and peace provide the substance of this healing (57:18b-19). Comfort, as Brueggemann insists, is not merely solace but also "a powerful intervention that creates new possibilities" (1998b:16). The phrase *creating . . . the fruit of the lips* invites interpretation. The intention seems to be speech that is healing rather than merely consoling. The Lord's word contends that peace lies at the heart of this healing. This peace (*šalom*) includes health, prosperity, and security as well as the absence of war.

The final stanza places an accent on the wicked, who stand in opposition to this peace (57:20-21). The tossing sea serves as an image of the wicked. The wicked, identified in 56:9–57:13, turn to practices leading to death. They churn up mud and mire! Peace does not belong to them. Peace belongs to those who choose healing with its roots in *šalom*.

THE TEXT IN BIBLICAL CONTEXT

Healing, Peace, Comfort

Isaiah 49–57 closes with a reflection on the reality of the Lord's anger toward human rebellion as well as his commitment to a process of restoration. The psalmists understand the seriousness of God's anger when they ask, "Will you be angry with us forever?" (Ps 85:5; cf. 74:1; 79:5; 80:4). In the OT the Lord's anger is proverbial. Willful human rebellion is the primary cause of it.

Alongside this anger lies God's mercy, mercy that takes account of human weakness (Isa 57:16). The Bible often speaks of the Lord as "merciful and gracious, slow to anger, and abounding in steadfast love and faithfulness" (Exod 34:6; cf. Num 14:18; Neh 9:17; Ps 86:15). The particular expressions of God's mercy in Isaiah 57 are his readiness to heal, his promise of comfort to those who mourn, and the gift of peace to those near and far.

God's readiness to heal appears at intervals throughout the OT. In Genesis 20 God heals Abimelech of an innocent mistake. Abraham serves as a prophet, who prays for Abimelech's healing. In 2 Kings 20 (= Isa 38) the Lord heals Hezekiah of an illness. There it is Hezekiah's prayer for healing that the Lord answers. The prophet Isaiah communicates the news to the king. The psalmist in Psalm 60 pleads with God to heal ("mend," NIV) the land (v. 2; Heb. v. 4), implying that God is ready and able to do so. The evidence of God's readiness to heal occurs often in the Gospels (cf. Matt 8:16; Mark 1:34; Luke 6:19; John 5). There Jesus is the agent of God's healing.

The promise of God's comfort appears in both Testaments. At times the promise is addressed to those who mourn, as in Isaiah 57:18. More often the promise refers to comfort in a more general sense, to give moral help to those confronting enemies (Ps 86:17) or to give spiritual strength to those who suffer (2 Cor 1:3-4).

The promise of peace to the far and near in Isaiah 57:19 is echoed in the declaration of Christ as *our peace* in Ephesians 2:11-22. Such a reinterpretation of the OT by the NT is commonplace. Those in the early church who wrote the NT knew the *source* of their faith to be in God's coming to them in Jesus the Messiah. But they understood the *roots* of their faith to be in the OT's testimony to God's relationship to his people in the millennia before the birth of Jesus.

THE TEXT IN THE LIFE OF THE CHURCH

Aliens and Foreigners

The call to include foreigners and eunuchs at the center of Israelite worship in Isaiah 56:3-8 foreshadowed the early church's debate about including Gentiles. Philip seems to have understood the logic of inclusion right away (Acts 8:26-40). Peter struggled with it (Acts 10; cf. Gal 2:11-12). Paul, after his conversion, understood himself to be an apostle to the Gentiles (Rom 11:13).

The debate came to a head in the controversy over whether Gentile believers had to keep the law of Moses as a condition of salvation (Acts 15:1). At the council of Jerusalem, it was decided not to impose these practices on Gentile followers of Jesus. They were exhorted, however, to abstain from four actions judged to be harmful to their new Christian spirituality: (1) *things polluted by idols*, (2) *fornication*, (3) *whatever has been strangled*, and (4) *blood* (Acts 15:20).

The question of including outsiders often troubles the church today. The criteria for admission into Israel's worship in Isaiah 56:3-8 provide clues for answering the question. In Isaiah 56 inclusion rested on faithfulness to central tenets of Israelite faith (Sabbath keeping, choosing to please God, holding fast to God's covenant, loving the Lord's name, being his servants).

The church would soon lose its integrity if outsiders could enter on their own terms and conditions. Problems arise, however, when outsiders are excluded on the basis of racial, cultural, or other criteria that are not central to the faith. Such criteria need to be examined so that all who come to faith may find refuge in the church. Agreeing on the criteria that are central to the faith can be a contentious issue. Carrying on the discussion in the spirit of Christ is more important than perfect harmony on every point.

Part 6
New Heavens and New Earth

Isaiah 58–66

OVERVIEW

The book of Isaiah draws to a conclusion in chapters 58–66 with an unabated onslaught of prophetic poetry coaxing and sparring with God's people to live a life worthy of their calling (paraphrasing Eph 4:1). Only at the end of the book, in Isaiah 66:17-24, does this poetry give way to a prosaic style in which promise follows judgment and blessing presides over curse.

The call to combine social ethics and personal piety dominates chapter 58. The complement to this call follows in chapter 59: upon their confession of injustice, the Lord comes as Redeemer to those who repent of their sin.

Chapters 60 through 62 form a trilogy of closely related reflections around a central theme. This theme may be stated as Jerusalem's righteousness founded on the Lord's redemption. Chapter 60 develops the Lord's coming as Redeemer (from chap. 59), seeing this coming as the Lord's glory rising upon his people as everlasting light. Everlasting joy and everlasting covenant in Isaiah 61 follow the good news of liberation. The Lord's salvation for Zion-Jerusalem concludes the trilogy in chapter 62.

Isaiah 63 and 64 belong together as contrasting pictures of God's judgment and salvation. Edom as the object of the Lord's judgment serves as a foil to Zion, the object of the Lord's salvation.

The last two chapters form a two-part conclusion to the book. The rebellious people are addressed with words of judgment in chapter 65, and the Lord's servants are addressed with words of promise in chapter 66.

Isaiah 58:1-14

Bona Fide Piety

PREVIEW

The contrast between genuine and counterfeit piety dominates the opening chapter of part 6 in the book of Isaiah. The chapter falls into five segments. The first four contrast rebellion and faithfulness assessed according to ways of fasting. The chapter opens with a general announcement of rebellion, with fasting as a specific instance of unfaithfulness (58:1-4). The next two segments reflect first on false fasting, then on true fasting, concluding with the spiritual fruit that matures from true fasting (58:5-6, 7-9a). The fourth segment includes conditions underlying bona fide piety that will, in turn, transform the one who implements them (58:9b-12). Throughout these segments the prophet does not mean to redefine the form that fasting takes but to correct its abuse. Guidance and restoration serve as the distinctive features of the Lord's blessing (58:11, 12).

Sabbath keeping, the fifth segment, appears at the end of the chapter (58:13-14). It is assumed that moral application, integral to the discipline of fasting, also applies to Sabbath observance.

OUTLINE

Sins of the House of Jacob, 58:1-4
The Lord's Purpose for Fasting, 58:5-6
Sharing Bread with the Hungry, 58:7-9a
Conditions of the Lord's Guidance, 58:9b-12
Nourished on the Heritage of Jacob, 58:13-14

EXPLANATORY NOTES

The contrasting themes of delighting in self-interest or in God-interest bind the chapter together. To delight in (ḥapeṣ) knowing God's ways and nearness appears in 58:2. Delighting in self-interest, however, defines the motive for fasting in 58:3. At the end of the chapter, abstaining from the pursuit of self-interest serves as the motive for Sabbath observance (58:13).

Isaiah 58:1-4 warns God's people collectively (using plural verbs) about rebellion in the form of bogus piety. Isaiah 58:5-14, on the other hand, exhorts God's people individually (using singular verbs) about the substance of bona fide piety.

Sins of the House of Jacob 58:1-4

An announcement of the sins of God's people is compared to a trumpeter using a ram's horn, raising the alarm of impending danger (58:1). An inventory of sins, however, does not immediately follow the command to announce them (cf. Joel 2:15, where the sound of the ram's horn announces a fast).

What appears to be a register of the people's faithfulness is stated in the next three stanzas (58:2ab, 2c-3a, 3b-4). They seek the Lord (58:2ab). The NRSV and NIV understand the text as irony and add *as if they were a nation* (*as a nation*, Heb.) practicing justice. The NIV also adds that *they seem eager* (*they are eager*, Heb.). It is not necessary to read into this stanza an accusation of hypocrisy against the people. Rather, the prophet sketches a picture of the people honestly seeking to know God's ways, oblivious to their own rebellion (Whybray: 212).

They are eager, they inquire, they long for God's nearness (58:2c-3a). The reality of their rebellion surfaces quite innocently, it seems, in a set of parallel questions formed as a complaint addressed to God:

> *Why do we fast, but you do not see?*
> *Why humble ourselves, but you do not notice?* (58:3a)

Should not God at least observe with appreciation the *form* that piety takes? No doubt the form that piety takes *is* noticed on high. But in God's design, form and substance belong together.

The separation of form and substance lies at the center of God's accusation (58:3b-4). The accusation opens with the interjection *hen* (*Look*, NRSV; *Behold*, RSV), calling the people to attention. The pursuit of self-interest lies in the exploitation of *workers*. The Hebrew word for workers is 'aṣabim, *sufferers*. Workers are exploited even as those who own the

Isaiah 58:1-14

material capital exhibit a piety separated from justice and righteousness. The same interjection (*hen*) continues the accusation, giving additional detail to this bogus piety. It is not clear whether fasting in which *quarreling and strife* (NIV) occur is internecine (among the owners) or directed by the owners to the workers, creating and extending their suffering. In any case, God does not sanction such quarrelsome behavior.

The Lord's Purpose for Fasting 58:5-6

Three rhetorical questions [*Literary Perspective, p. 446*] dominate the next stanza (58:5). The first two are clearly rhetorical; this means that the answer (No!) is already implied in the question. At issue is self-denial as an end in itself rather than as a means toward an end. Fasting as a means of calling attention primarily to the form of piety (*to humble oneself*) fails to address the substance of piety. The second question develops the theme of form to include three recognizable acts of piety: bowing down, wearing sackcloth, and applying ashes. Each of these calls attention to form and, by itself, does not meet the standard of fasting chosen by the Lord. The third question employs sarcasm, again calling into question fasting centered on form.

A new rhetorical question, this one inviting a positive response, is now put forward (58:6). The question begins on the first line and continues with a sequence of three infinitive clauses stating liberation from social oppression on lines 2 through 4 (*to loose, to undo, to let go free*). The various translations usually include the last line of the stanza (*and to break every yoke*) as part of the sequence, although its form is different in the Hebrew text. The stanza as a whole declares the soul of bona fide piety to be in implementing God's just order. What characterizes genuine fasting is not the pursuit of self-interest, but concern for the well-being of others.

Sharing Bread with the Hungry 58:7-9a

Another rhetorical question inviting a positive response begins the next segment (58:7). The specifics of liberation now emerge as caring for the impoverished and the destitute. The poor are not strangers and aliens but *your own kin*. Fasting as a spiritual resource for a social ethic that addresses the problems of poverty lies at the center of God's intention for his people.

Two uses of an adverb of time (*then*), signifying a fulfillment of the rhetorical question in 58:7, conclude the segment (58:8-9a). The first sign of this fulfillment comes in four parallel phrases (*your light, your healing, your righteousness,* and *your rear guard*, NIV), each phrase linked to a promise (58:8).

Your light refers to the clarity of insight that fasting is a spiritual resource for social action. This clarity rests on the authority of the speaker (the Lord) and not merely on human insight. *Your healing* indicates restoration of social health as an accompaniment of spiritual healing. *Your righteousness* (*vindication,* NRSV note) means right behavior as the vanguard of God's people. *Your rear guard* is none other than the Lord's glory itself, guarantee of safety and security. God is in the front and at the back, protecting the one who seeks him.

The second sign of this fulfillment, also introduced by *then,* comes in the form of the age-old promise of God's presence when his people call on him in their time of need (58:9a).

Conditions of the Lord's Guidance 58:9b-12

In the NRSV and NIV, the if-clause that opens this segment is taken as a new thought (58:9b-10; note the gap in the text between the two parts of v. 9). It is clear that the removal of the yoke, already mentioned in 58:6, means the yoke of injustice, particularly accusation and slander (Brueggemann, 1998b:191). The if-clause is completed in 58:10. Now the theme returns to the satisfaction of the hungry. In 58:7 sharing bread with the hungry constitutes a fast acceptable to the Lord. Here offering *yourself* to the hungry constitutes the appropriate response to God's presence. Satisfying the needs of the oppressed lies alongside this offering. When such selfless giving occurs, God's people experience illumination and the dissipation of gloom.

It is no accident that the promise of guidance and restoration follows the forging of the people's spirituality and social consciousness (58:11; cf. Hanson: 207). Guidance, satisfaction of needs, and strength represent blessings, although probably not in order of ascending importance, as Young suggests (1972:424). The pictures of a watered garden and a spring of water portray the prosperity of a people that receives God's guidance.

Reconstruction of ruins flows from the Lord's continual guidance (58:12). The *ancient ruins* may refer in general to the results of the Babylonian military campaign in Judah at the beginning of the sixth century BC, when Nebuchadnezzar's army ravaged the land (Whybray: 217). The titles *Repairer of Broken Walls* and *Restorer of Streets with Dwellings* (NIV) applaud the process of reconstruction.

Nourished on the Heritage of Jacob 58:13-14

A conditional sentence commending Sabbath keeping stretches over the last two stanzas of the chapter. The first stanza includes three subordinate clauses, each beginning with the conjunction *if* to introduce the conditional sentence (58:13):

> *If you keep your feet from breaking . . .*
> *from doing . . .*
> *if you call the Sabbath a delight*
> *and the LORD's holy day . . .*
> *if you honor it by not going . . .*
> *not doing . . . or speaking . . .* (NIV)

The theme of Sabbath-keeping departs from the chapter's focus on fasting. But the deeper intention of the chapter unites the two themes. At the beginning of the chapter, false piety is fasting alongside exploitation (doing *as you please*, 58:3 NIV). Here at the end of the chapter, true piety is Sabbath-keeping in order to honor the Lord's holy day (not *doing as you please*, 58:13 NIV). Bona fide piety includes spiritual disciplines. These disciplines attest to faith that embraces the form of piety (fasting, Sabbath-keeping) without abandoning the substance of piety (justice).

The adverb *then* opens the main clause of the conditional sentence (58:14). Having engaged in the spiritual discipline of Sabbath-keeping, the result is a wondrous relationship with the Lord. The Lord, in turn, honors the discipline and relationship with promises of well-being (Whybray: 219).

These promises echo the Song of Moses in Deuteronomy 32. There Jacob is described as the Lord's "allotted inheritance" (32:9), whom he made to "ride on the heights of the land" (32:13 NIV). Riding on the heights of the land in Isaiah 58 serves as a metaphor of prosperity. Such prosperity cannot be separated from the source of Israel's life, the faith of Jacob. The *inheritance of your father Jacob* (NIV) stands in contrast to the sins of the house of Jacob at the beginning of the chapter. The heritage continues to confront the sin. A final "signature," indicating the Lord's authority as speaker, closes the stanza (58:14).

THE TEXT IN BIBLICAL CONTEXT

Food, Shelter, Clothing

The Bible often exhibits the principle that a person's relationship to others reveals that person's relationship to God. In Isaiah 58:7 the principle finds expression in the call to distribute the resources of food, shelter, and clothing to those in need. Here, as Brueggemann says, is "a clear, radical statement of social ethics that is at the heart of Judaism" (1998b:189).

The principle that a person's relationship to others reveals that person's relationship to God appears in Deuteronomy 15:11, where open-handedness to the poor is commanded, and in 22:1-4, where helping a person in need is incumbent upon one who keeps the law. Ezekiel defines the righteous person as one whose life is characterized by right living that includes giving food to the hungry and clothing to the naked (18:5-9). Job asserts his integrity as a man of faith because of his regard for those in need (31:16-23). Throughout the OT the principle is reaffirmed.

The NT does not lose sight of the principle. Jesus' parable of the Good Samaritan demonstrates the importance of showing mercy (Luke 10:25-37). In Jesus' parable of the great judgment, compassion for the hungry, the thirsty, the stranger, the naked, the sick, and the prisoner is a key to God's blessing (Matt 25:31-46). Paul reflects this teaching when he writes that "the only thing that counts is faith working through love" (Gal 5:6). And James in his letter warns against faith in Christ that is unaccompanied by works of righteousness (2:14-26). Throughout Scripture, devotion to God is expressed in active concern for the welfare of fellow human beings.

Fasting

Fasting as a spiritual discipline occurs throughout the Bible. The Hebrew word for fasting (*ṣwm*) is used seven times in Isaiah 58. A corresponding Hebrew word (*'anah*), which means *to be bowed down* but in some cases means *to be humbled* by fasting, also occurs in Isaiah 58 (once each in vv. 3 and 5). The Day of Atonement is the only fast legislated in the law codes (D. Wright: 72-76). The so-called Holiness Code (Lev 19–26) includes a calendar of appointed festivals, including the Day of Atonement (Lev 23:26-32). The word *'anah* is used there to refer to self-denial, which is usually understood to mean fasting.

The occasions for fasting are varied in the OT. They include the fast of mourning after the death of Saul and Jonathan (1 Sam 31:13), David's fast when his child was ill (2 Sam 12:15-23), and Ahab's fast after Elijah's indictment (1 Kings 21:27). After the exile, fasts are proclaimed before the return to Jerusalem (Ezra 8:21-23) and as a support to Esther before her request to King Ahasuerus (Xerxes I; Esther 4:15-17). There are fasts of repentance in the books of Joel (1:14) and Jonah (3:5).

Jesus observed a forty-day fast after his baptism (Matt 4:1-11; Mark 1:12-13; Luke 4:1-13). His attitude toward this discipline is indicated in the Sermon on the Mount (Matt 6:16-21). Jesus assumed that fasting is a legitimate spiritual discipline. Yet his emphasis was not on its publicity but on its function to energize faithful living. Luke mentions fasting and prayer together in his account of the expansion of the early church (Acts 13:3; 14:23). In general, the NT is reserved about fasting, not excluding it but also not giving it a place of priority in the life of the church.

THE TEXT IN THE LIFE OF THE CHURCH

True Evangelical Faith

Menno Simons in his *Reply to False Accusations* (1552) gives an account of his evangelical faith, inspired in part by Isaiah 58:

> All those who are born of God, who are gifted with the Spirit of the Lord, who are, according to the Scriptures, called into one body and love in Christ Jesus, are prepared by such love to serve their neighbors, not only with money and goods, but also after the example of their Lord and Head, Jesus Christ, in an evangelical manner, with life and blood. They show mercy and love, as much as they can. No one among them is allowed to beg. They take to heart the need of the saints. They entertain those in distress. They take the stranger into their houses. They comfort the afflicted; assist the needy; clothe the naked; feed the hungry; do not turn their face from the poor; do not despise their own flesh. Isa 58:7, 8. (558)

Here Menno speaks for the church and to the church, urging the alliance of faith and love. Faith and love together do not refer primarily to feelings and sentiment but especially to a commitment that addresses needs beyond self.

Isaiah 59:1-21

The God Who Comes

PREFACE

The reality and confession of human rebellion against God receives graphic illustration in this chapter. Human failure dominates the first section, epitomized by a failure to discern the way of peace (59:1-8). In the second section this lamentable situation issues in a confession of sin (59:9-15a).

A turning point takes place in the third section (59:15b-21). The Lord intervenes as a warrior to reward faithfulness and punish offense. God is One who comes as Redeemer. The triad of his covenant, his spirit, and his words concludes the section and the chapter. The Lord's covenant, spirit, and words are durable and intergenerational (59:21).

OUTLINE

Human Failure, 59:1-8
    59:1-3   The Lord's Hand, the People's Hands
    59:4-8   Deeds and Thoughts of Wickedness
Confession of Sin, 59:9-15a
    59:9-11   Justice Is Far Away
    59:12-15a   Transgressions Are Near at Hand
The Lord's Coming, 59:15b-21
    59:15b-17   Absence of Justice and Truth
    59:18-20   Coming as Rushing River, as Redeemer
    59:21   The Lord's Spirit and Words

Isaiah 59:1-21

EXPLANATORY NOTES

Human Failure 59:1-8

59:1-3 The Lord's Hand, the People's Hands

The contrast between the Lord's hand and the people's hands provides the key to an interpretation of 59:1-3. The opening stanza asserts that the Lord's hand and ear are perfectly adequate to save and to hear respectively (59:1-2). A similar assertion about the Lord's hand appears elsewhere:

> Is my hand shortened, that it cannot redeem?
> Or have I no power to deliver? (50:2

In spite of the Lord's power to save and his willingness to hear, his people choose iniquities and so erect barriers in their relationship to the Lord. *Iniquity* ('awon) means belief and action that is opposed to what is morally right or justifiable. Such opposition to God's power to save and to hear means that God turns his face away and does not hear. Clearly, God is able to hear, but he now chooses not to hear by hiding his face.

After the initial assertion of the Lord's strength to save and his disposition to hear, the second-person plural form of address (English *you*) identifies the listeners as God's people. Their behavior stands as an impediment to an authentic relationship with God.

The direct address continues in the second stanza (59:3). Now the focus is on the people's hands. Hands and fingers together symbolize *acts* of violence. Lips and tongue follow close behind, symbolizing *speech* that cultivates violence. Acts and speech of violence constitute an assault on both God and humankind (cf. Brueggemann, 1998b:196).

59:4-8 Deeds and Thoughts of Wickedness

Five four-line stanzas continue the thought of the chapter's beginning, but in a new mode. Direct address gives way to third-person discourse in 59:4-8. The first stanza laments the perversion of the legal system (59:4). Empty arguments, lying, concocting devilry, and breeding wickedness displace the rule of law. The stanza enlarges on the spoken lies and muttered wickedness of 59:3.

The second and third stanzas illustrate the perversion of justice with a picture of poisonous eggs and treacherous webs (59:5, 6). The second stanza offers a composite metaphor in which hatching, weaving, and eating signify the concoction of wickedness in the previous stanza (59:5). The third stanza develops the imagery of weaving in the second stanza, but in a new direction (59:6). The spider's web, it now states, serves as a cover-up of perversity rather than as a trap. The poet insists that wickedness and violence cannot be covered up but need to be exposed for what they are.

The fourth stanza alters the imagery again (59:7). Now it is the feet and thoughts that carry out evil designs. Haste accompanies the intention to do violence, as if patience might be the occasion for second thoughts. It is in the region of the mind that the planning for death and destruction begins. The word *highways* at the end of the stanza completes the imagery of a road on which the feet run to carry out violence.

Knowing the way of peace characterizes the last stanza (59:8). The way of peace (in the first line) stands in stark contrast to the highways strewn with desolation and destruction at the end of the previous stanza. The way of peace serves as an antidote to all the wrongdoing enumerated in the previous stanzas. Behind the indictment that God's people do not know the way of peace is an invitation to consider this alternative way. The prophet, speaking God's Word, does not think of the way of peace as an impossible ideal. Rather, it is a challenge to those who call themselves realists to comprehend the realism of knowing peace.

The stanza serves as a fitting conclusion to 59:4-7 as well as an ending to the entire first section (59:1-8).

Confession of Sin 59:9-15a

In the second section the people speak in the first-person plural voice. The speech is a confession of sin but without a clear statement of repentance for sin.

59:9-11 Justice Is Far Away

The three stanzas that make up this part describe the present lamentable situation. The opening word *Therefore* indicates that the confession flows from the inability to grasp the way of peace (59:9). It is no surprise that justice and righteousness [*Justice and Righteousness, p. 445*] are remote if the way of peace is missing. The people confess to waiting for the light. *Light* surely refers to the way of peace. Watts is right in pointing out that while waiting is an appropriate religious exercise, simply waiting without addressing the issue of violence leads to hopelessness (1987:283).

The confession focuses on blindness in the second stanza (59:10). *Darkness* in the previous stanza seems to refer to the lack of knowledge that keeps justice and righteousness at a distance. Now it is also a question of *blindness*, a condition that prevents justice and righteousness from flourishing. The stumbling that results leads to death.

In the third stanza the confession turns to images of anger and despair (59:11). The picture of growling bears and mourning doves expresses an element of self-pity. The wait for justice and salvation seems to be vacant waiting, without a spirituality to nourish it. The text does not imply that such a spirituality is impossible, only that its potential has not been exploited.

59:12-15a Transgressions Are Near at Hand

The description of the present lamentable situation in 59:9-11 now gives way to general confession. The confession extends over three stanzas. The Bible's favorite words for wrongdoing (*transgressions, sins, iniquities*) are listed in the first stanza (59:12; cf. Lev 16:21; Ps 32:1-2). The confession that they know their iniquities recalls the accusation in 59:8 that they do not know the way of peace.

An elaboration of their wrongdoing takes place in the second stanza (59:13). Denial of the Lord at the beginning of the stanza merges seamlessly into speech of revolution in the social sphere at the end (cf. Whybray: 224). With its admission of wrongdoing, the entire confession can be compared to confessions, whether as genuine statements or as divine promptings, found elsewhere in the prophets (e.g., Jer 3:22b–4:2; Hos 14:2-3).

The parallel terms *justice* and *righteousness* introduce the last stanza (59:14-15a [*Justice and Righteousness, p. 445*]). As in 59:9 justice and righteousness are far away. Truth and honesty along with justice and righteousness form a quartet of standards for God's rule. Their absence indicates a community far from God. The final line of the stanza summarizes the level to which God's people have fallen. In 59:7 their feet run to evil (*ra'*). Here when they turn from evil (*ra'*), they are preyed upon (cf. NIV).

The Lord's Coming 59:15b-21

59:15b-17 Absence of Justice and Truth

The Lord's response to this confession without repentance is to take action, employing the tools of salvation and righteousness. The first stanza expresses the Lord's umbrage and intention to do something about it (59:15b-16). The word *displeased* fails to communicate the extent of the Lord's disappointment. The Hebrew phrase, literally translated, means *It was evil in his eyes that there was no justice*. The word *appalled* (better yet, *devastated*) evokes the full measure of the Lord's disapproval. In the Bible the arm of the Lord always refers to the Lord's power. Here the Lord's arm moves to restore salvation and righteousness where these, till now, have been kept at arm's length.

The language shifts to battle gear in the second stanza (59:17).

Paul employed this language in some of his epistles to describe the spiritual armor needed for protection against the powers of evil (TBC). In Isaiah the Lord's battle gear includes defensive armor (breastplate, helmet) and clothing symbolizing the determination to pursue the salvation of his people. His battle dress also includes reprisal and wrath, which provide the energy for punishment.

59:18-20 Coming as Rushing River, as Redeemer

Although the textual difficulties of 59:18 are considerable, the general sense of the stanza is reasonably clear. The Lord will discipline his enemies according to their deeds. God's enemies, including the evil-minded in Israel, will be punished (cf. Kaufmann: 183).

The Lord's coming forms the center of the second stanza (59:19-20). Those to the west and the east of Israel refer to the nations. They are the enemies, mentioned in the previous stanza, who now acknowledge the Lord's dominion (cf. Whybray: 227-28). There is an underlying theme in Isaiah that should be noted here, of the nations learning God's ways (2:1-5; 25:3; 42:1-4, 5-9; 45:14, 22-25; 49:6; 51:4-5; 52:10; 55:5; 60:1-5; 66:18-20).

The image of a rushing stream driven by the wind of the Lord signifies the Lord's irrepressible sovereignty. His coming as Redeemer to Zion-Jacob is tempered by the requirement of turning from transgression (cf. Brueggemann, 1998b:202). There is no blanket amnesty but one that requires a decision to repent of sin. A final declaration of the Lord (*says the LORD*) leaves no doubt about who is speaking.

59:21 The Lord's Spirit and Words

Modern translations cast 59:21 in a prose format, separating it from the previous text (cf. NRSV, NIV, JB). It makes more sense to see 59:21 in continuity with the foregoing subject matter by placing it in a poetry format (cf. Watts, 1987:285). I have placed this verse in two stanzas that form a continuous thought:

> [21a]*And me, this is my covenant with them, says the LORD:*
> *my spirit that is upon you,*
> *and my words that I have put in your mouth*
>
> [21b]*shall not cease from your mouth,*
> *or the mouth of your descendants,*
> *or the mouth of their descendants, says the LORD,*
> *now and into the future.* (AT)

The reference to the Lord's words in particular is intended as a contrast to the people's lying speech and speech of oppression and revolt earlier in the chapter (59:3, 13).

The first stanza gives voice to the enduring character of the Lord's spirit and words (59:21a). It recalls the cadence of Genesis 9:9 and 17:4, where covenant making is central. The sequence *my covenant, my spirit*, and *my words* in Isaiah 59:21a provides the key to the meaning of the stanza. The Lord's covenant *with them* refers to Zion-Jacob but also to the larger horizon of God's covenants with Noah and Abraham in Genesis 9 and 17. In the context of 59:20, this includes the former enemies from west and east who now acknowledge the Lord's dominion. The Lord's spirit and words refer to the mandate given to Zion-Jacob and, perhaps especially, to the prophets within Zion-Jacob. This mandate includes the Lord's spirit to bring justice to the nations (42:1) and the Lord's words to rehabilitate Jacob-Israel (51:16).

The second stanza guarantees the power of these words perpetually (59:21b). The Lord is not speaking here to Israel as a nation but to those in Israel who repent in the biblical sense of turning from their sin. The intention, Brueggemann argues, is to specify as faithful Israel those "who are visibly and easily contrasted with 'the transgressors' who do not care about torah obedience" (1998b:203).

THE TEXT IN BIBLICAL CONTEXT

God's Armor

The use of armor in battle is an ancient practice. In 1 Samuel 17 the Philistine Goliath wore a helmet of bronze and a coat of mail (breastplate). The Israelite David was fitted with the same armor but had to abandon it because it was too heavy. He opted instead for his sling and stones.

The figure of speech in Isaiah 59:17 has God putting on breastplate and helmet, representing righteousness and salvation, as well as other attire. The reference to a belt of righteousness around the waist and a belt of faithfulness around the hips of the *shoot* from *the stump of Jesse* in Isaiah 11:5 has a similar ring to it.

In the apocryphal book Wisdom of Solomon, the Lord also puts on righteousness as a breastplate and wears justice as a helmet (5:18). The Lord is said to "arm all creation to repel his enemies" (5:17). Still, it seems that the Lord's miracle does the repelling rather than humans carrying out a bloodbath on God's behalf.

The NT develops the figure of speech in a different direction. The classic text is Ephesians 6:10-20, which uses armor-of-God language. Yoder Neufeld notes that Ephesians employs the language of Isaiah 59 in order to be clear that although the armor belongs to God it is believers who wear it. Although vengeance and wrath are a component of God's armor in Isaiah 59, they are not stressed in Ephesians. Even so, the struggle against the spiritual forces of evil is no less real, and their defeat is no less certain (308-10). God's armor, both as metaphor and as reality, enhances the importance of living in the strength of God's power.

In 1 Thessalonians 5:8 Paul writes about putting on "the breastplate of faith and love, and for a helmet the hope of salvation." His argument there focuses on followers of Jesus being children of light and God's armor being available for their use.

Elsewhere in Paul's letters the imagery of God's armor comes into view. In Romans 13:12 Paul encourages his readers to "put on the armor of light." In 2 Corinthians Paul speaks about "the weapons of righteousness" (6:7) and "the weapons of our warfare" (10:4). These weapons refer to spiritual armament, and they exclude the swords and spears of ancient warfare.

The armor that God wears and furnishes is the armor of justice and righteousness. Prayer and alertness are the physical manifestations of this spiritual armor.

THE TEXT IN THE LIFE OF THE CHURCH

Human Intervention

Isaiah 59:16 (NIV) observes:

> [the LORD] saw that there was no one
> and was appalled that there was no one to intervene.

Synagogue and church have understood this to mean that humans serve as God's agents in the exercise of justice. The Lord's disquiet in the face of human injustice, writes Brueggemann, indicates the Lord's assumption "that some in Israel would accept responsibility for justice, which is Israel's great *raison d'être*. But no, none! Nobody cared; nobody bothered. Nobody took the trouble. The community is in a deeply sorry state" (1998b:200).

In his book *The Believers' Church*, Donald F. Durnbaugh includes a chapter (9) entitled "Mutual Aid and Service." This chapter enumerates personal, communal, social, and international dimensions of believers churches practicing mutual aid and service. The church's great *raison d'être*, alongside Israel's, is that responsibility for justice will be shouldered and not shrugged off.

Durnbaugh's many examples of mutual aid and service include the

Heifer Project. From his work of giving reconstituted milk to children during the Spanish Civil War, Dan West conceived the idea of bringing cows from North America to Spain, to supply milk on a long-term basis. Back in the United States he generated interest in the idea and began implementing it in 1944. The idea was that each person who received a cow would donate the first heifer to another needy person, creating a "chain reaction of love." This Brethren-sponsored program helped in the reconstruction of Europe after World War II by replacing depleted livestock herds.

Rural people in other North American denominations became interested in the practical wisdom of the Heifer Project, and the project soon became interdenominational. By the mid-1960s over a million animals had been shipped from North America to more than eighty-four nations (Durnbaugh: 280).

This way of shouldering justice and not shrugging it off continues to be the church's responsibility. Such a responsibility has its roots in texts such as Isaiah 59:16.

Isaiah 60:1-22

Everlasting Light

PREVIEW

Confidence and hope characterize the overall theme and cast of this chapter and the next two chapters. Isaiah 60 expands upon God's coming as Redeemer, stated as a promise in 59:17-21, by depicting this coming as the Lord's glory rising upon his people. As a result, this people becomes a peaceable kingdom, to which nations come.

Throughout the chapter, the Lord speaks. The second-person feminine addressee (*you, your*) refers to Zion, representing the city of Jerusalem, lying in ruins. The first part of the chapter calls on fallen Zion to rise (60:1-7). After rising, she becomes a gathering place for exiles and nations.

The second part of the chapter delineates the outline of a new community in a new Jerusalem (60:8-22). This new Jerusalem, in the book of Revelation, becomes "the holy city . . . coming down out of heaven from God, prepared as a bride adorned for her husband" (Rev 21:2). God, coming to redeem his people, moves in the direction of the whole earth's sharing God's salvation.

OUTLINE

The Lord's Light Rising, 60:1-7
    60:1-5   Appearance of the Lord's Glory
    60:6-7   Coming of the Nations

Isaiah 60:1-22

City of the Lord, 60:8-22
    60:8-12   Walls and Gates
    60:13-14   Sanctuary
    60:15-18   Walls of Salvation, Gates of Praise
    60:19-22   Everlasting Light

EXPLANATORY NOTES

The Lord's Light Rising 60:1-7

The first and shorter part of the chapter focuses on the Lord's light rising on fallen Zion, and on nations coming to that light. There are two clusters of verses. In the first cluster, nations come to Zion, upon whom the Lord's glory has risen (60:1-5) [*Glory, p. 443*]. The second cluster makes it clear that the nations come, not to Zion as such, but to the Lord, whose name and house are in Zion (60:6-7).

60:1-5 Appearance of the Lord's Glory

Back-to-back imperative verbs (*Arise, shine*) open the first stanza (60:1-2a). These verbs constitute a wake-up call because the Lord announces his favor, signified by his glory. The antecedent of *your* and *you* is Zion, mentioned in 59:20, and is generally understood to refer to the Jews who had been exiles in Babylon but who have recently returned to Palestine. Here Jerusalem, along with their hopes, lies in ruins (Whybray: 229). At the end of the stanza, intense darkness envelops the earth (60:2a). This is a deliberate contrast to the intense light of the Lord's glory. The darkness represents the extinguished hopes of earth's peoples: ignorance, disease, war, and suffering. The theme of the Lord's glory rising upon fallen Zion continues in the second stanza (60:2b-3). The result is that nations and kings come to Zion, which is illuminated by the Lord's light. The Lord comes to Zion as Redeemer in 59:20. Only then can Zion, upon whom the Lord's glory has risen, receive the nations. The reader will recall a similar text in Isaiah 2:1-5:

> Many peoples shall come and say,
> "Come, let us go up to the mountain of the LORD,
>   to the house of the God of Jacob. . . ." (2:3)
> O house of Jacob,
>   come, let us walk in the light of the LORD! (2:5)

In 2:1-5 the nations and peoples come to learn the Lord's law. In 60:1-5 nations and kings come to Zion's light, reflecting the Lord's glory.

The third stanza focuses on the gathering of Zion's sons and daughters (60:4). The first two lines quote 49:18a exactly, and the last two lines reflect the theme and some of the language of 49:22a. Here then, as also in the NT, earlier texts are brought together to make a new point (cf. Rom 15:9-12).

Not only are the exiles gathered to Zion; the wealth and abundance of the nations also come with them (60:5). Words of astonishment describe the feelings of happiness (lit., *to be radiant*), excitement (lit., *your heart shall be in awe*), and joy (lit., *your heart shall be enlarged*). It seems that a gathering of scattered and lost people would be enough. But now, like icing on the cake, the ways and means of rebuilding a ruined city are also at hand.

60:6-7 Coming of the Nations

As darkness covers the earth in 60:2, so camels cover Zion in 60:6. This refers, no doubt, to a profusion of camel caravans coming to Zion, bringing commodities of all sorts. Midian and Ephah, in northwest Arabia, used camels for transport. Sheba, recalling 1 Kings 10, where the queen of Sheba brings sumptuous gifts to King Solomon's court, here receives special mention as a source of wealth and homage. Genesis 25 names these nations (Midian, Ephah, Sheba) as offspring of Abraham and Keturah. Now their gifts of gold and frankincense accompany their proclamation of *the praise of the LORD*. The intention here is to point to a reconciliation of long-lost cousins who identify themselves as worshippers of the Lord. Kedar and Nebaioth, east of Palestine, provide sheep for the sacrificial altar at Zion (60:7). Genesis 25 names Kedar and Nebaioth as sons of Ishmael, grandsons of Abraham and Hagar. All of this indicates recognition by Abraham's family of the Lord's power and prestige.

City of the Lord 60:8-22

The rising of the Lord's glory (i.e., his favor, his radiance) upon fallen Zion at the beginning of the chapter gives rise to a radiant city at the end. A signal of this development is found in the question in verse 8. From that point onward, interest shifts to the raising up of the fallen city, and the vision becomes more clearly eschatological [*Day of the Lord, p. 443*].

60:8-12 Walls and Gates

The first two stanzas belong together as a continuous stream of consciousness (60:8-9a, 9b). The opening question indicates that the ships of Tarshish are not clearly visible from the shore. They appear as a flying cloud or doves alighting on their cotes. The islands looking to the

Isaiah 60:1-22

Lord (NIV) indicates a further gathering of scattered peoples, now coming from the west in ships.

The ships of Tarshish (see commentary at 23:1-3) bring Zion's children, along with resources for reconstruction of the ruined city. The concern here is for more than material resources. The ships bring Zion's children with their wealth, to honor the Holy One of Israel, who has once again liberated his people. The picture of coastlands waiting for God's coming echoes Isaiah 42:4.

The conjunction *for* joins the two halves of the third stanza (60:10). The first half declares that foreigners and their kings, former enemies presumably, contribute to Zion's reconstruction (cf. Zech 6:15). This is so because (*for*) although these enemies served as the Lord's agents to discipline his people, this discipline is now over, and the Lord is showing his mercy.

The next stanza features open gates instead of walls (60:11). Here the prophet envisions an open city, to which the nations bring their wealth. The question sometimes raised is whether the kings come under compulsion or on their own initiative (cf. Childs: 497). The passive form *led in procession* does not require compulsion.

The problem in the last stanza is whether judgment against the nations comes as a result of not serving Zion or because they refuse to serve the Lord (60:12). The verb *ya'abduk* with its second-person feminine singular suffix (*[they] will not serve you*) indicates that not serving Zion is meant. Such a reading could be interpreted in the direction of a new nationalism. Reading 60:12 in the context of the chapter as a whole, however, indicates that Zion is meant as the nucleus of the Lord's light rather than as the axis of a new nationalism.

60:13-14 Sanctuary

The Hebrew word translated *glory* defines the first stanza (60:13). *The glory of Lebanon* refers to its riches and reputation. Lebanon's timber resources serve to enhance the Lord's sanctuary, which the Lord will *glorify*. This second use of the Hebrew word for glory refers to this sanctuary as the place for the Lord's feet to rest.

Three plural verbs (*come, bow down, call*) distinguish the next stanza (60:14). The subject of these verbs is the nations and kings mentioned earlier in the chapter. Now, however, they do not bring only their wealth; they also come in a posture of humility. This humility is not abject submission, but it bears a dignity corresponding to the dignity of the Lord's sanctuary. And so they designate the place to which they come as *City of the LORD* and *Zion of the Holy One* of Israel. Here for the first time the antecedents of the pronouns *you* and *your* in the chapter are identified as Zion-Jerusalem.

60:15-18 Walls of Salvation, Gates of Praise

The four stanzas that make up this part of chapter 60 focus on the reversal of fortune for the Lord's city. In the first stanza, majesty and joy replace abandonment (60:15). The opening word of the stanza (Heb. *tahat*, "instead of"; *whereas* in NRSV, *although* in NIV) signals the theme of reversal. The same word is repeated in each line of the third stanza (60:17a).

The second stanza includes the curious picture of Zion nursing *at royal breasts* (60:16 NIV). Watts suggests that this picture gives a further explanation of the previous verse (1987:296): it speaks of joy in the promise insinuated in 60:15. But the figure of nourishment also continues the idea of being nurtured by the wealth of the nations (cf. 60:5). It may be a way of saying that the supply lines from abroad will continue.

The concluding lines of 60:16, then, exhibit the promise in classic terms. The people shall possess a knowledge of the Lord as Savior and Redeemer, the same Mighty One who revealed himself to the patriarch Jacob. As elsewhere in the Bible, this is not merely intellectual knowledge, but also knowledge of an experiential nature that enables faith, and faith that enables people to be "doers of the word" (James 1:22).

The third stanza returns to the opening word of the first stanza (*tahat*, here translated *instead of* and repeated on each line) and enlarges on the theme of reversal (60:17a). Four substances are mentioned, and each is surpassed with a substance of greater prominence (e.g., bronze is surpassed by gold, etc.).

The fourth stanza translates this reversal into both spiritual and material categories (60:17b-18), as shown in the following diagram:

> *gold* = Peace (your overseer)
> *silver* = Righteousness (your taskmaster)
> no more violence (in your land)
> no more ruin or destruction (in your borders)
> *bronze* = Salvation (your walls)
> *iron* = Praise (your gates).

The substances of greater prominence from the third stanza are in italics. The focus is on what these substances represent rather than on identifying the substances of lesser prominence. The whole stanza presents a vision of the peaceable kingdom as God intended for Zion. The two center lines proclaim an end to violence and destruction. These lines are flanked by the metallic symbols of this reality (gold, etc.) corresponding to the names that the Lord gives (Peace, etc.).

60:19-22 Everlasting Light

The chapter ends as it began, with a soliloquy on light. In the first stanza, sun and moon cease to provide light for the city (60:19). Instead, Zion assumes the marks of a heavenly city in which the Lord's perpetual light provides illumination (cf. Childs: 499).

The role of sun and moon becomes less clear in the second stanza (60:20). It is evident that in the heavenly city, mourning will come to an end, a theme mentioned elsewhere (cf. 25:8). And although the Lord magnifies his sanctuary in 60:13, this sanctuary does not appear in the exalted, eschatological Zion of 60:19-20.

Instead, Zion's people will display the Lord's magnificence (60:21). The central meaning of the stanza lies in the somewhat disputed phrase *neṣer maṭṭaʿaw* (lit., "the shoot of his planting"; *They are the shoot I have planted*, NIV). In spite of the various text traditions, the main point is understandable. Zion's reliance is to be upon the Lord for the source and the maintenance of its spiritual life (Young, 1972:456).

The final stanza abandons the chapter's feminine singular *you* and speaks in more general terms (60:22). *The least* and *the smallest* becoming a mighty nation alludes to the promise to Abraham and Sarah (Gen 18:18) and to the Israelites as a whole (Num 14:12). The recitation in Deuteronomy 26 recalls the few who went down to Egypt, becoming a mighty nation. These allusions reinforce the overall theme of 60:19-22 that in the restored Zion, the Lord will be glorified because he has the power to act.

THE TEXT IN BIBLICAL CONTEXT

The Lord as Perpetual Light

The suggestion of the Lord as perpetual light in Isaiah 60 calls attention to the Bible's association of light and deity. The two are often associated in both Testaments. God as the creator of light is established in the story of creation (Gen 1:1-5; cf. Isa 45:7). The Lord goes in front of the fleeing Israelites in a pillar of fire by night to give them light (Exod 13:21). The lighted lamp in the tabernacle symbolizes the presence of God (27:20-21).

Light as something that belongs to God (as opposed to something inherent in God) appears in Israel's wisdom literature (cf. Job 25:3; 29:3). The Lord's face is said to diffuse light (Pss 4:6; 44:3; 89:15; 90:8). The Lord is described as wrapped in light as a person might be wrapped in a garment (Ps 104:2). The house of Jacob is called to walk in the light of the Lord (Isa 2:5). Several prophets anticipate the Lord appearing as light (Isa 60:20-21; Mic 7:8). And in what is perhaps one of the most striking images of all, Habakkuk says that God's

brightness was like the sun;
>rays came forth from his hand,
>where his power lay hidden. (3:4)

It may be said that the OT associates light and deity in a variety of contexts and expressions but does not equate the two in any absolute sense.

The NT presents a more bold identification of light and deity. Matthew associates the beginning of Jesus' ministry with Isaiah's words about the people seeing a great light and light dawning upon them (Matt 4:16, quoting Isa 9:1-2).

The Johannine literature gives special attention to the light of God. The first half of John's Gospel, the so-called Book of Signs, identifies the light of God coming into the world as Jesus (John 1–12). Jesus refers to himself as "the light of the world" (John 8:12). The first letter of John states explicitly that "God is light" (1:5).

THE TEXT IN THE LIFE OF THE CHURCH

True Surrender (*Gelassenheit*)

The Chronicle of the Hutterian Brethren (vol. 1) includes five articles that distinguish Hutterite faith from other expressions of faith. These include (1) believers baptism, (2) the Lord's Supper, (3) *Gelassenheit* (yieldedness) and Christian community of goods, (4) the refusal to use force and the sword, and (5) the separation of believing and unbelieving marriage partners (251-94). The Chronicle gives the scriptural foundation for each article.

The supporting scriptural texts for *Gelassenheit* and Christian community of goods (art. 3) include Isaiah 23:18 and Isaiah 60:9. The *Chronicle* understands Isaiah 23:18 both as prohibition and as prescription. The prohibition against hoarding Tyre's merchandise is a warning, in the OT already, that "the church gathered in Christ" can take to heart. The prescription allotting Tyre's merchandise "to the citizens of the Lord and [to] supply food and lodging for the hungry and clothing for the old" (*Chronicle*) serves as a pattern for community of goods in the Hutterian branch of the Radical Reformation.

The same may be said of Isaiah 60:9. There the children of Zion come from afar with their silver and gold *for the name of the LORD your God*. The pertinent idea in this verse is the bringing of wealth and submitting it to the Lord. In this bringing and submission lies the central meaning of *Gelassenheit*.

Isaiah 61:1-11

Good News of Liberation

PREVIEW

A personal testimony to an endowment of the Lord's Spirit opens the chapter (61:1). The reader will recall two other similar references in the book of Isaiah, one in 11:2, where the Lord's Spirit rests upon an outgrowth from Jesse's root, and the other in 42:1, where the Lord himself speaks of putting his Spirit on his servant. God's Spirit is operative upon and among his people to bring about justice, righteousness, and peace.

In the four segments of this chapter, there is development without clear transitions from one segment to the next. The chapter opens with a proclamation of liberation in which the speaker, perhaps the prophet himself, is the bearer of good news to the poor, the brokenhearted, captives, and mourners (61:1-4). Those who hear this good news are probably repatriated exiles from Babylon, seeking to break free from their poverty and discouragement.

Next the prophet addresses these repatriated exiles, assuring them that their calling as priests and ministers will be accredited (61:5-7). The Lord's word then guarantees this assurance (61:8-9). Their blessing by the Lord will be known among the nations.

The prophet concludes with an ode to joy, which serves as a response to the Lord's promise (61:10-11). The emphasis on righteousness and praise at the beginning of the chapter is endorsed here in the prophet's own experience.

OUTLINE

Year of the Lord's Favor, 61:1-4
Everlasting Joy, 61:5-7
Everlasting Covenant, 61:8-9
Growth of Righteousness and Praise, 61:10-11

EXPLANATORY NOTES

Year of the Lord's Favor 61:1-4

The power and directness of the one who speaks at the beginning of this chapter impress themselves upon the reader. This advocate of the poor and the imprisoned has God's authority to speak and to act. When Jesus began his public ministry, he anchored his spiritual and political agenda to these credentials (Luke 4:14-21).

The notion of the Spirit of the Lord empowering people is widespread in the OT (cf. Vriezen: 250). Here the Spirit of the Lord *upon* the prophet inspires the announcement of good news. Such inspiration does not arise from nowhere or from just anywhere. It arises out of God's work as discerned in history.

That the prophet is *anointed* is unusual. Kings were anointed before the exile and high priests after it. Prophets, with the specific exception of Elisha (1 Kings 19:16), were not said to be anointed (but note the general exception in 1 Chronicles 16:22 = Psalms 105:15).

The message of the prophet endowed with the Spirit of the Lord charts a vision of redemption (Hanson: 224). This message is cast in the form of a series of infinitive clauses:

> [1b]*to bring good news* to the oppressed,
> [1b]*to bind up* the brokenhearted,
> [1b]*to proclaim* liberty to the captives, . . .
> [2a]*to proclaim* the year of the LORD'S favor, . . .
> [2b]*to comfort* all who mourn;
> [3a]*to provide* for those who mourn in Zion—
> [3a]*to give* them a garland. . . .

The clauses name groups burdened by hardship. The only exception to this is the fourth clause, which proclaims *the year of the LORD's favor* (61:2a). There is a recognizable parallel here to the year of Jubilee in Leviticus 25 (cf. Childs: 505; Yoder, 1972:36-40). The word *favor* (Heb. *raṣon*) does not appear in Leviticus 25 nor does the word *Jubilee* (Heb. *yobel*) appear in Isaiah 61. Nevertheless the similarity of theme and emphasis must be taken into account.

Isaiah 61:1-11

Central to the proclamation of a Jubilee year in Leviticus 25 is the notion of liberty for Israelites who have experienced loss of land and other economic hardship. In Isaiah 61 as well, liberty has a central place in the proclamation of the year of the Lord's favor. But beyond this specific reference to liberty in Leviticus 25 and Isaiah 61, there is an emphasis in both texts on a general amnesty for the impoverished and downtrodden.

Development of the message in Isaiah 61:1-4 moves through several stages. The first stanza introduces the speaker (*me*) and initiates the infinitive clause series with words of hope: *to bring good news, to bind up the brokenhearted,* and *to proclaim liberty* (61:1). The series of infinitive clauses continues in the second stanza (61:2-3a). The proclamation of *the year of the LORD's favor,* parallel to *the day of vengeance of our God,* opens the stanza. Although the English word *vengeance* usually means revenge and retaliation against enemies, the Hebrew (*naqam*) also has the positive sense of *rescue* (as here; cf. Whybray: 242). The final lines of the stanza focus on the replacement of sorrow with jubilation. The infinitives *to comfort, to provide,* and *to give* complete the series of infinitive clauses.

This vision of redemption closes with new names for the downtrodden at the beginning of the last stanza: *oaks of righteousness* and *planting of the LORD* (61:3b-4). These names signify the calling of the repatriated exiles rather than the hardship into which they have fallen. And beyond the significance of names, there is now a community (*oaks . . . a planting*) that is reconciled to the Lord. This community stands in sharp contrast to a captive, mourning, despairing people, and the transformation is pictured by the use of sturdy trees and the sowing of seed.

Three plural verbs (*they shall build up, they shall raise up, they shall repair*) conclude the stanza. *They* certainly refers to those who have experienced the liberty just announced (i.e., the community represented as *oaks of righteousness*). Their energy and vision for rebuilding depends on the good news of liberty, spiritual and material, that they have received (cf. Brueggemann, 1998b:215). Their work is now a service to the community. Those who have been liberated and transformed offer a "sacrifice of praise" by restoring what has been devastated.

These three stanzas at the beginning of Isaiah 61 bring the plan of redemption in Leviticus 25 up to date for the period of the exile and beyond it. Hanson has pointed out that Isaiah 61:1-3 in particular renews the message of the servant in Isaiah 42 for its own time and place (223-24). In Isaiah 42 and 61 the servant is presented as a pattern of Spirit-filled confidence in God, for the individual and the community, living out the call to be God's agent of redemption.

Everlasting Joy 61:5-7

The prophet continues to speak in 61:5-7, with a shift from rebuilding to office holding (61:5-6a). This shift indicates that alongside the repair of physical devastation is the ongoing need for spiritual formation.

Those who have experienced liberty are now addressed (*you, your*). It has been suggested that the rebuilding created a labor shortage and that outsiders were needed to supervise agricultural activity as the rebuilding took place (cf. Watts, 1987:304). The offices of priest and minister (where the responsibility for spiritual formation is lodged) fall to the newly liberated exiles.

The question is whether the offices are an entitlement complete with "economic privilege at the expense of others" (Brueggemann, 1998b: 216) or whether they are instruments of the good news of liberation. The priests and ministers seem to be those who have received the same *Spirit of the Sovereign Lord* (NIV) indicated at the beginning of the chapter.

As in 61:2-3a the topic of 61:6b-7 is the replacement of humiliation with joy. There is a curious shift from second person (*you*, pl.) to third person (*they*) in this stanza. The RSV changed all the third-person pronouns in 61:7 into second-person pronouns. The NRSV and the NIV go in the opposite direction and change the second-person pronoun at the beginning of 61:7 into a third-person pronoun (*their shame*), to give consistency to the verse. This uncertainty in translation indicates the textual difficulties of 61:7. It is my view that 61:6b-7 ought to be taken as a stanza rather than 61:7 by itself:

> ⁶ᵇ*You* shall consume the wealth of nations,
>   and *you* shall *boast* in their abundance;
> ⁷instead of *your* shame (you shall possess) double,
>   and (instead of) humiliation *they* shall exult in *their* lot;
> therefore *they* shall possess double in *their* land;
>   everlasting joy shall belong to *them*. (AT)

The shift from second to third person takes place in the middle of the stanza. The sense of the first three lines is that Israel will receive double (reward) from the nations for double punishment (cf. Isa 40:2). A question remains: To whom do the pronouns *they/their/them* refer in the last three lines? It makes the most sense to see the antecedents of these pronouns to be the nations, mentioned in the first line. The nations will not be dispossessed and humiliated by Israel. Instead, they will also receive double (plus everlasting joy!) as a result of their acceptance of the Lord's instruction (cf. Isa 2:3).

Everlasting Covenant 61:8-9

The prophet, Spirit-filled and anointed, has spoken in the first part of the chapter. Now the Lord speaks a word of promise, using the language of covenant faithfulness. In the first stanza the Lord describes his inward passions (loving justice [*Justice and Righteousness, p. 445*], hating robbery) and his outward actions (rewarding and covenanting with those who embrace his passions; 61:8; cf. Pss 85:10-13; 89:14-18; 97:10-12; Isa 5:7; Amos 5:21-24). The Lord states his love of justice here as a characteristic (perhaps *the* characteristic) of his own passion that he wishes his people (*them*) to imitate.

The NRSV adds *wrongdoing* (iniquity, NIV) to *robbery* as things that the Lord hates. Instead of the more generic *wrongdoing*, the Hebrew reads *with a burnt offering*. This places an emphasis on the travesty of worship and breach of commandment coexisting side by side (cf. Matt 5:21-26). If the pronoun *them* in Isaiah 60:8b refers to God's liberated people in 61:1-4, as I think it must, the word of promise is that the Lord's covenant faithfulness continues in and beyond the exile (cf. Brueggemann, 1998b:217).

The covenant with Abraham and Sarah in Genesis 12 lies behind the second stanza (61:9). The descendants of those who mourn in Zion will be the means by which "all the families of the earth shall be blessed" (Gen 12:3).

Growth of Righteousness and Praise 61:10-11

The prophet responds to the Lord's word of promise with an ode to joy at the end of the chapter. The first stanza exudes jubilation in the Lord (61:10). The clothing of salvation and righteousness portray the original purpose for God's people. The prophet wears this clothing as a sign that the promise is being fulfilled in him and through him to his people. What picture could better describe the joy of this sign than a bride and bridegroom at their wedding?

If the picture of bride and bridegroom fails to communicate joy, then perhaps earth's fruitfulness will do so (61:11). The righteousness of God's people in the sight of the nations continues to be a testimony calling the nations to receive the blessing lying in store for them.

The beginning (vv. 1-4) and end (vv. 10-11) of the chapter are concerned with an individual, anointed and clothed with God's purpose. But the center of the chapter (vv. 5-7, 8-9) is concerned with a community, God's own people and the nations side by side. The anointed individual is to wear a *robe of righteousness* (v. 10), and the community is to be called *oaks of righteousness* (v. 3). This righteousness, then, is not to be hidden under a bushel basket, so to speak, but shared with the nations.

THE TEXT IN BIBLICAL CONTEXT
Isaiah in Luke

Luke tells about Jesus' dramatic appearance in the synagogue in Nazareth at the beginning of his public ministry (4:16-30). In the synagogue service, Jesus was handed the scroll of the prophet Isaiah, which he was invited to read. He unrolled the scroll to chapter 61 and read from verses 1 and 2 of the chapter, including also a line from Isaiah 58:6. The quotation in Luke follows the Greek translation of the OT quite closely, and it ends with the proclamation of the year of the Lord's favor. The *year of the LORD's favor* (Isa 61:2) is widely assumed to be a reference to the year of Jubilee in Leviticus 25.

Here Jesus did not go on to speak about *the day of vengeance (naqam) of our God,* the line that immediately follows *the year of the LORD's favor* in Isaiah 61:2. The often-asked question is why Jesus stopped reading where he did. J. Massyngbaerde Ford takes Jesus' failure to read *the day of vengeance of our God* from Isaiah 61:2 as a signal that the Jubilee year he was announcing would be a good thing for both Jews and Gentiles. He renounced vengeance and began his ministry on a call for reconciliation with sworn enemies (Ford: 80-98).

This did not become fully clear, however, until Jesus referred to Elijah and Elisha in his synagogue sermon. It was a widow at Zarephath in Sidon, a Gentile, who gave refuge to Elijah when Ahab was searching for him. He found no refuge in Israel. It was Naaman the Syrian, a Gentile, who was cleansed of his leprosy when he followed Elisha's instructions. No Israelite lepers were cleansed. The synagogue congregation at Nazareth made the connection between his refusal to announce revenge on the Gentiles when he read Isaiah 61:2 and his examples of how God had cared for the Gentiles in the past. It was that connection that led to the eviction of Jesus from their synagogue.

THE TEXT IN THE LIFE OF THE CHURCH
Isaiah in the Lectionary

In the Common Lectionary, used for example in Episcopal, Lutheran, and Roman Catholic churches, Isaiah 61:1-4, 8-11 is read on the third Sunday of Advent alongside the Gospel reading from John 1:6-8, 19-28 (*PTCY:* Year B). It is odd that the connection is not made between Isaiah 61 and Luke 4, where Isaiah 61 is quoted. These two texts belong together and, taken together, belong at the inauguration of Jesus' public ministry. Isaiah 61 may be understood as corroborating evidence of Jesus' incarnation, but its central point lies elsewhere.

The central point in Jesus' interpretation of Isaiah 61 at the synagogue in Nazareth is the outward-looking and confrontational cast of this text. There is something confrontational in the announcement of good news to the poor and the proclamation of liberty to the captives. Oppositions to poverty and prisons are social and spiritual issues that evoke strong emotions.

Jesus read the Isaiah 61 text in order to confront the social conscience and the spiritual sensibilities of those in attendance at the Nazareth synagogue. He announced his good news of liberty and freedom by pointing to the widow of Zarephath in Sidon and the leprosy of Naaman the Syrian. The point at issue lay in Jesus' acclaim for Gentile openness to faith and his critique of Israelite wariness of those outside the established religious boundaries.

Isaiah 62:1-12

The Lord's Salvation

PREVIEW

As in chapters 60 and 61, the theme in chapter 62 has to do with the righteousness and salvation of Zion-Jerusalem. In the first segment of the chapter, Zion-Jerusalem is addressed as a woman, and the language of marriage is used to understand her redemption (62:1-5). The woman receives a new name, corresponding to her new status as the Lord's bride.

From marriage the imagery shifts to vigilance over the future of Jerusalem (62:6-7). Here the prophet as sentinel comes to the fore (TBC below). The Lord's oath forms the foundation of his promise to the inhabitants of Zion-Jerusalem (62:8-9). Harvesttime and temple festivity characterize the fulfillment of the promise.

The last segment, like the first, speaks of renaming God's people according to their vocation as a holy people (62:10-12). Here themes and language from Isaiah 40 are adapted to the new reality of the exiles living in Jerusalem.

It is not possible to say with certainty who is speaking in the chapter. I take the *I* in 62:1 and 6 to refer to God even though there is no introductory formula indicating this. In 62:8-9 and 11 it is clear that the Lord is the speaker. Elsewhere I understand the anointed one of 61:1-2 to be the speaker.

OUTLINE

Righteousness of Zion-Jerusalem, 62:1-5
Jerusalem, the Praise of the Earth, 62:6-7

Harvesting the Earth's Grain, 62:8-9
Coming Salvation, 62:10-12

EXPLANATORY NOTES

Righteousness of Zion-Jerusalem 62:1-5

Five four-line stanzas make up the first segment of chapter 62. In the first stanza the speaker resolves to speak unrelentingly on behalf of the salvation of Zion-Jerusalem (62:1). Two similes (*like the dawn, like a blazing torch,* NIV) give a vivid picture of Zion-Jerusalem lighting the way by her ethics and her spirituality.

The reference to nations and kings seeing the splendor of Zion-Jerusalem (62:2) recalls 52:13-15, where nations and kings seeing the Lord's servant are silenced because of the servant's marred appearance. In chapter 62 the Anointed One's refusal to be silent enables nations and kings to grasp the splendor of Zion-Jerusalem.

Alongside this understanding lies the anticipation of new names for Zion-Jerusalem, marking her new status. The old names, *Deserted* and *Desolate* (62:3-4b NIV), indicate a time of estrangement from the Lord. The new names, *Hephzibah* (*my delight is in her*) and *Beulah* (*married*) (62:4b NIV), indicate a restored relationship.

The crown and diadem in the Lord's hand seem to indicate that the Lord is about to wear Zion-Jerusalem as a crown on his head (for further comment, cf. Whybray: 247). Removal of the burdensome names *Deserted* and *Desolate* may be said to take place as the Lord holds crown and diadem in his hand (62:3-4a).

In the fourth stanza the new names are conferred (62:4b). The ideas of delight and marriage characterize the new status of Zion-Jerusalem. Both ideas employ the metaphor of wedlock. The name *Hephzibah* (*my delight is in her*) replaces the name *Deserted.* The Lord's brief abandonment of his wife—exilic Zion—is mentioned in 54:7. The retrieval of his wife is symbolized by her new name in 62:4b. The name *Beulah* (*married*) replaces the name *Desolate.* The desolation of the land is described already in 1:7 and echoed in 6:11. Now the security and emotional fulfillment of marriage replaces the distress of abandonment.

The wedlock metaphor appears again in the final stanza (62:5). The stanza's purpose is simply to accent the metaphor of marriage, describing the relationship between the Lord and his people.

Jerusalem, the Praise of the Earth 62:6-7

The prophet as sentinel/watchman governs the next segment of the chapter. In the first stanza the Lord (*I*) speaks as the "commanding officer" responsible for stationing sentinels on Jerusalem's walls (62:6a). The sentinels are stationed on the walls, where they are not to be silent.

The speaker in the second stanza may be understood as the prophet himself (62:6b-7). This speaker addresses the sentinels (*you*, plural) with the clarification that their assignment is to remind the Lord (their "commanding officer") of his promises to Jerusalem.

Harvesting the Earth's Grain 62:8-9

A new speech of the Lord is introduced in the first two lines of the first stanza (62:8). Now the feminine-singular pronouns *you* and *your* refer to Jerusalem. The sense of the text is not about refusal to share food even with enemies but about security from pillage by foreign invaders. It is the theme of security that links this stanza with the foregoing reference to sentinels and walls.

The same sentiment is expressed in the second stanza (62:9). The final line is translated *in my holy courts* in the NRSV and *in the courts of my sanctuary* in the NIV. Does this refer to a rebuilt temple in Jerusalem, or to a temple to be rebuilt in the future, or to no temple at all? Watts thinks *in my holy courts* refers to the restoration of temple worship (1987:319). Kaufmann doubts that it refers to the temple at all (214, n. 4). Whybray believes 62:9 refers to the practice of bringing firstborn cattle and firstfruits of grain and wine to the festivals for offering to God (250). It is my judgment, similar to that of Watts and Whybray, that *courts* ought to be understood as the courts of Solomon's temple (as in Isa 1:12). It is a reference to worship that flows out of adequate resources and adequate security.

Coming Salvation 62:10-12

A chain of seven imperative verbs distinguishes the first stanza (62:10). All seven imperatives direct the reconstruction *of the way for the people*. In 40:3 the way to be prepared is for the Lord, and those addressed are heavenly beings. But here the way to be prepared is for the people. The inhabitants of Jerusalem are charged with preparing the way for the returning exiles. Perhaps *the way* refers to *the way* alluded to in 57:14, indicating the way of loyalty to the Lord, which Zion's inhabitants must follow if their longing for peace is to be fulfilled (cf. Whybray: 250).

A word of the Lord, intended for the whole earth to hear, carries the thought of the previous stanza forward (62:11). The word to the daughter of Zion is that her salvation is coming. The allusion to 40:10 is an important clue to the interpretation here. In 40:10 the Lord comes as divine conqueror; the Babylonian deities have not displaced him. Here it is not the Lord himself who comes; it is *your salvation* that comes.

Nevertheless this salvation is guaranteed by the Lord's power to bring it about. *Reward* and *recompense* refer in particular to the Lord's compensation in the form of redemption [*Redemption, Redeemer,* p. 448] for his people with regard to their suffering in exile.

The renaming of God's people in the last stanza concludes the chapter (62:12). Four names are given: *The Holy People, The Redeemed of the LORD, Sought Out,* and *A City Not Forsaken.* Like the renaming at the start of the chapter, the names at the end of the chapter signal a new beginning for the daughter of Zion. The name *The Holy People* ('*am haqqodeš*) is found only here in the OT, although the idea of God's people assuming God's holiness is common. As in Exodus 19:6, the sense here is of a people "set apart in God's service" (Janzen, 2000: 239; cf. TLC below).

The Redeemed of the LORD recalls the prayer in Isaiah 51:9-11, where the Lord is addressed as the one who made a way through the sea for the redeemed to pass through. *Sought After* (NIV; *Sought Out*, NRSV) alludes to Israel's role as leader of the nations, of whom the nations inquire (cf. Isa 11:10). Finally, *A City Not Forsaken* reminds the reader of the promise in 62:4 that the Lord will delight in Jerusalem.

THE TEXT IN BIBLICAL CONTEXT

Prophet as Sentinel

The prophet as sentinel appears with some frequency in the prophetic literature of the OT. The closely related term *sentry* is a military term, meaning a soldier standing guard at a point of passage. In Isaiah 62:6, sentinels (*šomerim, watchmen,* RSV, NIV) remind the Lord of his promise to Jerusalem. Elsewhere in Isaiah, blindness and ignorance of the sentinels (*ṣopim*) indicate their disregard for the Lord's instruction (56:10). As a result they provide no teaching for God's people to use to ward off evil. On the other hand, the sentinels' voices have a positive function to announce the Lord's return to Zion (cf. 52:8).

In Jeremiah, sentinels (*ṣopim* and *noṣerim*) warn of disaster (6:17) and call people to revive their pilgrimages to Jerusalem (31:6). The book of Ezekiel provides the clearest understanding of the prophet as sentinel (cf. Lind, 1996:32-33). Ezekiel's commissioning as a sentinel (*ṣopeh*) in 3:17 includes the specific job description of warning the wicked about the consequences of their wickedness. The sentinel's responsibility is to sound the alarm, but as Ezekiel explains, it is incumbent on each person to respond to that alarm (33:1-9).

The prophet Hosea refers to the particular dangers encountered by the prophet in the role of sentinel (*ṣopeh,* 9:8). Rather than relying on the sentinel's warning, Ephraim repudiates the warning and disowns the sentinel (cf. Guenther: 161).

These instances employ a metaphor of the prophet that goes beyond the role as messenger. The prophet continues in the role as messenger and proclaimer of God's word, to be sure, but now the quality of alarm sounder receives special mention.

THE TEXT IN THE LIFE OF THE CHURCH
A Holy People

The idea of Israel as a holy people, set apart for service to God, has its roots in the Holiness Code (Lev 17–26) and is expressed elsewhere in the OT (e.g., Exod 19:6; Lev 11:44-45; Deut 7:6; cf. Isa 62:12). The NT, then, carries this idea forward. The first letter of Peter, in particular, quotes Leviticus 11:44-45 to argue for Christian conduct that reflects God's holiness (1 Pet 1:16; cf. 2:9).

At various times in its history, the church has embraced this understanding of being set apart. For example, the Czech separatist Peter Chelcicky (Petr Chelčický), nearly a century before the Reformation, believed that Christians belong to an order that is set apart, distinct, withdrawn. He protested the notion that church and world could ever be joined in some kind of partnership (Wagner: 91).

The Schleitheim Confession of 1527 affirmed the principle of separation from the world's evil (Yoder, 1973:37-38). In his *Hutterite Confession of Faith*, Peter Riedemann says:

> We have turned toward the church of Christ, not away from it. We have left the gatherings of profane and impure people, and we wish that everyone would do the same. That is why we call everyone to repentance and tell whoever is willing to hear, not to harden their hearts and thus bring the wrath of God upon themselves. If some will not repent and will not keep the true ordinances of God, but remain in sin, we must let them go on their way and leave them to God. (Riedemann: 123)

Magisterial Christianity has always looked upon separatism with disfavor. It may be said that the believers church position on separatism is akin to that of Peter Riedemann. That is, separatism is not an end in itself; it grows out of repentance and its main impulse is a turning toward the church of Christ.

An understanding of holiness as separation, therefore, is only partially true. Holiness also has to do with ethical behavior, and this is demonstrated in both Testaments where there is a call for God's people to be holy (e.g., Lev 19; 1 Pet 1:16, followed by 1:22–2:3). The modern call to discipleship

Isaiah 63:1–64:12

OUTLINE

Day of Vengeance, 63:1-6
    63:1-3   The Lord's Anger
    63:4-6   Vengeance and Redemption
Recital of Israel's Deliverance, 63:7-14
    63:7-9   The Lord's Gracious Deeds
    63:10-14   Israel's Faithlessness
Prayer of Petition, 63:15–64:12
    63:15-16   The Lord as Father
    63:17-19   Plea for Deliverance
    64:1-4   Plea for the Lord to Come Down
    64:5-7   Human Iniquity
    64:8-12   Turning Away from Anger

EXPLANATORY NOTES

Day of Vengeance 63:1-6

Strident language assaults the reader at the beginning of Isaiah 63. Isaiah 34 describes the Lord's judgment on Edom as a paradigm of God's judgment upon the nations. Now, at the beginning of chapter 63, the Lord is described as returning from this scene of judgment.

Isaiah 63:1-6 belongs to a literary form sometimes called War and Victory Songs (Gottwald, 1985:100). The song brings an answer to the plea in chapter 62 for the Lord to act (cf. Hanson: 232).

63:1-3 The Lord's Anger

Two opening questions pretend ignorance about the identity of a combatant returning in victory from a battlefield in Edom (63:1). The identity of the combatant becomes clear in the last two lines of the stanza. The speaker (*I*), in the larger context of Isaiah 63–64, is the Lord. His salvation and righteousness belong together.

The portrayal of God as a warrior returning from a bloody battle is troubling because of the reality of warfare's carnage. In describing the combatant's return, both the NIV and the NRSV emend the Hebrew *ṣ'h* (*stooping*) to *ṣ'd* (*striding* or *marching*). But the emendation is unnecessary and misleading. The stooping may indicate the weight of armor (Watts, 1987:321), but it is even more likely that it refers to the fatigue and dissipation of battle. There is less here of proud marching in victory than there is of grim bending in weariness.

The question-and-answer format is repeated in the second and third stanzas (63:2-3a, 3b). The question, addressed to the Lord as warrior, asks why the clothing of this warrior is stained red, as one would expect of a person treading grapes in a winepress (63:2). The first part of the Lord's reply indicates that the Lord acted alone and without associates (63:3a). That the Lord acts alone and without associates is generally assumed throughout the OT. It is often stated that in this case the point is that the Lord is not working with agents such as Cyrus or the servant (cf. Hanson: 233-35). But it is preferable to say that the phrase *from the peoples no one was with me* is a denial of human agency in general as a necessary accompaniment to God's work of judgment.

The Lord's further reply calls attention to the resemblance between the crushing of juice from grapes in a winepress and the spilling of blood in battle (63:3b). Of special importance in this reply is the Lord's anger [Wrath of God, p. 455], repeated in 63:4-6. Why is God angry? The answer lies in two observations. God's anger rises from his own righteousness and power to save (63:1). Justice and righteousness are the foundation of the Lord's earthly rule, and his anger descends on those who oppose this foundation (cf. Ps 97:1-5). But God's anger also rises because of human injustice, here specifically Edom's injustice (cf. Obad 10-14). The Lord expects that his people will do justice (Mic 6:8). And by his people's example of doing justice, the Lord intends that all peoples will do the same.

63:4-6 Vengeance and Redemption

Stridency of language continues, as the reason for the Lord's judgment on Edom becomes clearer. Three pairs of lines make up the first stanza (63:4-5). There is the pairing of *day of vengeance* and *year of my redemption* (63:4 NIV; cf. Isa 34:8; 61:2). Vengeance here means punitive action against Edom, but its larger meaning has to do with respite and restitution for God's people after a period of suffering (cf. Mendenhall: 99).

In the second pair of lines is a denial of anyone coming to the Lord's assistance (63:5a). This denial reflects back on the winepress analogy in 63:3, where the Lord treads the winepress alone (cf. Isa 59:15b-16). Although there is a denial of human agency in general as a necessary accompaniment to God's work, there is an invitation here and elsewhere for human participation in God's program (cf. 1 Sam 12:14-15; Jesus in the Gospels, where following is a sign of cooperation with God's work).

The third pair of lines accents the Lord's self-help (63:5b). The Lord's work of salvation recalls 63:1, where his power to save is emphasized. The Lord's arm is often used as a symbol of his strength (cf. the Lord's *outstretched arm* in Exod 6:6; Deut 26:8; Ps 136:12; Jer 27:5; et al.).

The theme of the Lord's anger is concluded in the second stanza (63:6). There is a wordplay on the Hebrew noun *niṣham* (lit., *their juice*). In 63:3 this word refers figuratively to the juice of grapes in the winepress. But in 63:6 it refers literally to the blood of those who have experienced the Lord's judgment.

Recital of Israel's Deliverance 63:7-14

It is often argued that Isaiah 63:7–64:12 belongs to a literary form in Hebrew poetry called the communal lamentation (Whybray: 255; cf. Anderson, 1974:57). In fact, 63:7–64:12 comprises a mixture of forms, for which the lament provides the most points of contact. There is an opening recital of the Lord's redemption and Israel's rebellion (63:7-14), followed by a prayer of petition (63:15–64:12). The prayer includes a confession of sin (64:5b-7) and a renewed petition for God to act (64:8-12; Whybray: 255).

63:7-9 The Lord's Gracious Deeds

The prophet (*I*) recounts the Lord's gracious deeds (*ḥesed*). The singular noun *ḥesed*, when used of God, may refer to his redemption from enemies (Gen 19:19; Exod 15:13) or from sin (Ps 25:7; 51:1-2). Here the noun is plural and refers to the Lord's historic displays of kindness to Israel (63:7).

The Lord expresses the hope that his people will remain loyal, followed by the prophet's tribute to the Lord's power to save (63:8-9a). The Lord's hope that his people will remain loyal is elsewhere part of a covenant promise, as in Ezekiel 11:20: "Then they shall be my people, and I will be their God" (NRSV). The prophet's tribute that the Lord *became their savior* indicates that the people did in fact fail (Isa 63:8b). But even in their failure, the Lord was with them (63:9a).

The third stanza begins with the unusual expression *the angel of his presence* (63:9b NIV). Although this expression is found only here in the OT, the Lord's presence represented by his angel or messenger (the same word in Hebrew) is not uncommon (Exod 23:20-23; 32:34; 33:2, 14, 15; cf. Childs: 523). God's love and redemption in the days of old recall the exodus and wilderness wanderings (Deut 1:31; 7:7-8; 32:10-12).

63:10-14 Israel's Faithlessness

Israel's rebellion is said to have grieved God's holy Spirit (63:10). The use of the lower case (holy spirit) by the NRSV and the upper case (Holy Spirit) by the NIV are both unfortunate translation choices. The NIV reads a NT understanding of God's Spirit into the OT. The NRSV treats *spirit* as a common noun rather than a proper noun and depreciates the OT's understanding of the God of Israel as an immanent and transcendent presence in the world (cf. Childs: 524). The KJV and the RSV read *holy Spirit*, acknowledging Spirit as a proper noun corresponding to God, whose holiness is a modifier rather than a title.

That the Lord fights against his own people when they rebel against him guarantees that the God of Israel is not a tribal god. When Israel became like the nations, the Lord fought against Israel (Lind, 1980:34).

The recollection that follows draws from the exodus and wilderness traditions, including Israel's memory of rest from her enemies after her settlement in the land (63:11; cf. Josh 21:44; 23:1). The questions beginning with *Where?* do not here exhibit Israel's unfaithfulness. Instead, they exhibit Israel's expectation that the Lord ought to make his presence known to his people (cf. Brueggemann, 1998b:230).

The questions continue in the next stanza (63:12-13a). Exodus language continues to dominate the recollection. Israel expects the Lord to make an *everlasting name* for himself as a witness among the nations (Watts, 1987:333).

The last stanza takes the exodus imagery one final step (63:13b-14). Now Israel's crossing of the sea is compared to a sure-footed horse in the wilderness, and Israel's guidance through the desert is compared to cattle entering a valley to graze (Whybray:259). The recital of the Lord's redemption and the people's rebellion ends with a confession of faith addressed to the Lord, confident in the Lord's leadership of his people and in his *glorious name* being made known among the nations.

Prayer of Petition 63:15-64:12

The lament form, introduced at the beginning of the previous section, usually includes a petition for God to help, often including a motive (for) to support the petition (Ps 44:23-26; cf. Anderson, 1974:57). The interrogatives (*Where?* 63:15; *Why?* 63:17; *Will you?*, 64:12) and imperatives (*Look down*, 63:15; *Turn back/Return*, 63:17; *Consider*, 64:9) distinguish the beginning and ending of the prayer in Isaiah 63:15-64:12. The center of the prayer focuses on an entreaty for God to come down (64:1-4) and a confession of human culpability (64:5-7).

63:15-16 The Lord as Father

The opening stanza combines petition and complaint (63:15). The first two lines form the petition. The plea to God is to pay attention. The last three lines form the complaint. The questions about the Lord's strength and mercy imply that he has not been paying attention. These lines are awkward in Hebrew. It seems best to take lines 3 and 4 as questions and line 5 as a final comment, following the NRSV. It is not necessary, as in the NIV, to emend the text to *from us* at the end of the stanza (*from me*, Heb.). The pronoun "me" refers to the one praying, perhaps the prophet himself.

The second stanza identifies the Lord as *our Father* (63:16). This identification is infrequent but not unknown in the OT (cf. Deut 32:6; Jer 3:4, 19; 31:9; Isa 64:8). The reference to the Lord as *our Father* here and in 64:8 argues for viewing the two chapters together (Smart: 272).

God is beyond gender distinctions in the OT. God is depicted as a mother (66:13) and compared to a woman nursing her child (49:15), yet the pronouns referring to God and the verbs with God as subject are (grammatically) masculine everywhere. What is more important, however, is that when Israel reflected on God, it was in terms of God's oneness and integrity rather than gender (cf. Gottwald, 1979:684-85).

The reference to Abraham and Israel (Jacob) not recognizing *us* (Israel during and after the exile) seems odd. The point is that whereas the patriarchs are somewhat distant and unapproachable, the Lord is accessible and present, a Redeemer with a long history.

63:17-19 Plea for Deliverance

The *Where?* question in 63:15, exhibiting the prophet's complaint, continues here with a *Why?* question: Why has God hardened his peoples' hearts? (63:17). The language about the hardening of the heart is well known from the exodus story (Exod 4–14). There as well as here it is not simply a matter of a hardening determined by God in advance. Rather, the hardening occurs because of "a mind-set in which human will and divine direction express themselves in a complex interplay" (Janzen, 2000:452). In Isaiah 63:17 the prophet urges the Lord to *turn back*, to repent (cf. Brueggemann, 1998b:232). The sense of God's turning back has to do with a changing of mind or reversal of direction rather than repentance of sin.

A brief historical reflection follows in the next stanza (63:18-19). The first part is difficult to translate, and various emendations have been suggested. The key words in the first two lines are '*am-qodšeka* (*your holy people*) and *miqdašeka* (*your sanctuary*). The contrast lies between God's people, who were in possession of the land, and the loss of God's sanctuary (temple), symbolizing the loss of land and monarchy. The last two lines of the stanza lament this state of affairs (63:19).

64:1-4 Plea for the Lord to Come Down

The interjection *Oh* or *O* expresses a deeply felt wish. Here the wish is expressed with the powerful image of tearing apart the heavens, creating an aperture to allow the Lord's descent to the earth (64:1-2). Elsewhere the verb *tear* (*qr'*) refers to the tearing of clothing to express grief and despair (Isa 37:1) or (figuratively) to the tearing away of kingship (1 Sam 15:28). But here the Lord is understood as hidden, and the plea is to tear open the heavens in order to reveal himself (cf. Whybray:262). Making his name known to his enemies (*adversaries*) means that these enemies will cease their hostility and worship in the Lord's presence (cf. Watts, 1987:335).

The theme of the Lord's coming down and the mountains shaking continues in the second stanza (64:3-4). The new element is the Lord's awesome deeds, which his people did not expect. The verb *expect* (*qwh*) means to look eagerly for something. The confession of faith here asserts that the Lord's awesome deeds took place "when they were least expected" (Whybray: 263). This confession goes on to assert the Lord's exclusive reign, echoing the first commandment: "You shall have no other gods before me" (Exod 20:3; cf. Childs: 525). This God honors those who wait patiently for him.

64:5-7 Human Iniquity

Now the lament turns more consciously to confession of sin. The first stanza addresses the Lord as one who reaches out to those who demonstrate faithfulness in work and worship (64:5). The last two lines of the stanza are difficult to translate. The form of the Hebrew verb *save* (*yš'*) in the last line suggests that salvation is possible even in the face of God's anger.

The confession of sin in the second stanza addresses the problem of being unclean before God (64:6; cf. "unclean lips" in 6:5). The bloodstained garment and the dried leaf are symbols of repentance, but there is a sense of hopelessness here as well. The possibility of salvation from the previous stanza casts its light, even if dim, on this hopelessness.

The hopelessness of the second stanza casts its shadow on the last stanza (64:7). Now the lament focuses on the absence of spiritual life. Without a spiritual life, God has become absent from them. The effect of evil and inattention to God's ways is not so much external calamity because of God's anger as it is God's withdrawal so that people cannot pray with integrity "since he is not there for them" (Smart: 272). The Hebrew verb for *melt* (*mwg*) is judged by both the NIV and the NRSV to be obscure and require emendation, as is also reflected in the Dead Sea Scrolls and other ancient versions. While it is unusual to say, *You (God) melted us*, it is not impossible. When the psalmist says, "The earth melts," the sense is that the earth is altered because of the disorder of nations and kingdoms (Ps 46:6). Here the people confess that God has altered them because of their evil ways.

64:8-12 Turning Away from Anger

The prayer of petition comes to an end in 64:8-12. The first stanza begins with the conjunction "yet" and confesses that in spite of human iniquity, God remains *our Father* (64:8). This divine parent is compared to a potter, who works and fashions a lump of clay into a useful vessel. There is here an appeal to the Lord not to smash what he has created (cf. Whybray: 265).

Confession turns to petition in the second stanza (64:9-10). Three imperatives open the stanza, the first two pleading for restraint in the Lord's anger and for limitation of the Lord's remembrance of human failure. The third imperative (*Oh, look upon us*, NIV; *Now consider*, NRSV) calls on God to take account of the physical ruin of Judah's cities and especially her capital city. Should this not inspire the Lord's compassion?

The prayer concludes with a lament over Jerusalem's temple, burned and broken (64:11-12). Historically, the Babylonian army destroyed Jerusalem and its temple in 587 BC. The questions in the last two lines wonder whether the Lord really will come down (64:1), show his face (64:7), and break his silence.

THE TEXT IN BIBLICAL CONTEXT

Rebellion and Redemption

The recital of the Lord's redemption and the people's rebellion in Isaiah 63:7-14 has points of similarity to the recital in Judges 2:6-16. The following comparison is instructive:

Judges 2:6-16	Isaiah 63:7-14
I. [2:6-10] the people worshipped the Lord **all the days** of Joshua and the next generation	[63:7-9] the Lord's salvation **all the days** of old
II. [2:11-13] the people **abandoned** the Lord	[63:10a] the people **rebelled**
III. [2:14-15] the Lord sold them into the power of **their enemies**	[63:10b] the Lord became **their enemy**

IV. ²:¹⁶the Lord raised up judges who delivered Israel **out of the power** of their plunderers	⁶³:¹¹⁻¹³ªWhere is the one who brought Israel up **out of the sea?**
V. ³:¹¹the land had **rest** (also 3:30; 5:31; 8:28)	⁶³:¹³ᵇ⁻¹⁴the Lord gave them **rest**

This pattern of rebellion and redemption in ancient Israel begins with a time of religious fervor (I), in which the people experience the Lord's works among them in a personal way. But in time this fervor yields to disillusionment, and subsequent loss of the faith and trust are once more evident (II).

A low point arrives when the Lord reciprocates by repudiating his people (III). Both Judges and Isaiah speak of the Lord not merely letting his people suffer the consequences of their rebellion but actually turning against them and unleashing his considerable power to their detriment.

A turning point comes when the Lord intervenes on behalf of his people in their distress (IV). The form of this intervention varies, but it often includes the raising up of leaders (Moses, judges) on whom rests the Lord's authority to save. The result of this intervention is rest (V). The Hebrew words for *rest* are not the same in Judges (*šaqaṭ*) and Isaiah (*nuaḥ*). But they are synonyms, and they indicate a cessation of the Lord's hostile campaign against his people and a restoration of his grace and favor.

THE TEXT IN THE LIFE OF THE CHURCH

All Have Sinned

The prayer of petition in Isaiah 63:15–64:12 includes a confession of human failure (64:5-7). In Christian worship the confession of sin has its roots in passages such as this. The NT writers were aware of the human condition and continued to emphasize it in the church. Paul in particular, as in Romans 3:23, declares the universality of human sin and failure.

One may ask whether sin is invariably fatal, or whether there may be a cure for it. Stated in more precise theological terms, the question is whether human beings are free to choose between right and wrong, or whether they are bound and determined to choose the wrong.

Among the church fathers, Augustine of Hippo (AD 354-430) championed a doctrine of the bondage of the will that has exerted a tremendous influence on the church in the West. This bondage is exhibited in Augustine's doctrine of original sin. He said that humankind was created with wondrous gifts, which were subsequently lost due to human disobedience (Gen 3). The result of this loss is that humankind lies under the control of inherited blame for original human disobedience. Humankind is characterized by this "original sin," although God has elected some for salvation. So Augustine could argue that infants who die without being baptized enter into everlasting destruction (*ODCC*: 123-30). Luther followed Augustine in broad outline, though not necessarily in detail, on the bondage of the human will (cf. *ODCC*: 1007-10).

While Anabaptists in the sixteenth century and since agree that all have sinned, they reject the Augustinian view of the bondage of the will and the assignment of unbaptized infants to perdition. In Pilgram Marpeck's *Vermanung* (*Admonition*) of 1542, he speaks to the question of original sin in his refutation of infant baptism.

> Original sin is inherited only when there is knowledge of good and evil. Adam and Eve, our father and mother, inherited it when, contrary to the command of God, they ate the fruit of the knowledge of good and evil. Such is the inheritance of [humans]. But, prior to the knowledge of good and evil, neither inherited sin or actual sin is reckoned before God. . . . [A person] may only be born anew by faith in Christ. . . . For the proclamation of faith in Christ captures the knowledge of good and evil . . . under the obedience of faith, to leave the bad and to choose the good (2 Cor 10:6). (*WPM*: 206-7)

Isaiah 65:1-25

Decision to Seek or Forsake the Lord

PREVIEW

Chapters 65 and 66 form a two-part conclusion to the book of Isaiah. The first part of the conclusion takes up the themes of judgment and promise so familiar in the book as a whole. Judgment and promise alternate in 65:1-16. The Lord's *servants* (pl.) appear prominently as the bearers of the Lord's promise (cf. 54:17; 56:6; 63:17; contrasting with servant [sg.] in Isa 41-53), while *a rebellious people* (*you*, pl.) appear as the unnamed bearers of the Lord's retribution, addressed with a word of judgment.

New creation and blessing dominate 65:17-25. Gone now is the word of judgment, replaced by a word of promise and ending on a note strongly reminiscent of Isaiah 11:6-9.

OUTLINE

Rebels Versus Servants, 65:1-16
    65:1-5   Rebellious People
    65:6-7   Repayment for Iniquities
    65:8-10   Not All Will Be Destroyed
    65:11-12   Destined to the Sword
    65:13-16   Servants of the Lord Spared
Transformation of Heaven and Earth, 65:17-25
    65:17-19   New Creation

| 65:20-23 | Building and Planting |
| 65:24-25 | Calling and Answering |

EXPLANATORY NOTES

Rebels Versus Servants 65:1-16

65:1-5 Rebellious People

The Lord speaks throughout the chapter, beginning with language of seeking and finding (65:1). Though not mentioned by name, the Lord has Israel in mind as those who did not inquire, did not seek him, did not call on his name. These three absolutely essential marks of the quest to know God's will are missing. This is so even though God was making his presence known all the while.

This people is designated as *a rebellious people* (65:2). Elsewhere people hold out (*paraś*) their hands to a faithful God as a gesture of prayer (cf. 1 Kings 8:22). But here it is the Lord who holds out (*paraś*) his hands to a rebellious people as a gesture of appeal (Whybray: 268). The indictment of rebellion returns the reader to chapter 1, where the same accusation is made (1:23).

The people's rebellious behavior is exhibited in a series of active participles, which English translations render as relative clauses introduced by *who*. Rebellion constitutes wrong choices of life paths and pursuit of wrongheaded thinking (65:2). To follow one's own ways is to substitute self for God, a basic form of idolatry. Moreover, rebellious people anger God by their deliberate breaking of the prohibitions concerning having and worshipping other gods than the Lord (65:3; cf. Exod 20:3-6).

Two further acts of rebellion are identified in the fourth stanza: necromancy and eating forbidden food (65:4). Necromancy consists of conjuring the spirits of the dead in order to reveal the future by magic. The people are described as sitting *inside tombs* and spending nights *in secret places*. This reference is to consulting spirits of the dead in order to find direction, a forbidden practice in the law (Deut 18:9-14; cf. Smart: 276). The eating of pork disqualifies the people from the mandate to seek and find the Lord (cf. Brueggemann, 1998b:240). The taboo on eating pork is found in Leviticus 11:7-8 and elsewhere.

A summary of rebellion is given by means of the peoples' own claim, in which they warn all and sundry of their "holiness" (65:5). The claim to holiness is based, however, on wrong worship, and it is devoid of repentance and conformity to the Lord's way (cf. Smart: 277). So the Lord repudiates this false holiness as *smoke in my nostrils*, recalling 2 Samuel 22:9 (= Ps 18:8).

65:6-7 Repayment for Iniquities

The statement of judgment that begins with the demonstrative *See!* draws attention to what follows: the Lord's resolution to repay the rebellious people for their wrong worship and wrong practices (65:6-7a). The reference to not being silent recalls the question at the end of chapter 64: *Will you keep silent and punish us beyond measure?* (NIV). Here the Lord says that he will not keep silent but will punish iniquity. This judgment includes the signature *says the LORD*, like the blessing at the end of the chapter.

Because they burned . . . and defied (NIV) gives a more precise reason for the judgment (65:7b). Illicit worship on mountains and hills appears elsewhere in the Law (e.g., Deut 12:2) and the Prophets (e.g., Jer 3:23; Ezek 6:13; Hos 4:13). The measuring of full payment means that rebellious Israel will receive her just deserts (cf. Brueggemann, 1998b:240).

65:8-10 Not All Will Be Destroyed

The contrast with the preceding sections (65:1-5, 6-7) is remarkable. There a rebellious people receive a word of judgment for their iniquities. Here a faithful people receive a word of blessing for their faithfulness. The reference in the first stanza to Israel as a cluster of grapes employs the well-known metaphor of God's people as a vineyard (65:8; cf. 5:1-7). The saying *Do not destroy it, for there is a blessing in it* means that the Lord will not destroy the whole of his people but will preserve clusters of them, his servants (G. E. Wright: 155).

The specific form of the blessing is revealed in the second stanza (65:9-10). Jacob and Judah serve as symbols of the original promise to Abraham of the land as an inheritance (TBC below). Here, however, the promise is limited to include only those who seek the Lord. The word *seek* (*drš*) repeats the same word from 65:1, but now in a context of affirmation. The allusion to Sharon on the Mediterranean coast and the *Valley of Achor* in the vicinity of Jericho signifies the restoration of cultivation and human occupation, perhaps after a time of abandonment and ruin.

65:11-12 Destined to the Sword

The rebellious people are addressed directly for the first time in 65:11 (*But as for you*, NIV). Four Hebrew participles summarize and itemize the rebellion (*forsaking, forgetting, setting, filling*, AT). The first two indicate the people's hostility toward the Lord. The last two indicate their partiality toward the deities Fortune (*gad*) and Destiny (*meni*). The significance of these gods is not well known. Apparently they were gods of fate with which Israel was familiar (Maier: 1992a, 1992b).

The second stanza assesses damages against the rebellious people (65:12). The verb *destine* (*manah*) is a wordplay with Destiny in the previous line. *Sword* and *slaughter* indicate some kind of inhumane death, probably in war. The reason for such a penalty lay in the people's obduracy when the Lord called them to faithfulness. Instead of embracing the Lord and choosing life, they renounced the Lord and chose death (cf. Deut 30:19-20).

65:13-16 Servants of the Lord Spared

In the final segment of the chapter's first part, the rebellious people continue to be addressed as the beneficiaries of the Lord's discipline, while the Lord's servants are presented as the beneficiaries of the Lord's favor.

This contrast is presented vividly in the first stanza, although neither the NRSV nor the NIV capture it fully (65:13). The following translation seeks to reproduce the force of the Hebrew text:

> Therefore thus says the LORD God:
> See here, my servants shall eat,
>   but you, you shall go hungry;
>
> see here, my servants shall drink,
>   but you, you shall go thirsty;
> see here, my servants shall rejoice,
>   but you, you shall be ashamed! (AT)

The *you* (pl.) is the same as the *you* (pl.) in 65:11. The antecedent of these plural pronouns is the rebellious people of 65:2.

The same *See here . . . but you* sequence introduces the second stanza (65:14-15). Now, however, the rebellious people hear the nature of the Lord's discipline in greater detail. The reference to *pain of heart* and *anguish of spirit* emphasizes the emotional suffering resulting from the discipline. The stanza focuses on the loss of the rebellious peoples' name and the gaining of *another name* (65:15 NIV) by the Lord's servants. The loss of name is surely the cause of the emotional suffering, although the identity of that name is not revealed. The new name, on the other hand, refers to a new identity and a new relationship (Brueggemann, 1998b: 244). It means a new beginning for the Lord's servants (cf. Isa 62:2-4).

The mood changes sharply in the third stanza (65:16). The blessing announced in 65:8 now concludes the section. The reference to *the God* of faithfulness (God of truth, NIV) is exceptional in the OT. The word faithfulness ('aman) recalls Isaiah 7:9, where the Lord's word to Ahaz is to stand firm in faith ('aman). In both places the Lord is the paragon of reliability. The troubles of the past, though not named, probably refer to the exile (Whybray: 276). The Lord's servants will forget them as they live inside the promise of their new name.

Transformation of Heaven and Earth 65:17-25

65:17-19 New Creation

The solemn introductory declaration concerning the future, *For I am about to create* . . . (65:17-18a), does not address the Lord's servants, but it is intended for them (Brueggemann, 1998b:245). The Lord declares his intention for the cosmos as a whole. The reference to erasing *former things* from God's memory provides a link with 65:16 (*past troubles*, NIV; *former troubles*, NRSV). But it is God's creation of *new heavens and a new earth* that is really startling. Is this a retreat from material reality? The answer depends in part on one's interpretive standpoint; I take it to be no retreat from material reality at all. Rather, it is God's projection of newness on the cosmic landscape, a newness that reflects God's intention for the cosmos. Whybray thinks of this newness as "a new radical theology" (276). Such a theology includes a new material reality infused with spiritual substance and meaning. This is to say that material and spiritual realities belong together. That is why there is the promise of new *heavens* and a new *earth*. It is not just new *heavens*, some kind of hope beyond earth's material limitations and frustrations. A new *earth* means that earth is also the domain of God's will. The stanza closes on a note of intense elation (65:18a). The plural imperatives may be understood as addressing the Lord's servants, and the time span is in the order of infinity (*forever*).

The second stanza begins, like the first, with the declaration, *For I am about to create* (65:18b-19; cf. v. 17). The mood of intense elation continues, but now on the landscape of terra firma. The Lord is about to create a Jerusalem and its people freed of the troubles of the past. The sense of the word *create* is not a restoration of something old to its former grandeur but a nativity, something utterly new (Whybray: 276). The Lord will share in the elation of his people and Jerusalem at this new creation. What is celebrated is the cessation of rebellion with its weeping and outcry.

65:20-23 Building and Planting

The next part commences with another *No more* (65:20; *Never again*, NIV). The theme here is the guarantee of long life (Brueggemann, 1998b:247). Infant mortality and premature death alike will be banished.

From the guarantee of long life, the poetry moves into the theme of economic stability (65:21-22a; cf. Brueggemann, 1998b:248). God intends a normal pattern of peaceful life, where there is enough for everyone: adequate housing and sufficient food.

The twin guarantees of long life and economic stability now receive a benediction (65:22b-23) that calls to mind Psalm 1, where the blessed are compared to a tree, and whose work prospers. The vision of new heavens and a new earth does not abandon material reality; it seeks to transform that reality by means of God's blessing.

65:24-25 Calling and Answering

The conclusion to the chapter echoes the beginning of the chapter: the Lord's presence is accessible even when his people do not want it (65:1), even before they request it (65:24)!

The final stanza echoes the beginning of the book. The vision of a peaceable kingdom there (11:7-9) is reaffirmed here in the elemental transformation of nature (65:24). The significance of this transformation lies in the Lord's commitment to a vision of transformed social reality. The vision is not an escape from reality but rather an undertaking to transform reality along the lines of the vision. *The serpent* in 65:25 does not appear to share the transformation evident in 11:7-9. But Watts points out that also in 65:25 the serpent acts "as a peaceful element of the newly created order" (1987:355). It is true that the serpent does not share its food with one of its traditional enemies. Nevertheless the serpent, like the *wolf* and the *lion*, does *not hurt or destroy* in God's new creation.

The reference to the serpent eating dust is almost certainly an allusion to Genesis 3:13-16, where part of the curse on the serpent is that it will eat dust. The serpent in Genesis 3 has the demeanor of danger and threat, whereas here in Isaiah 65 it is content with dust as its food (cf. Roth: 177).

THE TEXT IN THE BIBLICAL CONTEXT

Lion and Lamb

Isaiah 65:25 and 66:20 are often compared to Isaiah 11:6-9. The importance of this comparison lies in the relationship of the end of the book to its beginning. This bracketing underscores the importance of God's extended purpose:

> ¹¹:⁶The wolf shall live with the lamb,
>   ⁶⁵:²⁵**The wolf and the lamb shall feed together,**
> the leopard shall lie down with the kid,
> the calf and the lion and the fatling together,
>   and a little child shall lead them.
> ¹¹:⁷The cow and the bear shall graze,
> their young shall lie down together;
> and the lion shall eat straw like the ox.
>   ⁶⁵:²⁵**the lion shall eat straw like the ox;**
> ¹¹:⁸The nursing child shall play over the hole of the asp,
> and the weaned child shall put its hand on the adder's den.
>   ⁶⁵:²⁵**but the serpent—its food shall be dust!**
> ¹¹:⁹They will not hurt or destroy
> on all my holy mountain;
>   ⁶⁵:²⁵**They shall not hurt or destroy**
>   **on all my holy mountain, says the LORD.**
>   ⁶⁶:²⁰**They shall bring all your kindred from all the nations**
>   **as an offering to the LORD . . .**
>   **to my holy mountain Jerusalem, says the LORD . . .**
> for the earth will be full of the knowledge of the Lord
> as the waters cover the sea.

The vision of Isaiah in 11:1-9 links the prophet's messianic hope with the promise of an earth free of violence. Nowhere else is such a hope and a promise expressed with such extravagant originality. So it is not surprising that at the end of the book, this vision is revived for a new time and place. As the book draws to its conclusion a fresh "picture of creation restored to its God-intended wholeness" finds expression (Hanson: 247). Here it is no longer a new revelation but actually a declaration of what has already been said and needs to be said again. And it needs to be said again in order to fire the imaginations of all who read it.

THE TEXT IN THE LIFE OF THE CHURCH

Land as Inheritance

It is often said today that God gave Israel the Promised Land. Depending on the interpreter, this gift may be limited to the modern state of Israel, west of the Jordan River, or it may include a much larger territory extending from the Tigris-Euphrates River system to the Nile. The primary texts on which this gift of land rest are covenant texts found in Genesis 12 and 15 and at various places in Deuteronomy (e.g., 5:31; 11:17; 12:1; 15:7; 26:9).

exiles. The first stanza portrays the sudden birth of a new people (66:7-8a). The questions in the first two lines of 66:8 indicate disbelief that such a thing could happen (cf. G. E. Wright: 157).

The disbelief continues in the question that begins with *Can a country* (66:8b NIV). What seems to be implied in the phrase *brought forth in a moment* (NIV) is that Jerusalem's rebirth is miraculous and without precedent. Brueggemann sees this birth imagery as a reversal of the barrenness expressed in Isaiah 54:1 (1998b:256).

The two rhetorical questions that follow emphasize the Lord's power to do the unexpected (66:9). Each question is followed by a speech formula identifying the Lord as the speaker. A sense of the Lord's will-to-life and life-giving power lies behind the rhetorical questions.

Although the imagery moves away from the metaphors of childbirth in 66:10-11, it remains in the sphere of nativity and nourishment of the young. The plural imperatives *Rejoice! Be glad! Rejoice!* are now addressed to the residents of Jerusalem. The imperatives picture Jerusalem as the mother of her residents. The rebirth of Jerusalem inspires the same joy experienced at human birth (66:10).

The joy is not mere emotion; it results in the satisfaction and contentment a newborn child feels while nursing at its mother's breast. The satisfaction and contentment rest on an instinctive knowledge of abundance and well-being.

66:12-14 Peace and Comfort

The imagery of hope, introduced by a messenger formula, focuses on early childhood rather than on birth and infancy (66:12-14). Jerusalem as a mother is the recipient of abundance from the nations, an abundance that she conveys to her residents. The sum and substance of this abundance is that the Lord extends a river of *peace* (šalom) to Jerusalem (66:12 NIV). This peace mandate should not be understood, as Brueggemann points out, in a romantic and pious sense (1998b:256). But neither should it be understood as something optional and peripheral, a mandate to follow when it is convenient to do so. The image of peace *like a river* evokes a surging, unstoppable power underlying wholeness and security.

Two additional comparisons dominate the second stanza (66:13-14). In the first, the Lord compares his comfort of Jerusalem to the comfort of a mother for her child. The word *comfort* (nḥm) occurs three times in the first three lines of the stanza. The idea of comfort includes consolation and the easing of grief or trouble. In the second comparison the Lord thinks of the newfound prosperity of Jerusalem in terms of luxuriant grass. Both comparisons create a picture of sufficiency, in which life can be lived in peace. The last two lines provide a reassurance that in God's economy his servants experience God's presence and power while his enemies experience his dissatisfaction.

66:15-16 Fire and Sword

Here the word of judgment continues and completes the thought expressed in 66:5-6 (cf. Whybray: 283). Fire, though not mentioned earlier in the chapter, is now featured as the prescribed instrument of judgment (66:15). Comparing the Lord's chariots to a whirlwind indicates the hurricane force of his arrival. The same language is used in Jeremiah 4:13, where it depicts the coming of the Babylonian army (cf. Martens: 61-62).

The second stanza adds the sword as an instrument of judgment (66:16). Sword and fire together symbolize the Lord's determination to plead with humankind to *tremble at his word* (66:5). The fact that many die by fire and sword does not indicate the Lord's thirst for revenge. It indicates a human unwillingness to define meaning in terms of God's purposes.

Seeing the Lord's Glory 66:17-24

Although most of the book of Isaiah is presented in a poetic format, the last part of chapter 66 resists such a presentation and is more accurately presented as prose.

66:17 Abhorrent Practices

The theme of judgment characterizes the first paragraph (66:17). Entry *into the gardens* recalls Isaiah 1:29-31, which also denounces wrong worship associated with gardens (Sweeney: 471). The phrase *following the one in the center* is obscure. The plain meaning of the paragraph as a whole, however, lies in the disapproval of practices that refuse to place the Lord at the center of worship. The signature formula *ne'um-yhwh* (*declares the LORD*, NIV) resumes the formula from the beginning of the chapter (66:2), which serves to contrast the one who is humble and contrite in spirit with those who sanctify and purify themselves for false worship.

66:18-21 The Lord's Glory Among the Nations

The second paragraph leaves the domain of judgment and enters the domain of promise (cf. NIV, which sees two paragraphs in these verses: v. 18 and vv. 19-21). The Lord's coming results in the coming of the nations to see the Lord's glory (66:18). The reference to the Lord's glory indicates the Lord's presence in the temple, as in Ezekiel 10:1-22 and

The focus of the covenant described in Genesis 15 is God's promise of land. Millard Lind argues convincingly that this promise and Abram's response of trust have often been spiritualized but have seldom been comprehended as the foundation of a new political order. This new order, he says, constitutes "an alternative to violent political power" (1980:38). My argument for seeing God's gift of land to Abraham as a complex issue rather than to conceive of it as simple and easily explainable follows Lind's argument closely.

It is worth emphasizing that the issue is much more complex than is indicated by the simple statement of God giving the land to Israel. This complexity begins in the Bible itself. In Isaiah 65:9-10, for example, the Lord speaks of the descendants of Jacob as the inheritors of his mountains, where his servants shall settle. There, as in Genesis (15:7; cf. 28:4), the Hebrew word translated *inherit* and *possess* (*yaraš*) carries a great deal of meaning. Throughout the Bible, *gift* and *inheritance* are key words in the promise that God has for humankind.

If one trusts God's promise of grace, as Abram did, that God intends to give the land, then one need not fall back on works-righteousness by using violent political power to secure it. The Promised Land as the gift of God abolishes the principle of violent political power.

In the ancestral history (Gen 12–50) the inheritance of the land is usually described in terms of peace and negotiation rather than warfare. Abraham's purchase of the cave of Machpelah as a burial site for Sarah (Gen 23) is an illustration of this point. There are many other examples (e.g., the stories about Isaac in Gen 26). The ancestors of the Israelites lived as sojourners in the land. They trusted in the Lord's promise that the land was their inheritance, but they had no political power base in Canaan to demand that inheritance by means of violence. Nor does this appear to be their intention (cf. Jeschke: 25-28).

The focus of the ancestors' identity was their relationship to the God who called Abram, initially, to leave land and kindred and to seek the land that he would show him. The land as the Lord's gift, then, guided the ancestors in how it was possessed and used and defended. Stipulations for land use accompanied the gift.

To speak of the land as belonging to Israel simply because God gave it to them, therefore, needs to be revised by a more careful reading of the texts that reflect on the meaning of gift and giving.

Isaiah 66:1-24

Comfort and Hope

PREVIEW

Chapters 65 and 66 form a two-part conclusion to the book of Isaiah. Chapter 66, the second part of the conclusion, continues the themes of judgment and hope found in chapter 65, but in a different style. It is the rebellious people who are addressed in chapter 65. Here, however, the Lord's servants are addressed, although they are identified as *his servants* only once (66:14). Whereas messenger formulas and speech formulas appear infrequently in chapter 65, in chapter 66 they are abundant.

Comfort and hope for Jerusalem, within the larger context of judgment, is the subject of the first part of the chapter (66:1-16). A messenger formula introduces the first two clusters of verses in the chapter (66:1-2, 3-4). The structure of 66:5-16 may be understood as a text and commentary on hope (66:7-11, 12-14), enclosed by opening and concluding words of judgment (66:5-6, 15-16).

The Lord's glory, enhanced by the gathering of the nations, is the subject of the second part of the chapter (66:17-24). The style here, without warning, turns to prose (cf. NIV; NRSV presents 66:17-24 as prose, except vv. 22-23, which it exhibits as poetry). An opening paragraph denounces wrong worship (66:17). The second paragraph focuses on the Lord's glory and the gathering of the nations (66:18-21). The last paragraph ponders the prospect of the Lord's servants enduring for all time and his worship available for all people (66:22-24).

But the chapter ends on a note of judgment for rebellion (66:24). Judgment for rebellion has the last word in the book. This judgment serves

Isaiah 66:1-24

as a continuation of 66:17, its harshness mitigated only by the words of promise that precede it.

OUTLINE

Restoration of Jerusalem, 66:1-16
    66:1-2   Contrite in Spirit
    66:3-4   Choosing Their Own Ways
    66:5-6   Shame and Retribution
    66:7-11   Jerusalem's Rebirth
    66:12-14   Peace and Comfort
    66:15-16   Fire and Sword
Seeing the Lord's Glory, 66:17-24
    66:17   Abhorrent Practices
    66:18-21   The Lord's Glory Among the Nations
    66:22-24   Human Responses to New Heavens, New Earth

EXPLANATORY NOTES

Restoration of Jerusalem 66:1-16

66:1-2 Contrite in Spirit

Two pairs of lines follow the messenger formula in the first stanza (66:1). In the first pair, the heavens and the earth as the Lord's throne and footstool respectively evoke the language of 1 Kings (8:27), Lamentations (2:1), and several of the Psalms (11:4; 99:5; 132:7). The questions in the second pair of lines reflect the OT's refusal to confine God's presence to a specific location. Those addressed (*you*, pl.) would seem to be the Lord's servants (cf. v. 14), admonished and taught but not castigated.

A twofold repetition of *all these things* opens the second stanza (66:2). This refers to the heavens and the earth in the first stanza; they belong to the Lord. The contrast between the questions at the end of the first stanza (66:1) and the response at the end of the second stanza (66:2) is obscured in translation. The two questions at the end of 66:1 begin with the interrogative *Where?* (NIV) or *What?* (NRSV), *'e-zeh . . . 'e-zeh*. The questions can be translated:

> What is this? A house that you will build for me?
> What is this? A place for me to take my rest? (Smart: 287)

The response at the end of 66:2 begins with the phrase *But this . . . , we'el-zeh*. What is needed is not a resting place for the Lord, but people who tremble with wonder at the Lord's word. This is the meaning of being *humble and contrite in spirit* (TLC below).

66:3-4 Choosing Their Own Ways

The thought now turns to the combining of legitimate forms of belief with illegitimate forms of practice (66:3). There are four such combinations, each beginning with the pronoun *whoever*. The preposition *like* (NRSV, NIV) is not present in the Hebrew text, which simply places phrases side by side (*slaughtering an ox, killing a man*, etc.). The sense is that the legitimate act of worship (expressed first in each combination) is sabotaged by the illegitimate practice that follows. Those who worship are not observant of the ethical behavior that flows from true worship (cf. Brueggemann, 1998b:253). Idolatry nearly always masquerades as faithfulness, and people choose the forms of idolatry that they adopt.

There is a word of judgment in the six-line stanza that follows (66:4). In the first two lines the Lord's choice of punishment is a response to the people's idolatry. The reasons for the punishment, in lines 3 and 4, have to do with the refusal to answer or listen to God's voice. The last two lines repeat the people's choice of what displeased God, at the end of the previous stanza (66:3).

66:5-6 Shame and Retribution

Those who please God are now addressed as those who tremble at his word (66:5). A formula to introduce this word is employed: *Hear the word of the LORD* (cf. 2 Kings 7:1; Isa 1:10; Jer 2:4; Ezek 20:47; Hos 4:1). The Lord's servants (66:14) are pitted against the Lord's enemies who taunt them. The substance of the Lord's message to his servants is that their enemies will be disgraced.

Excited exclamations convey the emotion of those to whom the Lord's word is addressed (66:6). The Hebrew noun *qol* (*sound, voice*) appears as the first word on each of the first three lines:

> *The sound of an uproar from the city!*
> *The sound (of an uproar) from the temple!*
> *The sound of the LORD finishing*
>   *dealings with his enemies!* (AT)

There is vindication here for those who have pleased God by choosing God's ways.

66:7-11 Jerusalem's Rebirth

In a sudden shift of mood the prophet, still speaking the Lord's word, now employs the metaphors of labor and birth to describe Jerusalem's renaissance. Labor and birth serve as a text of hope for the returned

43:1-12 (cf. Whybray: 289) and more particularly in Isaiah 6:1-4. To see the Lord's glory and to declare this glory among the nations attests to a gathering beyond that of Israelite exiles (66:19). The rhetoric aims to welcome all who will embrace the Lord's instruction and the Lord's covenant (66:20; cf. Brueggemann, 1998b:258-59). The paragraph concludes with a speech formula (*says the LORD*) certifying and confirming this inclusiveness as the Lord's word and intention (66:21).

66:22-24 Human Responses to New Heavens, New Earth

The final paragraph serves as a kind of blessing and curse for all who read the book. The blessing comes with speech formulas that guarantee its credibility (66:22-23). It reflects earlier references to heavens and earth in the book of Isaiah (1:2; 13:13; 37:16; 40:12, 22; 42:5; 44:23-24; 45:8, 12, 18; 48:13; 49:13; 51:6, 13, 16; 55:9-10; 65:17; 66:1).

While the blessing comes with speech formulas that guarantee its credibility, the emphasis of the curse is not on the guarantee but on the consequences of rebellion against the Lord (66:24).

THE TEXT IN BIBLICAL CONTEXT

Wrong Worship

Worship is an important theme in the last chapter of the book of Isaiah (66:3, 17-24) as it is in the first (1:10-15, 27-31). The agenda of worship figures largely in the Bible as a whole. This is so because worship regulates the relationship between Creator and creature. The Bible characterizes this relationship as that of the creature's voluntary submission to the Creator's will.

Wrong worship and worship offered to false gods compromises this relationship between God and humankind. The warnings against having other gods than the Lord and making idols provide the clearest indicator of wrong worship in the OT (Exod 20:4-6 = Deut 5:8-10). Idolatry takes many forms in the Bible. Among them is the exalting of self-identity and self-interest by a person. When this happens, God is displaced and substituted by human self-will.

Alongside the displacement of God is the display and representation of deity by means of material objects (66:3). The purpose of this display and representation is manipulation. What a person makes by hand can be manipulated. This human interest in manipulating God stands in opposition to the creature's voluntary submission to the Creator's will.

At the heart of manipulation is the refusal to accept the ethical intention of worship and focusing instead on ritual. Worship that does not produce discipleship and obedience and justice and right living contributes to a religious experience focused on the human ego and gives rise to all the behavior that Paul lists as "the works of the flesh" (Gal 5:19-21).

THE TEXT IN THE LIFE OF THE CHURCH
Contrite in Spirit

The call to repentance in the first chapter of the book of Isaiah (1:16-20) is restated in the last chapter (66:1-2). In his confession of faith (known in German by its shortened title *Rechenschaft*), Peter Riedemann, a mid-sixteenth-century leader of the Hutterites in central Europe, refers to Isaiah 66:2 regarding repentance (Riedemann: 96).

True repentance, said Riedemann, means humbling oneself before God. This humbling includes a sense of shame for wrongdoing, and it brings about a sincere change of direction. Accompanying the change arising out of a sense of shame is a change of behavior. A person "begins to conquer his flesh," Riedemann says, "brings it into subjection, bridles it."

This is not a shallow contrition in which one fully expects to continue one's wrongdoing, each time repeating one's remorse. What God wants, Riedemann insists, is a person with a contrite spirit. This is not simply contrition *in intellect*, content with routine confession carried out mechanically. It is a deeper contrition *in spirit*, arising out of genuine remorse that is fully committed to addressing wrongdoing and bringing it into subjection. In such a person God can begin his work and perfect it.

Outline of Isaiah

Part 1: TESTIMONY AND TEACHING
Isaiah 1:1–12:6

Rebellion, Repentance, Redemption	**1:1-31**
The Lord's Rebellious Children	1:1-15
Rebellion	1:1-3
Woundedness	1:4-6
Devastation	1:7-9
Wrong Worship	1:10-15
Repentance and Redemption	1:16-31
Call to Repentance	1:16-20
Greed Has Displaced Justice	1:21-23
Threat and Promise	1:24-26
Redemption Versus Rebellion	1:27-31
Word of the Lord, Day of the Lord	**2:1-22**
Disarm and Dismantle	2:1-5
Nations and Peoples Come to the Lord's House	2:1-3a
Swords to Plowshares	2:3b-5
The Day of the Lord	2:6-22
Land Replete with Wealth, Weapons, Wizardry	2:6-8
The Lord's Terror and Glory (I)	2:9-10

Outline of Isaiah

The Day of the Lord	2:11-16
The Lord's Terror and Glory (II)	2:17-19
The Lord's Terror and Glory (III)	2:20-22

Corrupt Leadership and Its Replacement — 3:1–4:6

Removal of Support and Staff	3:1-15
Removal of Leadership	3:1-5
Defiant Tongues and Mutinous Deeds	3:6-7
Oppressed and Misled	3:9-12
The Lord's Judgment	3:13-15
Removal of Security	3:16–4:1
Pride and Penal Servitude	3:16-17
Removal of Finery	3:18-24
Lamentation and Mourning	3:25–4:1
The Lord's Security	4:2-6
The Lord's Branch	4:2-3
The Lord's Canopy	4:4-6

The Lord's Anger and Judgment — 5:1-30

The Vineyard	5:1-7
Song of the Vineyard	5:1-2
Appraising the Vineyard's Harvest	5:3-4
Removing the Vineyard's Defenses	5:5-7
Calamity	5:8-25
Woe! Greed	5:8-10
Woe! Spiritual Indifference	5:11-17
Woe! Deceptive Speech	5:18-20
Woe! Graft and Corruption	5:21-25
Seizing prey	5:26-30
An Invading Force	5:26-28
No Rescue	5:29-30

The Lord's Holiness and a Holy Offspring — 6:1-13

The Lord's Holiness	6:1-4
Confession and Forgiveness	6:5-7
Sending	6:8-10
Exile and Hope	6:11-13

Royalty and Remnant — 7:1-25

Wind and Fire	7:1-4

Outline of Isaiah

Trembling Before a Storm	7:1-2
Two Smoldering Stumps of Firebrands	7:3-4
Plot and Sign	7:5-17
Foiling the Plot	7:5-9
Countersign of Immanuel	7:10-17
Invasion and Survival	7:18-25
Dispatch of Assyria	7:18-20
Briers and Thorns	7:21-25

Call to Hope in the Lord — 8:1-22

Three Encounters	8:1-15
Name and Interpretation	8:1-4
Submerging Flood	8:5-10
Admonishment to Fear the Lord	8:11-15
Teaching and Testimony	8:16-22
The Lord, Cause for Hope	8:16-18
Hopelessness of Counsel from the Dead	8:19-20
Trespassing Teaching and Testimony	8:21-22

Judgment and Hope — 9:1-21

Passion for Justice	9:1-7
A Great Light	9:1-3
Boots and Uniforms Burned	9:4-5
Davidic Child with Divine Names	9:6-7
Passionate Anger	9:8-21
Pride Goes Before the Fall	9:8-12
Off with Their Heads!	9:13-17
Fuel for the Fire	9:18-21

The Lord's Power and Majesty — 10:1-34

Day of Infamy	10:1-19
Day of Visitation	10:1-4
Assyrian Bravado	10:5-11
Assyrian Brawn	10:12-15
Day of Burning	10:16-19
Day of Liberation	10:20-34
Return of a Remnant	10:20-23
Destruction of Assyria	10:24-26
Invasion Set in Motion	10:27-28
Invasion Halted	10:29-34

The Lord's Deeds Among the Peoples — 11:1–12:6

They Shall Not Hurt or Destroy	11:1-9
Delighting in the Fear of the Lord	11:1-3
Deciding with Justice	11:4-6
Declaring a Peaceable Kingdom	11:7-9
The Remnant	11:10-16
Recovery of a Remnant	11:10-11
Harmony of the Gathered Remnant	11:12-14
Return of the Remnant	11:15-16
The Lord's Salvation	12:1-6
Trust Without Fear	12:1-3
Call to Give Thanks	12:4-6

Part 2: THE NATIONS AND THE WHOLE EARTH
Isaiah 13:1–27:13

Nations Manifesto: Babylon — 13:1–14:32

Outcry Concerning Babylon	13:1-22
Marshaling Troops for Battle	13:1-5
The Day of the Lord Proclaimed	13:6-16
Babylon Overthrown	13:17-22
Parody on the King of Babylon	14:1-23
Prologue: Rest Versus Restitution	14:1-2
Downfall of the Autocrat	14:3-21
Epilogue: Babylon in Ruins	14:22-23
Oath Against Assyria	14:24-27
Outcry Concerning Philistia	14:28-32

Nations Manifesto: Moab — 15:1–16:14

Outcry Concerning Moab	15:1-9
Destruction of Moab	15:1-2
Lament for Moab	15:3-5a
Rampant Destruction	15:5b-6
Plight of the Survivors	15:7-9
Moabites in Judah	16:1-5
Compassion for the Moabites	16:1-4a
Davidic Rule	16:4b-5
Grieving for Moab	16:6-14
Hushing the Shout of Joy	16:6-11
Moab's Demise	16:12-14

Outline of Isaiah

PART 3: WEAL AND WOE
Isaiah 28:1–39:8

Woe, Ephraim!	**28:1-29**
Drunkards in Ephraim	28:1-13
Proud Crown	28:1-4
Crown of Glory	28:5-6
No One to Teach	28:7-10
Snared and Taken	28:11-13
Scoffers in Jerusalem	28:14-22
Covenant with Death	28:14-17
Overwhelming Scourge	28:18-22
Parable of the Farmer	28:23-29
Seedtime	28:23-26
Harvest	28:27-29
Woe, Ariel!	**29:1-24**
Conflict and Confusion	29:1-14
Ariel Besieged	29:1-4
Ariel's Enemies Dispersed	29:5-8
Deep Sedation	29:9-10
Vision Unrevealed	29:11-12
Lip Service	29:13-14
Understanding the Lord's Deeds	29:15-24
Illusion of Eluding the Lord	29:15-16
Day of Justice for the Poor	29:17-21
Jacob Comes to Understanding	29:22-24
Woe, Rebellious Children!	**30:1-33**
Rebellious People	30:1-18
Seeking Egypt's Shelter	30:1-5
Egypt's Worthless Help	30:6-7
Witness Against Rebellious Children	30:8-11
Breaking, Collapsing Wall	30:12-14
Remnant in Flight	30:15-18
The Lord as Teacher and Healer	30:19-26
The Lord as Teacher	30:19-22
Day of Healing	30:23-26
The Lord as Devouring Fire	30:27-33

Outline of Isaiah

Breathing Fire	30:27-28
Descending Blow	30:29-30
Assyria Shattered	30:31-33

Woe, Champions of Egyptian Help!   **31:1–32:20**

Idolatry of Military Power	31:1-9
Egyptian Powerlessness	31:1-3
The Lord's Protection of Jerusalem	31:4-5
Assyrian Collapse	31:6-9
Habitat of Peace	32:1-20
A King Ruling with Justice	32:1-8
Women at Risk	32:9-13
Righteousness and Peace	32:14-20

Woe, Destroyer!   **33:1-24**

The Lord's Salvation Open to View	33:1-6
Acknowledging the Lord's Might	33:7-16
Lament for People and Land	33:7-9
The Lord's Response	33:10-12
Right Living	33:13-16
Promise of Salvation	33:17-24
A Future Under a Righteous King	33:17-19
The Lord as King in Zion	33:20-22
Postscript	33:23-24

Edom and Zion   **34:1–35:10**

The Lord's Vengeance Destroying His Enemies	34:1-17
The Lord's Anger	34:1-4
Judgment on Edom	34:5-7
End of Edom	34:8-10
Edom Abandoned	34:11-15
Judgment Completed	34:16-17
The Lord's Vengeance Saving His People	35:1-10
Rejoicing in the Lord's Glory	35:1-4
All Nature Sings!	35:5-7
Everlasting Joy	35:8-10

Hezekiah's Face-Off with Assyria   **36:1–39:8**

Assyrian Advance and Retreat	36:1–37:38
Assyrian Advance	36:1-3

Outline of Isaiah

Sennacherib's Threat	36:4-22
Hezekiah's Appeal	37:1-4
Isaiah's Reply	37:5-7
Sennacherib's Threat	37:8-13
Hezekiah's Prayer	37:14-20
Isaiah's Reply	37:21-35
Assyrian Retreat	37:36-38
Hezekiah's Illness and Restoration	38:1-22
Impending Death and Bitter Weeping	38:1-3
Fifteen Years Added to Hezekiah's Life	38:4-6
A Sign for Hezekiah	38:7-8
Hezekiah Reflects on His Life	38:9-20
Of Figs and Figures	38:21-22
Envoys from Babylon	39:1-8
Hezekiah Shows All	39:1-4
Bondage in Babylon	39:5-8

PART 4: NEW DAY DAWNING
Isaiah 40:1–48:22

God's People Comforted	**40:1-31**
Prologue of Announcement	40:1-11
Revealing the Lord's Glory	40:1-5
All People Are Grass	40:6-8
The Lord Coming with Might	40:9-11
Ode to the Creator	40:12-31
God Without Equal	40:12-14
Pretension of Nations	40:15-17
God Without Image	40:18-20
Posturing of Princes	40:21-24
The Lord's Power	40:25-26
Power to the Faint	40:27-31
Cosmic Judicial Inquiry	**41:1-29**
Nations Called to Judicial Inquiry	41:1-20
Call and Query	41:1-4
Fear and Trembling	41:5-7
Israel's Servanthood	41:8-10
Enemies Disgraced and Scattered	41:11-16
Promise to the Poor	41:17-20

False Gods Called to Judicial Inquiry	41:21-29
Call and Query	41:21-24
No Answer	41:25-29

A Light to the Nations — 42:1-25

The Lord's Spirit upon His Servant	42:1-12
Justice in the Earth	42:1-4
Light to the Nations	42:5-9
Glory to the Lord	42:10-12
The People's Blindness and Disobedience	42:13-25
The Lord's Guidance	42:13-16
Calling Deaf and Blind to Account	42:17-20
The Lord's Guidance Spurned	42:21-23
Disobedience and Discipline	42:24-25

The Lord as Redeemer — 43:1-28

The Lord's Saving Presence	43:1-13
Redemption of Jacob-Israel	43:1-4
Gathering from East, West, North, South	43:5-7
The Lord's Witnesses	43:8-13
Doing a New Thing	43:14-28
The Lord as Redeemer	43:14-21
Burdened and Wearied	43:22-24
Sins Blotted Out	43:25-28

The Restoration of Jacob-Israel — 44:1-28

The Lord's Chosen Servant Jacob-Israel	44:1-8
Choice of Jacob-Israel	44:1-5
The Lord's Uniqueness	44:6-8
Ashes of Idolatry	44:9-20
Artisans of Idolatry	44:9-13
Raw Materials of Idolatry	44:14-17
Folly of Idolatry	44:18-20
The Lord's Redeemed Servant Jacob-Israel	44:21-28
Redemption of Jacob-Israel	44:21-23
The Lord Speaking as Redeemer	44:24-28

No Other God Apart from the Lord — 45:1-25

The Lord's Word to Cyrus	45:1-13
Cyrus as the Lord's Anointed	45:1-4

Outline of Isaiah

The Lord's Witness to Cyrus	45:5-7
Doxology and Disputation	45:8-10
Cyrus Summoned	45:11-13
The Lord's Word to the Exiles	45:14-25
Israel and the Promise of Salvation	45:14-17
Earth as Habitat for Humanity	45:18-19
No Other God Besides the Lord	45:20-21
Earth Called to Turn and Be Saved	45:22-25

Who Has the Power? — 46:1–47:15

Bel, Nebo, and the God Who Saves	46:1-13
Bel and Nebo as Burdens	46:1-2
Jacob-Israel Carried by the Lord	46:3-8
Remembering the Lord's Counsel	46:9-13
Lament over Babylon	47:1-15
Babylon Shamed	47:1-3a
Babylon Silenced	47:3b-5
Babylon's Lack of Mercy	47:6-7
Babylon Overtaken by Disaster	47:8-11
Taunting Babylon	47:12-13
Deriding Babylon's Astrologers	47:14-15

Listen to This! — 48:1-22

Hearing and Knowing	48:1-11
The Lord's Name	48:1-2
Former Things	48:3-5
New Things	48:6-8
For the Sake of the Lord's Name	48:9-11
Creation and Redemption	48:12-22
The Lord's Preeminence	48:12-13
The Lord's Speech	48:14-16a
The Lord's Way	48:16b-19
Redemption Aplenty	48:20-22

PART 5: SERVANT AND SCAFFOLD
Isaiah 49:1–57:21

A Covenant to the People — 49:1-26

Servant Song and Sequel	49:1-13

The Servant's Calling	49:1-3
The Servant's Mission	49:4-6
The Lord as Faithful One	49:7-11
The Lord's Comfort and Compassion	49:12-13
Redemption of Jacob-Israel	49:14-26
Not Forgotten	49:14-18
Children of the Exile	49:19-21
Signal to the Peoples	49:22-23
Savior Who Saves	49:24-26

Sustaining the Weary with a Word — 50:1-11

The Lord's Strength to Save	50:1-3
The Servant in Crisis	50:4-9
Gift of Speaking and Listening	50:4-6
Help Under Affliction	50:7-9
Call to Faithfulness	50:10-11

The Lord Will Comfort Zion — 51:1-23

Comforting the Lord's People	51:1-16
Tidings of Comfort and Joy	51:1-3
Everlasting Salvation	51:4-6
Righteousness and Salvation	51:7-8
Old Exodus, New Exodus	51:9-11
Fear and Forgetfulness	51:12-16
Loosening the Bonds of Oppression	51:17-23
Jerusalem Receives the Cup	51:17-20
Jerusalem's Enemies Receive the Cup	51:21-23

Crown Prince of God's Kingdom — 52:1–53:12

Messenger of Salvation	52:1-12
Jerusalem Freed of Chains	52:1-2
Knowing the Lord's Name	52:3-6
Salvation for Jerusalem	52:7-12
Servant Song	52:13–53:12
Demeanor and Disfigurement	52:13-15
The Servant's Suffering	53:1-6
The Servant's Death	53:7-10
Bearing the Sins of Many	53:11-12

Outline of Isaiah

Covenant of Peace — 54:1-17

Barren Woman Blessed	54:1-3
Widowed Woman Called	54:4-6
Covenant of Peace	54:7-10
Bejeweled City	54:11-14
Safety and Security	54:15-17

Everlasting Covenant and Sign — 55:1-13

Everlasting Covenant	55:1-3
The Lord's Ways and Intentions	55:4-9
The Lord's Word	55:10-11
Everlasting Sign	55:12-13

Access to the Lord's Holy Mountain — 56:1–57:21

Keeping Sabbath	56:1-8
Doing the Right Thing	56:1-3
Including Those Who Please the Lord	56:4-5
Including Those Who Love the Lord's Name	56:6-8
Practices Leading to Death	56:9–57:13
Corruption	56:9-12
Forced Removals	57:1-2
Sorcery and Child Sacrifice	57:3-5
Sexual Immorality	57:6-8
Idolatry	57:9-13
Comfort and Hope	57:14-21
The Lord as High and Holy	57:14-16
The Lord as Healer	57:17-21

PART 6: NEW HEAVENS AND NEW EARTH
Isaiah 58:1–66:24

Bona Fide Piety — 58:1-14

Sins of the House of Jacob	58:1-4
The Lord's Purpose for Fasting	58:5-6
Sharing Bread with the Hungry	58:7-9a
Conditions of the Lord's Guidance	58: 9b-12
Nourished on the Heritage of Jacob	58:13-14

The God Who Comes — 59:1-21

Human Failure	59:1-8
The Lord's Hand, the People's Hands	59:1-3
Deeds and Thoughts of Wickedness	59:4-8
Confession of Sin	59:9-15a
Justice Is Far Away	59:9-11
Transgressions are Near at Hand	59:12-15a
The Lord's Coming	59:15b-21
Absence of Justice and Truth	59:15b-17
Coming as Rushing River, as Redeemer	59:18-20
The Lord's Spirit and Words	59:21

Everlasting Light — 60:1-22

The Lord's Light Rising	60:1-7
Appearance of the Lord's Glory	60:1-5
Coming of the Nations	60:6-7
City of the Lord	60:8-22
Walls and Gates	60:8-12
Sanctuary	60:13-14
Walls of Salvation, Gates of Praise	60:15-18
Everlasting Light	60:19-22

Good News of Liberation — 61:1-11

Year of the Lord's Favor	61:1-4
Everlasting Joy	61:5-7
Everlasting Covenant	61:8-9
Growth of Righteousness and Praise	61:10-11

The Lord's Salvation — 62:1-12

Righteousness of Zion-Jerusalem	62:1-5
Jerusalem, the Praise of the Earth	62:6-7
Harvesting the Earth's Grain	62:8-9
Coming Salvation	62:10-12

God's Mercy Remembered — 63:1–64:12

Day of Vengeance	63:1-6
The Lord's Anger	63:1-3
Vengeance and Redemption	63:4-6
Recital of Israel's Deliverance	63:7-14
The Lord's Gracious Deeds	63:7-9

Outline of Isaiah

Israel's Faithlessness	63:10-14
Prayer of Petition	63:15–64:12
The Lord as Father	63:15-16
Plea for Deliverance	63:17-19
Plea for the Lord to Come Down	64:1-4
Human Iniquity	64:5-7
Turning Away from Anger	64:8-12
Decision to Seek or Forsake the Lord	**65:1-25**
Rebels Versus Servants	65:1-16
Rebellious People	65:1-5
Repayment for Iniquities	65:6-7
Not All Will Be Destroyed	65:8-10
Destined for the Sword	65:11-12
Servants of the Lord Spared	65:13-16
Transformation of Heaven and Earth	65:17-25
New Creation	65:17-19
Building and Planting	65:20-23
Calling and Answering	65:24-25
Comfort and Hope	**66:1-24**
Restoration of Jerusalem	66:1-16
Contrite in Spirit	66:1-2
Choosing Their Own Ways	66:3-4
Shame and Retribution	66:5-6
Jerusalem's Rebirth	66:7-11
Peace and Comfort	66:12-14
Fire and Sword	66:15-16
Seeing the Lord's Glory	66:17-24
Abhorrent Practices	66:17
The Lord's Glory Among the Nations	66:18-21
Human Responses to New Heavens, New Earth	66:22-24

Essays

APOCALYPSE The word *apocalypse* is sometimes used to refer to Isaiah 24–27 (the so-called Isaiah Apocalypse) because these chapters echo a manner of writing that occurs in later apocalyptic literature (e.g., Dan 7–12; Zech 1–8; and portions of Ezekiel in the OT; part of 2 Esdras in the Apocrypha; *2 Baruch* in the Pseudepigrapha; Mark 13; Matt 24-25; Luke 21; and the Revelation of John in the NT). This manner of writing includes symbolic visions (e.g., the vision of a ram and a goat in Dan 8) and mysterious numbers (e.g., the number of the beast in Rev 13) among other characteristics (Metzger and Collins: 362-63; cf. Gottwald, 1985:582-90).

The adjective *apocalyptic*, as it is applied to the Bible, refers to a type of literature in which God reveals messages through a heavenly mediator, who explains these messages to a visionary (Metzger and Collins: 362-63; cf. von Rad, 1965: 301-8). The messages concern judgment and salvation in the final climax of history.

The English noun *apocalypse* derives from the Greek noun *apokalypsis*, "revelation." The corresponding Greek verb is *apokalyptō*, "reveal" or "disclose"; or *anakalyptō*, "unveil" or "uncover." The Hebrew counterpart is the verb *galah*, "uncover" or "remove," which in its passive form means "to be revealed."

Although there are fifteen occurrences of the verb *galah* in Isaiah, only in 24:11 and 26:21 is *galah* used in a context that has apocalyptic overtones. These are intimations of an apocalyptic manner of writing, however, rather than true apocalypse. Elsewhere in Isaiah where *galah* means "to be revealed" (22:14; 53:1; 56:1; and probably 23:1) what is in view is simply God's communication of his will and way.

The best example of an apocalyptic manner of writing in the book of Isaiah outside of chapters 24–27 is in chapters 13 and 14 (Seitz: 175). In both places God's judgment on a cosmic scale is in view, yet without the more precise shape of apocalyptic writing.

How does the so-called Isaiah Apocalypse (chaps. 24–27) comply with the

Essays

biblical meaning of apocalypse and the broader contours of apocalyptic literature? It is best to say that Isaiah 24–27 is proto-apocalyptic rather than a full-fledged apocalypse. This means that in these chapters there is evidence of the beginnings (*proto*) of apocalyptic writing. For example, this may be seen in Isaiah 27:1, where the sea is a symbol of chaos and Leviathan a symbol of evil overthrown by the Lord (cf. Dan 7:1-3). But one has to look elsewhere for a more fully developed example of this kind of literature (e.g., Dan 7–12).

ATONEMENT The English word *atonement* translates the Hebrew word *kapar* in the OT, which portrays God's process for repairing what has gone wrong with creation. The human predicament is localized in broken relationships with God, with other people, and with the rest of the created order. This brokenness is described variously in terms of rebellion, legal violation, pollution, and shame, and it accumulates over time, leading to death (C. Wright: 69-71).

The contribution of Isaiah to this theme should be seen in the context of the OT as a whole [cf. *Redemption, Redeemer, p. 448*]. The main focus of OT atonement language is in the books of Genesis through Deuteronomy. Narratives and law codes alike highlight the importance of sacrifice and other rituals (e.g., Exod 29–30; Lev 1–7; and Num 15, 28–29, in which atonement involves the cleansing and removal of sin). In two especially notable passages, God addresses the healing of human wrong: the call of Abraham and Sarah to form a family to bless and be blessed (Gen 12:1-3), and the deliverance of Israel from Egypt. Intercessory prayer is an important means of human reconciliation to God, apparently negating the need for sacrifice at times (Gen 18; Exod 32–34; Deut 9).

Psalms of penitence reflect a deep awareness of sin, yet they contain almost no reference to atoning sacrifice. Most references to sacrifice occur in celebrations of thanksgiving or anticipations of such rather than in relation to confession of sin. Psalms 40, 50, and 51 indicate that for God, ritual unaccompanied by obedience has no integrity.

As with the Psalms, Israel's prophets grieved deeply over sins personal and corporate, yet also rejected the effectiveness of ritual apart from repentance. Jeremiah repeatedly calls people to "turn away from evil" (Jer 25:5) and to "turn to God" (Jer 3:22; cf. Joel 2:12-17; Ezek 18:30-32; 33:10-11). The prophets seek to restore broken covenants among the people and with God. Ultimately, restoration depends upon God's gracious character and upon the willingness of human beings to receive God's transforming forgiveness and restoration (Jer 33:8; C. Wright).

The Hebrew word *kapar* and related terms are used rarely in Isaiah. In 6:7 the prophet's sin is cleansed (*atoned*, NIV) by means of a burning coal touching his mouth (cf. Isa 22:14; 27:9; 28:18; 43:3; 47:11; 48:3). In the fourth servant song (52:13–53:12), however, a fuller view of atonement is conveyed. Though *kapar* is not used in this song, images of bearing infirmities, suffering for the transgressions of others, making intercession for sinners, and receiving punishment that makes others righteous suggest the atonement theme, accomplished this time through the life and death of the servant. In 53:4-6 it is stated that people (we) are made whole and healed (cf. Gold and Holladay: 940). Here the servant acts as mediator and reconciler between God and humankind. Atonement is brought about by the laying down of the servant's life (Vriezen: 297-99) [*Servant, Servants, p. 451*].

The New Testament writers looked to Isaiah's fourth servant song as an important source for understanding the meaning of Christ's work. Matthew, for example, quotes Isaiah 53:4 in his summary of Jesus' healing ministry (Matt 8:17; cf. also Isa 53:5, 9 in 1 Peter 2:22, 24; Isa 53:7-8 in Acts 8:32-33; and Isa 53:12 in Mark 15:28 and Luke 22:37). In the NT, no single Greek term covers as wide a range of meaning as *kapar*; instead, numerous metaphors—often with connections to the OT—are employed to depict how Christ's death is the means by which atonement takes place.

The church has never adopted one "official" explanation of what Christ's work has accomplished. Across the centuries, four major models have been constructed (*ODCC*: 122-24). (1) During the period of the church fathers (second to eighth centuries AD), the teaching in general was that in his death Christ ransomed us (Matt 20:28; Mark 10:45). Then, by his resurrection, Christ conquered the power of Satan and delivered humanity from bondage. In the twentieth century, Gustaf Aulén argued for this position as the most ancient and classical model, which he called *Christus Victor*.

(2) In the eleventh and twelfth centuries AD, Anselm of Canterbury (1033-1109) emphasized the idea of "satisfaction" as an explanation of Christ's redemptive work. Satisfaction was understood by Anselm as an act of compensation for violations of God's honor as lawgiver. Christ's death is a substitute that provides sufficient compensation on behalf of human beings for the sins of the world. This approach was later adapted to a legal framework, sometimes called "penal substitution."

(3) Abelard (1079-1142), a contemporary of Anselm, developed a "moral influence" approach, concluding that the effectiveness of Christ's death lies in the power of his loving actions. Sinners fear God, but Christ's death evokes a response of love in the sinner, who is then able to overcome this fear, be reconciled, and live a life of faithfulness. (4) With some similarity to Abelard, the Socinians (sixteenth century) viewed Christ's death as an energizing example to those who believed in him. They insisted that the cross had no power to atone for human sin, but through it people were motivated to faithfulness like that of Christ (*ODCC*: 122-24).

Sixteenth-century Anabaptists primarily employed *Christus Victor*, though some also referred to the moral influence and substitution models. In general, their approach to Jesus' work involved significant participation by believers and was shaped more by Jesus' life than was the case with other theologians of the period (Finger: 329-50).

In recent years a number of writers within the Anabaptist tradition have written about the atonement. They also tend to prefer *Christus Victor*, not as a precise model but as a biblical framework (Finger: 332, 364). They have especially sought to counter the influence of the penal substitution model for several reasons: to correct misperceptions of God's wrath; to give Jesus' life, teachings, and resurrection a more central place; to demonstrate the integration of ethics and atonement; and to counter the myth of redemptive violence (M. Baker, 2007:45).

John Driver (1986) sought a way through the impasse of the different atonement models in the variety of metaphors employed by NT writers. He identifies more than twenty images and motifs in ten groups, among which are conflict-victory-liberation, vicarious suffering, sacrifice, expiation, redemption, and adoption-family. These should not be assessed as contradictory perspectives but as overlapping messages that fill out the complex reality of God's atoning work in Christ. Each of the major atonement models prefers certain metaphors or emphases over others, and thus misses some of the atonement complexity. By itself, the sacrificial metaphor (taken up by the substitution model), for example, tends to devalue discipleship, and yet Jesus insisted that only those who obey his Father will enter the kingdom (Matt 7:21). Other atonement metaphors suggest the participation of the believer in Christ's work.

J. Denny Weaver (2001) adapts the classical *Christus Victor* model and calls it narrative *Christus Victor*. In a way that goes beyond the classical view, this adaptation stresses the life and work of Jesus alongside his victory over the evil powers of the world. Particularly concerned to reject the understanding of Anselm that God requires violent acts to satisfy divine justice, Weaver also critiques contemporary versions of Abelard's moral influence model. Yet his narrative *Christus Victor* has elements of both models: it involves "a forgiveness that is difficult and costly when visualized either from God's side or the side of sinful humanity." There was a cost for God and for the Son, and there is also a cost for believers, responding to violence with nonviolence, and thus giving their lives in God's service (Weaver: 215-16).

Thomas Finger likewise embraces the *Christus Victor* model with elements of moral influence (both "conflictive" and "transformative" dimensions), but he puts more emphasis on the Spirit and transcendence in the work of atonement and victory over the fallen powers of this world (358-59). Unlike some others, Finger finds positive elements in substitution imagery because it emphasizes that Jesus did things for us that we could not do for ourselves (361-62).

For Anabaptist writers, Isaiah's characterization of the servant—along with the royal images in chapters 7, 9, 11—represents both the unique ministry of Christ as suffering leader and the call of God's people to follow his example (see Finger: 331-65; M. Baker 2006; Green and Baker; essays in Swartley; and the literature cited).

COMPOSITION OF THE BOOK OF ISAIAH The book of Isaiah forms an organic unity. This means first and foremost that the book exhibits continuity from beginning to end. Unity also means that the various parts of the book have been ordered in such a way as to produce a whole.

The reader of the book may at first be surprised at the way in which themes and subjects shift, often abruptly, from one direction to another. This would seem to argue for disunity and discontinuity. It is important to say, therefore, that the organic unity is not a simple but a composite unity.

For a very long time both Jewish and Christian scholars have questioned whether chapters 1–39 were written by a different author than chapters 40–66. A clear break in historical background and literary style occurs between chapters 39 and 40 creating two main sections. (A further break between chapters 55 and 56 is sometimes suggested, creating a three-part structure of the book: chaps. 1–39, 40–55, 56–66.) An example of historical criteria supporting a two-part structure of the book is the reference to temple, land, and kingship as ongoing realities in chapters 1–39 but as things of the past in chapters 40–66. An example of literary criteria is the occurrence of the name *Isaiah* sixteen times in chapters 1–39 and never in chapters 40–66. Further comparison of the two parts indicates numerous differences of style and imagery. Among these differences are the introduction of the servant of the Lord after chapter 40 (in chaps. 41–53), recurrent imperatives (e.g., in chaps. 52–55), an explicit monotheism (e.g., chaps. 41–42), and a reinterpretation of the exodus traditions (e.g., chap. 43).

The subdivisions of the book, however valid they may be, should not be resolved into a simple chronological sequence except in a rather general way. It is better to think of the two or three parts as literary subdivisions rather than as time frames.

Two general approaches have been employed to consider the question of composition in Isaiah. One approach, founded on and growing out of Jewish and Christian belief systems, is dogmatic in its orientation. By "dogmatic" I do not necessarily mean rigid or static but rather an approach that employs principles or positions in a religious belief system. This orientation, for example, might take a statement from Isaiah in the NT introduced by "Isaiah said" (e.g., Matt 3:3, which quotes Isa 40:3) as an indication that the eighth-century BC prophet Isaiah wrote the entire book. Such a methodology for studying the Scriptures, it may be said, places primary emphasis on the face value of the text rather than taking the larger context of a book's meaning into consideration (cf. Gottwald, 1985:8-10).

Those who hold this approach contend that the thematic unity of chapters 1–39 and 40–66 is at least as significant as the differences. In addition, this method maintains that the testimony to Isaiah as author of the entire book bearing his name, in early Judaism and throughout the NT period and beyond, deserves serious attention. According to this view, it seems doubtful that a great prophet such as the one who wrote chapters 40–66 would be anonymous.

A second approach, heavily influenced by scientific method, is dialectic in its orientation. By "dialectic" I mean discussion and reasoning by means of dialogue as a method of intellectual investigation. This approach, often called historical-critical, includes widely diverse schools of thought, most of whom argue from literary and historical evidence for multiple authorship of the book of Isaiah over several centuries.

Which of these approaches one chooses affects the conclusions one draws about the composition of the book of Isaiah. A dogmatic approach wants to protect the Bible from the excesses of much modern thought, such as relativism or fragmentation of the text. A historical-critical approach wants to explore the Bible with tools available through the scientific method.

In this commentary I employ a blend of these approaches. I am interested in how the interpretation of the Bible is carried out and lived out today in communities of faith for whom the Bible is the foundation of faith and life. Such an interpretation, however, is not spoiled by the use of historical-critical tools. On the contrary, it is strengthened by these tools. The better we can understand how the prophetic word came to God's people in their own time and culture, the better we are prepared to hear it and receive it in our own time and culture.

My interest in the composition of Isaiah lies parallel to an interest in the notion of an exegetical consciousness in the prophets as a whole. There is an interpretive process in the book of Isaiah by which the messages Isaiah of Jerusalem gave for an eighth-century-BC audience were subsequently reinterpreted for the needs of later generations, particularly exilic and postexilic audiences in the sixth century BC and beyond. Such an interpretive process is not unlike preaching in the church today, where ancient texts are explained and expounded and brought up to date for communities of faith in the present.

The sixth century BC was a time of immense upheaval for the Judeans of the Southern Kingdom. There were the Babylonian threats followed by invasion and deportation in the first two decades of the century. Then Babylon itself fell in 539 BC, and under Cyrus the Persian the Judean exiles were given the opportunity to return to Judah and rebuild their temple. I assume, therefore, that the communities and the theological issues of the sixth century BC were different from those of the eighth century BC. I do not doubt that there was continuity between these communities, but the experience of invasion and deportation created new realities for the exiles in Babylon.

Two examples of the contrasting communities and issues of the eighth and sixth centuries exhibit these differing realities. In the Southern Kingdom of the eighth century BC, there were important social-justice issues that grew out of increasing affluence. So Isaiah of Jerusalem used the metaphor of a vineyard to denounce injustice and to warn about judgment (Isa 5:1-10). In the late sixth century, however, an heir of Isaiah's prophetic vision addressed repatriated exiles living under deprivation and need, speaking about a happy future when people would again plant vineyards and build houses (65:17-25; cf. Hanson: 186).

Again, in the eighth century there was a spiritual torpor in which the leaders of the Southern Kingdom were incapable of clear ethical decision making. The language for this is *a spirit of deep sleep* (Isa 29:10). Two centuries later the exiles were faced with a different kind of spiritual crisis: idolatry on a grand scale in Babylon. So a spiritual descendant of the eighth-century Isaiah presented an exposé of Babylonian idolatry addressed to exiles who, it is suggested, were using these images (Roth: 133). The argument against idols is another kind of deep sleep: *their eyes are shut, so that they cannot see* (Isa 44:18).

By way of summary, then, my solution to the question of composition begins with a consideration of the book of Isaiah as a whole and then looks for connections between the various parts that make up the whole (I. Friesen, 1990:23-26). In this process of composition, there were authors who wrote out of their different historical contexts and who were inspired to reinterpret for their own particular circumstances texts that were handed down to them.

DAY OF THE LORD The word *day* (*yom*) is used in Isaiah some 127 times in a variety of contexts. In the Hebrew Bible as a whole, the word occurs some 2,350 times (Lisowsky: 581-96). The idea that the Lord has a day on which judgment will occur is the leading theme of Isaiah 2:6-22. Closely allied to this is the *day of vengeance* found elsewhere in the book (e.g., Isa 34:8; 61:2; 63:4). Beyond the book of Isaiah, the *day of the LORD* is an important theme in Joel and Zephaniah and in most of the prophets.

Scholars usually include the day of the Lord under discussions of eschatology, a noun deriving from the Greek *eschaton*, meaning "last thing." Eschatology is the inquiry into the nature of the last things, and the day of the Lord is often seen as a final day of judgment.

The purpose of such a day cannot be separated from the biblical conviction that sin and misdeed have their consequences in loss and ruin. This is expressed by the prophet Amos in regarding the day of the Lord as a time of darkness and gloom (5:18-20). Isaiah sees it as a time of God's anger and destruction (13:6-16).

Nevertheless the prophets also view the day of the Lord as a time of renewal and redemption beyond judgment (Gottwald, 1985:362-63). This may be seen by the way in which promises of peace and restoration in Isaiah 2:1-5 and 4:2-6 provide the "framework" for the judgment that is announced in Isaiah 2:6–4:1 (cf. Seitz: 40-42).

GLORY The English noun "glory" occurs fairly often in both the Old and the NTs. The Hebrew verb *kbd* in the OT means "to be heavy" or "to be honored" and is sometimes translated "to glorify" when speaking about God (e.g., Ps 86:12). The noun form of *kbd* (*kabod*) is used frequently, alluding to God's self-revelation to humankind in a variety of ways. For example, God's glory is shown to Moses as a name, "The LORD" (Exod 33:17-23), and to Ezekiel as "something that looked like fire" (1:26-28). In the NT the glory (*doxa*) of the Lord visualized by the shepherds at the time of Jesus' birth is an angel (later angels) and something that shines (Luke 2:9).

The term "glory" is used theologically as "the outer aspect of God's true being" (Knight: 49). So in Exodus 40:34-38 the Lord's glory is represented by the cloud covering and filling the tabernacle. The Lord himself is not visible, but his glory, represented by the cloud, can be seen. Though God remains outside the empirical span of human perception, God reveals his glory to humankind in supernatural experience (Knight: 49).

The classic text concerning God's self-revelation in the book of Isaiah is in chapter 6. The Hebrew verb *ra'ah* (to see) is used to indicate normal seeing as well as visionary sight. Because of what is seen in Isaiah 6, it is clear that a vision is taking place, a particular kind of seeing (cf. Ezek 1:1; Amos 8:1; Zech 1:8, 18). "Isaiah saw the Lord, but in a vision" (Young, 1965:236). In this vision the Lord's *kabod* (*glory*) is said to fill the whole earth. Since God's holiness and glory are joined in Isaiah 6:3, it is clear that the main idea of God's glory lies in his holiness, eliciting surprise and readiness to serve among those who seek him (Isa 6:4-8), but consternation and apprehension among the arrogant and insolent (cf. Isa 2:10, 19, 21).

HEBREW POETRY There is an important distinction between prose and poetry in the Bible even though there is not a strict division between them. Prose may be defined as the ordinary language of speaking or writing, with a closer correspondence to the patterns of everyday speech. Poetry is the "elevated" language of speaking or writing, which wakens feeling and emotion and often has a rhythmical form (*COD*). These definitions of prose and poetry apply generally to biblical Hebrew, but a closer inquiry into the character of Hebrew poetry in particular is necessary.

For several centuries it has been recognized that Hebrew poetry consists of lines that often divide into two or three clauses parallel to each other. This analysis of Hebrew poetry continues to be discussed and debated among scholars. One view, for example, focuses mainly on syntax generating parallels at the level of words and lines (O'Connor).

Another view avoids a focus on syntax alone and stresses the combination of syntax and meanings (Kugel). In this view, parallelism means that *B continues line A* and *goes beyond it*. Another way to say this is that line *B seconds* or *supports* line *A* (for a synopsis of these views, cf. Gottwald, 1985:522-25, 657).

Hebrew poetry in fact exhibits several types of parallelism. There is synonymous parallelism, in which analogous ideas are expressed on adjoining poetic lines (e.g., *The ox knows its owner/and the donkey its master's crib//but Israel does not know/my people do not understand*; Isa 1:3). In antithetic parallelism there is a contrast between poetic lines (e.g., *The grass withers, the flower fades/but the word of our God will stand forever*; Isa 40:8).

There are other examples of parallelism that are not clearly synonymous or antithetic in which, for example, the relationship between poetic lines is not one of close correspondence at all but of unfolding thought (e.g., *All these things my hand has made/and so all these things are mine, says the LORD*; Isa 66:2). These examples indicate the richness of parallelism in Hebrew poetry.

There is also debate and discussion about the arrangement of poetic lines into larger clusters. The words "stanza" and "strophe" (often used interchangeably) may be employed to describe these clusters. In this commentary I use the noun "stanza" to designate a concise statement on a single topic usually distrib-

Essays

uted over three to six lines. The stanza in poetry has an approximate correspondence to the sentence in prose.

HOLY, HOLY ONE OF ISRAEL In modern usage the adjective "holy" suggests wholeness and refers to someone of pure or unblemished character (such as *Holy Spirit*, disclosure of God in Christ in human experience) or something of godlike quality (such as *Holy Scripture*, writing inspired by God).

The Hebrew adjective *qadoš* (from *qdš*) is usually translated "holy." Vriezen argues that the meaning of "holy" as it applies to God is "brilliance" so that humankind cannot view it (149). The lexical definition of God's holiness includes the idea of separation; God is understood as separate from human frailty and failing (cf. BDB: 872). God is not human, and humans are not God.

In the Bible, however, the adjective "holy" does not apply only to God. It is a shared quality with the people of Israel as in Isaiah 4:3 (cf. Lev 11:44-45; 19:2; and elsewhere). Israel is to take on something of the quality of holiness that derives from God (Isa 62:12; 63:18; cf. 35:8-10).

The use of *holy* as a noun in the book of Isaiah is especially notable with reference to God as *the Holy One of Israel*. This designation for God occurs some twenty-seven times in the book, appearing in all six sections (e.g., Isa 1:4; 5:19; 17:7; 29:19; 30:11, 12; 37:23; 41:14, 16; 47:4; 49:7; 55:5; 60:9, 14). Here the sense of *holy* is not simply "wholly other," in contrast to Israel, which is time bound and space limited. Holiness also has a moral character (cf. Knight: 36-37). In Isaiah 5:16, for example, there is the statement that God shows himself *holy by righteousness* (cf. 28:17; 30:18; 33:5; 61:8). This is evidence that, in Isaiah, ethics and holiness belong together in God's character. Not only do they belong together but righteousness also is one of the components of holiness.

JUSTICE AND RIGHTEOUSNESS The English word "justice" is a translation of the Hebrew noun *mišpaṭ*, built from the root word *špṭ*, meaning "to procure justice for" or "to decide" or "to settle" something (*HADOT*: 292). The English word "righteousness" is a translation of the Hebrew noun *ṣedeq/ṣedaqah*, meaning "what is right" or "what is just."

In the OT justice and righteousness are often found in tandem (e.g., Gen 18:19; 1 Kings 10:9; Pss 33:5; 72:2; 89:14; 97:2; Prov 8:20; Jer 9:24; Ezek 45:5; Amos 5:24). In these pairings justice and righteousness are understood both as something that God does and as something that God expects of his people.

In Isaiah and other OT prophets, justice is something that one *does* (Limburg, 1977:81-87). It is important to have the right attitude about justice, but unless one *does justice*, the right attitude means little.

In the courtroom, for example, the poor are not to be defrauded by laws written and enacted for the benefit of the rich (Isa 3:13-15). On the contrary, the elders and princes are to see to it that the poor are protected. Doing justice, however, extends beyond the courtroom and into everyday life (Isa 56:1). Political leadership must give evidence of doing justice, but in the end justice is the responsibility of everyone.

Justice and the love of justice are defining characteristics of God (Isa 5:16; 28:17; 30:18; 33:5; 61:8). But the Bible testifies that God's justice must be reflected in humankind, who is created in the image of God. In the words of Isaiah's vision, humankind is called upon to love justice and to do it (Isa 1:17).

Righteousness has to do with right relationships. When used of God, righteousness includes truthfulness in speech (Isa 45:19), covenant keeping (41:10), and delivering and guiding his people (e.g., Pss 5:8; 31:1; 72:2; 89:16). When used of people, righteousness includes what is ethically right: honesty (Gen 30:33), integrity (Deut 6:25), truthfulness (Zech 8:8). The application of ethics is to be found among judges, rulers, kings, and among God's people everywhere (cf. BDB: 841-42).

Von Rad's careful analysis of righteousness with reference to God and to Israel makes the important point that ṣedeq/ṣedaqah refers to relationships (1962:370-83). Righteous persons (ṣediqim) take seriously the claims laid upon them by their relationship to the Lord, who embodies justice and righteousness (cf. Isa 5:16). In the Hebrew Bible, God's righteousness is something that God is and does with a view toward shaping God's people in the same direction. It is at this point, in my judgment, that von Rad's analysis is inadequate. On the one hand he sees God's commands as entirely and even easily fulfilled. On the other hand he emphasizes the impossibility that humans can perform sufficient obedience to God. In this view there is an unwillingness to conceive of the human capacity by God's empowerment to do what is right.

The book of Ezekiel offers an example of the righteous person imitating God's righteousness. The underlying assumption in Ezekiel 18 is that the righteous person has the capacity to do "what is just and right" (v. 5 NIV). What this entails is a voluntary application of the Lord's ways rather than insisting on one's own way (cf. Lind, 1996:148-52). And the key for doing this in Ezekiel 18 is repentance, turning from evil and committing oneself to making relationships right.

LITERARY PERSPECTIVE The writers of the various books of the Bible shaped their compositions to provide clarity and interest. Such shaping can be seen at numerous places in the book of Isaiah.

Rhetorical questions in which no answer is expected or in which the answer is implied and obvious are found in the book. A good example is the Lord's word in Isaiah 10:15:

> *Does the ax raise itself above him who swings it,
> or the saw boast against him who uses it?* (NIV)

Metaphors and *similes* swarm through the literary landscape of the book of Isaiah. A *metaphor* is a figure of speech in which a word or phrase is employed for an object or idea to which it is not literally applicable. In Isaiah 6:13 and 11:1, for example, the figure of a tree (*stump*) symbolizes the remnant in the land after the exile (6:13) or the Davidic monarchy anticipating a messianic figure (11:1). A *simile* is also a figure of speech, but one in which two different things are indirectly compared by using the prepositions *like* or *as* to introduce the comparison. In Isaiah 28:2 an enemy's incursion is compared to a storm:

> *See, the Lord has one who is powerful and strong.
> Like a hailstorm and a destructive wind,
> like a driving rain and a flooding downpour,
> he will throw it forcefully to the ground.* (NIV)

Alliteration is the repetitive use of consonant sounds in adjacent syllables or words or phrases to add interest to poetic lines. Isaiah 43:19 offers an example of alliteration. The Hebrew text employs h and ḥ sounds as follows:

Essays

*h*inni 'oseh *h*adašah
    'attah tiṣma*h*
*h*alo' teda'u*ha*

Alliteration in the Hebrew text cannot easily be imitated in translation. It is more often the product of creative translation as in the sequence of new-now-not in Isaiah 43:19:

*I am about to do a **new** thing;*
    ***now** it springs forth,*
    *do you **not** perceive it?*

Chiasmus and *inclusio* are useful literary tools in the repertoire of the biblical writer. *Chiasmus* (Greek for "crosswise arrangement," from the Greek letter *chi*, which is shaped like an X) is an inverted relationship between phrases forming a mirror image, sometimes displayed as A-B-B'-A'. Such a mirror image is found in Isaiah 56:4-7, where the words *foreigner* and *eunuch* (v. 3, A-B) are inverted as *eunuchs* and *foreigners* (vv. 4 and 6, B'-A'). An *inclusio* (Latin for "locking up," which as a literary term means "bracketing") is a relationship between similar literary segments forming an "enclosure" or "envelope." It may be said, for example, that the beginning and end of the book of Isaiah form an *inclusio* because the similar theme of worship opens the book (esp. Isa 1:10-31) and closes it (notably Isa 66:17-24).

MESSENGER FORMULA The formula *Thus says the LORD* (e.g., Isa 37:6, *koh 'amar yhwh*) or variations on it occurs some fifty times in the book of Isaiah (cf. 7:7; 10:24; 18:4; 21:6; 28:14; 29:22; 30:15; 43:1; 50:1; 65:8). The pattern for this formula may be seen in Genesis 32:3-8, where Jacob sends messengers to Esau. The messengers speak in Jacob's name when they say, "Thus says your servant Jacob" (*koh 'amar 'abdeka ya'aqob*). The messengers use the first person singular *I* as they speak the message of Jacob. The speech of the Rabshakeh in Isaiah 36:4 follows the same pattern. The Rabshakeh speaks in the name of the king of Assyria when he says, "Thus says the great king . . . " By observing this use of diplomatic discourse, it is more easily possible to grasp the role of the biblical prophets as emissaries of "the Great King," who speak in his name.

By way of summary, then, when a prophet speaks in the Lord's name, the speech begins with the formula *Thus says the LORD*, followed by the prophet's use of the first-person singular I as the Lord's message is spoken. The prophet speaks in the Lord's name.

MESSIAH, MESSIANIC HOPE. The word "messiah" is derived from a Hebrew noun (*mašiah*) meaning "anointed." Elijah the prophet anointed Elisha as his successor (1 Kings 19:16). Elsewhere kings were anointed. Samuel anointed Saul (1 Sam 10:1) and David (16:13). Zadok the priest anointed Solomon (1 Kings 1:39). Prophets and kings were anointed with oil as a sign of being set apart for an office (BDB: 603).

The anointing of David in particular was viewed as a significant moment in Israel's history (cf. Anderson, 1974:131). Thus the promise to David (2 Sam 7:8-17) and the royal psalms (e.g., 2, 18, 110; cf. 89) testify to a developing messianic hope in ancient Israel. Originally these psalms were probably used in the reigns of specific Israelite kings. But later they came to be interpreted in terms of a messianic hope. This hope was that in the future God would raise up a descendant of King David, "his [the LORD'S] anointed" (*tou christou autou*; Ps 2:2 LXX), to restore and redeem his people. The royal psalms picture a model of kingship that blends strength and goodness.

In the two centuries before and the one after the birth of Christ, a number of understandings of Messiah and the messianic hope emerged in Judaism. The Dead Sea community at Qumran, often identified with the Essenes, mention two main messianic figures: the Messiah of Aaron, a priest, and the Messiah of Israel, a king. The kingly Messiah would be a Davidic prince who would defeat the Gentiles and bring the kingdom of God into being. The priestly Messiah would be an interpreter of the law, revealing the application of the Scriptures to events in the messianic age (Vermès: 86). The Zealots had a different view of the messianic hope. They were strongly anti-Roman in their outlook, and they anticipated a kingly Messiah who would free Israel from the grip of Roman rule (Organ: 37). The various Jewish teachings about the messianic hope in these centuries understood the Messiah as God's agent to deliver his people from oppression.

These teachings influenced Jesus' own self-understanding positively and negatively, as well as the perspective of the NT itself. It seems clear that Jesus understood himself standing in the tradition of this messianic hope (cf. Mark 14:62; Matt 26:64). That he was a different kind of Messiah, however, is indicated by his identification with the suffering servant of Isaiah (cf. Matt 12:15-21, which includes a quotation from Isaiah 42:1-4, the first servant song). All four Gospels present Jesus as a Messiah whose intention was not military victory but servant leadership in a new community (cf. the triumphal entry in Mark 11:1-10; Matt 21:1-11; Luke 19:29-40; John 12:12-19).

Those who knew Jesus of Nazareth and believed in him found the Jewish messianic hope fulfilled in him. Throughout the Gospels and in the Acts of the Apostles, Jesus is designated "Messiah," which in its Greek form *Christos* (Christ) serves as a personal name in the remainder of the NT. The NT invites its readers to see the messianic hope of the OT revealed and fulfilled in Jesus Christ.

REDEMPTION, REDEEMER In the OT three Hebrew verb stems in particular give color to the sum and substance of redemption. (1) The verb stem *kpr* means "cover over" (perhaps better "smooth," or "spread": cf. Vriezen: 287, n. 1) or "make atonement," as in Leviticus 17:11 (cf. *ward off*, Isa 47:11; "appease or pacify," Gen 32:20). In the OT it is understood that God himself covers over human sin, which humans of themselves cannot do. This is not a cover-up in the sense that sin is merely swept under the rug rather than swept out the door. Sin is covered over in the sense that it is not held against a person (Isa 6:7).

Since the human capacity to sin remains, the question is whether this capacity to sin constitutes slavery to sin, from which there can be no freedom, only incessant repentance and perpetual atonement. Such a treadmill approach to redemption is disproved by the spirit of the Psalms (e.g., Ps 51) and the prophets (e.g., Isa 1:16-20), if not by the law itself (e.g., Deut 21:8-9). The result is not a theology of perfection in which the capacity to sin can be rooted out once and for all. Rather, the idea is that through ongoing repentance and atonement, people who are committed to God's way will not only resolve to do the right thing but actually do it by God's power and grace within them [*Atonement, p. 439*].

(2) The verb stem *pdh* has the sense of "ransom" or "redeem." The meaning of this verb is to liberate someone from bondage by giving a ransom (cf.

Vriezen: 273, n. 1). The bondage may be violence and death (Pss 49:15; 130:8). It may be slavery (Deut 7:8) or exile (Isa 35:10; 51:11). In these examples it is God who ransoms his people from situations of despair and dashed hopes.

(3) Of the three verb stems, *g'l* is used most frequently in the book of Isaiah. This stem is often translated "redeem" and the noun *redemption* (*ge'ullah*) is derived from it in Isaiah 63:4 (*ge'ulay, my redemption*). The stem g'l reflects a kinship relation in which the relative of one person acts to save a member of the family from disgrace or to provide security for needy kinfolk (cf. the role played by Boaz in the book of Ruth). This kinship idea is extended to God's attachment to his people. When God acts to redeem, this implies a personal relationship to the one who is redeemed. Thus, individuals are redeemed from death (Ps 103:4), or Israel is redeemed from bondage in Egypt (Exod 6:6), or Israel is redeemed from exile in Babylon (Isa 41:14).

The English noun *redeemer* translates the Hebrew participle *go'el* in the OT. This noun is used as a designation for God thirteen times in the book of Isaiah, all in chapters 40 through 66 (41:14; 43:14; 44:6, 24; 47:4; 48:17; 49:7, 26; 54:5, 8; 59:20; 60:16; 63:16). In these texts, Redeemer is full of rich and varied meaning. God as Redeemer sends destruction on oppressors, acts as teacher and leader, takes care of his people with compassion, forgives, and saves. The collocation of *Redeemer* and *Holy One of Israel* indicates that God, who is "wholly other," nevertheless aligns himself with Israel, who is time bound and space limited.

REMNANT The noun "remnant" appears some seventy-six times in the OT, but only twice in the NT (*hypoleimma* in Rom 9:27; *leimma* in Rom 11:5). Several Hebrew roots are employed to express the remnant idea in the OT, especially š'r, which means "remain," and ytr, which means "be left over." The largest concentration of these words is in Isaiah (15 times) and Jeremiah (20 times).

The historical books (Joshua, Judges, Samuel, and Kings) speak of a minority in Israel who will survive God's judgment upon his people for their sins. In 1 Kings 19:18, for example, the Lord's word to Elijah that "I will leave [š'r] seven thousand in Israel" may be interpreted as a promise of the continuation of a faithful remnant.

Historical evidence and theological explanation merge in two summaries at the end of 2 Kings. In 2 Kings 17 there is a summary of the conquest of Israel (Northern Kingdom) by Assyria, with Judah alone left ('r) to keep the Lord's commandments. In 2 Kings 24–25 there is a summary of the conquest of Judah (Southern Kingdom) by Babylon. The exile of "the rest [ytr] of the people who were left [š'r] in the city" (25:11) is a reference to a remnant. The poorest people of Judah who were left (š'r) in the land as farmers constituted a further remnant.

The writing prophets (Isaiah, Jeremiah, Ezekiel, and the Minor Prophets) spoke of a remnant that would survive God's judgment. Isaiah in particular thought of the remnant as *a few survivors* (1:9) after judgment for sin in the form of an invasion. But the remnant was also thought of positively as the nucleus of a repentant people (Isa 10:20-22). From this repentant people, symbolized by *the stump of Jesse* (11:1) and *the root of Jesse* (11:10), would come a messianic king and a peaceable kingdom. Such a king and kingdom form the foundation of a strategy to bring peace on earth [*Messiah, Messianic Hope, p. 447*].

A general outline of this strategy may be developed from the "swords to plowshares" passage in Isaiah 2:1-5. I see the strategy moving through two fields of operation. The first identifies the place where the blessing of Abram on "all the families of the earth" (Gen 12:3) is lodged. This place is firmly rooted in the God of Jacob, whose ways and paths call for a world order resting on justice and peace. The calling of Jacob's descendants was not to imitate the main stream of Near Eastern power politics but to be free from this pattern of statecraft (cf. Lind, 1990:176). It is because of a fundamental trust in the Lord's integrity, however, that earth's peoples are willing and eager to be taught the Lord's justice and peace.

The second field of operation addresses five steps toward justice and peace. The first is the Lord's instruction that flows from Jerusalem. Jerusalem was not intended to be an isolated backwater but to guide the nations toward a political life with the Lord's instruction as their point of reference (cf. Lind, 1990:176). The second step is the Lord's arbitration in international disputes. The third, fourth, and fifth steps reflect the outcome of this arbitration: multilateral disarmament, cessation of warfare, and closure of military academies. The intention is that the Lord's instruction provides the framework that is to be implemented by his people. The house of Jacob—a remnant among the nations—is called to lead the way in this grand strategy of universal peace and justice.

RIGHTEOUSNESS (see **JUSTICE AND RIGHTEOUSNESS**)

SABBATH OBSERVANCE The observance of the Sabbath is indicated as a sign of the covenant between God and Israel in Exodus 31:12-17. It occurs in both versions of the Decalogue (Exod 20:8-11; Deut 5:12-15) although the motive for Sabbath observance differs in each. In Exodus the motive is centered on the narrative of creation and rest in Genesis 1:1–2:3. In Deuteronomy the motive is centered on the deliverance from slavery in Egypt.

At least since the time of the exile, Sabbath observance has distinguished Jews from their Gentile neighbors. Although the early Christians continued to observe the Jewish Sabbath (on the seventh day of the week), there was a gradual shift to worship as a celebration of Christ's resurrection (on the first day of the week; *NHBD*: 632-33). This is generally true even though there are examples of Sabbatarian movements in church history.

Although references to the Sabbath occur at the beginning and end of the book of Isaiah (1:13; 66:23), it is in chapters 56–57 and 58 that Sabbath observance is given specific emphasis (although the Sabbath is not mentioned in Isaiah 57, key practices are mentioned there that exhibit the absence of Sabbath keeping as taught in chapter 56). In these chapters Sabbath observance is defined as an inclusive rather than an exclusive practice. It is inclusive because it emphasizes proper motivation (choosing the things that please God, holding fast to God's covenant, foregoing self-interest) rather than proper ethnic identity as the foundation for keeping the Sabbath.

Sabbath observance became increasingly important after the exile. But even in Jeremiah (17:19-23), Ezekiel (20:8-12, 13-20), and Nehemiah (13:15-18, 19-22), where keeping the Sabbath is sometimes thought of as moving toward legalism, it remains an expression of worship in continuity with the instruction of Moses (cf. Childs: 458).

The proper observance of the Sabbath was a point of contention between Jesus and the Jewish leaders in first-century Palestine (Matt 12:1-8; Mark 3:1-6; Luke 13:10-17; John 5:2-18; etc.). Jesus' teaching is understood in the Gospels to be directed against a narrow legalism that took the joy out of Sabbath keeping.

Essays

SERVANT, SERVANTS The noun "servant" (*'ebed*) appears commonly throughout the OT. In the book of Isaiah it appears some 40 times, 16 times as a plural noun and 24 times as a singular noun. The great majority of these occurrences are in parts 4–6 of the book (chaps. 40–48, 49–57, 58–66).

The plural noun *servants* occurs mainly in part 6, where it refers to those who are faithful to the Lord. Chapter 65 in particular refers to *a rebellious people* (65:2) who are opposed to the Lord's servants.

The singular *servant* occurs mainly in parts 4 and 5. The use of *servant* as a singular noun has a special significance in Isaiah 41–53, where it appears twenty times. These chapters usually refer to *my servant*, meaning *the servant of the LORD*.

Ever since the late nineteenth century, when Bernhard Duhm identified four Servant Songs in Isaiah 40–55 (42:1-4; 49:1-6; 50:4-9, where the servant is implied; and 52:13–53:12), there has been discussion and debate about the identity of the servant and the relationship of the songs to their context. Duhm saw these songs as intrusions into the text from a later period. Many scholars since Duhm's time, however, have argued convincingly that the songs are integral to the context in which they are found (cf. Muilenberg: 406-15).

The question of the servant's identity is at least as old as the first century AD, when the Ethiopian official asked Philip about it (Acts 8:34). More recently some scholars regard the servant as an embodiment of the community (Israel; note Isa 49:3), some as an individual (Israelite), and some as both (cf. I. Friesen, 2003:64). Nevertheless the most helpful question to ask in understanding the servant in Isaiah is probably not *Who* is the servant? but instead *What* does the servant do? and *How* does the servant function? In this regard, Gottwald's suggestions are useful. The servant portrait includes the experience of conflict and torment in exile (cf. Gottwald, 1985:497-502). The servant clearly does God's work as teacher among God's people and among the nations. As such, the servant functions as God's emissary, bearing God's light to the nations.

In the servant as an individual, the NT writers saw the exemplar of Jesus as Messiah. The servant in the Servant Songs helped these writers understand Jesus' life and death as having redemptive significance for humankind as a whole (Phil 2:6-11). This servant is characterized by obedience and undeserved suffering, which leads to death. His death, in fact, is the means of taking away the sin of his people and making many people righteous (Isa 53:11) [*Atonement, p. 439*].

SHALOM In the OT, the Hebrew noun *šalom* means more than simply the absence of war, and its meaning is variegated rather than uniform (cf. P. B. Yoder; see esp. chap. 2, pp. 10-16). The most frequent use of *šalom* is as an indicator of well-being or success, as in Genesis 29:6, where Jacob asks the shepherds of Haran about the well-being of Laban; or in the blessing of Aaron in Numbers 6:26, where "the Lord . . . give you peace" indicates a hope that the Israelites will be successful in what they do.

Another use of *šalom* is in the arena of social relations, where it comes closest to the English word "peace." In social relations *šalom* is often closely associated with justice and righteousness (cf. Isa 9:7; 32:15-20; 59:4-8). *Šalom* portrays the presence of good relationships characterized by justice between persons or nations. In covenant relations it indicates the kind of community to which God's people are called.

A third use of *šalom* is in the domain of ethics and morality. Here the emphasis is on integrity or innocence, or honesty in contrast to deceit (cf. Ps 35:20).

The noun *šalom* in Hebrew derives from the root *šlm*, which conveys the sense of being complete or sound (BDB: 1022). This noun occurs some twenty-nine times in the book of Isaiah, referring at times to soundness of body (38:17, *welfare*), at times to peace or contentment (32:17-18), at times to wholesome relationships (59:8), and at times to the absence of war (39:8).

The common translation of *šalom* as *peace* takes the notion of completeness or soundness and gives to it the sense of harmony in human relationships and, alternatively, of yieldedness in the human encounter with God. To be at peace with God in this sense means to give precedence to God or to acknowledge God's superiority. The pleasant vineyard (God's people) in Isaiah 27:5, for example, is invited to *make peace* with the Lord. The prosperity (peace) of God's people, if they had yielded to the Lord's commandments, is compared to *a river*—not a river in destructive flooding, but a river providing nourishment for land and crops—in Isaiah 48:18.

STEADFAST LOVE The noun *ḥesed* (usually *steadfast love*, NRSV; or *unfailing love*, NIV) occurs some 245 times in the Hebrew Bible. Slightly over half of these occurrences are in the Psalter. The noun *ḥesed* occurs eight times in the book of Isaiah (16:5; 40:6; 54:8, 10; 55:3; 57:1; 63:7, 7). The substance of *ḥesed* is loyalty and solidarity, perhaps especially as it is expressed in concern for the good of others (cf. Prov 14:22).

Steadfast love (*ḥesed*) in the OT is a relational term (Baer and Gordon: 211). When it is used of God, it refers to his kindness in the preservation of human life from death (Ps 6:5) and in redemption from sin (Ps 51:3). This kindness is described as abundant (Lam 3:32) and great in extent (Num 14:19; Ps 36:5).

When steadfast love refers to kinship love, its dependability is exhibited in family relationships (Gen 20:13), in the bond of friendship (1 Sam 20:8), and in the affiliation between monarch and people (1 Kings 2:7; Baer and Gordon: 212). Steadfast love refers to human kindness at the level of personal ethics (1 Sam 20:15) as well as at the level of social ethics (Hos 12:6).

Although *ḥesed* does not occur frequently in Isaiah, its usage there is well-defined. In Isaiah 16:5 (the only occurrence in the first three parts of the book) steadfast love is equated with peace and prosperity in a restored Davidic monarchy (Clements: 154). In Isaiah 40–66 there is a stress on the durability and reliability of the Lord's steadfast love (54:8, 10; 55:3; 63:7). As a plural noun *ḥesed* refers to the Lord's displays of steadfast love in Israel's history, especially as this is related to the covenant (Isa 63:7).

WAR, WARFARE The book of Isaiah was forged in the struggle among empires—Assyrian, Babylonian, and Persian—who won their dominance through military supremacy. Facing the fact of empires, the book offers an alternative perspective on the course of imperial history, on the involvements in that history borne by Israel, and on the divine purpose for both Israel and the empires. In Isaiah the rule of God overwhelms all human empires and the power of militarism, by which they acquire and sustain their sovereignty. Such a religious and political perspective provides a vantage point from which to understand the complexity of warfare within the book of Isaiah.

Isaiah's stance toward warfare both embraces imperial reality and transcends it. In the eighth century BC, God's people faced the Assyrian threat and, in particular, the invasion of Judah by an alliance of Syria and Israel (734-732 BC) as well as an anti-Assyrian rebellion (713-711 BC). Judean kings Ahaz and Hezekiah were prominent players in those struggles (Isa 7; 36–39).

In the first of these, the war policy of Ephraim-Samaria (Northern Kingdom of Israel) is to cooperate with Damascus in an alliance against Assyria (2 Kings 16; 2 Chron 27–28; Isa 7–12). Yet the Lord has a plan to employ Assyria as a tool of judgment against the pride, the unjust practices, and the covenant disloyalty of God's people. Even in the face of judgment and the arrogance of Assyrian might, Isaiah counsels, *Do not fear* (7:4). Although it appears that the Lord is *hiding his face from the house of Jacob* (8:17), the Lord also has a subsequent plan to bring down the imperial pride and power of Assyria (10:12; 14:24-27). Even in the midst of these judgments, therefore, God's people are counseled not to be afraid, for God will do again what God has done for Israel at the exodus (10:24-27).

In the face of Ahaz's "I can do it myself" approach, Isaiah's alternative counsel is to trust the Lord (7:4; 12:2), the only God and Sovereign, whose rule brings about the end of imperial power and human pride. Only the Lord's alternative strategy will bring about the end of warfare by means of a new "imperialism" of justice with righteousness (9:1-7), within which violence will come to an end (11:1-9). So in the face of war, Isaiah counsels trust (*baṭaḥ*; 12:2; 26:3-4; 30:12; 31:1; 36:4-9, 15; 42:17; 47:10; 50:10). Such a strategy is possible because the Lord's plan transcends empires and their might. It can be imagined that even Egypt and Assyria might become God's people (19:23-25). With such a prospect, why *rely on horses* or *trust in chariots* (31:1)? The particular means by which God will accomplish this defeat of Israel's enemies is not mentioned by the prophet, perhaps because God's people need not participate in it.

Similar dynamics appear in the second struggle, the anti-Assyrian rebellion during Hezekiah's time (Isa 36–39; cf. 2 Kings 18:13–20:19). Sennacherib's envoy seeks to undermine Hezekiah's trust in the Lord. Again the term *baṭaḥ* is important, occurring seven times in Isaiah 36:4-15 and translated *confidence* (noun, NRSV, NIV), *rely* (verb, NRSV), and *depend*, *trust* (verb, NIV). The envoy asks, in effect, "Do you think that mere words are strategy and power for war?" (36:5). The claim, of course, is that Isaiah's counsel is "mere words." Isaiah says again, "Do not be afraid" (37:6), to which the Assyrian envoy gives the theological retort that Assyria's military strength is undergirded by its gods. None of the other nations' gods have ever delivered them! Nevertheless Hezekiah stands firm, asserting that there is only one God, who is sovereign over *all the kingdoms of the earth* (37:16). Again, the Lord issues a verdict against Sennacherib's pride and war machine (37:23-24); yet the Lord has another plan (37:26). Although Hezekiah's rash exposure of his treasures to the Babylonians (39:1-8) foreshadows Judah's defeat by Babylon, it is the Lord's plan that unfolds and prevails in chapters 40–66.

Isaiah contains no narrative of conquest by Babylon, yet the book addresses the context of Babylonian exile by continuing the same narrative pattern. Isaiah's alternative in the context of war is *Do not fear* (41:8-13, 14-15; 43:1-4, 5-7; 44:1-5). Isaiah's alternative embraces a vision of world (imperial) history that is driven, not by the pride of empires and emperors, but by a vision of God's universal judgment, which will result in a new era of peace and salvation.

Assyrian armies deported Israel's population. Babylonian armies devastated Jerusalem and deported thousands. To many it seemed that the Assyrian and Babylonian gods must be stronger. Yet in the midst of warfare and its consequences, the book of Isaiah offers a new kind of sovereignty mediated by a king who rules with justice (chaps. 9, 11), and a servant who suffers (Isa 42:1-4; 49:1-6; 50:4-9; 52:13–53:12). Although God is celebrated as a warrior (chap. 63), human warfare is not glorified, nor is it the last word in Isaiah. Although God uses the king of Assyria (Isa 7) and Cyrus the Persian (45:1-6, 13) for his purposes, God also provides comfort in the midst of oppression (40:1; 51:12) and makes possible a new political order in which violence itself is vanquished (chaps. 9, 11). This God is unlike the imperial gods, who undergird the ideology of warfare. For those who think in conventional militaristic categories, the Lord's ways remain hidden (40:27; 45:15; 49:14; 44:8; 55:8). Yet God, beyond all human imagining, wants to do a new thing (42:5-9; 43:19; 48:6) by introducing a new kind of politics and a new kind of power. God's purpose and plan come to fruition, says Isaiah, in the full end of warfare and its terrors (2:2-4; 43:16-19).

There are at least three ways in which the book of Isaiah speaks of warfare. (1) Some texts speak of God/the Lord as a *warrior*. The most common name for God in Isaiah is *LORD of hosts* (i.e., armies). This identification occurs fifty-eight times in the book of Isaiah (out of 245 times in the Old Testament). The predominance of this name serves to highlight the sovereignty of God over all creation and all human warfare. This is most clearly seen in Isaiah 42:13, but it is also evident in 13:3-4, where the Lord musters an army against Babylon (cf. 19:2). The Lord acts as warrior against Assyria (30:27-33) and Edom (chap. 34). The Lord acts as warrior against his own people (63:10) but also on their behalf (31:1-5). Isaiah's warfare theology (clearly articulated in 31:1-5) depends on the paradigm of warfare presented in the book of Exodus: it is not human combat with God's help, but God's help alone, rendering human combat unnecessary (Lind: 1980).

(2) Other texts in Isaiah speak of warfare simply as a fact of reality rather than judging it from an ethical perspective. The soldier, for example, is mentioned among other leadership roles in Judean society (3:2). Battlefield conditions are known to produce stress (21:15). The Assyrian field commander (Rabshakeh) speaks of the strategy of war (36:5). Warfare is described in a matter-of-fact way as a part of reality (20:1).

(3) Still others offer a negative reflection on the practice of war. For example, in Isaiah 2:2-4 is the vision of an end to war and an end to the preparation for war. The prophet Isaiah addresses the threat of war with a call to stand firm in faith rather than taking up arms (7:1-9; cf. 41:11-13). The theology here is one in which warfare is understood as lacking the power to produce the desired effect. Judah's search for military solutions is understood as faithlessness (30:15-17), and human fighting is understood to be counterproductive.

The book of Isaiah includes broad evidence, therefore, that warfare is not part of God's ultimate plan for humankind. The faith that mobilizes Isaiah is a trust in God that eschews sword and military academy (2:4). "Hold firmly to Yahweh," Berrigan (37) paraphrases Isaiah 7:9; "no other lifeline will hold." The book of Isaiah does not encourage the participation of God's people in war.

In the New Testament, where Jesus embodies the theological and political stance of Isaiah's *servant*, God remains the cosmic Lord, who asserts his sovereignty over every empire that trumpets itself as universal (Rev 13) and every emperor who heralds himself as lord and savior (Luke 4:1-14; 22:25). The prophetic vision of eschatological peace, Jesus' embodiment of love of enemy (Matt 5:43-48; Luke 23:34), Paul's assertion that the dividing walls of hostility have been brought down in God's new era (Eph 2:14), John's affirmation that love is the true test of God's presence in people (1 John 2:5), and the conquest of evil in the book of Revelation by the death of the Lamb that was slain (Rev 17:14)—all these point to God's rejection of human warfare, to God's determination to do a new thing, and to God's inviting our participation in that newness by taking the path of peace even when nations plan otherwise.

In much, though not all, of its history, the church has incorporated war and military service into its belief system (cf. *CCW*: 5-10). Isaiah's witness encourages us to acknowledge that although empires will always wage war, God's purpose is for all people to *beat their swords into plowshares* and to stop preparing for war (2:4). By acknowledging God's universal empire, human empires are overwhelmed as all people become *the work of my hands* (19:25).

WOE ANNOUNCEMENT Two Hebrew interjections, *'oy* and *hoy*, are employed in the book of Isaiah as expressions of despair, discontentment, or displeasure. Translated variously as *woe* or *alas* or *ah*, they usually imply denunciation of some kind (Isa 55:1 is an exception). The interjection *'oy*, used four times in Isaiah (3:9, 11; 6:5; 24:16), indicates grief and distress (BDB: 17).

The interjection *hoy*, used twenty-one times in Isaiah, often introduces an announcement of judgment (BDB: 222-23). Waldemar Janzen (1972) understands *hoy* to be addressed to those who act in self-reliance, independent of the Lord (61). These addressees are brought face-to-face with the certainty that the Lord will humble their independence. This is often brought about, Janzen says, by "reversal of imagery," as in Isaiah 5:8-10, where the amassing of houses and fields brings about a decimating of houses and vineyards.

Clusters of *hoy* announcements are found in Isaiah 5 (vv. 8, 11, 18, 20, 21, 22) and again in Isaiah 28–33 (28:1; 29:1, 15; 30:1; 31:1; 33:1). In each of these cases the interjection *hoy* introduces a verdict against a strategy or an inner conviction that contravenes God's will and way for his people.

WRATH OF GOD Though it may prompt discomfort for some, the "wrath of God" is a significant biblical concept in both the Old and New Testaments. In Isaiah, God's anger is a prominent theme, serving to emphasize the sovereignty of God within and beyond Israel, particularly in relation to the experience of exile. Here divine anger serves a significant purpose, to discipline Israel as well as to express guidance and correction; indeed, in the book of Isaiah, God constantly guides and corrects his people (Macgregor: 59-60).

A number of terms in the Hebrew Bible carry the basic idea of "anger," including *'np*, *z'm*, *z'p*, *ḥrh*, *yḥm*, *'br*, and *qṣp*. The noun *'ap* (from *'np*) alone occurs twenty-seven times in Isaiah, many of these attesting to God's anger. As is often the case elsewhere in the OT (cf. Jer 52:3 // 2 Kings 24:20), God's wrath is associated with exile in Isaiah. The metaphor of the vineyard in Isaiah 5, for example, concludes with the beloved vowing to remove the hedge of protection and allowing the vineyard to be devoured. After a description of what has gone wrong, the result is announced: houses and vineyards will be demolished (5:8-10). This prediction is then explained: *For all this his* [i.e., *the LORD's*] *anger has not turned away, and his hand is stretched out still* (Isa 5:25). Subsequent passages further outline the drastic changes Israel is to experience, with the same phrase appearing four more times (9:12, 17, 21; 10:4).

Reference to God's wrath is significant because it affirms God's sovereignty despite impressions to the contrary [*War, Warfare, p. 452*]. In the polytheistic context of the ancient Near East, where a plethora of gods were worshipped and many were linked to specific peoples or empires, people commonly assumed that the gods of a victorious nation were stronger than the gods of the peoples they had conquered. Isaiah claims something radically different: the Assyrians do not emerge victorious over Israel because their gods are more powerful, but because the Lord uses Assyria to discipline Israel! This is emphatically stated in chapter 10, where Isaiah identifies Assyria as *the rod of my anger* (v. 5) and then clarifies that it would be a mistake to confuse the instrument of God's wrath (Assyria the ax) with the lumberjack who wields the ax (the Lord; vv. 15-16). Indeed, God will even punish Assyria for its arrogance (10:5-15). This understanding that the exile reflects the Lord's punishing God's own people is not limited to Isaiah but is a very significant concept for the prophets in general.

Thus, the "wrath of God" provides the avenue to make the remarkable assertion that Israel's God is sovereign over *all* nations, and uses them to enact the divine will. The audacity of this claim in a polytheistic context is brought to the surface when the Assyrian emissary mocks Israel for thinking that their God will save them, given that Assyria has already conquered many other peoples without such interference (chap. 36). Isaiah subverts this logic by rejecting the idea of different nations with tribal gods in favor of the Holy One of Israel, who controls even foreign powers.

Nevertheless God's wrath does not have the last word in Isaiah. Chapter 12 already points to a time in an undetermined future when the tables will be turned: *You will say on that day: I will give thanks to you, O LORD, for though you were angry with me, your anger turned away, and you comforted me* (12:1, emphasis added). This statement reverses the repeated refrain identified previously and replaces it with a word of comfort *on that day*. In effect, Israel will go through a period of punishment, discipline, or even refinement, but hope remains that comfort will eventually come. Interestingly, this progression is reflected in the structure of the book itself. In the initial chapters *comfort* is in short supply, but it becomes more prominent later; indeed, the two occurrences of this term in Isaiah 40:1 matches its number of appearances in the first 39 chapters of the book (Isa 12:1; 22:4)! Isaiah 40 proclaims that the "day" has finally arrived: the period of God's anger is over, and a new day has come. The people will experience a new exodus, only this time from Babylon rather than Egypt (Isa 43). God has not forsaken Israel, and a remnant shall return to the land.

Discomfort with the idea of God's wrath sometimes prompts people to contrast the "God of wrath" of the OT with the "God of love" in the NT. It is worth identifying two common misconceptions that give rise to such a view. First, while it is true that anger is often attributed to God in the Old Testament, this is not the only or even the dominant perspective in these documents. God's wrath often responds to human sin and injustice, particularly in the context of God's covenant with Israel (cf. the Decalogue in Exod 20:1-17 and Deut 5:6-21 and many other expressions of the covenant in the law). Blessings or curses are the consequences of obedience or disobedience to the law (Deut 28). At the same time, many passages qualify God's anger and place it within a broader perspective. For instance, the Lord's self-description in Exodus 34:6-7 identifies God as "slow to anger," with steadfast love (ḥesed) extending to a thousand generations, while punishment only lasts for three or four. God's persistent care and merciful response to the people's cry, despite their repeated rejection and rebellion, proves central in Nehemiah 9. The book of Jonah extends God's mercy beyond Israel to concern for Nineveh, the hated capital city of Assyria. Against Jonah's explicit desire, God accepts Nineveh's repentance and foregoes punishment. In fact, it is Jonah's knowledge of God's character as one who is "merciful and slow to anger" that initially prompts him to flee in the opposite direction, presumably so that Nineveh would *not* be delivered from divine anger (chaps. 3–4)! Thus, while it is true that God's wrath is a significant element within the portrayal of God in the OT, it is inaccurate to describe "the God of the OT" uniformly in this way.

Second, God's wrath is not unique to the Old Testament but proves significant in the NT as well. For instance *orgē*, the common Greek term used for anger or wrath in the NT, appears in connection with God in each of the four Gospels, including Jesus' judgment parables (cf. Matt 18:34; 22:7) and passages about his rejection (cf. John 3:36). It is also a significant concept for Paul; *orgē* is linked to salvation in 1 Thessalonians (1:10) and is a major theme in Romans (cf. 1:18). The term is also used in Revelation, including the remarkable concept of the "wrath of the Lamb" (Rev 6:16).

The preceding sampling of instances where God is linked to love in the OT and wrath in the NT could be multiplied; these examples warn against simplistic characterizations of either Testament. The root of this issue, however, lies in a negative view of the wrath of God; it is worth considering how the "wrath of God" can function as a significant theological resource rather than as a problem needing to be solved.

In both the OT and the NT, the wrath of God is a theologically rich concept that reflects an understanding of a God who cares, hears, and responds to the plight of those facing oppression and tribulation. As such, the "wrath of God" is closely linked to God's mercy, where wrath represents the fierce face of love, in which God intervenes against certain powers, frequently on behalf of their victims (cf. Exod 22:21-24). Whether reflected in the immediate threat of national exile (Isaiah) or in a delayed end-times judgment (Paul), the "wrath of God" reflects more than the inevitable consequences of actions turning against themselves. Rather, this concept represents the caring attention of God for world and people.

In the New Testament as well as the Old, God requires commitment and obedience, shows persistent care and patience in the face of disobedience and even rebellion, but also holds people to account. God's wrath functions as an energizing force in God's character, a force precipitated by compassion rather than driven by retribution. The focus of this energy is to make wrongs right and to generate change toward what is good. God's wrath—though at times expressed in acts of judgment and destruction—is ultimately not inconsistent with God's kindness or mercy but rather functions as an extension of it. A healthy respect for God's wrath is particularly important for those who live within the military and economic equivalents of Assyria and Babylon.

ZION The first time that Zion is mentioned in the OT is in 1 Samuel 5:7, where there is an account of David's entry into and defeat of the Jebusite stronghold of Zion, which he renamed "the city of David." This is the site, then, to which David moved the ark of God from the house of Abinadab in Kiriath-jearim some years later (2 Sam 6; cf. 1 Chron 13). The ark resided inside a tent in the city of David.

The second mention of Zion is in 1 Kings 8, after the completion of the temple early in the reign of David's son Solomon. Here the ark is brought from "the city of David, which is Zion" (1 Kings 8:1), into the inner sanctuary of the newly constructed temple in Jerusalem.

Zion, therefore, became not only a place name of importance to the people of Israel but also, and more importantly, a symbol of the Lord's presence among his people. In Isaiah the term *Zion* occurs some forty-seven times throughout the six parts of the book. In his monograph entitled *Zion, the City of the Great King*, Ben Ollenburger argues that the essential component of Isaiah's message of salvation is that the Lord aligns himself with Zion "as the place of security and peace for those who do not attempt to secure their own or Jerusalem's defense through 'practical,' military means," (116) leaving the concern for security confidently in the hands of the Lord.

Central to Zion as a symbol of the worship tradition in Jerusalem is the conviction that the Lord is present among his people. And it is not *just* that the Lord is present among his people; he also is present among his people as *king* (Ollenburger: 23; cf. Pss 24, 68, 72).

One of the implications of this kingship in the context of Israelite faith and practice is that it is exclusive; it is not shared with anyone else. Ollenburger refers to this as the Lord's "exclusive prerogative" (81). In the book of Isaiah this prerogative may be seen at a number of places and nowhere more clearly than in Isaiah 30:1-5 and 31:1-3. Here Israel's rebellion is pinpointed for its readiness to take refuge in Egyptian power rather than in the Lord (30:1-5). Israel relies on Egyptian military help rather than consulting the Holy One of Israel (31:1-3). In the Zion symbol, Isaiah contrasts this behavior with the call to trust the Lord for security and refuge.

Outline of Isaiah

Nations Manifesto: Damascus — 17:1–18:7

Outcry Concerning Damascus — 17:1-14
  Remnant of Aram — 17:1-3
  Remnant of Jacob — 17:4-6
  Too Little, Too Late — 17:7-11
  Rebuking the Peoples — 17:12-14
Woe, Land of Whirring Wings — 18:1-7
  Go, Swift Messengers! — 18:1-2
  Listen, Earthlings! — 18:3-7

Nations Manifesto: Egypt — 19:1–20:6

Outcry Concerning Egypt — 19:1-15
  Civil War in Egypt — 19:1-4
  Drying Up the Nile — 19:5-7
  Fishers and Weavers Lament — 19:8-10
  Sages and Princes Deceive Egypt — 19:11-15
Egypt's Repentance and Blessing — 19:16-25
  Terror in Egypt — 19:16-18
  Egypt's Repentance — 19:19-22
  Blessing on Egypt, Assyria, and Israel — 19:23-25
Warning to Egypt and Ethiopia — 20:1-6
  Parable of Sackcloth and Sandals — 20:1-2
  Egypt and Ethiopia in Captivity — 20:3-4
  Judah's Plight — 20:5-6

Manifestos of Doom — 21:1–22:25

Outcry Concerning the Desert by the Sea (Babylon) — 21:1-10
  News of an Invasion — 21:1-5
  Observing the Invaders' Arrival — 21:6-7
  Fall of Babylon Announced — 21:8-10
Outcries Concerning Desert Regions — 21:11-17
  Dumah — 21:11-12
  Tema and Kedar — 21:13-17
Outcry Concerning the Valley of Vision (Jerusalem) — 22:1-25
  Empty Joy — 22:1-4
  Bitter Weeping — 22:5-8a
  Pointless Preparations — 22:8b-11
  Reveling Instead of Repentance — 22:12-14
  Shebna's Banishment — 22:15-19
  Transfer of Authority to Eliakim — 22:20-25

Nations Manifesto: Tyre — 23:1-18

Outcry Concerning Tyre	23:1-14
News of Tyre-Sidon's Demise	23:1-3
Anguished Response to the News	23:4-5
Plan Behind the News	23:6-9
Destruction of Sidon	23:10-14
Testimonial for Tyre	23:15-18
Tyre Forgotten	23:15-16
Tyre Remembered	23:17-18

Whole Earth Manifesto — 24:1-27:13

Desolation Everywhere	24:1-13
Earth Laid Waste	24:1-3
Earth's Inhabitants Decimated	24:4-6
City of Chaos	24:7-13
Trembling of Earth's Foundations	24:14-23
Singing and Pining	24:14-18a
Treachery and Terror	24:18b-20
Called to Account	24:21-23
A Feast Prepared	25:1-12
Hymn of Praise to the Lord	25:1-5
A Great Banquet	25:6-8
Hand, Hands	25:9-12
Song of Trust	26:1-6
Strong City Exalted	26:1-3
Lofty City Humbled	26:4-6
Confession of the Lord's Work	26:7-27:1
Waiting for the Lord	26:7-11
Acknowledging the Lord's Name	26:12-15
Confession of Failure	26:16-19
The Lord's Judgment	26:20-27:1
Root of Jacob	27:2-13
Vineyard Song	27:2-6
Jacob's Atonement	27:7-11
Great Gathering	27:12-13

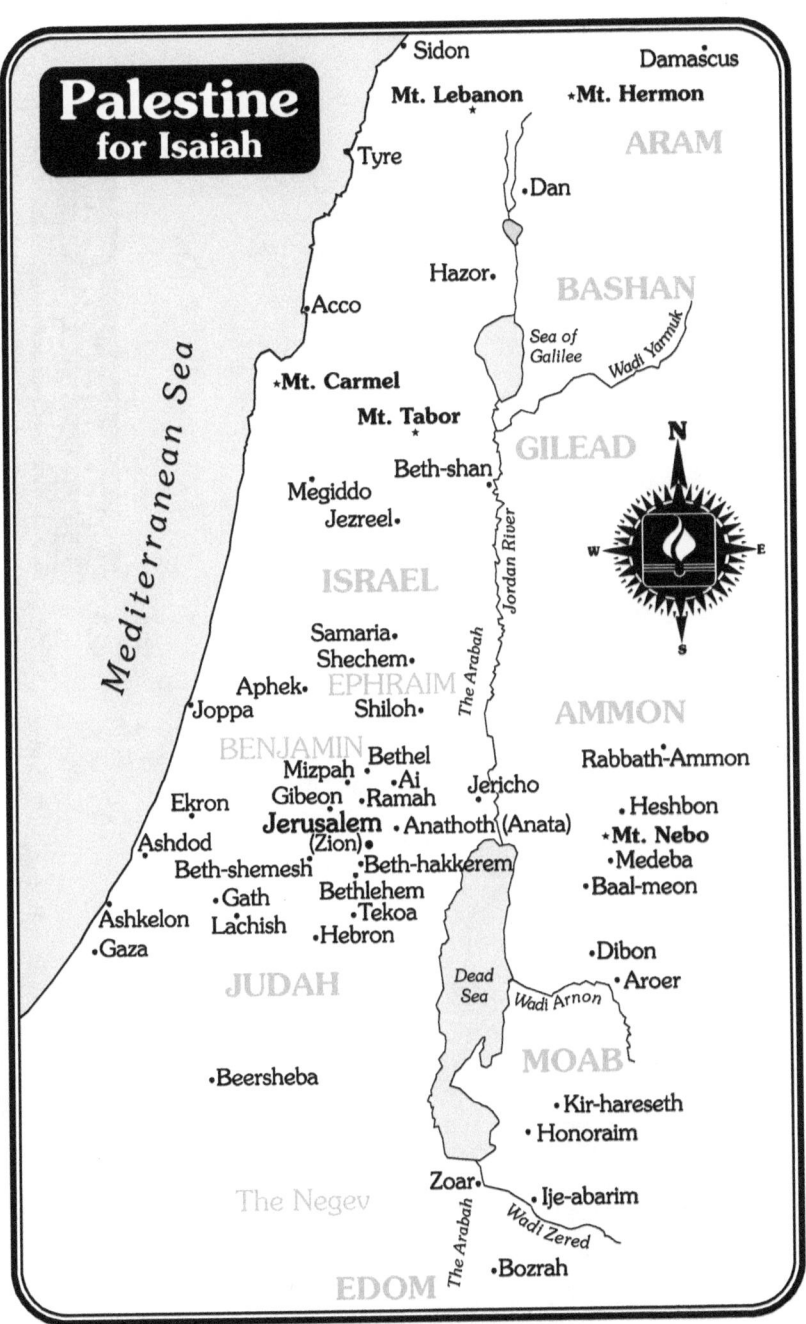

During the Time of the Prophets (9th through the 6th Centuries BC)

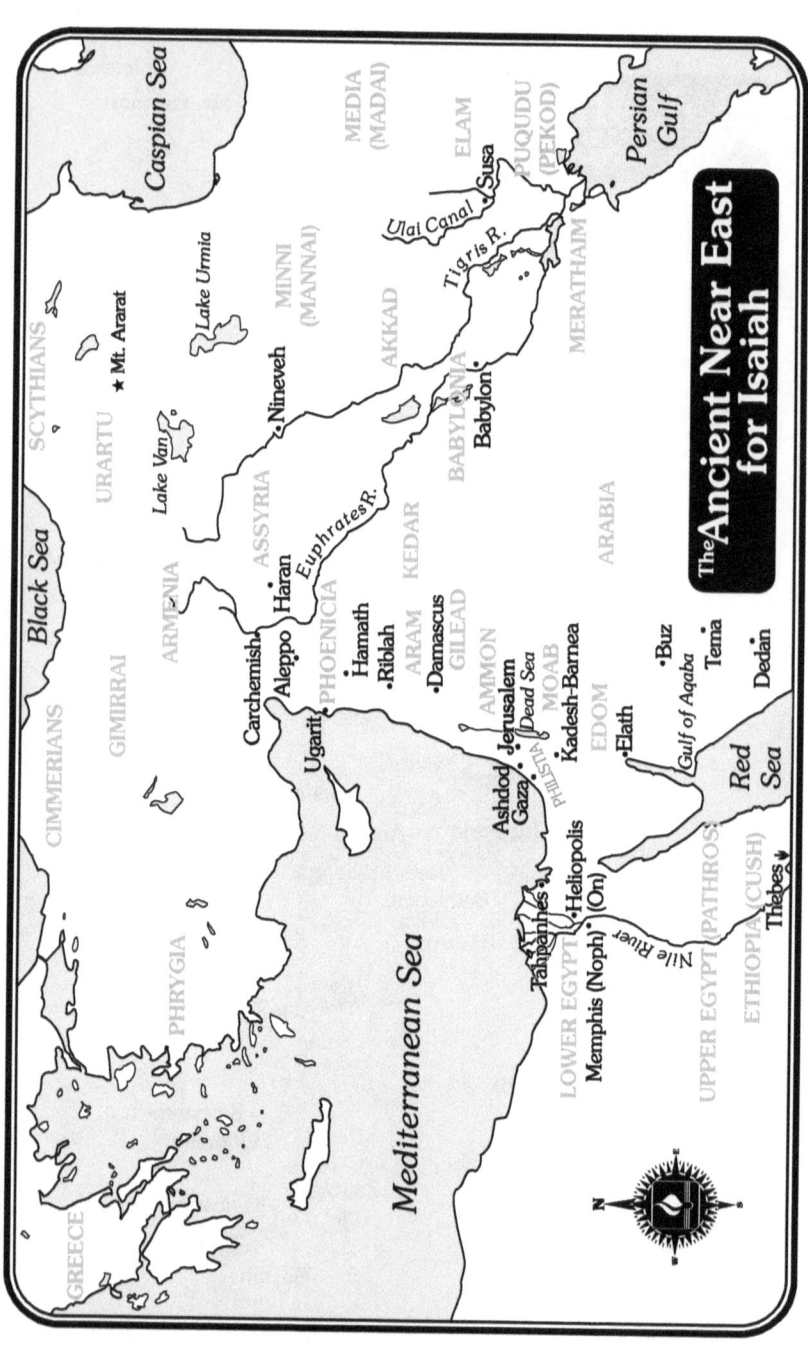

During the Rise and Fall of the Israelite Monarchy

Bibliography

Albright, William Foxwell
    1957   *From the Stone Age to Christianity*. Garden City, NY: Doubleday.
Anderson, Bernhard W.
    1974   *Out of the Depths: The Psalms Speak for Us Today*. Philadelphia: Westminster.
    1986   *Understanding the Old Testament*. 4th ed. Englewood Cliffs, NJ: Prentice-Hall.
Aulén, Gustaf
    1969   *Christus Victor*. New York: Macmillan.
Baer, D. A., and R. P. Gordon
    1997   "ḥâsad II, ḥesed II, ḥâsîd." Pages 211-19 in vol. 2 of *New International Dictionary of Old Testament Theology and Exegesis*. Edited by William A. VanGemeren. Grand Rapids: Zondervan.
Bailey, Wilma Ann
    2003   "Isaiah 2:2-5 and Micah 4:1-4: Learning the Ways of the God of Jacob." Pages 51-61 in *Beautiful upon the Mountains: Biblical Essays on Mission, Peace, and the Reign of God*. Edited by Mary H. Schertz and Ivan Friesen. Elkhart, IN: Institute of Mennonite Studies; Scottdale, PA; and Waterloo, ON: Herald Press.
Baker, David W.
    1992   "Ophir." In *ABD*, 5:26-27.
Baker, Mark D.
    2006   ed., *Proclaiming the Scandal of the Cross: Contemporary Images of Atonement*. Grand Rapids: Baker Academic.
    2007   "How the Cross Saves." *Direction* 36 (Spring): 43-57.
Barton, John
    1997   "Ethics in the Book of Isaiah." Pages 67-77 in vol. 1 of *Writing and Reading the Scroll of Isaiah: Studies of an Interpretive Tradition*. Edited by Craig C. Broyles and Craig A. Evans. Leiden: Brill.

Berrigan, Daniel
    1996   *Isaiah: Spirit of Courage, Gift of Tears.* Minneapolis: Fortress.
Bonhoeffer, Dietrich
    1955   *Ethics.* London: SCM.
Braght, Thieleman J. van
    1886   *Martyrs Mirror.* Translated by Joseph F. Sohm from the original Dutch-language edition of 1660. Scottdale, PA: Herald Press.
Brueggemann, Walter
    1982   *Living Toward a Vision.* New York: United Church Press.
    1998a   *Isaiah 1–39.* Louisville, KY: Westminster John Knox.
    1998b   *Isaiah 40–66.* Louisville, KY: Westminster John Knox.
Brunk, Conrad G.
    1982   "Law and Morality: Tensions and Perspectives." Pages 107-38 in *The Bible and Law.* Edited by Willard M. Swartley. Occasional Papers 3. Council of Mennonite Seminaries. Elkhart, IN: Institute of Mennonite Studies.
Childs, Brevard
    2001   *Isaiah.* The Old Testament Library. Louisville, KY: Westminster John Knox.
The Chronicle of the Hutterian Brethren.
    1987   Translated and edited by Hutterian Brethren. Vol. 1. Rifton, NY: Plough Publishing. Translated from *Das grosse Geschicht-Buch der Hutterischen Brüder.* 1580-81.
Chupp, Kryss
    1997   "CPT Delegation Visits Violent Chiapas Region." In *Canadian Mennonite* 1, no. 2 (September 29, 1997): 22-23.
Church Hymnal
    1951   Edited by J. D. Brunk and S. F. Coffman. Scottdale, PA: Mennonite Publishing House.
Clements, Ronald
    1980   *Isaiah 1-39.* New Century Bible Commentary. Grand Rapids: Eerdmans.
Confession of Faith in a Mennonite Perspective
    1995   Scottdale, PA; Waterloo, ON: Herald Press.
Conrad, Edgar W.
    1991   *Reading Isaiah.* Minneapolis: Fortress.
Curtis, Edward M.
    1992   "Idol, Idolatry." In *ABD,* 3:376-81.
Day, John
    1992   "Leviathan." In *ABD,* 4:295-96.
Dekar, Paul R.
    1979   "Baptists and Peace." In *The Believers' Church in Canada.* Edited by Jarold K. Zeman and Walter Klaassen. Brantford, ON: The Baptist Federation of Canada; and Winnipeg, MB: Mennonite Central Committee (Canada).
Delitzsch, Franz
    1891–92 *Biblical Commentary on the Prophecies of Isaiah.* Translated by James Denney from the 3rd German ed. 2 vols. London: Hodder & Stoughton.
Driver, John
    1986   *Understanding the Atonement for the Mission of the Church.* Scottdale, PA: Herald Press.

Bibliography

Duhm, Bernhard
    1902   *Das Buch Jesaja.* 2nd ed. Handkommentar zum Alten Testament. Göttingen: Vandenhoeck & Ruprecht.

Durnbaugh, Donald F.
    1968   *The Believers' Church: The History and Character of Radical Protestantism.* London: Collier-Macmillan.

Eichrodt, Walther
    1961   *Theology of the OT.* Translated by J. A. Baker. Vol 1. Philadelphia: Westminster.
    1967   *Theology of the OT.* Translated by J. A. Baker. Vol. 2. Philadelphia: Westminster.

Erlandsson, Seth
    1970   *The Burden of Babylon: A Study of Isaiah 13:2–14:23.* Lund: CWK Gleerup.

Finger, Thomas N.
    2004   *A Contemporary Anabaptist Theology.* Downers Grove, IL: InterVarsity.

Ford, J. Massyngbaerde
    1983   "Reconciliation and Forgiveness in Luke's Gospel." Pages 80-98 in *Political Issues in Luke-Acts.* Edited by Richard J. Cassidy and Philip J. Scharper. Maryknoll, NY: Orbis Books.

Fretheim, Terence
    1984   *The Suffering of God.* Philadelphia, PA: Fortress.

Friesen, Ivan
    1990   "Composition and Continuity in Isaiah 1–12." PhD diss., University of St. Michael's College and the Toronto School of Theology.
    2003   "Light to the Nations in Isaiah's Servant Songs." Pages 63-74 in *Beautiful upon the Mountains: Biblical Essays on Mission, Peace, and the Reign of God.* Edited by Mary H. Schertz and Ivan Friesen. Elkhart, IN: Institute of Mennonite Studies; Scottdale, PA; Waterloo, ON: Herald Press.

Friesen, Rachel Hilty
    1990   "A History of the Spiritual Healing Church in Botswana." Master's thesis, Knox College and the Toronto School of Theology.

Gardner, Richard B.
    1991   *Matthew.* Believers Church Bible Commentary. Scottdale, PA; Waterloo, ON: Herald Press.

Gold, Victor R., and William L. Holladay
    1991   "Isaiah." In *NOAB* (OT): 866-959.

Goncalves, Francolino J.
    1992   "Isaiah Scroll, The." In *ABD,* 3:470-72.

Gottwald, Norman K.
    1958   "Immanuel as the Prophet's Son." *Vetus Testamentum* 8:36-47.
    1979   *The Tribes of Yahweh: A Sociology of the Religion of Liberated Israel, 1250-1050 B.C.E.* Maryknoll, NY: Orbis Books.
    1985   *The Hebrew Bible: A Socio-Literary Introduction.* Philadelphia: Fortress.

Gray, George Buchanan
    1912   *A Critical and Exegetical Commentary on the Book of Isaiah I-XXVII.* International Critical Commentary. Edinburgh: T&T Clark.

Green, Joel B., and Mark D. Baker
   2000   *Recovering the Scandal of the Cross: Atonement in New Testament and Contemporary Contexts.* Downers Grove, IL: InterVarsity.
Guenther, Allen R.
   1998   *Hosea, Amos.* Believers Church Bible Commentary. Scottdale, PA; Waterloo, ON: Herald Press.
Hanson, Paul D.
   1995   *Isaiah 40-66.* Interpretation: A Bible Commentary for Teaching and Preaching. Louisville, KY: John Knox.
Hayes, John H., and Stuart A. Irvine
   1987   *Isaiah, the Eighth-century Prophet: His Times and His Preaching.* Nashville: Abingdon.
Hillers, Delbert R.
   1969   *Covenant: The History of a Biblical Idea.* Baltimore: Johns Hopkins University Press.
Holsopple, Mary Yoder, Ruth E. Krall, and Sharon Weaver Pittman
   2004   *Building Peace: Overcoming Violence in Communities.* Geneva: WCC Publications.
Janzen, Waldemar
   1972   *Mourning Cry and Woe Oracle.* Berlin: Walter de Gruyter.
   2000   *Exodus.* Believers Church Bible Commentary. Waterloo, ON; Scottdale, PA: Herald Press.
Jeschke, Marlin
   2005   *Rethinking Holy Land: A Study in Salvation Geography.* Scottdale, PA; Waterloo, ON: Herald Press.
Jones, Douglas
   1955   "The Tradition of the Oracles of Isaiah of Jerusalem." *Zeitschrift für die alttestamentliche Wissenschaft* 67:226-46.
Juhnke, James C.
   1979   *A People of Mission: A History of General Conference Mennonite Overseas Missions.* Newton, KS: Faith & Life.
Junker, H.
   1959   "Die literarische Art von Is 5, 1-7." *Biblica* 40:259-66.
Kaiser, Otto
   1974   *Isaiah 13–39.* Old Testament Library. Philadelphia: Westminster.
   1983   *Isaiah 1–12.* 2nd ed. Old Testament Library. Philadelphia: Westminster.
Katzenstein, H. J.
   1992   "Philistines." In *ABD*, 5:326-28.
Kaufmann, Yehezkel
   1970   *The Babylonian Captivity and Deutero-Isaiah.* New York: Union of American Hebrew Congregations.
Klaassen, Walter
   1973   *Anabaptism: Neither Catholic nor Protestant.* Waterloo, ON: Conrad.
Knight, George A. F.
   1984   *Servant Theology: A Commentary on the Book of Isaiah 40–55.* Edinburgh: Handsel.
Kraus, C. Norman
   1993   *The Community of the Spirit.* Grand Rapids: Eerdmans.
Kugel, James L.
   1981   *The Idea of Biblical Poetry: Parallelism and Its History.* New Haven, CT: Yale University Press.

Bibliography

Lacheman, Ernest
    1968-69 "The Seraphim of Isaiah 6." *Jewish Quarterly Review* 59:71-72.
Lasserre, Jean
    1962   *War and the Gospel*. Scottdale, PA: Herald Press.
Lederach, Paul M.
    1994   *Daniel*. Believers Church Bible Commentary. Scottdale, PA; Waterloo, ON: Herald Press.
Limburg, James
    1977   *The Prophets and the Powerless*. Atlanta: John Knox.
    1997   "Swords to Plowshares: Text and Contexts." Pages 279-93 in vol. 1 of *Writing and Reading the Scroll of Isaiah: Studies of an Interpretive Tradition*. Edited by Craig C. Broyles and Craig A. Evans. Leiden: Brill.
Lind, Millard
    1980   *Yahweh Is a Warrior*. Scottdale, PA; Kitchener, ON: Herald Press.
    1990   *Monotheism, Power, Justice: Collected Old Testament Essays*. Text-Reader Series 3. Elkhart, IN: Institute of Mennonite Studies.
    1996   *Ezekiel*. Believers Church Bible Commentary. Scottdale, PA; Waterloo, ON: Herald Press.
Lisowsky, Gerhard
    1981   *Konkordanz zum Hebräischen Alten Testament*. 2nd ed. Stuttgart: Deutsche Bibelgesellschaft.
McDonald, Patricia M.
    2004   *God and Violence: Biblical Resources for Living in a Small World*. Scottdale, PA; Waterloo, ON: Herald Press.
Macgregor, George H. C.
    1954   *The New Testament Basis of Pacifism and The Relevance of an Impossible Ideal*. Rev. ed. Nyack, NY: Fellowship Publications.
Maier, Walter A., III
    1992a "Gad." In *ABD*, 2:863-64.
    1992b "Meni." In *ABD*, 4:695.
Martens, Elmer A.
    1986   *Jeremiah*. Believers Church Bible Commentary. Scottdale, PA; Kitchener, ON: Herald Press.
Mendenhall, George E.
    1973   *The Tenth Generation: The Origins of the Biblical Tradition*. Baltimore: Johns Hopkins University Press.
Menno Simons
    1956   *The Complete Writings of Menno Simons, c. 1496-1561*. Translated by Leonard Verduin. Edited by John C. Wenger. Scottdale, PA: Herald Press.
Merton, Thomas
    1949   *Seeds of Contemplation*. New York: Dell.
Metzger, Bruce M., and John J. Collins
    1991   "Apocalyptic Literature." In *NOAB* (NT): 362-63.
Moravian Book of Worship.
    1995   Bethlehem, PA, Winston-Salem, NC: Interprovincial Board of Publications and Communications of the Moravian Church of America.
Muilenburg, James
    1956   "15. The Servant of the Lord." Pages 406-14 in vol. 5 of *The Book of Isaiah, Chapters 40–66*. The Interpreter's Bible, New York and Nashville: Abingdon Press.

Noss, John B.
: 1963 *Man's Religions*. 3rd ed. New York: Macmillan.
Noth, Martin
: 1966 *The Old Testament World*. Translated by Victor I. Gruhn. Philadelphia: Fortress.
O'Collins, Gerald G.
: 1992 "Salvation." In *ABD*, 5:907-14.
O'Connor, Michael Patrick
: 1980 *Hebrew Verse Structure*. Winona Lake, IN: Eisenbrauns.
Ollenburger, Ben C.
: 1987 *Zion, the City of the Great King: A Theological Symbol of the Jerusalem Cult*. Journal for the Study of the Old Testament: Supplement Series 41. Sheffield: Sheffield Academic.
Oosterbaan, Johannes A.
: 1967 "Word and Spirit." Pages 9-17 in *The Witness of the Holy Spirit*. Edited by Cornelius J. Dyck. Proceedings of the Eighth Mennonite World Conference, Amsterdam. Nappanee, IN: Evangel.
Organ, Barbara E.
: 1996 *Judaism for Gentiles*. N. Richland Hills, TX: BIBAL Press.
Oswalt, John N.
: 1986 *The Book of Isaiah: Chapters 1–39*. New International Commentary on the Old Testament. Grand Rapids: Eerdmans.
: 1997 *The Book of Isaiah: Chapters 40–66*. New International Commentary on the Old Testament. Grand Rapids: Eerdmans.
Pitard, Wayne T.
: 1992 "Damascus." In *ABD*, 2:5-7.
Rad, Gerhard von
: 1962 *Old Testament Theology*. Translated by D. M. G. Stalker. Vol. 1. New York: Harper & Row.
: 1965 *Old Testament Theology*. Translated by D. M. G. Stalker. Vol. 2. New York: Harper & Row.
Rempel, Henry
: 2003 *A High Price for Abundant Living*. Waterloo, ON; Scottdale PA: Herald Press.
Riedemann, Peter
: 1999 *Peter Riedemann's Hutterite Confession of Faith*. Translated from the 1565 German ed. and edited by John J. Friesen. Waterloo, ON; Scottdale, PA: Herald Press.
Rignell, Lars G.
: 1957 "Isaiah Chapter I. Some Exegetical Remarks with Special Reference to the Relationship Between the Text and the Book of Deuteronomy." *Studia theologica* 11:140-58.
Roth, Wolfgang
: 1988 *Isaiah*. Knox Preaching Guides. Atlanta, GA: John Knox.
Search for Peace in the Middle East
: 1970 London: Friends Peace and International Relations Committee and Friends Service Council.
Seitz, Christopher R.
: 1993 *Isaiah 1–39*. Interpretation: A Bible Commentary for Teaching and Preaching. Louisville, KY: John Knox.
Simons, Menno. *See* Menno

Bibliography

Smart, James D.
 1965 *History and Theology in Second Isaiah*. Philadelphia: Westminster.
Smith, George Adam
 1966 *The Historical Geography of the Holy Land*. New York: Harper Torch.
Solomonow, Allan, ed.
 1972 *Toward Middle East Dialogue: Responses to the Quakers' Search for Peace in the Middle East*. New York: Committee on New Alternatives in the Middle East.
Swartley, Willard, ed.
 2000 *Violence Renounced: René Girard, Biblical Studies, and Peacemaking*. Telford, PA: Pandora Press U.S.
Sweeney, Marvin A.
 1988 *Isaiah 1–4 and the Post-Exilic Understanding of the Isaianic Tradition*. Beihefte zur Zeitschrift für die alttestamentliche Wissenschaft 171. Berlin and New York: Walter de Gruyter.
Tillich, Paul
 1951 *Systematic Theology. Vol. 1, Reason and Revelation, Being and God*. Chicago: University of Chicago Press.
 1957 *Systematic Theology. Vol. 2, Existence and the Christ*. Chicago: University of Chicago Press.
 1963 *Systematic Theology. Vol. 3, Life and the Spirit: History and the Kingdom of God*. Chicago: University of Chicago Press.
Toews, John E.
 2004 *Romans*. Believers Church Bible Commentary. Scottdale, PA; Waterloo, ON: Herald Press.
Ullmann, Richard K.
 1959 *Between God and History: The Human Situation Exemplified in Quaker Thought and Practice*. London: George Allen & Unwin.
Unterman, Jeremiah, and Gary S. Shogren
 1992 "Redemption." In *ABD*, 5:650-57.
Vaux, Roland de
 1961a *Ancient Israel. Vol. 1, Social Institutions*. New York: McGraw Hill.
 1961b *Ancient Israel. Vol. 2, Religious Institutions*. New York: McGraw Hill.
Vermès, Géza, trans., ed.
 1997 *The Complete Dead Sea Scrolls in English*. New York: Allen Lane/Penguin Press.
Vriezen, Theodorus C.
 1966 *An Outline of Old Testament Theology*. Oxford: Basil Blackwell.
Wagner, Murray L.
 1983 *Peter Chelcicky, A Radical Separatist in Hussite Bohemia*. Scottdale, PA; Kitchener, ON: Herald Press.
Wallis, Jim
 1981 *The Call to Conversion*. San Francisco: Harper & Row.
Watts, John D. W.
 1985 *Isaiah 1–33*. Word Biblical Commentary. Waco, TX: Word.
 1987 *Isaiah 34–66*. Word Biblical Commentary. Waco, TX: Word.
Weaver, J. Denny
 2001 *The Nonviolent Atonement*. Grand Rapids: Eerdmans.

Weiser, Artur
    1961   *The Old Testament: Its Formation and Development*. Translated by Dorothea M. Barton. New York: Association.

Wesley, John
    1951   *The Journal of John Wesley*. Chicago: Moody.

Westermann, Claus
    1969   *Isaiah 40–66, A Commentary*. Old Testament Library. Translated by D. M. Stalker. Philadelphia: Westminster.

Whybray, Roger N.
    1975   *Isaiah 40–66*. New Century Bible Commentary. Grand Rapids: Eerdmans.

Wink, Walter
    1993   *Holy Week: Interpreting the Lessons of the Church Year*. Proclamation 5, Series B. Minneapolis: Fortress.

With One Voice: A Lutheran Resource for Worship.
    1995   Minneapolis: Augsburg Fortress.

Woolman, John
    1971   *The Journal and Major Essays of John Woolman* [1720-1772]. Edited by Phillips P. Moulton. New York: Oxford University Press.

Wright, Christopher J. H.
    2008   "Atonement in the Old Testament." Pages 69-82 in *The Atonement Debate*. Edited by Derek Tidball, David Hilborn, and Justin Thacker. Grand Rapids: Zondervan.

Wright, David P.
    1992   "Day of Atonement." In *ABD*, 2:72-76.

Wright, G. Ernest
    1964   *The Book of Isaiah*. Layman's Bible Commentary. Richmond, VA: John Knox.

Yeatts, John R.
    2003   *Revelation*. Believers Church Bible Commentary. Waterloo, ON; Scottdale, PA: Herald Press.

Yoder, John Howard
    1972   *The Politics of Jesus*. Grand Rapids: Eerdmans.
    1973   *The Legacy of Michael Sattler*. Classics of the Radical Reformation 1. Scottdale, PA: Herald Press.
    1994   "Peace Without Eschatology?" 1954. Reprint, pages 143-67 in *The Royal Priesthood: Essays Ecclesiological and Ecumenical*. Edited by Michael G. Cartwright. Grand Rapids: Eerdmans.

Yoder Neufeld, Thomas R.
    2002   *Ephesians*. Believers Church Bible Commentary. Waterloo, ON; Scottdale, PA: Herald Press.

Yoder, Perry B.
    1987   *Shalom: The Bible's Word for Salvation, Justice, and Peace*. Newton, KS: Faith & Life.

Young, Edward J.
    1965   *The Book of Isaiah*. Vol. 1 (chaps. 1–18). New International Commentary on the Old Testament. Grand Rapids: Eerdmans.
    1969   *The Book of Isaiah*. Vol. 2 (chaps. 19–39). New International Commentary on the Old Testament. Grand Rapids: Eerdmans.
    1972   *The Book of Isaiah*. Vol. 3 (chaps. 40–66). New International Commentary on the Old Testament. Grand Rapids: Eerdmans.

Zehr, Howard
    1990 *Changing Lenses: A New Focus for Crime and Justice*. Scottdale, PA; Waterloo, ON: Herald Press.

Index of Ancient Sources

OLD TESTAMENT

Genesis–Kings
.........................225

Genesis.................89
1–2..............256, 277
1:1......................236
1:1-5....................383
1:1–2:3.................450
1:2 ....104, 210,
       235, 254, 268
1:3-5....................347
2:21.....................181
3.........................406
3:13-16.................413
6–8......................340
6–9......................158
6:11-12.................158
7:11.....................157
8:2......................157
9 ....338, 340, 347
9:9......................375
9:12-13, 17 71
9:15-16.................158
9:16..........156, 158,
              345, 347
12 ....389, 414
12:1-3 ....18, 41,
            163, 321, 439
12:2.............18, 129
12:3 ....18, 87, 273,
              275, 353,
              389, 450
12–50..................415

15 ....72, 414-15
15:1.....................268
15:7.....................415
15:12...................181
16–17..................141
17........................347
17:4.....................375
17:4-6, 16 128
17:7.....................345
17:7, 13, 19 348
18.......................439
18–19...................32
18:14...................318
18:17-19................18
18:18 ....41, 383
18:19 ....18, 445
19:19...................401
20.......................358
20:13...................452
21.......................311
22:15-18................18
22:15-19................41
22:17....................94
23.......................415
24........................72
25 ....141, 311, 380
25:1......................32
26.......................415
26:1-5...................18
26:3.....................261
26:4......................41
26:28...................261
27.......................311
28:4.....................415
28:14....................41
29:6.....................451

30:33...................446
32:3-8..................447
32:12....................94
32:20...................448
32:22-32..............256
35.......................244
36.......................209
37.......................311
37:34...................119
39.......................261
46:3.....................242
49:24....................77

Exodus
2..........................72
3 ....160, 187
3:6, 14 241
3:7-8...................222
3:12.....................261
3:13-15................287
4–14....................403
6:2......................241
6:6 ....91, 201, 271,
          300, 400, 449
7–12 ....64, 135
7:4......................300
7:20-24................316
9:24.....................129
10:21-23..............316
13:21...................383
13:22...................331
13–14....................50
14.......................150
14–15....................89
14:13...................204
14:16....................95

Index of Ancient Sources

14:19 331
14:21-22 316
15 .... 260, 335
15:2 103
15:13 .... 271, 300, 401
15:21 103
17:1-7 299
18:8 300
19:6 .... 31, 129, 395-96
20 .... 19, 62
20:1-6 287
20:1-17 456
20:3 ...... 198, 282, 404
20:3-6 409
20:4 235
20:4-6 .... 269, 296, 421
20:5 251
20:8-11 450
20:13 319
22:21-24 457
23:1-3, 6-8 180
23:20-23 401
24 157
24:9-11 61
27:20-21 383
28:33-34 61
29–30 439
31 348
31:12-17 450
32–34 439
32:34 401
33:2, 14-15 401
33:17-23 443
33:20 61-62
33:23 61
34:6 357
34:6-7 .... 340, 456
34:10 129
40:34-38 444

Leviticus
1–7 .... 32, 62, 439
5:1-13 62
11:7-8 409
11:44-45 ..... 396, 445
16:21 373
17–26 .... 62, 396
17:11 448

19 396
19:2 445
19:9-18 55
19:15-18 180
19:18 161
19:26 39
19:31 80
19–26 368
20:6, 27 80
22 355
23 49
23:26-32 368
25 .... 271, 386-87, 390
25:44 129
26:26 49
26:40 49
27:32 92

Numbers
6:26 451
13:33 236
14:9 261
14:12 383
14:15 129
14:18 357
14:19 452
15 439
20 243
21:6 61
21:10-12 120
22–24 118
23:9 245
24:2 254
25:12 342
28–29 .... 355, 439
31:7 193

Deuteronomy
1:31 401
4:6 129
4:7–8 31
4:9, 23 129
4:9-20 190
4:19 157
4:29 179
5 .... 19, 62
5:6-21 456
5:7 198
5:8 190
5:8-10 .... 296, 421

5:9 251
5:12-15 450
5:17 319
5:31 414
6:12 129
6:25 446
7:6 396
7:7-8 401
7:8 449
7:19 .... 71, 315
8:11, 14, 19 129
8:15 61
9 439
10:1-2 79
10:12-22 55
11:17 414
12:1 414
12:2 .... 245, 410
15:6 129
15:7 414
15:11 368
16:18-20 180
17:3 157
17:14-20 196
17:18 79
18:9-14 .... 80, 409
18:9-22 272
18:10, 14 39
18:10-11 272
19:15-21 180
21:8-9 448
22:1-4 368
23:1 352
26 383
26:8 ...... 71, 201, 400
26:9 414
26:15 58
28 456
29:3 71
30 345
30:15-20 33
30:19-20 411
31 137
31:6 261
31:17 137
32 .... 30, 126, 367
32:1 30
32:4 .... 55, 77
32:15, 18, 30-31 ... 77
32:6 .... 30, 403
32:10-12 401

32:13..............367	14:47-48..........118	19:18................449
32:15..............266	15:28................404	20:31................119
32:18..............129	16:13 ....104, 447	21......................342
32:35..............161	17......................375	21:27................368
33:2..................233	20:8..................452	22:19-23............63
33:5, 26 266	20:15................452	22:48................149
33:15..............245	22:3-5................118	
34:11..................71	26:12................181	**2 Kings**
	28........................80	225
Joshua	31:13................368	2........................342
..........................449		6:30..................119
1:5....................261	**2 Samuel**	7:1....................418
2:1, 3 185	3:31..................119	15:29..................83
3:17..................129	5:17-21............173	16......................453
6:17, 23, 25 185	6........................457	16:3....................67
10:1-15............173	7........................197	16:5....................67
11:6..................242	7:8-15..............348	16:10-16............75
15:8..................126	7:16..................197	17 ....83, 449
21:44................402	8:2-12..............118	17:36................201
23:1..................402	12........................54	18:13–20:19......225, 453
24:19................251	12:15-23..........368	18:2....................75
	22:9..................409	18–19..............145
Judges	23......................348	18–20..............225
..........................449	23:3....................77	19:34................204
2:6-16............405-6	23:5 ......345-46, 348	19:35-37..........220
3:9....................134		20......................358
4:21..................181	**1–2 Kings**	21:6....................80
6–7....................84	449	23:10 ....189, 354
6:34..................104		23:24..................80
7:25....................95	**1 Kings**	24:20................455
8:23..................335	1:39..................447	24–25..............449
13:22..................61	2:7....................452	25:11................449
20:15: 21, 26, 35, 46	5:1....................152	
..........................137	7:10..................175	**1–2 Chronicles**
	7:13-14............152	225
Ruth	8........................457	
................118, 449	8:1....................457	**1 Chronicles**
4........................300	8:22..................409	13......................457
4:7......................77	8:27..................417	16......................348
	8:41-43..............41	16:17................348
1–2 Samuel	8:42..................201	16:22................447
..........................449	9:11-12............152	29:10-19............197
	10......................380	
1 Samuel	10:9..................445	**2 Chronicles**
2:1-11..............160	10:22................149	273
8:5, 20 130	14:22................251	2:3, 11, 14 152
8:7....................335	17–19................342	9:21..................149
9:16..................204	18 ....41, 343	13:12................262
10:1..................447	19......................175	27–28..............453
10:10................254	19:15, 18 343	29–32..............225
12:14-15............400	19:16 ....386, 447	

Index of Ancient Sources

32.............................225
32:1-31......................225
36.............................273
36:17-21...................282
36:32-33...................273

Ezra
.................................273
1:1, 7, 8 273
3:7..............................273
4:3, 5 273
5:13-17.....................273
6:3-5, 14 273
8:21-23.....................368

Nehemiah
4:15...........................116
9................................456
9:1..............................119
9:17............................357
13:15-18, 19-22
.................................450

Esther
4:15-17.....................368

Job
.................................231
4:13............................181
9:8..............................237
21:22..........................234
25:3............................383
26:12..........................323
29:3............................383
31:16-23...................368
33:15..........................181
38:4-41......................234
38:8-1........................237

Psalms
.................................439
1................................413
2 ....128, 447
2:2..............................448
4:6..............................383
5:8..............................446
6:4..............................204
6:5..............................452
7:1..............................204
8..................................77
11:4............................417

16:6............................211
18...............................447
18:8............................409
19:5..............................49
21:11..........................116
22...............................122
22:21..........................204
23:4............................262
23:5............................345
24 ....159, 458
25:1............................198
25:3, 5, 21 204
25:7............................401
25:11..........................299
27:1............................268
27:14..........................204
31:1............................446
31:14..........................198
31:24..........................204
32:1-2.........................373
33:4-5..........................55
33:5............................445
33:10..........................116
35:13..........................119
35:20..........................451
36:5............................452
37:3............................198
37:7, 9, 34 204
38:15..........................204
39:7............................204
40...............................439
42-43..........................122
44:3............................383
44:6-7.........................198
44:23-26....................402
46...............................128
46:2............................268
46:6............................405
46:8, 12 262
47...............................336
49:15..........................449
50...............................439
51 ....439, 448
51:1-2.........................401
51:3............................452
55:22..........................343
56:3-4, 9-11 198
60 ....336, 358
66:6............................316
68...............................458
71:2............................446

72...............................458
72:1..............................55
72:1-4.........................197
72:2............................445
72:3............................245
72:9............................310
74:1............................357
74:14..........................323
79:5............................357
80:4............................357
80:8-18........................58
80:8-19........................47
83...............................128
85:5............................357
85:10-13....................389
86:12..........................443
86:15..........................357
86:17..........................358
89 ....201, 447
89:10..........................323
89:14 ....55, 175, 445
89:14-18....................389
89:15..........................383
89:16..........................446
89:26............................77
89:29..........................348
90:2............................237
90:8............................383
91:5............................268
92:2............................198
93...............................336
95...............................282
96...............................336
97...............................336
97:1-5.........................400
97:2 ....55, 445
97:10-12....................389
99 ....336, 338
99:4..............................55
99:5............................417
102:25........................175
102:25-27..................237
103..............................336
103:4..........................449
103:6-14......................88
104:2 ....236-37, 383
105..............................104
105:8-22....................348
105:10........................345
105:15........................447
106:8..........................299

106:9 316	2:32 129	31:10-14 237
110 447	3 33	31:13 237
114:4, 6 245	3:4, 19 403	31:22 262
115 198	3:21 129	31:31-34 263
118:6 268	3:22 439	31–34 262
118:14 103-4	3:22b–4:2 373	32 .... 137, 300
125:1 198	3:23 .... 245, 410	32:40 .... 345. 348
130:5 204	4:8 119	33:8 439
130:8 449	4:24 245	33:15-16 197
132:7 417	5:9, 29 129	35:1-19 137
136:12 .... 201, 400	5:23 190	36:4-8 79
137:9 111	6:28 190	40:11-12 257
139 122	7:5 351	43:1-7 257
140:2 116	7:21-26 32	43:8-13 137
145 157	7:28 129	46–51 109
145:17 55	7:31-32 354	48:32 121
146 336	8:4-7 35	48:43-44 157
147:4 237	9:1, 18 121	49:7-22 .... 211, 213
147:5 237	9:8 129	49:20 116
148:9 245	9:24 445	49:30 241
148:13 104	12:17 129	50:5 348
	13:1-11 137	50:6 129
Proverbs	13:25 129	50:18 114
3:5 198	16:1-9 137	50:35-38 96
8:15-16 197	17:2-3 245	50:36 272
8:20 445	17:13 349	50:45 116
8:22-31 234	17:19-23 450	51 146
8:25 245	18 .... 96-97, 180	51:7, 24, 37 146
14:22 452	18:11 116	51:12 116
14:35 197	18:13-17 356	51:20 96
16:12 197	18:15 129	51:37 272
16:18 170	19:1–20:6 137	51:59-64 137
19:21 116	19:7 116	52:3 455
25:5 197	22:13-17 47	
26:18 318	22:18-19 114	**Lamentations**
29:14 197	23 .... 272, 353	2:1 417
30:19 72	23:1-4 234	3 122
	23:5-6 197	3:32 452
Song of Solomon	23:26-27 129	4:21 324
2:8 245	25 .... 36, 324, 353	5 122
3:11 47	25:3-7 315	
	25:5 439	**Ezekiel**
Jeremiah	25:11-12 151-52,	...... 35, 190, 438, 449
.... 449	282	1:1 444
1:5 306	25:15-29 96	1:3 77
1:8 242	27:1–28:17 137	1:26-28 443
1:8, 19 262	27:5 .... 201, 400	2:2 254
2:4 418	29:10 ..... 151-52, 282	2:6 242
2:4-13 30	29:10-14 116	3:4-11 64
2:13 349	29:13 179	3:9 77
2:21 58	31:9 403	3:12-15 104

Index of Ancient Sources

3:14................77
3:14, 22 77
3:17...............395
4:1–5:17..........137
4:16................49
6:3................245
6:13...............410
7:11................92
8:1.................77
10:1-22............420
10:4................62
11:20..............401
14:23..............237
15:1-8..............58
16..................33
16:49...............47
16:54..............237
16:60 ....345, 348
17:11-21...........196
18.................446
18:4...............214
18:5-9 ....351, 368
18:10-13............47
18:23..............214
18:30-32...........439
18:32..............297
19:10-14............58
20.................300
20:8-9, 44.........297
20:8-12, 13-20 450
20:33, 34 201
20:47..............418
21:21..............271
22:6-12............356
22:29...............47
23.................324
25:12-14...........209,
              211, 213
25–32..............109
26–29..............152
27:3...............292
27:15, 20..........142
27:31..............119
32:17-32...........113
33:1-9 ....141, 395
33:10-11...........439
33:22...............77
34 ....234, 272,
                  353
34:23-24...........197
34:25..............342

35.................213
35:5-7.............213
35:8...............245
36.................300
36:1-15............213
36:4, 6 245
37:1................77
37:24-28...........197
37:26 ....342, 348
40–48...............87
40:1................77
43.................233
43:1-12............421
43:15..............178
45:5...............445

Daniel

...................273
1:21...............273
10:1...............273
10:9...............181
11:35..............297
12:2-3.............162
12:10..............297
6:29...............273
7–12 438-39
7:1-3..............439
7:14................87
8..................438
8:18...............181
9:1-2, 24-27 282
9:2................151
9:2, 24 152

Minor Prophets

...................449

Hosea

1–3.................33
1:8-9..............164
1:10...............164
2:13...............129
2:18, 20, 22 137
2:18-20............104
4:1................418
4:6................129
4:13 ....245, 410
4:16...............190
6:4-6...............32
8:14...............129
9:8................395

10:8...............245
12:6 ....204, 452
13:6...............129
14:2-3.............373

Joel

...................443
1:14...............368
2:12-17............439
2:15...............364
2:16................49
3:4-8..............257
3:10................41
3:18 ....245, 349

Amos

1–2................109
1:11-12............213
2:12...............186
2:6-8...............62
5...................36
5:18...............111
5:21-24............389
5:21-25.............32
5:24...............445
5:27...............257
6:5-6...............56
8:1................444
8:3, 9.............137
8:4-6...............47
9:7................115
9:13...............245

Obadiah

1–21...............213
10–14..............400

Jonah

....................87
1:3................149
1:5-6..............181
3–4............456-57
3:5................368

Micah

1:8................121
2:2-3...............41
4:1................245
4:1-4...............41
4:1-5...............38
4:3.................43

4:12................116
6:1..................245
6:1-8.................30
6:6-8..........32, 180
6:8..................400
7:7..................204
7:8..................383
7:16-17......128, 310

Nahum
1:4..................316
1:5..................245

Habakkuk
2:2.............79, 237
2:14.................103
3:4..............383-84
3:6..................245

Zephaniah
........................443
2........................109
2:2......................88
3:8.................88, 204

Zechariah
1–8...................438
1:8, 18..............444
1:12...............151-52
2:11....................41
6:15...................381
7:5................151-52
7:8-14.................47
7:12...................104
8:8....................446
8:20-23................41
9:9-10...........41, 197
14:8...................349
14:12..................193

Malachi
1:2-5..................213
2:5.....................342
3:2-3......49, 62, 297

NEW TESTAMENT

Gospels
................400, 457

Matthew
......................336
1:2...................262
1:11, 12, 17......291
1:23....................72
2:1.....................35
3:2....................283
3:3.............238, 442
3:5.....................35
3:11-12................49
3:13-17...............253
4:1-11................368
4:15-16................87
4:16...................384
4:17...................283
4:25....................35
5:21-26..........32, 389
5:39...................161
5:43-48...............454
6:16-21...............368
7:21...................441
7:24-27...............175
8:16...................358
8:17...................440
9:14-17...............262
10:15...................42
11:22-24...............42
11:28..................349
12:1-8.................450
12:15-21..............448
12:36...................42
13:13-15...............64
13:52..................262
14:29-31..............349
14:72..................222
16......................147
16:18-19..............147
16:19..................146
18......................147
18:15-20...............14
18:34..................457
19:26..................319
20:28..................440
21:1-11...............448
21:33-46...............58
22:7...................457
23:37...................35
24......................42
24–25.............42, 438
25:31-46........58, 368

26:64.................448
28:19.................311
28:20.................262

Mark
.......................336
1:3....................238
1:5.....................35
1:9-11................253
1:10...................254
1:12-13................368
1:14-15...............238
1:15...................283
1:34...................358
2:18-22...............262
3:1-6..................450
3:8.....................35
4:12....................64
10:27..................319
10:32-34...............35
10:45..................440
11:1-10...............448
11:1-11...............137
12:1-12................58
13......................438
14:36..................319
14:62..................448
15:28..................440

Luke
.................25, 336
1:1-4...................79
1:13, 30..............242
1:28...................262
1:30...................268
1:32-33.................88
1:46-55...............160
1:79....................88
2:9....................444
2:25-35...............312
2:29-32...............311
3:4-6..................238
3:16-17................49
3:21-22...............253
4......................390
4:1-13.................368
4:1-14.................454
4:14-21...............386
4:16-30.........25, 204
5:17....................35

Index of Ancient Sources

5:33-39................262
6:17......................35
6:19....................358
6:46-49..............175
8:10......................64
10:25-28............198
10:25-37............368
13:10-17............450
13:20-21............307
15:11-32............356
18:7....................214
18:27..................319
19:9....................165
19:29-40............448
20:9-19................58
21........................438
21:20-21..............35
22:25..................454
22:37..................440
22:62..................222
23:34..................454
24:44-49............264
24:47....................42

John
1–12....................384
1............................89
1:6-8, 19-28........390
1:23....................238
1:29-34..............253
1:32....................254
2–11.................71-72
3:36....................457
4:10-11..............349
4:14....................344
5........................358
5:2-18................450
6:20....................242
7........................349
7:37....................344
8:12....................384
10........................35
12:12-19............448
12:40....................64
13:34-35............263
14:27..................268
15........................58
15:9-17................58
20:22..................254
20:30-31..............79

Acts
1:4......................204
1:7-8..................264
1:8........................35
2:1-18, 38..........254
2:14......................35
2:23....................116
2:38....................283
3:19....................283
5:38-39..............116
7:43....................291
8:1........................35
8:26-40..............358
8:34....................451
10......................358
10:39....................35
11:1-2..................35
11:21..................262
11:26....................26
11:27-29..............35
13......................312
13:3....................369
13:47..................312
14:23..................369
15........................35
15:1....................358
15:20..................358
18:9....................268
21:7-14..............137
26:23..................311
28:26-27..............64

Romans
..........................25
1:18....................457
2:5........................42
3:23....................406
6........................198
7:21-25..............198
8:23....................204
8:31....................262
8:39....................262
9:20-21................96
9:24-26..............175
9:27....................449
9:27-28..............175
9:29....................175
11......................175
11:5....................449
11:8....................181
11:13..................358
12:2......................36
12:19...........88, 161
12:19-21............214
13:12..................376
14......................282
14:10-12......281-82
15:9-12................25

1 Corinthians
1:7......................204
2:9......................398
3:11....................176
3:11-15..............175
9:10......................79
12:3....................104
15:22..................226

2 Corinthians
1:3-4..................358
1:14......................42
10:4....................376
10:6....................407
5:16–6:2............311
5:16-21..............263
5:19....................166
6:7......................376

Galatians
1:15....................306
2:11-12..............358
5............................58
5:5......................204
5:6......................368
5:19-21.......36, 422
5:22-26................36

Ephesians
1:10....................116
2:11-22..............358
2:14....................454
3:9......................116
4:1......................362
4:22-24..............263
6:10-20..............375

Philippians
1:6; 10..................42
1:28....................246
2........................282
2:7......................304
2:10-11..............282

2:12............................165
2:16..............................42
2:6-11 ....281, 451

Colossians
3:5-11..........................263

1 Thessalonians
1:10............................457
2:16..............................88
5:2, 4 42
5:8..............................376

1 Timothy
1:4..............................326
1:10............................246
4:7..............................326
6:11-15........................166

2 Timothy
3:14-17..........................79
4:4..............................326

Titus
1:14............................326

Hebrews
1:10-12........................237
8:8-13..........................263
9:15-22........................263
10:30............................161
10:32-39......................264
11:1-40........................264
12:18-24......................263

James
1:22............................382
2:14-26........................368
5:13-16........................191

1 Peter
1:16............................396
1:22–2:3......................396
2:9..............................396
2:22, 24 440
5:8..............................246
5:13............................291

2 Peter
1:16............................326

1 John
1:5..............................384
1:5-7............................42
2:5..............................454
2:7-11..........................263

Revelation
..............25, 438, 457
1......................................72
3....................................146
3:7-8............................146
5:6..................................25
6:1..................................25
6:16 ....88, 457
7:9..................................25
11:18..............................88
13 ....291, 326, 438, 454
13:8................................25
14:1................................25
14:8..............................291
14:10..............................88
17:14 ....25, 454
18:2..............................291
19:9................................25
21–22............................349
21:2..............................342
21:5-6..........................349
21:14..............................25
21:18-21......................341
22:1................................25
22:16-17......................349
22:17............................344

APOCRYPHA

2 Esdras 438
Wisdom of Solomon
5:17-18..........................375

PSEUDEPIGRAPHA
2 Baruch..............438

ANET
67, 130-31 326
132..............................132
137-38..........................162
284-86..........................279
286..............................135
287..............................218
288..............................218
290..............................289
293..............................136
303, 306, 311 286
313-14..........................142
316 ....273, 276
412-25..........................133
443..............................234

OTHER SOURCES
Apostles' Creed....254, 273
Augustine of Hippo.....
    254, 326, 406-7
Basil of Caesarea ...254
Clement of Rome...146
Dead Sea Scrolls 25, 404
Origen..................254
Tertullian 254

The Author

Ivan Friesen received a call to Christian ministry as a young adult and has engaged in academic studies and teaching, as well as service and pastoral ministries, in North America and in several international contexts. He was director of Mennonite Central Committee programs in the Middle East (West Bank) from 1968 to 1971. He taught at Swift Current Bible Institute, Swift Current, Saskatchewan (1976-80); Department of Theology and Religious Studies, University of Botswana, Gaborone (1986-92); and Shaw Divinity School, Raleigh, North Carolina (1996-99).

He and his wife, Rachel Hilty Friesen, served as copastors at Mennonite congregations in North Carolina and South Dakota from 1993 until 2007. He was a member of the Freeman Network for Justice and Peace. Ivan and Rachel are the parents of three adult children: Amal Ruth, Sena Margaret, and Philip Hilty.

Friesen did his undergraduate studies at Freeman Junior College and Goshen College (BA, 1964). He earned a degree in biblical studies at Associated Mennonite Biblical Seminaries (BD, 1967), including a year as an exchange student at the Interdenominational Theological Center in Atlanta. His graduate studies in the Old Testament were at San Francisco Theological Seminary (ThM, 1973) and at the University of St. Michael's College in Toronto (PhD, 1990). Ivan and Rachel coauthored a series of Shalom Pamphlets on the Christian peace witness (Herald Press, 1981). In addition, Ivan Friesen coedited with Mary Schertz *Beautiful upon the Mountains* (Institute of Mennonite Studies and Herald Press, 2003). He contributed an essay to that volume: "Light to the Nations in Isaiah's Servant Songs."

Friesen's family roots are in the settlement of Germans from Russia at Henderson, Nebraska. He was born there 58 years after the immigration of his Mennonite forebears from the Ukraine. Ivan and Rachel Friesen are now retired and living at Bluffton, Ohio, where Rachel grew up. They are members of Grace Mennonite Church in Pandora, Ohio.

Isaiah 63:1–64:12

God's Mercy Remembered

PREVIEW

Isaiah 63 and 64 belong together in a way that may be compared with Isaiah 34 and 35. In both cases the association of chapters rests on contrasting pictures. In each case Edom is the object of the Lord's judgment, followed by portrayal of God's salvation of Zion. Relationships of contrast often characterize the book of Isaiah.

Isaiah 63–64 falls into three main parts. The first part, employing a question-answer format, focuses on the Lord's verdict against Edom (63:1-6). This part is often understood to be independent and unrelated to its context (Whybray: 252). Nevertheless the underlying themes of God's salvation and redemption in 63:1-6 continue to receive emphasis in 63:7–64:12.

The second part recounts the Lord's salvation of his people in spite of their faithlessness (63:7-14). Lament and complaint are part of this recital.

Recital yields to a prayer of petition in the last part (63:15–64:12). The petition becomes most poignant in 64:1-4, where there is a plea for the Lord to come down and make his name known to his enemies. In 1 Corinthians 2:9 Paul paraphrases Isaiah 64:4 to explain the lack of understanding on the part of the first-century political leaders concerning God's plan in Jesus.

The verses in the Hebrew Bible from 63:19b–64:11 correspond to the English 64:1-12 (see NRSV footnote). The commentary will follow the English verse structure.

may come closer to what is meant by holiness than the "separateness" that earlier leaders advocated. This separateness was a movement toward faithfulness and yet incomplete.

www.ingramcontent.com/pod-product-compliance
Lightning Source LLC
Chambersburg PA
CBHW051240300426
44114CB00011B/824

Servant Song 52:13-53:12

The beginning and end of the fourth servant song indicate that through the servant's witness the nations will see the power of nonviolence, which undergirds God's reign and is the condition for peace on earth (52:13-15; 53:11-12). The description of the servant's suffering and death occupies the center of the song. This suffering and death illustrate the power of one person, solidly obedient to God's will, inspiring future generations to faithfulness (53:1-10).

52:13-15 Demeanor and Disfigurement

Two contrasting impressions etch themselves on the reader's consciousness at the beginning of the song: the servant's demeanor and the servant's disfigurement. By *demeanor* I mean the outward manner in which the servant bears himself in the face of aggression and brutality. The Lord's word, spoken by the prophet, presents the servant's demeanor in terms of prosperity and dignity (52:13). The meaning of the Hebrew verb *śakal* (*prosper*; *act wisely*, NIV) is *to have insight* or *to have success*. Such is the demeanor of royalty. So kings and nations are astonished that a mere servant should exhibit prosperity and dignity. Nevertheless the reader is invited to interpret the song with the servant's demeanor in mind.

The disfigurement provides an image, a preview really, of what the servant experienced under due process (52:14-15). Kings and nations express surprise at the sight of the Lord's servant disfigured yet resolute. His mission to the nations rests on the shock effect of a royal figure submitting to suffering rather than inflicting it. Kings and nations represent the sentinels of law and justice. What they see and understand, however, shocks them into silence (52:15). They are shocked because they realize that in this disfigured servant lies the power of God to bring healing and forgiveness and reconciliation to the world (cf. Hanson: 154-55). But does this new awareness lead to behavior characterized by a change of heart? The history of kings and nations suggests otherwise.

53:1-6 The Servant's Suffering

The *we* section of the fourth song portrays the suffering of the Lord's servant as perceived by a collective voice (53:1-6). Who might this be? The answer is not obvious. Two possibilities present themselves in 52:13-15. One is the *many who were appalled* (52:14 NIV), which may be an oblique reference to Israel's collective voice. The second is the *many nations* and *kings* in Israel's peripheral vision (52:15). They would be attentive to the growth and development of a royal figure. At the same that the God of Israel controls history and the forces of nature. This is good news in Israel's immediate situation because it means that there are limits to exile and punishment. It is also good news in a universal sense because it offers humankind, along with Israel, a foundation for salvation and peace on earth.

The second stanza pictures sentinels awaiting the messenger's arrival (52:8). They give a ringing cry when they see the Lord's return to Zion [*Zion, p. 457*]. What does this part of the vision mean? The prophet perceives that the Lord's presence in Zion has, until now, been restricted. The banishment of the people in exile and the withdrawal of the temple vessels indicate this restriction. The lifting of the restriction, therefore, occurs when news arrives of the impending return of temple vessels and long-lost exiles. It is not as if the Lord is limited by time and space, but that the Lord's presence is recognized in the presence of his people and the temple artifacts.

First the sentinels give a ringing cry; now the ruins of Jerusalem are instructed to give a ringing cry (52:9). Since the Babylonian destruction of Jerusalem in 587 BC, the city has lain in ruins. The *ruins of Jerusalem* may also refer to residents of the city despairing of a future (cf. Brueggemann, 1998b:139). They also are part of the redemption story. In his vision the prophet sees these ruins breaking into a song of joy because of the Lord's renewed presence in the city. The word *comfort*, as in 51:3 and 40:1, means to make new life possible for God's people. The comfort of God's people and the redemption of Jerusalem appear in parallel lines.

Isaiah 52:9-10 serves as a two-stanza praise hymn. The call to worship at the beginning of 52:9 gives way to the motive for worship in 52:10. The baring of the Lord's holy arm (a metaphor of power) before the nations indicates that Jerusalem's salvation is a public event. The Lord discloses himself to the nations through his redemption of his people.

The concluding stanzas recall the beginning of the chapter (52:1-2; cf. Childs: 406-07). There it is Zion-Jerusalem who is instructed with a double imperative to *Awake, awake!*. Here a double imperative *Depart, depart!* instructs the exiles to vacate the city and country of their exile. The instruction addresses in particular those who carry the emblems of the Lord's presence (52:11). They are to observe the purity rituals associated with those emblems.

Like the old exodus from Egypt, the Lord goes before (Exod 13:22) and behind the people (14:19) in the new exodus from Babylon (Isa 52:12). Unlike the old exodus with the Hebrews leaving in haste ahead of the pursuing Egyptians, however, the new exodus does not take place in haste. The initiator of the new exodus authorizes the exiles to go. The Lord's protection assures them that they are safe.